W9-CZN-662

The Nature of the Nonprofit Sector

The Nature of the Nonprofit Sector

edited by

J. STEVEN OTT

UNIVERSITY OF UTAH

A Member of the Perseus Books Group

Copyright © 2001 by Westview Press, A Member of the Perseus Books Group

Additional copyright information appears on p. 433 and is an extension of information on this page.

Published in 2001 in the United States of America by Westview Press, 5500 Central Avenue, Boulder, Colorado 80301–2877, and in the United Kingdom by Westview Press, 12 Hid's Copse Road, Cumnor Hill, Oxford OX2 9JJ

A CIP card is available from the Library of Congress for this book.
ISBN 0-8133-6785-9

The paper used in this publication meets the requirements of the American National Standard for Permanence of Paper for Printed Library Materials Z39.48-1984.

10   9   8   7   6   5   4   3   2

Contents

Part 1 Introduction to the Nonprofit Sector   1

Part 2 The Nonprofit Sector's Distinctive Values and Contributions to Society   47

Part 3 Historical Evolution of the Nonprofit Sector   89

Part 4   The Rationale for Tax Exemption   143

Part 5   Overview Theories of the Nonprofit Sector   157

Part 6   Economic and Political Theories of the Nonprofit Sector   179

Part 7   Social and Community Theories of the Nonprofit Sector   233

Part 8   Organization Theories of the Nonprofit Sector   267

Part 9   Giving Theories of the Nonprofit Sector   311

Part 10   The Blending and Blurring of the Sectors   355

Part 11   Challenges Facing the Nonprofit Sector   411

Foreword

This volume is a welcome—indeed a much needed—addition to the field of nonprofit studies. In the more than ten years since its predecessor, *The Nonprofit Sector: Essential Readings* (edited by David L. Gies, J. Steven Ott, and Jay M. Shafritz) was published, the field has exploded.

The primary scholarly organization in the field, Association for Research on Nonprofit Organizations and Voluntary Action (ARNOVA), has grown from fewer than 300 members in 1989 to more than 1,000 and now counts members from eighteen disciplines and fifty-five different nations. Its most recent annual conference in 1999 showcased more than 350 papers and panel presentations on the sector and attracted close to 600 participants, compared to 91 papers and 127 participants in 1989. A second scholarly organization, the International Society for Third-Sector Research (ISTR) has formed and launched another journal and a series of biannual conferences.

The number of journals, publishers, Web sites, and Internet discussion groups devoted to the field is expanding rapidly as well. There have been major advances in research on the sector, thanks in large part to the pioneering efforts of Independent Sector and the National Center for Charitable Statistics (the latter now housed in the Center for Philanthropy and Nonprofits at the Urban Institute). Indeed, the nonprofit sector has its own source of support for scholarly research in the Aspen Institute's Nonprofit Sector Research Fund with more than $7.5 million awarded by the fund for research on the sector since 1991.

The number of Ph.D. dissertations on topics related to philanthropy or the nonprofit sector shows similar trends. A conservative count suggests that the number grew by 539 during the 1990s, more than had been produced during the previous one hundred years (467), with most of those (356) completed during the 1980s (Peter Hall, personal communication). A more inclusive count confirms the explosion in dissertations but puts the number of new dissertations in the field above 1,400 for the 1990s to reach a cumulative total of more than 2,800 for the 1870–1999 period (Frances Huels, personal communication).

Similarly, the number of academic programs that offer at least three graduate level courses in the nonprofit sector has also grown, from seventeen in 1990 to eighty-six in 1999. These programs are located in a variety of academic homes, from freestanding programs and institutes, to traditional academic disciplines in the social sciences and humanities, to those that have become areas of specialization within existing professional degrees, such as the MPA, MBA, and MSW. The recent development of detailed guidelines for nonprofit management training through the collaborative efforts of the National Association of Schools of Public Affairs and Administration (the major accrediting body for MPA programs) and the Nonprofit Academic Centers Council, and the inclusion of nonprofit management in degree specializations ranked by *U.S. News and World Report* are just a few indicators of the extent to which the field of nonprofit studies has grown, matured, and become institutionalized.

These trends reflect a number of underlying forces, perhaps most obviously the growth of the sector itself—by an estimated 25,000 organizations per year according to IRS registration data and a doubling of its share of both paid employment and gross domestic product since the late 1970s—fueled largely by the growth in government spending over that period. Indeed, the sector is increasingly recognized as an economic, political, and social force in U.S. society. Devolution and privatization have encouraged policymakers to look to nonprofit service agencies as alternatives to direct government provision and have highlighted the role of local area service networks (in which nonprofits play prominent roles). At the same time, other types of nonprofits—membership and civic organizations that promote social capital and civic engagement—are thought to have declined, raising questions about the future of these key functions in democratic society.

The task of understanding the sector is indeed of major proportions, as this volume makes clear. Although the sector has grown and become more visible as indicated above, it is surprisingly difficult to comprehend how pervasive, ubiquitous, and complex the sector is. As a test, try reading your own local newspaper carefully from front to back, including announcements, obituaries, and want ads—everything in the paper. If your experience is like mine and that of my students, you will most likely be surprised to find that nonprofits surface everywhere—in 90 percent of the obituaries, in about one-quarter of reports on national and international news, and in the majority of items on local developments and events. Nonprofits appear both as the subject matter of newspaper reports, as commentators on specific issues, and as participants in or the site of events that are listed in the paper. But you need to know something about the sector to take this test—that all associations and churches are nonprofit, that social service agencies are mainly nonprofit as are some health organizations (but not all), and so forth.

Developing a cognitive map of the sector is difficult—but essential if we are to understand its capacities as well as its limitations. How are we to accomplish this? By analyzing the underlying puzzles of why people give money, goods, and time to strangers, of how such giving is structured, of the roles nonprofit institutions play in society, or what accounts for variations

in these dimensions across social groups, time, and space? By examining the sector's functions and the variety of tasks it performs for the overall society (enhancing innovation, pluralism, integration, and preservation), the policy process (providing negative feedback, societal support, and latent resources), or the individual (experiencing play, mystery/the sacred, and personal development)? By looking at the major fields of activities in the sector (by economic function or by primary purpose) and how these fields relate to the political economy? By disciplinary perspective (various social sciences and humanities)? By comparing the sector with those in other societies or in other time periods? By comparing it with the other sectors: business, government, and private households and how boundaries between the sectors shift over time?

The latter question gets to one of the key issues addressed in this volume: What is distinctive about the nonprofit sector? I would emphasize five major elements—all addressed by the readings in one way or the other. First, the sector operates under private, not public, auspices. That has important implications for how accountability is structured and carried out. Second, the sector operates under a particular ownership structure in which there are no formal ownership rights, with corresponding implications for the exercise of property rights, access to equity finance, and to a variety of revenue streams. Third, the sector is rooted in voluntarism. That means that the sector is inextricably intertwined with all the complexities associated with diverse values, motivations, incentives, and the vagaries of human behavior. It also means that the sector is centrally involved in confrontations, negotiations, and dispute resolutions. Fourth, the sector's purpose involves substantive rationality—the achievement of particular missions and substantive goals—not just profit for the sake of profit or reelection to political office for the sake of power. But substantive goals change over time and reflect environmental conditions, especially the political economy. What is a problem today may not be a problem fifty years from now or even ten years from now, because problems reflect the values and experiences of particular stakeholders along with their abilities to mobilize networks and cultural capital at a particular point in time.

Finally, the nonprofit sector operates with a particular type of technology. By and large, it does not produce things or process cases or transactions but seeks to change people—their views, values, behaviors, and/or knowledge. Thus, the nonprofit sector finds itself deeply immersed in uncertain causal structures—what, after all, does cause people to change their behavior or values, at least in the absence of coercive institutions? How do we transmit knowledge effectively? But changing people is difficult, interrupts routines, and is therefore painful for them and their surroundings. The nonprofit sector is composed of millions of organizations that experiment with those challenges.

I have emphasized these five elements because I believe they convey both the complexity and the importance of understanding the nonprofit sector. This volume of essential readings on the nonprofit sector, carefully edited to be accessible to students, professionals, and scholars alike, both reflects the important developments that

the sector has seen in recent years and is a major contribution in its own right. J. Steven Ott has succeeded in identifying, selecting, and editing a set of readings that takes us a long way toward making sense of the sector's complexity and recognizing its distinctive roles in the U.S. society. Although many scholars in the field will have a favorite selection that did not make it into the volume, everyone, whether specialist scholar, beginning student, or seasoned professional will benefit from a careful reading of the selections that are included. The introductory sections to the various parts of the book are of enormous help.

As someone who has taught both graduate and undergraduate courses in the field, I am painfully aware of the difficulty of developing a list of engaging readings that covers the major concepts and theories in the field. We owe the editor a major debt of gratitude for having produced this volume.

Kirsten A. Grønbjerg
School of Public and Environmental Affairs
Indiana University–Bloomington

Preface

Americans conduct almost all of their formally organized religious activity and many cultural and arts, human service, educational and research activities through private nonprofit organizations. American nonprofits have always received substantial support from local, state, and federal governments, and from fees paid by those who use their services, but they have also always relied on donations and voluntary service. . . . How did the United States come to rely so heavily on nonprofits? Why has it continued to do so? What are the consequences?

—David C. Hammack, *Making the Nonprofit Sector in the United States*

This book, *The Nature of the Nonprofit Sector,* is about the sector whose organizations engage in a surprisingly wide array of activities and provide an enormous range of services mostly for the purpose of improving aspects of the quality of life in the United States—or preventing their deterioration. *The Nature of the Nonprofit Sector* includes some of the most insightful, interesting, and useful readings to be found about the sector's nature, scope, history, theories, and the challenges it faces. All of its essays and readings present partial answers to two defining questions:

- What is "distinctive" about the nonprofit sector?
- What has caused it to be distinctive?

The Nature of the Nonprofit Sector is concerned only with "macro-level" issues and theories. It examines issues related to the existence, form, and functions of the sector, groups of organizations in the sector, and—at the lowest unit of analysis—individual organizations. In contrast, "micro-level" issues have as their unit of analysis the behavior of individuals and groups within organizations. Micro-level issues

are the sole focus of a companion book, *Understanding Nonprofit Organizations,* which I also edited.[1]

In attempting to provide "rich answers" to its two central questions, *The Nature of the Nonprofit Sector,* in effect, defines the nonprofit sector in a variety of ways. It does so by examining various elements and aspects of the sector from different perspectives. Each part of the book examines the sector from a specific point of view and emphasizes distinctive variables or factors in its analysis.

Part 1, "Introduction to the Nonprofit Sector," provides an overview of the sector's size, scope, and structure, including its largest subsectors, its myriad revenue sources, and the importance of voluntarism as an underlying value and as a human resource for many organizations in the sector.

Part 2, "The Nonprofit Sector's Distinctive Values and Contributions to Society," deals with the questions, "What is distinctive about the sector?" and "How and why is the nonprofit sector different from the public sector (government) and private sector (business), its foundational values and its role in and contributions to the sociopolitical economy of the United States?

Part 3, "Historical Evolution of the Nonprofit Sector," shows how the nonprofit sector is partially a product of its history. The historical development of the sector thus provides a third slant on its distinctiveness.

Part 4, "The Rationale for Tax Exemption" examines the influences of tax policy on the distinctiveness of organizations in the sector. It has been argued that the nonprofit sector is a "creation" or a "product" of our tax laws, codes, and rules. If so, the sector can be understood by learning about tax policy. This argument has some validity even though the approach is too limited for many purposes.

Parts 5 through 9 present important theories of the nonprofit sector, theories that explain its existence, forms and structures, and functions, including Part 5, "Overview Theories"; Part 6, "Economic and Political Theories"; Part 7, "Social and Community Theories"; Part 8, "Organization Theories"; and Part 9, "Giving Theories."

Part 10, "The Blending and Blurring of the Sectors," examines several pervasive political and economic changes that are taking place in the environment around the nonprofit sector, the responses of nonprofits to these changes, and some of the important effects these changes could have on nonprofits, the people they serve, government agencies, and perhaps on civil society in the United States.

Part 11, "Challenges Facing the Nonprofit Sector," continues the themes introduced in Part 10. Change always opens new opportunities, but for the nonprofit sector at the start of the twenty-first century, it also is creating challenges of near crisis proportions.

The nonprofit sector as we know it is a particularly unique democratic phenomenon. In some respects it is the most capitalistic approach to meeting community needs and providing public goods. In other societies with more centralized government systems, similar types of needs are met through tax-supported government programs and services. Yet, as several chapters in this book emphasize, the lines between the nonprofit sector, government, and business are blurring and blending. As we enter the new century, the nonprofit sector faces monumental challenges.

Criteria for Selection

Several criteria were used to make the final selection of readings included in this book. First, the reading needed to affirmatively address the following three questions:

- Should the serious student of the nonprofit sector be expected to be able to identify the authors and their basic themes—the crux of their arguments?
- Does the reading provide a reason or reasons why the nonprofit sector exists in its current form and/or why organizations in the sector engage in (or refrain from engaging in) particular types of activities?
- Does it help to explain how the sector developed, how it fits into the sociopolitical economy of U.S. society, its distinctive characteristics and contributions, or the paramount challenges that it faces?

The second criterion was related to the first. Each reading had to make a statement that represented a line of thinking that has persisted over the years. This criterion did not eliminate controversial readings—quite the contrary. Citations and quotations often are used as the justification for or the lead-in to opposing arguments. This criterion simply required that a reading must take a position—make a statement—that could not be ignored. The newly written readings are exceptions to this criterion. Obviously, new articles have not been cited or quoted as extensively as those written ten, twenty, or thirty years earlier. Thus, I had to be more subjective when making editorial decisions about inclusions and exclusions of recent publications. In my judgment, the newly penned selections that are included will fare well against the test of time.

Third, the article had to be readable. Students who have already had reason to peruse the literature of nonprofit organizations will appreciate the importance of this criterion.

Finally, the reading had to fit in this volume. It had to address issues or ideas that are important to the nonprofit sector, nonprofit organizations as entities that make up the sector, or nonprofit organizations as elements in networks or systems. Because this book is about "macro-issues" and "macro-theories"—not "micro-issues" and "micro-theories"—many interesting readings about the internal structures and workings of nonprofit organizations have been included in the companion book, *Understanding Nonprofit Organizations.* Most readings that I reviewed fit rather cleanly in either one book or the other. Decisions as to where they belonged were easy to make. In a few areas, though, the line is not absolutely clear. Readings about contracts and relationships between organizations in different sectors were perhaps the most difficult to place.

The placement of readings into specific parts was not always as easy as I had expected. For example, philanthropy represents an integral part of the sector's distinctive foundational values. The history of philanthropy is inexorably intertwined with the history of the sector. Tax policy in the United States both influenced and was influenced by the history of philanthropy. Thus, finding the "right home" for a reading about the history of philanthropy or the history of tax policy presented a challenge. In several cases, I had to simply make a decision, but I could have easily placed some readings in any of several parts.

Acknowledgments

I truly wish that I could acknowledge everyone who contributed ideas, insights, support, challenges, and constructive criticisms during the creation and development of this volume. Space and propriety, however, require that I limit my statements of appreciation to those who played central roles in shaping my early vision and preliminary ideas into a cohesive anthology. Among those whose intellectual contributions absolutely must be acknowledged are Stephen Block, Denver Options and the University of Colorado–Denver; William Boise, New York University; Kirsten Grønbjerg, Indiana University–Bloomington; Kevin Kearns, University of Pittsburgh; Naomi Wish, Seton Hall University; Jacquelyn Thayer Scott, University College of Cape Breton; and Albert Hyde, The Brookings Institution. Jared Bennett and Brigham Daniels, of the University of Utah, provided invaluable assistance with several chapters. Frederick Lane, City University of New York, graciously took the time several years ago to offer suggestions about how to improve the organization of a book to fit better with a graduate course on nonprofits.

Gary Scrivner, University of Arizona Foundation, graciously agreed to rewrite and update his historical analysis of tax policy changes and their effects on charitable organizations. Dr. Scrivner's original version was published in the 1990 book *The Nonprofit Organization: Essential Readings.*[2] Thanks also to dozens of graduate students at the Universities of Utah, Maine, and Pittsburgh who critiqued many of these readings as course assignments over the years.

Finally, I owe a special debt of gratitude to David Gies, Animal Assistance Foundation, Denver, Colorado, and to Jay Shafritz, University of Pittsburgh, my collaborators in editing the 1990 book *The Nonprofit Organization: Essential Readings.* Their forward thinking and insight helped shape my thinking about the sector, and thus contributed to the concepts for this book.

J. Steven Ott
University of Utah

Notes

1. J. Steven Ott, ed., *Understanding Nonprofit Organizations* (Boulder: Westview Press, 2001).

2. David L. Gies, J. Steven Ott, and Jay M. Shafritz, eds., *The Nonprofit Organization: Essential Readings* (Fort Worth, Tex.: Harcourt Brace, 1990). Brooks/Cole, of Pacific Grove, California, originally published this book. It is now out of print.

PART 1

INTRODUCTION TO THE NONPROFIT SECTOR

Defining the Nonprofit Sector by What It Is Not and What It Does Not Do

In many respects, the easiest way to describe or define the nonprofit sector is to identify what it *is not* and what it *does not do.** For example, making money *is not* the central purpose for organizations in the nonprofit sector. It isn't that making money is unimportant to nonprofits—quite the contrary. It is the relative importance of making money that distinguishes the nonprofit sector from the private or business sector. In the private sector, making money—or, more precisely, making profits—comes first. In the nonprofit sector, making money is necessary but *not* primary. Achieving other ends comes first. Revenues are resources, *not* the end purpose.

However, the same is true in the public sector. Revenues are resources used by government to advance the public good—not ends in themselves. What then separates the nonprofit sector from the public sector? Quite obviously, government raises revenue through taxes that are imposed on individuals and businesses, and nonprofits *do not* have taxing power. They raise revenue from a number of sources. Historically, the largest revenue sources for the nonprofit sector have been the millions of individuals and corporations who decide voluntarily to support the missions and activities of nonprofits through donations of time, effort, and money.[1] Although advancement of "the public good" usually is the central purpose for both nonprofit and public sector organizations, nonprofits *are not* government and, until recent decades, *had not been* "government-like."

Also, many organizations in the nonprofit sector *do not* pay federal, state, or local taxes, and individuals and corporations who give money (or other assets) to some types of nonprofits are

---

*Portions of this essay were written by David L. Gies and were published originally in David L. Gies, J. Steven Ott, and Jay M. Shafritz, eds., *The Nonprofit Sector: Essential Readings* (Ft. Worth, Tex.: Harcourt Brace, 1990), pp. xxiii–xxv. Mr. Gies currently is with the Animal Assistance Foundation, Denver, Colorado.

permitted to deduct the gift from their federal and state income taxes and thus *do not* pay taxes on that amount of their income.

However, trying to define the nonprofit sector by what it is not is neither very useful nor satisfying. Nonprofits are much more than what they are not. The sector's distinctive aspects and its invaluable contributions to society cannot be "captured" by defining it only in negatives. The proclivity of some authors to define the nonprofit sector by what it is not caused Roger Lohmann to write an article aptly titled "And Lettuce Is Nonanimal," in which he muses:

> Virtually all nonprofit management theories explicitly or implicitly begin with this negative accent and contribute to the paradoxical consensus position that nonprofit action has no independent basis. Nonprofits arise only from the failures of other institutions but are themselves inefficient, unproductive, poorly managed or mismanaged, and inadequately controlled.[2]

Defining the Nonprofit Sector in Positive Terms

Stating what the nonprofit sector *is* and *does* in positive terms, and why, is a considerably more difficult task. In this attempt, I have drawn upon the thinking of economists, sociologists, historians, organization theorists, political scientists, political economists, accountants, social workers, philanthropists, nonprofit executives, and public administrators. I have also tried to define the sector in positive terms by examining the distinctiveness of the fundamental challenges facing it today and the likely consequences of the ways in which the sector faces up to these challenges.

In some respects, the nonprofit sector is a particularly unique product of the democratic capitalistic governmental systems that have evolved in the United States. From this perspective, it is a means for reacting to marketplace failures by filling economic voids with volunteer time and charitable contributions and for filling voids left by government agencies that cannot or will not adequately serve citizens in need. In other respects, it is a product of the colonial era—a time and set of circumstances in which survival was possible only if neighbors banded together into voluntary associations for mutual assistance. It is in this aspect of the sector's distinctiveness that voluntarism and voluntary associations emerge as defining forces for the nonprofit sector.

> In few countries is the system of aid [for persons in need] more complicated and confusing, however, than in the United States. Reflecting a deep-seated tradition of individualism and an ingrained hostility to centralized institutions, Americans have resisted the worldwide movement toward predominantly governmental approaches to social welfare provision, adding new governmental protections only with great reluctance, and then structuring them in ways that preserve a substantial private life.[3]

People everywhere respond to problems by coming together out of mutual caring, organizing their efforts, and initiating activities and programs to ameliorate, remedy, or "pick up the pieces" behind society's problems or nature's disasters. Poverty, ignorance, illiteracy, child and spousal abuse, birth defects, genetic defects, prejudice, physical and mental illnesses, hurricanes, tornadoes, earthquakes, floods—the list goes on endlessly. Different strategies are used to deal with these causes and cases: Some associations provide services to individuals or groups in need; others try to eliminate the causes of the needs.

People also come together for positive uplifting reasons, such as to worship together and to create and share art, history, literature, and poetry. Still others gather to preserve a part of their history or culture, to advance the standing of their professions or industries, or simply to enjoy themselves.[4]

Repeatedly throughout the history of the United States, citizens have recognized a need and then built a nonprofit constituency that was committed to ameliorating, solving, or eliminating it, even though the issue or the people associated with it often were socially undesirable at the time. In instance after instance over the decades and centuries, this voluntary process has been used to change public policy and government support—or tolerance—for what was originally a politically unacceptable cause, case, or issue. The provision of services to people with mental retardation, mental illness, and related disabilities is a widely cited example. Prior to the 1960s, very little was done for people with chronic mental illness or developmental disabilities beyond the efforts of parents and relatives who struggled through mazes of limited, disconnected, and segregated services. Large state institutions—or warehouses, depending on one's point of view—were the dubious exceptions. What few community services there were typically had been established by or through organizations established and operated voluntarily by parents and other relatives. Over time, parents who shared concerns about the lack of services and access to them established organizations for mutual support, advocacy, and public information.

This type of organization gave members strength and power to speak their views of "the general welfare" and "domestic tranquillity" needs of their children and themselves. A small sampling of typical organizations' names communicates this point vividly: the Alliance for the Mentally Ill, ARC, Alzheimer's Association, Big Brothers/Big Sisters, Child Abuse Prevention Center, Citizens Against Physical and Mental Abuse, Community Treatment Alternatives, Disabilities Law Center, Everyone Should Have a Home, Gay and Lesbian Community Center, Help for Kids, Homeless Children's Foundation, Independent Living Center, Intermountain Therapy Animals, Make-a-Wish Foundation, Literacy Action Center, and People with AIDS Coalition.[5] Many programs such as these were initiated by faith-based organizations, often in response to pleas from their members.

Primarily because of grassroots campaigns conducted by parents of people with mental retardation, all state legislatures passed laws in the early 1960s establishing and funding systems of services. In most states, nonprofit organizations became the leading providers of direct community-based services, working in the seams—the crevices—between government agencies and for-profit enterprises. Similar sagas could be told about services for people with chronic mental illness, Alzheimer's disease, muscular dystrophy, multiple sclerosis, and cystic fibrosis; individuals who have suffered strokes and physical, psychological, and/or sexual abuse; who live in poverty; who are homeless. The same is true for myriad art appreciation programs, symphony orchestras, museums, zoos, and botanical gardens. Each of these public assets was started by individuals coming together voluntarily in associations to advance their cause or case.

Early in the nineteenth century, Alexis de Tocqueville documented his amazement at the degree of shared control and responsibility for efforts to meet community needs that existed in the United States.[6] Tocqueville observed that in contrast with the U.S. experience, throughout Europe the "secondary power"—the ability of the nobility, cities, and provincial bodies to represent local affairs—had been relinquished to the centralized authorities. Such centralization eliminated the need for the development of philanthropy in Europe. Tocqueville wrote:

> My object is to remark that all these various rights which have been successively wrested, in our time, from classes, guilds, and individuals have not served to raise new secondary powers on a more democratic basis, but have uniformly been concentrated in the hands of the sovereign. Everywhere the state acquires more and more direct control over the humblest members of the community and a more exclusive power of governing each of them in his smallest concerns.
>
> Almost all the charitable establishments of Europe were formerly in the hands of private persons or of guilds; they are now almost all dependent on the supreme government, and in many countries are actually administered by that power. The state almost exclusively undertakes to supply bread to the hungry, assistance and shelter to the sick, work to the idle, and to act as the sole reliever of all kinds of misery.[7]

Tocqueville's "secondary power" is what we refer to today as activities that serve the public good. Indeed, Tocqueville's discussion continues today where it is focused on concepts of the *public good, common goods,* and *private goods.* (See Parts 5 and 6 for more about these concepts.) Who is responsible for what? What is to be held as a common good? What are the limits of self-interest? It is also focused on the concept of *social capital,* networks of trust, goodwill, and obligations that are created as a by-product of people working together to achieve one end and that can be called upon in the future to achieve other ends. (See Part 7.)

There is no supreme government agency that is responsible for services to homeless people or individuals with HIV/AIDS. Services to people with HIV/AIDS became a national topic only after local groups, often church-related, recognized the need and organized to do something—despite angry opposition and threats from most neighbors, many churches, and politicians. As the means to meet new needs becomes more apparent, volunteers organize under the auspices of nonprofit organizations; grant applications are submitted to private foundations and government agencies; "special events" are sponsored to raise funds; programs develop and community awareness of the problem expands; and communities respond with new or adapted public social programs. Often, the need is redefined and articulated as communities gain experience in dealing with it. In time, new patterns of services are created. In some cases, the unpopular cause and the people affected directly by it, begin to regain public acceptance. If so, government may step forward with financial assistance. Secondary power thereby affects the community and national consciousness, philosophy, and programs. This is pluralism at its best—freedom helping to preserve social order.[8]

The Subsectors: Defining the Nonprofit Sector by Its Purposes

The Internal Revenue Service Codes identify and define about thirty types of nonprofit organizations. The IRS Codes provide a glimpse of the types of purposes and activities that are characteristic of nonprofit organizations. They include qualified pension and profit-sharing trusts; individual retirement accounts (IRAs); publicly supported charitable organizations, including religious, scientific, educational, and similar-purpose organizations, and private foundations; civic leagues and social welfare organizations; labor, agricultural, and horticultural organizations; business leagues, chambers of commerce, and boards of trade; fraternal beneficiary societies; benevolent life insurance associations; cemetery companies; state-chartered credit unions and mutual reserve funds; cooperative crop financing organizations; veterans' organizations; black lung benefit trusts; cooperative hospital services organizations; farmers' cooperatives; political organizations; homeowners' associations; and charitable remainder trusts.

In 1989, Michael O'Neill proposed a useful set of categories of subsectors that illustrates the types of purposes, issues, and causes that engage nonprofit organizations.[9]

- Religious organizations
- Private education and research
- Health care
- Arts and culture
- Social services
- Advocacy and legal services
- International assistance
- Foundations and corporate funders
- Mutual benefit organizations

These subsectors are, in effect, "fields of interest"; they identify the functional reasons why organizations in the nonprofit sector exist and what they do. These are the clusters of causes and cases that engage the attention and the emotions of volunteers, donors, and grantors. They are the sources of energy, the purposes that activate individuals and groups to form or join nonprofit associations, give of themselves and their money, and *do something.*

Corporatized Nonprofits: Are They in the Sector?

Many nonprofits do not look, feel, or act very much like the mental images that most of us have of nonprofit organizations. Some large nonprofit health care (including many hospitals), insurance, financial services, and mutual benefit companies are not—and do not begin to resemble—voluntary associations.[10] Many of the highly commercial or *corporatized nonprofits* originated as voluntary associations but have long since changed into large businesslike organizations in almost all respects. The Blue Cross/Blue Shield insurance organizations, credit unions, and the American Association for Retired Persons (AARP) are prime examples. These nonprofits (and many others) are all but indistinguishable from the for-profit firms that are in the same lines of business. Likewise, nonprofits that depend heavily on government contracts to fund the services they provide (particularly in the human services) can be difficult to identify as "nonprofit organizations"—in the sense that most of us use the words. Many have become almost indistinguishable from the government agencies with which they contract.

Although the corporatized nonprofits technically are in the nonprofit sector, they are "on the edge" of it. They make it difficult to explain the sector in positive rather than negative terms. It may be that the only way to define the sector so that it reasonably includes the corporatized nonprofits is to take a purely legalistic approach: An organization is a nonprofit if it meets criteria set forth in the tax laws and tax codes. This approach, though, is not particularly useful for most purposes, and it certainly is not uplifting. The legalistic approach also opens the door for the Congress and state legislatures to change the laws—to enact legislation that restricts the activities of corporatized nonprofits and alters the tax codes to stiffen eligibility requirements for tax exemption.[11] The corporatized nonprofit organizations also represent a potential danger for others in the sector, who could be affected by any legislative actions that are "aimed at" them.

Readings Included in This Part

The readings that are reprinted in this part introduce three complementary views of the nonprofit sector that explore different dimensions of its existence and activities.

Virginia Hodgkinson and Murray Weitzman, with their associates at the Washington, D.C.–based Independent Sector, have collected data regularly over the past two decades and produced statistical profiles of the sector and its place in the U.S. economy and society. "The State of the Independent Sector" is a summary of their 1995–1996 report, which describes the sector's size, shape, revenues, and composition. Hodgkinson and Weitzman present numerous trends including the sector's share of the U.S. economy, its sources of revenue (for the sector in total and for each of the major subsectors), changes in the number of charitable nonprofit organizations, and the formation of new nonprofits. "The State of the Independent Sector" also includes statistical series on variables such as the average age and size of nonprofits, the average number of employees, and employee diversity. A few interesting trends reported by Hodgkinson and Weitzman include the following:

- In 1992, the most recent year for which data were available, there were 1.03 million nonprofit entities with total annual funds of $509 billion.
- The number of publicly supported charitable nonprofit 501(c)(3) organizations registered with the IRS grew by 4.7 percent annually and nearly doubled between 1977 and 1992.
- "The most remarkable change [in revenue sources] over this period [1977 to 1992] was the decline in the share of total annual funds represented by private contributions and the increase in the share represented by government sources. In 1992 private contributions were 18 percent of total funds, down from 26 percent in 1977. Government payments represented 27 percent of total annual funds in 1977, and 31 percent in 1992."
- The sector's income grew rapidly from 1977 to 1994. The nonprofit sector's annual growth was about 3.7 percent, whereas the increase in all sectors combined was only 2.2 percent.
- Most nonprofit organizations are quite small. Forty-one percent of the nonprofits that filed annual reports with the IRS in 1993 had annual expenses less than $100,000.
- Paid employment in the sector grew by 3.3 percent annually between 1977 and 1994, to 15.1 million employees.
- The nonprofit sector is more diverse than the other two sectors. In 1994, 68 percent of all paid employees in the nonprofit sector were women and 15 percent were African American, compared with 44 and 10 percent respectively in the other sectors.
- The number of private foundations increased by 70 percent to 37,571 between 1980 and 1993.

Lester Salamon's "Scope and Structure: The Anatomy of America's Nonprofit Sector" provides a comprehensive and multidimensional overview of the nonprofit sector, often using data provided by Hodgkinson and Weitzman. In this introduction to the sector, Salamon "seeks to make some sense of the vast array of institutions that comprise the American nonprofit sector, to examine the basic anatomy or architecture of this sector and the scope and scale of some of its constituent parts." Salamon thus explores sector characteristics such as public-serving versus member-serving organizations; nonprofits as funding intermediaries; and the size, shape, revenue sources, and expenditures in the major subsectors.

"Voluntary Sector," by Jacquelyn Thayer Scott, moves the focus of this part away from data and to the nonprofit sector's history, theories, and challenges. Her essay is about the voluntariness of the sector—the nonprofit sector's bedrock values of philanthropy, charity, and volunteering (see also Parts 2 and 9). Scott explains:

> Activities in this [voluntary] sector are usually conducted by formal organizational entities that are incorporated and governed by boards of directors and operate under a non-distribution constraint (i.e., profits or residual earnings of the organization may not be distributed to individuals who control the entity). . . . When formally incorporated or registered [as charitable nonprofits], organizations in this sector must have clearly designated public-benefit purposes—usually related to religion, health, education, or social welfare—and partisan political activities by the entity are either prohibited or severely curtailed.[12]

Scott cautions that the task of defining the nonprofit sector by "the nature of its purpose, governance, and source or distribution of its funding . . . has proven quite complex." Thus, she approaches this task instead by examining its history, theories, and most important challenges. Scott concludes with a note on issues and concerns that are common to voluntary sector organizations in other nations: "Common challenges [across cultures] are identified as including promoting individual participation in voluntary activity, guaranteeing freedom of association, strengthening managerial capacity, and maintaining independence and political viability for voluntary organizations."

Notes

1. The readings by Hodgkinson and Weitzman and by Salamon that are included in this part and all of Parts 6 and 10 expand on this trend. The percent of the nonprofit sector's total revenues from private donations has decreased over the past two decades as government's share and fees-for-services have increased. The trend has affected organizations in various subsectors quite differently.

2. Roger A. Lohmann, "And Lettuce Is Nonanimal: Toward a Positive Economics of Voluntary Action," *Nonprofit and Voluntary Sector Quarterly* 18 (4), Winter 1989, p. 368.

3. Lester M. Salamon, *America's Nonprofit Sector: A Primer,* 2nd ed. (New York: Foundation Center, 1999), p. 1.

4. David Horton Smith, "The Impact of the Volunteer Sector in Society," in D. H. Smith, *Voluntary Action Research* (Lexington, Mass.: Lexington, 1973); and Lester M. Salamon, "The Contributions of the Nonprofit Sector," in L. M. Salamon, *Holding the Center: America's Nonprofit Sector at a Crossroads* (New York: Nathan Cummings Foundation, 1997).

5. These organization names were selected from the Utah Nonprofits Association's 1999 roster of members.

6. Alexis de Tocqueville, *Democracy in America* (New York: Knopf, 1840).

7. Ibid., vol. 2, pp. 303–304.

8. Robert N. Bellah, Richard Madsen, William M. Sullivan, Ann Swidler, and Steven M. Tipton, *Habits of the Heart: Individualism and Commitment in American Life* (Berkeley: University of California Press, 1985).

9. Michael O'Neill, *The Third America: The Emergence of the Nonprofit Sector in the United States* (San Francisco: Jossey-Bass, 1989). For his book, *America's Nonprofit Sector: A Primer,* 2nd ed. (New York: Foundation Center, 1999), Lester Salamon reduces O'Neill's list to six "key subsectors": health care; education; social services; arts, culture, and recreation; advocacy, legal services, and international aid; and religion.

10. There are differences, but they can be difficult to identify and are not always viewed as important enough to warrant favorable tax treatment. See Parts 4 and 10.

11. See Parts 4, 10, and 11.

12. Jacquelyn Thayer Scott, "Voluntary Sector," in Jay M. Shafritz, ed., *International Encyclopedia of Public Policy and Administration* (Boulder: Westview Press, 1998), p. 2361. By limiting her discussion to the "voluntary sector," Scott is deliberately excluding the corporatized, commercial-like nonprofits.

References

Bellah, Robert N., Richard Madsen, William M. Sullivan, Ann Swidler, and Steven M. Tipton. *Habits of the Heart: Individualism and Commitment in American Life.* Berkeley: University of California Press, 1985.

Gies, David L., J. Steven Ott, and Jay M. Shafritz, eds. *The Nonprofit Sector: Essential Readings.* Fort Worth, Tex.: Harcourt Brace, 1990.

Hansmann, Henry. *The Ownership of Enterprise.* Cambridge, Mass.: Belknap Press, 1996.

Hodgkinson, Virginia A., and Murray S. Weitzman. *Nonprofit Almanac, 1996–1997: Dimensions of the Independent Sector.* San Francisco: Jossey-Bass, 1996.

Lohmann, Roger A. "And Lettuce Is Nonanimal: Toward a Positive Economics of Voluntary Action." *Nonprofit and Voluntary Sector Quarterly* 18 (4), Winter 1989, 367–383.

O'Neill, Michael. *The Third America: The Emergence of the Nonprofit Sector in the United States.* San Francisco: Jossey-Bass, 1989.

Pennock, J. Roland, and John W. Chapman, eds. *Voluntary Associations.* New York: Atherton, 1969.

Salamon, Lester M. *America's Nonprofit Sector: A Primer,* 2nd ed. New York: Foundation Center, 1999.

_____. *Holding the Center: America's Nonprofit Sector at a Crossroads.* New York: Nathan Cummings Foundation, 1997.

_____. *Partners in Public Service: Government-Nonprofit Relations in the Modern Welfare State.* Baltimore: Johns Hopkins University Press, 1995.

Scott, Jacquelyn Thayer. "Voluntary Sector." In Jay M. Shafritz, ed., *International Encyclopedia of Public Policy and Administration,* pp. 2358–2362. Boulder: Westview, 1998.

Smith, David Horton. *Voluntary Action Research.* Lexington, Mass.: Lexington, 1973.

Tocqueville, Alexis de. *Democracy in America.* New York: Knopf, 1840.

Van Til, John. *Mapping the Third Sector: Voluntarism in a Changing Social Economy.* New York: Foundation Center, 1988.

CHAPTER 1

Overview:
The State of the Independent Sector

Virginia Ann Hodgkinson and
Murray S. Weitzman

The independent sector (or the nonprofit, third, or voluntary sector) includes a diverse array of organizations serving public purposes. These include organizations in health, human services, arts and culture, foundations and federated fund-raising organizations, religious organizations, educational and research institutions, and advocacy organizations. They range in size from the high school band booster club, church soup kitchen, or choirs to the great hospitals, universities and museums. As with the government and business sectors, the independent sector is influenced by a host of factors, including the state of the national economy, the status of changing populations and various public policies. But, perhaps, unique to the independent sector are some of its sources of support—voluntary time and contributions. This volume documents the various changes and developments in the independent sector over the last third of a century and reveals some of the aspirations, accomplishments and shortcomings of society.

The Independent Sector and Its Share of the U.S. Economy

The independent sector, with few exceptions, expanded faster than other sectors of the econ-omy. For nearly two decades, the independent sector has continued to grow as an important part of the service economy. Much of this growth can be attributed to federal legislation providing support for Medicare and Medicaid, education grants, programs of support in housing, job training and other social welfare programs. Many new organizations were founded to meet human needs and accomplish societal goals.

National data series reveal this growth. The annual rate of change in the national income accounts shows that the increase for all sectors of the economy was 2.2 percent from 1977 to 1994. In the independent sector, the annual increase, including the assigned value for volunteer time, was 3.7 percent, compared with 2.1 percent in the for-profit business sector and 2.3 percent in government. Over this same period, the annual rate of change in total nonagricultural employment was 1.9 percent. The annual rate of increase in total employment in the independent sector was 3.3 percent, compared with 1.9 percent in the business sector and 1.4 percent in government.

In 1992, the most recent base year, the independent sector had total annual funds of $509 billion. The sector included 1.03 million institutions, 4.2 percent of all entities. Approximately 6.5 percent of national income was generated in the independent sector, up from 5.8 percent in 1987. It employed 15.1 million people in 1994—9.7 million full and part-time employees and 5.5 million full-time employee equivalent volunteers. From 1977 to 1992, the annual rate of growth in paid employment in the independent sector was 3.4 percent. Combined, paid employees and full-time equivalent volunteers represented nearly 11 percent of total employment in the U.S. economy in 1992, up from 8.5 percent in 1977. From 1992 to 1994, the growth in the independent sector began to decline. Total annual funds were estimated at $568 billion in 1994, and the annual rate of growth in paid employment grew at 2.9 percent. As a result, the sector's share of national income in 1994 declined to 6.3 percent (Table 1.1).

Other statistical series also point to the growth of the independent sector within the service economy. Between 1960 and 1993, current operating expenditures of the nonprofit sector as a percentage of gross domestic product

more than doubled from 3.6 percent in 1963 to 7.9 percent in 1993.

From 1977 to 1994, the growth rate of the independent sector was greatest between 1977 and 1982 and between 1987 and 1992. Between 1982 and 1987, the sector grew at a slower rate that resulted from a round of federal budget cuts aimed at reducing the growth of federal funding. However, by the mid-1980s the growth in Medicare and Medicaid entitlement funding offset some of the earlier federal budget cuts. In addition, Congress did not further cut the growth rates in other domestic federal programs. Other major events and changes in public policy occurred during the 1980s and early 1990s that had an impact on the independent sector; these included a major recession during the early 1980s and again in the early 1990s; significant growth in the stock market in the early 1980s and again in the 1990s; a major reduction in inflation; a massive transformation in the corporate sector of the economy; a significant increase

TABLE 1.1   Summary for the Independent Sector, 1977–1994 (dollars in bilions, numbers in thousands)

Independent Sector	1994(p)	1992	1977
Numer of entities in the U.S.	NA	24,456	15,944
Independent sector	NA	1,030	739
Percentage independent sector	NA	4.2%	4.6%
National income including value of volunteer time	$4,491.3	$4,989.6	$1,705.1
Percentage independent sector	6.3%	6.5%	4.9%
Total U.S. employment	143,108	137,388	103,933
Independent sector	15,118	14,628	8,791
Paid employees (full and part-time)	9,656	9,128	5,520
Volunteers (full-time employee equivalent)	5,462	5,500	3,271
As a percentage of total U.S. employment	10.6%	10.6%	8.5%
Paid employees (full and part-time)	6.7%	6.6%	5.3%
Volunteers (full-time employee equivalent)	3.8%	4.0%	3.1%
Total annual funds—independent sector	$568.4	$508.5	$111.1
Health services	NA	51.4%	46.2%
Education/research	NA	18.6%	24.7%
Religious organizations	NA	11.5%	12.2%
Social and legal services	NA	10.9%	9.3%
Civic, social and fraternal organizations	NA	2.9%	3.8%
Arts and culture	NA	1.6%	1.5%
Foundations	NA	3.1%	2.3%

SOURCE: *Nonprofit Almanac 1996–1997.*

(p) = Preliminary.

NA = Not available.

in personal wealth, particularly among the top 2 percent of the population; and a continuing erosion in real wages and household income among workers and their families in 80 percent of households. All of these changes affected the various sectors of the economy differently.

Trends in Annual Sources of Funds

The composition of the major sources of funding for the independent sector changed significantly from 1977 to 1992. The combination of private contributions, private payments, and government grants and payments constituted 89 percent of the total sources of funds in the independent sector in 1992. The most remarkable change over this period was the decline in the share of total annual funds represented by private contributions and the increase in the share represented by government sources. In 1992, private contributions were 18 percent of total funds, down from 26 percent in 1977. Government payments represented 27 percent of total annual funds in 1977, and 31 percent in 1992. In 1992 private payments, primarily in the form of

dues, fees and charges constituted 39 percent, up from 38 percent in 1977.

One of the major reasons for variation in revenue composition was the changing annual rate of change for the various sources of funds over this period. Private contributions had an annual rate of increase of 2.7 percent; private payments of 5.4 percent; and government payments of 6.3 percent. In summary, while the annual rate of increase in total annual funds for the independent sector was 5.1 percent, the annual rates of growth by source of funds varied throughout the period (Figure 1.1).

The annual rate of change in private contributions varied between 1977 and 1992. Private contributions grew at a rate higher than that of government only between the years of 1982 and 1987 (5.7 percent compared with 4.5 percent). Between 1987 and 1992, private contributions grew at an annual rate of 1.3 percent, compared with an 8.3 annual rate of increase in funding from government. Private contributions increased at an annual rate of 3.5 percent between 1992 and 1994. Rates of increase in private contributions are affected by changes in the economy and tax policy. The greatest rate of increase in charitable contributions occurred between

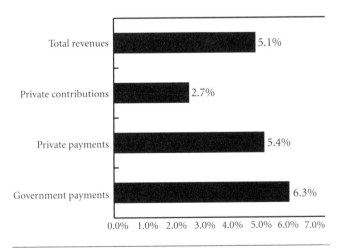

FIGURE 1.1   Annual Rates of Change for Selected Sources of Funds for the Independent Sector, 1977–1992

SOURCE: *Nonprofit Almanac 1996–1997*

1982 and 1987 and can be attributed to the concurrent growth in the stock market and reduction in inflation. Lower rates of change from 1987 to 1992 are attributed to the 1990 recession and changes implemented by the 1986 Tax Act which lowered tax rates and changed the valuation of appreciated property on gifts. With the changes made in the 1993 Tax Act which returned the full valuation for gifts of appreciated property and the growing strength of the stock market and the economy, private contributions increased more substantially between 1992 and 1994.

Much of the increase in government funding can be attributed to the growth rate in entitlement funds, such as Medicare and Medicaid, as well as price increases in general health care. These entitlement programs grew to respond to an aging population, increased access to Medicaid for people with various types of disabilities; an increase in poor children, in both number and proportion of the total population; and an increase in the proportion of the population below the poverty line.

Trends Among the Major Subsectors of the Independent Sector

The two subsectors that demonstrated the highest rate of growth from 1977 to 1992 were the health services subsector and the social and legal services subsector. The health services subsector increased its share of total annual funds of the independent sector from 46 percent in 1977 to 51 percent in 1992. This subsector dominated the independent sector in people employed, revenues and current operating expenditures. The social and legal services subsector increased its share from 9 to 11 percent (Figure 1.2).

One major reason for the various changes in the proportion of total funds represented by the major subsectors was their variable rates of growth. The social and legal services subsector had the highest annual increase at 6.3 percent, followed by the health services subsector at 5.9 percent. The education subsector had the lowest annual growth at 3.2 percent. In 1977, the edu-

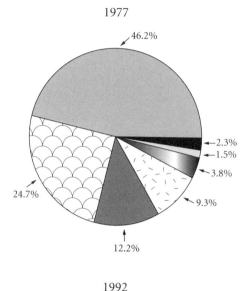

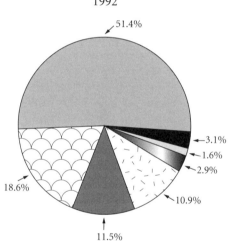

Health services
Education/research
Religious organizations
Social and legal services
Civic, social and fraternal organizations
Arts and culture
Foundations

FIGURE 1.2 Share of Total Funds for Selected Subsectors in the Independent Sector, 1977 and 1992

SOURCE: *Nonprofit Almanac 1996–1997.*

cation subsector represented nearly 25 percent of total annual funds for the independent sector; by 1992, it represented just under 19 percent. The religion and civic, social and fraternal subsectors also had a lower annual rate of change, each at 3.3 percent. The arts and culture subsector had an annual rate of change of 5.5 percent (Figure 1.3).

Health Services

In 1992, total annual funds in the health services subsector were $261 billion, representing 51 percent of total annual funds for the independent sector. This subsector, which is dominated by hospitals, also includes nursing and personal care facilities, and other health services—such as home health care, kidney dialysis services,

and outpatient alcohol and drug treatment—grew for a variety of reasons, including: an aging population; an increase in persons, especially children, in poverty; and increases in the cost of health care. The annual rate of change in funds from government was 7.5 percent from 1977 to 1992. This annual rate of change increased in the later years; for example, the annual rate of change was lowest from 1982 to 1987 at 4.7 percent, then increased to 9.9 percent between 1987 and 1992. Government payments accounted for 32 percent of funds in 1977 and 41 percent in 1992. The change was a result of, primarily, increased payments from Medicare and Medicaid. During this same period, private contributions to this subsector experienced an annual rate of change of 0.5 percent.

These figures do not reveal that, compared with other components of the health services

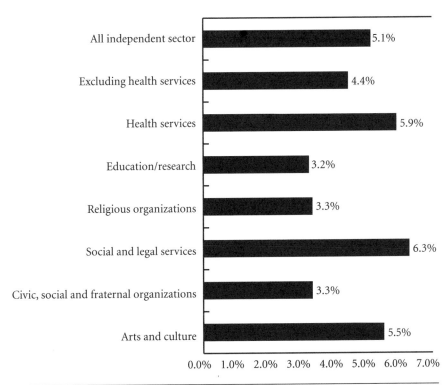

FIGURE 1.3   Annual Rates of Change for Total Revenue, Independent Sector and Selected Subsectors: 1977–1992

SOURCE: *Nonprofit Almanac 1996–1997.*

subsector, growth in hospitals slowed down over this period, or that the whole health care subsector's composition was changing. While there was little change in the position among the independent sector's hospitals over this period, and an actual decline in the total number of hospitals, the real changes in the health sector were the rapid growth in nursing and personal care facilities and other health services components. From 1982 to 1992, the independent sector increased its share of total institutions in the nursing and personal care facilities component from 21 to 28 percent and its share of total revenues from 27 to 31 percent. In another component—other health services—the for-profit sector demonstrated major growth. From 1982 to 1992, the independent sector's share of this component declined from 43 to 31 percent of total institutions, and from 54 to 39 percent of total revenues.

The health services sector of the economy revealed the major restructuring occurring in the delivery of health services in our society. In terms of the share of each of these major components of the health services sector from 1982 to 1992, the independent sector increased its share of total revenues from hospitals by 4.1 percent among the three sectors of the economy, and by 15 percent in the nursing and personal care component. In the other health services component, however, its share of total revenues declined by 27 percent, indicating a much higher rate of growth within this area in the for-profit sector of health care. From 1977 to 1992, this subsector increased its share of the total revenues in the independent sector from 46.2 to 51.4 percent.

Social and Legal Services

In 1992, the social and legal services subsector had $56 billion in total revenues, representing 11.0 percent of total revenues for the independent sector. This subsector includes the major components of legal services, individual and family services, job training and related services, child day care services, residential care, and social services not elsewhere classified (n.e.c.). The

social and legal services subsector experienced an annual increase in total revenues of 6.3 percent a year from 1977 to 1992. The total composition of funds in this subsector varied over the years. By 1992, a smaller proportion of funds was coming from private contributions and government, and a larger proportion from private payments. The largest change, however, was in private contributions, falling from 32.0 percent of total funds in 1977 to 20.0 percent in 1992. Government payments represented half of all revenues in this subsector in 1992. From 1977 to 1992, this subsector increased its share of total annual funds in the independent sector from 9.3 to 11.0 percent.

The annual rate of change in total revenues for this subsector varied over the years. It was higher from 1987 to 1992 (7.5 percent) than between 1982 and 1987 (5.8 percent). The composition of sources of funds for this sector also changed over this period. From 1982 to 1987, after a cut in growth in federal funding in 1982, the annual change in private contributions was 5.6 percent compared with 3.0 percent from government payments. During this period, private payments grew at 10.5 percent a year. From 1987 to 1992, these growth rates reversed. The annual rate of change in private contributions dropped to 3.0 percent and in private payments to 5.9 percent, but government payments increased to 8.4 percent a year (Figure 1.2). Much of the increase in government payments during this period is attributed to government contracts for services and increases in Medicaid payments.

While the social and legal services subsector had the highest annual rate of increase among all other subsectors in the independent sector, its rate of change was exceeded by the other two sectors of the economy. Both in terms of numbers of institutions and revenues, social services grew faster in other sectors of the economy, particularly in the for-profit sector. In 1982, the independent sector had 66 percent of all institutions, 85 percent of all revenues and 80 percent of total employees in the social services sector of the economy. In 1992, the independent sector had 58 percent of all social services institutions, 80 percent of all revenues and 74 percent of total employees. Therefore, the independent sector's share of social services compared with other sectors of the economy declined 11 percent in number of institutions, 5 percent in total revenues and 8 percent in total employees. The component of social services where independent sector lost its greatest percentage share between 1982 and 1992 was child day care services.

Education/Research

The education/research subsector includes higher education, elementary and secondary schools, correspondence schools, libraries, other educational services and research institutes. Growth in total revenues was the slowest in this subsector compared with the rest of the independent sector. It annual percentage change in total revenues was 3.2 percent from 1977 to 1992. As a result, its share of total revenues in the independent sector declined from 24.7 percent in 1977 to 18.6 percent in 1992 (Figure 1.2).

The subsector was unique, however, in the composition of its funding in comparison to most of the other subsectors and the independent sector as a whole. The education/research subsector was the only subsector in which private contributions increased as a proportion of total funds, from 9 percent in 1977 to 13 percent in 1992. The annual rate of change in private contributions was highest in this subsector at 5.7 percent. Private payments as a portion of total annual funds increased from 53 to 57 percent, as did payments from government, from 18 to 20 percent.

The sector is dominated by governmentally owned institutions especially in elementary and secondary schools, and in higher education, particularly by community colleges. New schools of higher education tend to be created in the public or for-profit sector and, particularly, in the component of vocational and correspondence schools. As a result, the independent sector lost share of most of the components of the education/research subsector. In higher education, its share in terms of number of institutions declined by 11 percent over this period, even

though it increased its percentage share of total revenues by 8 percent.

Religious Organizations

In 1992, the total revenues of the religion subsector were $58 billion, nearly 12 percent of total revenues of the independent sector. Similar to the education/research subsector, the religion subsector showed a lower annual percentage change in total funds from 1977 to 1992 than other subsectors. The annual rate of change in total revenues was 3.3 percent, compared with private contributions at 2.7 percent. Since these institutions are dependent on private contributions for most of their revenue, the percentage of revenues donated by religion for other purposes declined. Generally, religious organizations try to collect more contributions than they use for their internal operations and contribute the excess to various programs and causes. For example, private contributions in 1977 were estimated to exceed total revenues by 25 percent. By 1992, private contributions were at 94 percent of total revenues, indicating that religious institutions—which spend about 70 percent of their revenues on current operating expenditures—had far less to provide in donations to denominational programs, individuals or other organizations.

Arts and Cultural Organizations

In 1992, the arts and culture subsector had approximately $8 billion in total revenues, and represented under 2 percent of the independent sector. Arts and cultural organizations had their greatest growth between 1977 and 1982. Growth occurred during this time in all forms of income, including private contributions, government support and private payments. During that five year period, the annual rate of change in total revenues was nearly 14 percent. The annual rate of increase by major sources of funds were: private contributions, 13 percent; private payments, 13 percent; and government payments, 22 percent. However, from 1982 to 1992, there was a great downturn in the growth in the arts and cultural subsector. The annual rate of change in revenues fell to 1.7 percent. The annual rate of change by source of funds was: private contributions, 1.9 percent; private payments, 1.7 percent; and government payments, 0.8 percent. Arts and cultural organizations are highly dependent upon private contributions. In 1992, private contributions were 40 percent of total revenue; private payments represented 24 percent; and government payments, 15 percent.

Most of the components of the arts and cultural subsector, with the exception of museums and zoological and botanical gardens, are dominated by other sectors of the economy. In 1992, the independent sector represented over 90 percent of the revenues in the museums and zoological and botanical gardens component. However, it represented only about one quarter of the producers, orchestras and entertainers component, and 3 percent of the radio and TV broadcasting component.

Trends in Individual and Household Contributions and Volunteering

Private support in the forms of contributions and voluntary time are important sources of funding to the independent sector. While some voluntary time and contributions are given to government, particularly to schools and colleges, the bulk of contributions and voluntary time are contributed to institutions in the independent sector. As such, these forms of support serve as a barometer of public trust in the sector. Over the years, we have noted the importance of both voluntary time, household contributions and private contributions from foundations and corporations.

Despite the fact that the level of some of these forms of support varies with the condition of the economy, tax policies and other public policies, the percentage of the population engaged in giving and volunteering has proven to be an important indicator of public support and en-

gagement in the sector and on a variety of issues. One of the most positive findings in recent surveys on giving and volunteering in the United States is that nearly three-quarters of all households report charitable contributions. This percentage has remained stable for nearly a decade. Average household contributions and household income have declined in real terms since 1989. Even during recessions and periods of increased unemployment, Americans contribute to a variety of causes. Rather than eliminating contributions, households just give less. A more disturbing finding, as reported on in *Independent Sector*'s biennial survey on giving and volunteering, is the change in the percentage of Americans who worry about having enough money in the future. In 1994, when the economy had improved and unemployment was decreasing, the percentage of Americans reporting that they were worried about the future increased to 73 percent, up from 67 percent in 1990. It is also becoming more evident that giving is slowly increasing among affluent households which have experienced increases in their household income and can claim charitable deductions on their income tax returns. Among the 75 percent of households that have not experienced much change in household income, the percentage of income given to charity has declined somewhat.

Volunteering is important to charitable organizations. In 1994, volunteer time provided 36 percent of total employment to the independent sector but represented only 9 percent of total employment in government and a negligible percentage in business. Some subsectors of the independent sector could not survive without volunteer employment. Volunteers in 1992 provided 71 percent of total employment in the religion subsector; 60 percent in the arts subsector; and 56 percent in civic, social and fraternal organizations. Volunteers provided 22 percent of the employment in the education subsector and 16 percent in the health services subsector.

In 1994, 48 percent of all American adults volunteered at an average rate of 4 hours per week. This was down from a high of 54 percent in 1989, however, still higher than the 45 percent in 1987. In 1994, an estimated 89 million adults contributed over 19 billion hours. In terms of full-time equivalent employment, this translated into 8.8 million employees whose assigned value was $182 billion. Survey findings have shown that worrying greatly about having enough money in the future also affects volunteer participation rates. One very positive trend, however, is the increased rates of volunteering among retirees.

Giving and volunteering surveys have consistently shown that behavioral habits are very important predictors of not only present, but future volunteering and contributing patterns. These behavioral characteristics include membership and regular attendance at religious institutions and membership in community, voluntary and professional associations. Participation also increases by level of education. Having been a member of a youth group and having had a volunteer experience when young have a major influence on the level of volunteering of an individual as an adult. However, one of the most important factors is that members of organizations are more likely to be asked to give and volunteer than non-members, this increases their likelihood to contribute or volunteer.

Other data series provide a view of total contributions from all sources. Recently, the greatest growth in total contributions and individual giving, per capita, was between 1980 and 1986. After adjusting for inflation, total contributions, per capita, grew 21 percent. During this same period, individual contributions per capita, increased 16 percent. In constant (1987) dollars, individual giving actually declined after 1986 and did not reach its 1986 high again until 1993. This decline can be attributed to multiple factors, including major changes in the 1986 Tax Law, the recession in the early 1990s and a general restructuring of the economy.

Other Trends

- In 1993, there were 37,571 foundations, up from 22,088 in 1980. Thus, from 1980 to 1993, the number of foundations increased by 70 percent. The average annual number of foundations formed with as-

sets of $1 million or more, or grants of $100,000, was 308 during the 1980s, greatly exceeding the average annual formation of foundations (186) in the previous largest decade of growth, the 1950s. In 1993, the total assets of foundations were $189 billion. Foundation assets have nearly quadrupled since 1980. Grants given by foundations over this period more than tripled. In comparison, the founding of corporate foundations grew at a much slower rate in the 1980s and 1990s than in the 1970s. Similarly, corporate contributions grew less rapidly since 1987 than previously. In 1993, company-sponsored foundations increased their contributions by 1.4 percent, which represented an actual decline after inflation.

- The number of charitable 501(c)(3) organizations registered with the Internal Revenue Service (IRS) nearly doubled from 1977 to 1992. The annual rate of change in numbers of these organizations was 4.7 percent. In comparison, the annual rate of change in the formation of religious organizations was 0.1 percent, and for 501(c)(4) public benefit organizations, 0.6 percent.

- Most charitable organizations are very small. In 1993, out of the approximately 494,000 501(c)(3) organizations, excluding religious organizations and private foundations, that provided information to the IRS, only 33 percent of independent sector organizations filed a 990 return with financial information. Of these 164,247 filers, 41 percent had expenses of less than $100,000; 31 percent between $100,000 and $500,000; 9 percent between $500,000 and $1 million; 12 percent between $1 million and $5 million; 3 percent between $5 million and $10 million; and 4 percent over $10 million. The top 6 percent (9,901 organizations) controlled 80 percent of total assets, 61 percent of total public and private support and 85 percent of total expenses for this sector.

- Nearly three quarters of all charitable 501(c)(3) organizations, excluding most religious organizations and private foundations, have been founded since 1970, 38 percent between 1970 and 1984, and 34 percent between 1985 and 1992.

- Older charitable organizations are more likely to have expenses over $10,000,000 than those founded more recently. Of the organizations founded before 1940, 16.0 percent had expenses of $10,000,000 or more, compared with 1.2 percent founded between 1985 and 1992.

- Employment in the nonprofit sector grew at an annual rate of 3.3 percent from 1977 to 1994, higher than the service component of the for-profit sector (3.0 percent). From 1992 to 1994, the annual rate of change in employment in the independent sector slowed down to 2.9 percent while the service component of business increased to 3.2 percent.

- The composition of employment in the independent sector by gender and race varies substantially from other sectors of the economy. In 1994, 68 percent of paid employees were female compared with 44 percent among employees in other sectors of the economy. Fifteen percent of the employees in the sector were black compared with 10 percent among the other sectors. Employed persons of Hispanic origin were the exception. Nine percent of paid employees in the other sectors of the economy were of Hispanic origin compared with 6 percent in the independent sector.

Future Prospects

After 1992, in terms of overall revenues and employment rates, trends in the *Nonprofit Almanac 1996–1997* reveal a slowing down in the growth of the sector. Growth in the sector will be further curtailed, particularly after 1997, by the changes in federal funding proposed by both the Administration and Congress. Proposals by the Administration and Congress dictate a slowdown in growth in government funding, both in non-defense domestic programs and various entitlement programs, such as food stamps, Medicare and Medicaid. In programs, such as those in community and regional development, the cuts are both in nominal and real terms in both budgets.

Depending upon what proposals are enacted in the areas of welfare reform, Medicare and Medicaid, major changes could occur in both the health services sector and support programs for people in poverty. The locus of administration for many of these programs will continue to be shifted to state and local governments. There will be greater opportunities for citizens to participate more fully in the decision making processes affecting their communities. This may lead to more inventive solutions provided that adequate resources are made available. While many new efficiencies could occur in the use of federal funds, it may take many years to determine under which different programs and in what localities, low income individuals are best served.

The congressional budget resolution and the president's deficit reduction proposals would have different impacts on the nonprofit sector. A recent analysis indicates that the six-year reductions called for in the congressional plan would be 1.4 times greater than the president's plan. Under the congressional plan, federal funding to nonprofit organizations would decline by 18 percent, or $89 billion, between 1996 and 2002, using 1995 as the base year. Under the president's plan, the cumulative decline would be 12 percent, or $65 billion. Cuts in federal funding will affect all nonprofit organizations, and some subsectors disproportionately, particularly in the areas of community and regional development, international affairs and social services (Abramson and Salamon, 1996). Both plans seek outright reductions and reduced growth rates in funding and assume a growing economy. If a serious economic recession occurs, little room exists in these budgets to account for worker dislocation or severe unemployment. In such a scenario, governments, at all levels, and charitable organizations would not have the capacity to meet major increases in new need.

Current trends to provide waivers to states to experiment with new service delivery plans for welfare benefits and Medicaid funding structures could lead to new efficiencies in the delivery of welfare and health services. Evidence from some states that are currently experimenting, such as Hawaii and Tennessee, reveal that more uninsured people can receive access to health care. Programs that move retirees and Medicaid recipients to health maintenance plans may also lead to some efficiencies. Should these trends continue, it is expected that the nonprofit health, and part of the human services, subsectors will shrink over time. Many of these services will be provided by the for-profit sector. The question remains, however, about how much real need will be met and how much pressure will be put on charitable organizations to meet the needs for services to individuals no longer eligible for welfare.

Competition between nonprofit and for-profit organizations at the state level in contracting for a variety of services will accelerate in the areas of health services, job training, family services and residential care. At the same time, as government funding declines, competition among nonprofits for private contributions will accelerate. Private foundations will come under pressure to fund more immediate needs rather than to serve as institutions that provide seed money for new and experimental programs. It is clear that even a doubling of total private contributions could not replace the cumulative loss in projected government spending at both the federal and state levels through 2002. Even if contributions did double, there is no assurance from past history that these contributions would be targeted to meet new human needs. Private contributions to the social services subsector grew at a slower rate than giving to other types of charities and comprised a much smaller percentage of total annual funds in that subsector in 1992 than in 1977. Trends are similar for contributions to the health services subsector, and particularly, hospitals. Accelerating competition for contributions among independent sector organizations and for contracts for services at the state and local levels with for-profit businesses may lead nonprofits to form coalitions at the local level, to merge, and in some cases, to close.

As organizations compete for private contributions and government funds, accountability and performance will become increasingly more important. Organizations will have to demonstrate the efficient use of funds and positive outcomes from the use of funds more than ever. Independent sector organizations will be required to produce quantifiable measures of program achievement and effectiveness to donors, foundations and government funding agencies.

Finally, the great challenge for communities, government and business will be to determine the roles and responsibilities of governments and charitable organizations in order to provide necessary services to communities and the nation. In a recent article, Brian O'Connell (1996) argued that the fundamental question is not the level of private contributions, fees for service among those who can afford to pay or the delivery of services among the sectors, but rather "whatever funding patterns are appropriate and possible, making certain that essential services are in fact funded is ultimately government's responsibility" (O'Connell, 224).

Trends in Private Contributions and the Capacity to Increase Individual Giving

There is no question that there has been a great increase in the wealth of this nation since 1980. However, increases in both wealth and income have not been distributed equally to the whole population. In a recent analysis of the changes in levels of wealth and income among the population, Edward N. Wolff (1995) revealed the dimensions of the growing income gap between the upper 20 percent of households and the rest of the population. The share of wealth among the top 1 percent was 48 percent in 1989, up from 43 percent in 1983. The share of income for this group in the same period grew from 13 to 17 percent. For the next lower 19 percent, its share of wealth declined from 48 to 46 percent and its share of income remained the same at 39 percent. The bottom 80 percent of the population's, share of wealth declined from 9 to 6 percent, and its share of income from 48 to under

45 percent. The growth in real financial wealth for each of these groups from 1983 to 1989 was 66 percent among the top 1 percent, 37 percent among the next 19 percent, and a loss of 3 percent for the final 80 percent.

These trends confirm some trends found in other studies and data series. The *Independent Sector* biennial surveys on giving and volunteering show a declining capacity to increase giving among households with eroding incomes. However, the evidence also shows that household contributions and volunteering increase when there is a decline in unemployment and an increase in wages. While upper income taxpayers have increased their giving, these increases have been small and do not correspond to the increase in wealth. Growing wealth also reveals an enhanced capacity to increase contributions and bequests. In a recent analysis of the capacity of giving among taxpayers who itemized on their income taxes in 1991, Claude Rosenberg (1994) estimated that itemizers could have given $100 billion rather than the $60 billion actually given. This would be possible if persons of wealth considered their real capacity to give, including both income and earning assets. He estimated that the top income group, those with an adjusted gross income of $1 million or over, gave 40 times what low income earners gave. However, if one includes their earning assets, they had a capacity to give 450 times what the low income earner could give. While earnings on assets could be related to the condition of the stock market and their individual situations, he did show that from 1980 to 1991, real family income increased 80 percent in this group, compared with an increase of less than 5 percent of the median family income. This reveals a much enlarged capacity to increase charitable contributions (Rosenberg, 15).

There also is a great capacity to increase charitable bequests. Only 19 percent of the wealthiest one and a half percent of individuals leave a charitable bequest. While the amount of money left at death by that 19 percent has increased by 79 percent in real terms since 1977, the amount left in charitable bequests has increased by only 23 percent. The potential to increase giving in bequests is great over the next decade as the World War II population that achieved wealth dies. However, tax policy that reduces taxation at death could lead to a further decline in the amount left in charitable bequests. The challenge for foundations and voluntary organizations will be to convince these wealthy individuals to reinvest in their own communities and special causes.

Progress on Data Acquisition About the Independent Sector

Since the first edition of this series was published in 1984, much progress has been made in building the necessary infrastructure for data collection about this sector. The greatest progress has been made through the development of a national classification system—the National Taxonomy of Exempt Entities—and its implementation by the Internal Revenue Service (IRS). Data collection, in the form of institutional samples and universe files, by the IRS has greatly improved over the past decade. While not all pertinent data needed to adequately describe the independent sector or the effects of important public policy decisions are available from the 990 tax returns, progress is being made to provide a crosswalk between the IRS data and information available through other agencies via the Standard Industrial Code. As this wider system of information becomes available in the next century, developing trend line analysis from longitudinal data series of institutions, with the notable exception of religious institutions, will become possible. At that point, the size, scope and dimensions of the independent sector can be assessed based on an integrated set of data series, rather than separate estimates from several incomplete and incompatible data sources.

There are, however, two major areas of weakness in data collection that seriously hamper the full and accurate analysis of this sector and its place in the economy and society. These include data collection on private contributions from individuals and institutional information on religious institutions. In some ways, these two major weaknesses in data go together; over 90 percent of the total revenues of religious institutions come from individual contributions. In this series, and our reports on trends, the weakest link is of our estimates in the area of private contributions. Since we maintain that what is unique to the independent sector is the relative importance of individual contributions and volunteer time as sources of revenue, it is regrettable that little investment or progress has been made in constructing a reliable data series on individual giving based upon solid data collection over time.

Our estimates still rely on the incomplete picture of giving by itemizers from IRS data. This data provides the aggregate amount of charitable deductions, but no information on which organizations receive the gifts. Since itemizers represent only slightly more than one quarter of all taxpayers, we must rely on survey data or models with little backup data to estimate giving among the rest of the population. Although household surveys on giving are useful, they cannot be used as a replacement for the verifiable data of a longitudinal data series. Some recent studies that attempt to analyze patterns of giving among the wealthy, while very interesting, are flawed because they are not real random samples. The last survey of the upper two percent of the wealthy was in 1973 and was commissioned by the Commission on Private Philanthropy and Public Needs in cooperation with the U.S. Department of the Treasury. Total giving can now be verified through institutional data, but cannot be disaggregated by individuals. It is this discrepancy between what institutions record on their 990 returns and other estimates of total contributions that calls for a much more intense and serious attempt to build a reliable series of data. Until there is progress made in this critical area, figures about total individual giving and its designation are subject to gross estimates.

Trends in Voluntary Service

There are some positive indicators stating that service to the community will increase. While volunteering among adults has declined since 1990, it is still higher than it was in 1980. Data from a series of polls and studies are showing that volunteering among young people has increased after a decline during the early 1980s, and parental participation in schools is increasing. There has been little decline in church membership or other group membership organizations for over two decades and participation in social services activities is increasing. Three quarters of Americans still report annual household contributions.

More and more Americans and associations are using interactive technology, such as the Internet and local cable television, to keep in touch and to engage in discourse about public issues. At a time when there is concern that there is a civic decline in America, Everett C. Ladd (1996) concluded in a recent review of the research on citizen participation that "America in its post-industrial era is a vigorously civic America." (Ladd, 1). While the future presents challenges about government, continued services and maintaining the quality of life in this country, there are signs that the levels of participation and voluntary association and service will increase. There is the possibility for citizens to renew their commitments to community development and engage in the kinds of public discussion that make possible wise decisions about their future course. At the very heart of the independent sector and its voluntary associations is enhanced citizen participation, voluntary service and responsibility. Such is one of its unique roles and with this role lies its future.

References

Abramson, Alan J., and Lester M. Salamon. "The Federal Budget and the Nonprofit Sector: FY 1996 and FY 1997." A report prepared for *Independent Sector*. July 1996.

Hodgkinson, Virginia A., Murray S. Weitzman, and The Gallup Organization, Inc. *Giving and Volunteering in the United States:* Volumes I & II, 1994 Edition. Washington, DC: Independent Sector.

Ladd, Everett C. "The Data Just Don't Show an Erosion in 'Social Capital.'" *The Public Perspective: A Roper Center Review of Public Opinion and*

Polling, Volume 7, Number 4 (June/July 1996), 1–36.

O'Connell, Brian. "A Major Transfer of Government Responsibility to Voluntary Organizations? Proceed with Caution." *Public Administration Review,* Volume 56, Number 3 (May/June 1996), 222–224.

Rosenberg, Jr., Claude. *Wealthy and Wise: How You and America Can Get the Most Out of Your Giving.* Boston: Little, Brown and Company, 1994.

Wolff, Edward N. *Top Heavy: A Study of the Increasing Inequality of Wealth in America. A Twentieth Century Report.* New York: The Twentieth Century Fund Press, 1995.

CHAPTER 2

Scope and Structure: The Anatomy of America's Nonprofit Sector

LESTER M. SALAMON

To say that nonprofit organizations share certain common characteristics and a common rationale is not, of course, to suggest that all nonprofit organizations are identical. To the contrary, the complexity and diversity of this sector is one of the major factors that has diverted attention from it over much of its history. Indeed, nonprofit organizations are so diverse and so specialized that some observers question whether it is appropriate to consider this group of institutions a "sector" at all—a point that could be raised about the "business sector" as well, of course.

Complicating things further is the fact that significant portions of the nonprofit sector are largely informal in character and therefore difficult to capture in empirical terms. This reflects the fact that under American law organizations are not required to incorporate, or even to seek formal recognition by the tax authorities, in order to function as tax-exempt nonprofit organizations. This organizational fluidity is, in fact, one of the prized features of this sector, enabling groups of people to meet together to pursue common purposes without having to seek official approval or even acknowledgment. At the same time, however, it makes it exceedingly difficult to gauge the size of this sector with any real precision.[1]

While recognizing these problems, this chapter seeks to make some sense of the vast array of institutions that comprise the American nonprofit sector, to examine the basic anatomy or architecture of this sector and the scope and scale of some of its constituent parts. In the process, it seeks to strip away some of the confusion and misperception that too often characterize popular understanding of what the nonprofit sector really is and how it functions in American life.

To do so, we first examine the overall scale of this sector and then look in more detail at some of the sector's major components, focusing particularly on what we refer to as "public-benefit service organizations," the portion of this sector that most people have in mind when they refer to the "nonprofit sector." Given the limitations of available data, our focus is inevitably on the more formal and institutionalized organizations, although, as we will see, the line between these and the rest of this sector is far from clear.

Overview: Basic Dimensions

The nonprofit sector is not only a quite important, but also a quite sizable, presence in American society:

- As of 1995, this sector included approximately 1.6 million identifiable organizations, or more than 6 percent of all organizations of all types (nonprofit, business, and government) in the country.[2]
- These organizations had revenues as of 1996 of $670 billion, which is equivalent to nearly 9 percent of the U.S. gross domestic product. In fact, if the U.S. nonprofit sector were a separate country, it would exceed the gross domestic products of most of the countries in the world, including Australia, Canada, India, the Netherlands, and Spain.[3]
- These organizations are also an important source of employment. Nearly 11 million people worked as employees of nonprofit organizations in 1996, or approximately 7 percent of the nation's workforce. This was more than three times the number employed in agriculture and larger than the number employed in construction, in transportation and communication, and in finance, insurance, and real estate.[4]
- In addition to the paid employment, nonprofit organizations also employed the equivalent of 6.3 million full-time volunteers, boosting their workforce to 17.2 million workers, or about 11 percent of all paid and volunteer employment in the U.S. economy.[5]

A Basic Division: Public-Serving Versus Member-Serving Organizations

Included within these figures, however, are two very different categories of organizations.

Member-Serving Organizations

The first are what we may refer to as *primarily member-serving* organizations. These are organizations that, while having some public purpose, primarily exist to provide a benefit to the members of the organization rather than to the public at large. As reflected in Figure 2.1, the member-serving organizations include social

clubs, business and professional associations (e.g., chambers of commerce, the American Bankers' Association, local bar associations, labor unions), mutual benefit and cooperative organizations (e.g., farmers cooperatives, benevolent life insurance associations), and political organizations (e.g., political parties and political action committees). Approximately 400,000 such organizations were officially registered with the Internal Revenue Service as of 1995 and a far larger number probably exist more informally. These member-serving organizations account for about 10 percent of all nonprofit employment.

Public-Serving Organizations

The second category of nonprofit organizations are *primarily public-serving* in character. These are organizations that exist primarily to serve

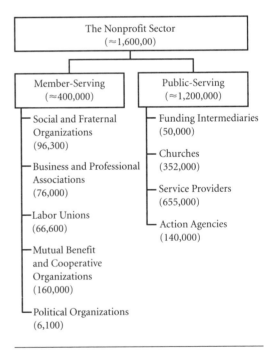

FIGURE 2.1   Anatomy of the Nonprofit Sector

NOTE: Estimates of numbers of organizations here include only the more visible and formal parts of the nonprofit sector.

SOURCE: See Endnote 2.

the public at large rather than primarily the members of the organization. They may do so in a variety of ways, however—providing health and education services, sponsoring cultural or religious activities, advocating for certain causes, aiding the poor, financing other non-profits, and many more. Altogether, at least 1.2 million such organizations exist at the present time and they account for 90 percent of the sector's employment.

Treatment in Tax Law

This distinction between primarily member-serving and primarily public-serving nonprofit organizations is far from perfect, of course. Even the member-serving organizations produce some public benefits, and the public-serving or-ganizations often deliver benefits to their members. Yet the distinction is significant enough to find formal reflection in the law.

In particular, public-serving organizations are the only ones entitled to tax-exempt status under Section 501(c)(3) of the federal tax law. What makes this so important is that this gives such organizations a tax advantage not available to other nonprofit organizations. In particular, in addition to being exempt from taxes them-selves like all nonprofit organizations, 501(c)(3) organizations are also eligible to receive tax-deductible gifts from individuals and corpora-tions; that is, contributions that the individuals and corporations can deduct from their own in-come in computing their tax liabilities. This gives the individuals and corporations a finan-cial incentive to make contributions to these 501(c)(3) organizations because they can deduct the gifts from their taxable income. The justification for this is that the organizations are serving purposes that are public in character and that government might otherwise have to support through tax revenues.[6]

To be eligible for this status, organizations must operate "exclusively for religious, charita-ble, scientific, literary, or educational purposes."[7] The meaning of these terms is rooted in English common law, however, and is quite broad, essen-tially embracing organizations that promote the general welfare in any of a wide variety of ways.[8]

Included, therefore, are not only agencies pro-viding aid to the poor, but also most of the edu-cational, cultural, social service, advocacy, self-help, health, environmental, civil rights, child welfare, and related organizations that most peo-ple have in mind when they think about the nonprofit sector. The one major exception are public-serving organizations heavily engaged in direct political action (campaigning and lobby-ing for legislation), for which a special section of the tax code [Section 501(c)(4)] exists.[9]

Focus on Public-Serving Organizations

Because of their essentially public character, the public-serving nonprofit organizations are the ones that most observers have in mind when they speak about the "nonprofit sector" in the United States. These are therefore the organizations that will be the principal focus of this "primer."

What is not widely appreciated, however, is that this public-serving component of the non-profit sector contains four very different types of organizations, as shown in Figure 2.1. The first are funding intermediaries, that is, organiza-tions that function chiefly to provide funds for other parts of the nonprofit sector. The second are religious congregations, that is, organiza-tions that principally engage in religious wor-ship (e.g., churches, synagogues, mosques). The third are various service-providing organiza-tions, that is, organizations that provide health care, education, counseling, adoption assistance, etc., or that advocate for particular causes. The fourth are the public-benefit political action agencies noted above, which devote a significant portion of their effort to supporting or oppos-ing particular pieces of legislation. Let us look briefly at each of these types, focusing particu-larly on the first and third.

Funding Intermediaries

Among the public-serving nonprofit organiza-tions in the United States, probably the least well understood, are the *funding intermediaries*. These are organizations whose sole, or prin-cipal, function is to channel financial support, especially private charitable support, to other nonprofit organizations.

The Scope of Private Giving

The existence of these funding intermediaries reflects the highly specialized and developed character of the U.S. nonprofit sector, which has led to the emergence of organizations that are dedicated exclusively to fundraising and fund distribution. But it also reflects the importance of private charitable giving in the United States and the scale that such giving has attained. In 1996, for example, Americans contributed an estimated $139 billion to various charitable causes.[10] This represented about 2.2 percent of personal income, considerably higher than for most other countries.[11]

Of this $139 billion, about 85 percent came from individuals, about 9 percent from foundations, and about 6 percent from corporations. The largest share of this support (an estimated $66 billion, or almost half) went to religious organizations, mostly for sacramental religious activities. Another $12.7 billion went to public or governmental institutions, particularly higher education institutions. This left an estimated $45.5 billion for all the rest of the private, nonprofit service organizations (see Table 2.1).[12]

Although, as we shall see, private charitable giving is by no means the only, or even the largest, source of support for American nonprofit service organizations, it is nevertheless quite important because of the role it plays in helping to ensure the sector's independence and autonomous character.

The role of the funding intermediaries is to help generate this private funding, to manage it once it is accumulated, and to make it available for use by the other organizations in the sector. Broadly speaking, as shown in Figure 2.2, three distinct types of such funding intermediaries exist: (a) foundations, (b) federated funders, and (c) professional fundraisers. Let us look briefly at each.

Foundations

Private foundations (e.g., the Ford Foundation, the Rockefeller Foundation, the W.K. Kellogg

TABLE 2.1   Private Charitable Giving in the U.S., 1996, by Type of Recipient and Purpose

Type of Recipient	Amount ($ billions)	Percent
Religious congregations	$66.3	48%
Government agencies	12.7	9
Foundations	8.3	6
Nonprofit Service Providers	45.5	33
Education	15.0	11
Health	11.2	8
Social/legal services	9.5	7
Arts, culture	4.2	3
Civil	5.6	4
Other Nonprofit	6.1	4
Total	$138.9	100%

SOURCE: See Endnote 10.

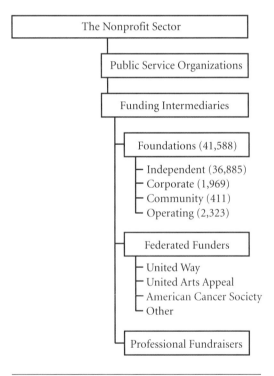

FIGURE 2.2   Nonprofit Funding Intermediaries

SOURCE: Foundation data from Loren Renz et al., *Foundation Giving* (New York: Foundation Center, 1998), p. 5.

Foundation) are among the most visible components of the nonprofit sector—so much so that there is a tendency to overstate their role and confuse them with the public-serving nonprofit sector as a whole. This latter problem is particularly acute among overseas observers because the term *foundation* is used quite differently in many other countries. In particular, there is often little distinction between foundations and other parts of the nonprofit sector elsewhere, whereas in the United States the term foundation is typically reserved for organizations with the more specialized function of making grants to other nonprofit organizations, typically out of the earnings from an endowment.[13]

Altogether, as noted in Table 2.2, there were over 41,000 foundations in the United States as of 1996, with total assets of $267.6 billion.[14] These foundations take four different forms, however.

Independent grantmaking foundations. The most important type of foundation by far are the so-called independent grantmaking foundations. These are nonprofit organizations set up to administer an endowment typically left for charitable purposes by a single individual, and to distribute all or some of the earnings from that endowment to nonprofit organizations pursuing public purposes. Of the more than 41,000 foundations in existence as of 1996, almost 37,000, or nearly 90 percent, were independent foundations, as shown in Table 2.2. These independent foundations controlled 85

percent of all foundation assets and accounted for 77 percent of all foundation grants.

Corporate foundations. Somewhat different from the independent foundations are the corporate or company-sponsored foundations. Unlike the independent foundations, which receive their endowments from wealthy individuals, corporate foundations receive their funds from business corporations that want to avoid the fluctuations that come from financing corporate charitable activities from current income alone. By creating corporate foundations, corporations are able to maintain more professional and stable giving programs because the foundations can receive excess funds during years of corporate prosperity to build up endowments for use when corporate profits are lower. Altogether, there were nearly 2,000 corporate foundations in 1996 and they controlled 4 percent of all foundation assets and accounted for 13 percent of all foundation grants. This excludes, of course, the amounts that corporations give to charitable purposes directly, rather than through separate foundations.

Community foundations. A third form of foundation is the community foundation. Where both independent and corporate foundations receive their funds from a single source, community foundations receive them from a number of sources in a given community. The basic concept of a community foundation is that wealthy individuals in a community, rather than tying their bequests to particular organizations that may go out of business or become less relevant over time, can pool them through a community foundation and put a board of local citizens in charge of deciding what the best use of the resources might be at a given point in time. Altogether, 411 community foundations were in existence in 1996, and they accounted for nearly 6 percent of all foundation assets and over 7 percent of all foundation grants—up from 5 percent in 1989.

Operating foundations. Finally, although most American foundations specialize in grantmaking, there were 2,323 foundations in 1996 that

TABLE 2.2   U.S. Grantmaking Foundations, 1996 ($ billions)*

Type	Number	Assets	Grants
Independent	36,885	$226.6	$10.7
Corporate	1,969	9.5	1.8
Community	411	15.9	1.0
Operating	2,323	15.7	0.3
Total	41,588	$267.6	$13.8

SOURCE: *Foundation Giving* 1998, p. 5.

*Figures may not add due to rounding.

functioned both as grantmakers and operators of actual charitable programs, a pattern that is much more common overseas. These so-called operating foundations accounted for 6 percent of foundation assets and 2 percent of all foundation grants.

The Relative Position of Foundations

Because of the scale and recent growth of the American foundation universe—the number of foundations has nearly doubled over the past decade and a half and the real value of their assets has increased two and a half times—there is often a tendency to exaggerate the role that foundations play and the contribution that they make. It is therefore important to bear a number of crucial facts in mind in assessing their position in the American nonprofit sector.

- In the first place, although the number of American foundations is quite large, most foundations are quite small. In fact, the top 1 percent of all foundations—645 institutions in all—controlled 70 percent of all foundation assets as of 1996. By contrast, those with less than $10 million in assets represented 94 percent of all foundations but accounted for only 15 percent of all the assets. In other words, it is only a relative handful of foundations that account for the vast majority of foundation resources. (See Table 2.3 for a list of the top ten foundations in terms of assets.)
- In the second place, although the overall scale of foundation assets seems quite large, it pales in comparison to the assets of other institutions in American society. Thus, compared to the $268 billion in foundation assets, U.S. money market funds had assets of $891 billion (3 times as much), U.S. life insurance companies had assets of $2,239 billion (8 times as much), U.S. mutual funds had assets of $2,349 billion (8 times as much), U.S. pension funds had assets of $3,031 billion (11 times as much), U.S. commercial banks had assets of $3,349 billion (12 times as much),[15] and U.S. nonfinancial

corporations had financial assets of $5,327 billion (20 times as much). In other words, while private foundations control significant assets, they hardly represent a major force in the American economy.

- Finally, private foundation grants, while important, hardly represent the dominant share even of the private philanthropic support that American nonprofit organizations receive. Foundations (including corporate foundations) accounted for only about 10 percent of the $138.9 billion in private philanthropic contributions that Americans made in 1996. Even when we focus exclusively on the giving that flows to nonprofit service organizations of the sort that foundations support, and exclude giving to religious congregations, the foundation share of the total is still less than 20 percent. Since private charitable contributions represent only slightly over 10 percent of the total income of these nonprofit organizations, moreover, this means that the foundation share of total nonprofit income is only about 2 percent.[16]

In short, the United States has an extraordinary number of private, charitable foundations. These foundations control significant assets and

TABLE 2.3   Ten Largest U.S. Foundations, 1996

Name	Assets ($billions)
Ford Foundation	$8.2
W. K. Kellogg Foundation	7.6
David and Lucille Packard Foundation	7.4
J. Paul Getty Trust	7.2
Lilly Endowment Inc.	6.8
Robert Wood Johnson Foundation	5.6
The Pew Charitable Trusts	4.0
MacArthur Foundation	3.4
Robert W. Woodruff Foundation	3.0
The Rockefeller Foundation	2.7
Total	$55.9

SOURCE: *Foundation Giving* (1998), p. 73.

make important contributions to the American nonprofit sector. Nevertheless, it would be wrong to exaggerate the role that these organizations play. They are by no means the dominant source of charitable donations and represent an even smaller share of the overall income of American nonprofits.

Federated Funders

Beyond the foundations, a second broad group of "funding intermediaries" in the American nonprofit sector are so-called federated funders. These are organizations that collect private donations on behalf of a number of service organizations. Examples here would be the United Jewish Appeal, the Lutheran social services network, the American Cancer Society, the American Heart Association, federated arts appeals, and the like.

Perhaps the best known of these federated funding organizations is the United Way. United Way is a network of some 1,900 local "community chests" that raise funds from individuals and corporations on behalf of a number of local social service agencies. What is distinctive about the United Way system, however, is its use of a particular mode of fundraising, namely, "workplace solicitation." This essentially involves a direct charitable appeal to workers in their workplace coupled with a system allowing employers to deduct the pledged contributions made by their employees automatically from the employees' paychecks each pay period. In order to ensure employer support, United Way has typically involved the corporate community actively in the organization of each year's United Way "campaign," and has historically restricted the distribution of the proceeds of the campaign to a set of approved United Way "member agencies." This latter feature has come under increasing attack in recent years, however, with the result that many local United Ways have established "donor option" plans, which permit donors to designate which agencies will receive their contributions.

Because of its obvious efficiencies, United Way's workplace campaigns have been quite effective, so much so that many other federated fundraising organizations have sought to break the monopoly that United Way has long had on the workplace as a solicitation site.[17] In 1997, for example, local United Ways throughout the United States collected a total of $3.25 billion in contributions.[18] While this is quite significant, it represented just over 2 percent of all private charitable donations to American nonprofit organizations, or a fourth as much as is provided by foundations. In the human service field in which it focuses, United Way provides closer to 25 percent of all the charitable support, but it is still important to remember that charitable support is just one of the sources of nonprofit income, and by no means the largest source.

While United Way is the best known of the federated funding organizations, it is by no means the only one. Also prominent are the numerous united health appeals organizations, such as the American Cancer Society, the American Heart Association, the American Diabetes Association, and others. These organizations sponsor public appeals through mail, by telephone, or via house-to-house solicitations to generate funds for use in health research and related purposes. The American Heart Association, for example, raised $345.2 million in 1995/6 from a combination of direct public appeals, special events, and bequests which it then used to support medical research, public health education campaigns, and medical education.[19]

Recent years have witnessed an expansion of the role of federated fundraising, even as individual nonprofit organizations have increased their direct appeals as well. Federated fundraising minimizes costs, especially for direct mail and related types of campaigning, but it also creates serious challenges in figuring out how to distribute the proceeds of federated campaigns and how to create donor identification with the causes and agencies being supported.

Professional Fundraisers

A final group of financial intermediaries of great importance to the nonprofit sector are professional fundraisers, the individuals and firms professionally involved in raising private contributions on behalf of private, nonprofit organizations. Larger nonprofit organizations typically employ one or more professional fundraisers on their regular staffs, and the typical large university or cultural institution may have a "development office" that employs 50 or more fundraisers. These professional fundraisers have their own professional association, the National Society of Fund-Raising Executives (NSFRE), as well as extensive networks of workshops and training courses. As of 1997, NSFRE had over 17,000 members throughout the United States.[20] In addition, a significant number of for-profit fundraising firms exist. For example, the American Association of Fund-Raising Counsel, Inc. represents approximately 25 of these firms. Such firms work on retainers from nonprofit organizations to manage fundraising campaigns.

Summary

In short, the American nonprofit sector contains a significant number of major institutions whose principal function is to serve as financial intermediaries, generating philanthropic contributions from the public, managing philanthropic asset pools, and transferring the resulting proceeds of both activities to other nonprofit organizations for their use. The existence of these organizations is at once a reflection of the maturity and specialization of the American nonprofit sector and of the premium that is placed on private, charitable support for it. But it can also be a source of confusion for those unacquainted with this class of organization.

Religious Congregations

In addition to the funding intermediaries, a second broad class of public-serving nonprofit organizations are the numerous sacramental religious organizations. Included here are the close to 350,000 religious congregations—churches, mosques, synagogues, and other places of worship—as well as an assortment of conventions of churches, religious orders, apostolic groups, and religious auxiliaries.[21]

The placement of these religious organizations in the primarily "public-serving" category is, of course, open to question. Although they often engage in a variety of service functions, re-

ligious congregations really exist primarily to serve the needs of their members rather than the public more generally. They are grouped in the public-serving category here because of the favored position they occupy in American law: They are the only organizations that are automatically entitled to tax exemption under Section 501(c)(3) of the tax code, and thus to the receipt of tax-deductible donations, without even having to file an application for formal recognition from the Internal Revenue Service. They are also exempt from the reporting requirements that the law places on all other types of 501(c)(3) organizations.

This favored position reflects the strong separation of church and state built into the American constitution.[22] Because the power to tax is the power to destroy, it is felt that to require religious congregations to secure approval from government to be incorporated or exempted from taxation would be to give government too much potential control over them. A self-declared religious congregation is therefore automatically treated as a 501(c)(3) organization exempt from taxes and eligible to receive tax-deductible gifts.

What constitutes a religious congregation or church for this purpose is open to dispute, however. Federal authorities have historically been loath to define the term very precisely in view of the First Amendment's prohibitions on any laws regarding the establishment of religion or the free exercise thereof. But the appearance of various self-styled religious organizations that turn out to be fronts for nonexempt activities has led the courts and the Internal Revenue Service to be somewhat more precise. Thus, churches and religious organizations are expected, among other things, to have some recognized creed or form of worship, to be sacerdotal in character, to have regular religious services, and to operate, like other 501(c)(3) organizations, for other than private gain.[23]

Service Providers

We come now to what in many respects is the heart of the public-serving nonprofit sector: the broad assortment of organizations that are neither funding intermediaries nor sacramental religious congregations, but rather service-providing organizations, broadly conceived. Included are providers of health services, education, day care, adoption services, counseling, community organization, employment and training assistance, shelter, food, arts, culture, music, theater, and hundreds of others. Also included, however, are organizations engaged in research, advocacy, information-sharing, civic action, and overseas relief and development. These organizations account for 40 percent of the known nonprofit organizations but 80 percent of total nonprofit employment.

To make sense of this welter of organizations, it is useful to group them into five basic categories:[24]

- health care, including hospitals, clinics, nursing and personal care facilities, home health care centers, and specialty facilities (e.g., kidney dialysis units);
- education, including elementary and secondary education, higher education, libraries, vocational schools, noncommercial research institutes, and related educational services;
- social and legal services, including individual and family social services, job training and vocational rehabilitation services, residential care, day care, and legal aid services;
- civic, including advocacy organizations, civil rights organizations, neighborhood-based organizations; and
- arts and culture, including bands, orchestras, theater groups, museums, art galleries, and botanical and zoological gardens.

Service Versus Action Organizations

Legally, two broad classes of these service organizations exist. The principal distinction between these two classes is the extent to which they engage in active legislative "lobbying," i.e., actively promoting the passage or defeat of specific pieces of legislation.[25] The first class includes organizations that are primarily service providers and that can engage in "lobbying" activities only as a subsidiary activity. Such organi-

zations are recognized as tax-exempt under Section 501(c)(3) of the tax code as "charitable" organizations. The second class is composed of organizations that are primarily engaged in lobbying and other legislative activity. Such organizations must register under Section 501(c)(4) of the tax code as "social welfare organizations." As such, they are not eligible to receive tax-deductible gifts from corporations or the general public.

Because of this restriction, many 501(c)(3) organizations, restricted from engaging "substantially" in lobbying activities themselves, organize (c)(4) "political action" affiliates to handle their lobbying activities for them without jeopardizing the tax-deductible status for the rest of the organization's operations. For purposes of our discussion here, however, we will treat both the primarily service organizations and the primarily "action" organizations as service providers.

Numbers of Organizations

Solid data on the scope of this nonprofit service sector, or of its constituent parts, are difficult to piece together and sensitive to differences in record-keeping (e.g., some organizations treat their branches as separate organizations and others as integral parts of a single parent organization; many organizations carry out a multitude of activities and cannot easily be classified in one category). Based on the available data, however, it appears that there were approximately 760,000 active nonprofit, public-benefit service organizations as of 1996, the latest date for which data are available.[26] As noted earlier, most of these are quite small, and many may be inactive.[27] At any rate, detailed information is available only on those with at least one paid employee or that file the required Form 990 with the Internal Revenue Service. As of 1992, there were approximately 170,000 such organizations.[28]

These organizations are not distributed evenly among the various service fields. Rather:

- *The social service agencies* are the most numerous. Close to 40 percent of all nonprofit service organizations fall into this category. Included here are child day-care centers, individual or family counseling agencies, relief agencies, job training and vocational rehabilitation facilities, residential care institutions, and the like.

- The next largest group of nonprofit service organizations are *educational and research institutions,* including private elementary and secondary schools as well as private universities and colleges, libraries, and research institutes. Close to 38,000 such nonprofit educational institutions exist and they comprise 22 percent of the sector's institutions.

- The third most numerous type of nonprofit agencies are the *civic organizations,* which include neighborhood associations, advocacy organizations, community improvement agencies, civil rights organizations and the like. Seventeen percent of nonprofit service organizations take this form.

- *Health organizations,* including hospitals, nursing homes, and clinics, comprise 14 percent of the organizations.

- The smallest component of the nonprofit service sector in terms of numbers of organizations is the arts and recreation component, which includes symphonies, art galleries, theaters, zoos, botanical gardens, and other cultural and recreational institutions. Together, these cultural and recreational organizations represent 8 percent of the known nonprofit organizations.

Expenditures: A Major Economic Force

Because of the growth of government spending in recent decades and the prominence given to government policies, it is widely believed that this nonprofit service sector has shrunk into insignificance. Yet nothing could be further from the truth. To the contrary, in addition to their social value, nonprofit organizations are also a major economic force. In particular, these nonprofit public-benefit service organizations had expenditures in 1996 of approximately $460 bil-

lion, or over 6 percent of the country's gross domestic product and more than 30 percent of total expenditures on services.[29] In many local areas, in fact, the expenditures of the nonprofit sector easily outdistance those of local government. For example, a recent study of the nonprofit sector in Baltimore, Maryland, revealed that nonprofit expenditures in this metropolitan area exceeded the total expenditures of the city government and the five surrounding county governments.[30]

The distribution of expenditures differs widely, however, from the distribution of organizations. In particular:

- *Health dominance.* The health subsector, composed in part of huge hospital complexes, accounts for the lion's share of the sector's total resources even though it comprises a relatively small proportion of the organizations. In particular, with 14 percent of the organizations the health subsector accounts for 62 percent of all nonprofit service-organization expenditures.

- *Significant education presence.* The education subsector accounted for another 21 percent of the expenditures. Health and education organizations alone thus make over 80 percent of the sector's expenditures.

- *Balance of the sector.* By contrast, the social service, civic, and arts and recreation organizations, which represent altogether two out of every three (65 percent) of the organizations, accounted for only 17 percent of the expenditures.

Quite clearly, this is a sector with a great deal of diversity in the size of its component organizations.

Where Do Nonprofit Service Agencies Get Their Funds?

Compared to their $460 billion in operating expenditures, America's nonprofit, public-benefit service organizations had revenues in 1996 of approximately $515 billion.[31] Included in the revenue figure are sums that were spent for non-operating expenses such as capital equipment and buildings, as well as fund balances.

Where did these resources come from? What are the major sources of nonprofit revenues?

Unfortunately, there is a great deal of misunderstanding about the answer to this question. One common belief has been that large charitable foundations provide most of the income of America's nonprofit sector. Another is that charitable contributions as a whole, including individual and corporate gifts as well as foundation grants, account for the bulk of nonprofit service-organization income.

As we saw earlier in this chapter, however, private foundations account for only 10 percent of the private charitable contributions that are given in the United States. And total charitable contributions amounted to only $45.5 billion in income to nonprofit service organizations in 1996, $54 billion if estimated indirect contributions through churches are included.[32] Compared to total revenues of $515 billion this means that private giving from all sources constituted only 9 percent of nonprofit income, 10 percent if estimated contributions through churches are included. Clearly, important as private charitable support may be to the independence of the nonprofit sector, it hardly comprises the major source of income.

What, then, are the major sources of income?

- *Fees, service charges, and other commercial income.* The major source of support of America's nonprofit public-benefit service organizations are fees, service charges, and other commercial income. Included here are college tuition payments, charges for hospital care not covered by government health insurance, other direct payments for services, and income from investments and sales of products. This source alone accounts for 54 percent of all nonprofit service-organization revenues.
- *Government.* The second most important source of income of America's nonprofit public-benefit service organizations is government. Government grants, contracts, and reimbursements account for 36

percent of nonprofit service-organization income. This reflects a widespread pattern of partnership between government and the nonprofit sector in carrying out public purposes, from the delivery of health care to the provision of education.[33]
- *Private giving.* The 10 percent of total income that nonprofits receive from private giving makes this only the third largest source of nonprofit service-organization income.

Variations by Subsector

Not only are fees, charges, and other commercial income the major source of support for America's nonprofit public-benefit service organizations overall, but also this source is the major source of support for four of the five different types of organizations. At the same time, some variations are also apparent. In particular, as shown in Figure 2.3:

- *Clear fee dominance in health and education.* The health and education portions of the nonprofit sector, which are by far the largest, receive the overwhelming preponderance of their income from fees and charges. This source accounts for 54 percent and 65 percent, respectively, of the income of these two types of nonprofit organizations. In the case of health, however, government is also a significant source of support, providing 41 percent of total revenue, whereas in the education field private giving plays a somewhat larger role.
- *Heavy reliance on fees in social services and arts and recreation.* Fees also turn out to be the major source of income in the fields of arts and recreation (45 percent) and social services (43 percent). In the former, however, private giving is a close second, whereas in the latter, government support plays this role.
- *Government support in community development and civic organizations.* In only one field—community development and civic—are fees and service charges not the

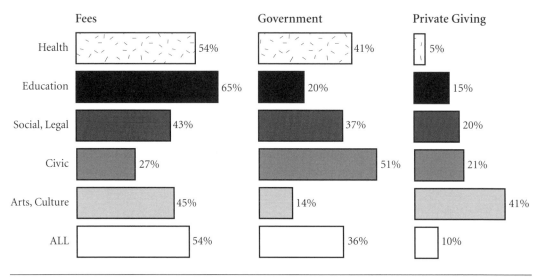

FIGURE 2.3   Sources of Nonprofit Organization Revenue, by Type of Agency, 1996

SOURCE: See Endnote 31.

major source of nonprofit income; here government support performs this role, with fees and private giving in second and third place, respectively.

In short, in none of the major fields of nonprofit activity is private giving the major source of income. Needless to say, this does not mean that particular agencies may not get the preponderance of their income from private giving. But for the sector as a whole, and for the major classes of organizations, such giving now lags behind fees and government support as a source of nonprofit income.

Volunteer Time

In addition to the cash income they receive, nonprofit service organizations also have access to the services of numerous volunteers. Recent estimates indicate that 95 million Americans volunteered an average of 4.2 hours per week to various charitable and other organizations in 1995, and public-serving nonprofit service organizations are the beneficiaries of a significant portion of this.[34] In fact, the volunteer labor available to these organizations translates into the equivalent of almost five million full-time

employees. If these organizations had to hire such employees, the cost would be over $100 billion.[35] Therefore, it is possible to consider this volunteer time as contributing another $100 billion to the revenues of the public-benefit service sector, of which half goes to social services and civic organizations, and nearly the other half to health, education, and arts organizations. Thus, including the assigned value of volunteers brings the total revenue of these organizations to $618 billion in 1996 and boosts the share represented by private contributions of time and money to 25 percent. In some fields, moreover, the inclusion of volunteers changes the picture even more dramatically. In social services, for example, the share of total support coming from philanthropy jumps from 20 percent to 56 percent once the value of volunteer time is factored in. For civic organizations it climbs to 48 percent, and for arts and recreation organizations to 78 percent.

Comparison to Other Countries

The scale of the nonprofit sector is larger in the United States than in most other countries. At the same time, however, measured as a share of total employment, the American nonprofit sector is hardly the largest in the world. At least four countries are known to exceed it in relative size—the Netherlands (12.4 percent), Ireland (11.5 percent), Belgium (10.5 percent), and Israel (9.2 percent) compared to the 6.9 percent in the U.S.[36]

Clearly, while America may have a particularly highly developed nonprofit sector, similar organizations are very much present in other parts of the world as well. Indeed, a veritable "global associational revolution" appears to be under way, a significant upsurge of organized, private, voluntary activity in virtually every corner of the globe.[37]

Summary

Four principal conclusions flow from this overview of the American nonprofit sector:

1. *The nonprofit sector is composed of many different types of organizations.* Some of these are essentially member-serving organizations, and others are primarily public-serving. Among the public-serving organizations, a great deal of specialization also exists. Some organizations are essentially funding intermediaries, others are places of sacramental religious worship, and others provide the human and other services for which the sector is best known.

2. *The nonprofit sector is much larger than is commonly believed.* America's nonprofit, public-benefit service organizations had operating expenditures in 1996 that were the equivalent of 6 percent of the gross national product. In many locales, the expenditures of the nonprofit sector outdistance those of all local governments.

3. *Private giving comprises a much smaller share of the income of the nonprofit sector than is commonly recognized.* Important as private giving is to the vitality and independence of the nonprofit sector, it is hardly the largest source of nonprofit service-organization revenue. Rather, most of the income of this sector comes from

fees and service charges, with government a close second.

4. *While the American nonprofit sector is larger than its counterparts elsewhere in absolute terms, it is not in relative terms.* Nonprofit organizations have long been present in other countries as well, and their role and scope appear to be on the rise almost everywhere.

Notes

1. One recent estimate puts the number of informal grass-roots organizations in the United States as of the early 1990s at 7.5 million, or about 30 per 1,000 inhabitants, though this is based on rather rough projections. By comparison, the number of organizations formally registered as tax-exempt entities under any of the 26 relevant provisions of the Internal Revenue Code was approximately 1.164 million as of 1995. See: David Horton Smith, "The Rest of the Nonprofit Sector: Grassroots Associations as the Dark Matter Ignored in Prevailing 'Flat Earth' Maps of the Sector," *Nonprofit and Voluntary Sector Quarterly*, Vol. 26, No. 2 (June 1997), p. 118. Internal Revenue Service data from: U.S. Internal Revenue Service, *1995 Data Book* (Washington: U.S. Treasury Department), p. 25.

2. The estimate of 1.6 million identifiable nonprofit organizations noted here was derived by adding to the 1,164,789 organizations listed as registered tax-exempt organizations on the Internal Revenue Service's Exempt Organization Master File two categories of organizations known to be underrepresented in the IRS records: the approximately 300,000 out of 375,000 religious congregations that exercise their right not to register with the Internal Revenue Service or to file the information return required of all other registered organizations; and the approximately 25 percent of all other charitable nonprofit organizations that are not recorded in IRS records but that prior research has documented to exist in communities throughout the country.

The IRS data were derived from *IRS Data Book: 1995*, p. 25. Data on the number of churches was compiled from several sources: *Yearbook of American & Canadian Churches*, Kenneth B. Bedell, ed. (New York: National Council of Churches, 1996), pp. 250–256 for Christian churches; television interview of Adburahman Alamoudi, Executive Director of American Muslim Council, National Public Radio, September 15, 1997, for Islamic mosques; Council of Jewish Federations for Jewish synagogues. The number of churches listed voluntarily with the IRS was derived from Mr. Ron Williams, IRS Personal Interview, October 27, 1997. The estimate of the number of 501(c)(3) organizations other than churches not listed with the Internal Revenue was based on survey work conducted by the present author in cooperation with a team of colleagues in sixteen American cities of various sizes in the early 1980s. See: Lester M. Salamon, *Partners in Public Service: Government-Nonprofit Relations in the Modern Welfare State* (Baltimore: Johns Hopkins University Press, 1995), p. 59, n.1.

The list of 1.164 million organizations provided by the Internal Revenue Service itself very likely includes numerous defunct, inactive, or informal organizations.

3. Revenue data derived from Independent Sector, *America's Nonprofit Sector in Brief* (Washington, D.C.: Independent Sector, Spring 1998) and U.S. Census Bureau, *1996 Census Annual Survey* (June 1998). Data on gross domestic products of foreign countries from U.S. Census Bureau, *Statistical Abstract of the United States: 1997,* p. 838.

4. Employment data derived from estimates prepared by Independent Sector, *America's Nonprofit Sector in Brief* (Washington, D.C., 1998) and from data in U.S. Department of Labor, Bureau of Labor Statistics, *Employment and Earnings,* 1996 (Washington, D.C., 1998).

5. Volunteer data derived from *Giving and Volunteering in the United States, 1996 Edition* (analyzed by Virginia A. Hodgkinson and Murray S. Weitzman), (Washington, D.C.: Independent Sector, 1996), p. 1–30. The nonprofit share of total volunteers was estimated from computer tapes made available by Independent Sector.

6. The justification for tax exemption in the case of religious organizations is naturally different from this, resting on the First Amendment's bar against any law that might prohibit the "free exercise" of religion. Taxation of churches has been judged to involve the kind of excessive entanglement of government with religion that the First Amendment has been interpreted to prohibit. Bruce Hopkins, *The Law of Tax-Exempt Organizations,* 6th edition. (New York: John Wiley and Sons, 1992), pp. 202–3.

7. The formal language of the law is somewhat more complex than this. Section 501(c)(3) status is available for: "Corporations, and any community chest, fund or foundation, organized and operated exclusively for religious, charitable, scientific, testing for public safety, literary, or educational purposes, or to foster national or international amateur sports competition (but only if no part of its activities involve the provision of athletic facilities or equip-

ment), or for the prevention of cruelty to children or animals."

8. The English Statute of Charitable Uses of 1601, which is the basis of the legal definition of the term charitable, specifically included the following activities within the term charitable: ". . . relief of aged, impotent, and poor people; . . . maintenance of sick and maimed soldiers and mariners; schools for learning, free schools, and scholars in universities; repair of bridges, ports, havens, causeways, churches, seabanks, and highways; . . . education and preferment of orphans; . . . relief, stock or maintenance of houses of correction; . . . marriages of poor maids; supportation, aid, and help of young tradesmen, handicraftsmen and persons decayed; relief or redemption of prisoners or captives; aid or ease of any poor inhabitants concerning payments of fifteens, setting out of soldiers and other taxes." For further detail, see: Hopkins, *The Law of Tax-Exempt Organizations* (1992), pp. 69–108.

9. The reason for this is that Section 501(c)(3) of the Internal Revenue Code law puts certain restrictions on the extent to which organizations can engage in "lobbying" activities, that is, activities intended to affect the passage or defeat of particular pieces of legislation. Organizations that intend to devote a substantial part of their activities to influencing legislation must seek tax-exempt status under Section 501(c)(4) of the Internal Revenue Code, which is reserved for "civic leagues or organizations not organized for profit but operated exclusively for the promotion of social welfare. . . ." Like "charitable" organizations exempted under section 501(c)(3), the "welfare organizations" granted exemption under section 501(c)(4) must be primarily public-serving and not member-serving in orientation, but they are allowed to be more action-oriented in political terms. In return, however, they cannot receive tax-deductible gifts. We have therefore depicted these organizations in Figure 2.1 in a special category. For more detail on the similarities and differences between 501(c)(3) and 501(c)(4) organizations, see Hopkins, *The Law of Tax-Exempt Organizations* (1992), pp. 564–568.

10. This estimate is a composite of estimates of bequest, foundation, corporate, and individual giving.

11. Comparable data for the United Kingdom, for example, reveal that private giving represents at most only about 1.4 percent of gross domestic product. Charities Aid Foundation, *Charity Trends.* 13th edition. (London: Charities Aid Foundation, 1990), p. 10.

12. See note 7 above for the derivation of the individual, bequest, foundation, and corporate giving to-

tals. The allocation of giving among recipient types is based largely on data provided by Murray Weitzman of Independent Sector. The estimate of charitable contributions received by foundations comes from: *Giving USA 1997,* p. 201. The estimate of giving to government agencies (e.g., higher education institutions) is derived by subtracting the estimates of giving to other independent sector organizations from total estimated giving.

13. While foundations in their present form have existed since the turn of the century, they were given legal definition only in 1969, with the passage of the Tax Reform Act. This Act differentiated foundations from other nonprofit institutions that have endowments and imposed extra restrictions on the foundations. The key defining feature of a foundation as opposed to other nonprofit institutions is that they typically receive their support from a single individual and utilize their resources chiefly to make grants or other "qualifying distributions" to other nonprofit organizations. To be treated as other than a foundation, nonprofit organizations must therefore meet a "public support test," demonstrating that they receive their support from multiple sources. "Community foundations," which, as noted below, receive their support from multiple sources also, fall into a special category in the law.

14. Loren Renz, Crystal Mandler, and Rikard Treiber, *Foundation Giving,* 1998 Edition. (New York: The Foundation Center, 1998), p. 5. All data on foundations here come from this source. (Cited hereafter as *Foundation Giving,* 1998).

15. U.S. Bureau of the Census, *Statistical Abstract of the United States,* 1997, 117th edition (Washington, DC: U.S. Government Printing Office, 1997), p. 510.

16. See note 7 for the source of the estimates of the various sources of giving. The estimates of foundation and corporate giving here differ from those mentioned in note 7 and the accompanying text in that the foundation figure includes giving by corporate foundations and the corporate giving figure is correspondingly reduced. This was done to make the estimates consistent with Foundation Center usage, which is the basis for all other foundation data here. Data on corporate foundation giving for 1996 were derived from *Foundation Giving 1998,* p. 5. Giving to religion was estimated by deducting from overall private giving to religious congregations an estimate developed by Independent Sector of the gifts these congregations made to other nonprofit organizations. It was assumed that all of the giving to religious congregations originates with individuals. I am grateful to Murray Weitzman of Independent Sector for sharing these estimates with me.

17. During the Carter Administration, several alternative funds, such as the Black United Fund and the United Health Appeal, secured permission to solicit contributions in the federal workplace. This was later revoked by the Reagan Administration, provoking a legal battle that has ended with a broadening of the access to the federal workplace and a greater willingness of the United Way to accept the donor option approach. For this and other features of United Way, see: Eleanor Brilliant, *The United Way: Dilemmas of Organized Charity* (New York: Columbia University Press, 1991).

18. United Way Press Release, August 18, 1997.

19. American Heart Association, World Wide Web Site, January 20, 1998.

20. World Wide Web site, www.nsfre.org, January 5, 1998.

21. Included here are an estimated 345,170 Christian churches, 1,500 Islamic mosques, and 1,859 Jewish synagogues. Data on churches from: *Yearbook of American and Canadian Churches,* 1996. Edited by Kenneth B. Bedell, (New York: National Council of the Churches of Christ in the United States, 1996), pp. 250–256. Data on mosques from American Muslim Council. Data on synagogues from Council of Jewish Federations. For a discussion of the definitions of these various types of religious organizations, see: Hopkins, *The Law of Tax-Exempt Organizations* (1992), pp. 270–272. The 350,000 religious congregations included here do not include the religiously affiliated service organizations offering day-care, family counseling, and other services, such as the agencies that are part of the Catholic Charities network or the Lutheran Social Services network. These agencies are included among the service agencies discussed later.

22. The First Amendment to the U.S. Constitution declares, "Congress shall make no law respecting an establishment of religion, or prohibiting the free exercise thereof."

23. Organizations that are church-related but that would be eligible for tax-exempt 501(c)(3) status for other than religious reasons (e.g., church-affiliated educational organizations, hospitals, orphanages, old-age homes) are required to be recognized under these other provisions and are not treated as churches. Typically such organizations must therefore secure separate tax-exempt status and are not covered by the exemption accorded the church *qua* church. Reflecting this, we do not treat them here as religious congregations, but rather as service organizations. On the treatment of churches and church-related charitable organizations, see: Hopkins, *The Law of Tax-Exempt Organizations* (1992), pp. 775–77.

24. This classification follows *U.S. Census of Service Industry* usage and is embraced here for convenience sake. The chapters in Part 2 of this volume separate out legal aid from other social services and group it with political action and international aid.

25. Lobbying is thus different from "advocacy." Advocacy includes the generation of information about public problems, the education of policymakers and the general public about such problems, and responses to inquiries from policymakers. Where advocacy crosses the line to become "lobbying" is when it is focused on a particular piece of legislation or administrative action. Organizations exempt under Section 501(c)(3) of the Internal Revenue Code are not limited in the extent of advocacy they can carry out, but they are limited in the extent of "lobbying" in which they can engage. Such lobbying cannot be a "substantial" part of the organization's activity, which has been interpreted to mean that it cannot absorb more than 20 percent of the organization's expenditures. For further detail, see: Hopkins, *The Law of Tax-Exempt Organizations* (1992), pp. 300–326, and Chapter 10 below.

26. This estimate was developed by subtracting from the 765,677 organizations registered as 501(c)(3) or 501(c)(4) organizations on the Internal Revenue Service's Master File of Exempt Organizations the estimated 78,866 churches that choose to register with the Internal Revenue Service even though they are not required to, and the approximately 51,330 funding intermediaries, and then adding the 25 percent of organizations that prior research has identified to exist locally but not to be included in the IRS listings. For further detail, see note 2 above. IRS data are from U.S. Internal Revenue Service, *Annual Report of the Director* (1997).

27. Reflecting this, only about a third of these organizations file the Form 990 that the Internal Revenue Code requires for all tax-exempt organizations with at least $25,000 in expenditures.

28. Included here are 129,956 organizations identified by the U.S. Census Bureau in its 1992 Census of Service Industries in the categories that meet our definition of public-benefit service organizations, plus 28,924 schools, colleges, and universities identified in the *Digest of Education Statistics,* and 14,288 civic organizations identified from the IRS records. Supplementation of the census data is necessary because the census did not cover schools and colleges in 1992. Deleted from the census data are certain member-serving organizations that do not meet our definition. In addition, the census tally of civic organizations groups these organizations with social and fraternal organizations that fall into the member-serving category in our grouping. Accordingly, we drew on IRS data to estimate the number of such civic organizations. For further information, see: U.S. Census Bureau, *1992 Census of Service Industries* (Washington: U.S. Government Printing Office, 1996); and U.S. Department of Education, National Center for Education Statistics, *Digest of Education Statistics,* 1997, Table 5.

An alternative estimate of the number of nonprofit public-benefit service organizations is available from data assembled by the Internal Revenue Service from the information forms (Form 990) that nonprofit organizations are required to file with the IRS. Only organizations with expenditures of $25,000 or more are required to file these forms, however. As of 1993, there were 152,186 such organizations that met our definition of a public-benefit service organization. Included here are all 164,247 501(c)(3) organizations that filed Form 990 in 1993 except for 5,345 philanthropic intermediaries and 6,716 religious-support organizations. (*Nonprofit Almanac 1996/97,* pp. 247–250). For a variety of reasons, the Census data appear more reliable and complete than the IRS Form 990 data. What is more, the classification of organizations in the IRS data differs from that used by the Census Bureau and other economic data agencies, making it difficult to line up the number of agencies with the extent of expenditures using the IRS data.

29. Nonprofit expenditure data provided by Murray Weitzman, Independent Sector, Washington, D.C., 1998. These data were adjusted to fit the definitions used here using data drawn from U.S. Bureau of the Census, Current Business Reports BS196, *Service Annual Survey: 1996* (Washington, D.C.: U.S. Government Printing Office, 1998). (Cited hereafter as Census Bureau, *Service Annual Survey: 1996*). In particular, social and fraternal organizations were deleted and Social Services Not Elsewhere Classified treated as part of civic. Excludes religious organizations and foundations. Data on gross domestic product and personal consumption expenditures on services from *Economic Report of the President* (February 1997), p. 300.

30. Lester M. Salamon, David Altschuler, and Jaana Myllyluoma, *More Than Just Charity: The Baltimore Nonprofit Sector in a Time of Change* (Baltimore: The Johns Hopkins Institute for Policy Studies, 1990), p. 9.

31. Computed from estimates provided by Murray Weitzman, Independent Sector, December 1997, adjusted to reflect the definitions used here as detailed in Endnote 29. Social service organization revenue

sources computed from special tabulations of Form 990 data supplied by the National Center for Charitable Statistics.

32. This assumes that approximately 12 percent of all religious contributions find their way to non-sacramental service organizations. Based on data provided by Murray Weitzman, Independent Sector, December 1997.

33. For more detail on this government-nonprofit financial link, see Lester M. Salamon, *Partners in Public Service: Government-Nonprofit Relations in the Modern Welfare State* (Baltimore: Johns Hopkins University Press, 1995.)

34. *Giving and Volunteering in the United States. 1996 Edition.* Virginia Ann Hodgkinson and Murray S. Weitzman. (Washington, D.C.: Independent Sector), p. 1–30.

35. The estimate of 4.7 million full-time equivalent workers and $103 billion in imputed value from volunteer inputs is based on applying to the 1995 estimates of total full-time equivalent volunteer workers of 9,233 million and total imputed value of volunteer work of $201.5 billion the estimated share of total volunteer time that is devoted to public-benefit service organizations. This latter was derived from data tapes generated from a 1996 survey conducted by the Gallup organization for Independent Sector. According to our own calculations, religious activities absorbed 24.4 percent of all volunteer time, for-profit organizations and governments 21.5 percent, professional organizations 3.0 percent, and other charitable nonprofit organizations 51.1 percent. Aggregate figures on the amount of volunteer time were derived from Independent Sector, *Giving and Volunteering in the United States, 1996 Edition,* (Washington, D.C.: Independent Sector, 1996). Full-time equivalent conversion was based on a full-time work-year of 1,700 hours. Volunteer time was valued at the average hourly wage for nonagricultural workers.

36. Lester M. Salamon and Helmut K. Anheier, *The Emerging Sector Revisited: A Summary* (Baltimore: MD: Johns Hopkins Institute for Policy Studies, 1998), p.8.

37. Lester M. Salamon, "The Rise of the Nonprofit Sector," *Foreign Affairs,* Vol. 73, No. 4 (July/August 1994), pp. 109–122.

▶ CHAPTER 3

Voluntary Sector

JACQUELYN THAYER SCOTT

Voluntary Sector. A term often used to describe the nonprofit, independent, or third, sector (in addition to the government and private economic enterprise) of the social economy; the preferred usage in Canada and the United Kingdom. The term has been most closely associated with numerous publications by American sociologists David Horton Smith (1972, 1973) and Jon Van Til (1988). Activities in this sector are usually conducted by formal organizational entities that are incorporated and governed by boards of directors and operate under a non-distribution constraint (i.e., profits or residual earnings of the organization may not be distributed to individuals who control the entity). Many of these incorporated organizations are also registered as charities and have tax-exempt status; that is, they do not pay income taxes on their earnings and donors receive some tax benefit (a deduction or a credit) for their financial contributions to the entity. When formally incorporated or registered, organizations in this sector must have clearly designated public-benefit purposes—usually related to religion, health, education, or social welfare—and partisan political activities by the entity are either prohibited or severely curtailed. However, the use of the term "voluntary sector" (as opposed to the more specific "nonprofit sector," especially in the United States) may include infor-mal and unorganized activity by persons and groups for charitable or broadly inclusive mutual benefit purposed, so long as voluntary action is evident in governance, provision of direct services, and/or financial support.

Historical Background

Although individuals voluntary activity within and between family and clan groups likely has been characteristic of human history since the earliest times, voluntary associations appear to have been around for only about 10,000 years. Robert Anderson (1973) reports that associations arose during the Neolithic period (7,000 or 8,000 B.C.E.), with the development of villages that were not integrated into complex political and economic systems. Earliest associations were religious societies, often of a secret nature, playing important roles in conserving traditions, and building bonds and alliances across family and tribal structures. In preindustrial states, association activity expanded to include the merchant associations of Greece, China, Rome, and Egypt, and the craft guilds of medieval Europe. The rise of the industrial nation-state coincided with the spread of democracy and the growth of bureaucratic techniques in government, leading to increased formalization of electoral and bureaucratic procedures in voluntary associations—statutes of incorporation, bylaws, an executive structure—devoted to more efficiency in making decisions and taking action. Anderson (1973) added that in modern societies, voluntary associations have acquired important sociological functions, including contributing to social stability by mediating between the individual and the community, especially in support of social change, "to adapt individuals for modern participation" (p. 22).

Voluntary association and sector activity in North America had historical roots in Elizabethan England and royalist France. Charitable purposes—relief of poverty, advancement of education, advancement of religion, or other charitable purpose beneficial to the community—were first set out in the Elizabethan Poor Law (1601), although distribution of charity to the destitute was left in the hands of municipal authorities or appointed overseers. In French Canada, a state Bureau of the Poor was established in 1685, funded through a combination of crown subsidies, fines from felonies and misdemeanors, and voluntary alms-giving. Thus, in both principal North American historical traditions, public institutions (or the church) were the principal recipients of private largesse. This was echoed in the earliest English colonial charitable organizations, Harvard College and local hospital societies in both the colonial United States and Upper Canada. Peter Dobkin Hall (1987, 1994) has written extensively on the suspicion with which Americans viewed the power of individuals incorporating and holding property in order to pursue their private interests, however charitable. It was not until the latter part of the nineteenth century, in both the United States and Canada, that a clear role for private institutions in the democratic state was set out in legislation. In 1874, President Charles Eliot of Harvard successfully defended the university's tax exemption to the Massachusetts General Court on the grounds of demonstrable public benefits being derived from private charitable institutions. The Massachusetts legislature subsequently expanded the range of tax-exempt institutions, and this law was seen as a model by other states. Also in 1874, the Charity Aid Act of

Ontario regularized state subsidies for religious, fraternal, and patriotic organizations operating hospitals, orphanages, and homes for unmarried mothers. This act also established government authority to inspect these private institutions and approve their management policies.

Voluntary sector associations and institutions continued to grow through the end of the nineteenth century and during the early part of the twentieth century. In the United States, this period was characterized as the "Golden Age of Philanthropy," when industrial giants like Andrew Carnegie and John D. Rockefeller parcelled out large fortunes to libraries, churches, and universities. They also established the first private grant-making foundations for charitable purposes. This period was also noted for establishment of community charitable foundations and united community fund-raising campaigns—the "Red Feather" drives, which evolved into the United Way—in both Canada and the United States.

The period of greatest growth in voluntary associations and the sector in North America, however, was after World War II. According to Hall (1994), "More than 90 percent nonprofit organizations currently in existence" (p. 3) in the United States were founded in this period. In Canada, this growth spurt peaked later, with the total number of registered charities growing by 40 percent during the 1980s (Scott 1992). These organizations are involved in a wide range of activities, including the direct delivery of services (often contracted for by the state), education of the public (including popular or moral education about public issues of the day), and advocacy for social change.

In recent years, scholars have devoted much energy to analyzing why the voluntary sector exists, what it includes (or excludes), and what factors affect its growth and structure. The theories about "why" it exists could be grouped as economic, religious, and sociopolitical. Economic theorists have been most plentiful, and a number of useful summary overviews of their work have been published. Henry Hansmann (1987) suggested economic theories of the sector can be divided into two types: theories about the role of voluntary institutions and theories about their behavior. "Role" theorists suggest that voluntary organizations serve as private producers of public goods because government or business cannot produce collective goods as well ("market failure"); or they offer a service (such as day care) where consumers may wish to "patronize a service provider in which they place more trust than they can in a proprietary firm" (p. 29) ("contract failure"); or they exist because the availability of government subsidies enables them to proliferate and compete with for-profit firms. "Behavior" theorists base their theories on the assumption that voluntary institutions cannot distribute their profits or residual earnings to those who control them. Thus, most of these theories are classical economic optimizing models: voluntary organizations will seek to maximize their budgets to enhance the importance of the organization or its managers; or they will be inherently inefficient (and fail to minimize costs) because their owners/managers do not benefit financially from efficient performance. These—and other—economic theories of the sector are important because they influence key public policies that affect it, such as tax exemption or the disallowance of for-profit firms in designated activities (such as day care or nursing homes).

Many have also written about the religious motivation for voluntary sector activity, particularly in the United States. Robert Bellah *et al.* (1985), in their landmark book *Habits of the Heart: Individualism and Commitment in American Life* wrote about the importance of the religious tradition in fostering activity that is other-oriented. Simplistically, these links can be summarized as flowing from the individual's belief that such behavior is (1) necessary for salvation and spiritual growth or harmony and (2) commanded by a "Higher Power."

Sectoral Boundaries

Implicitly, it would seem, voluntary sector activity is easily defined by the nature of its purpose, governance, and source or distribution of its funding. In fact, the task of "mapping" the sector has proven quite complex. Four sophisticated attempts have been undertaken to more clearly define the sectoral boundaries—by Russy Sumariwalla (1983), Ralph Kramer (1984), Franklin Gamwell (1984) and Jon Van Til (1988). Sumariwalla (1983) visualizes two principal divisions in the sector, private "nonbusiness" entities, operating either in the public interest or in an "all other" subcategory. In an alternate construct, he described the voluntary sector as "nonbusiness, nongovernmental," comprised of public interest and "all other" activities and organizations. Kramer (1984) focused his three-sector schematic on the delivery of personal and social services, and the interrelationships among profit making, governmental, and voluntary organizations. He identified the five possible relationships among sectors as reprivatization, empowerment, pragmatic partnership, governmental operation, and nationalization—a linear continuum that moves from private-sector predominance (of reprivatization) to voluntary-sector dominance (of empowerment) to increasing levels of governmental predominance (from pragmatic partnership through to nationalization). Gamwell (1984) draws on the philosophies of John Dewey and economist Milton Friedman in drawing two differing maps of the voluntary sector, before developing his own construction. The "Dewey map" defines the voluntary sector as "community-regarding," further subdividing it into "nonpublic interest" and "public interest" subsectors. The "Friedman map" subdivides the voluntary sector into "charitable" and "public service" categories. Gamwell's own map divides voluntary sector or "public-regarding" organizations on the basis of exclusively into "less inclusive" and "more inclusive" groupings. "More inclusive" groups are either "nonpolitical-regarding" or "political-regarding."

Van Til (1988) suggested a social science analog to natural science cartography. The voluntary sector (which he distinguishes from the household or informal sector) is subdivided into "public-regarding or charitable" associations and membership benefit" associations. His meteorological, or climatic, map looks at the three categories of values in the voluntary sector: basic democratic values as articulated by the eighteenth century French chronicler Tocqueville, the specter of privatism (Bellah *et al.*

1985), and cultural influences that come from associational life itself (which he derives from the work of sociologist Emile Durkheim). Finally, Van Til (1988) constructed a tectonic map, seeking to understand underlying forces affecting the shape and nature of sectoral activities: bureaucratization, mass democratization, power and oligarchical control, economic concentration, and the interpenetration of sectors.

As to which organizations and activities, precisely, are in the voluntary sector, the ultimate decision is made by the state and/or by the membership of the voluntary entity itself. In the United States, the state's determination is generally made by the Internal Revenue Service (IRS), which confers tax-exempt status and classifies voluntary organizations by subsections of the Tax Code. In 1991, the IRS listed 1,055,545 tax-exempt organizations, but this number includes a wide variety of organizations with a public purpose, such as mutual insurance companies and multiemployer pension plans. Most, however, would consider the core of the voluntary sector to be those organizations that are qualified for tax-exemption under Section 501(c)(3)—those generally known as the "charitable" nonprofits, serving broad public purposes that transcend interests of their members or benefactors.

In Canada, Revenue Canada determines tax-exempt status, and voluntary sector "charitable" organizations are divided into categories for welfare, health, education, religion, benefit to community (libraries, museums, historical sites, community foundations and trusts, recreation, protection of animals, etc.) and other (service clubs, employees' charity trusts, amateur athletic associations, etc.). During the high-growth period between 1974 and 1986, the greatest growth occurred in voluntary associations concerned broadly with public education (e.g., self-help and cultural, social, or public issues), rising from 9 to 14 percent of total charities.

A Sector Under Challenge

In both the United States and Canada, the voluntary sector is seen to be under challenge. The U.S. challenges were summarized by Hodgkinson and Lyman (1992) as including (1) identification of the sector and its members (an issue also dealt with extensively by Lohmann 1992), (2) widespread understanding and acceptance of the roles and functions, missions and practices of voluntary organizations, (3) the crisis in financing as governments restructure to meet global competitive needs, (4) lack of good research information about the sector and appropriate education about the role the sector plays in U.S. society. The challenges to the Canadian sector were set out by Jacquelyn Thayer Scott (1992), who saw issues of role acceptance and financing as associated with deeper changes in the Canadian public philosophy of the state, with which the voluntary sector is highly interactive. The proliferation of voluntary organizations during the late 1970s and 1980s was consistent with uncertainty about maintenance of the social welfare state and the rise of neocorporatism and the postindustrial global economy—but voluntary organizations were shaken as they moved to adjust from a focus on membership, constituency, and functional program direction (in a period dominated by pluralism) to concern for management efficiency (in a period increasingly dominated by neocorporatism). With indications that Canada's public philosophy of the state was moving in the 1990s toward communitarianism—a variant of democratic theory, which intentionally links individual values, needs, and aims with those of the larger community (in contrast to liberalism's historic emphasis on rights-based individualism)—Scott (1992) argued that the voluntary organization must adjust to this new reality by focusing on governance, decisionmaking processes, and values of its mission.

The interactivity of the voluntary sector with the state and its theoretical political underpinnings has been made by Kramer (1990) and Salamon (1987), as well. Lester Salamon (1987) suggested a theory of government-nonprofit partnership that recognizes the voluntary sector is limited in its ability to generate adequate resources and is vulnerable to particularism, the favoritism of the wealthy, amateurism, and self-defeating paternalism—but this corresponds well with government's strengths in generating resources, setting priorities through democratic processes, establishing quality-control standards and rights to access. Since voluntary organizations are more capable than government of personalizing service provision, operating on a smaller scale, and adjusting to the needs of clients, collaboration between government and nonprofits is more logical than replacement of one by the other, Salamon (1987) argued.

Most scholarship on the voluntary sector globally continues to be local or national case studies with few comprehensive, comparative works. The best-known of these latter are Benjamin Gidron *et al.* (1992) and Kathleen McCarthy *et al.* (1992). Common challenges are identified as including promoting individual participation in voluntary activity, guaranteeing freedom of association, strengthening managerial capacity, and maintaining independence and political viability for voluntary organizations.

Bibliography

Anderson, Robert T., 1973. "Voluntary Associations in History: From Paleolithic to Present Times." In David Horton Smith, ed., *Voluntary Action Research: 1973.* Lexington, MA: Lexington Books, 9–28.

Bellah, Robert N., Richard Madsen, Steven M. Tipton, William M. Sullivan, and Ann Swidler, 1985. *Habits of the Heart: Individualism and Commitment in American Life.* New York: Harper and Row.

Bowen, William G., Thomas I. Nygren, Sarah E. Turner, and Elizabeth A. Duffy, 1994. *The Charitable Nonprofits.* San Francisco, CA: Jossey-Bass.

Douglas, James, 1987. "Political Theories of Nonprofit Organization." In Walter W. Powell, ed., *The Nonprofit Sector: A Research Handbook.* New Haven, CT: Yale University Press, 43–54.

Gamwell, Franklin I., 1984. *Beyond Preference: Liberal Theories of Independent Associations.* Chicago, IL: University of Chicago Press.

Gidron, Benjamin, Ralph M. Kramer, and Lester M. Salamon, eds., 1992. *Government and the Third Sector: Emerging Relationships in Welfare States.* San Francisco, CA: Jossey-Bass.

Hall, Peter Dobkin, 1987. "A Historical Overview of the Private Nonprofit Sector." In Walter W. Powell, ed., *The Nonprofit Sector: A Research Handbook.* New Haven, CT: Yale University Press, 3–26.

———, 1994. "Historical Perspectives on Nonprofit Organizations." In Robert D. Herman, ed., *The Jossey-Bass Handbook of Nonprofit Leadership and Management.* San Francisco, CA: Jossey-Bass, 3–43.

Hansmann, Henry, 1987. "Economic Theories of Nonprofit Organization." In Walter W. Powell, ed., *The Nonprofit Sector: A Research Handbook.* New Haven, CT: Yale University Press, 27–42.

Hodgkinson, Virginia A., and Richard W. Lyman, eds., 1992. *The Future of the Nonprofit Sector.* San Francisco, CA: Jossey-Bass.

Hodgkinson, Virginia A., Murray S. Weitzman, and Arthur D. Kirsch, 1988. *From Belief to Commitment: The Activities and Finances of Religious Congregations in the United States.* Washington, DC: Independent Sector.

Joseph, James A., Edgar C. Reckard, and Jean A. McDonald, 1985. *The Philanthropy of Organized Religion.* Washington, DC: Council on Foundations.

Kramer, Ralph M., 1984. *The Economic Illusion: False Choices Between Prosperity and Social Justice.* Boston: Houghton Mifflin.

———, 1990. "Voluntary Organizations in the Welfare State: On the Threshold of the '90s." *The Centre for Voluntary Organizations Working Paper 8.* London: London School of Economics and Political Science.

Lohmann, Roger A., 1992. *The Commons.* San Francisco, CA: Jossey-Bass.

McCarthy, Kathleen D., Virginia A. Hodgkinson, Russy D. Sumariwalla, eds., 1992. *The Nonprofit Sector in the Global Community: Voices from Many Nations.* San Francisco, CA: Jossey-Bass.

Salamon, Lester M., 1987. "Partners in Public Service: The Scope and Theory of Government-Nonprofit Relations." In Walter W. Powell, ed., *The Nonprofit Sector: A Research Handbook.* New Haven, CT: Yale University Press, 99–117.

Scott, Jacquelyn Thayer, 1992. "Voluntary Sector in Crisis: Canada's Changing Public Philosophy of the State and Its Impact on Voluntary Charitable Organizations." Ph.D. dissertation, University of Colorado at Denver. Ann Arbor, MI: University Microfilms.

Smith, David Horton, ed., 1972. *Voluntary Action Research: 1972.* Lexington, MA: Lexington Books.

Smith, David Horton, 1973. "The Impact of the Voluntary Sector on Society." In David Horton Smith, ed., *Voluntary Action Research: 1973.* Lexington, MA: Lexington Books, 387–400.

Sumariwalla, Russy D., 1983. "Preliminary Observations on Scope, Size, and Classification of the Sector." In Virginia A. Hodgkinson, ed., *Working Papers for the Spring Research Forum: Since the Filer Commission.* Washington, DC: Independent Sector, 433–449.

Van Til, Jon, 1988. *Mapping the Third Sector: Voluntarism in a Changing Social Economy.* New York: Foundation Center.

PART 2

THE NONPROFIT SECTOR'S DISTINCTIVE VALUES AND CONTRIBUTIONS TO SOCIETY

Many values and contributions of the nonprofit sector are distinctive. On the other hand, the wide range in organizational sizes, purposes, functions, sources of income, levels of hierarchy, structural formality, managerial sophistication, degree of commercialization, and extent of reliance on volunteers makes it difficult to speak in generalities about the distinctiveness of the nonprofit sector. There are probably as many varieties of nonprofits as there are types of businesses. And all nonprofits share at least some aspects of their structures, processes, and commitment to the public good with organizations in the public and private sectors. Thus it is difficult to see or "feel" differences between some nonprofits and for-profits that have similar purposes and functions, for example, between most large hospitals in the two sectors. Employees and patients may not be able to sense any difference at all. The policies and procedures of some nonprofits that are heavily dependent on government contracts for revenue are virtually indistinguishable from the government agencies with which they contract. Thus, the term *distinctive* is approached with caution in this chapter, and the term *unique* has been avoided completely.

Despite these caveats and cautions, virtually all nonprofit sector organizations can claim some degree of distinctiveness in most of the following respects:

1. Their origins and histories are based on the values and practices of *philanthropy*—defined broadly to include *volunteerism, charity,* and *altruism.*
2. They exist primarily for the purpose of making some aspects of their "world" better—or preventing it from becoming worse.
3. Historically, organizations in the nonprofit sector have been financed largely through a *charitable* or *grants economy.*
4. They share *a commitment to the underlying values of individualism and pluralism* with for-profit businesses, more so than the values of equity and justice that serve as the foundations of the public sector.

5. Their perception of how the *public good* is defined differs substantively from the public sector.
6. They are "pathways to participation," the "vehicles" people use to gain access to, to participate in, and to establish links in their communities.[1]
7. They are the essence of community.[2]

Philanthropy

Philanthropy, the nonprofit sector's first distinctive pillar, is "voluntary giving, voluntary serving, and voluntary association to achieve some vision of the public good [and] includes charity, patronage, and civil society."[3] Thus, *philanthropy* is a broader term than *charity,* which means "relieving or alleviating specific instances of suffering—aiding the individual victims of specific social ills." With philanthropy, a return is expected from the donation in some form of improvement in the public's welfare or general benefit. *Philanthropy* attempts to eliminate the causes of problems that *charity* seeks to alleviate. *Voluntarism* is "actions undertaken freely by individuals, groups, or organizations that are not compelled by government, or directed principally at financial or economic gain, regarded as beneficial by participants or the larger society."[4]

The study of the nonprofit sector begins and ends with philanthropy, which is an area of applied ethics or applied moral philosophy. Philanthropy, including voluntarism, collectively organized and enabled through nonprofit sector organizations, is the primary means that has developed in our society for making individual choices among value preferences.

Voluntary action for the public good begins with individuals taking the initiative to improve the lives of others. Since the Reformation, two predominant forms of giving and assisting for the benefit of others have been evident in Western civilizations: individual and associational. This book focuses on associational philanthropy—the nonprofit sector and nonprofit organizations that enable and support philanthropy—including voluntarism.

Although many good things happen when individuals volunteer to give time or money to people in need or to causes, many more good things happen for longer periods of time when individuals join together, form associations, and collectively attack social or environmental ills or aid their victims. Associational philanthropy thus is the essence of *social capital formation,* "those bonds of trust and reciprocity that seem to be pivotal for a democratic society and a market economy to function effectively."[5] And giving—of time, energy, and money—is the "fuel" that energizes associational philanthropy.

Not all nonprofit organizations are recipients of or conduits for philanthropy. (See Part 1, "Introduction to the Nonprofit Sector.") Many nonprofits rely on fees for services and government contracts for the majority of their revenues, and many do not utilize volunteers. Yet an enormous number of others do rely on philanthropy, particularly in the subsectors of religion, the arts and humanities, advocacy, private education, environmental protection, and to a lesser extent, health and human services. Although many government agencies also are recipients of philanthropy, including fire departments, elementary schools, public libraries, and even occasionally the Internal Revenue Service, these exceptions do not diminish the distinctiveness of philanthropy for the nonprofit sector.

Nonprofit Organizations Exist Primarily to Improve the Quality of Life

Nonprofits and the people who work in them are allowed to make money—legally and morally. Personal gain, however, is not the primary purpose for nonprofits. The most fundamental reason why the nonprofit sector exists is to encourage and enable the benevolent donation of money, property, and time and effort to eliminate or prevent the causes of social problems and injustices and to otherwise improve the quality of life around us. This is true whether the organization exists primarily to promote the arts and humanities, help terminally ill persons die with dignity, advocate for environmental protection or gay rights, or advance a set of religious beliefs.

In recent decades, the nonprofit sector has become the object of high expectations among elected officials and a large segment of the general public. During the "social welfare reform" era of the late 1990s and early 2000s, nonprofits were expected to serve as the "safety net" for individuals and families who had exhausted their access to public supports but who were not self-sufficient. The nonprofit sector is expected to be the means for solving (not simply ameliorating) deep social problems by rebuilding "community" through its ability to generate *social capital*. George Bush (Senior), for example, often espoused the importance of the "thousand points of light" as voluntary solutions to societal problems, first as a presidential candidate in the late 1980s and subsequently as president. Thus, we have broadly come to expect our nonprofit sector to right myriad societal wrongs—and to "pick up the pieces" when the "system" fails.

Charitable or Grants Economy

Although the sources of revenues have changed noticeably in recent decades (see Part 1), organizations in the nonprofit sector have been financed largely through a charitable or *grants economy*. In contrast, government is financed primarily through a *coercive economy* (its primary revenue sources are taxes) and businesses through the *market economy*. (See Part 6, "Economic and Political Theories.")

The Sector's Core Values of Individualism and Pluralism

The values of *equity* and *justice* are the bedrock foundations for government. Government's overriding concern for equity and justice has been the primary cause for the proliferation of policies, procedures, and rules (and inflexibility) that attempt to ensure that everyone receives equal treatment. In this era of government downsizing, reinvention, and reengineering, unwavering government concern for equity and justice has been declared inadequate. Flexible responsiveness to individual client needs, circumstances, and preferences has been replacing equity and justice as the values we want emphasized in solving social problems. "One size does not fit all."[6]

The values of *individualism* and *pluralism* therefore are central to the existence and the essence of the nonprofit sector. The sector's history is in essence a long-standing record of voluntary giving for causes and cases that appeal to people individually and collectively through voluntary associations. Philanthropy and voluntarism, collectively organized and enabled through nonprofit sector organizations, are the primary means in our society for making individual choices among value preferences.

The nonprofit sector shares its core values of individualism and pluralism with the for-profit or business sector, because these same values are essential to the functioning of a market (or capitalistic) economy. Thus, although they are an essential part of the nonprofit sector's distinctiveness, they are not unique to this sector.

A Different Approach to Defining the "Public Good"

Many of us have our own visions of *the public good,* visions that we believe are compelling enough that others should share them—particularly elected officials and candidates for public office. Fortunately or unfortunately, however, *the public good* is an elusive concept because it is a socially constructed reality—a subjective, individualistic point of view or set of preferences.[7] And implementation of a vision of the public good usually requires collective action and an allocation of resources. Thus *some* collective definition of the public good is required in order to advance a vision into solution strategies. Otherwise our vision remains nothing more than a dream.

Government defines the public good through legislative actions that apply to everyone (almost). Tax revenues are allocated by the legislature among competing values, priorities, and projects through the appropriations process. In contrast, the nonprofit sector defines the public good by the willingness of individuals, families, corporations, foundations, and the government to donate, volunteer, or contract with nonprofit organizations to support the accomplishment of their particular missions. Thus, universal definitions of the public good are rarely sought in the nonprofit sector. Instead, operational definitions of the public good evolve piecemeal from the voluntary individual and collective giving of people and organizations in all three sectors.

Nonprofits as "Pathways to Participation"

Nonprofit organizations are the means—the "vehicles"—that individuals, families, and friends use to become active participants in their communities. Few problems can be solved or opportunities capitalized upon by people working alone. Nonprofits are voluntary associations of people who *decide individually* to *work collectively* to achieve ends that they decide are important—to them. If the ends were not important to them individually, they would not participate—or at least would not continue to participate for very long. "In no country in the world has the principle of association been more successfully used or applied to a greater multitude of objects than in America. . . . A vast number [of associations] . . . are formed and maintained by the agency of private individuals."[8]

Nonprofits as "Manifestations of Community"

At the same time that a nonprofit association is helping to alleviate poverty or a theater group is practicing for a performance, other long-term benefits are also being achieved—indirectly and usually not consciously. First, the nonprofit organizations provide outlets for individuals to develop and express their creativity—while they solve community housing problems or provide new learning or recreational opportunities in their neighborhoods.

Second, community leadership capability is developed among individuals, which can be applied in organizations in all three sectors. Future government officials, business executives, and nonprofit board members develop leadership, political, networking, and managerial skills and values by participating in nonprofit organizations.

Third, while individuals are working together on problems, community "networks" are built, used, and "banked" for future use on different issues. *Social capital* is the term used to describe the established linkages among people in communities who share common cares and concerns. These linkages or networks are themselves "capital assets" of a community. When caring people share common concerns, a capacity is created (or expanded) to prevent or resolve a variety of social problems. And fourth, if sufficient numbers of people participate enough—if enough individuals give enough time or money to the problem or opportunity—the need for government funding (tax support) may be diminished or eliminated.

As "manifestations of community,"[9] nonprofits thereby serve at least five distinctive "public benefit" ends: The situation that was the cause for the participation is improved; individuals find outlets for their creativity and desire to participate; community leadership is developed; social capital is created; and reliance on government may be diminished. As Alexis de Tocqueville observed in 1834,

> When an association is allowed to establish centers of action at certain important points in the country, its activity is increased and its influence extended. Men have the opportunity of seeing one another; means of execution are combined; and opinions are maintained with a warmth and energy that written language can never attain.[10]

But the Sector Is Not Independent

Until a few decades ago, many of us liked to think of the nonprofit sector as *the independent sector,* a sector whose organizations were free to pursue missions and purposes unfettered by legislatively—and bureaucratically—imposed mandates and restrictions, and free from the need to chase profits with every activity undertaken. Indeed, one of the largest and best known "umbrella associations" in the nonprofit sector was optimistically named the Independent Sector. Unquestionably, the nonprofit sector has been an independent voice for progressive solutions to social ills and an independent source of creative approaches to complex problems. Nonprofit organizations always have been largely dependent on others for their revenue, however, and it is quite difficult for organizations to remain programmatically independent when they are financially dependent. Perhaps organizations in the sector were more independent in earlier years, when individual donations were the largest source of income. Furthermore, as the boundaries among the three sectors have grown increasingly blurry over the past three decades, the independence of organizations in the nonprofit sector has diminished. It is doubtful that the label "independent" fits the nonprofit sector at the turn of the twenty-first century—if it ever did.

Readings Included in This Part

The article, chapter, and encyclopedia entries that are reprinted in this part expand on the distinctive aspects of the nonprofit sector that are discussed above. Although the historical development of the nonprofit sector and its philosophies is the topic of Part 3, several "historical" readings also are presented here—and several more are in Part 9, "Giving Theory." Quite obviously, the sector's history has influenced its distinctiveness, and giving—philanthropy—is an integral part of its history and its distinctiveness.

Jeffrey Brudney defines "voluntarism" in the reading reprinted in this part as "actions undertaken freely by individuals, groups, or organizations that are not compelled by biological need or social convention, mandated or coerced by government, or directed principally at financial or economic gain, regarded as beneficial by participants or the larger society."[11] Echoing most of Brudney's themes, John Van Til defines "voluntary action" as "freely chosen activity, usually directed toward the achievement of a long-term socially related goal and not merely a manifestation of biological, political, or economic drives."[12]

"The Gospel of Wealth," by Andrew Carnegie, the turn-of-the-twentieth-century steel baron whose personal saga is one of the greatest rags-to-riches models of industrial opportunity in the new world, was published originally in two 1889 journal articles under the simpler title "Wealth." It was renamed and republished as "The Gospel of Wealth" in 1900 and became the first compelling justification for a philosophy of philanthropy in the United States. It was eminently influential in establishing an early conceptual basis for philanthropy and against charity. Carnegie himself was a premier philanthropist who gave away most of his wealth to colleges and community libraries.

Concerned about communism, Carnegie viewed the democratic ideals of individualism, the right to hold private property, and the right to accumulate wealth as essential for humankind and this nation to evolve into a higher form. Carnegie was both pragmatic and philosophical. He advocated maintaining a spirit of competition and the higher result of human experience, and thereby preventing the spread of communism through (1) the redistribution of wealth by those who achieved it, (2) living a moderate lifestyle, and (3) not spoiling heirs by leaving them vast sums. Carnegie insisted that money should be used to help people help themselves. Not even a quarter should be wasted on a passing beggar to encourage "slothful behavior." Carnegie truly was concerned about possible struggles between the "haves" and the "have-nots." The rich, he believed, bear the obligation to "even things out" in society. Carnegie's "Wealth" should be read in order to understand a controversial point of view. It should not be accepted as "the gospel" of philanthropy.[13]

The "Filer Commission Report" is one of the best known and most articulate treatises on philanthropy and the nonprofit sector in modern U.S. history. The Filer Commission was established in 1973 by John D. Rockefeller to study the roles of philanthropic giving and the voluntary sector in the United States "at a time when [the nonprofit sector] was being attacked by hostile forces in the Richard Nixon administration and in the U.S. Congress."[14] John Filer, of the Aetna Life and Casualty Company, served as its chair. The 1975 report (which is reprinted here) carried the official title "The Report of the Commission on Private Philanthropy and Public Needs." Filer argued persuasively that the Tax Reform Act of 1969 had weakened and jeopardized the future of private foundations, the entire nonprofit sector, and thus also the nation. Prior to the 1969 act, there had not even been a definition of a private foundation in the IRS Tax Code. Indeed, the IRS did not have a way to identify organizations that were claiming tax-exempt status.

The events and the political climate leading up to the formation of the Filer Commission were interesting. Between 1950 and 1969, the U.S. Congress had become worried about the role of the nonprofit sector and the potential for foundation abuses. President Nixon and several influential members of Congress also were concerned about "liberal" faculty members at private universities and staffers at nonprofit "think tanks" who were outspoken opponents of the Vietnam War. The pressure for government regulation mounted as various congressional investigative hearings brought reports of abuses into public view. (Some reports were accurate, and some less than accurate.) Several nonprofits, mostly in higher education and health care, also raised ire for their failure to accept federal affirmative action guidelines, sexual as well as racial. The general public began to demand effective tax reform and control of private foundations. These multiple political pressures collectively culminated in passage of the watershed legislation for the regulation of private foundations, the Tax Reform Act of 1969. The 1969 act established distinctions between private foundations and public charitable organizations, placed new restrictions and taxes on private foundations, and gave the IRS expanded means and "teeth" to obtain information from foundations and other nonprofits. The act thereby redefined the entirety of the "playing field" and the rules of the philanthropy "game" in the United States.

By 1973, the effects of the Tax Reform Act of 1969 were unmistakably evident. The nonprofit sector was ailing. Private foundations were in particular danger. Public opinion, though, once again began to swing. Several studies were initiated in attempts to reestablish a balanced perspective on the roles and functions of private foundations in particular and nonprofits in general. The Filer Commission was the most notable of the many study groups that were formed in the early 1970s to review the sector's structure, contributions to society, functions, and worth—and its health. The 1975 Filer Commission Report concluded that the nonprofit sector is a distinctive element in the structure of society in the United States. The report also noted several of the most valuable "distinctive contributions" of the nonprofit sector, including the following: (1) the nonprofit sector initiates new ideas that government and businesses are unwilling to support; (2) it develops public policy leadership; and (3) it helps decrease feelings of alienation and powerlessness caused by interactions with ever larger, more impersonal government and business institutions. The Filer Commission Report indeed was an eloquent statement that caught the favorable attention of the public and the Congress. Whether or not it influenced long-term public policy is an open question.[15]

David Horton Smith's chapter, "The Impact of the Volunteer Sector on Society," continues to be the most frequently cited statement about the nonprofit sector's distinctive social contributions to U.S. society. Others have documented the sector's contributions, but his list remains (arguably) the most richly comprehensive.[16] Smith emphasizes the nature of nonprofit organizations in a three-sector environment and the nonprofit sector's ability to provide social risk capital, ideological innovation, social buffering, social integration, and preservation of traditions and ideas.

In defining the distinctive roles that nonprofits fill, Smith also expands our understanding of individual motivations for involvement with nonprofit sector organizations and their activities. Smith explains that in the 1970s, nonprofits were "safe havens" for post-1960s change and reform and, at the same time, keepers of America's traditions. Smith also was ahead of his time in urging for more evaluation of voluntary action to determine the effectiveness of voluntary organizations and movements.

Notes

1. Steven Rathgeb Smith and Michael Lipsky, *Nonprofits for Hire: The Welfare State in the Age of Contracting* (Cambridge: Harvard University Press, 1992), chapter 2, "Nonprofit Organizations and Community."

2. Lester A. Salamon identifies six distinctive characteristics of organizations in the nonprofit sector: formal, private, non-profit-distributing, self-governing, voluntary, and of public benefit. Lester A. Salamon, *America's Nonprofit Sector: A Primer,* 2nd ed. (New York: Foundation Center, 1999), pp. 10, 11.

3. Warren F. Ilchman, "Philanthropy," in Jay M. Shafritz, ed., *International Encyclopedia of Public Policy and Administration* (Boulder: Westview, 1998), p. 1654.

4. Jeffrey L. Brudney, "Voluntarism," in Jay M. Shafritz, ed., *International Encyclopedia of Public Policy and Administration* (Boulder: Westview, 1998), p. 2343.

5. Lester M. Salamon, *Holding the Center: America's Nonprofit Sector at a Crossroads* (New York: Nathan Cummings Foundation, 1997), p. 9. See also Darcy Ashman, L. David Brown, and Elizabeth Zwick, "The Strength of Strong and Weak Ties: Building Social Capital for the Formation and Governance of Civil Society Resource Organizations," *Nonprofit Management and Leadership* 9 (2), Winter 1998, pp. 153–171.

6. See, for example: chapter 1 in David Osborne and Ted Gaebler, *Reinventing Government* (Reading, Mass.: Addison-Wesley, 1992); and part 1 in Michael Barzelay, *Breaking Through Bureaucracy* (Berkeley: University of California Press, 1992).

7. Peter L. Berger and T. Luckmann, *The Social Construction of Reality* (Garden City, N.Y.: Doubleday, 1966).

8. Alexis de Tocqueville, "Political Associations in the United States," *Democracy in America,* vol. 1 (The Henry Reeve text as revised by Francis Bowen, now further corrected and edited by Phillips Bradley) New York: Vintage Books, 1945, p. 198.

9. Chapter 4 in Steven Rathgeb Smith and Micheal Lipsky, *Nonprofits for Hire: The Welfare State in the Age of Contracting* (Cambridge: Harvard University Press, 1992).

10. Tocqueville, "Political Associations," p. 199.

11. Brudney, "Voluntarism," pp. 2343–2349.

12. John Van Til, "Voluntary Action," in Jay M. Shafritz, ed., *International Encyclopedia of Public Policy and Administration* (Boulder: Westview, 1998), p. 2349.

13. For more on Carnegie's philosophy and for a comparison between the philanthropic beliefs of Carnegie and his contemporary John D. Rockefeller, see Milton Goldin's article "The Founding Fathers of Modern Philanthropy," reprinted in Part 9.

14. Erna Gelles, "Filer Commission," in Jay M. Shafritz, ed., *International Encyclopedia of Public Policy and Administration* (Boulder: Westview, 1998), pp. 885–887.

15. For more information about the Filer Commission and its report, see "100 Years of Tax Policy Changes Affecting Charitable Organizations, by Gary N. Scrivner, which is reprinted in Part 3.

16. See, for example, Lester A. Salamon's chapter, "The Contributions of the Nonprofit Sector," in *Holding the Center: America's Nonprofit Sector at a Crossroads* (New York: Nathan Cummings Foundation, 1997); and to an extent, Peter Dobkin Hall, "Inventing the Nonprofit Sector," in *Inventing the Nonprofit Sector* (Baltimore: Johns Hopkins University Press, 1992) (reprinted in Part 3); and Steven Rathgeb Smith and Michael Lipsky, "Nonprofit Organizations and Community," in *Nonprofits for Hire: The Welfare State in the Age of Contracting* (Cambridge: Harvard University Press, 1993) (reprinted in Part 7).

References

Ashman, Darcy, L. David Brown, and Elizabeth Zwick. "The Strength of Strong and Weak Ties: Building Social Capital for the Formation and Governance of Civil Society Resource Organizations." *Nonprofit Management and Leadership* 9 (2), Winter 1998, 153–171.

Barzelay, Michael. *Breaking Through Bureaucracy.* Berkeley: University of California Press, 1992.

Berger, Peter L., and T. Luckmann. *The Social Construction of Reality.* Garden City, N.Y.: Doubleday, 1966.

Brudney, Jeffrey L. "Voluntarism." In Jay M. Shafritz, ed., *International Encyclopedia of Public Policy and Administration,* pp. 2343–2349. Boulder: Westview, 1998.

Carnegie, Andrew. *The Gospel of Wealth: And Other Timely Essays.* New York: Century, 1900.

_____. "Wealth." *North American Review* 147, June 1889, 653–664; and 149, December 1889, 682–698.

Coleman, James S. "Social Capital in the Creation of Human Capital." *American Journal of Sociology* 94 (Supplement), 1988, S95-S120.

Filer, John H. "The Filer Commission Report." *Giving in America: Toward a Stronger Voluntary Sector.* Washington, D.C.: National Commission on Private Philanthropy and Public Needs, 1975.

Gelles, Erna. "Filer Commission." In Jay M. Shafritz, ed., *International Encyclopedia of Public Policy and Administration,* pp. 885–887. Boulder: Westview, 1998.

Gies, David L., J. Steven Ott, and Jay M. Shafritz, eds. *The Nonprofit Organization: Essential Readings.* Fort Worth, Tex.: Harcourt Brace, 1990.

Goldin, Milton. "The Founding Fathers of Modern Philanthropy." *Fund Raising Management* 99, June 1988, 48–50.

Hall, Peter Dobkin. *Inventing the Nonprofit Sector.* Baltimore: Johns Hopkins University Press, 1992.

Ilchman, Warren F. "Philanthropy." In Jay M. Shafritz, ed., *International Encyclopedia of Public Policy and Administration,* p. 1654. Boulder: Westview, 1998.

Osborne, David, and Ted Gaebler. *Reinventing Government.* Reading, Mass.: Addison-Wesley, 1992.

Powell, Walter W., and Elisabeth S. Clemens, eds. *Private Action and the Public Good.* New Haven: Yale University Press, 1998.

Putnam, Robert D. "Bowling Alone: America's Declining Social Capital." *Journal of Democracy* 6 (1), January 1995, 65–78.

_____. "The Prosperous Community: Social Capital and Public Life." *American Prospect* 13, 1993, 35–42.

Salamon, Lester M. *America's Nonprofit Sector: A Primer,* 2nd ed. New York: Foundation Center, 1999.

_____. *Holding the Center: America's Nonprofit Sector at a Crossroads.* New York: Nathan Cummings Foundation, 1997.

Scrivner, Gary N. "100 Years of Tax Policy Changes Affecting Charitable Organizations." In David L. Gies, J. Steven Ott, and Jay M. Shafritz, eds., *The Nonprofit Organization: Essential Readings,* pp. 126–137. Fort Worth, Tex.: Harcourt Brace, 1990.

Smith, David Horton. "The Impact of the Volunteer Sector on Society." In D. H. Smith, *Voluntary Action Research.* Lexington, Mass.: Lexington Books, 1973.

Smith, Steven Rathgeb, and Michael Lipsky. *Nonprofits for Hire: The Welfare State in the Age of Contracting.* Cambridge: Harvard University Press, 1992.

Tocqueville, Alexis de. "Political Associations in the United States." In *Democracy in America*, vol. 1 (The Henry Reeve text as revised by Francis Bowen, now further corrected and edited by Phillips Bradley). New York: Vintage Books, 1945.

Van Til, John. "Voluntary Action." In Jay M. Shafritz, ed., *International Encyclopedia of Public Policy and Administration*, p. 2349. Boulder: Westview, 1998.

CHAPTER 4

Voluntarism

JEFFREY L. BRUDNEY

Voluntarism. Actions undertaken freely by individuals, groups, or organizations that are not compelled by biological need or social convention, mandated or coerced by government, or directed principally at financial or economic gain, regarded as beneficial by participants or the larger society.

As suggested by the complexity of this definition, the study of voluntarism is not for those who insist on precise terms, crisp distinctions, and tidy categories. Jon Van Til (1988) has devoted an entire book to elucidating the construct and untangling it from related concepts, such as freedom, philanthropy, volunteering, and voluntary association. Most research on the subject concentrates on either the organizational aspects of voluntarism, such as the origin, history, role, and management of not-for-profit institutions, or the voluntary behavior of individuals, particularly the motivations that lead people to donate their time and/or money to preferred causes, and the implications of such gifts for the giver and the recipient. The definition of voluntarism offered here embraces—and attempts to unify—both principal foci.

On the one hand, voluntarism encompasses behavior as micro and seemingly insignificant (from a societal point of view) as helping a friend move, leading a church choir, contributing time to a homeless shelter, or attending a meeting of an arts club or self-help group. It includes many thousands of informal groups and grassroots associations that may meet only sporadically, have no paid personnel, rarely accumulate a respectable treasury, and struggle merely to survive, let alone pursue objectives.

On the other hand, voluntarism is concerned with the founding, operation, governance, and impacts of many of America's preeminent educational, medical, and cultural institutions, which qualify as nonprofit organizations (for example, Harvard University, Princeton University, American Cancer Society, Cedars of Lebanon Hospital, the Metropolitan Museum of Art, and the Boston Symphony Orchestra). Also included in the voluntary sector are numerous organizations that have contributed to profound changes in society, such as religious congregations and major foundations and grantmaking institutions (for example, the Rockefeller Foundation, Ford Foundation, and the Carnegie Corporation). Voluntarism is responsible for launching and sustaining vanguard social and political movements whose effects continue to reverberate in important areas, for example, civil rights, women's rights (and the women's suffrage movement that preceded it), consumer protection, environmental preservation, mental health, public health, progressive governmental reform, assistance for the needy, and numerous others (O'Neill 1989, pp. 9–122). "The accomplishments of American business and government have been awesome," acknowledges Michael O'Neill (1989), "but many of the social and moral advances in American history have come from nonprofit advocacy efforts" (p. 113).

Development of Voluntarism as a Field of Study

Although voluntarism enjoys a history as lengthy as civilization itself, so great a range is spanned by these institutions, organizations, and activities that it may have diverted attention from the field, delayed academic recognition, and prompted controversy over the meaning of the sector (Salamon 1992, p. 13; Salamon and Anheier 1992, pp. 125–128). Only since the 1970s has the nonprofit sector become recognized as a distinctive academic enterprise or professional pursuit.

In 1973, philanthropist John D. Rockefeller initiated the Commission on Private Philanthropy and Public Needs, usually identified as the Filer Commission after its chairman John Filer, to heighten awareness, appreciation, and study of voluntarism. At about the same time (1972), the first professional association dedicated to scholarly inquiry in the field was organized, now known as the Association for Research on Nonprofit Organizations and Voluntary Action (ARNOVA), and began publication of a quarterly journal. In 1977, Yale University established the first academic program in the United States for study of the voluntary, nonprofit sector, the Program on Nonprofit Organizations (PONPO). In the succeeding years, interest in the field has mushroomed: At this writing, more than 30 universities worldwide have centers or other programs devoted to voluntarism, and two more journals have begun publication. Many of the schools offer a master's degree in administration, management, and/or leadership of nonprofit organizations.

Scholarly inquiry in this area is decidedly interdisciplinary, attracting rich scrutiny and contributions from a great variety of academic traditions, including sociology, social work, political science, public administration, management, economics, psychology, anthropology, history, law, and numerous others.

Voluntarism: Between Market and State

Voluntarism can be understood as individual, group, or organizational behavior located in that sizable chasm between the marketplace and economic enterprise on the one hand (business, commerce, profitmaking, and the like) and government and the state on the other (authority, law, compulsion, and so forth), outside of the family or household. Although huge in scope and importance, this sphere is typically characterized as a "residual" category, supplementing ("following") the two predominant sectors of society: the private (the market and economic gain) and the public (government and the force of law) (Wuthnow 1991, pp. 5–8; Van Til 1988, pp. ix–x, 5–6). The sector comprises a wide variety of institutions, such as charities, research institutes, religious organizations, private colleges and universities, cooperatives, associations, foundations, hospitals, day care centers, youth organizations, advocacy groups, neighborhood organizations, and many more.

The most common name given to this group is the "third sector." In order to ease problems of comparability in law, custom, and definition across nations, international research often incorporates this term to describe organizations that are neither profit-oriented businesses nor governmental agencies or bureaucracies (for example, Seibel and Anheier 1990, p. 7). Other titles used regularly for the same purpose include the "nonprofit" or "voluntary" and, to a lesser extent, the "independent," "charitable," "philanthropic," or even the "tax-exempt" sector.

Origin of the Third Sector

Numerous scholars have speculated regarding the reasons for the origin and continued existence of a third, voluntary sector in society. Salamon (1992, pp. 7–10) summarizes five cogent explanations. The explanations are complementary, rather than mutually exclusive, and together offer a rationale for the birth and maintenance of the voluntary sector.

Historical Explanation

In an age in which citizens have routinely come to expect government to act in their interest in social and economic life, it may be difficult to recall that in most countries, society preceded the establishment of the state. In the absence of governmental institutions or agencies, individuals had to deal with common concerns and problems on their own. They often found it advantageous to join with other people to do so in voluntary groups, associations, and organizations. The result was the provision of services to meet a wide variety of community needs, such as charity, housing, culture, health, adoption, fire, and others, through a voluntary, nonprofit sector. Although desirous of help from the state, citizens nonetheless remain wary of government involvement. Thus, even after governments emerged, the nonprofit sector persisted to mobilize citizens, advocate for preferred causes, and help governments address needs through direct service activities.

Market Failure

Economists point out that the marketplace works admirably to produce goods and services that are consumed individually, such as clothing and toothpaste. For goods and services that are consumed collectively by groups of people, however, problems can arise with reliance on the market: Individuals have strong economic incentives to act as "free riders," that is, to let their fellow citizens pay for the provision of collective or public goods on the knowledge that once such goods have been created, they can share in their enjoyment whether they pay for them or not. Since all economically rational individuals will make the same calculation, however, the result will be inadequate production of collective goods, such as community safety and security,

clean streets and neighborhoods, and park lands and nature preserves, to the detriment of the larger society.

The best-known mechanism for overcoming market failure is government, which through the levy of taxes compels all citizens to assume the cost of providing collective goods. Another solution is the nonprofit sector: In nonprofit organizations, groups of individuals can pool their resources to produce goods or services they mutually want but cannot convince a majority of their fellow citizens to support. Using this mechanism, groups linked by common cultural, social, or economic characteristics or interests can provide the kinds and levels of collective goods desired in the absence of majority endorsement or government involvement.

Government Failure

Despite the capability to surmount problems of market failure, democratic governments encounter difficulties in providing collective goods. In the first place, mobilizing the majority support necessary for public action can be a long and arduous process; the existence of a voluntary sector allows groups of individuals with common motives or interests to begin addressing needs that have yet to command this level of approbation or that may never succeed in doing so. Second, even when governmental action has won authorization in a particular policy domain, citizens often find fault in the size, cost, ponderousness, and unresponsiveness—in short, the "bureaucracy"—they attribute to the undertaking. Regardless of the empirical validity of such complaints, citizens may prefer that a nongovernmental mechanism, such as nonprofit organizations, actually deliver the services and respond to the needs identified, with financing provided by the public sector. Often advocated by political officials, this preference has fueled a worldwide movement for governments to contract with outside organizations for the delivery of services, one form of "privatization." The culmination has been a very complex pattern of cooperation and interdependence between the public and nonprofit sectors, especially in the United States, for the production of governmentally financed services, and a blurring of the sectors has occurred.

Pluaralism/Freedom

While the first three explanations describe instrumental reasons for the existence of a nonprofit sector, such as offering an alternative means for the production of collective goods and efficiencies in the delivery of services, the last two reasons focus on expressive aspects of the sector. From this point of view, the nonprofit sector develops in a society to give voice to the great diversity of needs and preferences felt by the citizenry, for example, for gun control as well as the right to bear arms, for more open immigration policy as well as more vigorous enforcement of national borders, for ordinances banning smoking in public places as well as greater toleration of this habit, for safer automobiles and industrial equipment as well as less regulation of business, for greater freedom of choice in reproductive rights as well heightened concern for the rights of the unborn, for increased provision of child care as well as policies that encourage women to remain in the home as primary caregivers, for more tax benefits to nonprofit organizations as well as against "unfair competition" between the sector and profitmaking firms, and so forth. From civil rights to the Conservative Coalition, the nonprofit sector has spawned most of the major reform movements in the United States (O'Neill 1989). Even were governments to possess decided instrumental advantages over nonprofit organizations in the delivery of services, a voluntary sector would remain vital to secure liberties and ensure pluralism in beliefs and their articulation.

Solidarity

The final reason for the existence of the third, voluntary sector is that it preserves a capacity for joint action among citizens. As Alexis de Tocqueville observed, in democratic societies especially, equality of conditions can render individuals relatively powerless (see Salamon 1992, pp. 9–10). To overcome this tendency, they can come together to pursue common purposes in voluntary groups, associations, and organizations. Without a nonprofit sector to facilitate and activate the expression of these shared interests, much less progress would be possible across all realms of human endeavor.

Types and Purposes of Organizations in the Third Sector

As discussed previously, great diversity characterizes the voluntary, nonprofit sector with respect to both organizational form and mission. This section elaborates the types of entities and the range of purposes embraced by them.

Classifying Voluntary Organizations

Although many types of organizations inhabit the voluntary, nonprofit sector, useful commonalities exist for categorizing them and making sense of the constituent elements. The most basic classification is the distinction between "public-serving" and "member-serving" nonprofit organizations. The voluntary sector is best known for the former, or "public benefit" organizations: private nonprofit agencies founded to serve some general public, philanthropic, or charitable purpose, or to advance a like cause. This group includes schools, colleges, universities, hospitals, arts and cultural organizations, social service agencies, community development groups, legal service organizations, social action movements, research institutes, foundations, religious congregations, and others. In addition to these entities, a huge number of organizations exist primarily for the benefit of their own members rather than to advance some broader public purpose. Examples of these "mutual benefit," or "member-serving," organizations include professional associations, business associations, economic cooperatives, labor unions, member cooperatives, service organizations, fraternal organizations, veterans' organizations, pension trusts, ethnic societies, political parties, hobby groups, and sports and country clubs (O'Neill 1989, pp. 156–159).

Within the public benefit category, nonprofit organizations can be further divided into four types: funding intermediaries, religious institutions, service providers, and political action agencies (Salamon 1992, pp. 15–24). Funding intermediaries exist to generate funds and distribute them to other nonprofit organizations. This group includes both foundations and federated funders. In the United States, foundations make grants to other nonprofit organizations, usually financed through earnings on endowments, whereas federated funders collect and allocate private donations on behalf of service-providing organizations normally linked by common or allied purposes (for example, the American Cancer Society and the United Way).

A second type of public benefit, nonprofit organization consists of religious congregations, orders, and auxiliaries. These institutions engage in sacramental religious observances, and include churches, synagogues, mosques, and other places of worship. A third category of public benefit organizations are those that provide direct services. This group encompasses nonprofit agencies working in a very broad array of functional areas, such as education and library, health and personal care, culture and the arts, employment and training, counseling and rehabilitation, neighborhood and community programs, and foreign aid and development. The service providers are probably what most people have in mind when they refer to the nonprofit sector.

The final type of public benefit, nonprofit organization is the political action agencies, those that are engaged primarily in advocacy, campaigning, lobbying, and other legislative activity. Nonprofit service providers may also undertake advocacy and public education activities, but in the United States to qualify as a charitable organization under Section 501 (c)(3) of the Internal Revenue Service (IRS) tax code and receive all consequent tax advantages, advocacy must be a subsidiary function. Although all U.S. nonprofit organizations are exempt from the federal income tax, only those meeting the standards of Section 501 (c)(3) are eligible to receive tax deductible gifts from corporations and the general public (that is, contributions that can be de-

ducted from the tax liabilities of donors). A separate provision of the IRS tax code, Section 501 (c)(4), applies to the political action agencies ("social welfare organizations"). Since the tax deductibility of gifts gives firms and organizations a powerful incentive to make them, many 501 (c)(3) service providers establish auxiliary 501 (c)(4) action agencies for lobbying and advocacy purposes so as not to jeopardize their tax status (Salamon 1992, pp. 14–15, 23–24).

Classifying Voluntary Activity

Beginning in the mid-1980s, substantial progress has been made in classifying the variety of purposes motivating organizations in the voluntary, nonprofit sector. The National Center for Charitable Statistics (NCCS) at the INDEPENDENT SECTOR organization has taken a leading role in this effort; INDEPENDENT SECTOR, a nonprofit coalition of over 850 corporate, foundation and voluntary organization members with national interest and impact in philanthropy and voluntary action, strives to encourage volunteer and non-for-profit initiative. In cooperation with the Statistics of Income Division of the United States Internal Revenue Service, NCCS has developed a comprehensive scheme for classification, entitled the "National Taxonomy of Exempt Entities" (NTEE) (Hodgkinson *et al.* 1992, pp. 181–184).

The detailed NTEE classification of purposes lists 26 categories. For ease of presentation and statistical analysis, this large number is often collapsed into 9 major groupings. By this accounting, nonprofit organizations are active in the areas of arts, culture, and the humanities; education; environment and animals; health; human services; international and foreign affairs; public societal benefit; religion; and membership/mutual benefit (Hodgkinson *et al.* 1992, pp. 593–613).

Voluntarism and Individuals: Donating Money and Time

Treatments of voluntarism typically devote greatest attention to nonprofit organizations and to the sector as a whole. As the definition of the term emphasizes, however, a strong individual element pervades voluntarism. This element consists of the giving and volunteering behaviors that make the work of the voluntary sector possible.

As discussed earlier, charitable giving is not the only or even the largest source of funding for nonprofit organizations. Nevertheless, in 1990, total private contributions reached US$122.6 billion in the United States, or 2.77 percent of national income and 2.19 percent of personal income. Approximately 90 percent of giving came from individuals, chiefly living persons (83 percent), with a much smaller amount from personal bequests (6.4 percent); the remainder came from foundations (5.8 percent) and corporations (4.8 percent) (Hodgkinson *et al.* 1992, pp. 60). Just over half of private charitable giving (54 percent) went to religious congregations (Salamon 1992, p. 15). About three-fourths of American households make charitable contributions. Giving money and volunteering time are closely interrelated: People who make charitable contributions are much more likely to volunteer, and the incidence of volunteering increases dramatically with the percentage of income given (Hodgkinson and Weitzman 1994, pp. 27–30).

The study of volunteering behavior has stimulated considerable interest. Beginning in 1981, the INDEPENDENT SECTOR organization has commissioned a series of national surveys on volunteering in the United States, conducted at two-year intervals since 1985. Over this period, the percentage of Americans stating that they have spent time "working in some way to help others for no monetary pay . . . over the past twelve months" has hovered at around half the population. According to the results of the most recent survey at the time of this writing, in 1993, 47.7 percent of Americans volunteered an average of 4.2 hours per week. Projected to the population, these statistics indicate that nearly 90 million people (89.2 million) volunteer, the equivalent of about 9 million full-time employees (8,839,200). If the fortunate organizations that are the recipients of this labor had to pay for it, the price tag would have been a staggering

US$182.3 billion (Hodgkinson and Weitzman 1994, p. 23).

Throughout the 1980s, the reliance of all three sectors, for-profit, government, and nonprofit, on volunteer labor increased (Hodgkinson *et al.* 1992, pp. 18–19). The voluntary sector remains the prime beneficiary of this huge reservoir of time and talent. Converted to a full-time equivalent basis, of all volunteer time contributed in 1989, 69 percent went to the nonprofit sector, which also accounted for a like percentage of all volunteer work assignments (66 percent). As Jeffrey Brudney (1990) has shown, U.S. governments are markedly dependent on volunteer labor as well, in service domains such as fire and public safety, culture and the arts, health and emergency medical, education and recreation, food and homelessness. In 1989, about one-quarter of all contributed time (26 percent) and 28 percent of volunteer work assignments went to government. For-profit firms are responsible for the remainder (about 6 percent of both volunteer time and assignments). Although the number of full-time equivalent volunteers as a proportion of total employment is negligible in the for-profit sector (far less than 1 percent), volunteers constitute 40.4 percent of total employment in the U.S. nonprofit sector and 10.2 percent in government (Hodgkinson *et al.* 1992, pp. 7, 18–19, 29).

Two recent studies, the doctoral dissertation of Gabriel Berger (1991) and a review article by Smith (1994a), attempt to synthesize the results of the voluminous research on the determinants of volunteering. Based on a 1990 national survey of giving and volunteering behavior in the United States, Berger (1991) concluded that the strongest factor leading one to volunteer is to have been the target of recruitment efforts, a finding corroborated in many other surveys (e.g., Hodgkinson and Weitzman 1994). He also found that making philanthropic contributions is closely associated with volunteering to organizations (see earlier). The level of formal education received is the individual characteristic with the strongest impact on volunteering. Smith (1994a) concurred with these findings and identified other variables important to volunteering, such as higher socioeconomic status and participation in other forms of social activity. Smith's research also illustrates the complexity of volunteer behavior: A complete explanation must take into account the context or environment of the individual (e.g., size of community), the individual's social background (e.g., gender), personality (e.g., sense of efficacy), attitudes (e.g., liking volunteer work), situation (e.g., receiving services from the organization), and social participation (e.g., neighborhood interaction). While Smith's (1994a, p. 256) review shows that "we know a lot about why people participate in volunteer programs and voluntary associations," because studies have not been able to incorporate such an imposing range of variables, our understanding of volunteering behavior must be limited.

Bibliography

Berger, Gabriel, 1991. "Factors Explaining Volunteering for Organizations in General, and Social Welfare Organizations in Particular." Doctoral dissertation. Heller School of Social Welfare. Brandeis University.

Brudney, Jeffrey L., 1990. *Fostering Volunteer Programs in the Public Sector: Planning, Initiating, and Managing Voluntary Activities.* San Francisco, CA: Jossey-Bass.

Brudney, Jeffrey L., and Teresa K. Durden, 1993. "Twenty Years of the *Journal of Voluntary Action Research/Nonprofit and Voluntary Sector Quarterly,* An Assessment of Past Trends and future Directions." *Nonprofit and Voluntary Sector Quarterly,* vol. 22 (Fall) 207–218.

Cnaan, Ram A., and Peter D. Hall, 1994. "Book Reviews: *Government and the Third Sector: Emerging Relationships in Welfare States* and *The Nonprofit Sector in the Global Community: Voice from Many Nations." Nonprofit and Voluntary Sector Quarterly,* vol. 23 (Spring): 79–85.

Hodgkinson, Virginia A., and Murray S. Weitzman, 1994. *Giving and Volunteering in the United States: Findings from a National Survey, 1994 Edition.* Washington, D.C.: INDEPENDENT SECTOR.

Hodgkinson, Virginia A., Murray S. Weitzman, Christopher M. Toppe, and Stephen M. Noga, 1992. *Nonprofit Almanac, 1992–1993: Dimensions of the Independent Sector.* San Francisco, CA: Jossey-Bass.

Lohmann, Roger A., 1995. "Commons: Can This Be the Name of 'Thirdness'?" *Nonprofit and Voluntary Sector Quarterly,* vol. 24 (Spring): 25–29.

O'Neill, Michael, 1989. *The Third America: The Emergence of the Nonprofit Sector in the United States.* San Francisco, CA: Jossey-Bass.

Salamon, Lester M., 1992. *America's Nonprofit Sector: A Primer.* New York: Foundation Center.

Salamon, Lester M., and Helmut K. Anheier, 1992. "In Search of the Non-Profit Sector. I: The Question of Definitions." *Voluntas,* vol. 3 (August): 125–151.

Seibel, Wolfgang, and Helmut K. Anheier, 1990. "Sociological and Political Science Approaches to the Third Sector." In Helmut K. Anheier and Wolfgang Seibel, eds. *The Third Sector: Comparative Studies of Nonprofit Organizations.* Berlin, Germany: Walter de Gruyter.

Smith, David Horton, 1994a. "Determinants of Voluntary Association Participation and Volunteering: A Literature Review." *Nonprofit and Voluntary Sector Quarterly,* vol. 23 (Fall): 243–263.

_____, 1994b. "The Rest of the Nonprofit Sector: The Nature and Magnitude of Grassroots Associations in America." Paper presented at the Annual Meeting of the Association for Research on Nonprofit Organizations and Voluntary Action. Berkeley, CA, October 20–22.

Van Til, Jon, 1988. *Mapping the Third Sector: Voluntarism in a Changing Social Economy.* New York: Foundation Center.

Wuthnow, Robert, ed. 1991. *Between States and Markets: The Voluntary Sector in Comparative Perspective.* Princeton, NJ: Princeton University Press.

CHAPTER 5

The Gospel of Wealth

A N D R E W   C A R N E G I E

The problem of our age is the proper administration of wealth, so that the ties of brotherhood may still bind together the rich and poor in harmonious relationship. The conditions of human life have not only been changed, but revolutionized, within the past few hundred years. In former days there was little difference between the dwelling, dress, food, and environment of the chief and those of his retainers. The Indians are to-day where civilized man then was. When visiting the Sioux, I was led to the wigwam of the chief. It was just like the others in external appearance, and even within the difference was trifling between it and those of the poorest of his braves. The contrast between the palace of the millionaire and the cottage of the laborer with us to-day measures the change which has come with civilization.

This change, however, is not to be deplored, but welcomed as highly beneficial. It is well, nay, essential for the progress of the race, that the houses of some should be homes for all that is highest and best in literature and the arts, and for all the refinements of civilization, rather than that none should be so. Much better this great irregularity than universal squalor. Without wealth there can be no Mæcenas. The "good old times" were not good old times. Neither master nor servant was as well situated then as to-day. A relapse to old conditions would be disastrous to both—not the least so to him who serves—and would sweep away civilization with it. But whether the change be for good or ill, it is upon us, beyond our power to alter, and therefore to be accepted and made the best of. It is a waste of time to criticise the inevitable.

To-day the world obtains commodities of excellent quality at prices which even the generation preceding this would have deemed incredible. In the commercial world similar causes have produced similar results, and the race is benefited thereby. The poor enjoy what the rich could not before afford. What were the luxuries have become the necessaries of life. The laborer has now more comforts than the farmer had a few generations ago. The farmer has more luxuries than the landlord had, and is more richly clad and better housed. The landlord has books and pictures rarer, and appointments more artistic, than the King could then obtain.

The price we pay for this salutary change is, no doubt, great. We assemble thousands of operatives in the factory, in the mine, and in the counting-house, of whom the employer can know little or nothing, and to whom the employer is little better than a myth. All intercourse between them is at an end. Rigid Castes are formed, and, as usual, mutual ignorance breeds mutual distrust. Each Caste is without sympathy for the other, and ready to credit anything disparaging in regard to it. Under the law of competition, the employer of thousands is forced into the strictest economies, among which the rates paid to labor figure prominently, and often there is friction between the employer and the employed, between capital and labor, between rich and poor. Human society loses homogeneity.

The price which society pays for the law of competition, like the price it pays for cheap comforts and luxuries, is also great; but the advantages of this law are also greater still, for it is to this law that we owe our wonderful material development, which brings improved conditions in its train. But, whether the law be benign or not, we must say of it, as we say of the change in the conditions of men to which we have referred: It is here; we cannot evade it; no substitutes for it have been found; and while the law may be sometimes hard for the individual, it is best for the race, because it insures the survival of the fittest in every department. Having accepted these, it follows that there must be great scope for the exercise of special ability in the merchant and in the manufacturer who has to conduct affairs upon a great scale. That this talent for organization and management is rare among men is proved by the fact that it invariably secures for its possessor enormous rewards, no matter where or under what laws or conditions. The experienced in affairs always rate the MAN whose services can be obtained as a partner as not only the first consideration, but such as to render the question of his capital scarcely worth considering, for such men soon create capital; while, without the special talent required, capital soon takes wings. Such men become interested in firms or corporations using millions; and estimating only simple interest to be made upon the capital invested, it is inevitable that their income must exceed their expenditures, and that they must accumulate wealth. It is a law, as certain as any of the others named, that men possessed of this peculiar talent for affairs, under the free play of economic forces, must, of necessity, soon be in receipt of more revenue than can be judiciously expended upon themselves; and this law is as beneficial for the race as the others.

Objections to the foundations upon which society is based are not in order, because the condition of the race is better with these than it has been with any others which have been tried. Of the effect of any new substitutes proposed we cannot be sure. The Socialist or Anarchist who seeks to overturn present conditions is to be regarded as attacking the foundation upon which civilization itself rests, for civilization took its start from the day that the capable, industrious workman said to his incompetent and lazy fellow, "If thou dost not sow, thou shalt not reap," and thus ended primitive Communism by separating the drones from the bees. One who studies this subject will soon be brought face to face with the conclusion that upon the sacredness of property civilization itself depends—the right of the laborer to his hundred dollars in the savings bank, and equally the legal right of the millionaire to his millions. To those who propose to substitute Communism for this intense Individualism the answer, therefore, is: The race has tried that. All progress from that barbarous day to the present time has resulted from its displacement. Not evil, but good, has come to the race from the accumulation of wealth by those who have the ability and energy that produce it. But even if we admit for a moment that it might be better for the race to discard its present foundation, Individualism,—that it is a nobler ideal that man should labor, not for himself alone, but in and for a brotherhood of his fellows, and share with them all in common, realizing Swedenborg's idea of Heaven, where, as he says, the angels derive their happiness, not from laboring for self, but for each other,—even admit all this, and a sufficient answer is, This is not evolution, but revolution. It necessitates the changing of human nature itself—a work of æons, even if it were good to change it, which we cannot know. We might as well urge the destruction of the highest existing type of man because he failed to reach our ideal as to favor the destruction of Individualism Private Property, the Law of Accumulation of Wealth, and the Law of Competition; for these are the highest results of human experience, the soil in which society so far has produced the best fruit.

We start, then, with a condition of affairs under which the best interests of the race are promoted, but which inevitably gives wealth to the few. Thus far, accepting conditions as they exist, the situation can be surveyed and pronounced good. The question then arises,—and, if the foregoing be correct, it is the only question with which we have to deal,—What is the proper mode of administering wealth after the laws upon which civilization is founded have thrown it into the hands of the few? And it is of this great question that I believe I offer the true solution. It will be understood that *fortunes* are here spoken of, not moderate sums saved by many years of effort, the returns from which are required for the comfortable maintenance and education of families. This is not *wealth,* but only *competence,* which it should be the aim of all to acquire.

There are but three modes in which surplus wealth can be disposed of. It can be left to the families of the decedents; or it can be bequeathed for public purposes; or, finally, it can be administered during their lives by its possessors. Under the first and second modes most of the wealth of the world that has reached the few has hitherto been applied. Let us in turn consider each of these modes. The first is the most injudicious. In monarchical countries, the estates and the greatest portion of the wealth are left to the first son, that the vanity of the parent may be gratified by the thought that his name and title are to descend to succeeding generations unimpaired. Even in Great Britain the strict law of entail has been found inadequate to maintain the status of an hereditary class. Its soil is rapidly passing into the hands of the stranger. Under republican institutions the division of property among the children is much fairer, but the question which forces itself upon thoughtful men in all lands is: Why should men leave great fortunes to their children? If this is done from affection, is it not misguided affection? Observation teaches that, generally speaking, it is not well for the children that they should be so burdened. Neither is it well for the state. Beyond providing for the wife and daughters moderate sources of income, and very moderate allowances indeed, if any, for the sons, men may well hesitate, for it is no longer questionable that great sums bequeathed oftener work more for the injury than for the good of the recipients.

Wise men will soon conclude that, for the best interests of the members of their families and of the state, such bequests are an improper use of their means.

It is not suggested that men who have failed to educate their sons to earn a livelihood shall cast them adrift in poverty. If any man has seen fit to rear his sons with a view to their living idle lives, or, what is highly commendable, has instilled in them the sentiment that they are in a position to labor for public ends without reference to pecuniary considerations, then, of course, the duty of the parent is to see that such are provided for *in moderation.* There are instances of millionaires' sons unspoiled by wealth, who, being rich, still perform great services in the community. Such are the very salt of the earth, as valuable as, unfortunately, they are rare; still it is not the exception, but the rule, that men must regard, and, looking at the usual result of enormous sums conferred upon legatees, the thoughtful man must shortly say, "I would as soon leave to my son a curse as the almighty dollar," and admit to himself that it is not the welfare of the children, but family pride, which inspires these enormous legacies.

As to the second mode, that of leaving wealth at death for public uses, it may be said that this is only a means for the disposal of wealth, provided a man is content to wait until he is dead before it becomes of much good in the world. Knowledge of the results of legacies bequeathed is not calculated to inspire the brightest hopes of much posthumous good being accomplished. The cases are not few in which the real object sought by the testator is not attained, nor are they few in which his real wishes are thwarted. In many cases the bequests are so used as to become only monuments of his folly. It is well to remember that it requires the exercise of not less ability than that which acquired the wealth to use it so as to be really beneficial to the community. Besides this, it may fairly be said that no man is to be extolled for doing what he cannot help doing, nor is he to be thanked by the community to which he only leaves wealth at death. Men who leave vast sums in this way may fairly be thought men who would not have left it at all, had they been able to take it with them. The memories of such cannot be held in grateful remembrance, for there is no grace in their gifts. It is not to be wondered at that such bequests seem so generally to lack the blessing.

The growing disposition to tax more and more heavily large estates left at death is a cheering indication of the growth of a salutary change in public opinion. Men who continue hoarding great sums all their lives, the proper use of which for public ends would work good to the community, should be made to feel that the community, in the form of the state, cannot thus be deprived of its proper share. By taxing estates heavily at death the state marks its condemnation of the selfish millionaire's unworthy life.

It is desirable that nations should go much further in this direction. Indeed, it is difficult to set bounds to the share of a rich man's estate which should go at his death to the public through the agency of the state, and by all means such taxes should be graduated, beginning at nothing upon moderate sums to dependents, and increasing rapidly as the amounts swell, until of the millionaire's hoard, as of Shylock's, at least

> "—The other half
> Comes to the privy coffer of the state."

This policy would work powerfully to induce the rich man to attend to the administration of wealth during his life, which is the end that society should always have in view, as being that by far most fruitful for the people.

There remains, then, only one mode of using great fortunes; but in this we have the true antidote for the temporary unequal distribution of wealth, the reconciliation of the rich and the poor—a reign of harmony—another ideal, differing, indeed, from that of the Communist in requiring only the further evolution of existing conditions, not the total overthrow of our civilization. Even the poorest can be made to see this, and to agree that great sums gathered by some of their fellow-citizens and spent for public purposes, from which the masses reap the principal benefit, are more valuable to them than if scattered among them through the course of many years in trifling amounts.

If we consider what results flow from the Cooper Institute, for instance, to the best portion of the race in New York not possessed of means, and compare these with those which would have arisen for the good of the masses from an equal sum distributed by Mr. Cooper in his lifetime in the form of wages, which is the highest form of distribution, being for work done and not for charity, we can form some estimate of the possibilities for the improvement of the race which lie embedded in the present law of the accumulation of wealth. Let the advocate of violent or radical change ponder well this thought.

We might even go so far as to take another instance, that of Mr. Tilden's bequest of five millions of dollars for a free library in the city of New York, but in referring to this one cannot help saying involuntarily, How much better if Mr. Tilden had devoted the last years of his own life to the proper administration of this immense sum; in which case neither legal contest nor any other cause of delay could have interfered with his aims. But let us assume that Mr. Tilden's millions finally become the means of giving to this city a noble public library, where the treasures of the world contained in books will be open to all forever, without money and without price. Considering the good of that part of the race which congregates in and around Manhattan Island, would its permanent benefit have been better promoted had these millions been allowed to circulate in small sums through the hands of the masses? Even the most strenuous advocate of Communism must entertain a doubt upon this subject. Most of those who think will probably entertain no doubt whatever.

Poor and restricted are our opportunities in this life; narrow our horizon; our best work most imperfect; but rich men should be thankful for one inestimable boon. They have it in their power during their lives to busy themselves in organizing benefactions from which the masses of their fellows will derive lasting advantage, and thus dignify their own lives. The highest life is probably to be reached, not by such imitation of the life of Christ as Count Tolstoï gives us, but, while animated by Christ's spirit, by recognizing the changed conditions of this age, and adopting modes of expressing this spirit suitable to the changed conditions under which we live; still laboring for the good of our fellows, which was the essence of his life and teaching, but laboring in a different manner.

This, then, is held to be the duty of the man of Wealth: First, to set an example of modest, unostentatious living, shunning display or extravagance; to provide moderately for the legitimate wants of those dependent upon him; and after doing so to consider all surplus revenues which come to him simply as trust funds, which he is called upon to administer, and strictly bound as a matter of duty to administer in the manner which, in his judgment, is best calculated to produce the most beneficial results for the community—the man of wealth thus becoming the mere agent and trustee for his poorer brethren, bringing to their service his superior wisdom, experience, and ability to administer, doing for them better than they would or could do for themselves.

The best uses to which surplus wealth can be put have already been indicated. Those who would administer wisely must, indeed, be wise, for one of the serious obstacles to the improvement of our race is indiscriminate charity. It were better for mankind that the millions of the rich were thrown into the sea than so spent as to encourage the slothful, the drunken, the unworthy. Of every thousand dollars spent in so called charity to-day, it is probable that $950 is unwisely spent; so spent, indeed, as to produce the very evils which it proposes to mitigate or cure. A well-known writer of philosophic books admitted the other day that he had given a quarter of a dollar to a man who approached him as he was coming to visit the house of his friend. He knew nothing of the habits of this beggar; knew not the use that would be made of this money, although he had every reason to suspect that it would be spent improperly. This man professed to be a disciple of Herbert Spencer; yet the quarter-dollar given that night will probably work more injury than all the money which its thoughtless donor will ever be able to give in true charity will do good. He only gratified his own feelings, saved himself from annoyance,—

and this was probably one of the most selfish and very worst actions of his life, for in all respects he is most worthy.

In bestowing charity, the main consideration should be to help those who will help themselves; to provide part of the means by which those who desire to improve may do so; to give those who desire to rise the aids by which they may rise; to assist, but rarely or never to do all. Neither the individual nor the race is improved by alms-giving. Those worthy of assistance, except in rare cases, seldom require assistance. The really valuable men of the race never do, except in cases of accident or sudden change. Every one has, of course, cases of individuals brought to his own knowledge where temporary assistance can do genuine good, and these he will not overlook. But the amount which can be wisely given by the individual for individuals is necessarily limited by his lack of knowledge of the circumstances connected with each. He is the only true reformer who is as careful and as anxious not to aid the unworthy as he is to aid the worthy, and, perhaps, even more so, for in alms-giving more injury is probably done by rewarding vice than by relieving virtue.

The rich man is thus almost restricted to following the examples of Peter Cooper, Enoch Pratt of Baltimore, Mr. Pratt of Brooklyn, Senator Stanford, and others, who know that the best means of benefiting the community is to place within its reach the ladders upon which the aspiring can rise—parks, and means of recreation, by which men are helped in body and mind; works of art, certain to give pleasure and improve the public taste, and public institutions of various kinds, which will improve the general condition of the people;—in this manner returning their surplus wealth to the mass of their fellows in the forms best calculated to do them lasting good.

Thus is the problem of Rich and Poor to be solved. The laws of accumulation will be left free; the laws of distribution free. Individualism will continue, but the millionaire will be but a trustee for the poor; intrusted for a season with a great part of the increased wealth of the community, but administering it for the community far better than it could or would have done for itself. The best minds will thus have reached a stage in the development of the race in which it is clearly seen that there is no mode of disposing of surplus wealth creditable to thoughtful and earnest men into whose hands it flows save by using it year by year for the general good. This day already dawns. But a little while, and although, without incurring the pity of their fellows, men may die sharers in great business enterprises from which their capital cannot be or has not been withdrawn, and is left chiefly at death for public uses, yet the man who dies leaving behind him millions of available wealth, which was his to administer during life, will pass away "unwept, unhonored, and unsung," no matter to what uses he leaves the dross which he cannot take with him. Of such as these the public verdict will then be: "The man who dies thus rich dies disgraced."

Such, in my opinion, is the true Gospel concerning Wealth, obedience to which is destined some day to solve the problem of the Rich and the Poor, and to bring "Peace on earth, among men Good-Will."

CHAPTER 6

The Filer Commission Report—
Giving in America:
Toward a Stronger Voluntary Sector

JOHN H. FILER

Few aspects of American society are more characteristically, more famously American than the nation's array of voluntary organizations, and the support in both time and money that is given to them by its citizens. Our country has been decisively different in this regard, historian Daniel Boorstin observes, "from the beginning." As the country was settled, "communities existed before governments were there to care for public needs." The result, Boorstin says, was that "voluntary collaborative activities" were set up to provide basic social services. Government followed later.

The practice of attending to community needs outside of government has profoundly shaped American society and its institutional framework. While in most other countries, major social institutions such as universities, hospitals, schools, libraries, museums and social welfare agencies are state-run and state-funded, in the United States many of the same organizations are privately controlled and voluntarily supported. The institutional landscape of America is, in fact, teeming with nongovernmental, noncommercial organizations, all the way from some of the world's leading educational and cultural institutions to local garden clubs, from po-

litically powerful national associations to block associations—literally millions of groups in all. This vast and varied array is, and has long been widely recognized as, part of the very fabric of American life. It reflects a national belief in the philosophy of pluralism and in the profound importance to society of individual initiative.

Underpinning the virtual omnipresence of voluntary organizations, and a form of individual initiative in its own right, is the practice—in the case of many Americans, the deeply ingrained habit—of philanthropy, of private giving, which provides the resource base for voluntary organizations. Between money gifts and the contributions of time and labor in the form of volunteer work, giving is valued at more than $50 billion a year, according to Commission estimates.

These two interrelated elements, then, are sizable forces in American society, far larger than in any other country. And they have contributed immeasurably to this country's social and scientific progress. On the ledger of recent contributions are such diverse advances as the creation of noncommercial "public" television, the development of environmental, consumerist and demographic consciousness, community-oriented museum programs, the protecting of land and landmarks from the often heedless rush of "progress." The list is endless and still growing; both the number and deeds of voluntary organizations are increasing. "Americans are forever forming associations," wrote de Tocqueville. They still are: tens of thousands of environmental organizations have sprung up in the last few years alone. Private giving is growing, too, at least in current dollar amounts.

Changes and Challenges

Yet, while the value of philanthropy and voluntary organizations, their past and present achievements, is hardly questioned by Americans, and while by international comparisons these two expressions of the voluntary spirit are of unmatched dimensions, a major overall conclusion of this Commission must be that there are profound, and in some areas troubling, shifts happening in the interrelated realms of voluntary organization and philanthropy, changes that reflect, as these quintessential elements in American society must, broader churnings in the society as a whole. These changes present both practical and philosophical challenges to established patterns of voluntary activity and philanthropy.

The practical challenges are suggested by the stark fact that while many new organizations are being born in the voluntary sector, since 1969 nearly 150 private colleges—representing one of the oldest and largest areas of voluntary activity throughout American history—have closed down. Among the philosophical challenges are those facing the main governmental encouragement of private giving—the charitable deduction in the federal income tax—which is being questioned on grounds of equity.

Findings

The Commission's findings—about both the enduring virtues of nonprofit activity and philanthropic giving and about current challenges to established patterns within these areas—can be summarized in four broad observations:

1. The voluntary sector is a large and vital part of American society, more important today than ever. But the sector is undergoing economic strains that predate and are generally more severe than the troubles of the economy as a whole. Recent tremors in the nation's governance have strengthened the deeply rooted American conviction that no single institutional structure should exercise a monopoly on filling public needs, that reliance on government alone to fill such needs not only saps the spirit of individual initiative but risks making human values subservient to institutional ones, individual and community purposes subordinate to bureaucratic conveniences or authoritarian dictates. Thus, the third sector's role as an addition to government and, in many areas, an alternative and even counterbalance to government, has possibly never been more important; the basic rationale of the third sector in the philosophy of pluralism has possibly never been more pertinent. Also, in a society increasingly dominated by giant and impersonal institutions of business and government, voluntary organizations, generally less giant and more personal, provide arenas within which the individual can exercise personal initiative and influence on the course of events around him or her.

Economic Strains

The vital role of the voluntary sector in today's society must be viewed, however, against a background of mounting financial and economic strains that threaten the sector's ability to adequately perform this role.

Acute crisis describes the state of many parts of the nonprofit sector today. The existence of whole areas within the sector may be threatened.

One Commission study asserts that it is not "idle speculation to talk of the disappearance of the liberal arts college." Another study says that "in the long run, if the economic trends continue, the vast majority of nonpublic schools seem doomed, the exceptions being schools enjoying the support of the well-to-do or heavy subsidies from a few remaining religious groups with conservative theologies or strong ethnic emphasis." Social service organizations have been slashing their budgets and reducing their staffs in order to stay afloat. In a number of cases, they have gone out of business entirely. And nonprofit arts organizations, in many cases, are surviving only through large infusions of government funds.

The prevailing financial pattern of the non-profit sector has become one not only of uncommonly higher costs, but of more resources required for old problems and new solutions, and of more users needing greater aggregate subsidies for the nonprofit services that they consume. In addition, new and less traditional groups, such as those oriented toward urban and racial problems, environmental and consumer organizations, and other politically and legally activist groups, have been adding their claim for pieces of the philanthropic pie. And the pie has not been growing in terms of the real purchasing power of private contributions.

2. Giving in America involves an immense amount of time and money, is the fundamental underpinning of the voluntary sector, encompasses a wide diversity of relationships between donor, donations and donee, and is not keeping pace.   Most giving—79 per cent in 1974—comes from living individuals, and the main focus of the Commission's research has been on such giving. In 1973, according to projections based on the respondents' answers, individuals may have given as much as $26 billion.

In addition, nearly six billion womanhours and manhours of volunteer work were contributed to nonprofit organizations in 1973, the survey indicates, and the total value placed on this contributed labor is another $26 billion. (Bequests accounted for $2.07 billion in 1974, foundations for $2.11 billion and corporations for $1.25 billion in direct dollar giving.)

Estimating the sources of giving by individuals is still more art than science, but even by conservative reckonings, $50 billion a year is the very large round-number total of the value of contributed time and money in the mid-1970's. A disproportionate amount of giving comes from contributors with the highest income, at least 13 per cent of individual giving from this 1 per cent of the population. Yet at the same time

the bulk of giving, more than half, comes from households with incomes below $20,000.

Not Keeping Pace

While philanthropy plays a far larger role in the U.S. than in any other country, a disturbing finding is that the purchasing power of giving did not keep pace with the growth of the economy through the expansive years of the 1960's and early 1970's and that in recent years it has fallen off absolutely when discounted for inflation.

The dropoff in giving is by no means uniform. Giving to religion has declined most of all, falling from 49 to 43 per cent of all giving between 1964 and 1974, paralleling a drop in church attendance and in parochial school enrollments. Meantime, giving to civic and cultural causes has actually risen. And volunteer work has gone up markedly according to government surveys conducted in 1965 and in 1974. The success of some causes in regularly raising large sums suggests that the spirit of giving may not be fading so much as shifting its focus, even if the level of giving, of money at least, clearly has declined, by virtually every barometer.

3. Decreasing levels of private giving, increasing costs of non-profit activity and broadening expectations for health, education and welfare services as basic entitlements of citizenship have led to the government's becoming a principal provider of programs and revenues in many areas once dominated by private philanthropy. And government's growing role in these areas poses fundamental questions about the autonomy and basic functioning of private nonprofit organizations and institutions.   As a direct supporter of nonprofit organizations and activities, government today contributes almost as much as all sources of private philanthropy combined. In 1974, Commission studies indicate, government contributed about $23 billion to nonprofit organizations, compared to $25 billion from private giving. In addition, government has absorbed many philanthropic functions or services, either through the spread of public institutions and agencies that are counterparts of private organizations or through social programs that render philanthropic services and functions obsolete or redundant.

The growing role of government in what have been considered philanthropic activities is evident at every turn in the nonprofit sector.

The most massive change has occurred in relation to the poor, the unemployed, the aged, the infirm—largely because of Social Security legislation enacted in the 1930's. The impact of this legislation can be seen in the fact that in 1974 more than $90 billion was dispensed in old-age, survivors, disability and health insurance, and various forms of welfare assistance. Private philanthropy, by comparison, distributed around $2.3 billion in the whole "social welfare" category.

Along with this change has come an ever increasing involvement of government in the finances of nonprofit organizations themselves. The nonprofit sector has, in fact, become an increasingly mixed realm—part private, part public—in much the same sense that the profit-making sector has; and this trend poses a major dilemma. On the one hand, government money is needed and may even be a matter of life or death for many organizations as the amount of their private funding has advanced slowly or even declined. On the other hand, government money comes with strings attached, however invisible or unintentional they may be. The more an organization depends on government money for survival, the less "private" it is, and the less immune to political processes and priorities.

The presence of a firm core of private support, however small, in a private organization that gets major public funding can be of crucial importance in determining whether the managers of the organizations regard themselves, and behave, as independent operators or as civil servants.

In stressing the importance of private giving, however, the Commission recognizes that giving itself is influenced by government through the tax system and that some of the most debated issues concerning relations of government and the voluntary sector revolve around how the tax system is structured and how it affects donors and donees.

4. Our society has long encouraged "charitable" nonprofit activity by excluding it from certain tax obligations. But the principal tax encouragement of giving to nonprofit organizations—the charitable deduction in personal income taxes—has been both challenged from some quarters in recent years on grounds of equity and eroded by expansion of the standard deduction. The charitable deduction has been part of the tax law since 1917, four years after the income tax itself became a basic fixture of American life. It was instituted to sustain the level of giving in the face of new steep tax rates and because it was held that personal income that went to charitable purposes should not be taxed because it did not enrich the giver. These remain the two principal rationales of the charitable deduction, under which a contributor can subtract the amount of yearly giving from income upon which income taxes are computed. In recent years, however, partly as a result of a growing tendency to look at tax immunities as forms of government subsidy, the charitable deduction has been criticized, along with other personal income tax deductions, as inequitable. This is because, under the progressive income tax, the higher the deductor's tax bracket, the greater the tax savings he or she receives from taking a deduction. Thus, high tax bracket contributors have a significantly greater incentive to give than those at the other end of the income scale.

At the same time that the charitable deduction is being challenged philosophically, it is being eroded, in very concrete terms, by liberalizations of the standard deduction, the income tax provision that allows taxpayers to deduct a set amount or a proportion of their income in lieu of taking specific, itemized deductions. The maximum standard deduction has increased greatly in recent years—from $1,000 for a couple in 1970 to $2,600 in 1975. This has so diminished the advantage of taking itemized deductions that as of 1975's returns less than one third of all taxpayers are expected to be taking the charitable deduction.

Recommendations

Such are the main dimensions, trends and issues that the Commission's extensive research has uncovered or illuminated. These findings provide the background for the Commission's recommendations, among the major ones of which are those below. They fall into three categories: proposals involving taxes and giving; those that affect the "philanthropic process," the interaction between donors, donees and the public; and a proposal for a permanent commission on the nonprofit sector.

I. Taxes and Giving

The Commission examined the existing governmental inducement to giving and considered several proposed alternatives, including tax credits for giving and matching grant systems. In doing so, it kept these six objectives in mind:

- To increase the number of people who contribute significantly to and participate in nonprofit activities.
- To increase the amount of giving.
- To increase the inducements to giving by those in low- and middle-income brackets.
- To preserve private choice in giving.
- To minimize income losses of nonprofit organizations that depend on the current pattern of giving.
- To be as "efficient" as possible. In other words, any stimulus to giving should not cost significantly more in foregone government revenue than the amount of giving actually stimulated.

A. Continuing the Deduction. In light of these criteria, the Commission believes that the charitable deduction should be retained and added onto rather than replaced by another form of governmental encouragement to giving. The Commission affirms the basic philosophical rationale of the deduction, that giving should not be taxed because, unlike other uses of income, it does not enrich the disburser. Also, the deduction is a proven mechanism familiar to donor and donee, easy to administrate and less likely than credits or matching grants to run afoul of constitutional prohibitions as far as donations to religious organizations are concerned.

The deduction has been shown, furthermore, to be a highly "efficient" inducement. Computerized econometric analyses based on available tax and income data were made for the Commission and they indicate that for every dollar of taxes uncollected because of the charitable deduction, more than one dollar in giving is stimulated. The Commission's sample survey of taxpayers also indicates that itemizers who take the charitable deduction give substantially more, at every income level, than nonitemizers.

The deduction is seen as inviting the least amount of government involvement in influencing the direction of giving. And, finally, eliminating the deduction or replacing it with a tax credit or matching grant system would significantly shift giving away from several current recipient areas at a time when these areas are already undergoing severe economic strains.

B. Extending and Amplifying the Deduction. The Commission recognizes that the charitable deduction is used by fewer and fewer taxpayers—now fewer than one third—because of the liberalized standard deduction. So, to broaden the reach of the charitable deduction and to increase giving, the Commission recommends:

That all taxpayers who take the standard deduction should also be permitted to deduct charitable contributions as an additional, itemized deduction.

This extension of the deduction would, it is calculated, provide an inducement to give to nearly 60 million nonitemizers, and would thereby result in increased giving, according to econometric projections, of $1.9 billion in 1976 dollars.

This amount is still relatively modest in terms of the amount of giving that would be needed to restore giving to its level in 1960 before its decline in relative purchasing power set in—an increase in giving, in current dollars, of around $8 billion would be required. Moreover, while extending the deduction to nonitemizers would provide many millions of taxpayers with some inducement to give, the inducement would still be tied to the progressive rate structure of the income tax and would be markedly lower at low- and middle-income levels than it is at upper levels. Therefore, the Commission recommends as an additional new incentive for low- and middle-income contributors:

That families with incomes below $15,000 a year be allowed to deduct twice the amount of their giving, and those with incomes between $15,000 and $30,000 be allowed to deduct 150 per cent of what they contribute.

The "double deduction" and the 150 per cent deduction would have the effect of doubling the proportion of tax savings for charitable giving for low-income families and increasing the proportion by one half for middle-income families and would thus appreciably narrow the range in savings between these brackets and high-income taxpayers. The amount of giving induced and the efficiency of inducing it might, moreover, be impressive.

C. Increasing Corporate Giving.   Corporate giving is still a relatively new element in American philanthropy; the corporate charitable deduction itself has been in effect only for forty years. And there are those on both the left and right who question whether corporations should be involved in philanthropy at all. While recognizing that such giving can only be a minor element in the corporation's role in society, the Commission also notes that only 20 per cent of corporate taxpayers in 1970 reported any charitable contributions and only 6 per cent made contributions of over $500. The record of corporate giving is an unimpressive and inadequate one, the Commission believes. Therefore, the Commission recommends:

That corporations set as a minimum goal, to be reached no later than 1980, the giving to charitable purposes of 2 per cent of pretax net income, and that further studies of means to stimulate corporate giving be pursued.

II. Improving the Philanthropic Process

The social benefit that flows from giving and nonprofit activity results from a process of interaction—between donors and donees and between both and the society at large. In order to function properly—and to reassure a public grown skeptical of its institutions—this "philan-

thropic process" requires considerable openness between donors and donees and the public; it requires open minds as well as open doors. The tax-exempt status of nonprofit organizations, moreover, entails an obligation to openness, an accountability to the public for actions and expenditures.

Yet the Commission's research, including meetings with and reports from representatives of donee organizations, indicates that the process is operating imperfectly at best. So a number of recommendations were decided upon with the aim of improving the philanthropic process; the following are among the major ones. They fall into four categories: accountability, accessibility, personal or institutional self-benefiting, and influencing legislation.

A. Accountability.   Demands for accountability that have been heard in the business and government worlds of late are also being sounded in the voluntary sector, reflecting the haphazard procedures for accountability that exist in the sector, the increasing use of public funds by nonprofit organizations, and the perception by some that private nonprofit organizations are too private. The Commission agrees that, with notable individual exceptions, the overall level of accountability in the voluntary sector is inadequate, and the Commission therefore recommends:

That all larger tax-exempt charitable organizations except churches and church affiliates be required to prepare and make readily available detailed annual reports on their finances, programs and priorities.

Annual reporting requirements that now apply to private foundations would, in effect, be extended to tax-exempt organizations with annual budgets of more than $100,000—including corporate giving programs but excluding religious organizations. These reports would have to be filed with appropriate state and federal agencies and be made readily available to interested parties upon request. Uniform accounting measures for comparable types of nonprofit organizations are recommended, and an accounting model is provided in the compendium of Commission research, which is published separately.

That larger grant-making organizations be required to hold annual public meetings to discuss their programs, priorities and contributions.

This requirement would apply mainly to foundations, corporations and federated fund-raising groups such as United Way, those with contribution budgets of $100,000 or more. Like the above requirement it would not apply to churches or church affiliates.

B. Accessibility. Greater accessibility by potential donees to donor institutions has frequently been espoused as a goal in the nonprofit sector, yet the evidence suggests that it has been a goal honored more in preachments than in practical pursuit. The Commission believes that greater accessibility can only enrich the philanthropic process, and it is concerned that because of insufficient accessibility, the process may not be fluid enough to respond to new needs. So, with the aim of encouraging and facilitating wider access to and greater venturesomeness by institutional philanthropy, the Commission recommends:

That legal responsibility for proper expenditure of foundation grants, now imposed on both foundations and recipients, be eliminated and that recipient organizations be made primarily responsible for their own expenditures.

The 1969 Tax Reform Act places on foundations and their officers "expenditure responsibility" for any grant that a foundation makes. This provision serves as a restraint on the openness and venturesomeness of foundations. It also puts foundations in a policing and surveillance role and thus undermines the autonomy of grantees. The provision creates both an unnecessary and undesirable duplication of responsibility, and should be repealed.

That tax-exempt organizations, particularly funding organizations, recognize an obligation to be responsive to changing viewpoints and emerging needs and that they take steps such as broadening their boards and staffs to insure that they are responsive.

All exempt organizations, especially those that serve to channel funds to other nonprofit groups, have a public obligation to be aware of and responsive to new attitudes and needs of all segments of society, and each organization should periodically broaden its board and staff if need be so that a wide range of viewpoints is reflected in the organization's governance and management.

The Commission rejects the notion that all voluntary organizations should be "representative" but observes that as more government funds flow into or through voluntary organizations they may have to consider inviting "public" members on their boards as an element of public access and control.

In addition to broadening existing organizations the Commission urges the establishment of new funding organizations and structural changes to broaden the spectrum of institutional philanthropy in general. An example is the "People's Trust" plan currently being explored in Atlanta; it would raise money in modest monthly pledges for projects close to the donors' homes.

C. Personal or Institutional Self-Benefiting. While tax-exempt charitable organizations are not allowed to make profits, situations have been uncovered in which personal money-making appeared to be the main purpose of the organization or of certain transactions made by the organization. Most notorious, perhaps, have been discoveries of instances where fund-raising and administrative costs have used as much as four out of every five dollars raised. The 1969 tax reform law placed stringent restrictions on self-benefiting by foundation personnel. The Commission believes that other tax-exempt organizations may be as open to such abuses, however, and it therefore favors extending the 1969 restriction to all exempt organizations, with appropriate modifications. Other remedies and restraints are considered desirable as well to insure public confidence that charitable nonprofit organizations do indeed serve only charitable nonprofit causes. The Commission recommends:

That all tax-exempt organizations be required to maintain "arms-length" business relationships with profit-making organizations or activities in which any principal of the exempt organization has a financial interest.

That a system of federal regulation be established for interstate charitable solicitations and that intrastate solicitations be more effectively regulated by state governments.

The Commission believes that the vast majority of charitable solicitations are conscientiously and economically undertaken. Nonetheless, cases of unduly costly or needless fund raising point to the absence of any focused mechanism for overseeing such activity and, if need be, applying sanctions. State regulation is weak and should be strengthened, but because many solicitations are spread over a number of states at once, federal regulation is needed.

The Commission recommends fuller disclosure requirements on solicitation costs and proposes that a special federal office be established to oversee solicitations and to take legal actions against improper, misleading or excessively costly fund raisings.

D. Influencing Legislation.   Since 1934, organizations that are eligible to receive tax-deductible gifts have been prohibited from devoting a "substantial part" of their activities to "attempting to influence legislation."

Yet, since 1962, any business organization has been able to deduct costs of influencing legislation that affects the direct interest of the business. The anti-lobbying restriction operates unevenly among charitable groups themselves because of the vagueness that surrounds the term, "substantial part." Large organizations can lobby amply, smaller ones risk treading over some ill-defined line. Furthermore, constitutional questions are raised by what can be viewed as an infringement on free speech and on the right to petition government.

The Commission feels that the restriction inhibits a large and growing role of the voluntary sector. As government has expanded in relation to the nonprofit sector, the influencing of government has tended to become an ever more important function of nonprofit organizations. For many "public interest" and "social action" groups, it is a principal means of furthering their causes. Therefore, the Commission recommends:

That nonprofit organizations, other than private foundations, be allowed the same freedom to attempt to influence legislation as are business corporations and trade associations, that toward this end Congress remove the current limitation on such activity by charitable groups eligible to receive tax-deductible gifts.

III. A Permanent Commission

The Commission's studies have, it feels, significantly advanced the state of knowledge about America's third sector and its philanthropic underpinnings. Yet such is the immensity and diversity of this area of American life and such has been the scarcity of information that has faced the Commission that it inevitably has had to leave depths unfathomed.

A new organization of recognized national stature and authority is needed, the Commission believes, to further chart and study, and ultimately to strengthen the nonprofit sector and the practice of private giving for public purposes. In a time when the sector is subject to both economic strains and political and philosophical questioning, when profound changes are taking place in its role and relationship to government, and when philanthropy has failed to keep pace with society, in economic and financial terms at least, the Commission believes that such an entity is necessary for the growth, perhaps even the survival, of the sector as an effective instrument of individual initiative and social progress.

This Commission, in terminating its own work, puts forward as one of its major recommendations:

That a permanent national commission on the nonprofit sector be established by Congress.

Several major tasks of any new organization already await it. Among these is examining philanthropic priorities in light of America's changing social perceptions, of government's growing role in traditional philanthropic areas, and of the inevitably limited resources of private giving. Also, examining and advancing means of insulating voluntary organizations from the political and bureaucratic pressures that tend to accompany public funds.

Among other purposes and roles of the commission would be continuous collection of data on the sources and uses of the resources of the nonprofit sector; exploring and proposing ways of strengthening private giving and nonprofit activity; providing a forum for public discussion of issues affecting, and for commentary concerning, the nonprofit sector; studying the existing relationships between government and the nonprofit sector and acting as an ombudsman in protecting the interests of the sector as affected by government.

It is proposed that half the commission's membership be named by the President, subject to senatorial confirmation, the other half by the presidential appointees themselves. Funding for the commission would come half from government, half from private sources. The commission would be established as a permanent body, subject, of course, to periodic congressional review and the commission's demonstrtion of its benefit to society.

CHAPTER 7

The Impact of the Voluntary Sector on Society

DAVID HORTON SMITH

Having now looked at a few facets of the impact of voluntary action from the level of the individual up to the level of social movements, let us take a final step up to the highest currently applicable level of impact of voluntarism—on society as a whole. In looking at impact on all of the previous system levels, it is all too easy to get lost among the "trees," thus losing sight of the "forest." In our view, the "forest" is the larger context of social meaning that voluntary action has in human society. By *social* we mean to include all aspects of social structure and culture here, and by *society* we mean to include not just American society or any other particular society, but all of mankind, past, present, and (hopefully) future.

The "voluntary sector" refers to all those persons, groups, roles, organizations, and institutions in society whose goals involve primarily voluntary action. Roughly speaking, it includes what one is neither made to nor paid to do, but rather what one does out of some kind of expectation of psychic benefits or commitment to some value, ideal, or common interest. The voluntary sector may be roughly delineated in a negative way by contrasting it with the commercial or business sector (sometimes called the "private sector") and with the government or public sector. Another way of describing the voluntary sector is by saying that it is the total persisting social embodiment (in the form of norms, expectations, customs, and ways of behaving) of voluntary action in society.

Our question here is, simply, what impact does the voluntary sector as a whole have on society? There is not sufficient research information to permit one to do an aggregate analysis, building up a picture of the whole by systematically combining the parts—the kinds of impacts of voluntary action at different system levels we have been examining in part in prior chapters. Instead, we can only do the very sketchiest global analysis, based on a loose inductive logic and general theoretical considerations. In making this very brief and simplistic analysis, we are again more interested in suggesting some lines of possible future research and theory than in being exhaustive or thorough.

Another way of looking at what we are calling the impacts of the voluntary sector is to see the processes behind these impacts and to term them the "functions" or "roles" of the voluntary sector. These processes are not necessary features of the voluntary sector in any given nation, let alone in all nations. But they do represent what the voluntary sector can do and often has done in the past in particular societies at particular times. This is an attempt to help delineate more clearly why there is a voluntary sector in society, much as one might elsewhere discuss the role of government institutions or business or even the family in society. Like all of the latter, of course, the role of the voluntary sector changes over time in a given society and even in human society as a whole. The impacts of the voluntary sector we discuss briefly below are suggested as very general aspects of the voluntary sector in human society, and hence they are present to at least some degree as long as there is a voluntary sector.

First, one of the most central impacts of the voluntary sector is to provide society with a large variety of partially tested social innovations, from which business, government, and other institutions can select and institutionalize those innovations which seem most promising. The independent voluntary sector is thus the prototyping test bed of many, perhaps most new social forms and modes of human relations. Where business and government, science and technology are active in the creation and testing of technological innovations, the independent voluntary sector specializes in the practical testing of social ideas. Nearly every function currently performed by governments at various levels was once a new social idea and the experiment of some voluntary group, formal or informal—this is true of education, welfare, care for the aged, building roads, even fighting wars (volunteer citizen militias).

In sum, the voluntary sector has tended to provide the social risk capital of human society. It has been sufficiently free of the kinds of constraints that bind business (the constant need to show a profit) and government (the need to maintain control and, in societies with effective democracies, the need to act in accord with a broad consensus) so that its component elements (particular voluntary groups or even individuals) can act simply out of commitment to some value or idea, without needing to wait until the payoffs for that kind of activity can be justified in terms appropriate to mobilizing economic or governmental institutions. It is thus the most "error-embracing" and experimental component of society (see Smith with Dixon 1973).

Second, another central impact of the voluntary sector on society has been the provision of countervailing definitions of reality and morality—ideologies, perspectives, and worldviews that frequently challenge the prevailing assumptions about what exists and what is good and what should be done in society. The voluntary sector is that part of society which, collectively, is most likely to say that "the emperor has no clothes." Voluntary groups of various kinds are distinctive among human groups in the extent to which they develop their own ideologies and value systems. If these definitions of reality and morality are sufficiently compelling to people, voluntary groups grow into huge social movements and can change the course of history, both within a given nation (e.g., the abolitionist movement in the early and middle nineteenth century of the United States) and across human society as a whole (e.g., Christianity, Buddhism, democracy, communism).

This kind of impact of the voluntary sector is related to the previous one, but where the former kind of impact emphasized experimentation with social innovation in practice, the present impact emphasizes instead ideological and moral innovation. Where the previous point focused on the social risk capital role of the voluntary sector in society, the present point focuses on the role of the voluntary sector as a gadfly, dreamer, and moral leader in society. Voluntary groups of various kinds are concerned with the generation and allocation of human commitment in the deepest sense. In the process of doing this, the voluntary sector as a whole provides moral and ideological leadership to the majority of human society, and often calls into question the existing legitimacy structures and accepted social definitions of reality of particular societies.

A third major impact of the voluntary sector on society is to provide the play element in society, especially as the search for novelty, beauty, recreation, and fun for their own sake may be collectively organized. Again because the voluntary sector is not constrained generally by such values as profit, control, and broad social consensus, voluntary groups can form in terms of literally thousands of different kinds of common interests. A full array of common interest groups (especially expressive rather than instrumental ones) in an elaborated but still evolving voluntary sector permits (in principle) nearly all individuals to find at least one group that will be satisfying to them. If there is no such group, one or more individuals may form one, if they wish, to reflect their own needs and vision of the play element. Such a group may be formal or informal, large or small, permanent or transient, open or closed, and so forth.

To speak of the play element here is not to speak of something trivial and unimportant. As society becomes increasingly complex and work activity is increasingly structured in terms of large bureaucracies, people's unsatisfied needs for play, novelty, new experience, and all manner of recreation tend to increase. The kind of easy interchange and blending of play and work that could be present in more traditional economies tends to be lost. Under such circumstances, voluntary groups often provide a window of variety and intrinsic satisfaction in an otherwise rather boring or at least psychically fatiguing world of work and responsibility.

Fourth, the voluntary sector also has a major impact on the level of social integration in society. Partly through directly expressive groups, whose aims are explicitly to provide fellowship, sociability and mutual companionship, and partly through the sociability aspects of all other kinds of collective and interpersonal forms of voluntary action, the voluntary sector helps in a very basic way to satisfy some of the human needs for affiliation, approval, and so on. In advanced industrial and urbanized societies, where the family and kinship as well as the local community and neighborhood play a markedly reduced role in providing social integration, affiliations based on common interests can become very important to the individual. Indeed, without the latter kind of voluntary sector-based common interest affiliations, the resulting rates of individual social isolation in society would lead to even more anomie, alienation, and a variety of attendant social and psychological problems than are now the case. Obviously, the voluntary sector has not been the whole solution to the root problem of social isolation in modern society, yet voluntary groups do play a demonstrable and important part in the solution. And with the feeling of being accepted as a person that the voluntary sector provides (or can provide) to a significant proportion of the population in modern societies goes the correlative provision of positive affect, a major component of human happiness and the quality of human life.

Another aspect of the role of the voluntary sector in providing social integration is the social adjustment "buffering" function that many kinds of voluntary groups provide. When numerous individuals of a certain social and cultural background are for some reason uprooted from their customary societal niches, new voluntary groups frequently emerge to provide these individuals with an insulated or "buffered" special environment for part of their time. Typical examples would be the numerous immigrant associations that sprang up in the United States as a result of successive waves of immigration from various countries (Handlin 1951) or the kinship oriented voluntary associations that emerged to ease the adjustment of rural West Africans to life in large cities (Little 1965).

These kinds of social adjustment oriented voluntary groups do not, however, emerge only in the case of physical/geographical changes on a large scale. The voluntary sector also provides a social adjustment "mechanism" to ease the shocks of social dislocations and rapid social changes of all sorts. The voluntary groups involved may cater to a former elite that has been disenfranchised or deprived of its former holdings (e.g., the association of maharajahs of India, which arose to fight for "maharajah's rights" when the Indian Congress stripped them of their traditional privileges and land, substituting a moderate annual stipend). Or the voluntary groups involved may represent a deprived category of persons who are attempting to adjust to changed social conditions that are more conducive to their sharing equitably in the good life as lived in their society (e.g., the early labor unions or black power groups, striving for recognition of their right to exist and to fight for the betterment of the conditions of their constituencies).

On another level, the voluntary sector plays an important integrative role by linking together individuals, groups, institutions and even nations that otherwise would be in greater conflict, or at least competition, with each other. (This and other impacts of voluntary groups are discussed further in Smith, 1966.) At the community level, a variety of voluntary associations will each tend to have as members a set of two or more individuals representing differing and often opposing political, religious, cultural, or social perspectives and backgrounds. The co-participation of this set of individuals in the same voluntary association can have significant moderating effects on the relationships among these individuals. Similar integrative effects can be found at national levels where several groups from different parts of the country and/or different social and cultural perspectives participate together in a common federation or other national voluntary organization. And at the international level, the joint participation of voluntary groups from otherwise conflicting nations in some transnational federative organization may well have important long range effects on the relations between the countries involved and on the possibilities of peace in the world.

A fifth kind of general impact of the voluntary sector involves the opposite of the first one, which dealt with the social innovation role of voluntarism. In addition to providing a wide variety of *new* ideas about social behavior, the voluntary sector also is active in preserving numerous *old* ideas. Voluntary action and voluntary organizations have played a major role in history in preserving values, ways of life, ideas, beliefs, artifacts, and other productions of the mind, heart, and hand of man from earlier times so that this great variety of human culture is not lost to future generations. For example, there are in the United States numerous local historical societies that specialize in preserving the history of particular towns and areas. There are nonprofit voluntary organizations that run local museums, libraries, and historical sites. And there are a number of voluntary organizations whose primary function it is to preserve the values of cultures or subcultures that no

longer have any substantial power or importance in American society, but that nevertheless represent a way of life of significant numbers of people at some period in history or somewhere around the world (e.g., American Indian groups, in some instances, or immigrant ethnic associations that persist long after the ethnic group involved has been thoroughly assimilated into American culture). The role of municipal, state, and national governments in supporting museums and historical sites grows from the roots of earlier non-profit, non-governmental support of such "islands of culture."

Another aspect of the belief/value preservation role of the voluntary sector involves voluntary associations as educational experiences, especially where these associations are attempting to pass on to their members or to the public at large some body of beliefs and values originating in the past. In part this would include many of the activities of most religious sects and denominations, especially insofar as one focuses upon their socialization and indoctrination activities (e.g., catechism classes, "Sunday schools," Hebrew day schools, etc.). In part this function also includes all manner of more strictly educational voluntary organizations, from Plato's Academy (see Peterson and Peterson 1973) to modern Great Books Discussion Groups and so-called "Free Universities."

The various levels of government in the contemporary world have largely taken over the task of education on a broad scale, yet voluntary organizations still are active in supplementing government-run educational systems by filling in the gaps and by prodding these systems to improve or take on responsibility for the preservation of additional knowledge or values. For instance, voluntary civil rights and black liberation organizations have taken the lead in educating both blacks and whites in the United States regarding black history and accomplishments. Gradually, under the pressure of such voluntary associations in the past several years, the public educational system in the United States has been changing to accommodate a more accurate and complete picture of black history, although the process is by no means finished yet. Similar examples could be given with regard to other content areas as well (e.g., women's history, American Indian history, etc.).

A sixth major impact of the voluntary sector is its embodiment and representation in society of the sense of mystery, wonder, and the sacred. Neither the business nor government sectors in modern society have much tendency to be concerned with such matters. Many would say that religion today *is* very much a big business; and both business and government support science in a substantial way. Yet precisely in those areas where religion and science almost meet, where the borders of religion are receding under the pressure of an ever-expanding science, the business and government sectors are often *least* involved. Voluntary associations and non-profit foundations/research organizations are the only groups experimenting seriously with new forms of worship, non-drug induced "consciousness expansion" and the "religious experience," the occult, investigation of flying saucers, extra-sensory perception, etc.

The "heretics" of both science and religion are seldom supported in their work directly and consciously by the business or government sectors. Only through voluntary action and the support of the voluntary sector have the major changes in man's view of the supernatural and its relation to the natural tended to come about in the past. The same has also been true, by and large, for major changes in man's view of himself and of the natural universe in the past. The dominant economic and political (and religious) systems of any given epoch are seldom very receptive to the really new visions of either the natural or supernatural world (e.g., Galileo and Copernicus; Jesus). Voluntary action is thus the principal manner in which a sense of the sacred, the mysterious, and the weird can be preserved and permitted some measure of expression in our otherwise hyper-rational contemporary society.

A seventh impact of the voluntary sector results from its ability to liberate the individual and permit him or her the fullest possible measure of expression of personal capacities and potentialities within an otherwise constraining social environment. All societies have their systems of laws, customs, roles, and organizations that box people in and limit their opportunities for personal expression and personal development. The full extent of societal limitations on people has just begun to be realized in recent decades, spurred in part by the "liberation" movements of women, blacks, the poor, the "Third World" and other disadvantaged or disenfranchised groups. The primary embodiments of these societal barriers and boxes have generally been the economic and governmental systems, although other major institutions of society have played a role as well (e.g., education, the family, religion, etc.).

Voluntary associations and groups, on the other hand, have long been a primary means of at least partially escaping these barriers and boxes. Through participation in voluntary action a wide variety of people have been able to find or to create special social groups that would permit them to grow as individuals. This kind of personal growth has many relevant aspects, but can be summed up generally as "self actualization," to use a term from Maslow (1954). For some this means intellectual development, the process of becoming increasingly analytical, informed, and self-conscious about the nature of one's life situation and problems. When this occurs for a whole category or group of people, the process is often referred to as "group conscienticization" or "consciousness-raising" (e.g., among blacks, women, the poor). Seldom does such special personal growth occur on a broad scale outside voluntary groups and movements.

For others, self-actualization through voluntary action takes the form of developing otherwise unused capacities, talents, skills or potentials of a more active and practical sort. For many kinds of people, depending on the stage of social, economic, and political development of a society, voluntary associations and voluntary action offer the only feasible opportunity for leadership, for learning to speak in public, for practicing the fine art of management, for exercising analytical judgment, etc. Until very recently in American society, for instance, neither blacks nor women nor the members of certain other disadvantaged groups could hope to develop fully their capacities through the occupational system of the economic or government sectors.

Only in voluntary groups of their own making could they seek any kind of fulfillment and self expression, bound as they were (and in part continue to be) by the prejudices and discrimination of the dominant white, male, Anglo-Saxon Protestants in our society. However, this situation is not unique to the United States. There are similar and even different forms of prejudice and discrimination in *all* other societies, varying only in degree and the particular social groups singled out for attention. And in all societies voluntary associations also offer the disadvantaged some chance of enhanced self-development, though these associations must sometimes meet in secret as underground groups if the society in which they are operating is oppressive and does not respect the right of free association.

Voluntary action potentially offers unique opportunities for personal growth and realization of personal potentials not only for those people whom society otherwise deprives, but also for *all* the members of society in certain directions. No matter how free, open, egalitarian, and highly developed the society, there are always limitations of some sort placed on the development of each person by his particular social environment. Any major decision to follow a certain line of personal occupational or educational development, for instance, automatically forecloses a number of other alternatives, or at least makes them highly unlikely. Voluntary associations, however, exist (or can exist) in such profusion and variety that they can provide otherwise missed personal development opportunities to almost any person at almost any stage of life. This is as true for the school teacher who always wanted to learn to fly (and who can join a flying club to do so even at age 60), as it is for the airline pilot who always wanted to write novels (and who can join a writer's club to work toward this end).

Of course, not every person will find the appropriate voluntary association for his or her personal growth needs to be available at the time it is needed. But the voluntary sector as a whole, nevertheless, still serves in some significant degree this general role of providing substantial numbers of individuals in society with otherwise unavailable opportunities for self actualization and self fulfillment.

An eighth major impact of the voluntary sector in society is one of overriding importance, relating directly to the first and second impacts discussed above. We are referring to the impact of the voluntary sector as a source of "negative feedback" for society as a whole, especially with regard to the directions taken by the major institutions of society such as government and business. Without "negative feedback," any system is dangerously vulnerable to destroying itself through excesses in one direction or another. Thus, however uncomfortable and irritating they may be at times, voluntary associations and the voluntary sector are absolutely vital to the continuing development of a society.

This systemic corrective role of the voluntary sector is, of course, not carried out by *all* voluntary associations, any more than all voluntary associations are concerned with the play element, value preservation, or the sacred. Yet the small cutting edge of the voluntary sector that does perform the role of social critic is extremely important, usually bearing the responsibility for the continued existence and future growth of the rest of the voluntary sector. In societies where a sufficient number and variety of voluntary groups are *un*able to play effectively their roles as social critics, the dominant governmental and economic institutions may well take over and suppress the entire voluntary sector (e.g., Allen 1965).

In the contemporary United States there are numerous examples of voluntary associations and groups playing this systemic corrective role. All of the cause-oriented, advocacy, and issue-oriented groups tend to fall into this category, from the environmental movement to the civil rights movement and women's liberation. The tactics and strategy of such groups cover a broad range from rather traditional lobbying, through demonstrations and "be-ins," to direct remedial action such as "ecotage" (sabotage of notable corporate polluters and other "environmental undesirables").

Some of the more imaginative and innovative approaches have been developed in an attempt to modify the business sector, rather than focusing solely on the government sector. For instance, there have been in-depth investigations by Ralph Nader and his associates of particular companies' practices and their relationship to the public interest (e.g., for First National City Bank of New York and for DuPont), counter-management stockholder activity in the public interest (e.g., Project G.M.), dissenting annual reports written to present a full public accounting of a corporation's activities harmful to the general public interest and welfare, class action suits brought by voluntary groups against manufacturers and developers, etc.

When looked at in the particular, such activities (which vary markedly in their success) often seem fruitless and doomed to failure, given the power of the organizations and systems being challenged. Yet when we see these activities of voluntary groups in a larger context, when we sum up these numerous activities attempting to modify and improve the dominant systems and organizations of our society, they take on a very important general meaning. Even if many or most of such system correction attempts by voluntary groups should fail, the continual and expanding pressure being brought to bear by the voluntary sector on the central institutions of society is still likely to have a salutary long term modifying influence. When the leaders of the business and governmental sectors *know* that "someone is watching," that they will eventually have to account to the public interest for their actions, this awareness encourages greater attention to the public interest rather than merely to narrow, private interests.

When for one reason or another the voluntary sector is not able to operate effectively as a systemic corrective (either because of its own inadequacies or the failure of the leaders of dominant institutions to listen and change accordingly), the usual result in human history has been a broad social revolution (not just a palace revolution or simple coup). When the dominant institutions of any society have ignored for too long or too often the voices of the public interest as expressed by elements of the voluntary sector, revolutionary and usually underground voluntary groups arise and make concrete plans to overthrow the existing system completely. The

American, French, Russian, Chinese, Cuban, and other revolutions all attest to this pattern.

Thus, when the voluntary sector cannot make itself heard adequately through the permissible communication and influence channels in a society, certain voluntary groups and movements tend to arise to revamp the whole system, establishing whole new institutional arrangements with their corresponding new channels of influence and communication. Not surprisingly, these new channels generally favor those kinds of persons and groups who were unable to be heard previously (although the kinds of people formerly dominant often end up in as bad a position or worse than that faced by the formerly disadvantaged prior to the revolution). This cycle will tend to repeat itself until a society reaches a point where it is effectively and continuously self-correcting, through the activities of a strong and social change-oriented voluntary sector, and where its major institutions are basically operating primarily in the public interest of *all* of its citizens (not just its white, male, Anglo-Saxon Protestants, or their equivalents in some other societies than the United States and the British Common-wealth).

The ninth major impact of the voluntary sector worth mentioning here is the support given by the voluntary sector specifically to the economic system of a society, especially a modern industrial society. Voluntary associations of many kinds provide crucial kinds of social, intellectual, and technical linkages among workers in numerous occupations: professional associations increase the effectiveness of most kinds of scientists, engineers, technicians, etc., just as manufacturers' and trade associations support the growth of whole industries. And various kinds of labor unions play their part as well, although many businessmen would question the degree to which they "support" the economic system. But labor unions only seem nonsupportive of the economic system when the latter is viewed narrowly from the point of view of an employer interested solely in profit maximization. Labor unions ultimately have to be deeply concerned with the viability of the economic system and the productivity of their own members if they are to survive.

This economic support role of the voluntary sector is usually lost sight of because so many people tend to view all kinds of economic self-interest and occupationally related voluntary associations as integral parts of the business sector. In fact, these kinds of voluntary organizations are quite distinct from the business sector itself, however close their relationship might be to business corporations and occupational activities. The primary purpose of business corporations is to make a profit for their owners, whether they are actually involved in running the corporation or not. On the other hand, economic self-interest voluntary associations have as their primary purpose the enhancement of the long term occupational and economic interests of their member-participants. While corporation employees and professionals are *paid* in salaries, wages or fees for their participation, the members of economic self-interest voluntary associations themselves *pay* for the privilege of belonging to and benefiting from these associations.

The tenth major impact of the voluntary sector we shall note is a rather subtle one: the voluntary sector constitutes an important *latent* resource for all kinds of goal attainment in the interests of the society as a whole. Put another way, the voluntary sector represents a tremendous reservoir of potential energy that can be mobilized under appropriate circumstances for broad societal goals. The role of the voluntary sector in revolutionary situations is but one example of this latent potential. The activity of voluntary association networks in more limited disaster situations is a more common example (Barton 1970). The voluntary sector and its component associations, groups, and channels of communication and influence make possible the mobilization of large numbers of people on relatively short notice for special purposes (usually in the common interest) without resorting to economic rewards or legal coercion as activating forces. Such a latent potential in the voluntary sector is especially important when neither economic nor political-legal forces can feasibly be brought to bear to resolve some widespread problem situation.

The latent potential of the voluntary sector can be viewed in another way as well. Voluntarism is based on a *charitable grants economy* (donations of time, money, etc.) as contrasted with the *coercive grants economy* (taxation) on which the government sector operates or the *market economy* on which the business sector operates. Both of the latter types of economy work well for certain kinds of purposes, but neither works well for the accomplishment of *all* kinds of purposes in society. In the same way, there are many kinds of purposes and activities (several of which are implicit in the nine major impacts of the voluntary sector reviewed above) for which the charitable grants economy tends to work best.

Now the important latent potential of the voluntary sector is that, under appropriately compelling circumstances (i.e., for the "right" value, goal or ideal), the money, goods, real property, and services mobilized by the voluntary sector through the charitable grants economy can completely overwhelm all considerations of the coercive grants economy and the market economy. For certain goals and ideals, a large majority of society can be induced to "give their all" and to do so gladly, willingly, and voluntarily. This does not occur very often, to be sure, nor does it last very long. But the latent potential is there in any society at any time. With the right spark—usually a charismatic leader with an idea and an ideal—the course of history can be changed in these brief, rare periods of almost total societal mobilization through the leadership of the voluntary sector.

The Negative Side

In describing the foregoing ten types of impact that the voluntary sector tends to have in some degree in any society, we have emphasized the positive contributions that voluntary action makes to society. However, as with any form of human group or activity, voluntary action and the voluntary sector are by no means always positive in their impacts. For every one of the ten types of impact we have noted, there can be negative consequences in certain circumstances and with regard to certain values. Thus, when voluntary associations experiment with new social forms, the failures can often be harmful to specific people and organizations. When alternative definitions of reality and morality are offered, these can be evil as in the case of Nazi Germany and its ideology as generated by the Nazi party, a voluntary association. When voluntary groups focus on the play element, their fun can become mischievous as in the case of a boys' gang that wrecks a school "just for kicks." When social clubs provide a warm and close sense of belonging to their members, they can also create deep dissatisfaction in people who would dearly like to belong but are excluded from a particular club or kind of club.

In the same way, voluntary groups striving to preserve some beliefs or values from the past may be holding on to anachronisms that would be better left to the pages of history books. Clubs whose members chase around seeking flying saucers and little green men from Mars might more profitably spend their time and energy elsewhere with more satisfying results. Organizations that arouse the full potentials of black people—who must then go out into the real world and face a harsh reality of bigotry and discrimination—may or may not be doing them a favor. The kinds of systemic corrections being suggested by cause-oriented and advocacy groups may not be conducive to the greatest good of the greatest number. Economic self-interest voluntary groups often tend to ignore the public interest in favor of an exclusive and self-ish private interest. And the latent potentials of the voluntary sector can be mobilized to do evil as well as to do good for one's fellow man.

References

Allen, William Sheridan. 1965. *The Nazi Seizure of Power.* Chicago: Quadrangle Books.

Barton, Allen H. 1970. *Communities in Disaster.* Garden City, New York: Anchor Books, Doubleday and Company.

Handlin, Oscar. 1951. *The Uprooted.* New York: Grosset and Dunlap.

Little, Kenneth. 1965. *West African Urbanization: A Study of Voluntary Associations in Social Change.* Cambridge, England: Cambridge University Press.

Maslow, Abraham H. 1954. *Motivation and Personality.* New York: Harper and Row.

Peterson, Sophia, and Virgil Peterson. 1973. "Voluntary Associations in Ancient Greece." *Journal of Voluntary Action Research* 2, no. 1, 2–16.

Smith, David Horton. 1966. "The Importance of Formal Voluntary Organizations for Society." *Sociology and Social Research* 50, 483–92.

Smith, David Horton, with John Dixon. 1973. "The Voluntary Sector." Chapter 7 in Edward Bursk, ed., *Challenge to Leadership: Managing in a Changing World.* New York: The Free Press, Macmillan and Co.

Smith, David Horton, Richard D. Reddy, and Burt R. Baldwin. 1972. "Types of Voluntary Action: A Definitional Essay." Chapter 10 in David Horton Smith et al., eds., *Voluntary Action Research: 1972.* Lexington, Mass.: Lexington Books, D.C. Heath and Co.

PART 3

HISTORICAL EVOLUTION
OF THE
NONPROFIT SECTOR

"Nonprofits pose almost insuperable problems for anyone who would presume to relate their history,"[1] because in order to understand the history of the nonprofit sector a person needs to appreciate the multiple contexts and cultural milieus through which it evolved over the history of modern civilization. For example,

- Accounts of collaborative voluntary action can be found dating all the way back in history to the origins of record-keeping.
- The philosophical roots of the nonprofit sector can be found among the early Greeks, Romans, Jews, and Christians and in the writings of the post–Industrial Revolution liberal democratic theorists, including John Locke and John Stuart Mill.[2]
- Our modern forms of institutional voluntary action trace their lineage to the Reformation's stimulation of freedom of association, increased interdependence, and reduced self-sufficiency that were caused by the Industrial Revolution's need for specialization, division of labor, and urbanization.[3]
- Much of the sector's legal and tax history was imported and adapted from England.
- The sector's distinctively "American associational character" and the central role of this "associational character" for the enactment of citizen democracy can be traced to the colonial era's harsh, survival-oriented context, as was documented extensively by Alexis de Tocqueville.[4]

Many of the sector's most important features and functions, however, did not develop until the last three or four decades of the twentieth century.

The sector's evolution in the United States has been neither consciously planned nor linear. It "happened" in response to events, evolving patterns and norms in the public and for-profit sectors, shifting cultural values, and societal changes at points in time. Patterns in its development are reflections of the richness of the political, social, demographic, economic, and cultural histories of the United States.[5] Several themes or dimensions, however, are easily identifiable by reviewing the historical evolution of the nonprofit sector, including its philosophical history, the history of choices among democratic values, associational philanthropy in the United States, and major changes in the relationships between nonprofits and the U.S. government.

Philosophical History

The Western tradition of voluntarism has its roots in two diverse ideological streams:

- The Greco-Roman heritage of emphasis on community, citizenry, and social responsibility. The Greco-Roman ideology rests on a foundation of social reform to relieve community social problems, or in other words, to improve the quality of life for all in the community.
- The Judeo-Christian belief that relationships with a higher power affect our choices and thus our decisionmaking. Our purpose is not to change people's lot in life but rather to alleviate the "preordained" suffering of others, particularly the poor. Under the Judeo-Christian tradition, we do not help others solely from concern for ourselves or our neighbors, but first and foremost because a deity has given us instructions to do so. We are told to love our neighbors as we love ourselves. We love our neighbor because we love God first and thus seek to obey.

The influence of these two distinct, historical ideologies has been replayed countless times and in countless ways through the history of the American nonprofit sector, and it is reflected in the following definitions of two types of voluntarism (see also the introductory essay in Part 2):

- *Philanthropy,* the giving of money or self to solve social problems. Philanthropy is developmental, an investment in the future, an effort to prevent future occurrences or recurrences of social ills.
- *Charity,* relieving or alleviating specific instances of suffering—aiding the individual victims of specific social ills. Charity is acts of mercy and compassion.

We tend to view these two forms of voluntary action as complementary dimensions of the nonprofit sector. We need philanthropy, and we need charity. This interdependence has not always been recognized, however. For example, Andrew Carnegie, the ardent philanthropist, abhorred charity. (Carnegie's philosophy of philanthropy is articulated in the "Gospel of Wealth," which is reprinted in Part 2). "It were better for mankind that the millions of the rich were thrown into the sea than so spent as to encourage the slothful, the drunken, the unworthy . . . so spent, indeed, as to produce the very evils which it hopes to mitigate or cure."[6] Yet from the Judeo-Christian charitable tradition, almshouses, charitable hospitals, orphan homes, and charitable organizations such as Catholic Charities, the Little Sisters of the Poor, the Salvation Army, the International Red Cross, and countless others have helped relieve untold instances of human suffering in the United States.

The History of Difficult Choices
Among Democratic Values

Part 2 introduced the two distinctive foundation values of the nonprofit sector, *individualism* and *pluralism*. These two values are as much a part of the democratic ideal in the United States as are *equity, justice,* and *fairness,* the values that serve as the primary foundations of the public sector. During the past twenty or thirty years of the twentieth century, the basic approach to alleviating domestic social problems, such as poverty, youth gangs, mental illness, developmental disabilities, and lack of access to affordable housing and employment, changed in the United States. Historically, the approaches for dealing with these types of social problems had developed from individual and family responsibility in the eighteenth and nineteenth centuries, to community problem solving as the nation urbanized in the nineteenth century, and to massive state and national government intervention in the twentieth century. Since about 1980, however, the trend has been reversed. This powerful movement has been *devolution*—the shifting of money and decisionmaking authority away from national and state action back toward community problem solving. Nonprofit organizations have reemerged as the primary focus of solution strategies for domestic ills. State government (often with federal support) is still the primary source of funding for social programs, but moral and practical responsibility (and quite a bit of the financial burden) for problem solutions and the direct delivery of services has returned to communities.[7]

Associational Philanthropy in the United States

During the first half of the nineteenth century, Alexis de Tocqueville, the astute French observer of American life, traveled through the colonies documenting his impressions of this nation's approach to shared control and responsibility for efforts to meet community needs. He observed the potent contributions that voluntary associations made to political and intellectual life in the United States:

> An association consists simply in the public assent which a number of individuals give to certain doctrines and in the engagement which they contract to promote in a certain manner the spread of those doctrines. . . . An association unites into one channel the efforts of divergent minds and urges them vigorously toward the one end that it clearly points out. . . . The second degree in the exercise of the right of association is the power of meeting.[8]

Tocqueville also noted that across Europe, the sharing of power and responsibilities had taken a different form. The *secondary power*—the ability of the nobility, cities, and provincial bodies to represent local affairs—had been relinquished to the centralized authority. Tocqueville's secondary power is what we refer to today as the activities that serve the public good and which also result in the formation of social capital.[9] In the early 1800s in the United States, social welfare needs often were met through the actions of voluntary associations, which, in turn, created the civic life that is the wellspring of democratic community life.[10] Tocqueville's issues are as timely now as they were then. Once again as a nation, we are engaged in similar debates about public and private goods, and the extent of government's responsibility for citizens versus the extent of citizens' responsibilities for helping others through voluntary associations.

Changes in the Relationship Between Nonprofits and the U.S. Government

As the end of the twentieth century approached, the historical barn-raising spirit of neighbors helping neighbors in good times and in bad began to reemerge as the foundation for domestic public policy. In the short span of about two decades, the underlying philosophy—or ideology— of programs for people moved a great distance from what they had been throughout most of the twentieth century. Several streams of events and philosophical currents led to this radical redefinition of U.S. social policy. This nation had been committed to and believed it could win the "War on Poverty" through "Great Society" programs in the 1960s and 1970s. In the 1980s and 1990s, however, two beliefs or understandings emerged as public policy "truths": social needs are endless, and government programs seldom can solve social problems.

In effect, the modern devolution era started with the administration of President Ronald Reagan. Reagan used his extraordinary communicative skills to change the nation's basic vision about how social problems and community needs should be addressed and how remedial and ameliorating activities should be funded. For Reagan, responsibility belonged at the local level. Thus, almost all decisions about the allocation of financial resources to nonprofit organizations now are determined through local governmental and private funding structures and decision processes.

The Reagan administration's devolution agenda coincided with—and was a component of— Reagan's "shrink government" agenda. Sources of government social funding were terminated at the same time that Congress and the public was being told that nonprofits would carry more of the burden. Thus since 1980, the nonprofit sector has been called upon to do more with less.[11] The devolution movement has altered the nonprofit sector's roles, funding sources, structures, power balances, and relationships with communities.

Although most of the recent attention to the effects of the devolution movement has centered on the human services, its effects have been felt in other subsectors as well. Programs and services in health care, the arts and humanities, and environmental protection have devolved out of Washington, D.C., into statehouses, counties, and municipalities. Many of them have been diffused out of government and into the nonprofit sector.

When the nature of the relationship between the nonprofit and public sectors changes, tax policy changes usually follow—and thus the sector's ability to raise and retain financial resources changes as well. When, for example, elected officials lose confidence, legislative attempts to "reign in" nonprofits inevitably follow—as Wright Patman, House Ways and Means Committee Chair, did with private foundations in the 1960s and as the House's "Republican freshmen" attempted to do in the mid-1990s to large nonprofits with powerful affiliated lobbying groups (such as the American Association of Retired Persons [AARP]).

Readings Included in This Part

Three readings are reprinted in this chapter. Each focuses on different periods in the sector's evolution or on different dimensions of the sector. The first two readings, "A History of the Discipline," by Stephen R. Block, and "Inventing the Nonprofit Sector," by Peter Dobkin Hall, focus on different eras and are written from diverse perspectives. Collectively they present a comprehensive historical overview that introduces the "rich" contexts and the broad spectrum of issues and events that have shaped the evolution of the sector. The third reading focuses on the history of a single dimension of the sector: tax policy changes.

The first reading, "A History of the Discipline," by Stephen R. Block, traces and analyzes the sector's development from the Babylonian Code of Hammurabi, through the English Poor Laws, and to the mid-1980s. "A History of the Discipline" is particularly helpful for understanding the sector's philanthropic history, associational voluntarism, and the early development of nonprofit management professionals. Block uses Carl Milofsky's six "influential traditions of American participation": Protestant patrician, urban ethnic, free professional, organizational professional, interorganizational coordination, and corporate philanthropic.[12]

The second reading, Peter Dobkin Hall's historical analysis, "Inventing the Nonprofit Sector," actually is only a section of a chapter by Hall. The portion that is included here focuses on the sector's historical development from 1950 to 1990.[13] In this section, Hall documents and analyzes the changing relationship between government and nonprofits, noting, for example, that

> recognition of the interdependence of public and private enterprise became a fundamental premise of American polity in the twentieth century. But the balance between the two was always at issue—and the status of voluntary and charitable organizations, especially those that were supported by the wealthy and that explicitly sought not only to provide services for the public but also to influence its opinions, continued to be the subject of intense, but periodic, public controversy.[14]

Hall interprets the effects of numerous events and movements on nonprofits, including the following:

- The anti-Communist "witch-hunt" led by Senator Joseph McCarthy during the 1950s
- The 1954 "Reece Committee," which was formed to investigate tax-exempt foundations
- The Tax Reform Act of 1969
- The reports produced by the Commission on Private Philanthropy and Public Needs, chaired by John Filer, the chief executive officer of Aetna Insurance Company in the 1970s
- President Ronald Reagan's attraction to the nonprofit sector as an alternative to government service delivery, but the fiscal damage his administration did to the sector because of his all-consuming drive to lower taxes
- President George Bush's announcement of the "1,000 Points of Light" with great flourish, but his continuation of the Reagan agenda that "promoted tax proposals that would eliminate or reduce incentives to charitable donors. . . . [The] combination of threatened cutbacks in direct and indirect federal support for nonprofits and privatization has encouraged nonprofits to become far more entrepreneurial."[15]

Gary Scrivner's "A Brief History of Tax Policy Changes Affecting Charitable Organizations" is more than a description of tax changes and their impacts on nonprofit organizations. It is also an explanation of how "heritage, morality, and special interests help to form and affect changes in the very nature of charitable organizations." Scrivner traces impacts and their likely causes — tradition, public policy, and special interests in particular — from their beginnings in the United States with the Tariff Act of 1894 (the first major tax legislation in the United States to specify the organizations that were subject to taxation). Scrivner concludes:

> There have been innumerable changes in tax policy over the past one hundred years, with just as many reasons why these changes have occurred. The three bases [of tax policy] — tradition, public policy, and special interests — have all played a part in shaping tax policy and, ultimately, the very nature of nonprofit organizations. It is likely these factors will continue to shape American tax policy affecting nonprofits.[16]

The history of the nonprofit sector is an integral part of its future.

Notes

1. Peter Dobkin Hall, "Historical Perspectives on Nonprofit Organizations," in Robert D. Herman, ed., *Jossey-Bass Handbook of Nonprofit Leadership and Management* (San Francisco: Jossey-Bass, 1994), p. 4.

2. For historical overviews of philanthropy, see Merle Curti, "Philanthropy," in Philip P. Wiener, ed., *The Dictionary of the History of Ideas* (New York: Charles Scriber's Sons, 1973); and Hank Rubin, "Philanthropy: Historical and Philosophical Foundations," in Jay. M. Shafritz, ed., *International Encyclopedia of Public Policy and Administration* (Boulder: Westview Press, 1998), pp. 1661–1667.

3. R. H. Cass and G. Manser, *Voluntarism at the Crossroads* (New York: Family Service Association of America, 1976).

4. Alexis de Tocqueville, *Democracy in America,* vol. 1 (The Henry Reeve text revised by Francis Bowen and further corrected and edited with a historical essay, editorial notes, and bibliographies by Phillips Bradley) (New York: Vintage Books, 1945). Also see, Whitney Pope in collaboration with Lucetta Pope, *Alexis de Tocqueville: His Social and Political Theory* (Beverly Hills, Calif.: Sage, 1986).

5. Thus Peter Dobkin Hall's claim that nonprofit organizations pose "almost insuperable problems for anyone who would presume to relate their history."

6. Andrew Carnegie, *The Gospel of Wealth: And Other Timely Essays* (New York: Century, 1900), p. 26. Also see Milton Goldin's article, "The Founding Fathers of Modern Philanthropy," which is reprinted in Part 9, "Giving Theories."

7. J. Steven Ott and Lisa A. Dicke, "Important but Largely Unanswered Questions About Accountability in Contracted Public Human Services," *International Journal of Organization Theory and Behavior* 3 (3 and 4), Summer 2000, 283–317.

8. Tocqueville, *Democracy in America,* vol. 1, p. 199.

9. See Part 7.

10. Steven R. Smith and Michael Lipsky, "Contracting for Services in the Welfare State," in *Nonprofits for Hire* (Cambridge: Harvard University Press, 1993).

11. For more information about the Reagan agendas and their impacts on nonprofit organizations, see Gary Scrivner's, "A Brief History of Tax Policy Changes Affecting Charitable Organizations," Chapter 10. Also see Lester M. Salamon, "Nonprofit Organizations: The Lost Opportunity," in J. L. Palmer and I. V. Sawhill, eds., *The Reagan Record* (Cambridge, Mass.: Ballinger, 1984), pp. 261–284.

12. Carl Milofsky, *Not for Profit Organizations and Community: A Review of the Sociological Literature* (PONPO Working Paper 6) (New Haven: Yale University, 1979).

13. Hall's complete chapter consists of seventy-one pages of text and thirty-seven pages of notes.

14. Peter Dobkin Hall, *Inventing the Nonprofit Sector and Other Essays on Philanthropy, Voluntarism, and Nonprofit Organizations* (Baltimore: Johns Hopkins University Press, 1992), p. 15.

15. Hall, *Inventing the Nonprofit Sector,* p. 80.

16. Gary N. Scrivner, "A Brief History of Tax Policy Changes Affecting Charitable Organizations," updates and refines an earlier article written by Scrivner, "100 Years of Tax Policy Changes Affecting Charitable Organizations," in D. L. Gies, J. S. Ott, and J. M. Shafritz, eds., *The Nonprofit Organization: Essential Readings* (Ft. Worth, Tex.: Harcourt Brace, 1990).

References

Block, Stephen R. "A History of the Discipline." In David L. Gies, J. Steven Ott, and Jay M. Shafritz, eds., *The Nonprofit Organization: Essential Readings,* pp. 46–63. Fort Worth, Tex.: Harcourt-Brace, 1990.

Carnegie, Andrew. *The Gospel of Wealth: And Other Timely Essays.* New York: Century, 1900.

Cass, R. H., and G. Manser. *Voluntarism at the Crossroads.* New York: Family Service Association of America, 1976.

Curti, Merle. "Philanthropy." In Philip P. Wiener, ed., *The Dictionary of the History of Ideas.* New York: Charles Scribner's Sons, 1973.

DiMaggio, Paul J., ed. *Nonprofit Enterprise in the Arts: Studies in Mission and Constraint.* New York: Oxford University Press, 1986.

Drucker, Peter. *The New Realities in Government and Policies.* New York: Harper and Row, 1989.

Gelles, Erna. "Filer Commission." In Jay M. Shafritz, ed., *International Encyclopedia of Public Policy and Administration,* pp. 885–887. Boulder: Westview Press, 1998.

Goldin, Milton. "The Founding Fathers of Modern Philanthropy." *Fund Raising Management* 99, June 1988, 48–50.

Hall, Peter Dobkin. "Historical Perspectives on Nonprofit Organizations." In Robert D. Herman, ed., *Jossey-Bass Handbook of Nonprofit Leadership and Management,* pp. 3–43. San Francisco: Jossey-Bass, 1994.

_____. *Inventing the Nonprofit Sector and Other Essays on Philanthropy, Voluntarism, and Nonprofit Organizations.* Baltimore: Johns Hopkins University Press, 1992.

_____. *The Organization of American Culture, 1700–1900: Institutions, Elites, and the Origins of American Nationality.* New York: New York University Press, 1982.

Hammack, David C., ed. *Making the Nonprofit Sector in the United States: A Reader.* Bloomington: Indiana University Press, 1998.

Karl, B. D., and S. N. Katz. "Foundations and Ruling-Class Elites." *Daedalus* 116 (1), 1987, 1–40.

McCarthy, Katherine. *Noblesse Oblige: Charity and Cultural Philanthropy in Chicago, 1849–1929.* Chicago: University of Chicago Press, 1982.

Milofsky, Carl. *Not for Profit Organizations and Community: A Review of the Sociological Literature* (PONPO Working Paper 6). New Haven: Yale University, 1979.

O'Neill, Michael. *The Third America: The Emergence of the Nonprofit Sector in the United States.* San Francisco: Jossey-Bass, 1989.

Ott, J. Steven, and Lisa A. Dicke. "Important but Largely Unanswered Questions About Accountability in Contracted Public Human Services." *International Journal of Organization Theory and Behavior* 3 (3 and 4), Summer 2000, 283–317.

Pope, Whitney, and Lucetta Pope. *Alexis de Tocqueville: His Social and Political Theory.* Beverly Hills, Calif.: Sage, 1986.

Putnam, Robert D. "Bowling Alone: America's Declining Social Capital." *Journal of Democracy* 6 (1), January 1995, 65–78.

Rubin, Hank. "Philanthropy: Historical and Philosophical Foundations." In Jay M. Shafritz, ed., *International Encyclopedia of Public Policy and Administration,* pp. 1661–1667. Boulder: Westview Press, 1998.

Salamon, Lester M. "Nonprofit Organizations: The Lost Opportunity." In J. L. Palmer and I. V. Sawhill, eds., *The Reagan Record,* pp. 261–284. Cambridge, Mass.: Ballinger, 1984.

Scrivner, Gary N. "100 Years of Tax Policy Changes Affecting Charitable Organizations." In D. L. Gies, J. S. Ott, and J. M. Shafritz, eds., *The Nonprofit Organization: Essential Readings,* pp. 126–137. Fort Worth, Tex.: Harcourt Brace, 1990.

Smith, Steven R., and Michael Lipsky. "Contracting for Services in the Welfare State." In *Nonprofits for Hire.* Cambridge: Harvard University Press, 1993.

Tocqueville, Alexis de. *Democracy in America,* vol. 1 (The Henry Reeve text revised by Francis Bowen, further corrected and edited with a historical essay, editorial notes, and bibliographies by Phillips Bradley). New York: Vintage Books, 1945.

Wall, J. F. *Andrew Carnegie.* New York: Oxford University Press, 1970.

CHAPTER 8

A History of the Discipline

STEPHEN R. BLOCK

Unlike the study of political science which can more easily be traced to Plato and Aristotle, or the field of medicine capable of being traced to Hippocrates of Cos, the lineage of nonprofit management is not as clear-cut and precise. The ancestry of nonprofit management descends from several areas. To understand the historical development of the discipline of nonprofit management, it will be essential to trace four of the field's major origins: (a) the roots of charity and philanthropy; (b) the development of the role of the volunteer; (c) the evolution of tax exemption; and (d) the adaptation of management technologies into the nonprofit sector. In addition to these four major areas, the nonprofit sector is steeped in the traditions of Americans' associating and joining in order to further a cause, to become integrated into a community or to form social and business ties. On this subject, Milofsky (1979) proposes that nonprofit organizations are rooted in at least six traditions of American participation. An examination of the philosophical and contextual differences between the six participatory traditions may shed some additional light on the foundation of nonprofit management knowledge, in addition to gaining an understanding of the remarkable fortitude of today's nonprofit organizations.

Knowledge about the organizations' historical participatory roots may also help us understand the contemporary nonprofit organization's management policy preferences, in addition to explaining why the nonprofit organization can become what Max Lerner (1983) has called a "collective expression which belies the outward atomism of American life" (p. 82).

There has been little, if any, self-scrutiny as a discipline and a dearth of information about the evolution of this emerging profession as a whole. However, there are many signs to suggest that charity, philanthropy, and volunteerism fit squarely in the evolutionary design of the discipline. There is less clarity or evidence of events that historically led to management technology transfers or the significance of tax exemption in the development of a nonprofit curriculum. Nevertheless, attention will be given to these areas as a "kind" of conceptual bridge leading from a vast arena of activities and interest in charity, philanthropy, and volunteerism to a new "promised land" marked by books, courses, degree programs, and research.

While it is important to describe the developmental phases that have helped shape the discipline, one limitation must be acknowledged. There do not appear to be clean boundaries, no clear line at which one stops and another begins, between these fields of concern. But the new discipline of nonprofit management did start from somewhere. Indeed, as we stand in the midst of volumes of books, courses, training programs, and development of university degree programs, it is possible to look back and trace the emergence of a discipline from the relative dominance of these core areas.

The Roots of Charity and Philanthropy

Ideologically, nonprofit organization management is derived quite centrally from the historical ethos of charity and philanthropy. Early precepts of giving and taking care of community needs are part of the evolutionary development of today's nonprofit organization (Academy for Educational Development, 1979). Even if a contemporary nonprofit organization is not directly concerned with the compassionate service program interests of charity and philanthropy, it cannot deny, as part of the voluntary sector, that its heritage includes accumulated contributions of those that served and gave to others in need.

Sir Arthur Keith (1949) suggests that the concept of charitable giving may have biological aspects. According to Keith, the concept of altruism is "both inborn and instinctive" (p. 451). While Keith's evolutionary notion is quite interesting, there is no biological human trait known as altruism. Perhaps Keith's idea is not too far afield, however, given the innate altruistic qualities which are known to exist among certain insect and animal groups (Kalmus, 1963). Nevertheless, it is more likely that the origins of charity and philanthropy began with early human civilizations. For pragmatic reasons, primitive societies were the first to develop and exhibit the concept of charity or philanthropy (Bakal, 1979). In these early societies, the welfare and preservation of individuals and families required the community to share in the tasks of food gathering, hunting, and providing shelter.

As ancient societies became more complex, the idea of sharing in order to help, protect, and preserve the community was also advanced through the incorporation of rules and struc-

ture. It is known, for example, that the Babylonians were instructed through their Code of Hammurabi to protect the less fortunate of the community (Harper, 1904). This Code instructed the community to care for the poor, the widows, and the orphans. In addition to the instructive charitable nature of the Code, George (1972) indicates that the Code is one of the earliest illustrations of management thought which is characterized by a set of inscribed laws relating to a variety of business practices.

Religious doctrines, ideology, and influences on giving, compassion, and personal sacrifice are a significant part of the heritage of charity and philanthropy which eventually resulted in the development of the nonprofit sector. The notion of blessed giving existed in ancient Egypt at least 2,300 years before the Christian era (Weaver, 1967). At that time, the Egyptian aristocracy would be buried with rich gifts for the gods as well as with records of gifts that were given to the poor and needy during the aristocrat's lifetime. Propitiating the gods with gifts and records of good deeds was an attempt to satisfy the gods and assure the preservation of a restful afterlife for the giver. On the other hand, charity in the pre-Christian Greek tradition was exemplified by a different type of giving. The Greek philosophy of charitable giving aimed to fortify the community by giving community-oriented gifts rather than to help individuals who were poor. In this respect, Weaver (1967) suggests that the Greek concept of giving is closer to the guiding philosophy of modern philanthropic foundations than to the Judeo-Christian concept of charity. For example, Greek benefactors were known to have given their cities gifts of theaters and stadiums, and modern philanthropists have similarly donated large community-oriented structures such as libraries, universities, and museums.

Ancient roots also appear to extend to Biblical and religious concepts of charity. The Old Testament, for example, in the Book of Deuteronomy, commands individuals to tithe a portion of their produce and share it with the widows and hungry children in one's own community and with transients. Similar to the early Jewish concept of community giving (Frisch,

1969), as outlined by Maimonides, the early Christian communities valued the idea of helping the infirm and the poor. In fact, the scriptures of Matthew detail the Christian expectation of sharing. These Christian expectations to help the poor and needy were exacerbated during a crisis period brought on by the Bubonic Plague, and also in response to the period of the Reformation. In fact, during the period of the Reformation, individual begging was looked on askance and organized community responses were developed not only to assist the poor and homeless, but also to deter individual almsbegging and almsgiving.

In England, the influence of the Reformation and the breakup of the feudal system were among the social changes that led to an organized response to the plight of the poor. Municipalities, responding to the discontent caused by the social instability of unemployment and vagrancy, created ordinances about begging and work expectations (Leonard, 1965). As problems controlling the begging behavior of the indigent poor and the able-bodied poor increased and were not fully deterred by the laws in the townships, the Parliament responded by the creation of the English Poor Laws in 1601. The Poor Laws of 1601 codified the following three principles for overseeing the plight of the poor: public responsibility, local responsibility, and relatives' responsibility (Leiby, 1978). The fundamental element in the poor laws was the expectation that individuals should work and take care of their individual needs and the needs of their families. In the event that an individual could not fulfill this work ethic, the community was obliged and responsible for providing, at least minimally, for the needs of these poor individuals. While the English Parliament was the first to establish these laws (Rose, 1971), the early colonial settlers adopted similar principles. The advance of the poor laws in the United States became guiding principles for the development of both charitable and philanthropic activity. In addition, the poor laws set a philosophy and community ethos for the eventual creation of government intervention in problems of welfare and American statutes on social welfare.

The early implementation of poor laws in the United States were mainly at the state level. In different communities, responsibility for looking after the poor was delegated to county officials. In some situations, local churches assumed this responsibility. As the population of the country grew, the ability to monitor the poor became unwieldy. This led to the development of almshouses (also known as the "poor-house" or sometimes referred to as "the workhouse"). These early prototypes to the modern concept of work-relief programs were intended to discourage loafers, and simultaneously to provide some adequate support to the real needy.

By the latter half of the nineteenth century, urban centers began to become overpopulated as a result of the industrial revolution and immigration of millions of people from Europe. During this period, the responsibility to oversee the poor was overwhelming and the ability to provide adequate care, services, or almshouse shelters was beginning to come under scrutiny. For example, members of the Conference of Charities and Correction reported on a variety of concerns and difficulties found in the state's role and ability to administer the almshouse. In many cases, admissions were made to the deplorable and harsh living condition in the almshouses (Bruno, 1957). In response to the recognition that there was a significant contrast in the quality of life for the rich and the poor, the charity organization and settlement movement began to flourish.

As with the poor laws, the concept of the settlement house was an English invention. In fact, many American settlement houses were modeled after the Toynbee House settlement in England, including Hull House in Chicago (Addams, 1910), the Neighborly Guild in New York, South End House in Boston, and Northwestern University Settlement House in Chicago (Bruno, 1957). The settlement house consisted of a home situated in poor neighborhoods whose residents consisted of more fortunate individuals, committed to working with community members and helping them to improve their situation. In fact, the goal of the settlement house was to provide social change through a community center of hope and opportunities, and to improve one's condition in life (Trolander, 1975). For example, many settlement houses offered day nurseries, playgrounds, lecture series, meeting places, and advice on civic matters. In addition, some settlement houses offered counseling services to promote the growth of individuals and families.

Concurrent with the settlement house movement, the Charity Organization Society movement, again an English invention, took hold in the United States. Originally, the advocates of this secular movement were inspired by clergymen who were committed to an effective system of private charity (Leiby, 1978). The framers of this movement advanced the concept of indiscriminate almsgiving to a rationalized approach where conscientious thought was given to long term consequences and outcomes. Indeed, this movement appears to have been the forerunner of the modern philanthropic foundation or corporate contribution, based on a rationale of purpose or philosophy to achieve a prescribed outcome. Furthermore, this movement attempted to be scientific by both collecting data about charitable agencies and by coordinating the effects of several of the charities. Members of a Charitable Organization Society, like the modern foundation, would review applications for financial assistance. In addition to providing some emergency relief, the society might arrange for a host of individuals to provide professional services to the poor, such as legal advice, spiritual guidance, and medical care. This movement became stronger after the turn of the twentieth century with growing interest and financial support among businessmen and chambers of commerce in addition to the traditional support of wealthy family contributors.

Support for the organized charities interested businessmen because they expected that private charities would be better administered than public charities. Following from this expectation, donors began to push for the development of a federated organization of charities that would regulate fundraising efforts and the distribution of monies. In addition, the federation would be able to oversee the quality of management of the charitable organizations. The development of the Cleveland Federation for Charity and Philanthropy in 1913 was one such example and also was a pioneering model for financial federations in other cities (Waite, 1960). The development of federations was also a critical step toward the creation of paid staff positions to manage the federations and the charitable organizations.

During the same developmental period, the creation of periodicals devoted to furthering knowledge about the charitable interests and the settlement house interests appeared. In 1909, Paul Kellogg produced *The Survey* with the financial underwriting of the Russell Sage Foundation. *The Survey* was a national magazine directed toward both the paid and volunteer charitable worker; it was intended that this magazine should envelop earlier periodicals which had a local, not a national, constituency. *The Survey* supplanted at least three periodicals: the Boston magazine *Lend-a-Hand;* the New York City publication, *Charities Review;* and the Chicago publication, *The Commons* (Chambers, 1971).

The Development of the Volunteer Role and Its Importance

While volunteerism has been said to be a very American tradition (Commission on Private Philanthropy and Public Needs, 1975), the rise and development of the concept and the practice of volunteerism parallels the evolution of charity and philanthropy. One way of viewing the Americanization of volunteerism is that it springs from the phenomena of early American community participation. In 1835, Tocqueville (1969), among the earliest observers of America's rich tradition of volunteerism, described voluntary association as uniquely American and influential for promoting America's democratic character. Tocqueville's astonishment with the Americans' propensity toward volunteerism is evident in his following quote:

> Americans of all ages, all stations in life, and all types of disposition are forever forming associations. There are not only commercial and in-

dustrial associations in which all take part, but others of a thousand different types—religious, moral, serious, futile, very general and very limited, immensely large and very minute. Americans combine to give fêtes, found seminaries, build churches, distribute books, and send missionaries to the antipodes. Hospitals, prisons, and schools take shape in that way. Finally, if they want to proclaim a truth or propagate some feeling by the encouragement of a great example, they form an association. In every case, at the head of any new undertaking, where in France you would find the government or in England some territorial magnate, in the United States you are sure to find an association. (Tocqueville, 1969, p. 513)

While its American heritage and evolvement may be similar to charity and philanthropy, volunteerism reflects some different and special aspects that deserve separate attention. Indeed, volunteers may be philanthropic or charitable but there is a wide range of voluntary activity open to individuals that goes beyond the intentions of charity. Manser and Cass (1976) define volunteerism as follows:

> those activities and agencies arising out of a spontaneous, private (as contrasted with governmental) effort to promote or advance some aspect of the common good, as this good is perceived by the persons participating in it. These people are volunteers—persons who, motivated by varying degrees of altruism and self-interest, choose to give their time and talents freely. (p. 42)

To differentiate the role of volunteerism from acts of charity or philanthropy is a difficult task. While all three activities require some form of action, the actions of charity and philanthropy may require little, if any, direct involvement with the beneficiaries. Volunteerism, on the other hand, is a very active process that requires active involvement with either the beneficiaries directly or an organization or group that serves a specific population. Unlike the action of charity or philanthropy, however, the activities in volunteerism do not necessarily benefit an un-

derprivileged, poor, or needy group. In fact, many associations, agencies, or groups that utilize the volunteer may be far from experiencing financial deprivation. . . .

Were it not for a long-standing American tradition of volunteerism, it would seem odd that, in an economic democracy that promotes capitalism, there are individuals who are willing to work for a voluntary cause/organization without financial compensation (Jones & Herrick, 1976). Marts (1966) suggests that the generosity and willingness of volunteers to give their time and energy is a result of the experiences and inspiration of American freedoms. This same concept was undoubtedly behind O'Connell's (1983) collection of readings entitled *America's Voluntary Spirit.* Bremner's (1960) view is a bit more sober. According to Bremner, the Americanization of volunteerism had its start in the colonization of the New World. The number of activities involved in the colonization required a variety of personal acts of benevolence: conversion of natives to Christianity, taming the wilderness, the cultivation of land and crops. Likewise, Max Weber spoke of the American tendency to participate in voluntary activities as a socially constructive process for bridging the Old World's hierarchical society to the New World's rugged individualism (Lerner, 1983). The joining process permitted individuals to form ties and develop positions of status in the community. Indeed, the idea of an individual joining and actually belonging to a voluntary association serves very important sociological and psychological needs.

Participation and Its Influences on the Nonprofit Sector

. . . Milofsky (1979) suggests that an examination of six American traditions of participation will reveal how their influences on America have rooted the nonprofit sector and nonprofit organizations. The six traditions of American participation include the Protestant patrician, urban ethnic, free professional, organizational professional, interorganizational coordination, and corporate philanthropic traditions.

The Protestant Patrician Influence

The Protestant tradition was first influential in America in the mid-1800s, during the development of a strong Protestant middle class. Protestant followers were interested in community reforms as reflected in their belief in the "Protestant Ethic." One aspect of this ethic was that individuals are responsible for developing their own Christian character and for assisting other individuals to develop as well. Furthermore, ecclesiastical authority associated with this ethic asserted that individuals have a moral responsibility to contribute their own personal skills and monies to help others in need. This resolve, or philosophy, created a framework and a sense of moral obligation for an individual to participate in voluntary efforts.

According to Seeley, Junker, Jones, Jenkins, Haugh, and Miller (1957), the Protestant tradition draws certain social boundaries around an individual's willingness to volunteer. Generally, individuals are willing to donate money or services that will assist others in need, but the volunteers would prefer not to become directly involved with those they assist. Verba and Nie (1972) explain this ideology as a typical expression of wealthy or upwardly mobile, powerful individuals. In other words, voluntary leadership in nonprofit organizations preserves or creates a civic leadership position consistent with Protestant ideas about civic association.

Milofsky (1979) characterizes the influences of the Protestant patrician tradition on nonprofit organization management to include a distinctive style of leadership. Leadership in this mode is strongly committed to a community-based model with an emphasis on resource development and concrete services to those in need, such as providing hot meals and shelter. In addition, this style of leadership is weakest in responding to organizational crises and will tend to replace managers rather than revise program services.

The Urban Ethnic Influence

Unlike the Protestant influences of concern for helping others, the urban ethnic tradition evolved as a reactive response by ethnic groups who believed they were being poorly treated in American society. To protect themselves, ethnic groups began forming their own nonprofit organizations in the form of mutual aid societies. In addition to preserving cultural traditions, mutual aid organizations were helpful in assisting community members with recreational events, religious celebrations, and personal crises, such as death or illness. The development of these ethnic-related nonprofit organizations appears to have been greatest during a surge of refugee resettlement after the turn of the century through the 1920s.

The emphasis on ethnic-related community development nonprofit organizations continues to play an important role in culturally diverse communities. Interestingly, the recognition that ethnic communities have played a valuable support and assimilation role in America accounts for more recent federal incentive grants to establish mutual assistance associations for America's newest pool of refugees from Southeast Asia (Office of Refugee Resettlement, 1986). However, there is a down side to ethnic-related service organizations. By providing services to members of only one type of cultural heritage or religious system, these organizations may unwittingly reinforce cultural separation and isolation from other ethnic groups. This may also account for a vast duplication of social services in a community.

In the ethnically oriented organization, management decisions may be strongly influenced by ethnic beliefs rather than by commonly held management principles. Even with the introduction of the professionally educated nonprofit manager into this work setting, the cultural traditions of the organization may still have prevailing influence on service delivery. This is surely the case with religion-affiliated nonprofit organizations that grew out of the ethnic urban tradition, such as Jewish Family Services, Lutheran Social Services, and Catholic Community Services. In addition, Berger and Neuhaus (1977) suggest that organized ethnic/cultural groups have a strong mediating role in society which can have a strong influence on the type of policy and services developed and offered by nonprofit and governmental entities.

The Free Professional Influence

Unlike the religious and sociopolitical needs of individuals, which influenced the Protestant tradition, or the need to protect cultural and ethnic identities, evidenced in the urban ethnic tradition, the free professional tradition extends beyond these distinctive dimensions and is characterized by individuals sharing similar professional interests. This tradition is representative of controls over educational and technical skills that have been defined as critical for entering into, belonging to, and practicing within a particular profession. For example, all attorneys must attend a law school and pass a bar exam and all physicians must attend medical school and serve an internship and residency in addition to passing exams.

As a response to the acquired skills and achievements that must be attained in order to become a member of a profession, many nonprofit organizations have been spawned to protect the distinctive interests of their professional members. In fact, many professionals join trade associations to protect the values of their discipline, to assist in their own definition of being a professional, and to receive special support and tangible products like journals and continuing education programs (Judd, Block, & Jain, 1985). The National Association of Social Workers, the American Society for Public Administration, and the American Medical Association are just three examples of nonprofit organizations that exist to protect the practice domain of its members. In addition to the influence on standards and policies that professionals have over their own professions, Milofsky (1979) suggests that professionals also have an influencing effect on the norms and policies of society by controlling reports of professional research and determining what will be considered acceptable performance criteria for delivering professional services.

The Organizational Influence

This participatory tradition is a direct outgrowth of the professionalization of occupations and is characterized by many of the larger nonprofit organizations that have had both staff and volunteer involvement. Furthermore, the organizations that can be described by this tradition are church organizations or sect-like groups that have a large constituency, such as the "Y." In this situation, professional staff are oriented toward their job out of professional/occupational and career interests. In contrast, volunteers affiliate with an organization based on a personal ideology or belief system. Frequently, policy decisions or management styles are reflected by the influences of the constituency served by the organization rather than by the leadership of the organization.

The Interorganizational Influence

After World War I, the successful development of the urban ethnic tradition's ability to create community support and social services organizations found itself in a conflict. Many organizations with similar service delivery missions were in competition with one another for funding. Rather than create a situation that could discourage "giving," the concept of the community chest was introduced. The community chest movement permitted agencies to focus on service delivery while the community chest organizers would specialize in the task of fundraising.

In the 1960s and 1970s, many specialized service delivery organizations embarked on their own resource development programs relying largely on government funded grant programs. In the 1980s, with severe cuts in federally funded grant-in-aid programs, the reliance on a community-based fundraising effort has become, once again, more predominant and necessary for many nonprofit organizations to survive.

The Corporate Philanthropic Influence

There are three important influencing factors that led to the development of American corporate philanthropy. One factor is represented by the personal giving philosophy of Andrew Carnegie (1900), who believed that philanthropic giving was a social obligation, akin to the Protestant patrician tradition, rather than a religious obligation. Carnegie's personal point of view is illustrated through his often cited remark that "The man who dies rich, dies disgraced." He was an adherent of providing philanthropic support to programs and special projects that would benefit and provide strength to the community. A second factor is characterized by the philanthropic philosophy of John D. Rockefeller, I (1908). Unlike Carnegie, Rockefeller followed a traditional, religious doctrine of giving. Both Carnegie and Rockefeller paved the way for large, organized, corporate giving.

The third important influencing factor was the development of tax credits and tax deductions which led to corporate incentives to give to tax-exempt nonprofit organizations. The practice of giving to nonprofit organizations benefits both the nonprofit organizations and the corporate giver (Galaskiewicz, 1986). The corporation gains important public relations and community benefits, while the nonprofit's financial capacity to deliver services is improved.

The Evolution and Impact of Tax-Exempt Status

Tax exemption is an essential element of the American economy and the advantages of obtaining the 501(c)(3) tax-exempt status for the nonprofit organization is an integral part of forming and maintaining charitable, educational, scientific, as well as religious organizations. In fact, the review provided by Clotfelter (1983) demonstrates the importance of tax deductions as incentives to giving to charitable causes. The relationship between tax credits and charitable giving is so strong that the contemporary nonprofit organization would adversely suffer if not for the benefit of not having to pay income taxes, as well as the incentives of the tax deduction given to its contributors (Clotfelter, 1983). While tax exemption is a popular inducement for present day charitable giving, the concept of tax exemption is not a twentieth-century phenomenon. In fact, Lashbrooke (1985) dates at least the implementation of tax exemption to the Old Testament in Ezra 7:24:

> . . . also we certify you, that touching any of the priests and Levites, singers, porters, Nethinim,

or Ministers of this House of God, it shall not be lawful to impose toll, tribute, or customs upon them. (p. 3)

In the modern era, government-endorsed tax exemption in the United States has been a common practice since the nation's founding (Hopkins, 1983). In fact, religious organizations have been spared the burden of paying taxes by statutory omission at all levels of government, and this practice was sustained during the first federal income tax that spanned 10 years from 1862 to 1872. It was not until 1894, however, that expressed tax exemption was defined in tax legislation and became the official policy of the United States (Smith & Chiechi, 1974). Section 32 of the Revenue Act of 1894, imposed a flat 2% tax on profitable income and complete tax exemption on charitable income. The 1894 statute also provided for the tax exemption of charitable, religious, educational, fraternal organizations, as well as certain savings and insurance institutions.

The 1894 act was overturned by a constitutional challenge to the rental income tax portion of the law which was not apportioned by population. Although the 1894 act was repealed, its influence on subsequent revenue legislation was measurable. Every revenue act since 1894 has bestowed tax-exempt status to religious, charitable, and educational organizations.

In addition to the historical precedent that established an unwritten rationale for tax exemptions for nonprofit organizations, Congress articulated a supporting rationale in its Revenue Act of 1909, exempting organizations which by their nature could not generate sufficient income. In seven revenue acts, Congress identified the many different types of organizations, noted in Table 8.1, which would be protected from tax liabilities. According the Gelb (1971), the Federal Government was concerned about the possible reduction of gifts to charitable organizations following the 1917 increase in individual income taxes to pay for the expenses of World War I. In response to their concern, the tax law was expanded to permit the deduction for an individual's gift to charitable organizations.

Another rationale that has supported the existence of tax exemption is the government's

TABLE 8.1   Organizations Protected from Tax Liabilities

Revenue Act by Year	Tax Exemption by Type of Organization
1894	Charitable, educational, and religious organizations
1909	Labor, horticulture, agriculture
1913	Business leagues, chambers of commerce, scientific organizations, social welfare organizations, mutual cemetery companies
1916	Public utilities, social clubs, land banks, title holding companies, farming associations
1918	Societies for prevention of cruelty to animals
1921	Foundations, community chest funds
1976	Homeowner associations, fishing associations, organizations promoting national and international sporting competition

SOURCE: E. C. Lashbrooke, *Tax Exempt Organizations* (Westport, CT: Quorum Books, 1985).

recognition that without tax-exempt organizations, the burden for many social programs undertaken by the nonprofit sector would need to be assumed by the government. . . .

Since 1954, tax exemption has been described best in the Internal Revenue Code 501(c)(3). Organizations that fit into this category agree to devote their net earnings to the mission of the organization and they further agree that individual directors and officers will not receive any part of the net earnings. Another common thread in all organizations with the 501(c)(3) status is the advantage of attracting deductible contributions. It is largely this "benefit" that adds to the unique management characteristic of the nonprofit organization and sometimes its preoccupation with fundraising events and grant proposal writing. In fact, in 1984, the nonprofit sector received $68 billion from private contributions and approximately an equivalent amount from all levels of government sources.

Clearly, the incentive for both the individual and corporate giver has been tied to the deductibility of tax-exempt gifts. . . .

There is agreement among nonprofit tax policy researchers that the level of an individual's after-tax income will have an important consequence on whether the individual gives, and how much, to charitable organizations in very active fundraising campaigns. In the situation of severe losses in charitable donations as projected by Lindsey, nonprofit organizations could point out to potential contributors the increased need for contributions as a result of drastic reforms. The outcome of such appeals is, of course, unpredictable. Beyond this, the impact on the creation or maintenance of private foundations is another area that is potentially affected by shifting tax liabilities. On this point, Odendahl (1985) reported that since the Tax Reform Act of 1969, there has been a decline in both the number of new grant-making foundations and the number of grant awards over $10,000.

In summary, a history exists that interweaves the development of the field of nonprofit management with the history of tax exemption and other tax policies that impact propensities toward charitable giving. In addition, there is a continued need for data collection to study the ongoing patterns of giving and its relationship to the effective management of nonprofit organizations.

From Management to the Emergence of Nonprofit Management

. . . The term "nonprofit management" is a singularly difficult one. It denotes a function of management in the nonprofit sector and implies a different type of "management" than the type found in business or in government. To understand the critical differences between nonprofit management, business management, and public management, and to learn more about the emergence of this younger (nonprofit management) practice field and discipline, it is imperative to trace its management roots beginning with the development of management as a professional field of business practice and as an academic discipline that grants degrees, such as the MBA and DBA. There is also a kinship to the field of public administration that requires identification.

Although the evolution of management is difficult to reconstruct (George, 1972), the activity of management is ubiquitous throughout the history of humankind. Some forms of management activities were a likely part of prehistoric civilization. When men hunted in bands, traveled in groups or developed tribes and villages, some form of division of labor and leadership surely marked the arrangement of management functions. According to George (1972), the imposition of taxes, the amassing of wealth, the management of major construction projects, such as pyramids, and the creation of city governments are examples of traceable practices of management during ancient civilizations.

Clearly, the advance of management tasks, functions, and management tools evolved over time. At the end of the Dark Ages, financial management and control tools such as record keeping and double entry bookkeeping were developed in response to the growth of commerce in the Mediterranean (Drucker, 1974). Shipbuilding and outfitting the ships during the Middle Ages also saw the development of business-related activities such as warehousing, assembly line practices, and personnel supervision. But it was the period of the Industrial Revolution, predominantly in England, that witnessed the introduction of improved manufacturing technologies and improved methods of production. These improvements were largely responsible for the shift from home-based production activities to the factory system and its need for a large labor pool. The need for factory employees influenced a shift from an agrarian society to an industrial one.

The development of the capitalistic system and a growing interest in economics were highlights of this era (Massie, 1979). Adam Smith stressed economic concepts in his 1776 publication *The Wealth of Nations* and contributed greatly to the fundamental management concept of "division of labor." There were other important economic and management concepts and practices that resulted from the boom in manufacturing. One such important practice included the idea of incorporating a business for the purpose of raising capital through the sale of shares in the business. This development in entrepreneurism also paved the way for later thinking about the functions of ownership as separate from the functions of management.

The impact of the new industrial methods was also felt in the United States by the mid-nineteenth century. America's growing reliance on a railroad system provided an opportunity for railroad investors to pursue profits, while engineers pursued the mastery of management over complex organizations. The administration of complex railroad organizations became the focus of information sharing and the subject of papers presented at meetings of the American Society of Mechanical Engineers (ASME).

At one of the ASME meetings in 1886, Henry R. Towne, president of the Yale and Towne Manufacturing Company, presented his paper on "The Engineer as Economist." Towne called for the recognition of industrial management as a science and equal in importance to that of engineering. Towne emphasized the need for management to be an independent field of study with its own professional literature and professional membership society. Towne's comments marked the beginning search for a science of management and is the one event that is most often referenced as the pioneering inspiration for the development of the scientific management movement (Bedeian, 1978).

A Philadelphia manufacturer, Joseph Wharton, recognized the need for a special management curriculum to educate and prepare individuals for a career in management. Acting on his belief, Wharton financed America's first school of management, the Wharton School, at the University of Pennsylvania. In 1898, 17 years after the Wharton School was started, the University of California and the University of Chicago launched their own business schools. A little more than a decade later the idea of business management education was becoming well institutionalized with at least 30 schools of business management in the country.

The promulgation of ideas about management as a profession inspired another Philadelphian, Frederick Taylor, to seriously question the role and responsibilities of management. As an engineer, Taylor became very interested in the idea of maximizing the performance of workers with a minimal level of stewardship. Taylor envisioned a system of cooperation and improved production through appropriate standards and rewards, a system also based on the harmonious relationship between worker and management. The development of these pioneering ideas gave Taylor recognition as the "father of Scientific Management" (Massie, 1979).

Aside from Taylor, the insight of other supporters of scientific management figured predominantly in the development of management thought, especially in areas of efficiency (Brandeis, 1914) and motion studies (Gilbreth, 1911). Henry L. Gantt (1916, 1919), for example, contributed to the ideas of pay plans and managerial leadership, but is probably best known for his development of a charting system (the Gantt Chart) for the planning and controlling of production tasks. Another staunch advocate of the scientific method was Harrington Emerson, best known for his book *The Twelve Principles of Efficiency* (1913). Emerson was among America's first management consultants (George, 1972) who attempted to guide managers to focus on the creation of wealth through the fulfillment of company objectives while preserving company resources through the use of conservation policies. Henry Fayol, a French industrialist, who also focused his study and writing on management principles, was among the first writers to classify different management functions. In 1916, he published *Administration Industrielle et Generale,* which was later translated into English in 1930 and 1949. In Fayol's schema, management was divided into five major functions, including planning, organizing, commanding, coordination, and control. In addition, Fayol developed fourteen management principles to emphasize the managerial functions (Fayol, 1949).

The first twenty years following the turn of the twentieth century were critically important for the development of management as a field of professional practice and as an emerging academic discipline. It was during this era that Towne's earlier dream of the creation of professional societies, books, and university programs was fulfilled. In 1911, for example, approximately 300 educators and practitioners assembled at Dartmouth College's Amos Tuck School of Administration and Finance. This meeting marked the first formal attempt to pave an academic direction for the field of management. Another academic first came in 1915, when Horace B. Drury of Columbia University published *Scientific Management: A History and Criticism.* This publication is considered to be the first doctoral dissertation in management (Mee, 1963), and, therefore, a hallmark for the fledgling academic discipline. During this same period, in 1914, the first professional management society was founded as the Society to Promote the Science of Management, later evolved into the Taylor Society, and eventually became the Society for Advancement of Management. The American Management Association, another bastion in the management field, was also formed during this developmental period. . . .

The decade between 1930 and 1940 witnessed further advances in management's understanding of human behavior in the work environment, including the psychological needs of the individual, the effect of motivation, and the role of executive leadership.

Movement away from the physical factors of scientific management continued between 1940 and the 1960s. The period marked the refinement of management techniques and principles that emerged during and following World War II. Drucker (1974) suggests that interest in management as a field of practice and an academic discipline was triggered by the performance of American manufacturing industry during World War II. It was during the mid-1950s that a significant increase in the number of professional management books and periodicals unfolded (Bedeian, 1978).

The cumulative development of the management field from the turn of the twentieth century into the 1970s eventually blended the concerns of the founders of scientific management efficiency and the concerns of the human relations behavioralists with the needs of the workers. Thus, the focus of the 1960s gave rise to organizational behavior and theory (Thompson, 1967), including matters of supervision (McGregor, 1960), leadership (Fielder, 1967), and motivation (Herzberg, 1959).

In the 1970s, two particular trends were identified as important to the development of management thought. The two integrative trends include the contingency approach and the systems approach (Huse, 1979).

The complexities of today's organizations also have required its managers to be more flexible and discriminating in applying management theory into practice. Thus, the contingency approach in management allows managers to be more eclectic in their style and to adapt to changing organizational needs and environments.

Management of the 1980s is characterized by future-oriented thinking and planning for future courses of action. . . . The modern organization has many competing interests and must pay attention to several conditions besides profit. These developments have led to an emphasis on learning about different management styles in order to maximize opportunities for success (Peters & Waterman, 1982). In addition, modern organizations have been primarily concerned about responding to the social pressures of the organization's internal and external environments. In the internal environment, management has attempted to satisfy the needs of employees through the management of benefits and creating satisfying working conditions. In the external environment, management is sometimes practiced to influence the opinions of consumers as well as the need to prevent circumstances that might lead to potential litigation against the company. Management in the modern organization has also been shaped by the demands of governmental regulatory agencies and the power of the mass media.

Management Technologies Applied to the Nonprofit Sector

. . . Examination of the development of management thought and practice provides the basis

for at least speculating about the development of management practice in the nonprofit sector.

Scientific management was just beginning to develop at the time that Congress passed legislation in 1894 creating a public policy supporting the tax exemption of nonprofit organizations. Although charitable and voluntary activity has always been a fundamental part of the history of the United States, it was this formal Congressional action on behalf of the nonprofit sector that can be considered a landmark for the beginning development of the contemporary practice of nonprofit management.

It was also during the early twentieth century that the establishment of foundations and national service organizations concerned with charitable activities were on the rise (Bakal, 1979).

An outgrowth of the scientific management movement was the development of management principles. The principles approach was also generalized to public sector management. It was hoped that the study of important public administration activities would yield the best way or "principles" of administrative practice. Perhaps the principles approach also influenced the operations of charitable and voluntary organizations. the special process of management that is required in the three sectors.

The disillusionment of the administrative management approach assisted the rise of the behavioral science approach, also known as the human relations movement, which evolved next in both the business and public sectors, and the nonprofit sector as well. The experience of the business sector in the 1950s was marked by the integration of social science into management practice. The fact that organizations appeared concerned about the humanistic needs and reactions of the individual may explain the climate of the period which supported the creation of tax-exempt legislation that gave definition to the contemporary charitable, 501(c)(3), organization.

In the 1954 establishment of Section 501 of the Internal Revenue Code, the statutory provisions for recognizing tax-exempt organizations were firmly put into place. In addition, certain collateral benefits were created through the adoption of Code 501(c)(3). By imposing certain requirements for recognition as a charitable organization, the boundaries between the three sectors became clarified, and management responsibilities were also further distinguished between organizations located in the nonprofit sector with those in the business or public sectors.

For the first time, the nonprofit organization was subject to meeting two different types of tests to either qualify or maintain the tax-exempt status of the 501(c)(3) organization—the organizational test and the operational test. First, the organizational test is one in which the organization's articles of incorporation and by-laws clearly limit the activities of the organization to one or more tax-exempt activities, such as educational, charitable, scientific, or religious activities. The second test, known as the operational test, is demonstrated by the organization's resources being primarily devoted to the activities that were outlined in the organizational test. Furthermore, the net earnings of the organization may not inure to the board of directors. Together, the operational and organizational tests provide quasi-guidelines concerning the administration of the nonprofit organization. In other words, the use of management technologies from the business or public sector must be adapted for use to further the tax-exempt mission of the nonprofit organization. In this context, the concepts that envelop management ideas of governance, marketing, financial management, planning, among other management tools, are applied to achieve different ends in the three sectors: In business, the aim of management practice is the achievement of profit; in government, the administration of laws and public policy are the end product; and, in the nonprofit sector, management is focused on the satisfactory accomplishment of the organization's service mission. Another distinction of management in the three sectors can be drawn from the target groups shown below in Table 8.2 to be served by the three sectors. In the private sector, organizations are managed in the interest of their stockholders. In the public sector, governmental entities are managed for the interest of the general public. In the nonprofit sector, organizations are managed to sometimes serve the

TABLE 8.2   Management Aims and Major Target Groups in the Three Sectors

Sector	Target Group	Aim
Public	General public	Administration of laws and public policy
Business	Stockholders	Generate profit
Nonprofit	General public or minority	Organizational mission

public interest and sometimes to serve only the interests of an unfortunate (or, sometimes, even an unpopular) few who are the clients or constituents that benefit from the organizational mission.

A little more than 30 years ago, IRS Code 501(c)(3) was created. Since that time more than two-thirds of all nonprofit organizations have been incorporated (Salamon, 1984). Following the rise in the number of new nonprofit organizations, the adaptation of management technologies have become evident in the nonprofit sector and identified in a blossoming professional literature on nonprofit management. The trend in the literature has shown that recognized management tools are being widely used in the nonprofit sector and applications of those tools are being modified to achieve different goals and objectives than in the business or public sectors.

References

Academy for Educational Development. (1979). *The voluntary sector in brief.* New York: Academy for Educational Development.

Addams, J. (1910). *Twenty years at Hull House.* New York: MacMillan.

Bakal, C. (1979). *Charity USA.* New York: Times Books.

Barnard, C. I. (1938). *The functions of the executive.* Cambridge: Harvard University Press.

Bedeian, A. G. (1978). Historical development of management. In L. R. Bittel (Ed.), *The encyclopedia of professional management* (pp. 645–650). New York: McGraw-Hill.

Berger, P. L., & Neuhaus, R. J. (1977). *To empower people: The role of mediating structure in public policy.* Washington, DC: American Enterprise Institute for Public Policy Research.

Brandeis, L. D. (1914). *Business: A profession.* Boston: Small, Maynard.

Bremner, R. H. (1960). *American philanthropy.* Chicago: University of Chicago Press.

Bruno, F. J. (1957). *Trends in social work, 1874–1956.* New York: Columbia University Press.

Carnegie, A. (1900). *The gospel of wealth and other timely essays.* New York: Century.

Chambers, C. A. (1971). *Paul U. Kellogg and the survey.* Minneapolis: University of Minnesota Press.

Clotfelter, C. T. (1983, May 3). Tax incentives and disincentives for charitable giving. In Independent Sector, *Working papers for spring research forum: Since the Filer commission* (pp. 347–367). Washington, DC: Independent Sector.

Commission on Private Philanthropy and Public Needs (Filer Commission). (1975). *Giving in America.* Washington, DC: Department of the Treasury.

Dahl, R. A. (1947, Winter). The science of public administration: Three problems. *Public Administration Review, 7,* 1–11.

Drucker, P. F. (1974). *Management-Tasks-Responsibilities-Practices.* New York: Harper & Row.

Emerson, H. (1913). *The twelve principles of efficiency.* New York: The Engineering Magazine.

Fayol, H. (1949). *General and industrial management.* Trans. C. Storrs. London: Sir Isaac Pitman & Sons.

Fielder, F. E. (1967). *A theory of leadership effectiveness.* New York: McGraw-Hill.

Frisch, E. (1969). *An historical survey of Jewish philanthropy.* New York: Cooper Square Publishers.

Galaskiewicz, J. (1986). The environment and corporate giving behavior. In Independent Sector, *Working papers for spring research forum: Philanthropy, voluntary action, and the public good* (pp. 141–154). Washington, DC: Independent Sector.

Gantt, H. L. (1916). *Industrial leadership.* New Haven: Yale University Press.

Gantt, H. L. (1919). *Organizing for work.* New York: Harcourt, Brace & Howe.

Gelb, B. A. (1971). *Tax-exempt business enterprise.* New York: The Conference Board.

George, C. S. (1972). *The history of management thought.* Englewood Cliffs, NJ: Prentice-Hall.

Gilbreth, F. B. (1911). *Motion study.* New York: Van Nostrand.

Gulick, L. (1937). Notes on the theory of organization. In L. Gulick & L. Urwick (Eds.), *Papers on the science of administration* (pp. 3–13). New York: Institute of Public Administration.

Hansmann, H. (1981). *The rationale for exempting nonprofit organizations from corporate income taxation.* PONPO Working Paper 23. New Haven: Yale University Press.

Harper, R. F. (1904). *The code of Hammurabi, king of Babylon.* Chicago: University of Chicago Press.

Herzberg, F. (1959). *Work and the nature of man.* New York: John Wiel & Sons.

Hill, L. B., & Hebert, F. T. (1979). *Essentials of public administration.* North Scituate, MA: Suxbury Press.

Hopkins, B. R. (1983). *The law of tax-exempt organizations.* New York: Wiley.

Hougland, J. G., & Shepard, J. M. (1985, April-September). Voluntarism and the manager: The impacts of structural pressure and personal interest on community participation. *Journal of Voluntary Action Research, 14* (2–3), 65–78.

Huse, E. F. (1979). *The modern manager.* St. Paul, MN: West.

Independent Sector. (1986b, October 8). *Projected loss of charitable giving.* Memo to Members, Attachment #7.

Jacoby, A., & Babchuk, N. (1963, July). Instrumental and expressive voluntary associations. *Sociology and Social Research, 47,* 461–471.

Jones, J. F., & Herrick, J. M. (1976). *Citizens in service: Volunteers in social welfare during the depression, 1929–1941.* Detroit: Michigan State University Press.

Judd, P., Block, S. R., & Jain, A. K. (1985, Fall). Who joins NASW: A study of graduating MSWs. *Arete, 10*(2), 41–44.

Kalmus, H. (1963, November 28). The evolution of altruism. *New Scientist,* London.

Keith, A. (1949). *New theory of human evolution.* London: Watts.

Lashbrooke, E. C. (1985). *Tax exempt organizations.* Westport, CT: Quorum Books.

Leiby, J. (1978). *A history of social welfare and social work in the United States.* New York: Columbia University Press.

Leonard, E. M. (1965). *The early history of English poor relief.* London, England: Frank Cass.

Lerner, M. (1983). The joiners. In B. O'Connell (Ed.), *America's voluntary spirit* (pp. 81–89). New York: The Foundation Center.

Manser, G., & Cass, R. H. (1976). *Volunteerism at the crossroads.* New York: Family Service Association of America.

Marts, A. C. (1966). *The generosity of Americans.* Englewood Cliffs, NJ: Prentice-Hall.

Massie, J. L. (1979). *Essentials of management.* Englewood Cliffs, NJ: Prentice-Hall.

Mayo, G. E. (1933). *The human problems of an industrial civilization.* Boston: Harvard Business School.

McGregor, D. (1960). *The human side of enterprise.* New York: McGraw-Hill.

Mee, J. F. (1963). *Management thought in a dynamic economy,* New York: New York University Press.

Merton, R. K. (1976). *Sociological ambivalence and other essays.* New York: Free Press.

Metcalf, H. C., & Urwick, L. (1942). *Dynamic administration: The collected papers of Mary Follett.* New York: Harper & Bros.

Milofsky, C. (1979). Not for profit organizations and community: A review of the sociological literature. PONPO Working Paper No. 6. New Haven: Yale University Press.

O'Connell, B. (Ed.). (1983). *America's voluntary spirit.* New York: The Foundation Center.

Odendahl, T. J. (1985, March 15). Private foundation formation, growth, and termination: A report on work in progress. In Independent Sector, *Giving and volunteering: New frontiers of knowledge, 1985 spring research forum* (pp. 513–524). Washington, DC: Independent Sector.

Office of Refugee Resettlement. (1986, January). *Assessment of the MAA incentive grant initiative.* Final Report, Contract Number 600–84–0231. Office of Refugee Resettlement, U.S. Department of Health and Human Services.

Palisi, B. J. (1972). A critical analysis of the voluntary association concept. In D. H. Smith, R. D. Reddy, & B. R. Baldwin (Eds.), *Voluntary action research: 1972.* Lexington, MA: D. C. Heath.

Peters, T. J., & Waterman, R. H. (1982). *In search of excellence.* New York: Harper & Row.

Radford, K. J. (1980). *Strategic planning: An analytical approach.* Reston, VA: Reston Publishing.

Rockefeller, J. D. (1908). The difficult art of giving. *The world's work.*

Roethlisberger, F. J., & Dickson, W. J. (1939). *Management and the worker.* Cambridge: Harvard University Press.

Rose, A. (1954). *Theory and method in the social sciences.* Minneapolis: The University of Minnesota Press.

Rose, M. E. (1971). *The English Poor Law: 1789–1930.* Newton Abbott, UK: David and Charles, Publishers.

Salamon, L. M. (1984, Autumn). The invisible partnership, government and nonprofit sector. *Bell Atlantic Quarterly, 1.*

Seeley, J. R., Junker, B. H., Jones, W. R., Jenkins, N. C., Haugh, M. T., & Miller, I. (1957). *Community chest.* Toronto: University of Toronto.

Sills, D. (1957). *The volunteers.* Glencoe, IL: Free Press.

Sills, D. (1968). Voluntary associations: Sociological aspects. In D. Sills (Ed.), *International encyclopedia of the social sciences,* Vol. 16. New York: MacMillan and Free Press.

Simon, H. (1946, Winter). The proverbs of administration. *Public Administration Review, 6,* 53–67.

Smith, C., & Freedman, A. (1972). *Voluntary associations.* Cambridge, MA: Harvard University Press.

Smith, W. H., & Chiechi, C. P. (1974). *Private foundations: Before and after the tax reform act of 1969.* Washington, DC: American Enterprise Institute for Public Policy Research.

Taylor, F. W. (1911). *The principles of scientific management.* New York: Harper & Bros.

Thompson, J. D. (1967). *Organizations in action.* New York: McGraw-Hill.

Tocqueville, A. de (1969). On the use which the Americans make of associations in civil life. In *Democracy in America,* Vol. 2 (pp. 513–517). New York: Doubleday, Anchor Books.

Trolander, J. A. (1975). *Settlement houses and the great depression.* Detroit: Wayne State University.

Verba, S., & Nie, N. (1972). *Participation in America: Political democracy and social equality.* New York: Harper and Row.

Waite, F. T. (1960). *A warm friend for the spirit.* Cleveland: Family Service Association of Cleveland.

Waldo, D. (1948). *The administrative state.* New York: Ronald Press.

Weaver, W. (1967). *U.S. philanthropic foundations: Their history, structure, management and record.* New York: Harper & Row.

Weisbrod, B. A. (1977). *The voluntary nonprofit sector.* Lexington, MA: D. C. Heath.

Zald, M. N. (1970). *Organizational change.* Chicago: The University of Chicago Press.

CHAPTER 9

Inventing the Nonprofit Sector: 1950–1990

PETER DOBKIN HALL

By the 1830s, foreign visitors such as Alexis de Tocqueville were describing voluntary organizations supported by private contributions as the quintessential American contribution to the democratic idea. Although such organizations had existed in one form or another since the mid-eighteenth century, they were neither ubiquitous nor universally important: in some places they were encouraged—indeed, favored—as instruments of public action, in others they were actively discouraged; to some groups in society, they were mechanisms of choice for collective action, and others preferred to act through government. Even where the organizations enjoyed public sanction and private support, their status in relation to government, in particular the question of whether they were private entities, remained unsettled for decades.

Nonprofit organizations only became a significant and ubiquitous part of the American organizational universe in the very recent past: in 1940, there were only 12,500 secular charitable tax-exempt organizations; today there are over 700,000. Most of this growth took place after 1960—and did not became significant enough to merit the compilation of regular annual statistical reports until late in that decade. The effort to treat nonprofits as an institutional sector in the National Income Accounts dates only from 1980.[1]

The effort to treat organizations delivering a wide variety of seemingly unrelated services—in the arts, education, health care, social welfare—as constituting a distinctive organizational sector, primarily on the basis of a set of technical criteria having to do with their status under the federal tax code, the sources and disposition of their revenues, and their manner of governance, is part of a complex process. On the one hand, this effort is part of the means by which organizations sharing these features are forging awareness of themselves as distinct and coherent, particularly with regard to their legal and regulatory status. On the other hand, this effort is part of the means by which society and governmental bodies recognize and devise mechanisms for dealing with these new entities.

Although the existence of a nonprofit sector and the distinctiveness of the organizations constituting it are grounded in the present, the debate over voluntary associations and other kinds of private institutions acting in the public interest dates back to the eighteenth century and, as such, appears to be a central part of a broader struggle to define democratic institutions. Democratic ideals are ambiguous with regard to how the people can best make known their will. From the beginning, Americans have argued about whether voluntary associations threatened democracy by permitting small groups of citizens, particularly the wealthy, to exercise power disproportionate to their numbers, or whether such bodies were essential to a citizenry that, without them, would be powerless to influence the state.

Over time, the terms of the debate, as well as the institutional mechanisms of voluntary action and private initiative for public purposes, became more elaborate and concrete. By the 1870s, some were arguing that democracy attains is fullest institutional expression not through government action, but through government encouragement of private action, including grants of incorporation, tax exemptions, tax regulations providing incentives to individuals who make donations to nonprofit organizations, and the ability to set property aside in perpetuity for charitable and educational purposes. Others argued with equal passion that leaving such essential public concerns as culture, education, health, and social welfare to the discretion—or to the neglect—of the few wealthy enough to concern themselves with such issues was as dangerous to democracy as leaving the banking, transportation, and communications systems unregulated.

Recognition of the interdependence of public and private enterprise became a fundamental premise of American polity in the twentieth century. But the balance between the two was always at issue—and the status of voluntary and charitable organizations, especially those that were supported by the wealthy and that explicitly sought not only to provide services for the public but also to influence its opinions, continued to be the subject of intense, but periodic, public controversy. This became more or less continuous after 1942, when income taxation became universal through the mechanism of withholding. With government claiming a significant share of everybody's income, questions of tax equity and, in particular, the costs to taxpayers of permitting certain institutions to be classified as tax exempt and extending special tax benefits to those who supported them reinvigorated the controversy. However, once again the perennial debate was framed by a peculiar

set of institutional circumstances. Although the American government grew in scale and scope after World War II, rather than creating elaborate bureaucracies to provide the cultural, educational, health, and welfare services the public demanded, it created incentives for private enterprises to do so. Because these grew incrementally in particular industries, it was decades before tax-exempt enterprises came to recognize their common stake either in the general public debate over taxing, budgeting, and regulating, or in the particular aspects of that debate which affected their interests. During the 1970s the common ground turned out to be not only highly technical issues of tax and regulatory policy but also perennial concerns about the place of private initiative in public life, which were heightened by Reaganism and its rhetorical emphasis on the evils of big government.

In the late 1980s, the need for historical understanding of nonprofit activity, however defined, was driven by a new set of concerns. The collapse of communism abroad and efforts to establish democratic governments and market economies raised fundamental questions about the place of nonprofits in modern institutional systems. Before this, scholars and policymakers could frame their concerns within a set of conditions relatively unique to American culture, in which individuals were socialized to responsible autonomy, modes of authority were geared to compliance rather than coercion, and financial and productive resources of individuals were subject to their discretionary disposal. By treating these conditions as givens, scholars and policymakers could overlook both the complex issues of interdependence and the uncomfortable issues of inequality that underlay the growth of nonprofit enterprise in the United States. But when they were faced with the task of building national institutional systems from the ground up, these questions inevitably resurfaced—reviving an awareness of the core ambiguities of democracy and capitalism.

In 1938, Frederick W. Keppel, president of the Carnegie Corporation, had deplored

the large number of foundations which make no public record of their activities whatsoever—

thereby failing to recognize their responsibility to the public as organizations enjoying exemption from taxation, a privilege shared with religious, educational, and charitable institutions. The instances in which it seems impossible to obtain pertinent information is disquietingly large. The question is not whether the funds of these silent trusts are put to useful purposes—indeed, some of the so-called family foundations are to the writer's knowledge making their grants with intelligence and discretion—it is rather whether public confidence in the foundation as a social instrument, a confidence which is in no small degree based upon the policy of complete publicity adopted by the better known foundations, may not be endangered.[2]

Ultimately, the threat came from the Right, as part of the broad realignment of political loyalties during World War II. As early as 1940, many isolationists had already identified what they saw as an internationalist conspiracy to draw the United States into the war and had begun to question the role of foundations and a variety of tax-exempt interest groups which advocated American intervention in Europe. However, these charges did not find legislative expression until 1944, when, in the context of a Senate debate over tax legislation, John A. Danahar of Connecticut proposed an amendment to restrict the amount of losses from secondary businesses which could be allowed as deductions.[3] On the face of it, the amendment was aimed at wealthy individuals who used expensive money-losing businesses to avoid taxation. But as the debate proceeded, it became clear that it was aimed at the activities of Marshall Field III, one of the nation's richest and most politically liberal businessmen and philanthropists. On the eve of the war, Field had recognized the problems that isolationist control of the press (by men such as Hearst and Robert McCormick) posed for internationalist efforts to prepare the nation for the inevitability of war. To combat the isolationists, he established two newspapers, *New York PM* and the *Chicago Sun-Times*. Although both newspapers consistently lost money, they were widely read and effectively promoted internationalism. But as the war drew to a close, the iso-

lationist coalition, a curious alliance of Irish-Americans and native-born Americans with populist roots, began to sharpen its knives. The former group, mostly Democrats, had never forgiven Roosevelt for coming to the aid of the British. The latter, mostly Republicans, had never forgiven the internationalists for depriving their candidate, Robert Taft, of the party's presidential nominations in 1940 and 1944.

The start of the Cold War, the breakup of wartime domestic and international political alliances, and the death of the nation's leading internationalists, Roosevelt and Wendell Willkie opened the door to an assault, which was cloaked in anti-Communist rhetoric, against liberal internationalism. The antisubversive movement, which included the activities of the House Committee on Un-American Activities and the Senate Internal Security Sub-Committee under Senator Joseph McCarthy, was directed in large part against the policy elites, as well as the private universities and foundations with which they were closely associated.

In April 1952, the Select (Cox) Committee of the House of Representatives began an investigation of "educational and philanthropic foundations and other comparable organizations which are exempt from federal taxation to determine whether they were using their resources for the purposes for which they were established, and especially to determine which such foundations and organizations are using their resources for un-American and subversive activities or for purposes not in the interest or tradition of the United States."[4]

Keele began his work by meeting privately with the heads of the largest foundations and urging their cooperation with the committee's work. This they agreed to do. In fall 1952, all foundations with assets of $10 million or more received a questionnaire covering virtually every aspect of their operations. Responses ran to book-length—for example, the Guggenheim Foundation's ran to over three hundred pages. As it turned out, the foundations' willingness to cooperate was generously rewarded. Keele allowed the foundations and their friends to present their case first—which they did with extraordinary effectiveness and vigor. After two weeks of hearing testimony from such notables as Henry Ford II, John D. Rockefeller 3rd, Alfred P. Sloan, and Vannevar Bush—as well as a handful of professional anti-Communists—the committee completed its work. Its final report, submitted to Congress in January 1953, ringingly endorsed the loyalty of the foundations. "So far as we can ascertain," it declared, "there is little basis for the belief expressed in some quarters that foundation funds are being diverted from their intended use."[5] The report concluded by recommending better public reporting and a re-examination of pertinent tax laws to encourage private individuals to make greater gifts to "these meritorious institutions."

Unhappy with the Cox Committee's conclusions, Congressman B. Carroll Reece pushed for a continuation of its work. In April 1954, the House authorized a Special Committee to Investigate Tax-Exempt Foundations and Comparable Organizations (the Reece Committee). Unlike its predecessor, which limited its attention to generalities, the Reece Committee mounted a comprehensive enquiry into both the motives for establishing foundations and their influence on public life. Although the promotion of internationalism and moral relativism by foundations concerned the committee, it saw their concentrated power as the more central threat. Even if benign, this power posed a threat to democratic government.[6]

The Reece Committee's report, submitted in the midst of the ultimately successful efforts to censure McCarthy, failed to attract much attention. McCarthy's fall led to a discrediting of all efforts that smacked of redbaiting. Once again, the foundations and the other organizations of the growing tax-exempt universe had a fortunate escape. Nevertheless, their vulnerability had been underscored—and their leaders set about to prepare for future congressional assaults by trying to create a public record of their activities.[7] Initiatives took several forms. In 1955, the Ford Foundation made its first grants to encourage scholarly investigations of the role of philanthropy in American life. In the same year, the Carnegie Corporation and the Russell Sage Foundation began planning the establishment of "a new organization [that] would be a strategic gathering place for knowledge about foundations"—the Foundation Library Center. The center's activities, which included the publication of a comprehensive directory of foundations and a bimonthly magazine, *Foundation News.*[8]

These efforts came none too soon. In July 1959, the Senate Finance Committee recommended a liberalization of tax-code provisions affecting unlimited deductions for charitable contributions. A minority on the committee—which included senators Russell Long, Albert Gore, Eugene McCarthy, and Clinton Anderson—issued a sharply worded minority report, which charged that "this bill is designed specifically to encourage a proliferation of foundations which would be established by individuals and families." "The tax base is being dangerously eroded by many forces," the minority warned, "among them tax-exempt trusts and foundations. Not only is the tax base being eroded, but even more harmful social and political consequences may result from concentrating, and holding in a few hands and in perpetuity, control over large fortunes and business enterprises. The attendant inequities resulting from the tax treatment of contributions, particularly in the form of capital, to foundations are being magnified daily." Noting that 87 percent of the thirteen thousand foundations had been created since 1940 and that approximately twelve hundred new ones were being created every year, the minority report warned that "at present rates of establishment, substantial control of our economy may soon rest in the 'dead hands' of such organizations." The minority report urged that "the social, political, and economic implications of the growth of foundations should be thoroughly studied," underlining the dangers of wealth "removed from ostensible ownership and from the free choices presented by the marketplace and by the democratic processes of a free government, free economy, and a free society."[9]

In May 1961, Texas Congressman Wright Patman took up the challenge suggested by the minority report, using the floor of the House to deliver a series of speeches on foundations and other tax-exempt organizations.[10] Briefly stated, Patman concluded:

I am at present concerned with first, foundation-controlled business competing with small businessmen: second the economic effect of great amounts of wealth accumulating in privately controlled, tax-exempt foundations; third, the problem of control of that capital for an undetermined period—in some cases in perpetuity—by a few individuals or their self-appointed successors: and fourth, the foundations' power to interlock and knit together through investments, a network of commercial alliances, which assures harmonious action whenever they have a common interest.[11]

He promised to continue examining "the economic consequences of the granting of tax exemption to privately controlled foundations" and to report "from time to time" to the House.

Patman's efforts over the next decade, conducted under the auspices of the Small Business Committee, focused not on subversion, but on economic issues, particularly the favorable treatment that philanthropy brought the very wealthy and the power of philanthropy over the economy.[12]

Patman's persistence, combined with rising taxes and inflation, which increased the tax sensitivity of the public, stimulated a rising demand for tax reform. In February 1969, the House Ways and Means Committee began hearings on the subject. The lead-off witness was Patman, who railed against the ways in which the foundations had "perverted" philanthropy, transforming "one of mankind's more noble instincts" into "a vehicle for institutionalized, deliberate evasion of fiscal and moral responsibility."[13]

Although they faced a common threat, the defenders of charitable tax-exempt organizations were remarkably *un*unified in their efforts to defend themselves. Even relatively well-institutionalized agencies such as the Foundation Center and the newly organized Council on Foundations, despite their calls for "stronger internal discipline and evaluation" and "friendly encouragement from government," were unable to present specific legislative recommendations when asked to so by the House Ways and Means Committee in 1965, because of lack of agreement among their members.[14]

Things had not much improved by 1969, when Congress began hearing testimony on proposed sweeping revisions in the tax code. The leaders of big foundations were unanimous in their opposition to any form of increased regulation.[15] The Carnegie Corporation's Alan Pifer defended the "honored place" of foundations and warned that "governmental control" of the sort embodied in the proposed tax reforms would "have far-reaching and extremely dangerous consequences for the American pluralistic system." The Ford Foundations's McGeorge Bundy echoed this theme, pointing out that the growing role of government increased the need for private philanthropy, which fostered diversity and pluralism. George Harrar and Dana Creel, representing the Rockefeller philanthropies, defended their institutions and urged against the passage of any regulations that would "act as dis-incentives for the creation and growth of foundations" or that would "discourage individual charitable giving."

The unyielding stance of the foundations won them few friends on the Hill. Bundy's testimony, described by some as arrogant, was marked by sharp exchanges with the committee over the foundation's political activities. including funding voter-registration drives and "fellowships" given to former members of Robert F. Kennedy's staff. By the time the hearings concluded, it was quite clear that Patman's charges had been largely accepted at face value and that major changes in regulations governing foundations and favoring their wealthy donors were inevitable.

Although the 1969 Tax Reform Act turned out to be less than a disaster for philanthropy, it once again underlined the vulnerability of the charitable tax-exempt universe.[16] Quite clearly, quoting Tocqueville to Congress would no longer serve as an effective defense. Future efforts would have to rely on the technical language of law and economics that had come to frame the creation of tax policy by the late 1960s.

One of the few figures to recognize how significantly philanthropy had changed since the war was John D. Rockefeller 3rd. His statements contrasted sharply with those of foundation executives, who, according to one congressman, expressed an "all or nothing" attitude, felt entitled to act outside the tax system, and left Congress no middle ground.[17] Rockefeller urged philanthropy and government to work together to reevaluate the place of foundations in modern society.[18] Rockefeller's call for a public-private partnership in the drafting policies affecting "private initiative in the public interest" acknowledged the complexities and uncertainties of the relationship between government and the private sectors that had developed since the war. On the most fundamental level, as the role of government grew, some in Congress wondered whether private philanthropy was needed anymore. Others were concerned about government support for private institutions whose policies on race and gender ran counter to public policy.

The current of hostility to foundations and other tax-exempt organizations did not end with the passage of the 1969 Tax Reform Act. Patman and other congressional leaders had watched with dismay as the act's provisions were progressively watered down by the I.R.S. In June 1972, Patman wrote to leading foundations demanding that they demonstrate their compliance with various sections of the act.[19] In spring 1973, the Treasury Department proposed further toughening of tax-law provisions affecting foundations and large donors.[20] And by the fall, the Subcommittee on Foundations of the Senate Finance Committee, chaired by Indiana's Vance Hartke, began a series of panel discussions on the issue.[21] Hartke was outspokenly hostile and disdainful to foundation representatives.

[In] the months before the hearings on the 1969 Tax Reform Act started, when John D. Rockefeller 3rd had convened a blue-ribbon panel, the Commission on Foundations and Private Philanthropy. Made up of individuals prominent in business, education, law, and the arts, the Peterson Commission, as it came to be known (after its chairman, Pete Peterson, president of Bell and Howell), set itself the task of studying "all relevant matters bearing on foundations and private philanthropy" in order to make "long-term policy recommendations."

The Peterson Commission report failed to have the desired impact, because not only was it completed after the passage of the 1969 Tax Reform Act but also little of the information it gathered was really new.

No sooner had the Peterson Commission disbanded than Rockefeller and his associates initiated conversations with Ways and Means Committee Chairman Wilbur Mills, Treasury Department officials, and others with regard to convening "a group of knowledgeable and concerned individuals to review and make recommendations in regard to tax incentives in the philanthropic field" and other matters relating to the well-being of "the whole private nonprofit sector."[22] With Mills' affirmative response, the effort to organize what was then called the Committee on Tax Incentives began in earnest, under the direction of Leonard Silverstein and Rockefeller's associates Howard Bolton and Datus Smith.[23] What had been conceived of as a relatively modest effort took on greater urgency and importance with the new year—the year of Watergate. One of the revelations in the impeachment hearings was a memorandum by presidential aide Pat Buchanan which laid out strategies for combating "the institutionalized power of the Left concentrated in the foundations that succor the Democratic party," mentioning the need for "a strong fellow running the Internal Revenue Division . . . and an especially friendly fellow with a friendly staff in the Tax-Exempt office."[24] This, combined with the Hartke hearings and the increasingly restrictive proposals from the Nixon administration, made it clear that philanthropy's best defense was to seize the policy initiative.

Patronage of scholarship played a crucial role in allowing philanthropy to shift the basis for advancing its claims for special status under the tax code. In the early 1960s, the 501(c)(3) Group, a loose network of tax lawyers and top officials of national donee organizations, had begun exchanging information about the technical dimensions of the tax code as it affected charitable tax-exempt organizations.[25] The group had been troubled about the ineffectiveness of pluralist rhetoric in the 1969 hearings and—with an eye to the emerging econometric literature on tax policy—were alarmed by the emergence of a scholarly literature that seemed to suggest there was no economic justification for such things as the charitable deduction.[26] "We all felt intuitively that taxes influenced giving," Hayden W. Smith, then chair of the group, later recollected. "But none of the available scholarship supported our viewpoint. We cast a net looking for economists who might look into this for us."[27] After rejecting various Washington-based economists as biased, the group learned of the work of Harvard economist Martin S. Feldstein, who had done important work in the 1960s on the economics of health care. Smith met with Feldstein, who, in January 1973, made a formal proposal for a research project on the effects of deductibility on charitable contributions and, more broadly, to produce "a more general analysis of the rationale and effects of the current tax treatment."[28] These studies would be directed to professional economists, tax lawyers, and government officials.

Feldstein began his study in February 1973, having agreed to keep the 501(c)(3) Group appraised of his preliminary findings. Within months, it became clear that his analysis strongly supported philanthropy—and he was given the go-ahead to complete the study, which he completed by December 1973. The importance of Feldstein's work, which created a compelling and academically credible rationale for the tax treatment of nonprofits, was suggested by the language of the *Philanthropy Monthly*'s "Outstanding Service Award" for 1974."

Feldstein's exciting findings put the work of Rockefeller's Committee on Tax Incentives into high gear. By May 1973, the committee, now renamed the Advisory Group on Private Philanthropy, had become a top priority with both the Rockefeller group and the Treasury Department, now led by William Simon.[29] By the end of the summer, a prestigious group—exquisitely balanced by geography, party, gender, race, occupation, and religious denomination—had been recruited under the chairmanship of John Filer, a corporate lawyer and the chief executive officer of the Aetna Insurance Company.[30] The joint effort of Congress, the Treasury Department, and the private sector would be "aided by a distinguished panel of experts including economists, sociologists, tax attorneys, and spe-

cialists in nongovernmental organizations." The commission's broad mandate would include consideration of: "(1) policy considerations respecting the present system of incentives to private philanthropic giving; (2) specific considerations relating to the present treatment of private contributors; (3) specific considerations relating to the present method of supervising, regulating, and classifying charitable institutions; and (4) alternative means of achieving the results sought by [the] present structure of private philanthropy in the United States."

The results of the Filer Commission's work were published by the Treasury Department in six weighty volumes in 1977.[31] This comprehensive multidisciplinary survey of every aspect of charitable tax-exempt organizations described and analyzed the role of nonprofits as employers, as sources of essential health, educational, welfare, and cultural services, and as forces in political life. The work also carefully considered the regulatory and tax issues affecting these organizations' well-being. Most importantly, the work gave substance to what, up to then, had been only an idea: that charitable tax-exempt organizations composed a coherent and cohesive "sector" of American political, economic, and social life. This unified conception of nonprofits as part of a "third," "independent," or "nonprofit"—or, as the commission preferred to call it, "voluntary"—sector lay the groundwork for establishing organizations that could give its common interests unified expression.

Initially, the majority and the commission had hoped to establish a permanent quasi-governmental agency—modeled on the British Charity Commission—within the Treasury Department. But hopes for this were dashed by the Carter administration, which not only questioned the propriety of such an industry presence within a government department, but also was engaged more broadly in a sweeping review of the regulatory process.[32]

Because the Filer Commission had failed in its main task—the creation of an agency that would have effectively removed public policy toward philanthropy from the political process—those in sympathy with the commission's recommendations had to try to devise alternate means of bringing the diverse and discordant elements of the tax-exempt universe—the third sector—into harmony. This would not be easy.

Conciliating these interests took almost four years. And even when agreement on a unified organization to serve all elements of the non-profit sector was finally reached, it was in effect an agreement to disagree. Repeatedly reminding itself of the diversity of the sector and its key role in preserving pluralism in American society, the new entity, Independent Sector (IS), pledged itself to address its mission "only by working through the vast network of organizations already extant," understanding that "the extent to which the new organization tries to overreach these groups and build separately, it will have neither an impact nor a future."[33] In considering the long-term dangers IS faced, organizers listed first and foremost "the danger of slipping into a spokesperson role. To do so not only will be a disservice to the sector and society, but will bring the wrath of the sector down on the organization. There are very few issues where the sector will ever speak with one voice or tolerate one voice speaking in its behalf."[34] Rather than serving as a spokesman, IS would, its organizers hoped, be a "common meeting ground" for all elements and all viewpoints within the charitable universe.

Nonprofits in the Reagan Era

The formation of IS coincided with the election of Ronald Reagan. The new president, who had proclaimed himself a friend of philanthropy and voluntarism, set about not only to increase its responsibilities—by cutting back federal spending and allowing localities and private charities to "take up the slack"—but also to highlight the need for greater support for non-profits. To stimulate higher levels of voluntary effort, the president convened a Task Force on Private Sector Initiatives, chaired by industrialist William Verity and directed by E. B. Knauft, chief of corporate contributions at Aetna and a former Filer Commission staffer.[35] After months of meetings, the commission failed to reach agreement on whether the private sector was up

to the task—a point brought home by the unwillingness of many major corporations to commit themselves to giving at even the 2 percent level (much less the 10 percent that was permitted under the new administration's tax legislation).[36] The most serious blow to the president's efforts came from policy analysts Lester Salamon and Alan Abramson of the Urban Institute, whose analysis of the Reagan budget proposals suggested that the nonprofit sector, by then so dependent on public funding, would be crippled by cutbacks in federal spending—which the scholars demonstrated as constituting between one-third and one-half of nonprofit revenues.[37]

Over the past decade, neither the government nor philanthropy's defenders have managed to articulate coherent policies toward the nonprofit sector. The Reagan and Bush administrations, though rhetorically supporting private initiative, have promoted tax proposals that would eliminate or reduce incentives to charitable donors. At the same time, conservative efforts to privatize public services, often through contracting them out to nonprofits, have encouraged the continuing growth in the number of nonprofit organizations.[38] This combination of threatened cutbacks in direct and indirect federal support for nonprofits and privatization has encouraged nonprofits to become far more entrepreneurial, reducing uncertainty by broadening their financial bases beyond charitable contributions to include a mix of grants, contracts, donations, and sales of services. Nonprofits responded by encouraging the professionalization of management, with skills in marketing, accounting, and planning, as well as in reinterpreting organizational missions to fit the new circumstances.[39] The professionalization of nonprofits management, the increasingly active presence of businesspeople on boards of trustees, and unprecedentedly high levels of corporate giving were the Reagan era's chief legacy to the nonprofit sector.[40]

As nonprofits achieved an influence and visibility in the 1980s that would have been unimaginable even a decade earlier, groups such as IS and the Council on Foundations found themselves increasingly stymied by changes in the sector. These national organizations were not geared to deal with local and regional organizations—the arenas in which most of the growth was taking place.

Certainly the greatest changes in the non-profit world have involved both vastly greater numbers of organizations and vastly broader public participation and support.[41] Mutual-benefit and advocacy organizations (including churches) aside, most nonprofits had been a relatively unruffled preserve of primarily Protestant community elites—people who knew one another, who shared the same values and goals, and who tended to dominate the major social and economic institutions of their communities. The mass availability of higher education and economic growth in the decades following World War II moved new elements—particularly people of non-Northern European and non-Protestant background—into positions of leadership in the private sectors. They brought with them a variety of new perspectives on communities, as well as their needs and how best to meet them.

By the end of the 1980s, charities such as the United Way were compelled to make major changes in their policies to accommodate the increasingly pluralistic nature of American communities and their leadership.[42] The increasing diversity of backgrounds and viewpoints of community leaders has found its most compelling expression in growing conflict among board members and between boards and managers over organizational missions, goals, and strategies. This conflict has led to growing attention to the broad issues of community leadership and how it should be recruited and trained.[43]

Conclusion

The debate continues over how a democracy can best do the public's business. Despite the growing recognition of nonprofits as a centrally important part of American life, doubts still remain about the wisdom of delegating public tasks to private groups. Some commentators, pointing out how few of the organizations enjoying tax exemption are actually concerned

with benefiting the needy, have urged a thorough overhaul of tax laws. Others have pointed to the ways in which philanthropy, despite the strictures of the 1969 Tax Reform Act, continues to serve the purposes of the wealthy far more than it does those of the population as a whole.

Perhaps the most significant shift in the debate has involved the Rights's decreasing hostility to nonprofit activity. As conservatives became a unified political force in the 1980s, they depended more and more on their own network of think tanks, foundations, and sympathetic academics. This influential counterestablishment, combined with the growing importance of foundations outside the Northeast, has helped to broaden the profile of philanthropy, making it less the creature of a small group of like-minded cosmopolitans with liberal proclivities.[44]

Accompanying the current broad acceptance of the activity of nonprofits has been a growth in concerns about their global dimensions.[45] On the one hand. American nonprofits are increasingly seeking support from overseas corporations, while foreign corporations doing business in the United States are increasingly eager to be good "corporate citizens." On the other hand, the collapse of communism and consequent efforts to put free-market economies and democratic polities in its place has, necessarily, suggested the need for third-sector organizations abroad as well. Despite forceful arguments in favor of establishing nonprofit sectors abroad, questions remain about what forms they might take.

The lack of unanimity on these issues, as well as the continuing debate over the mission, goals, and mechanisms of philanthropic, voluntary, and nonprofit organizations, has been disheartening to some. For others, the debate is an exciting intellectual adventure involving fundamental questions about the nature of human institutions, the possibilities of political, economic, and social organization, and the quality of our values and moral imagination.

Notes

1. For an especially incisive discussion of the distinctions between charitable and noncharitable non-

profits, see Henry Hansmann, "Economic Theories of Nonprofit Organization," in W. W. Powell, ed., *The Nonprofit Sector: A Research Handbook* (New Haven: Yale University Press, 1987), 27–42.

2. Quoted in Coon, *Money to Burn,* 334–35. See also Frederick Keppel's *The Foundation: Its Place in American Life* (New York: Macmillan Co., 1930).

3. Stephen Becker, *Marshall Field III: A Biography* (New York: Simon & Schuster, 1964), 241–48.

4. H. Res. 561, 82nd Congress, 2nd Session, "Resolution," in *Hearings before the Select Committee to Investigate Tax-Exempt Foundations and Comparable Organizations,* 1.

5. Select Committee to Investigate Foundations, 82nd Congress, 2nd Session, House Report No. 2514, *Final Report* (Washington. D.C.: Government Printing Office, 1953).

6. This is a summary of the "Introductory Material" in Special Committee to Investigate Foundations and Comparable Organizations (Reece Committee), 83rd Congress, 2nd Session, House Report No. 2681, *Tax-Exempt Foundations—Report* (Washington, D.C.: Government Printing Office, 1954), 1–14.

7. Andrews gives a detailed account of these responses in *Foundation Watcher.* They included the convening of the Princeton Conference in December 1955. This two-day meeting, underwritten by the Ford Foundation, brought together a group of leading scholars, led by historian Merle Curti, to define a strategy for studying—and thereby creating a place for—philanthropy in the historical and social-science literature. This meeting not only marked the beginning of nonprofits scholarship but also set the paradigm of grants-driven research which has characterized the field ever since. Working with Ford money, Curti and a number of his colleagues and students (including Irvin Wyllie, Daniel M. Fox, Howard Miller, David Allmendinger, and Paul Mattingly) produced valuable and important studies. But typically, when the money ran out, interest waned. On this important meeting, see *Report of the Princeton Conference on the History of Philanthropy* (New York: Russell Sage Foundation, 1956).

8. Andrews, *Foundation Watcher,* 175–94. See also Foundation Library Center, *Annual Reports,* 1956–, and *Foundation News—Bulletin of the Foundation Library Center* 1, no. 1 (September 1960): 1–3.

9. U.S. Senate, "Limitation on Deduction in Case of Contributions by Individuals for Benefit of Churches, Educational Organizations, and Hospitals—Report Together with Minority and Supplemental Views," 87th Congress, 1st Session, Report No. 585 (July 20, 1961), 7–8.

The Rockefeller Archives contain important material on philanthropy lobbying efforts in connection with this bill: see memorandum from F. Roberts Blair to Laurence S. Rockefeller, "Recent Proposed Federal Legislation on Unlimited Deduction for Charitable Contributions," October 1, 1959, Rockefeller Archives Center (Family, RG3, JDR3rd, Box 24, "Taxes—Unlimited Deduction"); F. Roberts Blair to John D. Rockefeller 3rd, "Federal Income Tax—Qualification for Unlimited Deduction for Charitable Contributions," October 8, 1959, in ibid.; Weston Vernon to John D. Rockefeller 3rd, "Re: Unlimited Charitable Deduction," February 24, 1961, in ibid.; F. Roberts Blair to John D. Rockefeller 3rd and Laurence S. Rockefeller,, "Unlimited Deduction Averaging Proposal," April 21, 1961, in ibid.; Weston Vernon to John D. Rockefeller 3rd, June 5, 1961, in ibid.; F. Roberts Blair to John D. Rockefeller 3rd, "Charitable Contributions H.R. 2244," in ibid. In the latter, Blair described the minority report as "interesting reading" and called attention to "the hostility that exists in the Committee to tax-exempt foundations and to measures which encourage contributions to charities."

10. On Patman, see Robert Sherill, "'The Last of the Great Populists' Takes on the Foundations, the Banks, the Federal Reserve, the Treasury," *New York Times Magazine,* March 16, 1969.

11. *Congressional Record,* August 7, 1961, 13751–56.

12. Patman's reports included *Tax-Exempt Foundations and Charitable Trusts: Their Impact on Our Economy,* Chairman's Report to the Select Committee on Small Business, House of Representatives, 87th Congress, December 31, 1962 (Washington, D.C.: Government Printing Office, 1962); *Tax-Exempt Foundations and Charitable Trusts: Their Impact on Our Economy,* Second Installment, Subcommittee Chairman's Report to Subcommittee No. 1, Select Committee on Small Business, House of Representatives, 88th Congress, October 16, 1963 (Washington, D.C.: Government Printing Office, 1963); ibid., Third Installment, March 20, 1964; *Tax-Exempt Foundations: Their Impact on Small Business,* Hearings Before Subcommittee No. 1 on Foundations, Select Committee on Small Business, 88th Congress, 2nd Session (Washington. D.C.: Government Printing Office, 1964); *Tax-Exempt Foundations and Charitable Trusts: Their Impact on Our Economy,* Fourth Installment, December 21, 1966; *Tax-Exempt Foundations and Charitable Trusts: Their Impact on Our Economy,* Fifth Installment, April 28, 1967; *Tax-Exempt Foundations: Their Impact on Small Business,* Hearings Before Subcommittee No. 1 of the Select Committee on Small

Business, House of Representatives, 90th Congress, 1st Session (1967); *Tax-Exempt Foundations and Charitable Trusts: Their Impact on Our Economy,* Sixth Installment, March 26, 1968.

13. Quoted in Andrews, *Foundation Watcher,* 253.

14. Andrews, *Foundation Watcher.*

15. The testimony of foundation leaders and other friendly witnesses are in *Foundations and the Tax Bill: Testimony on Title I of the Tax Reform Act of 1969 Submitted by Witnesses Appearing before the United States Senate Finance Committee, October 1969* (New York: Foundation Center, 1969); and House of Representatives, 91st Congress, Part 1, *Hearings before the Committee on Ways and Means* (February 18, 19, 20, 1969) (Washington, D.C.: Government Printing Office, 1969). The published testimony of the hearings, because it is edited and seldom reveals the jockeying behind the various positions taken by witnesses, only provides a partial documentation of the tension and turmoil in the world of philanthropy during this period.

16. Efforts to gauge the impact of the 1969 Tax Reform Act became a minor industry in the 1970s. A definitive study, the Project on Foundation Formation and Termination, was conducted in the mid-1980s by Yale's Program on Non-Profit Organizations, under the direction of Teresa Odendahl. Its findings appeared as Odendahl et al., *America's Wealthy and the Future of Foundations.* By the late 1980s, most philanthropic leaders conceded that the 1969 Tax Reform Act had done more good than harm.

Although is was ultimately possible to concede that the 1969 Tax Reform Act did not mark the beginning of the end for private philanthropy, the congressional hearings of 1969 left a deep scar on the consciousness of a whole generation of nonprofits executives. Most seriously, the trauma of the hearing impaired their capacity to tolerate either candid self-evaluation or criticism. This fearfulness had a major impact on the development of industry-funded research on nonprofits.

17. On John D. Rockefeller 3rd's controversial testimony at the 1969 Tax Reform Act hearings, see "Mr. R3 re Statement, Tax Reform Bill," unrevised stenographic minutes of testimony to the House Ways and Means Committee, February 27, 1969 (Family, RG3, JDR3, Box 37, "Tax Reform Bill/Statements"). See also Box 371, "Tax Reform Bill—Clippings," for responses to John D. Rockefeller 3rd's remarks.

18. John D. Rockefeller 3rd had been thinking along these lines as early as the mid-1960s—see "Thoughts on Philanthropy" (Family, RG3, JDR3,

Box 370, "Philanthropy—JDR3rd/Book"). His ideas along these lines were much stimulated by Alan Pifer's May 1968 speech "The Foundation in the Year 2000," in ibid. Pifer helped Rockefeller understand the fluidity of circumstances and the necessity for philanthropy to be able to respond to extraordinary change with flexibility—a view very much in contrast to the rigidity and defensiveness of most "philanthropoids" and wealthy donors in this period. John D. Rockefeller 3rd acknowledged his intellectual debt to Pifer by appointing him to the Filer Commission. He was the only foundation executive so honored.

19. See Henry C. Suhrke. "Foundation Replies: "Dear Mr. Patman," *Non-Profit Report* 5, no. 9 (September 1972).

20. "Peril in Treasury's Tax Proposals," *Non-Profit Report* 6, no. 5 (May 1973).

21. Henry C. Suhrke, "Foundations on the Senate Griddle," *Non-Profit Report* 6, no. 10 (October 1973): 1, 4–7.

22. John D. Rockefeller 3rd to Wilbur Mills, November 1, 1972 (Family, RG3, JDR3rd, Box 369, "Committee on Tax Incentives"); Wilbur Mills to John D. Rockefeller 3rd, November 8, 1972, in ibid., and Datus C. Smith to Mills, November 13, 1972, in ibid.

23. Memorandum from Datus C. Smith, Jr., to John D. Rockefeller 3rd, "Committee on Tax Incentives," December 7, 1972, in ibid. This memorandum summarizes the group's thinking about the committee's purposes, composition, program, and budget. Evidently, the effort was originally conceived as a modest effort—budgeted at only $80,000. By the time it completed its work in 1978, the committee—better known as the Filer Commission—raised and spent over $2 million! The original list of members was compiled by John D. Rockefeller 3rd's staff and congressional staffer Lawrence Woodward. On Woodward's involvement, see Datus Smith to Laurence N. Woodward, chief of staff, Joint Committee on Internal Revenue Taxation, November 13, 1972 (Family, RG3, JDR3rd, Box 369, "Commission on Philanthropy"). Interestingly, of the twenty-five proposed members, not one was a foundation executive.

24. Henry C. Suhrke, "Watergate Foundation Testimony," *Non-Profit Report* 6, no. 10 (October 1973): 34. In this issue, which also included coverage of the Hartke hearings, Suhrke speculated that Hartke, who was otherwise densely ignorant about philanthropy, was simply trying to cash in on public interest in Watergate.

25. I am grateful to Hayden W. Smith for his account of the origins of the 501(c)(3) Group, of which

he was a member from the early 1970s until its disbanding in 1987. According to Smith, the founders included Charles Sampson of the United Way, Jack Schwartz of the American Association of Fundraising Counsel, John Leslie of the American College Public Relations Association, and tax lawyers Connie Tytell and Stan Whitehorn. Hayden Smith was interviewed by the author on December 13, 1989.

26. This literature included William D. Andrews, "Personal Deductions in an Ideal Income Tax," *Harvard Law Review* 86, no. 2 (1972): 309–85; Boris I. Bittker, "The Propriety and Vitality of a Federal Income Tax Deduction for Private Philanthropy," in *Tax Impacts on Philanthropy* (Princeton: Tax Institute of America, 1972); R. Goode, *The Individual Income Tax* (Washington, D.C.: Brookings Institution, 1964); Harry C. Kahn, *Personal Deductions in the Federal Income Tax* (Princeton: Princeton University Press, 1960); Paul R. McDaniel, "An Alternative to the Federal Income Tax Deduction in Support of Private Philanthropy," in *Tax Impacts on Philanthropy,* 171–209; Paul R. McDaniel, "Federal Matching Grants for Charitable Contributions: A Substitute for the Income Tax Deduction," *Tax Law Review* 27, no. 3 (Spring 1972): 377–413; Joseph A. Pechman, *Federal Tax Policy* (New York: W. W. Norton & Co., 1971); David Rabin, "Charitable Trusts and Charitable Deductions," *New York University Law Review* 41 (1966): 912–25; Henry C. Simons, *Personal Income Taxation* (Chicago: University of Chicago Press, 1938); Stanley S. Surrey et al., *Federal Income Taxation* (Mineola, N.Y.: Foundation Press, 1972); William S. Vickrey, "Private Philanthropy and Public Finance," unpublished paper, 1973; William S. Vickrey, "One Economist's View of Philanthropy," in Frank Dickinson, ed., *Philanthropy and Public Policy* (New York: National Bureau of Economic Research, 1962), 31–56: Murray Weidenbaum, "A Modest Proposal for Tax Reform," *Wall Street Journal,* April 4, 1973, 18; Melvin White, "Proper Income Tax Treatment of Deductions for Personal Expense," in *Tax Revision Compendium,* Compendium of Papers on Broadening the Tax Base submitted to the Committee on Ways and Means, House of Representatives, U.S. Congress (Washington, D.C.: Government Printing Office, 1959), 1:370–71; and Department of the Treasury, *Tax Reform Studies and Proposals,* U.S. Congress, House Ways and Means Committee and Senate Finance Committee, 91st Congress, 1st Session, 1969.

27. Hayden W. Smith, interview with author, March 1990.

28. Feldstein formally presented his proposal to Hayden W. Smith, chair of the 501(c)(3) Group, in a letter of January 22, 1973 (Family, RG3, JDR3rd, Box 371, "Tax Reform Act of 1969").

29. Memorandum from William Howard Beasley III to Mr. [William] Simon, "Advisory Group on Private Philanthropy," May 11, 1973 (Family, RG3, JDR3rd Confidential Files, Box 14, "Commission on Philanthropy").

30. Memorandum from Porter McKeever to Howard Bolton and Leonard Silverstein, "Subject: John Filer," July 16, 1973 (Family, RG3, JDR3rd Confidential Files, Box 14, "Commission on Philanthropy"); and memorandum from Leonard Silverstein to Commission on Private Philanthropy Advisory Committee, untitled (to apprise the Advisory Committee of developments since its August 13 meeting), August 1973, in ibid. This important summary of the Filer Commission's preliminary discussions specifically details the range of its informational needs and policy concerns. Porter McKeever, author of the first memorandum, had replaced Datus Smith as John D. Rockefeller 3rd's point man on the philanthropy front. McKeever would be a key background figure in activities of the Filer Commission and in institutionalizing its legacy with the formation of Independent Sector.

31. The first volume was Report of the Commission on Private Philanthropy and Public Needs, *Giving in America: Toward a Stronger Voluntary Sector* (Washington, D.C.: Commission on Private Philanthropy & Public Needs, 1975). The six volumes of research papers were published as *Research Papers Sponsored by the Commission on Private Philanthropy and Public Needs* (Washington, D.C., Department of the Treasury, 1977).

32. Department of the Treasury, "Treasury Secretary Blumenthal Cuts Advisory Committees," press release, March 15, 1977; Advisory Committee on Private Philanthropy and Public Needs, "Minutes—April 7, 1977 Meeting"; John D. Rockefeller 3rd to Michael Blumenthal, April 7, 1977; Leonard Silverstein to Porter McKeever, April 18, 1977; memorandum from Leonard Silverstein to Commission Members [this untitled memorandum summarizes the status of the Treasury Committee on Private Philanthropy and Public Needs], April 18, 1977; Michael Blumenthal to Leonard Silverstein, April 27, 1977; memorandum from John D. Rockefeller 3rd to Porter McKeever, "Re: Conversation with Walter McNerney," June 22, 1977— all in Porter McKeever Papers, RG17, McKeever, Box 1, "Filer Commission." See also "PM Newsletter," *Philanthropy Monthly* 10, no. 3 (March 1977): 4.

33. Coalition of National Voluntary Organizations and National Council on Philanthropy. *To Preserve an

Independent Sector-Organizing Committee Report (Washington, D.C., 1979), vi.

34. Ibid., 23.

35. On the President's Task Force on Private Sector Initiatives (Verity Commission), see *Building Partnerships* (Washington, D.C.: Government Printing Office, 1982); *Corporate Community Involvement* (New York: Citizen's Forum on Self-Government/National Municipal League, 1982); and *Investing in America: Initiatives for Community and Economic Development* (Washington, D.C.: Government Printing Office, 1982). For a conservative critique of the task force, see Marvin Olasky, "Reagan's Second Thoughts on Corporate Giving," *Fortune,* September 20, 1983.

36. Conservatives charged that the Verity Commission was sabotaged by the liberal Knauft; see Marvin Olasky, "Reagan's Second Thoughts on Corporate Giving," *Fortune,* September 20, 1983. I am grateful to Burt Knauft for sharing his recollections of the commission with me.

37. Lester Salamon and Alan Abramson, "The Federal Government and the Nonprofit Sector: Implications of the Reagan Budget Proposals" (Washington, D.C.: Urban Institute, 1981). This research was funded by the 501(c)(3) Group. After Feldstein's 1973 study, it ranks as one of the most important single pieces of research ever done on the nonprofit sector.

38. According to "The Non-Profit World: A Statistical Portrait," *Chronicle of Philanthropy* 2, no. 6 (January 9, 1990): 8, the number of nonreligious nonprofits continued to grow through the 1980s: these 501(c)(3) and (4) organizations numbered 406,000 in 1977, 454,000 in 1982, 483,000 in 1984, and 561,000 in 1987—an increase of nearly 40 percent.

39. The best critical appraisal of these changes is Jon Van Til's *Mapping the Third Sector: Voluntarism in a Changing Social Economy* (New York: Foundation Center, 1988). Also valuable is Virginia A. Hodgkinson et al., eds., *The Future of the Nonprofit Sector* (San Francisco: Jossey-Bass Publishers, 1989).

While encouraged by circumstances, the professionalization of nonprofits management has been strongly encouraged by major nonprofit groups, including the United Way and Independent Sector. The chief spokesman for professional training of nonprofits managers is Dennis R. Young, who heads the Mandel Center for Nonprofit Organizations at Case Western Reserve University. Young's work in this area includes "Executive Leadership in Nonprofit Organizations," in Powell, ed., *The Nonprofit Sector,* 167–79; "Entrepreneurship and the Behavior of Nonprofit Organizations: Elements of a Theory," in Susan Rose-Ackerman, ed., *The Economics of Nonprofit Institutions: Studies in Structure and Policy* (New York: Ox-

ford University Press, 1986), 161; (with Lilly Cohen), *Careers for Dreamers and Doers: A Guide to Management Careers in the Nonprofit Sector* (New York: Foundation Center, 1989); and (with Michael O'Neill), *Educating Managers of Nonprofit Organizations* (New York: Praeger, 1988). For a valuable, if not somewhat outdated, critical overview of existing literature in this area, see Melissa Middleton, "Nonprofit Management: A Report on Current Research and Areas for Development," Working Paper no. 108 (New Haven: Program on Nonprofit Organizations, Yale University, 1986).

Although management schools and schools of public administration have generally resisted the effort to create degree programs—and even special courses—for nonprofit managers, the movement received significant encouragement recently from management guru Peter Drucker, who has decided that nonprofits represent a new managerial frontier. See Drucker, *The New Realities* (New York: Harper & Row, 1989), and *Managing the Nonprofit Organization: Principles and Practices* (New York: Harper Collins, 1990).

40. On these trends, see Miriam Wood's important "The Governing Board's Existential Quandary," Working Paper no. 150 (New Haven: Program on Non-Profit Organizations, Yale University, 1990); and Peter Dobkin Hall, "Conflicting Managerial Cultures on Nonprofit Boards," *Nonprofit Management and Leadership* 1, no. 2 (Winter 1990): 153–65.

41. On these changing patterns, see Anne Lowry Bailey, "Big Gains in Giving to Charity," *Chronicle of Philanthropy* 3, no. 1 (October 16, 1990), which reports on the publication of Virginia Hodgkinson and Murray Weitzman, *Giving and Volunteering in the United States, 1990* (Washington, D.C.: Independent Sector, 1990). The results of this survey point to major changes in patterns of giving and volunteering in the late 1980s. Especially notable is the downward shift in the age cohorts of givers.

42. United Way originally supported sets of organizations deemed by local leaders to best represent the interests of their communities. On this, see Seeley et al., *Community Chest.* A recently published reprint of this classic study includes an introduction by sociologist Carl Milofsky, which sheds valuable light on the relation between the traditional Community Chest and the modern United Way (New Brunswick, N.J.: Transaction, 1989), vii–xxi.

As communities became more pluralistic—and as previously unempowered constituencies, especially blacks and women, became more insistent in their demands for community services—United Way found it increasingly difficult to serve their needs. Moreover, it found itself facing competition from rival federated charities designed to serve minority interests. In the course of the 1980s, donor designations, which permitted contributors to target particular recipient organizations either positively or negatively, and program support supplanted earlier forms of institutional subvention.

43. 255. See Peter Dobkin Hall, "Understanding Nonprofits Trusteeship," *Philanthropy Monthly* 23, no. 3 (March 1990): 10–15; and the proceedings of the "Lilly Endowment Education Conference, December 3–4, 1990," which contains historical background on this midwestern foundation's developing interest in these issues and summaries of more than thirty different leadership/education projects currently funded by the endowment. Similar efforts are being underwritten by another important midwestern philanthropy, the Kellogg Foundation.

44. See Sidney Blumenthal, *The Rise of the Counter-Establishment: From Conservative Ideology to Political Power* (New York: Harper & Row, 1988). See also Smith, *The Idea Brokers.*

45. See Estelle James, ed., *The Nonprofit Sector in International Perspective: Studies in Comparative Culture and Policy* (New York: Oxford University Press, 1989); Virginia Hodgkinson, ed., *The Nonprofit Sector (NGO's) in the United States and Abroad: Cross-Cultural Perspectives–1990 Spring Research Forum Working Papers* (Washington. D.C.: Independent Sector, 1990); and James Joseph, *The Charitable Impulse: Wealth and Social Conscience in Communities and Cultures outside the United States* (New York: Foundation Center, 1989). For background on this sudden interest in international dimensions, see Anne Lowry Bailey, "Leaders of Philanthropy Call on Foundations to Join Forces, Seek Solutions to Global Ills," *Chronicle of Philanthropy* 2, no. 3 (November 1989); and Stephen G. Greene, "For U.S. Philanthropy, Opportunity in the Turmoil of Eastern Europe," *Chronicle of Philanthropy* 2, no. 4 (November 28, 1989).

CHAPTER 10

A Brief History of Tax Policy Changes Affecting Charitable Organizations

GARY N. SCRIVNER

Introduction—The Tariff Act of 1894: Just the Beginning?

Charitable organizations have historically been defined in large part by reference to their status as organizations exempt from taxation under specific provisions of the Internal Revenue Code including Sections 501, 521, 526, 527 and 528. While ". . . federal tax law is only one of several bodies of law that bear on nonprofits, its impact is particularly pervasive in terms of both positive encouragement and extensive regulation and oversight."[1] Initially this connection to the Tax Code most likely arose out of the necessity to define those entities subject to income, excise or other taxes. One commentator concluded: "While it is clear, in retrospect, that many of the exemption provisions have long outlived their historic justification, it is also clear in contemporary application that many of them continue to play a very crucial role in the law of tax exempt organizations."[2]

The law's evolution over the last century clearly was ". . . not the result of any planned legislative scheme . . . (but was) enacted . . . by a variety of legislators for a variety of reasons."[3] Nonetheless, over time the charitable sector has developed a kind of security in the Tax Code that allows it to pursue its charitable endeavors

and associations with some assurance as to the taxability thereof.[4] This may be due in part to American's belief in the power and responsibility of the individual; a desire for a wider variety of public goods and services than business or government can offer; the desire for maintaining rights of free association; the public's interest in tax reductions through charitable contributions; and a general distrust in big government and its ability to deliver many desired public goods and services in timely and economical way.

Viewed simplistically, there appears to be three basic reasons why these charitable entities continue to be entitled to tax exemption: "heritage," "morality" (or perhaps more correctly, public policy), and "special interests."[5] These reasons are not fully developed exemption theories, but merely describe this evolution. An examination of these reasons may aid in understanding how the charitable sector was formed and how the law effected changes in the very nature of charitable organizations. What follows therefore, is a review of tax law changes over the last one hundred plus years which will explain in large part why nonprofits' reliance on the tax law continues.

Charitable, religious and other types of nonprofit organizations obviously existed well before the Tax Code, thus most tax legislative efforts have recognized a preferred status for these organizations.[6] Exemptions for charity have existed at least since the British Statute of Charitable Uses of 1601.[7] The Tariff Act of 1894 was the first major piece of U.S. tax legislation enacted by Congress that specified the entities subject to taxation.[8] Prior to this, exemption existed merely by virtue of statutory commission. The Tariff Act of 1894, however, imposed a flat two percent tax on corporate income, forcing Congress to face the task of defining the appropriate subjects of tax exemption. Section 32 of the Act provided for exemption for nonprofit charitable, religious, and educational organizations, fraternal beneficiary societies, certain mutual savings banks, and mutual insurance companies. In addition, the income tax charitable contribution deduction originated in the 1894 statute. A year later though, the 1894 Act was declared unconstitutional thereby relegating exempt organizations to the pre-1894 statutory commission state of affairs.[9] Focusing only on charitable organizations as described in the present Internal Revenue Code Section 501(c)(3), the 1894 Act stated, "Nothing herein contained shall apply to corporations, companies or associations organized and conducted solely for charitable, religious or educational purposes."[10] This is not inconsistent with the older English common law concept of philanthropy, nor those concepts of almost any earlier civilization or religion. This illustrates the heritage reasoning for charitable organizations mentioned above. Our early legislators were not setting any precedent by exempting religious or charitable organizations.

The morality or public policy grounds upon which organizations are granted exemption are a derivative of the perception that these organizations perform functions that, in the organizations' absence, government would have to perform. Therefore government should be willing to forgo tax revenues for the public services rendered. In short, because we have a moral obligation to provide these services we should impose as few impediments (such as taxation) as possible on their provision. This is often called the "subsidy theory" of exemption.[11] Exemption is

justified because the qualified organization provides a public benefit, provides public type services to the general public (such as health care or education), or provides ordinary or generic services to a particularly needy public (such as housing or food for the poor or homeless). The Supreme Court has observed: "The State has an affirmative policy that considers these groups as beneficial and stabilizing influences in community life and finds this classification (exemption) useful, desirable and in the public interest."[12] Even as early as 1924, the Court noted: "Evidently the exemption is made in recognition of the benefit which the public derives from corporate activities of the class named, and is intended to aid them when not conducted for private gain."[13] In addition, in a frequently cited case from 1877, the Supreme Court stated: "A charitable use, where neither law nor public policy forbids may be applied to almost anything that tends to promote the well-doing and well-being of social man."[14] These cases illustrate not only the heritage of exemption but represent an affirmation by the courts of the public policy grounds for tax exempt status.

Another aspect of the public policy grounds for exemption is the *way* in which these organizations are formed and provide services: ". . . they are said to deliver goods and services more efficiently, more innovatively, or otherwise better than other suppliers."[15] This speaks to the issue of big government and its ability to provide or interest in providing public goods or services to diverse, geographically limited (or widely dispersed persons), or very small populations. For example, nonprofit groups formed to assist persons affected by a localized weather emergency might be granted exemption and could certainly respond to such an emergency more quickly and specifically than the federal government. In addition: ". . . charities' very existence is said to promote pluralism and diversity, which are taken to be either inherently desirable or intimately related to our liberal democratic values."[16] Exemption thus encourages the expression of our constitutionally guaranteed rights of freedom of intimate association (personal liberty) and expressive association (free speech).[17] In summary exemption is justified because these organizations provide important public services or mundane services to underprivileged populations, and they do so in ways which may be more efficient than government or forprofit business and more politically and constitutionally correct than if provided by government.

The special interest consideration underlying the concept of exemption, may be illustrated by examining some of the categories under Section 501, other than Section 501(c)(3), such as Section 501(c)(5) labor, agricultural, or horticultural organizations, Section 501(c)(6) business leagues, chambers of commerce, or trade associations. Section 501(c)(9) employee beneficiary societies, or Section 501(c)(19) veterans' organizations. Each of these types of entitles (and numerous others), are granted exemptions generally because of the political power these special interest groups represent or the legislature's feeling these groups (veterans particularly) should be rewarded for past services to the country. These classifications also lend credence to the diversity and free association argument for exemption mentioned above. The demographics of the nonprofit sector reflect this diversity. As of 1992, there were over 1,140,000 exempt organizations including some 546,000 Section 501(c)(3) organizations (excluding churches).[18] A mere one-percent of these organizations controlled approximately seventy percent of the total assets and expenditures of the entire sector.[19] Thus, there are literally hundreds of thousands of small community based groups often formed to support a special interest of that community. These issues have continued to play a part in tax policy affecting nonprofits throughout the twentieth century.

Revenue Act of 1913, to 1950

Although the 1894 Act succumbed to constitutional challenge, the Sixteenth Amendment to the Constitution was later ratified by the states paving the way for the federal income tax. The Revenue Act of 1913 contained measures comparable to the 1894 Act and permanently established tax exemption for certain organizations. At least one commentator has indicated Congress believed these organizations should

not be taxed and found that proposition sufficiently obvious as to not warrant extensive explanation.[20] This argument is supported by the fact that the Committee Reports for the 1913 Act contain no explanation for the inclusion of these provisions. To tax these entities in the same way as for-profit businesses would be to disavow a part of our nation's heritage. Alexis de Tocqueville commented on this heritage in his masterpiece *Democracy in America* first published in 1830:

> Americans of all ages, all conditions, and all dispositions constantly form associations. They have not only commercial and manufacturing companies, in which all take part, but associations of a thousand other kinds, religious, moral, serious, futile, general or restricted, enormous or diminutive. The Americans make associations to give entertainments, to found seminarys, to build inns, to construct churches, to diffuse books, to send missionaries to the antipods, in this manner they found hospitals, prisons and schools. If it is proposed to inculcate truth or to foster some feeling by encouragement of a great example, they form a society. Wherever at the head of some new undertaking you see the government in France or a man of rank in England, in the United States you will be sure to find an association.[21]

This comment was of course made some eighty years prior to the enactment of the Revenue Act of 1913. The issue of heritage was further discussed by John Stewart Mill in *On Liberty,* published in 1859:

> With individuals in voluntary associations there are varied experiments and endless diversity of experience. What the State can usefully do is to make itself a central depository, and active circulator and difusor, of the experience resulting from many trials. Its business is to enable each experimentalist to benefit by the experiments of others, instead of tolerating no experiments but its own.[22]

Exemption from taxation for certain types of not-for-profit organizations is clearly a principle larger than the Internal Revenue Code. Citizens combating problems and reaching solutions on a collective basis, in associations, are inherent in the very nature of American societal structure. Thus, the Revenue Act of 1913 did little to change the nature or existence of not-for-profit organizations, it merely served to define those organizations for the purpose of administrative convenience in the collection of an income tax. One major difference in the 1913 Act and the 1894 Act is that the statute in 1913 contained a reference to scientific purposes—an apparent byproduct of the Industrial Age. In addition, the prohibition concerning the inurement of net income to private persons was added by the 1913 Act.[23] Subsequent revenue acts continued expansion of the various charitable categories. The Revenue Act of 1918 added the prevention of cruelty to children and animals, and in 1921, community chest funds, foundations, and literary groups were also made tax exempt. Arguably this would not have been necessary had the term "charitable" been used in the English common law sense. Had Congress intended to rely on the common law definition of charity, there would have been no need to add to the statutory law at all as was done in 1913.[24]

The exemption requirements were generally carried forward to the Revenue Act of 1934 at which time a rule was added that no substantial part of the activities of an exempt organization can involve the carrying on of propaganda or attempting to influence legislation.[25] The Revenue Acts of 1936, 1938, and 1939 did little to affect the rules for exempt organizations, with two exceptions. The Revenue Act of 1936 made the charitable contribution deduction available to regular corporations.[26] In addition, the Revenue Act of 1938 stated: "The exemption from taxation of money or property devoted to charitable and other purposes is based upon the theory that the government is compensated for the loss of revenue by its relief from the financial burden which would otherwise have to be met by appropriations from public funds and by the benefits resulting from the promotion of the general welfare."[27] This is a direct reference to the subsidy theory mentioned above. It appears to have

been a long held and widely accepted justification for exemption.

The tax code was recodified by the 1939 Act in an attempt to bring together all income tax provisions scattered throughout federal law into one place and one code. The form of the exemption statute however, remained essentially unchanged. References to the tax code after 1939 were identified as "the 1939 Code." These references would change again following the 1954 Act and the 1986 Act as described further below. Tax legislative efforts were practically nonexistent during the war years and shortly thereafter. Obviously the Congress had more pressing matters to deal with. Thus, there were no significant changes to the law of tax exempt organizations during this time.

The Revenue Act of 1950

The feeder organization rules were added to the law in 1950 as a legislative mandate against the destination of income argument. Feeder organizations were separate trades or businesses owned by a nonprofit, and which turned over all their net income to, a nonprofit organization. Generally these trades or businesses were unrelated to the nonprofits purpose or activities. The destination of income argument viewed the use of these organizations income for charitable purposes to be of a greater consequence than the source of the funds. The principle problem with the destination of income argument was that it allowed exempt organizations to undercut forprofit business which, of course, must take taxes into account in pricing their goods and services. The House Ways and Means Committee Report accompanying the Revenue Act of 1950 concluded the feeder organization provision was intended: ". . . to deny exemption of a trade or business organization. . . . It appears clear to your committee that such an organization is not itself carrying out an exempt purpose. Moreover, it obviously is in direct competition with other taxable businesses."[28]

The Senate Finance Committee Report accompanying the corresponding Senate version of the bill states that the provision applies "to organizations operated for the primary purpose of carrying on a trade or business for profit, as for example, a feeder corporation whose business is the manufacture of automobiles for the ultimate profit of an educational institution."[29] This provision focused primarily on the deprivation of tax-exempt status to organizations whose primary purpose was a commercial one. In addition to the feeder organization rules, the unrelated business income tax rules were added in response to perceived unfair competition by nonprofits.[30] The primary objective of the unrelated business income tax was to eliminate this source of unfair competition by placing those unrelated activities on the same tax footing as the private business endeavors with which they compete. The House Ways and Means Committee Report on the Revenue Act of 1950 further observed:

> The problem at which tax on unrelated business income is directed here is that of unfair competition. The tax-free status of (exempt) organizations enables them to use their profit tax free to expand operations, while their competitors can expand only with the profits remaining after taxes. Also, a number of examples have arisen where these organizations have, in effect, used their tax exemption to buy an ordinary business. That is, they have acquired the business with no investment on their part and paid for it in installments out of subsequent earnings—a procedure, which usually could not be followed if the business were taxable.[31]

The taxation of unrelated income was seen as a more effective sanction in the long run for authentic enforcement of the requirements for tax exempt status than the denial of exempt status. Only if a substantial portion of an organization's income is from unrelated sources is an organization to be denied tax exemption. We will see this theme repeated in the 1990s discussed further below.

1954 to 1969

A major restructuring of the Code occurred in 1954, much like the one in 1939, resulting in a complete renumbering of all the sections of the Code to the system we continue to use to this day. When we talk of a Section 501(c)(3) organization we are referring to the number assigned by the 1954 Act. Thus, the 1954 Code has had a great deal to do with how we have defined exempt organizations over the past 40 plus years, how they were formed, and how the rules have been enforced. The Act also added some new rules to the exemption statute. The list of organizations was expanded to include organizations formed for the purpose of "testing for public safety," and Section 501(c)(3) organizations were forbidden to "participate in, or intervene in (including the publishing or distributing of statements), any political campaign on behalf of any candidate for public office."[32]

It wasn't until 1959 that the Treasury Department issued many of the regulations explaining the provisions of the 1950 Act and 1954 Code affecting exempt organizations.[33] At the time, these regulations were considered to be expansion of the definition of the term charitable to one more closely approaching the common law definition.[34] This definition has become the law on the subject.[35]

> The term "charitable" is used in Section 501(c)(3) in its generally accepted legal sense and is, therefore not to be construed as limited by the separate enumeration in (that section) of other tax exempt purposes which may fall within the broad outlines of charity as developed by judicial decisions. Such term includes relief of the poor and distressed or of the underprivileged, advancement of religion, advancement of education or science, erection or maintenance of public buildings, monuments or works, lessening of the burdens of government, and promotion of social welfare by organizations designed to accomplish any of the above purposes, or (i) to lessen neighborhood tensions, (ii) to eliminate prejudice and discrimination, (iii) to defend human and civil rights secured by law, or (iv) to combat community deterioration and juvenile delinquency."[36]

Expansion of the law continued into the 1960s with new exemption categories added in

1968 for "cooperative hospital service organizations" and "cooperative service organizations of operating educational organizations."[37] The beginnings of a distinction between private foundations and public charities first appeared in 1964 with the introduction of different percentage limitations for gifts of property based on 30 percent of adjusted gross income for gifts to public charities versus 20 percent for gifts to private foundations. While no other significant tax legislation affecting charitable organizations was passed until 1969, the sector remained under scrutiny during this period, most notably private charitable grantmaking foundations. Extensive congressional studies were conducted throughout the 1960s because it was thought that these organizations were being used to further private rather than public interests.[38] This too would be repeated in the 1990s.

The Tax Reform Act of 1969

Prior to the 1969 Act, Code Section 503 provided the basic standards of conduct for charitable organizations. The Tax Reform Act of 1969, however, repealed Section 503 and brought into law the most extensive and burdensome changes in tax policy affecting charitable organizations since the Code was first enacted. A series of restrictions, prohibitions, new filing and reporting requirements, and excise taxes were added aimed at deterring or eliminating perceived abusive transactions engaged in by charitable entities, particularly private foundations.[39] In fact, private foundations—as distinguished from public charities—were first clearly defined by the Act.

Generally, a public charity is one that, in connection with accomplishing its exempt purpose, receives a substantial amount of its annual support or revenue from the general public, or supports another charitable organization that does. A private foundation does not.[40] The restrictions on private foundations include limitations on transactions between the foundation and related parties, prohibitions against risky investments, lobbying and political action, and limitations on who the foundation may support.[41]

Some commentators have intimated the 1969 Act resulted in the demise of hundreds of foundations.[42] Despite the changes, however, private foundations appear to have flourished. More than 22,000 private grantmaking foundations now exist, owning assets in excess of $100 billion and making annual grants of over $7 billion.[43] The perceived abuses that led to the enactment of the restrictions contained in the Act, whether or not they existed in fact have been substantially eliminated, at least with respect to private foundations.[44] Perhaps this provides justification for the expansion of these rules to apply them to public charities. This issue will be hotly debated during the 1990s ultimately leading to the adoption of the "intermediate sanctions rules" described further below.

The Tax Reform Act of 1969 also redefined the percentage limitations for deductions of charitable contributions, providing a higher (50 percent) limit for gifts of cash; first enumerated many of the limits for noncash contributions; and restricted the deduction of gifts in trust. The tax laws surrounding charitable contributions and tax exemption have been inextricably linked since the 1969 Act.[45]

One court described these various sanctions as follows: "The language of the Act, its legislative history, the graduated levels of the sanctions imposed, and the almost confiscatory level of the exactions assessed convince us that the exactions in question were intended to curb the described conduct through pecuniary punishment."[46] The Joint Committee explanation of the Act goes on extensively in its listing of the restrictions and limitations.[47] It should be required reading for foundation executives, officers, directors, managers and trustees.

The Tax Reform Act of 1976

The late 1970s and early 1980s were prolific tax act times, many of which have had significant impacts on charitable organizations. The Tax Reform Act of 1976 specifically added to the list of charitable entities, organizations fostering "national or international sports competition (but only if no part of its activities involve the

provision of athletic facilities or equipment),"
and added the safe harbor rules on permissible
legislative activities [Section 501(h)]. These new
lobbying rules were intended to prevent "subjective and selective enforcement."[48] The Act
also exempted small hospitals from the unrelated business income tax rules for income
from certain services provided to other small
hospitals.[49]

The 1976 Act also contained a number of special interest provisions related to exempt organizations other than charitable organizations, including an expanded definition of the term
agricultural for Section 501(c)(5) organizations
and an exclusion from the unrelated business
income tax rules for certain income received by
retirement homes.[50] The adoption of Code Section 528 as part of the 1976 Act clarified the tax
treatment of homeowner's associations. The Act
also added a new category of tax-exempt organizations, commonly referred to as qualified
group legal services plans.[51]

The Revenue Act of 1978

Although the 1978 Act had fewer changes to the
rules affecting charitable organizations than the
1969 and 1976 Acts, the changes were certainly
not insignificant.[52] For instance, Congress believed that the 4 percent excise tax on private
foundations was far in excess of the resources
needed to administer the law of tax exempt organizations.[53] Thus, the tax was reduced from 4
percent to 2 percent for taxable years beginning
after September 30, 1977, and has remained at
this rate to today. However, Congress expressed
concern that the IRS might not be devoting adequate resources to auditing charitable and other
exempt organizations which is what the excise
tax on private foundations pays for.[54] The IRS
was directed to report to Congress on the extent
of its audit activities involving exempt organizations and to notify Congress of "any administrative problems experienced in the course of enforcement of the Internal Revenue laws with
respect to exempt organizations."[55] The Revenue
Act of 1978 also added a provision allowing
bingo game income realized by most exempt or-

ganizations to be exempt from the unrelated
business income tax rules.[56]

During the late 1970s and early 1980s, a number of pieces of legislation were introduced that
could have had significant impact on the structure and viability of the nonprofit sector. One of
the bills that failed to pass (the Tax Restructuring Act of 1979) would have eliminated charitable contribution deductions for 84 percent of
the taxpaying public.[57] This provision, as first
proposed in 1977 by President Carter, would
have narrowed the availability of the contribution deduction, effectively making it a tax shelter for the wealthy.[58] The belief that the charitable contribution deduction benefits only the
wealthy however, has been shown to be incor-
rect. Charitable giving is pervasive among all income levels with charitable giving proportion-
ately higher at lower income levels.[59]

The Economic Recovery
Tax Act of 1981

President Reagan signed the Economic Recovery
Tax Act of 1981 into law on August 13, 1981, and
for the first time individuals could avail themselves of the so-called above the line charitable
contribution deduction.[60] The term "above the
line" means the charitable contribution deduction is taken against gross income to arrive at
adjusted gross income—not from adjusted gross
income as an itemized deduction under the general rules. This treatment allowed taxpayers to
take charitable contribution deductions even if
they didn't itemize deductions. This addition to
the law appeared to be a major shift in tax policy
affecting charitable organizations and was
viewed by the nonprofit sector and Congress as
important to the future viability of the sector.

> It (the new legislation) would restore a bit more
> independence and vitality to the voluntary sec-
> tor. It will add a bit of the ability of ordinary
> working men and women to determine how
> and on what some of his or her money is spent.
> It will in some small measure retard the process
> that has been described as a slow but steady
> conquest of the private sector by the public. Ac-

companing a mounting wariness toward government, there is a widening appreciation by the American people that the unique and vital role played by private, nonprofit organizations in our nation's economy. This appreciation constitutes the fundamental rationale for this legislation first introduced in the 95th Congress. Moreover, it is familiar to every American as the basic principle of Federalism that the National Government should assume only those responsibilities that cannot satisfactorily be carried out by the states, the localities, and by the myriad private structures and organizations, both formal and informal, that comprise the American society.[61]

But, the government giveth and the government taketh away. Shortly after the passage of this favorable tax legislation, came a number of President Reagan's budget cuts that are thought to have resulted in a loss of revenue of $110.4 billion to the nonprofit sector during the years 1981 through 1984.[62]

A number of other important changes occurred, including one relating to annual income distribution requirements for private foundations. Prior to the 1981 Act, foundations were required to distribute the greater of their adjusted net income from investments or their so-called minimum investment return (generally defined as 5 percent of the fair market of the foundation's investment assets). This "greater of" requirement was eliminated by the Act, thus allowing foundations to distribute only their minimum investment return regardless of the amount of their net income. Any income in excess of 5 percent distribution required could be accumulated by the foundation.[63] Some authors have suggested that this change actually resulted in reduced distributions to charity, but the overall result appears to have been favorable by allowing foundations to perpetuate their existence for future charitable needs.[64]

Another change from the 1981 Act that was important to charity, particularly for scientific and educational organizations, was the addition of a tax credit for increasing research and experimentation activities. The Act contained a 25 percent tax credit for increasing expenditures

for research and experimentation in a trade or business. Since much of this type of research is contracted out by private businesses to charitable scientific and educational organizations, it became an important and greatly enlarged source of revenue. It appears that companies entered into research they may not have undertaken without the added incentive of a tax credit.[65] A number of other changes directly or indirectly benefited charitable organizations, not the least of which was a reduction in corporate tax rates, which coincidentally reduced the tax rates imposed on unrelated business taxable income.

Tax Equity and Fiscal Responsibility Act of 1982

As was previously mentioned, the Tax Reform Act of 1976 added to the list of exempt organizations those that foster national or international sports competition, but only if no part of their activities involve the provision of athletic facilities or equipment. TEFRA lifted the restriction on the provision of athletic facilities or equipment for certain sports organizations. It is conjectured that the change was made to facilitate the improvement of the U.S. Olympic Committee's training facility in Colorado Springs in preparation for the 1984 Los Angeles Olympics. Although this Act was intended to simplify and restructure the tax Code, this was really the only direct change of any significance affecting charitable organizations.

The Deficit Reduction Act of 1984

The Deficit Reduction Act of 1984 was one of the most comprehensive and complex revisions ever attempted of our tax system. While many of its provisions were aimed at cracking down on what Congress believed were tax-abusive transactions (such as tax shelters), the news for exempt organizations was generally favorable. The Act was in fact, two acts in one. The first part (Division A) was aimed at tax reform, and the

second part (Division B) was for spending reduction. The Act made a number of very favorable changes to the tax rules affecting private
foundations in an attempt to mitigate some of
the negative results resulting from the 1969 Tax
Reform Act. These changes included increasing
the limit on deductibility of contributions to
private foundations for certain gifts and allowing a five year carryforward period for excess
contributions where none previously existed;[66]
exempting certain "operating" foundations
(such as museums) from the 2 percent excise tax
on net investment income; liberalizing the definition of persons who are related to a foundation; reducing the 2 percent excise tax to 1
percent if the foundation makes additional
charitable distributions; limiting the amount of
administrative expenses a foundation may
claim; and, giving the IRS discretionary authority to abate certain excise taxes imposed by the
1969 Act. Although generally favorable, all of
these changes greatly complicated an already
complex area of the tax law.

The Act also changed reporting and disclosure requirements for exempt organizations and
individuals with respect to deductions for charitable contributions requiring appraisals, reports
for noncash gifts above a certain amount and
penalties for overvaluation. Other changes include the tax-exempt leasing provisions, which
virtually eliminated the sale-leaseback as a form
of financing for exempt organizations, changes
to the UBTI rules, and exemption for certain
childcare organizations. The liberalization expressed through these provisions indicates
a favorable shift in policy reflective of the
President's emphasis on self-sufficiency and
voluntarism.

The Tax Reform Act of 1986

As a result of continued pressure to address the
burgeoning deficit, President Reagan's tax proposals to the Congress for fairness, growth, and
simplicity were submitted to Congress on May
29, 1985. Most of these proposals found their
way into the Tax Reform Act of 1986. Interestingly, the 1954 Code was renamed the 1986

Code without any significant restructuring or
renumbering as had occurred in 1954. Some of
these changes however, were expected to have
significant adverse effects on charity. For instance, *The Chronicle of Higher Education* estimated that charitable contributions would decrease by at least 17 percent if the President's
proposals were adopted.[67] While there was disagreement about the effect a reduction in
marginal tax rates would have on charitable
contributions, it is now apparent that the sim-
plification efforts resulted in fewer people itemizing deductions and, for that reason, reduced
charitable deductions could have resulted.[68]

Other changes affecting charitable organizations included the elimination of trusts as income shifting devices, repeal of the deduction
for charitable contributions for non-itemizers,
limiting other itemized deductions, repeal of income averaging and research credits, and an
add-back of all itemized deductions for alternative minimum tax purposes.[69] The 1986 changes
in tax policy reflect a new emphasis in public
policy, mirroring public discontent with the di-
nosaur of a tax code that existed. The Code's
complexity and perceived inequity, despite the
implicit fairness of graduated tax rates, may
have resulted in frustration, anger, and, in some
cases, revolt. A simplified filing procedure, coupled with elimination of tax breaks for the
wealthy, was intended ultimately to result in increased revenue. Unfortunately the 1986 Act did
little to accomplish these goals. In fact, the Act
was the longest and most complex piece of tax
legislation ever considered and may have increased the frustration and confusion of the
general public.

The 1987 Revenue Act and the Omnibus Budget Reconciliation Act of 1989

One of the primary movements of the 1980s for
tax exempt organizations was the increased emphasis on self-sufficiency precipitated by declines in traditional funding sources and continued increases in demand for services. The Urban
Institute's Nonprofit Sector Project estimated

that federal support for the nonprofit sector declined by more than $110.4 billion between 1980 and 1984.[70] Yet the sector continued to experience exceptional growth. In fact, the 1980s and 1990s were periods of unparalleled prosperity for nonprofits. For example between 1977 and 1990, total expenditures for the sector grew some 240 percent from $114 billion to $389 billion, and total assets (excluding religious organizations) grew 427 percent from $134 billion in 1975 to about $707 billion in 1990.[71] Much of this growth has been financed through commercial ventures and other nontraditional sources of income. For example, there has been a dramatic increase in the use of taxable subsidiary corporations to assist in the management of for-profit enterprises and to protect the favored tax status of nonprofit organizations. The Internal Revenue Service issued some 593 private letter rulings to charitable organizations authorizing multi-entity structures between 1977 and 1986. In the prior decade, only eight such rulings were issued.[72]

The presumed increase in income-producing commercial activities is also supported by source of income data provided by the Treasury Department. Although contributions in total dollar amount rose, contributions as a percent of total revenue decreased from 17 percent to 13 percent—while other revenue (such as business receipts, interest, dividends, rents. royalties, and other income) grew from 57 percent in 1946 to 75 percent in 1978.[73] With the increased commercial activity by nonprofit organizations came increased scrutiny by business, Congress, and especially the Internal Revenue Service. In 1983, a coalition was formed called the Business Coalition for Fair Competition. Sponsored in large part by the U.S. Small Business Administration, the Business Coalition expressed its concern over competition from tax exempt entities through a 1984 SBA report, *Unfair Competition by Nonprofit Organizations with Small Business.*[74] U. S. Small Business Administration, (3rd ed., 1984). Competition was also on the agenda of the August 1986 White House Conference on Small Business and the subject of a special report by the Government Accounting Office to the Joint Committee on Taxation of the U. S.

Congress.[75] In 1987, hearings on commercial activities of nonprofit organizations began before the House Ways and Means Committee and included testimony by the Deputy Assistant Secretary of the Treasury for Tax Policy who offered recommendations and suggestions for further legislative debate.[76]

Much of the debate was over the unrelated business income tax (UBIT) statutes and their ability to eliminate or control unfair competition. The Revenue Act of 1987 originally contained a number of provisions that would have extended the scope of the UBIT, but the provisions did not make it into the final Bill. The Act did contain new taxes on excess lobbying and political campaign activities as well as fundraising disclosure requirements.[77]

The 1984 Small Business Administration report contained a number of suggested alternatives for dealing with the issue of inter-sector competition including:

1. A complete federal prohibition on all unrelated activities;
2. Higher tax rates for unrelated activities;
3. Fundamental changes to the definition of UBIT;
4. A percentage limit on permissible unrelated activities, and;
5. A repeal of some or all statutory exceptions to the UBIT.[78]

In a March 25, 1988 memorandum from House Ways and Means Oversight Subcommittee Chairman Pickle (D–Tex), many of these options for changes to the UBIT were discussed. Specific recommendations included restricting the use of taxable subsidiaries and joint ventures; elimination of various exceptions and exclusions to the UBIT; and application of the UBIT to specific commercial activities of nonprofits such as gift shop/bookstore sales, sales of medical equipment and devices, income from health and fitness programs, travel and tour services, food sales, certain veterinary services, hotel facility income, and advertising income. One of the most controversial proposals was the redefinition of unrelated business income, including modification or elimination of the substantially related test. Substitution of an "inherently commercial test" would have extended the UBIT to certain activities considered *per se* unrelated, such as the sale of goods and services.

The Oversight Subcommittee also considered a "directly related test" to replace the current statutory requirements. Under this approach, only income from directly related activities would have escaped taxation. In an April 15, 1988, letter from Assistant Treasury Secretary Chapoton to Congressman Pickle, Chapoton complained that a directly related test would "wreak administrative havoc among exempt organizations and, possibly, within the Internal Revenue Service."[79] The assistant secretary pointed out that such a basic change in the structure of the tax could have an adverse affect on legitimate activities and would require a complete "reexamination of all activities currently considered to be substantially related."[80] Similarly, Chapoton dismissed the "inherently commercial" concept as unclear and requiring a total review of exempt organization activity.

The Treasury Department was not the only one who opposed these options. Over 300 letters were received from nonprofit groups opposing these changes. In June 1987, IRS Commissioner Lawrence Gibbs told the subcommittee he did not want a piecemeal approach to amending the statutes. And, in testimony to the subcommittee on May 9, 1988, Chapoton made it clear that the Treasury Department did not want a major overhaul of the UBIT statutes. His sharpest criticisms were reserved for fundamental changes to the substantially related test in the current statute. Perhaps these comments and other testimony positively influenced the subcommittee, as Chairman Pickle made a point of indicating the subcommittee and Treasury are "moving in tandem on the UBIT issue" and essentially backed away from a fundamental change in policy.[81]

The substantiality test of the UBIT statute has been loosely interpreted by the courts and the IRS, but it appears to be the most acceptable legal model giving the courts sufficient flexibility to enforce public policy. It appears to be consistent with current legal theory in that it is up to the courts to evaluate individual facts and circumstances in making decisions about the nature, scope, and motivation of each nonprofit activity. Ultimately, the Oversight Subcommittee declined to back any fundamental change to the substantially related test of the statute. But, this is an area where exempt organizations can most likely expect significant future policy changes.

The 1989 Omnibus Budget Reconciliation Act contained little of interest to nonprofits. However, the Act did direct the Treasury Department to conduct a study of whether the public interest would be served by increased disclosure of financial information by nonprofits. This became an important topic of debate during the 1990s.

While the 1970s and early 1980s were prolific tax act times, changes made to the exemption and unrelated business income sections in 1976, 1978, 1981, 1982, 1984, 1986, 1987 and 1989 tax acts were relatively minor and did not affect the basic exemption requirements or UBIT rules. The question of so-called unfair competition had become one of the most hotly contested tax questions of the 1980s. For-profit businesses argued that nonprofits had a competitive advantage.[82] Nonprofits argued that for-profit business had encroached upon traditional nonprofit activities (such as health care, childcare, health, and fitness facilities). That is the ends justified the means.[83] This debate and the scrutiny of the sector it engendered would not go away.

The 1990s

The Revenue Reconciliation Act of 1990 and the Energy Policy Act of 1992 had almost no impact on nonprofits. The Omnibus Budget Reconciliation Act of 1993, like the 1989 Act with a nearly identical title, also contained little of interest or impact to the nonprofit sector. The 1993 Act however did introduce additional rules governing the deductibility of lobbying and political activity expenditures and expanded the disclosure rules for these activities for nonprofit associations.[84]

The major piece of tax legislation with respect to both complexity and impact on the nonprofit sector adopted during the 1990s was passed in 1996. In fact, four separate pieces of tax legislation were passed in 1996: the Small Business Job Protection Act; the Health Insurance Portability and Accountability Act; the Personal Responsibility and Work Opportunity Reconciliation (Welfare Reform) Act; and the Taxpayer Bill of Rights 2 Act, all of which contained provisions affecting nonprofits.[85] Although the lion's share of tax law changes were contained in the Small Business Job Protection Act, the Taxpayer Bill of Rights 2 (TBOR2) Act had the greater impact on nonprofits as you will see.[86] The Welfare Reform Act's primary tax impact was limited to making the earned income tax credit more difficult to claim, an issue of only tangential interest to nonprofits.[87] The Health Insurance Portability and Accountability Act added two new categories of exempt organizations: exemption was provided for state-sponsored organizations providing health coverage for high-risk individuals; and for state-sponsored workmen's compensation reinsurance organizations.[88] The Small Business Job Protection Act contained provisions expanding the reach of the UBTI rules to include income from foreign corporations; allowed certain nonprofits to hold stock in Subchapter S small business corporations; and provided tax exempt status for "qualified charitable risk pools" and "qualified state-sponsored prepaid tuition and educational savings programs."[89]

The provisions in the TBOR2 Act affecting nonprofits were extensive and resulted from a period of intense scrutiny and criticism of charitable organizations. Throughout the late 1980s and early 1990s numerous stories were reported of the failed, wasteful, ineffective, or rich and greedy nonprofit, or of the self-serving, greedy or downright dishonest nonprofit manager.[90] These were mainstream reports in such respected publications as *The Wall Street Journal, The Philadelphia Inquirer,* and *The Denver Post.*[91] The purported abuses were believed to be widespread and growing.[92] A legal and ethical crisis was believed by many to be gripping the sector.[93] Whether there was truly erosion of the ethics of the sector or merely a crisis of confidence stemming from a few highly publicized

anecdotes was apparently irrelevant to the Congress. Then Assistant Secretary of the Treasury for Tax Policy, Leslie Samuels, admitted the evidence supporting the change in law was anecdotal.[94] It was also implied at the time that the public hearings leading up to these changes were stacked with government "yesmen" and the nonprofit sector was under-represented.[95]

TBOR2 added new mandatory disclosures of financial data by nonprofits and most importantly, added new penalties for transactions with insiders called "intermediate sanctions."[96] The reason these rules were called "intermediate" is because they do not go as far as the ultimate sanction which is revocation of exemption when an illegal act by a charity or its related parties is to be punished. These new penalties and excise taxes (up to 200 percent of the amount of the illegal act) apply to Section 501(c)(3) charities and Section 501(c)(4) social welfare organizations and were aimed generally at any "excess benefit" provided to any related party.[97] Excess benefit includes any compensation in excess of reasonable compensation, and any transfer, lease, license, or loan of property to, for the benefit of, or from a related party if the related party underpays the charity or the charity overpays the related party. An excise tax at an initial rate of 25 percent is imposed on any insider engaged in these transactions. There is also an excise tax imposed on any organization manager who knowingly approves an excess benefit transaction.[98]

If intermediate sanctions are imposed that would be the IRS' sole sanction. That is, the IRS could not later revoke the organization's exempt status due to that specific violation. The law also made provision for abatement of the tax if the violation was corrected and the organization could demonstrate the violation was due to reasonable cause.[99]

There was surprisingly little opposition to the idea of intermediate sanctions in lieu of exemption revocations.[100] Regulations issued in 1999 answered many of the unasked and unanswered questions of the statute such as what standard would be used for determining whether an organization is paying reasonable compensation. These changes will have a long-lasting impact on the sector and it is believed, will usher in a new era of openness and accountability.[101]

The Taxpayer Relief Act of 1997 contained a number of changes, both favorable and unfavorable to nonprofits. The Act clarified the exempt status of state worker's compensation funds, and state-sponsored health care plans for high-risk individuals. It also liberalized the rules affecting cooperative hospital service corporations and the UBTI rules dealing with sponsorships and tightened the rules related to income from subsidiaries. There were other housekeeping changes expanding the homeowner's association exemption, clarifying abatement provisions in the intermediate sanctions statutes, and conforming reporting requirements to the related excise tax sections.[102]

The changes in tax law affecting nonprofits continued into 1998 with the Internal Revenue Service Restructuring and Reform Act of 1998.[103] Under this plan to restructure the IRS a separate component of the Service will serve tax-exempt organizations, employee plans and state and local governments. The intent is to provide greater access and oversight, improved compliance and responsiveness, more efficient operation and processing, and a process to identify legal and compliance issues.[104]

Conclusion

In a 1994 poll, the Daniel Yankelovich Group found for the National Civic League that public confidence in the voluntary sector had dropped substantially since 1990. The study indicated as much as 17 percent of the population had lost confidence in nonprofits and religious organizations and concluded, ". . . this loss of public confidence suggests citizens increasingly distrust all organized institutions as well as the people associated with them."[105] Similarly, in a Harris poll it was reported that in the 1960s approximately 61 percent of Americans placed a high degree of confidence in the people running higher education, while today, only 25 percent feel the same way.[106] The source of this increasing distrust is unclear. Surely problem organiza-

tions existed before the exposure of the few egregious examples of the 1980s and early 1990s. It is possible however, the reporting of these incidences has affected the public's perceptions of the sector as a whole.

Recently the *Wall Street Journal* reported the IRS had approved a record 46,887 exemption applications in 1995.[107] At least one author has suggested it has become easier and easier to obtain tax-exempt status perhaps adding to the growing distrust of voluntary organizations.[108] And in a Government Accounting Office Report the Service was sharply criticized as being too lenient in the granting of exemptions.[109] For 1992, the GAO reported the IRS received more than 57,000 exemption applications of which they approved nearly 44,000 (77 percent) and denied fewer than 1000 (2 percent). The others were either withdrawn or were still pending.

The sector has grown substantially in size and economic impact.[110] In fact, the charitable group was the fastest growing sector of the American economy from 1975 to 1995 increasing its proportion of the national income from 5.2 percent to 5.7 percent between 1975 and 1984 and jumping to an astounding 8 percent of gross domestic product by 1990. Gross domestic product as a whole grew some 52 percent during this period while total revenue for the charitable subset grew by more than 225 percent.[111] As of 1992 there were more than 1.1 million tax exempt organizations of which more than 550,000 were charitable organizations. In 1954 when the modern exemption statute was codified, there were fewer than 100,000.[112] This rapid unregulated growth is one of the reasons given for the scandals of recent years.[113] What this all means is:

> Current conditions indicate that the potential for conflict will not abate, and probably will intensify. The economic importance of the nonprofit sector has grown at a significantly increased rate. Nonprofits are increasingly undertaking new activities and adopting new methods of operation which warrant a reexamination of their societal role and the attributes of nonprofit status. . . . The wide range government-bestowed privileges for nonprofits, pres-

sures on lawmakers and regulators . . . and the decentralized system of agencies . . . employed to regulate specific aspects of the relationship between nonprofits and government . . . ensure fertile ground for controversy and conflict. . . . The increased pressures on nonprofits resulting from decreased government funding may suggest the need for closer monitoring of nonprofits to ensure that nonprofits are legitimately pursuing the public good in a manner that inspires public confidence.[114]

Thus there have been innumerable changes in tax policy over the past one hundred years, with just as many reasons why these changes have occurred. The three bases—tradition, public policy, and special interests—have all played a part in shaping tax policy and, ultimately, the very nature of nonprofit organizations. It is likely these factors will continue to shape American tax policy affecting nonprofits. It is also likely, given the public's apparent interest in increased accountability, that we will continue to see tax exempt organizations as the subject of subsequent tax legislation. The sector needs to decide whether to oppose further legislation out of hand or, "it follows that a wise approach is to coopt the regulatory process."[115]

Notes

1. Atkinson, Rob, *Major Legal Topics to be Covered in a Law School Course on Nonprofit Organizations,* Conference Proceedings, RESEARCH AGENDA: LEGAL ISSUES AFFECTING NONPROFIT CORPORATIONS, 3 (N.Y.U. School of Law, Nov. 10–11, 1989) (*hereinafter* RESEARCH AGENDA: LEGAL ISSUES).

2. McGovern, J., *The Exemption Provisions of Subchapter F,* TAX LAWYER, 29, 523.

3. *Id. See also,* Facchina, Bazil, Showell, Evan, and Stone, Jan E., PRIVILEGES & EXEMPTIONS ENJOYED BY NONPROFIT ORGANIZATIONS: A CATALOG AND SOME THOUGHTS ON NONPROFIT POLICYMAKING, 6, (N.Y.U. School of Law, 1993) (*hereinafter,* PRIVILEGES AND EXEMPTIONS) ("The privileges and exemptions granted nonprofits have evolved on an *ad hoc* basis. . . . Congress . . . has not proven an effective architect of comprehensive nonprofit policy. It has been unable even to articulate a clear policy for regulating non-

profits. Exemptions have been created based on the exigencies of the nonprofit sector.")

4. Odendahl, Teresa, *Independent Foundations and Wealthy Donors: An Overview, in* AMERICA'S WEALTHY AND THE FUTURE OF FOUNDATIONS, ed. Teresa Odendahl, 1987. (In a society suffused with taxes and reliant on them as engines of social and economic policy, the union of charity and taxes is in reality indissoluble—and controversy inevitable. Charity seems destined to be enmeshed in tax policy debate . . . because, over the years, we have come to entrust to the tax system a central role in the nourishment and regulation of the nonprofit sector.")

5. McGovern, J., *The Exemption Provisions of Subchapter F, supra,* note ii.

6. Belknap, J., *The Federal Income Tax Exemption of Charitable Organizations: History and Underlying Policy, in* COMMISSION ON PRIVATE PHILANTHROPY AND PUBLIC NEEDS (*hereinafter,* FILER COMMISSION REPORT), Department of the Treasury, *reprinted in* IV RESEARCH PAPERS, TAXES (1977). ("The functions of the Service with respect to philanthropy result from history and convenience, not rational design.")

7. Bittker, B., and Rahdert, T., *The Exemption of Nonprofit Organizations from Federal Income Taxation,* 85 YALE L. J. 3 (Jan. 1976).

8. Tariff Act of 1894, 28 Stat. 556.

9. *Pollock v. Farmer's Loan and Trust Co.,* 157 U.S. 428 (1895).

10. *Supra,* note vii.

11. Atkinson, RESEARCH AGENDA: LEGAL ISSUES, *supra,* note 1.

12. *Walz v. Tax Commissioner,* 397 U.S. 664,673 (1970).

13. *Trinidad v. Sagrada Orden de Predicadores,* 263 U.S. 578, 581 (1924).

14. *Ould v. Washington Hospital for Foundlings,* 95 U.S. 303 (1877).

15. Atkinson, RESEARCH AGENDA: LEGAL ISSUES, *supra,* note 1, at 11.

16. *Id.*

17. Hopkins, Bruce R., THE LAW OF TAX-EXEMPT ORGANIZATIONS, 5 (7th ed., 1998).

18. Hodgkinson, Virginia A., Weitzman, Murray S., Toppe, Christopher M., and Noga, Stephen M., NONPROFIT ALMANAC 1992–1993: DIMENSIONS OF THE INDEPENDENT SECTOR (1992) (*hereinafter* NONPROFIT ALMANAC).

19. *Id.*

20. Hopkins, THE LAW OF TAX-EXEMPT ORGANIZATIONS, *supra,* note xvii.

21. Toqueville, A. de, DEMOCRACY IN AMERICA (1830).

22. Mill, J.S., ON LIBERTY (1859).

23. Hopkins, THE LAW OF TAX-EXEMPT ORGANIZA-TIONS, *supra,* note xvii.

24. *Id.*

25. Revenue Act of 1934, 48 Stat. 700.

26. Revenue Act of 1936, 49 Stat. 1674.

27. Revenue Act of 1938, House Report 1438, 61st Congress, 1st Session (1939).

28. Revenue Act of 1950, House Report 2319, 81st Congress, 2nd Session (1950).

29. Revenue Act of 1950, Senate Report 2375, 81st Congress, 2nd Session (1950).

30. The term *unrelated business taxable income* is defined in the Internal Revenue Code (Sections 511–514) generally any "trade or business, regularly carried on which is not substantially related" to the organization's exempt purpose. This is a highly technical area of tax law. Further description and analysis of what constitutes an unrelated trade or business is believed to be beyond the scope of this analysis. However, the reader is referred to Hopkins, THE LAW OF TAX-EXEMPT ORGANIZATIONS, *supra,* note xvii.

31. House Report 2319, *supra,* note xxviii.

32. 68A Stat. 163 (Chapter 736).

33. Code of Federal Regulations, Title 26, Part I.

34. Hopkins, THE LAW OF TAX-EXEMPT ORGANIZA-TIONS, *supra,* note xvii.

35. While regulations generally do not have the force of law, subsequent rulings and court decisions have upheld the regulatory definition for the most part. Congress has had plenty of opportunity, yet has refrained from adopting a more concrete statutory definition.

36. Regulation Section 1.501(c)(3)–1(d)(2).

37. Revenue and Expenditure Control Act of 1968, 82 Stat. 269 (Act Title I, Section 109, 1968).

38. *See* Rep. W. Patman, *Tax-exempt Foundations and Charitable Trusts: Their Impact on Our Economy,* CHAIRMAN'S REPORT TO (HOUSE) SELECT COMMITTEE ON SMALL BUSINESS, 87th Congress, 1st Session, (1962); TREASURY DEPARTMENT REPORT ON PRIVATE FOUNDA-TIONS, Committee on Finance, U.S. Senate, 89th Congress, 1st Session (1963); Fremont-Smith, M., Conference Proceedings, FOUNDATIONS AND GOVERN-MENT (1965); Revenue Ruling 67–149, 67–1 C.B. 133.

39. Specific enumeration of these complex provisions is beyond the scope of this paper. The reader is referred to: Lashbrooke, E., PRENTICE HALL'S TAX EX-EMPT ORGANIZATIONS (1984) *and* Hopkins, THE LAW OF TAX-EXEMPT ORGANIZATIONS, *supra,* note xvii.

40. The public support test is contained in Code Section 509(a).

41. *See* Code Sections 4911 and 4940–4947.

42. American Association of Fundraising Counsel, GIVING USA (1982).

43. Hodgkinson, Weitzman, Toppe and Noga, NON-PROFIT ALMANAC, *supra,* note xviii.

44. Hopkins, THE LAW OF TAX EXEMPT ORGANIZA-TIONS, *supra,* note xvii.

45. Golden, W., *Charitable Giving in the 1970s: The Impact of the 1969 Act,* TAXES, 48, 787 (1970).

46. *In re. Unified Control Systems, Inc.,* 586 F.2d 1036 (5th Cir., 1978). *See also, Farrell v. U.S.,* 80–1 USTC 9833 (E.D. Ark., 1980).

47. Tax Reform Act of 1969, Joint Committee on Internal Revenue Taxation, GENERAL EXPLANATION OF THE TAX REFORM ACT OF 1969, 91st Congress, 2nd Session (1970).

48. Senate Report No. 94–938, 94th Congress, 2nd Session (1976).

49. Internal Revenue Code Section 513(e).

50. Internal Revenue Code Section 501(g) and pre–1976 Section 512(b)(14).

51. Internal Revenue Code Section 501(c)(20).

52. Public Law 95–600, and House Report 95–842, 95th Congress, 2nd Session (1978).

53. *Id.*

54. *Id.*

55. *Id.*

56. Internal Revenue Code Section 513(f)(2)(a).

57. Hopkins, THE LAW OF TAX EXEMPT ORGANIZA-TIONS, *supra,* note xvii.

58. *Id.*

59. Hodgkinson, Weitzman, Toppe and Noga, NON-PROFIT ALMANAC, *supra,* note xviii.

60. Public Law 97–34 (1981).

61. *Attributed to* Senator Patrick Moynihan, 127 Congressional Record S7962 (July 20, 1981).

62. Salamon, L., and Abramson, A., THE FEDERAL GOVERNMENT AND THE NONPROFIT SECTOR: IMPLICA-TIONS OF THE REAGAN BUDGET PROPOSALS, Urban Institute, May 1981, *reprinted in* Congressional Record S7964 (July 20, 1981).

63. Section 823, Economic Recovery Tax Act of 1981.

64. Hopkins, THE LAW OF TAX EXEMPT ORGANIZA-TIONS, *supra,* note xvii.

65. Section 44(f), Economic Recovery Tax Act of 1981.

66. Section 301(a), 1984 Tax Reform Act.

67. Palmer, S., *Charities Charge Gifts Would Drop 17 Percent Under Reagan Tax Plan,* CHRONICLE OF HIGHER EDUCATION, *vol. 30, no. 16.*

68. Clotfelter, C., TAX REFORM PROPOSALS AND CHARITABLE GIVING IN 1985 (1985).

69. _____, EXPLANATION FOR THE PRESIDENT'S TAX PROPOSALS TO CONGRESS FOR FAIRNESS, GROWTH AND SIMPLICITY, May 1985.

70. Salamon, L. and Abramson, A., THE FEDERAL GOVERNMENT AND THE NONPROFIT SECTOR: IMPLICATIONS OF THE REAGAN BUDGET PROPOSALS (1981), *reproduced at* 127 Congressional Record S7964 (July 20, 1981).

71. Hodgkinson, Weitzman, Toppe, and Noga, NONPROFIT ALMANAC, *supra,* note xviii.

72. McGovern, J.J., *The Use of Taxable Subsidiary Corporations by Public Charities—A Tax Policy Issue for 1988,* TAX NOTES, March 28, 1988, 1128 (*hereinafter* McGovern, TAX NOTES).

73. TAX POLICY: COMPETITION BETWEEN TAXABLE BUSINESSES AND TAX-EXEMPT ORGANIZATIONS, Report to the Joint Committee on Taxation, U.S. Congress, GAO/GGO–87–40B, Feb. 1987 (*hereinafter* COMPETITION).

74. U.S. Small Business Administration (3rd ed., 1984).

75. COMPETITION, *supra,* note lxxiii.

76. McGovern, TAX NOTES, *supra,* note lxxii.

77. Hopkins, THE LAW OF TAX-EXEMPT ORGANIZATIONS, *supra,* note xvii.

78. U.S. Small Business Administration, *supra,* note lxxiv.

79. Jones, P., *Treasury Objects to Fundamental Changes in UBIT,* TAX NOTES, May 2, 1988, 548.

80. *Id.*

81. Jones, P., *Treasury Advocates UBIT Fine Tuning: But UBIT Overhaul Not Needed,* TAX NOTES, May 16, 1988, 791–793.

82. *See for example, Nonprofits Drop the 'Non',* NEW YORK TIMES, Nov. 24, 1985; and *Cry of Unfair Competition Evokes Mixed Response,* WASHINGTON POST, Aug. 15, 1986.

83. *See for example,* Wellford, H., THE MYTH OF UNFAIR COMPETITION BY NONPROFIT ORGANIZATIONS (1985). *See also,* Taylor, S., *Taxing Public Charities Out of Business: A Solution in Search of a Problem,* TAX NOTES, May 8, 1988, 753–758.

84. Hopkins, THE LAW OF TAX-EXEMPT ORGANIZATIONS, *supra,* note xvii.

85. *Id.*

86. Suelzer, R.G., *et al.,* eds., 1996 TAX LEGISLATION: LAW AND EXPLANATION, CCH (1996).

87. *Id.*

88. Sections 341(a) and 342(a), 110 Stat. 1936, P.L. 104–191.

89. Suelzer, *et al.,* 1996 TAX LEGISLATION: LAW AND EXPLANATION, *supra,* note lxxxvi.

90. *See for example,* Glaser, Hohn, S., AN INSIDER'S ACCOUNT OF THE UNITED WAY SCANDAL: WHAT WENT WRONG AND WHY (1993); Barringer, J., *United Way Head Is Forced Out in a Furor Over His Lavish Style,* NEW YORK TIMES, Feb. 28, 1992; Tannenbaum, J.A., *Three Former United Way Aides Are Indicted on Fraud Charges,* WALL STREET JOURNAL, Sept. 14, 1994.

91. Connor, John, *White House Seeks Excise Tax to Fight Abuses by Charities,* WALL STREET JOURNAL, March 17, 1994; Gaul, Gilbert M., and Borowski, Neill A., *Warehouses of Wealth: The Tax Free Economy—A Series,* PHILADELPHIA INQUIRER, April 18–24, 1993; *Legislators Scrutinizing CU Foundation,* DENVER POST, March 28, 1988.

92. Kimmelman, John, *Too Charitable to Charities?—Why Congress Should Get Tough on America's $400 Billion Charity Industry,* FINANCIAL WORLD MAGAZINE, Sept. 1994.

93. *Id.*

94. Suhrke, H., *What's Wrong with Intermediate Sanctions,* PHILANTHROPY MONTHLY, Nov. 1993. *See also,* Carson, Marlis, and Streckfus, Paul, *EO Lawyers Get an Earful from the Government,* 9 EXEMPT ORGANIZATION TAX REVIEW 1231 (June 1994), quoting Kathleen Nies, tax counsel to the House Ways and Means Committee that their investigation of nonprofit practices relied on anecdotal information.

95. *Id.*

96. Suelzer, *et al.,* 1996 TAX LEGISLATION: LAW AND EXPLANATION, *supra,* note lxxxvi.

97. *See* Streckfus, P., *Summary of Treasury Intermediate Sanctions Proposal,* 9 EXEMPT ORGANIZATIONS TAX REVIEW 803 (April 1994).

98. Suelzer, *et al.,* 1996 TAX LEGISLATION: LAW AND EXPLANATION, *supra,* note lxxxvi.

99. Samuels, Leslie, *Proposal to Improve Compliance by Tax Exempt Organizations,* PHILANTHROPY MONTHLY (Nov. 1993).

100. Carson, Marlis, *Cerney Predicts Success for Intermediate Sanctions Proposal,* 9 EXEMPT ORGANIZATIONS TAX REVIEW 1203 (June 1994) ("Treasury's intermediate sanctions proposal will receive broad support"). *See also,* Suhrke, H., *Will Treasury's Proposal End Charitable Oversight as We Know It?* PHILANTHROPY MONTHLY (Nov. 1993) ("The casual observer . . . may remonstrate: how can one object to a more rational process of penalizing transactions which are by definition illegal?"); and Murawski, John, *Clinton Proposes to Let IRS Fine Charity Officials*

Who Reap Personal Gain, CHRONICLE OF PHILAN-THROPY, Sept. 7, 1995 ("Charities like the idea of adding fines because it spares them the threat of losing their tax exemption because of misconduct by one employee").

101. Schaffer, Scott, *Public Scrutiny: An Opportunity for Nonprofit Reform,* NONPROFIT TIMES, March 1994. *See also,* McIlnay, Dennis P., *The Public Accountability of Foundations: Private Organizations in the Public Interest,* PHILANTHROPY MATTERS, Spring 1993; and Herzlinger, Regina, *Can Public Trust in Nonprofits and Governments Be Restored?* HARVARD BUSINESS REVIEW, March/April 1996.

102. Luscombe, Mark A., *et al.,* eds., 1997 TAX LEGISLATION: LAW, EXPLANATION AND ANALYSIS (1997).

103. 112 Stat. 685, P.L. No. 105–26, 105th Congress, 2nd Session (1998).

104. Harani, J., *Exempt Sector Will See Regional Offices, Ultimately More Funding for Operations,* DAILY TAX REPORT (Nov. 23, 1998).

105. *Solving Public Problems: Where Citizens Place Their Confidence,* 7 CIVIC ACTION 2 (1994).

106. *Id. See also,* Roche, George, THE FALL OF THE IVORY TOWER (1994).

107. *Tax Report,* WALL STREET JOURNAL (Aug. 30, 1995).

108. Emshwiller, John R., *More Small Firms Complain About Tax Exempt Rivals,* WALL STREET JOURNAL (Aug. 8, 1995).

109. *United States General Accounting Office Briefing Report to Congressional Requesters,* GAO/GGD–95–84BR, Tax Exempt Organizations, Information on Selected Types of Organizations, Feb. 28, 1995, *reprinted in* 11 EXEMPT ORGANIZATION TAX REVIEW 739, 757 (April 1995).

110. Hodgkinson, Weitzman, Toppe, and Noga, NONPROFIT ALMANAC, *supra,* note xviii.

111. *Tax Watch,* CHRONICLE OF PHILANTHROPY, July 27, 1993.

112. *Id.*

113. Hall, Peter Dobkin, *The Best of Times, the Worst of Times: A Report on the State of Nonprofit Research,* PHILANTHROPY MONTHLY, Dec. 1992.

114. Fachina, B., Showell, E, and Stone, J., PRIVILEGES AND EXEMPTIONS ENJOYED BY NONPROFIT ORGANIZATIONS, *supra,* note iii.

115. Suhrke, H., *Nonprofit Regulation,* PHILANTHROPY MONTHLY, Jan./Feb. 1994.

PART 4

THE RATIONALE FOR TAX EXEMPTION

In order for a nonprofit organization to be eligible for tax exemption or for contributions to such an organization to be eligible for tax deduction, United States tax laws and Internal Revenue Service (IRS) Codes require it to be "organized for charitable or mutual benefit purposes." A wide array of nonprofits fall under this broad umbrella. When most people talk about nonprofit organizations, usually they are referring to "501(c)(3) publicly supported charitable organizations," organizations that are engaged in religious, scientific, charitable, educational, or similar-purpose activities.[1] The IRS Codes specify that no part of the net earnings of 501(c)(3) organizations may inure to the benefit of any private shareholder, and no substantial part of its activities may be for propaganda purposes or for influencing legislation or intervening in political campaigns.[2] "Publicly supported charitable organizations," or as they are most commonly known, "501(c)(3) organizations," are *tax-exempt* and contributions to such organizations are *tax-deductible.*

- Tax-exempt organizations do not pay corporate income taxes and in most states also are exempt from a variety of state and local taxes, including, for example, property, sales, franchise, and use taxes.[3] Many tax-exempt organizations also are eligible for lower U.S. Postal Service mail rates.
- Individuals and corporations who donate money and other items of value to 501(c)(3) nonprofit organizations are entitled to deduct the value of their gifts from their federal income taxes and, in most states, also from state income taxes.

The Rationale for Favorable Tax Treatment

Tax-exempt nonprofit organizations thus "cost" local, state, and the U.S. government lost tax revenue every year.[4] Contentious relationships sometimes develop between universities, museums, and other large nonprofits and the cities and counties whose public services they use, but to which tax-exempt nonprofits do not pay property or sales tax. For example, close to one-half of all real estate in the City of Boston is exempt from property taxes. Why then are units of government willing to grant favorable tax treatment to nonprofits that meet their criteria? Why are they willing to forgo the revenue that they could otherwise earn? Why are they willing to, in effect, "subsidize" this class of nonprofits?

In 1913, the Sixteenth Amendment was adopted, which permitted the establishment of the personal income tax. Four years later, Congress authorized tax deductions for charitable donations.[5] The reasons why Congress originally established public policy whereby nonprofit organizations and those who contribute to them could receive favorable tax treatment and why favorable tax treatment has continued as public policy for almost one hundred years are fundamental to the sector's existence. Government "subsidizes" nonprofits that provide "public goods" through favorable tax policies—government "pays for" services that contribute to the quality of life and to the well-being of communities, states, and the nation.[6] At least in concept, government agencies would otherwise need to provide these "public good" services themselves—or provide more of them than they do currently.

Public-Serving and Member-Serving Nonprofit Organizations

Nonprofits that provide services to a broad segment of the public receive more favorable tax treatment than nonprofits that primarily serve their own members. Public-serving and publicly supported charitable organizations—*501(c)(3) organizations*—receive the most favorable tax treatment. They are tax-exempt and contributions to such organizations are tax-deductible, which is an enormous advantage for nonprofit organizations that rely on donations for significant portions of their revenue.

Dozens of other types of nonprofits exist, though, that also receive some degree of favorable tax treatment from Congress and the IRS. Many of the other types of tax-exempt nonprofits fall into the broad category of *mutual benefit organizations,* including civic clubs, fraternal societies, credit unions, business and manufacturing associations, farmers cooperatives, labor unions, and professional associations such as the American Medical Association, the American Bar Association, the American Manufacturing Association, and the American Nursing Association.[7] "Even the member-serving organizations produce some public benefits, and the public-serving organizations often deliver benefits to their members."[8] The distinction thus is rarely "clean," and public-serving nonprofits and member-serving nonprofits both are usually viewed as community resources. "There is, therefore, a justification for subsidizing such organizations—provided that it is not excessively costly for regulatory authorities (currently the IRS) to monitor their actions to assure that they provide the public-type services expected of them."[9] The question is not whether public-serving and member-serving nonprofits should receive favorable tax treatment, the question instead is one of degree or "gradation."

Permitted and Restricted Activities

All types of tax-exempt organizations are permitted to engage in many activities but are limited or prohibited from engaging in others. Each "gradation" of tax treatment is associated with tighter or looser restrictions on activities. For example, 501(c)(4) "Civic Leagues and Social Welfare Organizations" may be involved actively in political campaigns and may attempt to influence legislation. The "price they pay" for the right to be politically active is ineligibility for tax-deductible contributions. Likewise, the other types of nonprofit organizations that are identified in the more than thirty IRS Code Sections all receive *some* favorable tax considerations—but all less than 501(c)(3) organizations. Examples of other types of nonprofit organizations identified in the IRS Code Sections that reflect the range of tax-exempt purposes include the following: labor, agricultural, and horticultural organizations, 501(c)(5); state-chartered credit unions, 501(c)(14); cemetery companies, 501(c)(14); benevolent life insurance associations, 501(c)(12); veterans' organizations, 501(c)(19); political organizations, 527(e); and homeowners' associations, 528(c).

One prohibition that is widely misbelieved to apply to nonprofits is making a profit. *A tax-exempt nonprofit organization is permitted to make a profit*—or, as they are called in nonprofit finance, a "surplus." Tax-exempt organizations are severely restricted, however, in what they can do with profits. Surpluses may be used, for example, to acquire new equipment, hire more staff, or rent a larger office—but only if these acquisitions advance the nonprofit's charitable, religious, scientific, educational, or other Tax Code–permitted purpose. Nonprofits do not have "owners" or "shareholders" and cannot distribute dividends as for-profit businesses routinely do.

Readings Included in This Part

The readings included here are short descriptions of nonprofit tax laws, IRS Code Sections, and statements of requirements that organizations must satisfy in order to be designated as tax-exempt by the IRS Exempt Organization Section.

Christopher Hoyt defines a "tax-exempt organization" as an organization exempt from income taxation because it operates to provide either broad social benefits to the public or mutual benefits to its members. Many organizations are also exempt from state and local income and property taxes, although the exemptions vary with each local jurisdiction.

Hoyt explains the justifications and legal requirements for tax exemption, provides an overview of the economic activities of tax-exempt organizations, and presents a comprehensive list (with short descriptions) of the various types of tax-exempt organizations. In 1995, charitable organizations represented 48 percent of all tax-exempt organizations in Section 501(c), followed by social welfare organizations at 14 percent, and fraternal organizations at 10 percent. Hoyt notes that many other nations have followed the United States' lead in establishing tax-exempt policies for social welfare and mutual benefit organizations.

Stephen Block's encyclopedia entry, "Nonprofit Organization," has been edited to include only information about tax-exempt nonprofit organizations. Block outlines the "tests" the IRS uses to make tax-exemption determinations, and he introduces the Federal Form 990, the end-of-year financial reporting form that tax-exempt organizations with annual revenues of at least $25,000 are required to file with the IRS. The IRS uses Form 990 information to help determine "whether the nonprofit has experienced adequate public support for the Internal Revenue Service's continued recognition of the organization as a tax-exempt entity. The 990 information [thus] can serve as the basis for invoking the 'public support test.'"

Notes

1. See the *United States Master Tax Guide,* published by Commerce Clearing House, Chicago; and the Internal Revenue Service's *IRS Statistics of Income Bulletin.*

2. See the *United States Master Tax Guide.*

3. Bruce R. Hopkins, *The Law of Tax-Exempt Organizations,* 7th ed. (New York: John Wiley & Sons, 1998); and Bruce R. Hopkins, *The Legal Answer Book for Nonprofit Organizations* (New York: John Wiley & Sons, 1996), particularly pp. 14, 15.

4. In the field of public finance, these lost tax revenues are known as "opportunity costs" or, more commonly, "tax expenditures." See Marcia L. Whicker, "Tax Expenditure," in Jay M. Shafritz, ed., *International Encyclopedia of Public Policy and Administration* (Boulder: Westview Press, 1998), pp. 2217–2219.

5. See Gary Scrivner, "A Brief History of Tax Policy Changes Affecting Charitable Organizations," reprinted in Part 3.

6. For excellent examples of "tax subsidies" in a variety of fields, see Henry Hansmann, *The Ownership of Enterprise* (Cambridge: Belknap Press of Harvard University Press, 1996).

7. Charles T. Clotfelter, "The Distributional Effects of Nonprofit Activities," in Charles T. Clotfelter, ed., *Who Benefits from the Nonprofit Sector?* (Chicago: University of Chicago Press, 1992), pp. 1–23.

8. Lester A. Salamon, *America's Nonprofit Sector: A Primer* (New York: Foundation Center, 1992), p. 14.

9. Burton A. Weisbrod, *The Nonprofit Economy* (Cambridge: Harvard University Press, 1988), p. 70.

References

Block, Stephen R. "Nonprofit Organizations." In Jay M. Shafritz, ed., *International Encyclopedia of Public Policy and Administration,* pp. 1509–1514. Boulder: Westview Press, 1998.

Clotfelter, Charles T., ed. *Who Benefits from the Nonprofit Sector?* Chicago: University of Chicago Press, 1992.

Cordes, Joseph J., and Burton A. Weisbrod. "Differential Taxation of Nonprofits and the Commercialization of Nonprofit Revenues." In Burton A. Weisbrod, ed., *To Profit or Not to Profit: The Commercial Transformation of the Nonprofit Sector,* pp. 83–104. New York: Cambridge University Press, 1998.

Fishman, James J., and Stephen Schwarz. *Nonprofit Organizations: Cases and Materials,* 2nd ed. New York: Foundation Press, 2000.

———. *Nonprofit Organizations: Statutes, Regulations, and Forms,* 2nd ed. New York: Foundation Press, 2000.

Hansmann, Henry. *The Ownership of Enterprise.* Cambridge: Belknap Press of Harvard University Press, 1996.

Hopkins, Bruce R. *The Law of Tax-Exempt Organizations,* 7th ed. New York: John Wiley & Sons, 1998.

———. *The Legal Answer Book for Nonprofit Organizations.* New York: John Wiley & Sons, 1996.

Hoyt, Christopher. "Tax-Exempt Organization." In Jay M. Shafritz, ed., *International Encyclopedia of Public Policy and Administration,* pp. 2214–2217. Boulder: Westview, 1998.

Salamon, Lester A. *America's Nonprofit Sector: A Primer.* New York: Foundation Center, 1992.

Scrivner, Gary. "100 Years of Tax Policy Changes Affecting Charitable Organizations." In David L. Gies, J. Steven Ott, and Jay M. Shafritz, eds., *The Nonprofit Organization: Essential Readings,* pp. 126–137. Fort Worth, Tex.: Harcourt Brace, 1990.

United States Internal Revenue Service. *IRS Statistics of Income Bulletin.* Washington, D.C., various years.
United States Master Tax Guide. Chicago: Commerce Clearing House.
Weisbrod, Burton A. *The Nonprofit Economy.* Cambridge: Harvard University Press, 1988.
Weisbrod, Burton A., ed. *To Profit or Not to Profit: The Commercial Transformation of the Nonprofit Sector.* New York: Cambridge University Press, 1998.

CHAPTER 11

Tax-Exempt Organization

C HRISTOPHER H OYT

Tax-Exempt Organization. An organization exempt from income taxation because it operates to provide either broad social benefits to the public or mutual benefits to its members. Many organizations are also exempt from state and local income and property taxes, although the exemptions vary with each local jurisdiction.

Reason for Exemption

In the United States, Congress determined that two categories of nonprofit organizations qualified for exemption from income taxation: social benefit organizations and mutual benefit organizations. Social benefit organizations operate to improve the quality of life in a community. Examples include charitable organizations and social welfare organizations. Mutual benefit organizations operate to promote the welfare of the members of the organization rather than the public at large. Examples include labor unions, trade associations, and social clubs.

An essential feature of both types of organizations is that they must not be organized to enrich investors. For example, a music school that is owned by a few teachers and investors will not qualify as a charity, whereas a similar school that is part of a college will. A privately owned restaurant cannot qualify for tax-exemption, whereas a private social club that restricts its dining facilities to its members can. Similarly, a privately owned business that gathers statistics about industry sales and sells it to purchasers will not qualify as a tax-exempt organization, whereas a nonprofit trade association that gathers and distributes similar information to its members will. Although the purpose of many mutual benefit organizations is to improve the economic vitality of their members, that is not considered a form of private benefit that will prohibit tax-exempt status.

Despite a general exemption from income tax, a tax-exempt organization will generally be liable for income tax on profits from unrelated business activities. This can arise from fundraising activities, such as selling holiday cards, or from certain investments, such as being a partner in a mining operation.

Economic Activity

The number of tax-exempt organizations in the United States has significantly increased in recent years, according to the Internal Revenue Service (IRS) Statistics of Income Bulletin issued August 1995. In 1990, there were 1,022,223 tax-exempt organizations, which is a 27 percent increase over the 806,375 organizations that existed in 1978. Over that time period, the assets of tax-exempt organizations increased by 150 percent to over US $1 trillion and their revenues increased by 225 percent to US $560 billion, whereas the nation's gross domestic product (GDP) increased by only 52 percent. In 1990, the revenue of tax-exempt organizations constituted nearly 10 percent of the nation's GDP, an increase from 6 percent in 1975. Charities alone accounted for more than 7 percent of GDP in 1990.

Charitable organizations comprise the largest category of tax-exempt organizations (48 percent of all tax-exempt organizations described in Section 501(c)), followed by social welfare organizations (14 percent), fraternal organizations (10 percent), labor and agricultural organizations (7 percent), business leagues (6 percent), and social clubs (6 percent). Certain segments of the tax-exempt sector are growing faster than others. Whereas the number of tax-exempt organizations grew by 27 percent from 1978 to 1990, the greatest growth was in the number of charities (67 percent), business leagues (45 percent), and social welfare organizations (14 percent). By comparison, the number of labor and agricultural organizations decreased by 18 percent.

Overview of Legal Requirements

Most state statutes specify procedures to establish a non-profit corporation or some other form of nonprofit organization, such as a cooperative or a benevolent association. Many statutes require the organization to specify in its organization documents (e.g., articles of incorporation, bylaws) whether it is a social benefit or a mutual benefit organization. Complying with these state laws does not ensure that an organization will be tax-exempt under the federal income tax laws. Instead, each organization's governing documents must also contain specific provisions that comply with the federal laws

that grant tax-exemption. Most organizations must apply to the IRS for tax-exempt status before they will be treated as tax-exempt, although churches are a notable exception.

Section 501(c) Organizations

The most important statute that grants tax-exemption is Section 501(c) of the Internal Revenue Code. It lists 25 types of tax-exempt organizations in relatively random order. In order to obtain tax-exemption, most organizations structure their legal documents and limit their operations to comply with the appropriate exemption. Many organizations can describe their operations to outsiders by simply referring to the appropriate paragraph of the statute.

The different types of tax-exempt organizations are listed here in the order that they appear in Section 501(c). For example, number (3) on the list corresponds to Section 501(c)(3). The number in brackets represents the number of that type of organization that existed in the United States in 1991, according to IRS records. The following types of organizations are exempt from federal income tax under Section 501(c):

1. A tax-exempt corporation organized by an act of Congress that is an instrumentality of the United States. Examples include the Federal Deposit Insurance Corporation (FDIC) and the Pension Benefit Guarantee corporation (PBGC). [9]
2. A corporation organized for the exclusive purpose of holding title to property, collecting income therefrom and turning over the entire amount, less expenses, to another tax-exempt organization. [6,408]
3. A charitable organization that engages primarily in charitable activities. [516,554 plus an estimated 340,000 churches for a total of 856,554]
4. A social welfare organization that promotes the general welfare of a community by bringing about civic betterments and social improvements. The statute also exempts certain local associations of employees, such as a local police relief association. [142,811]

5. A labor union, agricultural, or horticultural organization. A labor organization is an association of workers who have combined to promote their interests by bargaining collectively with their employers to secure better working conditions, wages, and similar benefits. An example is the United Auto Workers. An agricultural or horticultural organization operates to improve the economic conditions of agriculture or horticulture workers, the grade of their products, and the efficiency of production. [72,009]

6. A trade association, business league, chamber of commerce, real-estate board, board of trade, or professional football league. Examples include the American Medical Association and a city's Chamber of Commerce. [68,442]

7. A social club organized for pleasure, recreation, and other nonprofit purposes, provided that substantially all of its activities are restricted for such purposes. Although revenue paid by members as dues, service fees, and charges for meals will generally be tax-exempt, a social club will pay tax on its investment income. [63,922]

8. A fraternal benefit society, order, or association that operates under the lodge system or for the exclusive benefit of its members and provides for the payment of life, sickness, accident, or other benefits to its members and their dependents (compare with 10 below). [98,840]

9. A voluntary employees' beneficiary association (VEBA) that provides for the payment of life, sick, accident, or other benefits to the employee members of such association or their dependents. [14,708]

10. A fraternity, sorority, domestic fraternal society, order, or association that operates under the lodge system and devotes its net earnings exclusively to religious, charitable, scientific, literary, educational, and fraternal purposes and that does not pay life, sick, accident, or other benefits to its members and their dependents (compare with 8 above). [18,360]

11. A local teachers' retirement fund whose income consists solely of amounts received from public taxation, assessments on the teaching salaries of members, and income from investments. [10]

12. A mutual ditch or irrigation company, mutual or cooperative telephone company, or a local benevolent life insurance association; but only if 85 percent or more of the income consists of amounts collected from members for the sole purpose of meeting losses and expenses. [5,984]

13. A cemetery association or company that is owned and operated exclusively for the benefit of its members or is operated not for profit. [8,781]

14. Certain types of nonprofit credit unions that are organized and operated for mutual purposes and certain types of mutual associations (organized before 1958) that provide reserve funds and insure deposits at banks and savings and loan associations. [6,219]

15. Certain types of insurance company (other than a life insurance company) whose net premiums do not exceed US $350,000 in a year. [1,147]

16. A corporation to finance the ordinary crop operations of its members. [20]

17. A trust that provides supplemental unemployment benefits to employees. [644]

18. A trust created before June 25, 1959, that is part of a pension plan that is funded only by contributions of employees. [8]

19. A post or organization that has at least 75 percent of its members comprised of past or present members of the U.S. Armed Forces. [27,962]

20. An organization that is part of a qualified group legal services plan. [206]

21. A trust established to pay claims to miners and other victims of black lung disease. [23]

22. A trust established by sponsors of a multiemployer plan (usually a union-administered retirement plan) to pay certain pension plan withdrawal liabilities. [None]

23. An association to provide insurance and other benefits to veterans associations, but

only if the association was established before 1880. [2]

24. A trust to pay certain types of retirement income obligations. [None]

25. A corporation or trust that holds title to buildings and other real property for certain retirement plans, charities, or governmental subdivisions (maximum 35 beneficiaries of each organization). [181]

Other Tax-Exempt Organizations

1. A qualified retirement, pension, profit-sharing, and stock bonus plan is tax-exempt. Such a retirement plan will not pay tax on revenue from contributions from employers or from investment income, but it will be liable for tax on unrelated business income. Sections 401(a) and 501(a). [unknown]

2. A charitable remainder trust that distributes amounts annually to a person for life, or for a fixed number of years, and then terminates and distributes its assets to a charity. In 1995, the Tax Court concluded that a charitable remainder trust will lose its tax-exempt status in any year that it has unrelated business taxable income. [16,000]

3. A farmer's cooperative is tax-exempt (Section 521). Most cooperatives merely share costs among their members rather than operate a business for profit, and they are therefore generally exempt from taxation under Subchapter T of the Internal Revenue Code. [2,129; by comparison there were 3,219 taxable farmers' cooperatives]

4. Special rules apply to cooperative service organizations of hospitals (Section 501(e) [72 in existence]) and for a pooled investment fund of educational organizations (Section 501(f) [Only 1 in existence, "The Common Fund"]).

5. A political organization (political party, election committee, etc.) is tax-exempt with respect to the amounts it receives from contributions, member dues, and proceeds from fund-raising events. However, it must pay income tax at the highest corporate rate (currently 35 percent) on its net investment income. In addition, a political candidate will be liable for income tax if any amounts are diverted for his or her personal use (Section 527).

6. A homeowners association (an organization that manages a subdivision development or a condominium) is tax-exempt with respect to the amounts it receives as membership dues, fees, or assessments from owners of the managed property. However, it must pay a 30 percent income tax on its net investment income (Section 528).

Many nations have adopted similar policies to those of the United States and have exempted social welfare and mutual organizations from income, sales, and property taxes. Of course, the laws vary from nation to nation.

Bibliography

Internal Revenue Service, 1995. *IRS Statistics of Income Bulletin, Summer 1995.* Washington, DC.

CHAPTER 12

Nonprofit Organization

STEPHEN R. BLOCK

Nonprofit Organization. A grouping of individuals who collectively form a social unit—an organization—to accomplish some public or societal purpose.

Tax Exemption

When the term "nonprofit organization" is used, most individuals envision charitable [501(c)(3)], tax-exempt organizations. There are, however, approximately 30 types of nonprofit organizations that are classified as exempt from federal taxes. . . .

When an organization seeks federal tax-exempt status, the IRS may test the applicant's responses and attachments to Form 1023 to determine whether the nonprofit corporation fits the IRS code profile of a charitable, tax-exempt organization. There are at least three tests that can be used at this stage of the application process. One test determines whether the nonprofit organization's purpose and mission statement is compatible with the IRS codes categories of exempt organizations, which are as follows: charitable, education, science, health, human services, religion, testing for public safety, the prevention of cruelty to children or animals, or fostering national or international amateur sports competition (excepting the provision of athletic facilities or equipment).

In a second test, Form 1023 responses are used to determine whether the organization was formed to engage in political campaigns or ballot initiatives. Lobbying to influence public policy cannot be a central activity of the nonprofit that is recognized as a 501(c)(3). Although some legislative lobbying is permitted, an intent to engage in extensive organizational lobbying must be declared.

A third test determines whether the organization intends to distribute organizational assets to board members or other individuals. This test may include a review of the bylaws and/or articles of incorporation to ensure that a dissolution provision exists, stating that assets would be distributed to similar mission-oriented nonprofit organizations or to government entities. Unlike for-profit corporations, nonprofits may not distribute annual earnings to their directors; therefore, the IRS will be interested in responses to Form 1023 questions about the trustees' handling of excess revenues. The expectation is that excess revenues will be reinvested in staff salaries, operational expenses, safe investments, and program services.

All 501(c)(3) organizations must be categorized as either private foundations or public charities; organizational testing can be used to sort private foundations from publicly supported charities. Private foundations do not experience all of the same benefits as publicly supported charities. By law, the private foundation must annually distribute a percentage of its assets to other charitable organizations; it may be taxed on certain investments; and it is subject to very strict rules that subject its trustees and executive director to harsh fines for violations. Therefore, charitable organizations would want to avoid this private foundation classification (unless, of course, the organization is truly seeking a private foundation classification).

As part of the Form 1023 review, the IRS may ask for financial statements that report assets, liabilities, revenues, and expenditures, especially if the organization has been operating for a year or more. An existing organizational budget or a proposed budget will be reviewed to determine fund-raising projections and methods. The IRS is particularly interested in whether the organization plans to generate revenues mainly from public support or from fees for services. This distinction is used to further classify nonprofit organizations according to their primary means of generating revenues; publicly supported charities are classified as 501(c)(3), 509(a)(1), and organizations relying on fees for service are classified as 501(c)(3), 509(a)(2).

If the IRS is satisfied with the information in Form 1023, the organization will receive a ruling letter recognizing it as a tax-exempt organization. This status is retroactive only if Form 1023 was filed within 15 months of incorporation. If the form was filled after the 15-month period, recognition is granted from the date of the application, not the date of incorporation. Understanding the limited time frame may be important. Missing the 15-month deadline can adversely impact donors who expected deduction privileges for their gifts. Timing is also critical for the organization seeking exemption from taxes on revenues generated from the organization's inception through its 15-month filing deadline. If tax-exempt recognition occurs after the 15-month filing deadline, the nonprofit organization will have a tax burden on its income up until the date of tax-exempt recognition.

Organizations in which the missions are human service oriented and which have been in existence longer than 15 months may apply for recognition as a 501(c)(4), a social welfare organization. The 501(c)(4) has tax-exempt privileges, although it does not offer deduction privileges to donors. Receiving a 501(c)(4) ruling is advantageous for late application filers because the recognition is retroactive to the organization's inception. The 501(c)(4) nonprofit organization may be relieved of all prior tax obligations. Once excused of its tax burdens, the organization can file Form 1023 for recognition as a 501(c)(3) organization. If recognized, it can add donor deduction privileges to its fund-raising arsenal, effective as of the Form 1023 application date.

Other Forms of Tax Relief

IRS recognition does not guarantee tax exemption from any other taxing authority. Therefore, nonprofit organizations should also apply for tax relief from state, city, and county taxing authorities. Some states, cities, and counties have very narrow definitions of charitable organizations, making it difficult to secure tax exemption on organizational revenues, purchases, and property. Additionally, tax exemption may not excuse an agency from paying taxes on revenues if the income was derived from activities not directly related to the organization's purpose and mission. Earnings of US $1,000 or more from unrelated business usually create a tax liability, and earnings that exceed one-third of an organization's budget may even trigger examination by the IRS to determine whether the tax-exempt status should be revoked.

Similar to the obligations of for-profit businesses, nonprofits also have tax collection and tax payment obligations. The nonprofit organization, for example, is required to pay taxes for unemployment insurance programs, workers' compensation, social security, and medicare. Some states permit nonprofit organizations to purchase a bond or use a letter of credit in lieu of paying state unemployment taxes. Under these circumstances, the nonprofit would be responsible for reimbursing the state for any financial payments awarded by the state to former employees of the nonprofit.

Expenditures by nonprofit organizations for unemployment insurance and workers' compensation fees are usually affected by the number of claims made against the organization's insurance policies. Workers' compensation insurance fees are also calculated by a formula that considers number of employees, amount of annual payroll, and the type and degree of risks associated with employee job responsibilities.

Although nonprofit organizations may be exempt from paying taxes, its employees are not. Employees will have social security taxes, medicare taxes, as well as federal, state, and local income taxes withheld from their paychecks. As an employer, a tax-exempt nonprofit organization is not exempted from matching its employees' share of social security and medicare taxes.

Nonprofit, tax-exempt organizations have certain tax-reporting obligations. Specifically, the organization is required to file Form 990, an end-of-year tax return filed by organizations with annual revenues of at least US $25,000. Form 990 must be filed no later than five and a half months after the end of the organization's fiscal year.

Form 990 can be used by the Internal Revenue Service to review an organization's revenue base, source of revenues, fund-raising methods, lobbying expenditures, and major salary and benefit expenditures. It can also be used to help demonstrate whether the nonprofit has experienced adequate public support for the Internal Revenue Service's continued recognition of the organization as a tax-exempt entity. The 990 information can serve as the basis for invoking the "public support test."

With a minimum of four years of operating experience, the nonprofit organization may be scrutinized by the IRS seeking proof of public support under the organization's (509)(a) classification. Failing the support test can lead to the loss of tax-exempt recognition. There are two related tests: the one-third support test and the 10 percent support and facts and circumstances test.

An organization classified as a 501(c)(3), 509(a)(1) must demonstrate that during a preceding four-year period, at least one-third of its support came from the general public, or government, or a combination of public and government funding. In the calculation of support, a non-profit organization may not count any individual contribution to the extent it exceeds 2 percent of the organization's total support. This restriction severely limits the ability of the organization to pass the one-third test on the basis of a few large contributions.

If the organization fails the one-third test, it may be reviewed under a more subjective analysis, the 10 percent test, showing 10 percent of the organization's support coming from the general public. In addition, the IRS may look at other facts and circumstances. For example, the organization may evidence a large pool of community volunteers and board members from diverse backgrounds. The IRS has the authority to determine whether certain facts and circumstances can be evidence of public support.

Nonprofit organizations with 501(c)(3), 509(a)(2) designations have a similar obligation to demonstrate public support, proving that more than one-third of its public support is from contributions, fees, and program-related business income. Passing the public support test should be a matter of concern for any organization. If a nonprofit organization is unable to muster a diverse funding base, volunteer participation, or cross section of community representatives on its board of directors, it risks the loss of its special tax-exempt status.

Bibliography

Billis, David, 1993. "What Can Nonprofits and Businesses Learn from Each Other?" In David C. Hammack and Dennis R. Young, eds., *Nonprofit Organizations in a Market Economy.* San Francisco: Jossey-Bass, 319–343.

Block, Stephen R., and Katherine Carol, 1994. "From Visions to Reality: Transforming Community Through a Transformed Organization." In Cary Griffin, Katherine Carol, and Roger Van Lieshout, eds., *Vision, Innovation, and Competence: The An-*

nual Management Mentoring Monograph. Greeley, CO: Center for Technical Assistance and Training, University of Northern Colorado.

Block, Stephen R., and Jeffrey W. Pryor, 1991. *Improving Nonprofit Management Practice: A Handbook for Community-Based Organizations.* Rockville, MD: OSAP/Public Health Service, U.S. Dept. of Health and Human Services.

Bookman, Mark, 1992. *Protecting Your Organization's Tax-Exempt Status.* San Francisco: Jossey-Bass.

Dayton, Kenneth N., 1987. "Governance Is Governance." *An Independent Sector Occasional Paper,* Washington, DC: Independent Sector.

Hall, Peter Dobkin, 1994. "Historical Perspectives on Nonprofit Organizations." In Robert D. Herman, ed., *The Jossey-Bass Handbook of Nonprofit Leadership and Management.* San Francisco: Jossey-Bass, 3–43.

Hansmann, Henry, 1987. "Economic Theories of Nonprofit Organization." In Walter W. Powell, ed., *The Nonprofit Sector: A Research Handbook.* New Haven, CT: Yale University Press, 27–42.

Hodgkinson, Virginia Ann, et al., 1992. *Nonprofit Almanac, 1992–1993: Dimensions of the Independent Sector.* San Francisco: Jossey-Bass.

Milofsky, Carl, 1987. "Neighborhood-Based Organizations: A Market Analogy." In Walter W. Powell, ed., *The Nonprofit Sector: A Research Handbook.* New Haven, CT: Yale University Press, 277–295.

Ostrom, Elinor, and Gina Davis, 1993. "Nonprofit Organizations as Alternatives and Complements in a Mixed Economy." In David C. Hammack and Dennis R. Young, eds., *Nonprofit Organizations in a Market Economy.* San Francisco: Jossey-Bass, 23–56.

Van Til, Jon, 1988. *Mapping the Third Sector.* New York: Foundation Center.

_____, 1994. "Nonprofit Organizations and Social Institutions." In Robert D. Herman, ed., *The Jossey-Bass Handbook of Nonprofit Leadership and Management.* San Francisco: Jossey-Bass, 44–64.

PART 5

OVERVIEW THEORIES OF THE NONPROFIT SECTOR

For many readers, *theory* is an ugly, intimidating term that suggests irrelevance and impracticality.

—Roger A. Lohmann, *The Commons*

The word *theory* has such a mystique about it. We tend to talk about theory as researchers much like our forebears would have discussed theology: with a mixture of awe, fascination, and cynicism.

—Jacquelyn Thayer Scott, "Some Thoughts on Theory Development in the Voluntary and Nonprofit Sector"

This part and the four parts that follow introduce some of the most important and useful theories of the nonprofit sector. It is necessary to understand first, however, that there is no such thing as *the* theory of the nonprofit sector. Rather, there are many theories that attempt to explain why the sector exists in its current form and how nonprofit organizations and the people in and around them behave in varying circumstances. Theories also attempt to account for differences and similarities among nonprofits in the numerous, distinctly different subsectors, such as private education, health care, religion, international assistance, and mutual benefit organizations.

The theories presented in these chapters are "macro-level theories"—theories that try to explain and predict the existence, form, and functions of the sector, groups of organizations in the sector, or at the lowest level, individual organizations. In contrast, "micro-level theories" have as their unit of analysis the behavior of individuals or groups in organizations.[1]

Nonprofit Theories Reflect Diverse Perspectives

Some theories of the sector are compatible with and build upon others in what they try to explain or predict; the aspects of the sector or organizations they consider to be important; their assumptions about the sector, organizations, and the societal environment of which they are a part; and the methods that are used to study the sector and its organizations. These groupings of somewhat compatible theories and theorists tend to be associated with a variety of academic disciplines and fields of study. Theories of the nonprofit sector and its organizations draw significantly from economics, sociology, social psychology, cultural and social anthropology, philosophy and ethics, religion, history, public administration, and business administration. They also draw with less force, but still importantly, from political science, some fields of applied mathematics and statistics, and systems theory.

The question is not, Which of these theories or groups of theories are right? Each wrestles with different questions and incorporates different variables. Although these nonprofit sector theories individually represent a loosely knit community of diverse approaches and perspectives, collectively they form the intellectual base of the sector.

Theories of the nonprofit sector are as important for decisionmaking in the practice arena as they are in university classrooms. They are used frequently to provide justification for public policy decisions that affect, for example, tax-exempt status, favored treatment in government contracting, and restrictions on commercial activities by nonprofits that compete with for-profit businesses. Remember Kurt Lewin's astute observation: "There is nothing so practical as a good theory."[2]

Organization of the Next Five Parts

Because the nonprofit sector is so diverse, there cannot be a single definitive listing of "the most important" theories and theorists to include in this book. I readily admit that some highly significant contributors and contributions have not found their way into the sections that introduce the essential theories of the sector (Parts 5 through 9, and in reality, Part 10 also). I have tried, though, to include a representative collection of the essential theories. The theories that are reprinted in these chapters range from "old classics" to very recent contributions. They also represent the thinking and approaches of a variety of disciplines.

In order to help bring a sense of cohesion to the multiple perspectives and approaches, "somewhat compatible" groupings of theories are organized into parts that approximately represent the academic disciplines that have been most central to development of the sector's theories:

- *Part 6, Economic and Political Theories.* There are economic theories, political theories, and political-economy theories of the nonprofit sector. Some of these theories address both of the fields and perspectives, and others are neatly contained within one of the two fields. Some political theories of nonprofits were written by economists and sociologists, and vice versa. Almost all political and economic theories, however, are concerned with issues such as the "place of"—or the roles of—nonprofit organizations in a three-sector political economy; the types of revenue-generating activities nonprofits tend to engage in; the nature of relationships between nonprofit sector organizations and their revenue sources, particularly government agencies and businesses; the resulting effects of these relationships on organizations in all three sectors; and the effects of these relationships on civil society, democracy, the strength of the nonprofit sector, and the capitalistic system.

- *Part 7, Social and Community Theories.* Social and community theories attempt to identify and explain the "place" of nonprofits in communities and the complexity of relationships among nonprofit organizations, their numerous constituencies, and other community institutions. They often address the roles of community networks, niches, and the importance of community elites and influentials for the nonprofit sector.
- *Part 8, Organization Theories.* As the name implies, organization theories address questions such as, Why do nonprofit organizations make the strategic decisions they do? What causes nonprofits to act in certain ways? Why are organizations in the nonprofit sector designed and structured as they are? How *should* nonprofits be organized and thus managed? To what extent should nonprofit organization structures, processes, and controls "look like" government and business organizations?
- *Part 9, Giving Theories.* Why do people give their money, time, and effort to causes and to cases? Why do some people give more than others do? Why do people give more to some organizations and purposes than they do to others? To what extent is giving driven (or influenced) by sympathy, empathy, a sense of justice, to alleviate guilt, a desire for public recognition, or by rational calculation of "personal utility"? Is altruism (or egoism) a characteristic of human nature that emanates from genetic structure? Is giving an inherited personality trait or a "drive"? Or is altruism learned from others around us, developmentally over years? How and why do people's giving patterns differ at various life stages? How is philanthropy similar and different in other countries and cultures? These types of questions — and attempts to answers them — represent the essence and purpose of theories of giving.
- *Part 10, The Blending and Blurring of the Sectors,* introduces theory and practice issues of resource dependence, intersectoral interdependence, and corporatization or commercialization of the nonprofit sector. The nonprofit sector has always been positioned rather delicately between the business sector's profit motive and the government sector's drive to meet social needs. Although the trend toward "blurring and blending" is quite universally acknowledged, its implications are not clear for the business, nonprofit, and public sectors — indeed for democratic government and a civil society. Theories in this part address the changing complexities caused by intersectoral blurring and blending. For example, the privatization of human services raises a far more complex set of issues than simply involving the nonprofit sector in getting people off welfare. It also raises a disturbing array of questions about accountability, democracy, governance, and citizenship in this society.

The Readings Included in This Part

Before presenting theories that represent distinctive perspectives (in Parts 6 through 10), three readings are reprinted here that provide crosscutting introductory overviews of the sector: "What Is the Nonprofit Sector and Why Do We Have It?" by Lester Salamon; and a chapter from the book *The Commons,* in which Roger Lohmann articulates a "new theory" of the nonprofit sector.

"What Is the Nonprofit Sector and Why Do We Have It?" by Lester Salamon is a chapter from his insightful booklet *America's Nonprofit Sector: A Primer.*[3] Salamon opens with a short historical overview and a description of the sector and then turns to what he believes are the most fundamental theory issues confronting the sector, including the following:

- the distinction between philanthropy and the nonprofit sector;
- the defining characteristics of the sector; and

- the "rationale" for the sector and why it exists, including historical justification, market failure theory, government failure theory, the undergirding values of pluralism and freedom, and "a response to the need for some mechanism through which to give expression to sentiments of solidarity. This is particularly important in individualistic societies like the United States."

Salamon concludes:

While there is reason to question whether American nonprofit organizations always live up to the expectations that these theories assign to them, it seems clear that the existence of such a set of institutions has come to be viewed as a critical component of community life, a compelling and fulfilling way to meet community needs, and a crucial prerequisite of a true "civil society."

"A New Approach: The Theory of the Commons," is Roger Lohmann's attempt to present a "fresh, integrated vision of nonprofit organizations and voluntary action" that enables readers to understand "how diverse and disparate organizations within the sector, some with seemingly conflicting purposes, all share the basic characteristics of a commons—including free and uncoerced participation, a common purpose and shared resources, and a sense of fairness and mutuality among participants." In *The Commons*, Lohmann "seeks to talk generally (and interestingly) about the social, economic, and political structures and processes of nonprofit and voluntary action and at the same time to redraw some of the major internal and external boundaries of the field."[4]

Notes

1. A number of micro-level theories are included in the companion to this volume that I also edited: *Understanding Nonprofit Organizations* (Boulder: Westview Press, 2001).
2. A. J. Marrow, *The Practical Theorist: The Life and Works of Kurt Lewin* (New York: Basic Books, 1969).
3. Lester M. Salamon, *America's Nonprofit Sector: A Primer,* 2nd ed. (New York: Foundation Center, 1999). Chapter 2, "What Is the Nonprofit Sector and Why Do We Have It?" is reprinted here.
4. Roger A. Lohmann, "A New Approach: The Theory of the Commons," in Roger A. Lohmann, *The Commons: New Perspectives on Nonprofit Organizations and Voluntary Action* (San Francisco, Jossey-Bass, 1992), pp. 46–82.

References

Brown, Eleanor. "Altruism Toward Groups: The Charitable Provision of Private Goods." *Nonprofit and Voluntary Sector Quarterly* 26 (2), June 1997, 175–184.

Clary, E. Gil, Mark Snyder, and Robert Ridge. "Volunteers' Motivations: A Functional Strategy for the Recruitment, Placement, and Retention of Volunteers." *Journal of Nonprofit Management and Leadership* 2 (4), Summer 1992, 333–350.

Clotfelter, Charles T., ed. *Who Benefits from the Nonprofit Sector?* Chicago: University of Chicago Press, 1992.

Coles, Robert. "Satisfactions." In Robert Coles, *The Call of Service: A Witness to Idealism.* Boston: Houghton Mifflin, 1993.

DiMaggio, Paul J., and Helmut K. Anheier. "The Sociology of Nonprofit Organizations and Sectors." In W. Richard Scott and Judith Blake, eds., *Annual Review of Sociology* 16, pp. 137–159. Palo Alto: Annual Reviews, 1990.

Ferris, James M. "The Double-Edged Sword of Social Service Contracting: Public Accountability Versus Nonprofit Autonomy." *Nonprofit Management and Leadership* 3 (4), Summer 1993, 363–376.

Galaskiewicz, Joseph, and Wolfgang Bielefeld. *Nonprofit Organizations in an Age of Uncertainty.* New York: Aldine-DeGruyter, 1998.

Grønbjerg, Kirsten A. "Markets, Politics, and Charity: Nonprofits in the Political Economy." In Walter W. Powell and Elisabeth S. Clemens, *Private Action and the Public Good,* pp. 137–150. New Haven: Yale University Press, 1998.

Hansmann, Henry. *The Ownership of Enterprise.* Cambridge, Mass.: Belknap Press, 1996.

_____. "The Two Nonprofit Sectors: Fee for Service Versus Donative Organizations." In Virginia A. Hodgkinson and Richard W. Lyman, eds., *The Future of the Nonprofit Sector,* pp. 91–102. San Francisco: Jossey-Bass, 1989.

James, Estelle. *The Nonprofit Sector in International Perspective: Studies in Comparative Culture and Policy.* New York: Oxford University Press, 1989.

Lohmann, Roger A. *The Commons.* San Francisco: Jossey-Bass, 1992.

Mount, Joan. "Why Donors Give." *Journal of Nonprofit Management and Leadership* 7 (1), Fall 1996, 3–14.

Popielarz, Pamela A., and J. Miller McPherson. "On the Edge or In Between: Niche Position, Niche Overlap, and the Duration of Voluntary Association Memberships." *American Journal of Sociology* 101 (3), November 1995, 698–720.

Powell, Walter W. *The Nonprofit Sector: A Research Handbook.* New Haven: Yale University Press, 1987.

Powell, Walter W., and Elisabeth S. Clemens, eds. *Private Action and the Public Good.* New Haven: Yale University Press, 1998.

Putnam, Robert D. *Bowling Alone.* New York: Simon and Schuster, 2000.

Saidel, Judith. "Resource Interdependence: The Relationship Between State Agencies and Nonprofit Organizations." *Public Administration Review,* November-December 1991, 543–553.

Salamon, Lester M. "What Is the Nonprofit Sector and Why Do We Have It?" In Lester M. Salamon, *America's Nonprofit Sector: A Primer,* 2nd ed., pp. 7–19. New York: Foundation Center, 1999.

Scott, Jacquelyn Thayer. "Some Thoughts on Theory Development in the Voluntary and Nonprofit Sector." *Nonprofit and Voluntary Sector Quarterly* 24 (1), Spring 1995, 31–40.

Smith, Steven R., and Michael Lipsky. *Nonprofits for Hire.* Cambridge: Harvard University Press, 1993.

View, Jenice. *A Means to an End: The Role of Nonprofit/Government Contracting in Sustaining the Social Contract.* Washington, D.C.: Union Institute, 1995.

Weisbrod, Burton A. "The Future of the Nonprofit Sector: Its Entwining with Private Enterprise and Government." *Journal of Policy Analysis and Management* 16 (4), 1997, 541–555.

Weisbrod, Burton A., ed. *To Profit or Not to Profit: The Commercial Transformation of the Nonprofit Sector.* Cambridge: Cambridge University Press, 1998.

Wolf, Alan. "What Is Altruism?" In Walter W. Powell and Elisabeth S. Clemens, eds., *Private Action and the Public Good,* pp. 36–46. New Haven: Yale University Press, 1998.

CHAPTER 13

What Is the Nonprofit Sector and Why Do We Have It?

LESTER M. SALAMON

> Nothing, in my opinion, is more deserving of our attention than the intellectual and moral associations of America.
>
> —Alexis de Tocqueville, 1835

Few aspects of American society are as poorly understood or as obscured by mythology as the thousands of day-care centers, clinics, hospitals, higher-education institutions, civic action groups, museums, symphonies, and related organizations that comprise America's private, nonprofit sector.

More than a century and a half ago, the Frenchman Alexis de Toqueville identified this sector as one of the most distinctive and critical features of American life. Yet, despite a steady diet of charitable appeals, most Americans know precious little about the sector or what it does. Indeed, to judge from press accounts and national policy debates, it would seem as if the nonprofit sector largely disappeared from the American scene some 60 years ago, as both public and scholarly attention focused instead on government policy and the expansion of the State.

In fact, however, as the third century of the American democratic experiment begins, the private, non-profit sector remains at least as potent a component of American life as it was when de Toqueville observed it more than a century and a half ago.

What Is the Nonprofit Sector?

But what is this "nonprofit sector"? What is it that the organizations that are part of this sector have in common? Why do we have such organizations? What purpose do they serve?

A Diverse Sector

Unfortunately, the answers to these questions are somewhat complicated because of the great diversity of this sector. U.S. tax laws contain no fewer than 26 separate sections under which organizations can claim exemption from federal income taxes as non-profit organizations. Mutual insurance companies, certain cooperatives, labor unions, business leagues, as well as charitable and educational institutions are all eligible. Of these, the "religious, charitable, and educational" organizations eligible for tax exemption under Section 501(c)(3) are probably the best known—yet included even within this narrow span are a wide assortment of institutions:

- small, one-room soup kitchens for the homeless;
- massive hospital complexes;
- museums, art galleries, and symphony orchestras;
- day-care centers;
- foster care and adoption agencies; and
- advocacy and civic action groups bringing pressure on government and the private sector to clean the environment, protect farmers, promote civil rights, or pursue a thousand other causes.

A Crucial Distinction: Philanthropy Versus the Nonprofit Sector

The task of comprehending the nonprofit sector is further complicated by a widespread failure to recognize the important distinction between *philanthropy,* on the one hand, and t*he private, nonprofit sector,* on the other. In many accounts, these two terms are treated interchangeably when in fact one is really just a part of the other.

- The *private nonprofit sector,* as the term will be used here, is a set of organizations that is privately incorporated but serving some public purpose, such as the advancement of health, education, scientific progress, social welfare, or pluralism. The nonprofit sector thus includes thousands of daycare centers, private hospitals, universities, research institutes, community development organizations, foster care facilities, social service agencies, employment and training centers, museums, art galleries, symphonies, zoos, business and professional associations, advocacy organizations, and dozens of similar types of institutions.

- *Philanthropy* is the giving of gifts of time or valuables (money, securities, property) for public purposes. Philanthropy, or charitable giving, is thus one form of income of private nonprofit organizations. To be sure, some nonprofit organizations have the generation of charitable contributions as their principal objective.

Six Defining Characteristics

What, then, do the organizations that comprise the "nonprofit sector" have in common? What are the defining characteristics of this sector?

Broadly speaking, six characteristics seem most crucial.[1] In particular, as we will use the term here, the nonprofit sector refers to a set of organizations that are:

- *Formal,* that is, institutionalized to some extent. Purely ad hoc, informal, and temporary gatherings of people are not considered part of the nonprofit sector, even though they may be quite important in people's lives. At the same time, the nonprofit sector may include many organizations that are not formally incorporated. Typically, however, nonprofit organizations have a legal identity as corporations chartered under state laws. This corporate status makes the organization a legal person able to enter contracts and largely frees the officers of personal financial responsibility for the organization's commitments.
- *Private,* that is, institutionally separate from government. Nonprofit organizations are neither part of the governmental apparatus nor governed by boards dominated by government officials. This does not mean that they may not receive significant government support. What is more, government participation on nonprofit boards is not unheard of, as was the case with Yale University until the 1870s.[2] But nonprofit organizations are fundamentally private institutions in basic structure.
- *Non-profit-distributing,* that is, not dedicated to generating profits for their owners.

Nonprofit organizations may accumulate profits in a given year, but the profits must be plowed back into the basic mission of the agency, not distributed to the organizations' founders. This differentiates nonprofit organizations from the other component of the private sector—private businesses.

- *Self-governing,* that is, equipped to control their own activities. Nonprofit organizations have their own internal procedures for governance and are not controlled by outside entities.
- *Voluntary,* that is, involving some meaningful degree of voluntary participation, either in the actual conduct of the agency's activities or in the management of its affairs. Typically, this takes the form of a voluntary board of directors, but extensive use of volunteer staff is also common.
- *Of public benefit,* that is, serving some public purpose and contributing to the public good.

The Rationale: Why Do We Have a Nonprofit Sector?

Why does the nonprofit sector exist in the United States, or any other country? Why did such organizations come into existence, and why do we give these organizations special tax and other advantages?

Five major considerations seem to be involved.

Historical

In the first place, the nonprofit sector came into existence for reasons that are largely historical. In the United States, as well as in many other countries, society predated the state. In other words, communities formed before governmental structures, or governmental institutions, were in place to help deal with their common concerns. People therefore had to tackle problems on their own and often found it useful to join with others in voluntary organizations to

do so. The result was the creation of voluntary fire departments, schools, adoption societies, and many more. Even after governments came into existence, moreover, Americans were often reluctant to use them, fearing the rebirth of monarchy, or bureaucracy. Therefore, citizens still had to take matters into their own hands until they could persuade their fellow citizens that government help was needed. Once created, these organizations then often continued in existence even after government entered the scene, frequently helping government meet a need.

Market Failure

Beyond this historical reason, the creation of nonprofit organizations has been motivated by certain inherent limitations of the market system, which dominates the American economy.[3] Economists refer to these as *market failures.* Essentially, the problem is this: The market is excellent for handling those things we consume individually, such as shoes, cars, clothing, food. For such items, consumer choices in the marketplace send signals to producers about the prices that will be paid and the quantities that can be sold at those prices. By contrast, the market does not handle very well those things that can only be consumed collectively, such as clean air, national defense, or safe neighborhoods. These so-called public goods involve a serious "free-rider" problem because, once they are produced, everyone can benefit from them even if they have not shared in the cost. Therefore, it is to each individual's advantage to let his or her neighbor bear the cost of these collective goods because each individual will be able to enjoy them whether he or she pays for them or not. Because everyone will think the same way, however, the inevitable result will be to produce far too little of these collective goods and thus leave everyone worse off.

To correct for this, some form of nonmarket mechanism is needed. One such mechanism is government. By imposing taxes on individuals, government can compel everyone to share in the cost of collective goods. But another mechanism for overcoming market failure is the nonprofit sector. Nonprofit organizations allow groups of individuals to pool their resources to produce collective goods they mutually desire but cannot convince a majority of their countrymen to support. This can happen, for example, when particular subgroups share certain cultural, social, or economic characteristics or interests not shared by all citizens of a country. Through nonprofit organizations such subgroups can provide the kinds and levels of collective goods they desire.

A slightly different kind of market failure occurs where the purchasers of services are not the same as the consumers, a situation economists refer to as *contract failure*.[4] This is the case, for example, with nursing homes, where the consumers are often elderly people with limited consumer choice or ability to discriminate among products and the purchasers are their children. In such situations, the purchasers, unable to assess the adequacy of services themselves, seek some substitute for the market mechanism, some provider they can trust. Because nonprofits do not exist principally to earn profits, they often are preferred providers in such situations.

Government Failure

A third reason for the existence of a vibrant nonprofit sector springs from certain inherent limitations of government as a provider of collective goods. In the first place, in a democracy it is often difficult to get government to act to correct "market failures" because government action requires majority support. By forming nonprofit organizations, smaller groupings of people can begin addressing needs that they have not yet convinced others to support.

Even when majority support exists, however, there is still often a preference for some nongovernmental mechanism to deliver services and respond to public needs because of the cumbersomeness, unresponsiveness, and bureaucratization that often accompanies government action. This is particularly true in the United States because of a strong cultural resistance to the expansion of government. Even when government financing is viewed as essential, therefore, it is often the case that private,

nonprofit organizations are utilized to deliver the services that government finances. The result, as will be detailed later, is a complex pattern of cooperation between government and the nonprofit sector.

Pluralism/Freedom

A fourth reason for the existence of nonprofit organizations has less to do with the efficiency of these organizations or the service functions they perform than with the role they play in promoting a crucial social value—the value of freedom and pluralism. As John Stuart Mill pointed out in his classic treatise, *On Liberty,* "Government operations tend to be everywhere alike. With individuals and voluntary associations, on the contrary, there are varied experiments, and endless diversity of experience."[5] Nonprofit organizations encourage individual initiative for the public good just as the business corporation encourages individual action for the private good. Most of the major reforms in American society, in fact, have originated in this nonprofit sector—civil rights, environmental protection, workplace safety, child welfare, women's rights, and the New Right. Even if it were the case that government was far more efficient than the nonprofit sector in responding to citizen needs, Americans would still insist on a vibrant nonprofit sector as a guarantor of their liberties and a mechanism to ensure a degree of pluralism.

Solidarity

Finally, the nonprofit sector is a response to the need for some mechanism through which to give expression to sentiments of solidarity. This is particularly important in individualistic societies like the United States, as Alexis de Tocqueville pointed out in his seminal essay 150 years ago. In fact, it was this facet of the nonprofit sector that Toqueville had principally in mind when he argued, "In democratic countries the science of association is the mother of science; the progress of all the rest depends upon the progress it has made."[6] The reason, Toqueville observed, is that "... among democratic nations . . . all the citizens are independent and feeble; they can do hardly anything by themselves, and none of them can oblige his fellow men to lend him their assistance. They all, therefore, become powerless if they do not learn voluntarily to help one another."

Voluntary associations are thus needed especially critically in democratic societies to create artificially what the equality of conditions makes it extremely difficult to create naturally, namely, a capacity for joint action. It is for this reason that Toqueville finds it so noteworthy that "wherever at the head of some new undertaking you see government in France, or a man of rank in England, in the United States you will be sure to find an association." As he notes, "If men living in democratic countries had no right and no inclination to associate for political purposes, their independence would be in great jeopardy, but they might long preserve their wealth and their cultivation; whereas if they never acquired the habit of forming associations in ordinary life, civilization itself would be endangered."

Conclusion

In short, there is a vitally important set of institutions in American society that, despite many differences, all share certain common features. They are formally constituted, private, self-governing, non-profit-distributing, voluntary, and of public benefit. Together they comprise what we will call the nonprofit sector.

The existence of this set of organizations is partly an accident of history. But it has more concrete foundations as well—in the inherent limitations of the market in responding to public needs, in the inherent limitations of government as the sole alternative mechanism to respond to market failures, in the need that a democratic society has for some way to promote cooperation among equal individuals, and in

the value Americans attach to pluralism and freedom.

The rationale for the existence of a nonprofit sector is not peculiar to American society, of course. The same arguments apply to other societies as well, particularly those with democratic governmental structures and market-oriented economic systems. But there is no denying that these organizations have come to play a particularly important role in the American setting. While there is reason to question whether American nonprofit organizations always live up to the expectations that these theories assign to them, it seems clear that the existence of such a set of institutions has come to be viewed as a critical component of community life, a compelling and fulfilling way to meet community needs, and a crucial prerequisite of a true "civil society."

Notes

1. Maria Brenton, *The Voluntary Sector in British Social Services* (London: Longman, 1985), p. 9

2. John S. Whitehead, *The Separation of College and State: Columbia, Dartmouth, Harvard and Yale, 1776–1876* (New Haven, CT: Yale University Press, 1973).

3. This line of argument has been applied to the nonprofit sector most explicitly in Burton Weisbrod, *The Voluntary Nonprofit Sector* (Lexington, MA: Lexington Books, 1978).

4. This line of argument has been developed most explicitly in Henry Hansmann, "Why Are Nonprofit Organizations Exempted from Corporate Income Taxation," in Michelle J. White (ed.), *Nonprofit Firms in a Three-Sector Economy*, COUPE Papers (Washington, DC: The Urban Institute Press, 1981).

5. John Stuart Mill, *On Liberty*, quoted in Bruce R. Hopkins, *The Law of Tax-Exempt Organizations*, 5th Ed. (New York: John Wiley and Sons, 1987), p. 7.

6. Alexis de Tocqueville, *Democracy in America* [The Henry Reeve Text] (New York: Alfred A. Knopf, Inc., 1945), pp. 114–118.

CHAPTER 14

A New Approach:
The Theory of the Commons

ROGER A. LOHMANN

In the first issue of the *Journal of Voluntary Action Research,* Smith and others (1972) asked, "Can there be a theory of voluntary action, or must/should we pay major attention to theories and models about one or another aspect of voluntary action without attempting to put it all together for the moment?" (1972, p. 6). Clearly, the latter course proved the prudent one, and "the moment" lasted for twenty years.

Two decades later, voluntary action theory and its cognate, nonprofit theory, even with the various extensions identified in the preceding chapter, are still insufficient for clarity of understanding, policy, or practice.

My approach is to attempt to identify a set of interdisciplinary "first principles" rather than the more conventional residual approach, which, according to the introductory editorial statement of *Voluntas,* treats the voluntary sector "as what is left over once government and commercial agencies, and probably also the 'informal sector,' have been put to one side." Especially important in defining the sector in this way is value for comparative studies in the international domain (Anheier and Knapp, 1990).

I am not primarily concerned with all nonprofit organizations, all members of the legal category of nonprofit corporations, or all members of the subcategory of tax-exempt corpora-

tions. My primary concern is with eleemosynary or donative associations, organizations, and groups engaged in unproductive or volunteer labor, whether or not they are incorporated, recognized by the state, tabulated in national data, or made up of paid employees. This broad category of social organizations will be called *commons* for reasons that follow, and generalizations about these organizations will be said to constitute the theory of the commons.

Initial Premises and Assumptions

The following discussion sets forth nine basic assumptions upon which the theory of the commons is premised.

Social Action

One of the most interesting and challenging characteristics of nonprofit and voluntary services is their intangible character. Thus, a basic assumption of the theory of the commons is that nonprofit services and unproductive labors are composed of social action, or "substantively meaningful experience emanating from our spontaneous life based upon preconceived projects" (Schutz, 1970, p. 125). As Max Weber (1968, p. 4) puts it, "In 'action' is included all human behavior when and insofar as the acting individual attaches a subjective meaning to it." Ignoring or explicitly rejecting profit orientation, said by some to be the defining characteristic of nonprofit action, constitutes such a subjective attachment of meaning.

Action, in this sense, is social insofar as subjective meaning attached to it by acting individuals "takes account of the behavior of others and is thereby oriented in its course" (Weber, 1968, p. 4). Philanthropy as action for the good of humanity, charity as action for the good of others, altruism as action in the interest of others—all involve social action in this sense. Thus, the various organizations and structures of nonprofit and voluntary action will present predictable, recurring, and institutionalized as well as idiosyncratic patterns of social action (Billis, 1991).

Affluence

Under ordinary circumstances, overriding ethical considerations of philanthropic, charitable, and altruistic purposes discourage people from seeking personal gain and mandate that people in the commons deny, downplay, or ignore their own self-interests. The appropriateness of such self-denial, however, is conditional upon the absence of any immediate threats to the safety, security, health, or well-being of those people involved. (One cannot, for example, ethically demand of starving people that they take time out from the pursuit of food to aid others who may be ill or homeless.) We might ask, Under what circumstances is such self-denial reasonable? An answer to this question is offered by the condition of affluence.

Bona fide participation in the commons is available only to the affluent: those people whose individual and group survival and reproduction are sufficiently assured so that their own self-interest is not their paramount concern. Only those whose basic needs for survival and reproduction have been met are in a position to rationally choose or reject self-interested behavior. It is unreasonable to expect that peo-

ple who are starving, under siege or assault, or threatened with extinction should rationally choose to ignore their own interests or that any society or association can have a legitimate interest in encouraging them to do so.

Under conditions of affluence, when the problems of material, human, and social reproduction are overcome, even momentarily, the choice of whether to engage in maximizing profit or some other nonprofit activity is, itself, a rational choice. In the United States, the creation of a tax-exempt, nonprofit 501(c)(3) corporation signifies the creation of a commons, and individuals knowingly accepting the legal obligations of board membership for such an organization indicate a willingness to abide by its standards.

Authenticity

The theory of the commons also assumes that actors operating in nonprofit and voluntary settings are *authentic;* that is, they are what they appear to be to informed others also operating in the same context (Etzioni, 1968). Affluent actors who seek to pursue their own self-interest in the commons or whose individual or organizational goals include maximizing utility are operating under false pretenses and are subject to penalty or expulsion from the commons. Norms of authenticity may not be universally or consistently invoked, but when they are invoked, the result is usually consistent and convincing, as in the collapse of various empires of television evangelists in the past decade. State charity fraud statutes throughout the United States seek to enforce such norms of authenticity.

Although it may appear to be somewhat pretentious or moralistic, the norm of authenticity points up the fundamentally ethical core of common social action and encapsulates numerous examples of actual empirical practices in the commons. For example, professional oaths in helping professions usually prohibit placing the professionals' own interests above those of the clients, and scientists in most disciplines are subject to severe sanctions for falsifying research data or results. Thus, although its enforcement may be complex and problematic, there is little doubt of the importance of the assumption of authenticity in nonprofit and voluntary action.

Continuity

Charitable, philanthropic, and altruistic action and other common action is also associated with consistent life-style choices. The experience of others in nonprofit and voluntary action is an ongoing one, characterized by past, present, and future and a sense of connectedness between them. The experience of continuity offers a basis for explanation and prediction.

Continuity in nonprofit and voluntary action is often experienced in the form of tradition. I (and others) will continue to exist in a known and knowable world through the repetition of time-honored ceremonies and habitual and familiar ritual acts. The continuity of present experience may also be experienced as rational. We will act in the appropriate manner because it is reasonable, predictable, or productive of desirable consequences to do so. Occasionally the experience of continuity even takes the form of transformative, "inexplicable," or other charismatic experiences.

Practical questions of an intergenerational nature often arise with respect to the appropriate division of an individual's estate between heirs and the commons. Legal issues of this type are among the oldest, most long-standing, and thorniest of issues of the law as it relates to common goods.

Rationality

We shall assume that actors in the commons, engaged in acts of philanthropy, charity, and altruism, act rationally in the sense of observable consistency between the intentions they announce to themselves and others and the results they hold up to be successful outcomes. The rationality of actors in the commons is a practical rationality, concerned with the exercise of reason in solving the problems that arise in the conduct of daily affairs. It is often also a prosocial rationality, devoted to solving problems primarily affecting others, engaging in various forms of presentation, and obtaining

the resources necessary to carry out these pursuits.

The rationality of the commons is not merely a matter of moment-to-moment consistency of thought or behavior. The term *rational* refers, instead, to the philosophical sense of having (and following) a life plan (Rawls, 1971). Practical rationality, in this context, involves the day-to-day decisions that must be made in consistent pursuit of a life plan.

Near-Universality

Commons are assumed to be near-universal cultural forms, known in some manner in most, possibly all, human cultures (Brown, 1991). But the degree to and exact ways in which the theory of the commons transcends the U.S. cultural context and history remain to be determined. Research has already shown that commons exist in a variety of countries and cultures.

Nonprofit corporations and philanthropic foundations are the distinctive products of Anglo-American legal traditions. U.S. voluntary associations are the unique inventions of an open society devoid of a long heritage of intermediate institutions and intent upon creating an open society. Both nonprofit corporations and philanthropic foundations are members of a larger class of related groups, organizations, and institutions to which the name commons is applied.

In all known cultures, self-defining collectives of people voluntarily associate and act jointly outside of markets and households and independent of the state in pursuit of common purposes. Even among itinerant hunter-gatherers and farming and fishing cultures, leisure time not spent in subsistence activities can be devoted to group participation in common activities.

Autonomy

Organized action in the commons is assumed to be autonomous in the sense that actors in the commons are capable of acting independently and exercising both individual and group self-control. Such autonomy may merely be assumed or may take institutional form as freedoms of speech and association. Under repressive conditions, people may deliberately seek this autonomy by engaging in covert actions or secret societies.

Actors in the commons are assumed to be able to create and sustain autonomous social worlds. Although this idea is most evident in the case of certain social movements and religious zealots, it is also implicit in everyday clubs and associations of bird watchers, stamp collectors, and peace or environmental activists (Cavan, 1977; Cummings, 1977; Ross, 1977). The ability to act with others to create and sustain an autonomous social world is one of the most fundamental characteristics of nonprofit and voluntary action.

Intrinsic Valuation

The proper way to evaluate an autonomous common world is assumed to be on the basis of the values arising within it. Following Garfinkel, the theory of the commons refuses to give "serious consideration to the prevailing proposal that efficiency, efficacy, effectiveness, intelligibility, consistency, planfulness, typicality, uniformity, reproducibility of activities—i.e., that rational properties of practical activities—be assessed, recognized, categorized, described by using a rule or standard outside actual settings within which such properties are recognized, used, produced and talked about by settings' members" (quoted in Mitchell, 1978, p. 143).

Ordinary Language

An assumption related to that of intrinsic valuation is that a satisfactory theory of nonprofit and voluntary action must be stated in language that philanthropic, charitable, and altruistic actors can recognize and understand. Terms such as *endowment, benefit, gift, patron, legacy, heritage,* and *treasury* are among those borrowed from common usage and applied in the theory of the commons.

Terms and Concepts

On the basis of the previous assumptions, we can now look more closely at the basic vocabulary of the theory of the commons. In particular, we need an adequate summary term to describe the range of nonprofit and voluntary action usually grouped together in law, statistics, and tradition and to set it apart in a general sense from other human endeavors. In the following discussion, a set of related terms are set forth as fundamental to an understanding of nonprofit and voluntary action. These terms are *benefit, benefactory, commons, endowment, civilization, socialization, technique, search, treasury, collection, repertory, regime,* and *patronage.* Together, they provide a basic theoretical language for discussing nonprofit and voluntary action.

Benefit and Benefactory

The largest, most important, and most definitive subclass of nonprofit organizations are those 501(c)(3) nonprofit corporations that are exempt from federal taxation on the basis of their charitable purposes. Such organizations are part of a larger class of service organizations in which no tangible product is produced, marketed, or sold and no individual or group of owners or stockholders should legitimately expect to profit.

The term *benefactory* is used here as a play on the economic terms *factor* and *factory* and is intended to highlight the central role of deliberate and organized distribution of benefits. A benefit can be defined as an advantage, useful aid, or financial help (Gifis, 1991). Benefit, in general, involves enhancing or advancing the interests of any person or group by increasing wealth, health, well-being, safety, or security. A benefactory, then, is any network of organized social relations established for the purpose of aiding, assisting, helping, improving, supporting, comforting, enabling, or in other ways benefitting other persons or groups.

Obviously, charities such as soup kitchens or free counseling centers would be benefactories in this sense. However, the term can also be extended to encompass churches, symphony orchestras, experimental theatre groups, dance companies, museums, galleries, and all types of artistic and athletic events in which a performance or presentation by one group (actors, athletes, priests, political candidates, and others) has as its purpose enhancing the interests of other people (congregations, audiences).

Based on the assumptions of autonomy and authenticity discussed earlier, two tests can determine whether or not an organization should be considered a benefactory. First, there is the test of authenticity: is the potential benefactory what it appears to be, or is it merely a front for some other type of nonbenefactory? This is the test ordinarily applied by legal authorities in prosecution of charity scams and telephone solicitation "boiler rooms," in which false charitable claims are made. Second, there is the test of purpose: does the structure of the organization identify classes of benefactors and beneficiaries, and are the goals or purposes of the possible benefactory actually designed to benefit individuals or groups other than the benefactors?

As organizations, benefactories are distinct from firms, government bureaus, and families. If we follow the logic of Blau and Scott (1962) and Smith (1991), benefactories are also intrinsic, extrinsic, and mixed. *Intrinsic benefactories* include self-help groups, social and recreational clubs, membership associations, fraternal societies, trade associations, and employees' beneficiary associations, which focus their benefits upon members. *Extrinsic benefactories* include charitable organizations, foundations, civic associations, legal aid societies, and other groups that focus their benefits upon nonmember clients. *Mixed benefactories* engage in both intrinsic and extrinsic benefactions. Most churches, for example, combine ecclesiastical and missionary efforts.

Commons

The concept of benefactory as employed here corresponds with many uses of the generic term *organization*, albeit with an explicit emphasis on the dispensing of benefit to designated target groups. It necessarily implies a second level of relations between the benefactors (or patrons), beneficiaries, and those who may be acting as benefactors to the benefactor. This complex of intrinsic and extrinsic organized relations is one of several related meanings I will attach to the term *commons*.

The main characteristics of what I intend by the concept of commons are encompassed by the Greek term *koinonia*. According to the historian M. I. Finley (1974b), the ancient Greeks had five prerequisites for koinonia: (1) participation must be free and uncoerced; (2) participants must share a common purpose, whether major or minor, long term or short term; (3) participants must have something in common that they share such as jointly held resources, a collection of precious objects, or a repertory of shared actions; (4) participation involves *philia* (a sense of mutuality, often inadequately translated as friendship); and (5) social relations must be characterized by *dikiaon* (fairness). This five-part definition encompasses all of the major elements sought by advocates of nonprofit, voluntary, independent, and third-sector terminology and does so in a simple and elegant manner.

If it is defined in this manner, the commons is an explicitly interdisciplinary concept that links under a single rubric the separate concerns of the nonprofit organization and voluntary labor perspective and the voluntary action perspective, which is concerned with associations and groups. Definitions of groups tend to emphasize stable patterns of interaction and feelings of unity and shared consciousness that parallel the shared purpose and mutuality in the definition of koinonia/commons (Smith and Preston, 1977; Vander Zander, 1977). Defining organizations as groups "deliberately formed to achieve a specific goal or set of goals through a formalized set of rules and procedures," Smith and Preston (1977, p. 536) connect purpose with a specific set of means. Uncoerced participation is ordinarily indicated by placing the word *voluntary* before the word *group, organization,* or *association*. Thus, any set of related social acts characterized by uncoerced participation, common purpose, shared resources, mutuality, and fairness can be characterized as common, and social organizations and institutions in which such norms predominate can be called commons.

A commons can be thought of as an economic, political, and social space outside the market, households, and state in which associative communities create and reproduce social worlds. Associative social worlds are composed of the images, meanings, and sense of reality shared by autonomous, self-defining collectivities of voluntarily associating individuals.

A basic characteristic of social action in commons is the norm of mutual reciprocity. Participants in markets and states feel no such mutuality. Instead, market participants are usually governed by the norm of quid pro quo (give and take), and concepts of the democratic state place emphasis on equity—in particular, the equality of citizens before the state. Social relations in the commons are governed by the basic norm of fairness. Market relations are governed by caveat emptor (let the buyer beware), and social relations in the state are governed by law (including rules, as in the Weberian model of bureaucracy [Weber, 1968]).

As commentators since Adam Smith and Alexis de Tocqueville have noted, commons include some of the most intrinsically interesting of human endeavors. These endeavors include religious celebrations, ceremonies, rituals, and observances; dialogue and contemplation; basic scientific research; literary criticism and hermeneutics; the arts; amateur athletics; counseling and psychotherapy; and care of abused or neglected children and adults, the dying, and the disadvantaged. We might even include political activities such as electoral campaigns, legislative or administrative advocacy, political parties and caucuses, labor unions, and trade associations in this list, insofar as their immediate goals are noncommercial.

Commons in art, religion, philosophy, and athletic games are found in diverse forms in all human societies. In addition, achievements in these commons are frequently among the elements cited as hallmarks of the attainment of high civilization.

Wherever and whenever commons are found, we see the coordinated social action of benefactors, intermediaries, and beneficiaries. Indeed, commons are inherently social. The existence of a community—a plurality of mutually interested and interacting persons—is a fundamental precondition of religion, athletic games, ceremonies, art, science, social service, and all true commons.

The essential character of commons rests in their role in the presentation and dramatization of profound symbols of community; that is, in the affirmation of the most fundamental human values of the community through human communication (Goodman and Goodman, 1960; Hillary, 1963; Warren, 1963). No civilization can afford to ignore or deny this role of the commons without trampling underfoot its most sacred values. To see a U.S. Fourth of July celebration only as an activity of state, for example, is to miss much of its fundamental character as a celebration of the nation—itself a kind of commons.

Commons are not places any more than are markets or states. Commons consist of sets of complex social acts that are basic, universal, and not reducible to more fundamental categories of social behavior. The mutual, collective purposes, ends, or objectives that participants in these complex acts share (regardless of their rationality or irrationality as perceived by outsiders) constitute the common goods that are the real economic products of the commons.

Significant common acts include worship, contemplation, help, inquiry, self-expression, and play (the latter often dignified as leisure, recreation, or athletics). Each of these acts is a fundamental human activity at least as basic as production, consumption, or exchange and not reducible to them. Any theory of economics that reduces common goods to the basic categories of production, consumption, and exchange is reductionistic and misleading.

Although a commons is not primarily a physical place, it may include a place, as in the case of temples and other common spaces. A commons can be any social space for interaction within a community. Common space may be a committee room, a conference center, a restaurant dining room, or almost any other public or private space. It may also be the social space of a newspaper, scientific journal, or electronic bulletin board. The commons can be anywhere in the community where the baseline assumptions discussed earlier are played out.

It is evident as well by the frequency with which community terms such as *fellowship, congregation,* and so on are used in describing such communities.

It is useful, therefore, to locate the commons alongside the marketplace and the state, with its distinctive concerns for the authoritative allocation of values. The metaphor of the commons is particularly appropriate in the context of U.S. history. Important historical cities as diverse as Boston, New Haven, Philadelphia, and Santa Fe have commons even today. The town square is a major feature in many smaller communities as well. Similarly, most associations have an annual meeting or conference whose function, at least formally, illustrates the potential for open dialogue in the commons.

Commons are fundamentally "universes of discourse." They are composed of groups of people who understand one another, speak common languages, and evolve specialized terminology and language over time. Such discursive universes are a type of commons whose shared understandings have become known as cultures (Urban, 1991), communities (Schwartzman, 1992), or paradigms (Berger and Luckmann, 1966; Bernstein, 1983; Kuhn, 1962). In this sense, *philosophers, librarians, physicists, Roman Catholics, philatelists, joggers,* and *social workers* are all terms for such commons, and *realism, information science,* and *Copernican cosmology* are the names of particular paradigms.

Commons tend to be organized both informally, through use of common languages and a common worldview, and formally, through associations and other noncoercive groups. The structure of a commons consists of a community of one or more benefactories and related basic institutions. Two such institutions are most basic: language and education.

Common language is essential because without it meaningful common activities would be literally impossible. The existence of all types of common activities on a significant scale requires substantial language ability. This is particularly the case with commons in which the community functions as a reference group to set and reinforce attitudes and values, a process that occurs primarily through the medium of spoken and written language.

Another set of institutions basic to the commons are those necessary for the education, training, and socialization of participants. Because knowledge, as the combination of available meanings and information, is a key element in the commons, ways and means of passing knowledge among members of the community and from one generation to another are basic to any commons. Ways of passing on knowledge include the socialization rites by which primitive youths are initiated into the mysteries of tribal dance and legends, the apprenticeships of medieval cathedral builders, and the management training programs of the modern private nonprofit settlement house.

In the United States, ongoing associations of all types tend to be incorporated because of the explicit tax concessions and limits on participant liability offered by incorporation. Incorporation, however, represents a legal adaptation in a particular society and not a fundamental defining characteristic of commons.

Democratic self-governance has evolved as one of the basic characteristics of the autonomous commons, in which participants are free to leave if they wish. The model of the self-governing association is characterized by a special vocabulary. *Bylaws* are rules adopted by a group to regulate its own actions.

Meetings are official gatherings, sessions, or assemblies of the group. *Plenary* means full, complete, entire, or unqualified. A *plenary session,* such as an annual meeting, is a meeting that is open to the full or entire membership.

A *committee* consists of "a person or persons to whom the consideration or determination of certain business is referred or confided" (Gifis, 1991, p. 82). The *board of directors* or *trustees* is a special committee, elected by rules or procedures held by the group to be fair and usually spelled out in the bylaws or articles. In most state law, boards are held responsible for the overall management of the affairs of the association or corporation (Oleck, 1980).

Civilization

Hill's treatment (1983) of what he calls the "concept pool" offers a useful pointer to the concepts of civilization and paradigm as human endowments. Every commons is endowed with a dowry of jointly held resources, some created by its benefactories; some received from markets, states, and households; and some handed down from benefactors of previous generations (and thus constituting its heritage). For example, the rituals and practices of *The Book of Common Prayer* are part of the endowment of the Church of England, and the collection of books in a college library are part of the resource endowment of the school.

Some portion of every endowment consists of public goods for the simple reason that any good that is available equally to everyone will be as available in the commons as it is elsewhere. Thus, the Library of Congress is part of the resource endowment of every U.S. school, thanks to the interlibrary loan system. Current economic arguments notwithstanding, however, the production of public goods is not a fundamental objective in most commons. Members of religious groups, lodges, fraternities, sororities, and other social groups do not indiscriminately seek to share participation and mutual relations with every other social organization but only with others of similar affiliation (and presumably similar outlook).

I shall employ the term *common goods* for the goods shared in commons. Private goods can also be made available to the commons by donation. The bulk of common goods, however, are characterized by the rather remarkable fact that while they may not be universal in the same sense as public goods, they are treated as universal within the commons. This is one of the most difficult concepts to realize or implement when money and market goods enter the commons. Perhaps some examples will help.

The system of metric measurement is a common good. Metric measurement is not yet a public good in the United States because it is not indivisible, in that some people can practice it while others cannot, and it is not universal. Yet in scientific communities in which any type of exact measurement is important, the metric system is a common good. It is in precisely this sense that metric measurement (indeed, mathematics as a whole) is an important component of the endowment of modern science, and presumably a part of its legacy to future scientific development.

In this same sense, the astronomical observations and calculations of a great many ancient civilizations were part of their endowments.

The particular legacy of Western civilization that we call humanism, humanitarianism, or, more recently, the much derided secular humanism, is another such resource endowment that is especially important in the modern private nonprofit world.

It is the role of the commons in preserving, restoring, and utilizing the heritage of a civilization that is unique. Commons apply resources of our heritage to solve what might be called the puzzles or mysteries offered by a particular cultural heritage—whether religious, scientific, or modern-day attacks upon social problems.

The value of a particular endowment may be realized only in dramatizing, presenting, and thereby preserving it. This is as true of jazz musicians seeking to preserve their legacy in after-hours jam sessions as it is of the concert halls, museums, and theaters of the culture industry. The endowment of the Latin language was irreversibly transformed when it ceased to represent the resource of a living language. Until the advent of writing, literature, myth, and lore could only be preserved through the oral tradition of retold tales. In a similar way, prior to visual recording techniques and systems of choreographic notation, dance could only be preserved through actual regular performance.

The sum total of the values of a civilization (its social capital, so to speak) may include a great many artifacts that are neither purely privately held nor universally accessible. It is that portion of a civilization which we can call its endowment. In a larger sense, a civilization itself represents a common endowment as it is passed down from one generation to the next.

Socialization, Technique, and Search

A good deal of the social action of sustaining cultural continuity occurs within the commons. Much of that action consists of three fundamental processes: *socialization,* or learning; *technique,* or performing learned skills and demonstrating repertories and thereby revitalizing them in the present; and *search,* or consciously seeking to solve established problems or identify new ways of doing things. The learning and presentation of repertories, which often take routine disciplines or ritual forms, can constitute an important study in itself.

Socialization, technique, and search are fundamentally important processes in any commons, market, or state. Socialization is a social and psychological process related to voluntary participation. The role of socialization in the formation of commons and in the admission of new participants to commons has not been widely explored, however.

Treasury

A *treasury* is generally the best known and most clearly understood set of common resources held by a benefactory. Treasuries consist of closely measured funds of identifiable assets; that is, resources that can be measured by accounting systems and reported in financial statements of an association or corporation. Treasuries seem to have been important in nonprofit institutions long before the modern age. In addition to the ark of the covenant, the original temple at Jerusalem contained a temple treasury (de Vaux, 1965). The treasury is also a standard feature in the architecture of Greek temples (V. Scully, 1991).

Repertory

The resource endowment of a commons that is the most difficult of all to deal with is the intangible *repertory*—the symbolic gestures, rituals, and ceremonies of religious bodies; the skillful, nuanced performances of actors, singers, musicians, and other performers; the occult body of specialized knowledge and practical wisdom, whether scientific, magical, religious, artistic, political, or otherwise, that communities have built up over years, decades, and in some instances centuries.

A repertory is, in this sense, any set of acts that an individual or group is prepared to perform. It may be the set of discrete but related skilled behaviors necessary to rescue a community of disaster victims or the set of unique patterned motions and utterances that compose a performance of *Hamlet.*

Repertories are often built up of sequences of related problem-solving strategies. Some repertories involve straightforward applications of if-then reasoning: if the victim is choking then perform the Heimlich maneuver. This maneuver and numerous others constitute the repertory of emergency medical technicians.

Although we may be unaccustomed to thinking of them as resources, performance repertories are also among the key resources of the commons. They often constitute the uniqueness and relative advantage of the commons that money cannot buy. This is as true of charitable and religious organizations as it is of artistic performances and athletic competitions. For example, the twelve-step method of Alcoholics Anonymous describes a repertory that is distinctive and unmistakable.

Economists, accountants, and managers have shown virtually no interest in repertories as key resources of nonprofit corporate benefactories. Contemporary financial statements and annual reports not only fail to list estimates of the value of repertories, they usually even fail to note their existence. Such are the exigencies of contemporary concern with the accountability of nonprofit groups.

Regime

According to Ostrander, Langton, and Van Til (1988), we need new ways of thinking about the interdependence and interaction of the state, for-profit organizations, and nonprofit organizations. It may be possible, however, to use existing concepts in new ways to produce what represents, in effect, such new ways of thinking. One approach, for example, is to use the interdisciplinary model of urbanism, with its distinction between core and periphery, as a matrix for spelling out the links between sectors.

The concepts of core and periphery as they have evolved in urban and regional theory can be used to distinguish the defining, or central, characteristics of the sectors from other peripheral functions that they may serve. Thus in the traditional terms of the theory of civil society, the recognized core of the state involves those coercive powers usually identified as police powers. It is a conventional axiom of political theory that legitimate governments may justly deprive others of their liberty and property through the exercise of these powers. Yet modern governments also clearly involve a variety of public (that is, tax-supported) functions in which coercion is replaced by compassion, community, or some other public virtue.

The political concept of regime can be broadened and usefully applied for this purpose. A *regime* may be said to be a network of related formal and communal organizations across sectors. We already have names for some such combinations. *Democracy* is the term we ordinarily apply to a regime in the control of elected officials. Oligarchy, fascism, and monarchy are other types of regimes.

The literatures on participatory democracy, coproduction, and collaboration also conjure up quite distinct core regimes. At the heart of the Reagan revolution was the vision of a market-centered, family-centered regime, with a restricted state and a vibrant commons on its periphery.

As a regime may be said to consist of a specific set of relations between commons, markets, states, and households, a civilization may be said to consist of a set of relations between regimes. Medieval Western civilization, for example, was built upon the primacy of a particular set of religious commons, and modern Western civilization is to a high degree built upon the civil society model of the supremacy of the constitutionally limited nation-state (Cohen and Arato, 1992).

Patronage

The core of the commons, as noted earlier, consists of social relations between patrons, agents, and clients. *Patronage* occurs between a *patron* (someone with some type of good) and a *client* (someone who is seeking that same good).

The central focus of patronage theory in the commons is on voluntary (uncoerced) hierarchies—of power, influence, wealth, status, information, knowledge, or other resources—and the circumstances leading to the emergence and continuation of inequalities in this sense. This focus accounts in part for the strong emphasis on negation in terminology of the commons. The absence of kinship as a requirement of asso-

ciation membership, for example, points up the nonfamilial nature of the commons as a pure type. Apparent exchange asymmetries (or the absence of fair and equal exchanges by buyers and sellers in a competitive environment) for grants of all types point up the nonmarket nature of the commons. The absence of legitimate control or domination by a single actor (the "monopoly of force") points up the nonstate nature of the commons.

Patronage relationships may be seen in different ways by different parties; relations can be seen as coercive, remunerative, or normative by either party.

Note that many patronage relationships are asymmetric in another sense: they do not involve equitable exchange in its traditional sense. The teacher who gives knowledge, information, or skill to a student does not receive the student's ignorance in exchange. The patron who gives money to a charity or directly to the poor presents a much more complex case. Although the patron may not expect an equitable return, some reciprocation in terms of recognition, status, and gratitude may be involved. The current view that all common relations involve exchanges is thus one requiring a good deal of close examination.

Conclusion

Ordinary English contains a robust vocabulary for speaking of non-profit and voluntary action. Terms like *benefit, benefactory, commons, endowment, socialization, technique, search, treasury, collection, repertory, regime,* and *patronage* provide a conceptual matrix for denoting and explaining nonprofit and voluntary action. Moreover, they provide a vocabulary that places emphasis where many have argued it belongs— on the uncoerced cooperation of peers. For the most part, we may talk of issues and matters of common concern by using long-standing English terms like *commons, beneficiary,* and *endowment.* In other cases, there are no existing terms for important ideas, and we need to apply well-understood principles of language construction to coin terms like *benefactory.* In both cases, the robustness of our language serves us well.

References

Anheier, H. K., and Knapp, M. "Voluntas: An Editorial Statement. *Voluntas,* 1990, *1*(1), 1–12

Berger, P. L., and Luckmann, T. *The Social Construction of Reality: A Treatise in the Sociology of Knowledge.* Garden City, N.Y.: Anchor, 1966.

Bernstein, R. *Beyond Objectivism and Relativism: Science, Hermeneutics and Praxis.* Philadelphia: University of Pennsylvania Press, 1983.

Billis, D. "The Roots of Voluntary Agencies: A Question of Choice." *Nonprofit and Voluntary Sector Quarterly,* 1991, *20*(1), 57–70.

Blau, P. M., and Scott, W. R. *Formal Organizations.* San Francisco: Chandler, 1962.

Brown, D. *Human Universals.* Philadelphia: Temple University Press, 1991.

Cavan, R. S. "From Social Movement to Organized Society: The Case of the Anabaptists." *Journal of Voluntary Action Research,* 1977, *6*(3–4), 105–111.

Cohen, J. L., and Arato, A. *Civil Society and Political Theory.* Cambridge, Mass.: MIT Press, 1992.

Cummings, L. D. "Voluntary Strategies in the Environmental Movement: Recycling as Cooptation." *Journal of Voluntary Action Research,* 1977, *6*(3–4), 153–160.

de Vaux, R. *Ancient Israel.* Vol. 2: *Religious Institutions.* New York: McGraw-Hill, 1965.

Etzioni, A. *The Active Society: A Theory of Societal and Political Processes.* New York: Free Press, 1968.

Finley, M. I. "Aristotle and Economic Analysis." In M. I. Finley (ed.), *Studies in Ancient Society.* New York: Routledge & Kegan Paul, 1974b.

Gifis, S. H. *Law Dictionary.* (3d ed.) New York: Barrons, 1991.

Goodman, P., and Goodman, P. *Communitas: Means of Livelihood and Ways of Life.* New York: Vintage, 1960.

Hill, L. E. "The Pragmatic Alternative to Positive Economics *Review of Social Economics,* 1983, 1–11.

Hillary, G. *Communal Organizations: A Study of Local Societies.* Chicago: University of Chicago Press, 1963.

Kuhn, T. S. *The Structure of Scientific Revolutions.* Chicago: University of Chicago Press, 1962.

Mitchell, J. N. *Social Exchange, Dramaturgy and Ethnomethodology.* New York: Elsevier Science, 1978.

Oleck, H. L. *Non-Profit Corporations and Associations.* (4th ed.) Englewood Cliffs, N.J.: Prentice-Hall, 1980.

Ostrander, S., Langton, S., and Van Til, J. *Shifting the Debate Public/Private Sector Relations in the Modern Welfare State.* New Brunswick, N.J.: Transaction, 1988.

Rawls, J. *A Theory of Justice.* Cambridge, Mass.: Harvard University Press, 1971.

Ross, J. C. "Arnold Rose on Voluntary Associations." *Journal of Voluntary Action Research,* 1977, *6*(1–2), 7–17.

Schutz, A. *On Phenomenology and Social Relations: Selected Writings.* Chicago: University of Chicago Press, 1970.

Schwartzman, S. *A Space for Science: The Development of the Scientific Community of Brazil.* University Park: Pennsylvania State University Press, 1992.

Scully, V. "The Greek Temple." In *Architecture: The Natural and the Manmade.* New York: St. Martin's Press, 1991

Smith, D. H. "Four Sectors or Five? Retaining the Member-Benefit Sector." *Nonprofit and Volunteer Sector Quarterly,* 1991, *20*(2), 137–151.

Smith, D. H., and others. "Major Analytical Topics of Voluntary Action Theory and Research: Version 2." *Journal of Voluntary Action Research,* 1972, *1*(1), 6–19.

Smith, R. W., and Preston, F. W. *Sociology: An Introduction.* New York: St. Martin's Press, 1977.

Urban, G. A. *Discourse Centered Approach to Culture: Native South American Myths and Rituals.* Austin: University of Texas Press, 1991.

Vander Zander, J. W. *Social Psychology.* New York: Random House, 1977.

Warren, R. *The Community in America.* Skokie, Ill.: Rand McNally, 1963.

Weber, M. "Economy and Society: An Outline of Interpretive Sociology." (G. Roth and C. Wittich, eds.) New York: Bedminster Press, 1968.

PART 6

ECONOMIC AND POLITICAL THEORIES OF THE NONPROFIT SECTOR

Most economic and political theories try to answer questions about the roles of nonprofit sector organizations and the functions they serve in a three-sector political economic society.* Some theories, for example, seek to explain why nonprofits exist—or exist in a particular form—in a society with a unique blending of political dynamics, entrepreneurial capitalism, and a government that organizes, provides and regulates many services. Numerous economic role theories have examined the "failures" of the market, of government, and of contracts as justifications for the existence and characteristics of the nonprofit sector.[1] Political scientists, economists, and sociologists alike have used *niche theories* to explain why some nonprofits cluster in certain functional and geographical areas.[2] At a different level, theorists and researchers have used *rational choice theories*, *principal-agent theories*, and *transaction cost theories*, among others, to help explain why government agencies prefer to contract for services instead of provide services directly, why government contracts for the provision of some types of services with organizations in the nonprofit sector instead of with for-profit businesses, and why government does not appear to have a preference between nonprofits and for-profits when it comes to other services.

Answers to questions such as these are of major importance to practitioners in all three sectors as well as to university teachers and researchers. As Kurt Lewin wisely reminded us several decades ago, "There is nothing so practical as a good theory."[3]

There are many more economic theories of the nonprofit sector than political or political-economy theories. Economic theories of the sector may be loosely divided into two categories: role theories—theories that try to explain why the sector and its organizations exist in the economic,

---

*E. Brigham Daniels made major contributions to this chapter. I am grateful for his sage advice, uniformly useful suggestions, gentle but accurate criticisms, and for his drafts of portions of this introductory essay.

political, and/or political economy system; and *functional theories*—theories that attempt to explain what it is that organizations in the nonprofit sector do, how they function, and why.

Most political scientists remained largely unaware of the importance of the nonprofit sector for politics and government until the last decade of the twentieth century. Meanwhile, theorists from other fields ventured into the nonprofit political void. Political, economic, and political-economy theories have been written by economists, sociologists, psychologists, scholars from business and public administration, and a few by political scientists. This part presents a balanced representation, but obviously some important theories and theorists had to be omitted.

Economic Theories

All discussions about economic theories that apply to the nonprofit sector can be traced to concepts first introduced by Adam Smith. Smith, who is widely acknowledged as being the "father" of modern economics, divided all labor into two categories: *productive labor* and *unproductive labor*. According to Smith, productive labor "adds to the value of the subject upon which it is bestowed."[4] Unproductive labor does not add value. Prior to the 1980s, most economists tended to dismiss activities in the nonprofit sector as unproductive labor and therefore the sector as not value-producing. The sector had been viewed by many mainstream economists as being outside the realm of rational economics, because it was not profit-driven, and thus it was largely ignored.[5]

Changes in Nonprofit Revenue Sources During the 1960s and 1970s

The nonprofit sector entered a period of major changes in revenue sources during the late 1960s and 1970s. Nonprofit organizations (particularly in some subsectors) that had relied heavily on donated funds began to turn more to contracted services and funding from government agencies. The changes caught the attention of the economists.[6] These revenue source changes became evident first in the fields of mental health and developmental disabilities but spread rapidly in other areas of the human services, health care, and to an extent in community development and housing.[7] The revenue source changes affected almost all aspects of nonprofit organizations' missions, structures, and operations. The effects of the changes extended to less obvious dimensions, such as the professionalism of management, the roles of boards of trustees, and the relationship between nonprofits and their communities.[8]

At the same time that many nonprofits continued to grow more reliant on government contracts during the 1970s, 1980s, and 1990s, many also turned aggressively to a second alternative revenue source. They started to become more "corporatized." They were surprisingly successful at learning to be more competitively entrepreneurial in their business strategies. Many competed directly for business with for-profit firms.[9]

Overall, the shifts in funding that have characterized the nonprofit sector for the past thirty to thirty-five years have dramatically altered the identities, roles, activities, and arguably the character of many organizations in the nonprofit sector.[10] As more and more nonprofit sector organizations were looking and acting like for-profit businesses, the economists' interest in them peaked. At the same time, theorists in other social sciences (and a few economists)[11] were asking whether government contracting and commercialization had irreparably damaged the long-term value, social contributions, and integrity of the sector.[12]

Nonprofits and Mainstream Economic Theory

Nonprofit organizations provide an interesting challenge for mainstream economic theory. For example, according to mainstream economic theory, the market establishes housing prices through interactions between the supply of houses and apartments on the market and consumers' (potential buyers' or renters') demand for housing. Because high housing prices make it difficult for low-income persons to enter the housing market, nonprofit and government organizations often provide housing subsidies. Nonprofit organizations, such as Habitat for Humanity, cobuild homes with the future occupants and sell them to the cobuilders at far less than the prices they could command on the open market. Government might also regulate the market using any of the many regulatory policy tools available to it. From the perspective of mainstream economic theory, nonprofit and government actions such as these that "artificially influence" the "natural" working of the market disturb its functioning and decrease its efficiency.

What economic theorists have found most compelling about nonprofit organizations—particularly the rapidly growing number of "professional" or "commercial" nonprofit organizations that look and act like private businesses—is that they exist *at all*.[13] The central question for mainstream economic theory thus leads back to Adam Smith's distinction between productive and unproductive labor: What can nonprofit organizations offer that profit-seeking firms cannot provide more efficiently? For decades, the economists' response to this question relied mostly on several "failure theories." *Failure theories* explain the existence or actions of one phenomenon by the failure of another phenomenon. In the housing example above, the presence in and actions of nonprofit organizations in the market are explained by the failure of the market to satisfy the demand for housing and by the failure of government to alleviate the problem. Nonprofit organizations have a presence in the housing market and function as they do because the market and government have failed to satisfy needs in communities for low-cost housing.

Economic Models

The argument that the sum of individual choices leads to the aggregate good is a controversial position. The failure of markets to meet this idealistic view does not invalidate the usefulness of economic models that attempt to predict economic behavior. Models are built to simplify complex sets of relationships and to explain the interactions among the most meaningful factors. They are not intended to explain all minute details, and it would be unfair to hold them to a standard of precise accuracy. Despite the limitations of economic models—which usually are publicly declared by their authors—economic models are highly useful for testing economic theories and for explaining or predicting the effects of government and business policies and the actions of individuals and organizations in the market. Occasionally, reality differs too much from the assumptions built into an economic model, effects differ dramatically from predictions, and it becomes necessary to factor in conditions that cause the model to fail.

Market Failure Theory

Markets usually fail for one of two reasons.[14] First, as noted in the housing example above, markets fail when something interferes with them. Even in an "ideal world" where a market mirrors what is best for both individuals and society, when markets lose their competitive edge, the suppliers of goods and services gain leverage to raise prices. Reduced competition allows firms to charge higher prices than they would in a more competitive market. If the suppliers of the good or service exercise this leverage, the market "fails" to operate as it should, and society's well-being is reduced.

The second cause of market failure is the behavior of consumers. In a perfectly competitive market, the individuals who "value" particular goods or services the most pay more than anyone else, and the resulting aggregate allocation of goods also benefits society more than any other allocation. Quite obviously, this lofty set of assumptions often falls short of what happens in the real world. Factors that cause goods to be allocated in less than "optimal" ways (i.e., as defined by economic theory) cause the second type of market failure.

When the market fails, opportunities are created for nonprofit organizations to enter the market, and the effectiveness of for-profit businesses is diminished. Although market failures take many forms, the four failures that are most useful for helping to explain the existence, roles, and functions of organizations in the nonprofit sector are transaction costs, information asymmetries, externalities, and public goods.

Transaction costs are the costs associated with market exchanges ("transactions"), including the costs of obtaining the information needed to participate wisely in a transaction, transporting the goods or services and the buyers to and from the place where the transaction will occur, pooling resources, and holding both parties to the terms of a contract ("enforcing" a contract). Economists assume that transaction costs do not exist in a "perfect market." In reality, some transaction costs almost always exist, but they are seldom high enough to disrupt or prevent market transactions. When they are disruptive, government in effect is "invited" in to correct ("regulate") the market failure or nonprofits are invited in to offset the effects of its failure.

Nonprofit organizations may reduce or help consumers or sellers overcome a variety of transaction costs. The cost of obtaining information is a good example. Sometimes information is important but isn't "valued" in the market, and nonprofits move in to fill the void or "niche." Many nonprofit organizations thus collect, analyze, and provide information to educate people about how to make decisions in the market. Better Business Bureaus,[15] consumer credit counseling services, Consumers Union, and mutual benefit nonprofits that serve communities of immigrants or the aging are all examples.

Also, many nonprofits exist to help pool resources to acquire common goods or to achieve shared purposes. Pooling resources allows many individuals to donate relatively small amounts of money or time to help create, preserve, or expand a community asset. Pooling resources, however, can be costly. Thus, some nonprofits "absorb" the costs of pooling the resources needed to create community centers, parks, Little League baseball fields, places of worship, and to protect nature. A few examples of the latter include the Nature Conservancy, the Wildlife Federation, Ducks Unlimited, and the Sierra Club.

Information asymmetry costs are one of several causes of information asymmetry—a second variety of market failure that helps to explain the existence, roles, and functions of nonprofit organizations. An information asymmetry occurs when the producer or seller of a good has more knowledge about the good than the consumer does. Asymmetries may be related to a good's cost, quality, or quantity. Three factors are associated with information asymmetries: the complexity of goods, incompetence of those who receive goods, and goods that are consumed by people other than those who purchase them.[16] Information asymmetries lead to contract failures when consumers believe that they cannot judge a good or service, and their discomfort prevents a transaction that would have otherwise occurred.[17] In addition to reducing the costs of information, nonprofit organizations help in preventing or overcoming market failure by creating trust.

Medical care and higher education are frequently cited examples of complex goods, the second cause of information asymmetries. It is difficult—if not impossible—to judge the quality of these goods or services. In the absence of information about quality, consumers tend to be more trusting of organizations that do not have profits as their prime motivation. Examples of information asymmetries that involve the incompetence of those who receive goods include services to individuals with developmental disabilities, mental illness, and services to the impaired elderly. The third type of information asymmetries, goods that are consumed by people other than those who purchase them, include services paid for by third parties, for example, long-term health care, international relief organizations, and arrangements whereby individuals receive vouchers for food, housing, or education.

Externalities are the indirect effects of a transaction that are not reflected in the market price.[18] Sometimes persons who are not party to a transaction either suffer or benefit from the transaction, but the "cost" of their suffering (or benefit) is not included in the transaction. Pollution created in a production process often is used to illustrate negative externalities. People and towns downriver from a paper mill "pay" part of the cost of producing paper in many ways. They pay to clean up the river water in lowered housing valuations and in lost tourism because fish cannot live in the water.

When a person has her house painted, trash cleared out of the yard, or plants a garden, positive externalities have been created. Her neighbors benefit from the improved environment, and the value of their houses increases. Externalities are a category of market failure because the total costs and benefits of the transaction are not limited to—do not accrue to—the buyer and seller. The market "doesn't work" as it is supposed to.

Some nonprofit organizations exist to discourage negative externalities and others to encourage positive externalities.[19] Advocacy nonprofit organizations are prime examples of the former. Examples include environmental nonprofit organizations dedicated to stopping air and water pollution or the destruction of animal habitat. Examples of nonprofit activities that create positive externalities include adult education programs that raise the employability and literacy of unemployed citizens, and community center volunteer groups that provide recreation opportunities to help keep at-risk youth "off the street." In both cases, others benefit—in addition to the direct recipients of services.

"A *public good* is a commodity or service whose benefits are not depleted by an additional user and for which it is generally difficult or impossible to exclude people from its benefits, even if they are unwilling to pay for them."[20] Examples of public goods include national defense, clean air, and scenery. Public goods cannot be divided, and people cannot be excluded from using them. If one citizen benefits, all other citizens will also. In most cases, it is absurd to think about restricting or regulating the use of public goods. Even if some people could be charged for "consuming" a public good, for example, looking at the scenery out their windows, other "free riders" could not be excluded from looking also. Because public goods are difficult to monitor and are available to "free riders" as well as people who might be willing to pay for them, public goods tend to be undersupplied and abused in a free market.[21] Abuses of public goods cause negative externalities—a market failure. Thus, many nonprofit organizations exist to provide public goods that are undersupplied in the market or to discourage abuse of public goods that already are present.[22]

Government Failure Theories

When the market fails, economists look to government or, increasingly, to nonprofit organizations to respond to the demands left unsatisfied by the market. *Government failure theory*, however, carries the market failure logic to another level. When government fails to respond satisfactorily to a market failure, demands are left unsatisfied. Some organizations in the nonprofit sector exist because they have "stepped forward" to satisfy unmet needs caused by failures of both the market and government.

Government failure theory holds that nonprofit organizations and governments do not compete to provide goods and services. Instead, the nonprofit sector exists to *complement* government in meeting demands for goods and services. The three most frequently cited rationales for government failure are the following: (1) individuals and minority groups demand goods or services beyond the norm or beyond the demands of the majority group; (2) officerholders have shorter time horizons than the long-term public interest requires; and (3) government fails to have essential information, and/or citizens fail to come forward to educate the government.[23] Although government failure theories are relatively new in their formal sense, in a less formal sense they have been a part of the nonprofit literature for centuries.[24]

Criticisms of the Failure Theories

Prior to the emergence of economic theories of the nonprofit sector, most explanations for the sector's existence and roles relied on "giving theories"—psychological, sociological, anthropological, and religious theories of altruism, philanthropy, voluntarism, and compassion (see Part 11). Economic theories have enlightened, but they also have created contention. The "failure theories" in particular have been criticized more for what they ignore—the values that are the sector's strength—than for their assumptions that markets and governments are not "perfect."

At the abstract level, various explanations of society's demand for goods and services that are used in economic theories incorporate values such as altruism and compassion. Critics counter that this is not sufficient. Instead of participating in the normative evaluation of the intentions that fuel the nonprofit sector, economists have "glossed over" this issue and have remained narrowly focused on microeconomic and macroeconomic efficiency. In sum, the critics argue, the nonprofit sector cannot be understood when attention is limited to the failures of other institutions and when the values and contributions that are central to the existence and roles of the nonprofit sector are ignored.

Some scholars have rejected the "failure theories" entirely. Roger Lohmann, for example, argues that economic failure theory distorts reality in order to make the roles and behaviors of the nonprofit sector conform to economic theory.[25] Failure theories "tell us more about what the nonprofit sector is not than they do about what it is."

Political Theories

The best-known political theories of the nonprofit sector have attempted to explain public policy—and changes in public policy—on economic dimensions, such as tax exemption and tax deductible contributions in general (see Part 4), Unrelated Business Income Tax (UBIT) and other aspects of competition with businesses, restrictions on private foundations that were enacted in 1969, initiated referendums to eliminate tax exemption for religious organizations, such as in Colorado in the mid-1990s, and the unsuccessful but highly publicized bills introduced in Congress during the mid-1990s to restrict nonprofits' informational activities (under the umbrella label "Istook Amendments").[26] By and large, nonprofit political theories have in effect emerged from economic issues and economic theory, and indeed some have been written by economists.[27]

A few political theories of the nonprofit sector have examined the roles of nonprofits in the development and maintenance of civil society, with particular emphasis on opportunities for community political participation and civic leadership development. (See also Part 11.)

Readings Included in This Part

In "Contract Failure," Dennis Young, emphasizes the importance of contract failure in market failure theory. Young identifies information asymmetries as the primary form of contract failure that affects the behavior of nonprofit organizations. In a related reading, Young uses James Douglas's "five sources of constraints on governmental action that create unsatisfied demands for public service to which private nonprofits may respond" to explain "Government Failure." Young explains that the essence of government failure theory is that when government and markets do not satisfy the demands of individuals, people organize to "do something about it." Thus government failure theory provides insights about how nonprofit organizations operate "in reality." The interfaces and interactions among nonprofits, government, and individuals represent components of the informal infrastructure that we refer to as "community." (See also Parts 7 and 10.)

Despite the not-so-subtle humor in the title, Roger Lohmann's article, "And Lettuce Is Nonanimal: Toward a Positive Economics of Voluntary Action," is a serious critique of mainstream economic theories of the nonprofit sector and is particularly critical of the "failure theories."[28] Lohmann notes the erroneous assumptions and the limitations of economic theories that use "public goods" as their basis. He argues instead that economic theories should use a "common goods approach" or "endowment theory," which allows "a positive conception of voluntary action as a unified type of economic activity, grounded in human group experience and based on autonomous, self-defining and self-regulating communities of nonmarket actors with shared mutual interests in identified common goods." A common goods approach permits theorists to use more appropriate criteria for judging the activities and roles of organizations in the nonprofit sector than, for example, the historic economic criteria of efficiency, maximization, and Pareto-optimality. "It is possible to identify a rational choice model that resembles actual nonprofit settings and defines a set of standards and criteria for evaluating choices in those settings. . . . The most fundamental of these positive statements is that actors in the commons need not be held to the standards of [for-profit] buyers."

James Douglas's chapter is the sole reading reprinted here that focuses directly on "Political Theories of Nonprofit Organization."[29] Douglas acknowledges that economic theory has identified conditions and criteria for for-profit enterprises criteria but adds: "We need something that will serve the same function in political theory that market failure and its related concepts serve in economic theory. . . . There is no similar single measure that can be applied to political institutions." The central question addressed in this reading thus is key for "centering" the political economy of the nonprofit sector: Why, given the extensive range of services provided by the public (or government) sector, do we need to supplement them by private endeavors that are not accountable through the same political channels? Although this question may sound similar to an economist's, the concepts incorporated in analyses by Douglas and other political scientists differ in emphasis and approach.

In answering this question, Douglas notes the coercive power of the state—a power that allows government to tax and thereby to avoid the "free-rider problem" associated with all public goods (and common pool goods) and thus with market failure. But, in identifying the conditions when a service should be left to voluntary provision, Douglas introduces political variables that separate his analysis from the economist's. "In a pluralist democracy . . . the work of voluntary organizations can be viewed as a private analog to the making and implementation of public policy." Government services are subject to a "categorical constraint" that does not apply to the nonprofit sector—political feasibility. When a service is provided through voluntary action, "the question of political feasibility [that constrains government] does not arise. . . . Similarly, the question of the justice of the imposition of the cost does not arise so long as the service is provided voluntarily." Douglas concludes with a theme that has been repeated frequently in this part (and a theme that dominates Part 10): "Although I have written of three distinct sectors—government, business, and voluntary—. . . these are artificial and academic distinctions imposed on what is, in reality, the seamless web of the institutional fabric of society. . . . The third sector has tended to be neglected by the social sciences. Yet it touches on both of the others. . . . Increasing concern with the third sector . . . follows logically from the academic trend to return to the older conception of a political economy, in which economy and polity are seen as all of a piece."

In an insightful overview of the political economy of the nonprofit sector, "Markets, Politics, and Charity: Nonprofits in the Political Economy," Kirsten Grønbjerg, a sociologist, examines how the distinctive relations among nonprofits and government and private sector organizations affect the specific nature of intersectoral relationships in the social services and community development industries.[30] Although "state and market organizations exercise significant control over nonprofit financial resources . . . and shape other aspects of the organizational environment in which nonprofits operate," nonprofits "can and do advance their own interests, creating an iterative process of strategic action and response." Grønbjerg concludes:

> First, nonprofits are not passive targets for market or public sector interests but take active roles in shaping their environment and resource opportunities. Second, over time, the division of labor among the three sectors will shift as some strategies are more effective than others. Third, in the process of pursuing organizational self-interests, a good deal of public goods are delivered, although not necessarily in the most efficient manner or in ways that assure effective attention to major social issues.

Notes

1. See particularly, "And Lettuce Is Nonanimal," by Roger Lohmann; "Markets, Politics, and Charity," by Kirsten Grønbjerg; and "Contract Failure" and "Government Failure," both by Dennis Young. All are reprinted in this part.

2. In addition to the readings reprinted in this chapter, also see Pamela Popielarz and Miller McPherson, "On the Edge or In Between: Niche Position, Niche Overlap, and the Duration of Voluntary Association Memberships," reprinted in Part 8.

3. A. J. Marrow, *The Practical Theorist: The Life and Works of Kurt Lewin* (New York: Basic Books, 1969).

4. Adam Smith, *Wealth of Nations* (1776; reprint, New York: Penguin, 1973).

5. For more information on this topic, see the readings reprinted in this part by Grønbjerg and Lohmann.

6. See Parts 1, 5, and 10 for more about privatization of government services through contracting of services.

7. The changes in revenue sources were closely associated with the "de-institutionalization movement" in mental health and developmental disabilities in the late 1960s and early 1970s and to distrust of local government among members of the Richard Nixon administration.

8. See Part 7 for more about the relationship between nonprofits and communities, and the multiple roles nonprofits play in communities.

9. U.S. Small Business Administration, *Unfair Competition by Nonprofit Organizations with Small Business: An Issue for the 1980s,* 3rd ed. (Washington, D.C.: U.S. Government Printing Office, June 1984); and James T. Bennett and Thomas J. DiLorenzo, *Unfair Competition: The Profits of Nonprofits* (Lanham, Md.: Hamilton Press, 1989).

10. Steven Rathgeb Smith and Michael Lipsky, *Nonprofits for Hire* (Cambridge: Harvard University Press, 1993); Ralph M. Kramer, "Voluntary Agencies and the Contract Culture: 'Dream or Nightmare?'" *Social Science Review* 68 (1), 33–60; James M. Ferris, "The Double-Edged Sword of Social Service Contracting," *Nonprofit Management and Leadership* 3 (4), Summer 1993, 363–376; Melissa Middleton Stone, "Competing Contexts: The Evolution of a Nonprofit Organization's Governance System in Multiple Environments," *Administration and Society* 28 (1), May 1996, 61–89.

11. Burton A. Weisbrod, ed., *To Profit or Not to Profit: The Commercial Transformation of the Nonprofit Sector* (Cambridge: Cambridge University Press, 1998).

12. Smith and Lipsky, *Nonprofits for Hire.*

13. Smith and Lipsky, *Nonprofits for Hire;* Weisbrod, *To Profit or Not to Profit.*

14. Robert S. Pindyck and Daniel L. Rubinfeld, *Microeconomics,* 3rd ed. (Englewood Cliffs, N.J.: Prentice Hall, 1995).

15. The nonprofit organization that publishes *Consumer Reports* and provides product price and quality information by telephone and the Internet.

16. Dennis R. Young, "Contract Failure," in Jay M. Shafritz, ed., *International Encyclopedia of Public Policy and Administration,* pp. 516–518 (Boulder: Westview Press, 1998), reprinted in this part.

17. Henry B. Hansmann, "Economic Theories of Nonprofit Organization," in Walter W. Powell, ed., *The Nonprofit Sector: A Research Handbook*, pp. 27–42 (New Haven: Yale University Press, 1987); Henry B. Hansmann, "The Role of Nonprofit Enterprise," *Yale Law Journal* 89 (5), 1980, 835–902.

18. Pindyck and Rubinfeld, *Microeconomics*.

19. Robert Scott Gassler, *The Economics of Nonprofit Enterprise: A Study in Applied Economic Theory* (Lanham, Md.: University Press of America, 1986).

20. William J. Baumol and Alan S. Blinder, *Economics: Principles and Policy* (San Diego: Harcourt Brace Jovanovich, 1991), p. 617.

21. Baumol and Blinder, *Economics: Principles and Policy;* Pindyck and Rubinfeld, *Microeconomics.*

22. Weisbrod, *The Nonprofit Economy.*

23. James Douglas, *Why Charity?* (Beverly Hills, Calif.: Sage, 1983); Young, "Government Failure," pp. 1006–1008. (Young is reprinted in this part.)

24. Recall Tocqueville's "theory" that nonprofit associations thrived in colonial United States due to the lack of established institutions, particularly government (Parts 2 and 3).

25. Roger A. Lohmann, "And Lettuce Is Nonanimal: Toward a Positive Economics of Voluntary Actions," *Nonprofit and Voluntary Sector Quarterly* 18 (4), 367, reprinted in this part.

26. Peter J. Van Hook, "Ethics in Nonprofit Organizations," in Jay M. Shafritz, ed., *International Encyclopedia of Public Policy and Administration*, pp. 796–802 (Boulder: Westview Press, 1998).

27. Jacquelyn Thayer Scott, "Voluntary Sector," in Jay M. Shafritz, ed., *International Encyclopedia of Public Policy and Administration*, pp. 2358–2362 (Boulder: Westview Press, 1998), reprinted in Part 1. Also see the readings reprinted in this part by Kirsten Grønbjerg and James Douglas.

28. Lohmann, "And Lettuce Is Nonanimal."

29. James Douglas, "Political Theories of Nonprofit Organizations," in Walter W. Powell, ed., *The Nonprofit Sector: A Research Handbook*, pp. 43–53 (New Haven: Yale University Press, 1987).

30. Grønbjerg, Kirsten A., "Markets, Politics, and Charity: Nonprofits in the Political Economy," in Walter W. Powell and Elisabeth S. Clemens, *Private Action and the Public Good*, pp. 137–150 (New Haven: Yale University Press, 1998).

References

Douglas, James. "Political Theories of Nonprofit Organization." In Walter W. Powell, ed., *The Nonprofit Sector: A Research Handbook*, pp. 43–53. New Haven: Yale University Press, 1987.

Grønbjerg, Kirsten A. "Markets, Politics, and Charity: Nonprofits in the Political Economy." In Walter W. Powell and Elisabeth S. Clemens, *Private Action and the Public Good*, pp. 137–150. New Haven: Yale University Press, 1998.

Hammack, David C., and Dennis R. Young, eds. *Nonprofit Organizations in a Market Economy*. San Francisco: Jossey-Bass, 1993.

Hansmann, Henry B. "The Two Nonprofit Sectors: Fee for Service Versus Donative Organizations." In Virginia A. Hodgkinson and Richard W. Lyman, eds., *The Future of the Nonprofit Sector*, pp. 91–102. San Francisco: Jossey-Bass, 1989.

_____. "Economic Theories of Nonprofit Organizations." In Walter W. Powell, ed., *The Nonprofit Sector: A Research Handbook*, pp. 27–42. New Haven: Yale University Press, 1987.

_____. "The Role of Nonprofit Enterprise." *Yale Law Journal* 89, 1980, 835–901.

_____. "The Role of Nonprofit Enterprise." *Yale Law Review* 89 (5), April 1980, 835–901.

James, Estelle, ed. *The Nonprofit Sector in International Perspective: Studies in Comparative Culture and Policy*. New York: Oxford University Press, 1989.

Kramer, Ralph M. "Voluntary Agencies and the Contract Culture: 'Dream or Nightmare?'" *Social Science Review* 68 (1), March 1994, 33–60.

Lohmann, Roger A. "The Economics of Common Goods." In Roger A. Lohmann, *The Commons: New Perspectives on Nonprofit Organizations and Voluntary Action*, pp. 158–176. San Francisco: Jossey-Bass, 1992.

_____. "And Lettuce Is Nonanimal: Toward a Positive Economics of Voluntary Action." *Nonprofit and Voluntary Sector Quarterly* 18 (4), Winter 1989, 367–383.

Salamon, Lester M. *Partners in Public Service: Government-Nonprofit Relations in the Modern Welfare State*. Baltimore: Johns Hopkins University Press, 1995.

Smith, Steven Rathgeb, and Michael Lipsky. *Nonprofits for Hire: The Welfare State in the Age of Contracting*. Cambridge: Harvard University Press, 1993.

Weisbrod, Burton A., ed. *To Profit or Not to Profit: The Commercial Transformation of the Nonprofit Sector*. Cambridge: Cambridge University Press, 1998.

_____. "The Future of the Nonprofit Sector: Its Entwining with Private Enterprise and Government." *Journal of Policy Analysis and Management* 16 (4), 1997, 541–555.

_____. *The Nonprofit Economy*. Cambridge: Harvard University Press, 1988.

Young, Dennis R. "Contract Failure." In Jay M. Shafritz, ed., *International Encyclopedia of Public Policy and Administration*, pp. 516–518. Boulder: Westview Press, 1998.

_____. "Government Failure." In Jay M. Shafritz, ed., *International Encyclopedia of Public Policy and Administration*, pp. 1006–1008. Boulder: Westview Press, 1998.

CHAPTER 15

Government Failure Theory

DENNIS R. YOUNG

Government Failure. A segment of economic theory that explains the conditions under which governmental provision of public goods and services is inefficient. Charles Wolf, Jr. (1979) described a variety of circumstances under which government intervention in the private economy to correct market failures may produce new inefficiencies and conditions under which government may over- or underproduce public services or provide them at too high of a cost.

Government failure is an important component in the theory of private nonprofit organizations. In particular, this body of theory has been used to explain why private nonprofit organizations arise to provide public goods and services on a voluntary basis, even in the presence of governmental provision. Government failure theory applied to nonprofit organizations focuses on the limitations of government and how private nonprofit organizations may fill in the niches left unserved by governmental action (Hansmann 1987).

James Douglas (1983, 1987) identified five sources of constraint on governmental action that create unsatisfied demands for public service to which private nonprofits may respond:

1. The "categorical constraint" results from the necessity of governments to provide goods and services on a uniform and universal basis. This constraint implies that the demands of individuals whose preferences for public services differ from the norm will go unsatisfied. This situation creates niches for nonprofit organizations to provide additional public services on a voluntary basis. Moreover, since government must provide its services universally to all its citizens, it is limited in its ability to experiment on a small scale with new programs, which creates another niche for private nonprofit organizations.

2. The "majoratarian constraint" of government reflects the fact that in a diverse population there may be multiple conception of the public good and what government should be doing. If government responds to the majority, it leaves niches for private nonprofit organizations to respond to minority issues and demands.

3. The "time horizon" constraint of government reflects the relatively short tenures of government officeholders and their consequent incentive to focus on short term-issues and results. This constraint leaves another area of action for private nonprofit organizations—the addressing of long-term societal issues and concerns.

4. The "knowledge constraint" connotes that government bureaucracies are organized in a relatively monolithic, hierarchical way and, hence, cannot be expected to generate all of the relevant information, ideas, and research needed for intelligent decisionmaking on public issues. This, too, creates a niche for private nonprofit advocacy groups, research centers, and other institutions.

5. The "size constraint" reflects the view that government bureaucracy is typically large and intimidating, thus, it is difficult for ordinary citizens to engage government. This situation creates a niche for nonprofit organizations to serve as "mediating institutions" between government and the citizenry (see Berger and Neuhaus 1977).

Burton Weisbrod's (1975) seminal economic theory of nonprofit organizations focuses essentially on James Douglas's categorical constraint. Weisbrod considers the implications of government as a provider of a particular public service to constituents with diverse preferences (demands) within a given political jurisdiction. The service is assumed to be a classical "pure public good," which is simultaneously consumed in the same quantity by all constituents once it is provided, and from which no one can be excluded. The government finances this good by imposing the same "tax-price" per unit of output on all citizens, no matter how much or little each values the good. Moreover, the government is assumed to use a voting mechanism to decide how much of the good to provide. For example, the use of majority voting would lead the government to provide an amount of the good that would correspond to the preferences of the "median voter," that is, the voter whose preferences fell in the middle of the distribution of voter preferences for this good.

The particular voting mechanism utilized is beside the point. The essential result is that one particular level of public goods provision will be selected and consumed by all voters, no matter what their individual preferences. Some voters may thus find the marginal value of the good less than the imposed tax-price and, hence, would prefer less of the good, and others may find the marginal value more than the tax-price and would prefer the government to provide more. Only those voters whose preferences resembled that of the median voter would be relatively satisfied. Thus, government is seen to be potentially inefficient in its provision of the good because it provides too much of it to some citizens and too little of it to others.

Weisbrod (1975) has considered various mechanisms available to correct such inefficiency. For example, he noted that people can move to different jurisdictions, where their preferences more closely match those of their neighbors (Tiebout 1956). He has also pointed out that private goods can be purchases as partial substitutes when citizens desire more than government provides. For example, people can buy watchdogs and install burglar alarms to make up for a lower-than-desired level of police services. Finally, Weisbrod pointed out that when mobility and private consumption fail to fill the gap, nonprofit organizations can arise to provide public goods on a private, voluntary basis. For example, neighborhood watch organizations may arise to supplement governmental police services.

One of the important predictions of the Weisbrod theory of government failure is that it suggests that the nonprofit sector will be most active where citizen populations are most diverse, and that nonprofit organizations are important for satisfying the service needs of political minorities. Thus, the theory gives us insights into the important role of nonprofit organizations in a democracy in accommodating the needs of diverse groups and averting conflicts over government service policy (Douglas 1987). It also helps to explain, at the international level, why some countries more than others rely on the nonprofit sector to provide public services. Estelle James (1987), for example, noted that the cultural diversity of such countries as Holland and Belgium helps to explain why these countries, have more significant nonprofit sectors than more homogeneous countries such as Sweden.

Other evidence of the utility of government failure to understand the role of private nonprofit organizations derives from examination of the sources of funding of these organizations (Weisbrod 1988). In particular, Weisbrod presumes that if the function of the nonprofit sector is to provide public goods on a voluntary basis then a substantial fraction of their financing should derive from charitable contributions, gifts, or grants, rather than revenues from sales or membership fees. He thus created a "collectiveness index" from the ratio of contributions, gifts, and grants to that of the total revenues of nonprofit organizations in a variety of fields. The ratio was found to vary widely among industries in which nonprofit organizations participate, but substantial evidence was found to support the notion that nonprofit organizations classified as charitable (501 (c) (3) by the Internal Revenue Service enjoyed relatively high collectiveness indices (typically in the range of 20% to 40%) and hence were indeed providing collective goods on a voluntary basis.

Bibliography

Berger, Peter L., and Richard J. Neuhaus, 1977. *To Empower People*. Washington, D.C.: American Enterprise Institute.

Douglas, James, 1983. *Why Charity?* Beverly Hills, CA: Sage.

_____, 1987. "Political Theories of Nonprofit Organization," chap. 3, pp. 43–54. In Walter W. Powell, ed., *The Nonprofit Sector: A Research Handbook*. New Haven: Yale University Press.

Hansmann, Henry, 1987. "Economic Theories of Nonprofit Organization," chap. 2, in pp. 27–42. In Walter W. Powell, ed., *The Nonprofit Sector: A Research Handbook*. New Haven: Yale University Press.

James, Estelle, 1987. "The Nonprofit Sector in Comparative Perspective," chap. 22, pp. 397–415. In Walter W. Powell, ed., *The Nonprofit Sector: A Research Handbook*. New Haven: Yale University Press.

Tiebout, Charles, 1956. "A Pure Theory of Local Government Expenditure." *Journal of Political Economy* (October): 414–424.

Weisbrod, Burton A., 1975. "Toward a Theory of the Voluntary Non-Profit Sector in a Three-Sector Economy." In Edmund S. Phelps, ed., *Altruism, Morality, and Economic Theory*. New York: Russell Sage Foundation.

_____, 1988. *The Nonprofit Economy*. Cambridge: Harvard University Press.

Wolf, Charles, Jr., 1979. "A Theory of Nonmarket Failure: Framework for Implementation Analysis." *Journal of Law and Economics*. (April): 107–139.

CHAPTER 16

Contract Failure Theory

DENNIS R. YOUNG

Contract Failure. An economic theory that helps to explain the existence of nonprofit organizations in a market economy. It is a particular aspect of the more general economic theory of "market failure" that specifies conditions under which unfettered competition among profit-making firms fails to provide particular goods or services efficiently.

The condition of contract failure is said to occur where consumers feel unable to judge competently the quality or quantity of services they are receiving (Hansmann, 1987). In this circumstance, consumers will be reluctant to purchase the goods and services they need, for fear of being cheated. Hence, markets composed solely of unregulated profit-making firms will fail to allocate economic resources to their most highly valued uses.

The basic source of contract failure is a condition called "information asymmetry" where producers have more accurate knowledge of the quantity, quality, and cost of services delivered than do consumers. There are three basic causes of information asymmetry. First, certain goods and services may be inherently complex or their quality may be difficult to judge. The technical and multifaceted natures of medical care or higher education illustrate this case. Second, the consumer himself or herself may simply not be

competent to evaluate the services he or she is receiving. Preschool care or services to the mentally ill or the impaired elderly are examples of this type. Third, certain services may not be purchased by the same individual that consumes them. In this instance, the purchaser does not experience the service directly and may not be in a position to obtain good information from the consumer. Again, day care for young children purchased by parents, or nursing home care purchased by children of elderly parents, illustrates this condition. Another example is international relief services financed by donors in one country to help victims in another country distant from the first. (Note, for purposes of this discussion, donors can be considered one variety of consumer of nonprofit organization services.) One or more of these conditions may characterize a particular service, creating conditions of contract failure that inhibit the efficient functioning of normal markets because consumers may fear the possibility of exploitation.

The utilization of nonprofit organizations is just one possible remedy to conditions of contract failure. Other potential remedies include licensing and regulation of profit-making providers such as in the case of automobile repair; standards of practice and oversight by professional associations or accrediting bodies as in dentistry or teaching; or purchasing control by expert third parties, such as doctors who behave as consumer proxies for hospital care or insurance companies that oversee medical care purchases.

There is no clear-cut theory for determining which of the latter solutions best fits each circumstance of contract failure or when the participation of nonprofit organizations provides the best remedy. However, some sense of the latter can be discerned from the premises that underlie different theoretical approaches to the question of why participation of nonprofit organizations serves as a correction to contract failure. There are basically three streams of thought that purport to explain how nonprofit organizations help overcome the problems of contract failure and hence provide particular services more efficiently than profit-making firms. The most prominent explanation, developed by Hansmann (1980), is that the nondistribution constraint governing nonprofit organizations creates a disincentive for nonprofit organizations to exploit their customers or patrons. In essence, the nondistribution constraint prohibits those who control the organization (managers, trustees) from distributing financial surpluses (profits) for their personal benefit. If this constraint is effectively policed, for example by government authorities, then nonprofits will allocate all of their resources to the promulgation of their missions, and will have little incentive to cheat those who finance or consume its services. In this context, consumers and donors will find nonprofit organizations "trustworthy" and will exhibit less reluctance to utilize and pay for their services.

A second stream of theory, advanced by Young (1983) and Hansmann (1980), postulates that nonprofits become trustworthy by a different mechanism: the selection and screening of leaders. In this framework, executive leaders of organizations come to their positions with a variety of different motivations ranging from self-interested income and power seeking to the pursuit of personal beliefs and public ideals. The differences between profit-making and nonprofit organizations, including the presence of the nondistribution constraint for nonprofits,

cause the pool of potential leaders to sort itself out among the sectors according to motivational differences, with the public service-oriented executives going into the nonprofit sector and the more wealth-seeking executives clustering in the profit sector. The result of this motivational sorting is to make the nonprofit sector more trustworthy by virtue of the kinds of people attracted to it, providing consumers and supporters with the confidence they require to overcome contract failure.

A third line of theory focuses less on the nondistribution constraint and more on other structural aspects of the nonprofit form that allow consumers and supporters to have greater control over service provision. Easley and O'Hara (1983) postulate that a nonprofit firm is distinguished from a for-profit firm by the fact that its managers accept a fixed amount of compensation and promise to devote all other resources to the costs of producing its services. In contrast, a for-profit firm contracts only on the basis of producing a given output for a given price. In this model, although the output of the nonprofit organization is difficult to measure, its expenditures on executive compensation and other inputs can be monitored and policed, helping to assure that the organization delivers what it has promised.

Ben-Ner (1986) takes still another view of nonprofits, arguing that they are distinguished by the fact that their donors and consumers play a more intensive role in governance of the nonprofit organization than they would in a for-profit organization. In this view, the nonprofit is a kind of consumer cooperative in which production and consumption of a service are integrated within the organization. This resulting close control by consumers overcomes information asymmetry by giving consumers an insider's view.

Each of these strands of theory suggest that under conditions of information asymmetry, the nonprofit form will serve consumers by promising that such organizations behave in more trustworthy fashion. Weisbrod (1988) elaborates on how more trustworthy behavior should manifest itself. In particular, he makes the distinction between "type 1" and "type 2" attributes of a good or service. A type 1 attribute, such as the physical appearance of a nursing home, is easily observable; a type 2 attribute, such as the caring nature of the relationship between attendants and elderly nursing home patients, is difficult for the outsider to observe. Weisbrod argues that if contract failure theory is correct, nonprofits should be superior to for-profits in the provision of type 2 attributes, but no different than for-profits in providing type 1 attributes. He points out, however, that verifying this hypothesis through research is intrinsically challenging: "Gathering data is difficult. If differences in type 2 dimensions of behavior persist across institutions, they must be difficult to discern—for analysts as well as consumers" (p. 147).

Nonetheless, empirical research has been carried out with some success (Steinberg and Gray, 1993). For example, surveys provide some evidence that people do distinguish between nonprofit and for-profit institutions and that they express more confidence in nonprofits. Studies of behavioral differences between nonprofits and for-profits within particular industries also provide some verification. For example, Weisbrod (1988) studied long-term care facilities for elderly, mentally handicapped, and psychiatric patients, finding that nonprofits were more likely than for-profits to provide family members with detailed information, less likely to sedate their patients heavily, and more likely to achieve higher levels of expressed satisfaction by patients' families. He interprets these data cautiously to suggest that nonprofits, especially those that are religiously affiliated, offer a more trustworthy alternative to for-profits in industries where type 2 attributes prevail.

While providing a powerful framework for understanding why nonprofits exist in certain areas of the economy, the theory of contract failure is not a comprehensive theory and leaves some unanswered puzzles (Steinberg and Gray, 1993). Most obvious is the fact that the theory does not fully distinguish between private, nonprofit organizations and government agencies, which are also technically nonprofit in a financial sense and which presumably should also engender greater trustworthiness than for-profit

firms. Thus, a separate segment of theory has developed to explain why private nonprofits exist alongside government and are more efficient than government in some circumstances. However, an interesting sidelight to this question is the issue of governmental contracting with nonprofit organizations for the provision of public services.

Here the question also arises as to whether the government should utilize the services of for-profit firms or restrict its contracting to nonprofits (Smith and Lipsky, 1993). If government as consumer/contractor also suffers the problem of information asymmetry, then the theory of contract failure can provide insight on its selection of nonprofit verses for-profit suppliers under various circumstances (Brodkin and Young, 1989). For example, if a service such as garbage collection is primarily of a type 1 variety, there is less reason for the government to prefer nonprofit contractors. However, for services such as children in foster care, contract failure provides a stronger rationale for nonprofit contractors. Moreover, the governmental choice of contractors is presumably influenced by the mechanism through which government chooses to finance privately supplied public services. If that mechanism is direct contracting with a few suppliers, government officials may be more able to police contractor behavior, whether profitmaking or nonprofit. But if the mechanism is subsidy of consumers who must make the choice of suppliers and monitor the services they receive, but are limited in their abilities to do so, the theory of contract failure suggests a preference for utilizing nonprofits.

Another lacuna in the theory of contract failure is that it does not directly address the puzzle of why we observe "mixed industries," such as day care for children or nursing homes for the elderly, in which profit-making and nonprofit organizations coexist. If nonprofits are more efficient in certain industries characterized by information asymmetry, why do they not drive for-profits in those industries out of business? While this question is unresolved, contract failure theory contains within it one source of explanation: If consumers vary in their levels of understanding and information about service quality, they might choose to utilize a variety of types of institutions. Well-informed consumers, confident in their ability to discern whether or not they were receiving a good bargain, might choose a for-profit provider, especially if it were cheaper or provided a variety of service closer to their personal preferences. A less competent consumer, or one who didn't have the time to gather sufficient information, might prefer to rely on a nonprofit organization in which he or she could place greater trust.

A related puzzle, however, is that if nonprofits enjoy greater trust in certain situations, why wouldn't some for-profit businesses disguise themselves as nonprofit organizations in order to exploit consumers' fears and drain away resources for their own benefit through various indirect means such as inflated salaries and sweetheart contracts with suppliers? Clearly the answer to this question depends on the effectiveness with which the nondistribution constraint or other structural aspects of the nonprofit form are assumed to police such behavior. If "for-profits in disguise" can successfully infiltrate the nonprofit sector, analysts have shown that this could seriously undermine confidence in nonprofits in general, destabilizing mixed industries and driving nonprofits out unless other means were implemented to ensure the survival of honest nonprofits (Steinberg, 1993).

Contract failure is not just of interest to theorists, or to policymakers wishing to discern within what areas of the economy nonprofits should be encouraged to operate. This concept also highlights an important principle for managers and trustees of nonprofit organizations: the essential currency of nonprofit organizations is trust. When that is undermined, nonprofits lose an important reason for their existence and the confidence of those who support them or utilize their services.

References

Ben-Ner, Avner, 1986. "Non-Profit Organizations: Why Do They Exist in Market Economies?" In Susan Rose-Ackerman, ed., *The Economics of Nonprofit Institutions.* New York: Oxford University Press, pp. 94–113.

Brodkin, Evelyn Z., and Dennis Young, 1989. "Making Sense of Privatization: What Can We Learn from Economic and Political Analysis?" In Sheila B. Kamerman and Alfred J. Kahn, eds., *Privatization and the Welfare State.* Princeton, NJ: Princeton University Press, pp. 121–154.

Easely, David, and Maureen O'Hara, 1983. "The Economic Role of the Nonprofit Firm." *Bell Journal of Economics,* 14:531–538.

Hansmann, Henry, 1980. "The Role of Nonprofit Enterprise." *Yale Law Journal,* 89:835–901.

Hansmann, Henry, 1987. "Economic Theories of Nonprofit Organization." In Walter W. Powell, ed., *The Nonprofit Sector: A Research Handbook.* New Haven: Yale University Press, pp. 27–42.

Smith, Steven R., and Michael Lipsky, 1993. *Nonprofits for Hire.* Cambridge, MA: Harvard University Press.

Steinberg, Richard, 1993. "Public Policy and the Performance of Nonprofit Organizations: A General Framework." *Nonprofit and Voluntary Sector Quarterly,* 22:13–32.

Steinberg, Richard, and Bradford H. Gray, 1993. "The Role of Nonprofit Enterprise in 1993: Hansmann Revisited." *Nonprofit and Voluntary Sector Quarterly,* 22:297–316.

Weisbrod, Burton A. 1988. *The Nonprofit Economy.* Cambridge, MA: Harvard University Press.

Young, Dennis R. 1983. *If Not For Profit, For What?* Lexington, MA: D.C. Heath and Company.

And Lettuce Is Nonanimal: Toward a Positive Economics of Voluntary Action

ROGER A. LOHMANN

Negative Theory

Existing economic and financial theories of nonprofit organizations are based on an extensive and rather remarkable set of negations and negative comparisons of voluntary action with the market or for-profit sector. These negations tell us far more about what the nonprofit sector is *not* than they do about what it is. They also proceed rather consistently from the charming, but completely unwarranted, assumption that all nonprofit activity is somehow a deviant form of commercial enterprise. As a result, the professed usefulness of recent nonprofit economic theory to those with a substantive interest in voluntary action (Rose-Ackerman, 1986, p. 15) falls far short of the mark.

The intent of this paper is to stimulate further debate among market-oriented economists, voluntary-sector management theorists, and others over appropriate models of resource allocation and decision making in the voluntary sector. A suitable starting point for this discussion is the remarkably negative tone of extant nonprofit economic theories and associated work in accounting and management science. Anthony and Young (1984, p. 38) define a nonprofit orga-

nization as one "whose goal is something other than earning a profit for its owners." They also include the absence of a profit measure and inadequate management controls among a list of characteristics that identify nonprofit organizations. Many others share their view of nonprofit organizations as inherently inefficient owing to the lack of profit motivation and inadequate management controls (for example, Steinberg, 1987, p. 134; Zaltman, 1979).

Hansmann (1980, 1987) finds the basis of an economic model of nonprofit action in a phenomenon he terms "contract failure." Weisbrod (1977) places the negative accent not in the nonprofit sector but rather in the public sector. Nonprofit action, he argues, tends to serve a gap-filling role vis-à-vis governmental enterprise, meeting demands for public services that are not met by governmental provision. The first two sections of Rose-Ackerman's (1986) book on nonprofit economics are entitled "Government Failure" and "Contract Failure."

Virtually all nonprofit management theories explicitly or implicitly begin with this negative accent and contribute to the paradoxical consensus position that nonprofit action has no independent basis. Nonprofits arise only from the failures of other institutions but are themselves inefficient, unproductive, poorly managed or mismanaged, and inadequately controlled.

The remarkably negative accent of literature that concentrates on the economics and management of nonprofits is marked contrast to the positive statements of most noneconomic sources that deal with the voluntary sector.

Why is the economic treatment of voluntary action so uniformly and distinctly negative? One possible answer, of course, is a theoretical bias against nonprofit action by economists, accountants, management scientists, and business leaders—a simple preference for market and profit-oriented activity or a distaste for nonprofit ventures.

A Classification Anomaly

An equally plausible explanation is that all of this negativism results from the failure of economic theory to adequately explain noncommercial voluntary action. The very concept of "nonprofit" (or "not-for-profit") activity as a unit of analysis may well be a classification anomaly resulting from the observable existence of voluntary action outside the range of concepts covered by existing economic and financial theories. Thus, the term "nonprofit" functions as a linguistic marker for various rhetorical extensions and clever analogies that serve to bring these phenomena back within the analytic and descriptive range of established economic theory. Such restoration efforts, while interesting from the vantage point of existing theory, do remarkably little to adequately describe or explain the basis of rational choice in voluntary action. But through this inadequacy the restoration efforts do suggest that noncommercial voluntarism is outside the bounds of existing economic concepts, thus necessitating those remarkable negations. Classifying lettuce as a mammal produces approximately the same effect. Lettuce is a non-fur-bearing, non-milk-producing, non-child-bearing, and non-warm-blooded nonanimal. Further, as a mammal, lettuce is highly ineffective, being sedentary and not warm-blooded. All other mammals are

much faster! Lettuce is also remarkably nonagile and fails to protect its young. On the whole, lettuce is a miserable excuse for a mammal!

In a similar way, nonprofit action has increasingly been misclassified as a very deficient form of productive enterprise. The full burden of this classification anomaly is to equate formally organized nonprofit activities, such as services for the homeless, community orchestras, and intercollegiate lacrosse and rugby competitions, with completely unrelated commercial ventures, such as the manufacture of shoes and automobiles. In the process, the very nature of nonprofit action is transformed and distorted solely in order to make it fit theory.

The reasons for this misclassification are not difficult to discern. First, some types of contemporary American nonprofit services do look and act a good deal like commercial ventures, and the current trend indicates that some of them will move even further in that direction in the future. We are in danger of forgetting, however, that a very large portion of voluntary action does not look or act anything like commercial enterprise, and nonprofit economics has been virtually mute on these efforts.

Clues that "nonprofit organizations" are actually of two basic types are scattered throughout the existing literature. Hansmann (1980), for example, differentiates mutual, entrepreneurial, donative, and commercial types in a two-by-two table. In a similar vein, Anthony (1978, pp. 8–10) distinguishes between "Type A" nonprofits, which rely on revenues (entrepreneurial and commercial), and "Type B" nonprofits (mutual and donative), which do not. In one of the fundamental, formative documents of economic theory, for example, Adam Smith classified many common activities, today called "voluntary," as "nonproductive" and set them entirely, and perhaps permanently, outside the bounds of economics. The theoretical basis of this perspective is itself a negation: Smith's concept of "unproductive labor."

Mainstream economics has continued to hold this position to the present day.

The indifference of economic theory is well documented. A brief check on the volumes of economic theory shelved in any library will confirm that terms such as nonprofit, voluntary, gifts, charity, philanthropy, and even services occur rarely and peripherally in economic theory. Voluntary action, it would seem, was written out of the economic corpus at the beginning and has, at best, only recently sneaked back in at the far corners. And, perhaps as a price for readmission, the main body of voluntary action has remained beyond the analytical limits of economic theory.

Important questions can be raised about whether an economic theory of voluntary action is even possible. Smith did not appear to believe so. Yet, if by "economics" one means formal and logical analysis of rational collective action, certainly the answer would appear to be yes. And if by "economics" one means the wholesale application of abstract mathematical models to empirical problems encountered in voluntary-action situations, based on rather loose analogies and metaphors, the answer certainly appears to be yes. But if one seeks fundamental and consistent explanations of rational allocative choice in voluntary action, or the contribution of voluntary action to the national wealth, the picture is considerably less clear. The technology of contemporary economic analysis is very powerful. But whether the results of those applications have any meaning except as logical exercises is another question entirely.

Equally unclear is whether nonprofit economic theory must be grounded in philosophical utilitarianism. It would appear that distinct economic criteria are implicit in virtually every major philosophy, belief system, scientific discipline, or other "thought system" and way of life represented in the nonprofit world. These represent alternative evaluative systems, at least as well grounded as the utilitarian concepts of economic theory.

There is nothing particularly rational about the view that adherents of these diverse schools of thought must adhere to the logic and standards of nineteenth-century English utilitarians as the price of access to and use of economic resources in otherwise free and unconstrained voluntary institutions. The preferred approach of a genuine, nonprofit economic theory should allow for the intrinsic establishment of group standards ("minimally satisfactory alternatives") rather than the imposition of utility maximization as a universal criterion.

Toward Positive Theory: An Alternative Model

The main body of this paper is devoted to a number of speculative comments about the nature of an economic theory of voluntary action, with particular emphasis on "Type B" or donative-mutual associations, societies, congregations, groups, and other similar forms of collectivities.

Key Questions

The present aim is to address in an affirmative manner the following questions: What is the nature of economic action outside the market, the household, and the state? What it is not has already been established. What other than earning a profit energizes those who operate in the voluntary sector or commons? Are there any recognizable rational economic criteria employed by voluntary-sector actors who frankly acknowledge the absence or inappropriateness of profit measures such as maximization, Pareto-optimality, and efficiency?

The perspective set forth as common goods, or endowment theory, is deeply rooted in philosophical pragmatism and sociological interactionism.

The Economics of Common Goods

The first task is to establish some suitable nomenclature. As a fundamental term, nonprofit is inadequate, although not noticeably more so than such dated terminology as charity, philanthropy, or even eleemosynary. In the following discussion, the term *commons* is used to signify the economic dimensions of a large and diverse set of voluntary collective action by service clubs; artistic, scientific, and amateur athletic societies; social and political movements; religious and philosophical groups; and other groups that form the core of the voluntary sector in the United States and in other countries.

In all known human cultures, self-defining collectivities of voluntarily associating individuals operate jointly and independently outside of markets, households, and the state in social spaces that can be called commons. There they pursue mutually agreed-upon purposes along joint lines of action and on the basis of economic criteria unique and intrinsic to the commons. Those mutual purposes constitute common goods. An economic commons and associated common goods arise whenever an association or group is formed simply because it is a virtual impossibility that any collective action can or will occur without resort to money or economic resources.

The economic objective of joint action in the commons is the creation of common goods, which includes such phenomena as religious worship, contemplation, scientific inquiry, helping and charity, artistic expression, play, and many other desirable projects of voluntary-action groups. These common goods are easily and readily distinguished from both market commodities and public goods. Exclusion is typically possible with common goods, and they are, therefore, unlike public goods. However, since both the costs and the benefits of common goods accrue to pluralities without division, they are not private goods either. Further, because they do not involve large numbers of buyers and sellers and any known or recognizable price mechanism, they cannot be considered market goods without resort to extraordinary theoretical devices or deus ex machina.

Common goods are best viewed as an entirely separate category of economic goods, with their own unique characteristics. One of the most intriguing traits of common goods, for example, is the two-way transformation of economic values (money and commodities) into noneconomic values (religious, philosophical, scientific, artistic, and charitable meanings) and back again.

Perhaps the most universal, clearly observable, and easily understandable example of the common goods process is the transformation of gold, other precious metals and gems, and even ordinary objects into religious icons and sacred objects.

The central economic facts of the commons are episodes of communicative interaction. The reason is quite simple: services are primarily social acts and not physical objects. Those philosophers and social scientists who have studied social acts generally agree that such acts involve communication. This is one of the key departures of twentieth-century American social science from nineteenth-century materialism, a departure that any nonprofit economic theory must accommodate.

Although there is no fully satisfactory term for the economic aspects of this communication process, *discretion* might be used (as in "discretionary grants" or "discretionary purchases"). Here, however, the common phrase of "rendering a service" is seen as pertinent and hence the process is called *rendition*.

Renditions are elementary, basic social acts that cannot be reduced to allegedly more fundamental activities such as production, consumption, or exchange. Rendition of common goods is thus quite distinct from economic production. In fact, rendition involves a process of simultaneous "production" and "consumption" that is easily observed: It is a central fact of common goods that they cannot be inventoried, warehoused, or traded, for the simple reason that their "production" and "consumption" are simultaneous.

Diverse economic and noneconomic sources working in the theoretical no-man's-land of common goods have struggled with the resulting inapplicability of economic dualisms such as production and consumption to social action. A recent trend is to speak of the "coproduction" of common goods (Austin, 1981). Overall, it seems preferable to abandon the dualistic language of production entirely.

In further contrast to economic production, rendition of common goods involves a symbolic process that blends *information* and *meaning*, neither of which adheres to ordinary economic assumptions of scarcity (Ilchman and Uphoff, 1968).

Information involves communication of novelty, freshness, spontaneity, and unpredictability in discretionary situations. When an astrophysicist searching for the edge of the universe makes a discovery, when a performer offers a new interpretation of a familiar work of art, and when a social worker begins working with a new client, the research finding, the presentation, and the new case are heavily informational. In the same vein, the new perspective offered here is intended to be informative for readers.

In contrast, meaning addresses the certainty, order, redundancy, and predictability of communication. New research findings must be placed in the context of previous research to be understood. Likewise, the artistic presentation is judged against previous interpretations, and the dramatic script, musical score, and client problems are interpreted within a respective body of established theory.

Because they consist of information and meaning, common goods are symbolic and unaffected by either economic scarcity or physical laws. Furthermore, the consumption (or extinction of value) associated with acts of rendition is never entirely complete because of memories, written accounts, artifacts, and other meanings. Any fund of surviving meanings and of new information that functions as a resource for further voluntary action is here termed an *endowment*. The economics of the commons treat money as a symbolic medium, along with other resources. Money is, however, only one of the media of the commons.

One process with important consequences for the economic value of an endowment in the commons involves the process of *learning,* the economic importance of which involves taking value away from a situation. The complementary process to learning is *technique,* which is one of two forms of bringing value into a situation. An accumulated set of learned techniques possessed by a person or a group is a special set of meanings that can be termed a *repertoire.* Thus, establishment of a musical or theater group, for example, often hinges on hiring seasoned performers with solid repertoires, able to draw upon and to teach their techniques. The same can also be said for a monastic order, an athletic team, or a research laboratory.

The other major way to bring value into the commons involves *search,* which is the primary way in which information is brought into the commons. Philosophical contemplation, scientific research, and artistic creation are important forms of search, as are some types of religious activity, such as quests for more profound religious experience, and some types of athletic activity.

Because of the characteristics of action, information, and meaning, time is a key to economic measurement in the commons. It is also problematic.

Common goods also require an alternative to atomic individualism. Many rendered acts, such as baptisms, weddings, and initiation rites, as well as scientific conferences and athletic competitions, are only possible as collective actions. (If this characteristic is not immediately clear, try marrying yourself or conducting your own funeral!)

The fact that, in American culture at least, many (perhaps most) types of voluntary action can also be pursued commercially is not especially important for common goods theory. Commercial potential reveals only that in an open society the borders between the commons and the market are open, and that economic actors are free to move back and forth. For our purposes, we need only assume that economic actors, possessed of perfect knowledge in the marketplace, retain their knowledge when they enter the commons. Rational actors who move from "nonprofit" to "commercial" activity, or vice versa, will be aware of their situations, as will most of their associates in the commons.

The application of the perfect knowledge assumption to the commons has several interesting implications. For example, it provides a rational basis for membership and legitimacy in the commons. Artists, scientists, philanthropists, and amateur athletes who have "gone commercial" constitute a well-known and well-recognized phenomenon in all areas of voluntary action. In this vein, rational actors engaged in acts of common good will know that they are acting outside of markets, households, and the state and are motivated by ends other than profit.

In the case of the commons, ends other than those of profit (that is, common goods) are a condition of admission to and the basis for continuation in the commons. A self-interested posture seeking personal gain immediately takes a consistent, rational actor out of the commons. Thus, a scientist guilty of fabricating data for profit or career advancement may suffer various forms of removal from that particular commons, including negative publicity, sanctions, expulsion from an organization, or dismissal from an appointment or position. Defrocking, excommunication, suspension, and probation are other forms of such removals.

Important economic roles in the commons include, for example, *patrons* who obtain or provide material and symbolic resources.

In the commons, patrons are not just those who give money but also those who give meanings. The benefactor and the composer of sacred music thus share a common status as patrons. Patrons typically operate from a complex of motives and derive a range of economic and noneconomic values from their acts.

Values in the Commons

It is possible to tentatively set forth some value premises that at least partially model the empirical world of voluntary action. Because the rendition of common goods is a process of symbolic interaction rather than material fabrication, the pattern of role assignments can be seen as the ultimate basis of the economic value of common goods. While the study of other, noneconomic aspects of role definition in the voluntary sector is relatively advanced, little attention has been given to the manner in which actors assume "appropriate" roles and initiate the complex patterns of learning, search, and technique by which economic values are created and sustained.

In fact, this process is so central that we can speak of the *role-taking theory of value* as basic to the commons. Common goods are of value to actors in the commons because they are mutually valued among members of the commons. This leads to what might be called the *principle of economic ethnocentrism:* Because economic value arises within the commons and is a part of large clusters of information and meaning, eval-

uation of common goods must occur within the commons on the basis of those socially shared values. It is not reasonable or consistent to take values and standards from another context and superimpose them on groups operating in the commons. This ethnocentric principle is greatly threatened by present trends in nonprofit economics, in which the standards of one commons—professional economists—are being inappropriately imposed on a wide range of other commons in the name of scientific neutrality and objectivity.

Consistently rational participants in the commons whose basic needs have been met will, as a result, have no rational reason to prefer pursuit of personal gain over other objectives. If they chose personal gain as a discretionary act, they necessarily remove themselves from the commons. This is consistent with the nondistribution clause found in all nonprofit corporate statutes and the associated legal and ethical tradition.

"Maximization" as a criterion of rational action is irrelevant in the commons. Actors who have not entered the commons under false pretense will simply have no utility to calculate or to maximize. This situation is a result of both the affluence assumption and the formal, content-empty status of utility in modern economic theory. Since Edgeworth, economists have held that utility is a formal concept without subjective meaning—a construct of market behavior, devoid of subjective connotations of happiness or pleasure and not possessed of any meaning beyond its operational definition. Thus, if utility is a purely formal characteristic of market situations, then actors in situations explicitly defined as nonmarket and nonprofit can hardly be expected to have any utility!

Can a nonutilitarian economics exist without maximization and utility? From an economic standpoint, how is it possible to summarize the diverse values and ends of actors in the commons without resort to these concepts? First, the possibility must be acknowledged that, indeed, there may be no single universal standard to summarize motives and ends in the commons, even though in the Western tradition terms such as happiness, pleasure, actualization, satiation, welfare, health, and utility are all commonly used for this purpose.

Steinberg (1987, p. 134), for one, is forthrightly skeptical about whether there can be a general, formal, theoretical objective in the commons.

Whether or not there is such a universal standard for at least some common goods, rational choice appears to be guided by a nonutilitarian criterion called *satisfaction.* An alternative is said to be satisfactory if (1) there exists a set of agreed-upon criteria that describe minimally satisfactory alternatives and (2) the alternative in question is agreed to meet or exceed all of these criteria in the view of the decision makers (March and Simon, 1958, p. 140). Note that the first of these criteria conforms closely to the definition of meaning given earlier, while determination of the second would introduce new information into the situation.

Satisfaction, in this sense, is not a utilitarian counting principle, and it is not to be confused with a utilitarian pleasure-pain calculus. It is, instead, itself an act, an observable moment or event in the interaction of members of the commons. Thus, satisfaction is attained when search is suspended and technique and attention are shifted elsewhere. Exactly this criterion can be observed in the governance of many associations.

In the commons, choice seldom involves exact calculations or precise predictions. Instead, when consensus is reached that an agreed-upon satisfactory objective has been realized, discourse, simply shifts to another topic. Such satisfaction is the primary criterion of rational choice in the commons and also governs economic decisions there.

By itself, satisfaction only operates as a "termination rule," telling us when it is rational to end predecision discussion. It says nothing about the distributive rationality of common goods that may occur as a result. However, satisfaction often occurs concurrently with a fundamental principle of distribution in the commons. That criterion is *proportion,* and it occurs in a situation when no rational actor with the standing to do so acts to gain additional resources except from uncommitted endowments.

In the commons, proportion is almost always a preferred alternative to Pareto-optimality for settling issues of distribution. The criterion of Pareto-optimality, which is often also referred to as an "efficiency" measure, suggests that a decision is optimal if no one loses and at least one person gains.

Taken together, these criteria offer the beginning of an economic value theory appropriate to the analysis of common goods. Some aspects of market-based nonprofit economics will undoubtedly prove provocative and troublesome. For example, it would appear that analysis of real allocations of common goods is primarily a logical, rather than a quantitative, process. Thus, much of the apparatus of economic analysis has little to offer the study of common goods. Not only does the isomorphism of the production model not apply, as has been suggested, but also the actual actors in the commons, past or present, seldom engage in detailed mathematical analysis of their alternatives. Thus, there are real and important questions about whether an economic theory of common goods is, in fact, nonquantitative. It could be argued, for example, that the theory is most appropriately seen as a branch of interdisciplinary collective choice theory. If so, the methods of modern symbolic logic may be more suitable than calculus and indifference curves as the basis of analysis of common goods.

Conclusion

It is possible to identify a rational choice model that resembles actual nonprofit settings and defines a set of standards and criteria for evaluating choices in those settings. Common goods or endowment theory appears to offer an approach to the allocation of resources in the nonprofit sector that respects the integrity of voluntary action without inappropriately reducing such action to the categories of the marketplace. Moreover, it is highly probable that many of the most interesting and provocative findings of nonprofit economics can be incorporated into endowment theory and stated in positive terms.

The economics of the voluntary sector need not be treated exclusively as a series of negations.

Positive statements can be made about collective action in the commons, just as they can be made about economic action in the market, household, and state. The most fundamental of these positive statements is that actors in the commons need not be held to the standards of buyers and sellers in order for their behavior to be treated as economically rational. To attempt such application of mainstream economic theory is to fall victim to the limits of the same inappropriate classification whereby lettuce is nonanimal.

References

Anthony, Robert N. (1978). *Financial Accounting in Nonbusiness Organizations: An Exploratory Study of Conceptual Issues.* New York: Financial Accounting Standards Board.

Anthony, Robert N., and David W. Young. (1984). *Management Control in Nonprofit Organizations* (3rd ed.). New York: Irwin.

Austin, David M. (1981). The Political Economy of Social Benefit Organizations: Redistributive Services and Merit Goods. In Herman D. Stein (ed.), *Organization and the Human Services* (pp. 37–88). Philadelphia: Temple University Press.

Hansmann, Henry. (1980). The Role of Nonprofit Enterprise. *Yale Law Journal, 89,* 835–901.

Hansmann, Henry. (1987). Economic Theories of Nonprofit Organizations. In Walter W. Powell (ed.), *The Nonprofit Sector: A Research Handbook* (pp. 27–42). New Haven, CT. Yale University Press.

Ilchman, Warren, and Norman Uphoff. (1968). *The Political Economy of Change.* Berkeley and Los Angeles: University of California Press.

March, James, and Herbert Simon. (1958). *Organizations.* New York: Wiley.

Rose-Ackerman, Susan (ed.). (1986). *The Economics of Nonprofit Institutions: Studies in Structure and Policy.* New York: Oxford University Press.

Steinberg, Richard. (1987). Nonprofit Organizations and the Market. In Walter W. Powell (ed.) *The Nonprofit Sector: A Research Handbook* (pp. 118–140). New Haven, CT: Yale University Press.

Weisbrod, Burton. (1977). *The Voluntary Nonprofit Sector.* Lexington, MA: D. C. Health Books.

Zaltman, Gerald. (1979). *Management Principles for Non-Profit Agencies and Organizations.* New York: American Management Association.

Political Theories of Nonprofit Organization

James Douglas

The fields of activity we most readily associate with nonprofit organizations include health care, education, religion, the arts, and a vast array of social welfare services. In medieval times, these activities would have come primarily within the jurisdiction of the church rather than the state. After the Reformation, they were brought within the purview of civil as distinct from canon law. In 1601, the English Parliament enacted the Statute of Charitable Uses (43 Eliz. I c4), which has been described as "the starting point of the modern law of charities" and remains to this day one of the bases for the definition of charity in both English and American law.[1]

Thus history accounts for the fact that a charitable nonprofit sector exists independent of the government. It does not explain, however, why some fields of activity remain in this sector, whereas others either have been taken over by government (like the maintenance of bridges,[2] for example, or the care of prisoners) or are normally carried out by for-profit business enterprises. Institutions, like other organisms, are subject to the laws of natural selection. What we need to identify are the characteristics of the "environmental niche" in which nonprofits thrive.

Private nonprofits are subject to competition for survival from three other forms of social or-

ganizations—the family, commercial for-profit enterprises, and government-run services. Competition from any family unit beyond the nuclear has been weakened by deep-seated social and economic trends for at least a century. However, a recent study of voluntary organizations (Wolfenden Committee 1978) sees as a strength of the nonprofit sector its ability to work easily with and supplement the resources of family and informal networks of friends and neighbors.

Economists have developed a considerable body of theory that enables us to identify the conditions most appropriate to for-profit enterprises—their environmental niche. The environmental niche for government services remains ill defined. We need something that will serve the same function in political theory that market failure and its related concepts serve in economic theory.

The task of devising a political analogue to market failure bristles with difficulties. At a fundamental level economists have a common criterion or measuring rod—that of "utility"—for judging the desirability of a form of organization. They can say that market failure occurs when pursuit by individuals of their own utility is calculated not to result in maximum utility for society. But there is no similar single measure that can be applied to political institutions. We can say that a government agency should promote both welfare and efficiency—two criteria subsumed in the economic concept of utility. But they cannot be the only criteria. Government action must also be based on publicly defensible criteria of justice, and it must in some measure respond to the values and choices of the majority of citizens, although not in a way that infringes on the rights of minorities. This age-old problem of reconciling the will of the majority with the rights of minorities is only one of the cases of contradictory criteria encountered when one tries to define a good polity. The economic good, for all its ultimately unquantifiable aspects, remains a much tidier concept than the political good.

At a less fundamental level, economists have acquired a mass of empirical data against which they can test their theories, and these theories in turn have stimulated more empirical studies. In examining the boundary between the state and the autonomous nonprofit sector, however, we have no comparable wealth of empirical data upon which to draw. In this chapter I shall suggest some normative hypotheses in the hope that this will stimulate others to test them empirically.

Yet another difficulty is presented by the very term *nonprofit organization*. We use the legal form of incorporation as a basis of classification because it is convenient. Yet the term includes a wide variety of organizations, and the legal form of incorporation may tell us little about their nature.

In this chapter, I shall confine my attention to private nonprofit organizations carrying out a public function. This, broadly speaking, is the legal definition of a public charity. The question I will discuss is why, given the extensive range of services provided by the public (or government) sector, we need to supplement them by private endeavors that are not accountable through the same political channels.

The most obvious distinctive characteristic of a state service is that it can invoke the coercive power of law. Nowadays, this power is most frequently used to commandeer money through compulsory taxation. Organizations in the pri-

vate sector have no such power to commandeer the resources they need. They must either exchange something they own (or to which they have some form of title) for something they need or rely on tapping some vein of generosity. Exchange of the specific kind usually referred to as a quid pro quo transaction is, of course, the basic mechanism used in the marketplaces of the commercial sector. Both the quid and the quo must be identifiable, and it must be possible to transfer some form of exclusive title to them. Failing these two characteristics, market transactions simply cannot take place. The power of the state and access to the power of coercion are, of course, also necessary to market transactions. A market economy could not exist without the power of the state and the legal framework it provides in a variety of forms, not least the law of contract.

Exchange also plays a part in the transactions of the voluntary nonprofit sector. Indeed if we use the term *exchange* in a sufficiently broad sense, it can be made to cover even the most altruistic of voluntary endeavors. The problem arises when benefits from a transaction cannot be confined to those who have contributed to the exchange and there is nothing to stop noncontributors from taking a free ride on the backs of the contributors.

The Free-Rider Problem

Even when those who contribute to a voluntary enterprise—whether labor, goods, or money—receive in return no exclusive benefit for themselves, we have to assume that they derive some satisfaction from their contribution; they're getting something in return whether it is a psychic reward or a share in a collective good. But because that benefit is not exclusive, the link between their contribution and the benefit it helped create is weak.

To take a typical example of a public good, all citizens in a given state benefit from national defense. This is a benefit that cannot be made exclusive: if you are being protected from invasion by a foreign power, then I too am being protected from the same danger. This is not to say that all citizens place the same value on national defense, only that it is a value that cannot be assessed by market forces. The relative value to be placed on, and hence resources to be devoted to, national defense can be only politically determined. As a citizen of the United Kingdom, I may want to live in a society that provides free health care to those in need. (Note that this is not the same as saying that I want to be able to get free health care.) But the costs of maintaining the National Health Service are vast and my contribution to those costs is not going to make much difference one way or the other, so why should I bother to add my petty contribution?

Only the state, by using the coercive power of law, can avoid free riders, and thus hopes it will achieve a distribution of resources that more closely approximates the collective interests of the community. What the free-rider argument suggests, then, is that the distribution of resources that most closely approximates what the community really wants—the Pareto optimum—will not be reached so long as individuals can avoid contributing to the cost of a collective good and still benefit from it. The possibilities both of taking a free ride oneself and of others taking a free ride will deter individuals from contributing voluntarily to the cost of a collective good. To return to the case of the National Health Service, it is manifestly more rational for me to pay my contribution to its cost if I know that all others are contributing their share than if I have no way of knowing how many others are going to skip their contributions and take a free ride.[3] Considerations of both equity and efficiency will thus tend to shift services from the voluntary to the state sector as the demand for the service becomes more widespread.

Olson (1971) develops an argument along these lines for determining when a service can be left to voluntary provision. Relatively small groups can form viable organizations for providing collective goods because the individual members will be aware that their failure to contribute their share of the cost will have a significant effect on the provision of the collective good they all want. The link between their contribution and the benefit is close and apparent.

On the other hand, a large group will have much more difficulty establishing such an organization because each member is likely to feel his contribution will make little difference and will thus be more tempted to take a free ride. Such large groups, Olson argues, are unlikely to succeed without some form of compulsion or some selective benefit for their members.

Olson is concerned primarily with self-seeking motives for collective action, but the same logic may apply to more altruistic motives. A self-seeking motive might be some privilege or benefit for members of a professional body, in which case the collective good is the privilege achieved by the members' collective action. However, the collective good might reflect some social value the members have in common. For example, imagine a group of relatively wealthy citizens who believe that better housing should be provided for the poor. In this case, the good they collectively want is an altruistic one, but Olson's logic will still apply. If the group is small and knows that its views are not widely shared, it may set up a voluntary organization to provide housing for the poor—realizing that this is the only way the good it wants can be attained. Many such organizations were in fact set up toward the end of the nineteenth century and in the early years of this century. On the other hand, if many people share this view (or the group believes they do), they will seek to invoke the coercive power of the state and press for public housing subsidized from taxation.

In a pluralist democracy both government and voluntary organizations provide public goods. Some authorities have even argued that the work of voluntary organizations can be viewed as a private analogue to the making and implementation of public policy (Mavity & Ylvisaker 1977). Frequently voluntary and state services run side by side. The relationship of private philanthropic activities to the state and the services it provides varies from country to country, but the freedom to form voluntary organizations to serve a public purpose is characteristic of all democracies.

Dahl (1982) presents a balanced picture of the merits of pluralist democracies in which more or less autonomous voluntary organizations play a part in the provision of public goods and in the development of public policy. First, and more important, the organizations present a mechanism through which conflicts of values, interests, and views can, if not be resolved, be at least accommodated.

Dahl argues that because each group prevents the others from making changes that might seriously damage its perceived interests, the system exerts a stabilizing and conservative influence.

There are basic differences between the characteristics of a voluntary service and those of a public service. As I have indicated above, the principal advantage enjoyed by public services run by government agencies and financed by compulsory taxation is that the scale of the service and the resources devoted to it are not limited by the free-rider problem. There are limits, however, to the use of public services run by government agencies.

The Categorical Constraint

As soon as we invoke the coercive power of law, ordinary principles of democratic freedom and justice require restraints that are not applicable to a purely voluntary service. If we ask ourselves why such and such a voluntary service should not be made statutory and financed through compulsory taxation, several normative constraints will occur to us immediately. These constraints of political feasibility and political justice are not entirely clear-cut. Is the state entitled to compel those who disapprove of abortion to pay for it by compulsory taxation? What about those who disapprove of various kinds of defense expenditures—MX missiles or CIA activities in Latin America? Nor can we resolve the issue simply by saying that in such cases the minority must bow to the wishes of the majority.

Constraints that must exist when a service is provided by the state will not exist when a service is provided by voluntary action. There are clearly many services of the need for which a large proportion of the population is unconvinced and yet are not seen as positively harmful. This is an area that voluntary organizations are free to explore.

Similarly, if we look at the service from the point of view of the benefits it provides, a democratic state is more constrained to ensure that benefits are distributed fairly and equitably than is a voluntary organization. The democratic state has to treat all its citizens equally, which is what we mean by equality before the law. Furthermore, the state's distribution of benefits must not only be equitable; it must be *seen* to be equitable. One of the things we mean by political accountability is that state officials can be made to justify why they provide a benefit to one citizen and deny it to another. State action has to fit a pattern of rules. Voluntary action can be more spontaneous and even, if need be, aleatory. Spontaneity, in turn, can release that style of human warmth and loving care that a generalized pattern of defensible rules tends to crush. At its best, voluntary action can be based on true charity; ultimately state action has to be based on justice.

Reviewing the historical record and the impact of voluntary organizations on the development of state services, the Nathan Committee (1952) concluded, "Historically, state action is voluntary action crystallized and made universal." The constraints on the use of government agencies implicit in this universalizing process are, I believe, the nearest we can get to the constraints on the use of market mechanisms implicit in the market failure concepts of welfare economics. Because universality seems to me a more important characteristic than formality—law has to be a categorical imperative—I call these the categorical constraints.

Diversity

We can divide the categorical constraints into several sub-classifications. The private sector may comprise both prolife groups opposed to abortion and prochoice groups favoring it, but the state must ultimately choose. Similarly, it cannot simultaneously oppose the teaching of religion in its schools and encourage it. Within any given jurisdiction, contradictory policies on the same subject must be avoided. This presents no problem when the policy adopted reflects virtually unanimous views, but far more often, this aspect of the categorical constraint prevents the policy and law of the state from reflecting the full diversity of views and values it is the objective of pluralist democracy both to tolerate and to respect.[4]

The classic pluralist argument is that a voluntary nonprofit sector permits a greater diversity of social provisions than the state itself can achieve.

This pluralist argument for diversity, which I have developed more fully elsewhere (Douglas 1983), is probably the most important from the point of view of political theory, for it addresses the central paradox of democracy—that the people are sovereign but many: there is not one will of the people but several, sometimes contradictory wills.

It is probably for this reason that a healthy voluntary sector is characteristic of a democracy. We lack comprehensive systematic comparative data, but anecdotal evidence (such as the suppression of free trade unions in Communist-bloc countries) suggests that autonomous voluntary organizations are among the first casualties of a totalitarian regime whether of the Right or of the Left. Where tensions are less severe and less violent, a voluntary sector seems to provide the desired diversity. James's comparison of Sweden, a relatively homogeneous society, and Holland, a relatively heterogeneous one, supports the hypothesis that cultural heterogeneity is positively associated with provision of services through nonprofit organizations (1982).

Denominational education provides another illustration of the diversity argument.

The distinctive factor is that the social value the contributors place on the service is not shared by all. In a state in which all citizens were of the same denomination and placed the same value on denominational education, a state service financed from taxation would presumably be the solution adopted.

In a much debated report, Coleman, Hoffer, and Kilgore (1982) provided evidence that private schools, and Catholic schools in particular, produced what they call "better cognitive outcomes" than do public schools. It would be rea-

sonable to suppose that this would lead people to support such schools, and, indeed, the argument is often met in conversation. On the other hand, they also found that denominational schools led to more segregation not only on expected religious lines but also on social, income, and ethnic lines. Here we can see the way a voluntary sector permits the expression of differing social values.

In the case of research and higher education, distrust of too great a governmental influence is partly an attempt to achieve a greater diversity of approaches under a mixed regime of partly voluntary, partly statutory provision than in an entirely state-run system.

Weisbrod (1975) has provided an elegant model showing how voluntary nonprofit provision enables those who believe in a greater degree of social provision to supplement the level the politicians believe their constituents will accept. Weisbrod's basic point that voluntary organizations permit those who want to do more than they are legally compelled to do remains valid. The diversity argument applies just as much to those who want to provide more of a public good as it does to those who want to provide different kinds of public goods.

Experimentation

Closely allied to the diversity argument is the greater facility for experimentation possessed by the voluntary nonprofit sector. Before a democratic government can embark on any course of action, the case for it must be accepted by a relatively large section of the population. If the approach has already been tried by a voluntary body and proved viable, government can then follow using the experience and evidence gained by the voluntary organization. Voluntary bodies not infrequently adopt a course of action precisely in order to make a case for subsequent government action on the same lines. One well-known example is the "green revolution" pioneered by the Rockefeller Foundation, subsequently supported by other private foundations, and now primarily financed by governmental and intergovernmental agencies. It is extremely unlikely that governments would have embarked on this trail if it had not been blazed by the Rockefeller Foundation.

Even if a government has been persuaded to adopt an experimental policy, the requirement of equal treatment will present special problems. Let us take a hypothetical example, again from the field of education.[5] A public education authority wants to find out the most cost-effective student-teacher ratio. The obvious way to do this would be to set up classes with different ratios—ten students per teacher, twenty, perhaps a hundred—and measure performance against cost in each case. It is not difficult to imagine the political reaction to this strategy!

Experimentation involves not only trying things that have not been proven; it involves also abandoning experiments when the results show them to be unjustified. Here again government is at a disadvantage as against both the for-profit sector and the private nonprofit sector. Precisely because governments cannot easily admit to an experimental approach, it is more difficult for a government, which has invested political capital as well as taxpayers' money, to recognize that an experiment is no longer worth pursuing. The checkered history of sunset legislation is testimony to the difficulty governments experience in abandoning a project once it has been embarked upon.

The voluntary sector has fulfilled the role of experimenter and initiator with distinction in the past. Almost without exception every major social service was originally undertaken by the voluntary sector.[6] But does the sector still fulfill this role? Again we lack empirical data. We may be too close in time to recognize the true significance of the current work of the philanthropic sector; nevertheless it often seems to lack the pioneering and innovative character of earlier endeavors. Thus the roles of government and the voluntary sector have become more difficult to distinguish. Yet this may be no more than an impression derived from the media's presentation of the sector's activities. We need much firmer empirical evidence before we can determine how the sector is fulfilling its initiating and experimental role in social policy.

In one way the voluntary sector still seems to cater to the diversity of values in a complex society: the sector as a whole covers a wide spectrum of political and religious values. Politically we find voluntary organizations from the far Right to the far Left with almost every shade of opinion represented. Similarly most Christian denominations have their own relatively strong voluntary organizations, as does a wide variety of Jewish organizations. What is not clear is whether political and religious values are represented by these organizations proportionate to their incidence in society.

Is it true, for example, that the political Right is better represented in the voluntary sector than the Left because it has easier access to money? Arnove edited a collection of essays (1980) that develops the more subtle argument that one section of the voluntary sector, the big foundations, have tended to support a sophisticated conservatism (with a small *c*). These foundations were established and endowed by successful men operating in a competitive economy, and they have continued to be controlled for the most part by those whom the status quo has served well. Not surprisingly, therefore, they have tended to support changes, both in the United States and internationally, that make the status quo more acceptable and efficient rather than altering it radically.

Fisher's chapter in Arnove's book is a carefully documented and detailed case study of the development and influence of the Rockefeller Foundations' policies regarding the social sciences in England during the interwar years. Fisher found that the Rockefeller administrators, although committed to capitalist democracy, recognized that there was something fundamentally wrong about the levels of poverty and unemployment of the time. His case study revealed attitudes that were probably representative of those of the big foundations at the time: mainstream thinking, moderate progressiveness, an emphasis on research, and faith in the ameliorative potential of improved knowledge. Balance, however, is not necessarily a desirable objective in the voluntary sector: enabling the unpopular, the eccentric, and the heterodox to survive and lend their vitality to mass society is not the least of its functions.

Bureaucratization

The diversity argument emphasizes the extent to which a service is made universal when it is transferred to the government sector, thus inevitably sacrificing some diversity. But the categorical constraint also springs from the way a service is formalized when transferred to the public sector; it becomes accountable to the public or the public's representatives. It must treat equals equally and it must show that it is doing so. These needs—to ensure equality of treatment throughout a jurisdiction and to be able to defend its actions politically—together, generate the morass typical of bureaucratic red tape. The irony is that those who complain most about red tape are often those who are most vociferous in their demands for public accountability. What exactly constitutes bureaucratic red tape, as is the case with many such disparaging phrases, is rarely defined.

Voluntary organizations themselves are of course not totally free of bureaucratic constraints; there is always someone—be it trustees or contributors—to whom their executives are accountable. But they are usually freer than government agencies, partly because the scale of operations typically is smaller and partly because those to whom they are accountable are less numerous so that conditions of trust are more easily established. But, above all, those who contribute voluntarily to an enterprise have a safeguard that those who are compelled to contribute do not possess. The former can stop contributing; the latter cannot.

The voluntary sector achieves diversity through the very diversity of its institutions, but it may also achieve a measure of freedom from bureaucratic red tape even within its constituent institutions.

Let us say, for example, that a denominational school is as committed as a public-sector school to providing the most promising students with an education their parents can afford (or what-

ever may be the rule by which its mission is defined). But the public school will have to do this in a way it can defend publicly and politically. Thus it is likely to develop fairly rigid rules. The private school, on the other hand, because it is not legally and politically bound to its rules in the same way, can be more flexible. It can rely on more subjective criteria and trust more in the judgments of its officials.

In the matter of costs, the more elaborate administration of the public-sector institution inevitably is more expensive. But an economic price is paid, too, for the diversity achieved by fulfilling functions through voluntary endeavors. There is the cost of carrying free riders and the cost of fund-raising activities designed to reduce their numbers. On the other hand, the voluntary sector's relative freedom from accountability results in a savings and enables a greater proportion of available resources to be devoted to the institution's primary mission. There is clearly a trade-off here that will vary from case to case. An empirical study would be useful to ascertain whether voluntary organization in any given field actually leads to a more economical service.

The relative freedom of the private voluntary sector from bureaucratic constraints is so well established that governments frequently use the device of subsidizing existing voluntary bodies (or establishing new ones) to carry out functions somewhat protected from the usual requirements of political accountability. Kramer and Terrell (1984) conducted an extensive survey of the use of voluntary bodies by government agencies in the San Francisco Bay area. A significant proportion of the social services in the area are provided by private organizations under contract to government agencies. From their survey emerged a clear picture of the perceived advantages and disadvantages of services paid out of taxation and provided by voluntary organizations.

The advantages most often mentioned by government officials were greater flexibility—a program could be initiated (or terminated) more easily when the government agency did not itself have to engage staff—and a saving in costs—volunteers could be used and staffs given lower salaries and fewer fringe benefits. The claimed advantage in cost, however, was not universally accepted. Kramer and Terrell, in effect, returned a verdict of "not proven" because of the difficulties of comparing costs in the public and private sectors. Advantages less frequently mentioned were perhaps more interesting. The private agencies were seen as having greater competence in certain specialized areas—for example, providing day and residential care for adults, dealing with violence in the family, running suicide prevention centers, and maintaining sheltered workshops. It was also easier to use private agencies for controversial programs like family planning services. Voluntary bodies could make contact more easily with certain classes of clients, such as ethnic and cultural minorities and drug and child abusers, where a social stigma is attached to receiving services from government agencies.

The major disadvantage seen by public officials in using private agencies was the difficulty of achieving the degree of accountability required. Government managers also complained of inadequate management in the private agencies, poor personnel practices, weak budgeting (*virement*, anathema in public-sector budgeting, is almost meaningless in the private sector), and inadequate record keeping. They also complained of political pressures and attempts to avoid complying with contractual requirements. The general impression left by Kramer and Terrell fits our model of a trade-off between accountability in the public sector and flexibility and diversity in the private sector.

Three Classes of Nonprofit Organizations

The nonprofit organization set up to provide a public benefit from private funds is the most interesting from a theoretical point of view. This form of nonprofit organization is, in a real sense, an alternative to government, permitting a greater diversity of social provision than the state itself can achieve. Thus it constitutes a dis-

tinctive element in the Western liberal democratic tradition. It is not the only or even the most common form of nonprofit organization, however. We can identify at least two others: the mutual benefit organization—which is established to provide collective benefits more or less exclusively for its members—and the pressure group, or political action organization—which aims not to provide benefits itself but to persuade government to do so.

The distinctions among these three classes of nonprofit organizations are somewhat artificial and arbitrary. Actual organizations often straddle the classes to a greater or lesser extent. Mutual benefit organizations whose benefits seem at first sight exclusive to their members, such as motoring or golf clubs, may on closer examination be shown to provide forms of benefit to those who are not members. Motoring clubs usually seek to represent the interests of all motorists whether members or not, and golf clubs frequently have a beneficial effect on the value of properties in their vicinity. Similarly, the distinction between a charity and a political action organization may be difficult to discern. Charities frequently feel that their commitment to their clients requires them not only to provide the specific benefits for which they were founded but also to defend the interests of their clients in terms of public policy. For example, a charity established to provide financial assistance to impoverished senior citizens will find it a natural and almost inevitable extension of its role to lobby on questions of their social security.

The problem created by this blurring of categories is one with which lawyers have had to wrestle and have resolved in different ways in different countries. The resolution is rarely very satisfactory. Organizations that common sense suggests should be seen as charitable (such as Gingerbread, and English mutual benefit organization for single-parent families) are sometimes excluded by the legal definition. Conversely the legal definition occasionally includes organizations that do not seem particularly charitable. Charities seeking to remain within the legal definition frequently complain that their activities are unduly restricted.

Mutual Benefit Organizations

Mutual benefit organizations range from elitist social clubs to trade unions. In many ways these are closer to the for-profit sector than to the philanthropic. There is frequently very little altruism about the motivation of their members. They differ from the typical commercial for-profit enterprise in providing goods or services for their members collectively rather than on a quid pro quo transaction basis, which usually is why the nonprofit form is adopted.

Trade unions, for example, negotiate collectively for their members. As wages and working conditions are usually determined for a whole class of working people, they cannot charge clients individually for their services in the same way as, say, a lawyer or a doctor might do. Although they often represent individual members as a lawyer might do, their central activity cannot be organized on a commercial quid pro quo basis, and this determines the form of organization adopted.

Sporting and social clubs, another common form of mutual benefit organizations, typically provide premises and facilities for which theoretically members could be charged individually each time they were used. This, however, would be an expensive way of organizing things. It is cheaper and more satisfactory to make facilities available to the members collectively in return for membership fees—an example of the way the economic case for a nonprofit organization can be made in terms of "transaction costs." The concept of transaction cost was developed by Williamson (1979) originally to elucidate the economic reasons for-profit firms adopt different commercial strategies in such matters as deciding whether to subcontract or manufacture their own components, whether to maintain their own retailing organization or sell on the open market to retailers, and so on. The key element in the concept involves shifting attention from the subject of the transaction to the transaction itself. The concept is readily applicable to the distinctions among for-profit, nonprofit, and government forms of organization.[7]

In the case of social clubs, the cost of organizing things on a quid pro quo basis (the cost of this form of transaction) is higher than the cost of organizing them on a collective basis, and the higher transaction cost is not compensated by any significant advantages. This does not wholly explain why the nonprofit form is adopted, however.

I suspect that in this case the explanation lies in the greater control the nonprofit form gives to the customers/members. It compensates for the weakening influence of "exit" when goods are provided collectively by a strengthening of "voice."

Political Nonprofit Organizations

The class of nonprofit organizations that have public policy objectives is crucially important to the workings of democratic government. Political parties are themselves members of this class, but, even apart from them, it is almost impossible to imagine the workings of a modern democratic system without a whole constellation of lobbies, interest groups, and the like to articulate the range of interests and values that must be reconciled by the political system.

Although a wide spectrum of interests is represented by pressure groups and lobbies, it is generally recognized that all interests do not get equally represented. For example, producers find it easier to organize than consumers do, and a wealthy industry can deploy more resources in creating a pressure group to lobby on its behalf than a poor section of the community can. Here political norms of equity come into conflict with the spontaneity and randomness—the general untidiness—of the nonprofit sector.

It should be noted that these characteristics of the nonprofit sector are not mere accidental by-products to be corrected by systematic legislation ensuring equal representation of varying interests. Any attempt by the state to tidy up the nonprofit sector would necessarily interfere with freedom of association and thus would undermine an essential source of vitality for the sector. There is a seeming irrationality in encouraging the formation of two voluntary organizations with mutually incompatible goals (for example, pro- and antiabortion groups), but to suppress one or both would be gravely to restrict democratic freedom. Either we must follow Rousseau in his condemnation of partial societies and allow nothing between the state and the individual or we must accept that the nonprofit sector will reflect some of the differences in power that exist within our society.

In general, the institutions of the political nonprofit sector facilitate the nonviolent resolution of conflicts within society. They form part of the system by which conflicting interests are represented, expressed, and reconciled. This reconciliation is normally achieved by a process of bargaining, in which negotiators represent a sufficiently wide range of interests to be able to concede in one direction in return for concessions in another. In negotiations between management and labor, for example, concessions on hours or wages might be traded against concessions on staffing. The existence of representative voluntary organizations greatly helps this process. Management and labor negotiations would be virtually impossible without voluntary organizations in any large industry with hundreds of firms employing tens of thousands of employees. Similarly, a point of view widely scattered throughout the population can be made effective only after it has been gathered together by a voluntary organization, which represents that point of view in the legislative process and frequently confronts representatives of other points of view. The environmental lobbies are examples of this process.

Voluntary organizations, however, may sometimes impede rather than help the process of reaching societal decisions—for example, when voluntary pressure groups represent too narrow a range of interests. The tendency in recent years to develop single-issue groups rather than the older pattern of class-interest groups has accentuated this danger. It is difficult to see how any basis for agreement could be reached between, say, a group that believes all nuclear power stations are anathema and one that believes nuclear power is the safest, most economical, and most socially desirable way of generating electricity. The difference lies in the specificity with which the issue is defined.

When beliefs are held so intensely that compromise is impossible, the process of making societal decisions may break down. How can agreement be reached between a group that believes that any form of abortion under any circumstances is murder and a group that sees abortion as the inalienable right of women? Instead of facilitating compromise and negotiation between different elements of society, pressure groups like these may serve to accentuate differences, as they not only reflect the view of their constituent members but reinforce them. The process of organizing a group, bringing it together, holding meetings, and the like tends both to reinforce the members' views and to develop an adversary relation with groups representing different interests. Moreover, as Michels (1966) long ago recognized (in relation to political parties), the officials of such a group acquire a vested interest in its survival. They are not necessarily eager to recognize that their activities have resolved the problems that led to the establishment of the group or that a satisfactory modus vivendi has been established with their erstwhile adversaries.

Although I have written of three distinct sectors—government, business, and voluntary—and of different classes of nonprofits within the last sector, these are artificial and academic distinctions imposed on what is, in reality, the seamless web of the institutional fabric of society. The study of two of these sectors—business and government—developed into the disciplines of economics and political science. The third sector has tended to be neglected by the social sciences. Yet it touches on both of the others and is not only interesting in itself but a good vantage point from which to study the other two. Increasing concern with the third sector, which the issuing of this volume demonstrates, follows logically from the academic trend to return to the older conception of a political economy, in which economy and polity are seen as all of a piece. It is also appropriate that we should explore more fully the strengths and weaknesses of the third sector at a time when the public is becoming increasingly disillusioned with both government and business.

Notes

1. Today we tend to distinguish such private non-profit organizations as churches, private universities, and schools from charitable institutions. Yet they all come within the legal definition of a charity.

2. The care of bridges was a common charitable purpose of monastic foundations. The term *pontiff* originally derived from a builder of bridges.

3. Note that in this formulation I implicitly assume both that there is a general desire for a national health service and that the tax system is "fair." Both these assumptions will vary from country to country and from one period to another.

4. The abortion issue shows that even the private sector cannot always permit reflection of the full diversity of values, especially when both factions wish to engage the coercive power of the state. The pro-life groups want to engage the coercive power to forbid abortion, and the prochoice groups want to engage the coercive power by compelling those who consider abortion to be murder to pay for it through taxation.

5. I am indebted to Martin Landau for this hypothetical example.

6. Many schools, universities, and hospitals were established in medieval times (see Jordan 1959). It is a moot semantic point whether these should be classed as voluntary organizations. But certainly by the beginning of the seventeenth century, they had come under the rubric of charity. The eighteenth century saw a great proliferation of humanitarian charities, and the nineteenth century saw the establishment of many organizations both to combat poverty and to systematize and coordinate charitable endeavors. In the same century we find movements to spread education and improve housing for the laboring classes. In contrast, the state was not greatly involved in providing any of these traditionally philanthropic services until toward the end of the century (see Owen 1964; Bremner 1975). Thus, if we take education, health, housing, and welfare as the main contemporary social services of the state, their origins in all cases lie in the voluntary sector (see Nathan Committee 1952).

7. The application of transaction cost analysis (and other techniques drawn from the economics of organization) to political institutions is reviewed by Moe (1984).

References

Archer, M., ed. 1982. *The Sociology of Educational Expansion.* Beverly Hills, Calif.: Sage Publications.

Arnove, Robert, ed. 1980. *Philanthropy and Cultural Imperialism.* Boston: G. K. Hall.

Arrow, Kenneth. 1963. *Social Choice and Individual Values.* New Haven: Yale University Press.

Berry, Jeffrey M. 1984. *The Interest Group Society.* Boston: Little, Brown.

Brennan, G., and Buchanan, J. M. 1980. *The Power to Tax.* New York: Cambridge University Press.

Bremner, Robert H. 1975. "Private Philanthropy and Public Needs: Historical Perspective." In *Research Papers,* sponsored by the Commission on Private Philanthropy and Public Needs. Washington, D.C.: Department of the Treasury.

Coleman, James; Hoffer, Thomas; and Kilgore, Sally. 1982. *High School Achievement.* New York: Basic Books.

Crotty, William, 1984. *American Parties in Decline.* 2d ed. Boston: Little, Brown.

Dahl, Robert A. 1982. *Dilemmas of Pluralist Democracy.* New Haven: Yale University Press.

Douglas, James. 1983. *Why Charity?* Beverly Hills, Calif.: Sage Publications.

Fisher, Donald. 1980. "American Philanthropy and the Social Services." In *Philanthropy and Cultural Imperialism,* edited by Arnove, 1980.

Hirschman, Albert. 1970. *Exit, Voice and Loyalty.* Cambridge, Mass.: Harvard University Press.

James, Estelle. 1980. "The Non-Profit Sector in International Perspective: The Case of Sri Lanka." Yale University, Program on Non-Profit Organizations Working Paper no. 28.

———. 1982. "The Private Provision of Public Services: A Comparison of Sweden and Holland." Yale University, Program on Non-Profit Organizations Working Paper no. 60.

Jordan, W. K. 1959. *Philanthropy in England, 1480–1660.* London: Allen & Unwin.

Kaufman, Herbert. 1977. *Red Tape.* Washington, D.C.: Brookings Institution.

Keefe, William. 1980. *Parties, Politics and Public Policy in America.* 3d ed. New York: Holt, Rinehart & Winston.

Kramer, Ralph, and Terrell, Paul. 1984. *Social Service Contracting in the Bay Area.* Berkeley, Calif.: Institute of Governmental Studies.

Levy, Dan. 1982. "The Rise of Private Universities in Latin America and the United States." In *The Sociology of Educational Expansion,* edited by Archer, 1982, 93–132.

Mavity, Jane H., and Ylvisaker, Paul N. 1975. "Private Philanthropy and Public Affairs." In *Research Papers,* sponsored by the Commission on Private Philanthropy and Public Needs, vol. 2, pt. 1, 795–836. Washington, D.C.: Department of the Treasury.

Michels, Robert. 1966. *Political Parties.* New York: Free Press.

Moe, Terry M. 1984. "The New Economics of Organization." *American Journal of Political Science* 28, no. 4: 739–77.

Nathan Committee. 1952. *Report of the Committee on Law and Practice Relating to Charitable Trusts.* (Cmd. 8710). London: HMSO.

Nielsen, Waldemar. 1972. *The Big Foundations.* New York: Basic Books.

Olson, Mancur. 1971. *The Logic of Collective Action.* Cambridge, Mass.: Harvard University Press.

_____. 1982. *The Rise and Decline of Nations.* New Haven: Yale University Press.

O'Malley, Padraig. 1983. *The Uncivil Wars.* Boston: Houghton Mifflin.

Owen, David. 1964. *English Philanthropy, 1660–1960.* Cambridge, Mass.: Harvard University Press.

Picarda, Hubert. 1977. *The Law and Practice Relating to Charities.* London: Butterworths.

Pomey, Michel. 1980. *Traité des foundations d' utilité publique.* Paris: Presses Universitaires de France.

Schattschneider, Elmer E. 1975. *The Semi-Sovereign People.* New York: Holt, Rinehart & Winston.

Sorauf, Frank. 1984. *Party Politics in America.* 5th ed. Boston: Little, Brown.

Thurow, Lester C. 1980. *The Zero-Sum Society.* New York: Basic Books.

Truman, David. 1971. *The Governmental Process.* New York: Alfred A. Knopf.

Weisbrod, Burton. 1975. "Towards a Theory of the Non-Profit Sector." In *Altruism, Morality and Economic Theory,* edited by Edmund S. Phelps. New York: Russell Sage Foundation.

Williamson, Oliver. 1979. "Transaction-Cost Economies: The Governance of Contractual Relations." *Journal of Law and Economics* 22: 233–61.

Wolfenden Committee. 1978. *Report of the Future of Voluntary Organizations.* London: Croom Helm.

CHAPTER 19

Markets, Politics, and Charity: Nonprofits in the Political Economy

KIRSTEN A. GRØNBJERG

State and market organizations exercise significant control over nonprofit financial resources in the United States and shape other aspects of the organizational environment in which nonprofits operate. The political economy of the United States creates enduring institutional patterns which determine the structural opportunities for relations among the three sectors in a particular industry. Nonprofits, however, have both strategic and dynamic relations to the public and for-profit sectors and do not play a passive role in compensating for general shortcomings in the political or market systems, as most observers implicitly assume. Nonprofit, public, and market actors can and do advance their own interests, creating an iterative process of strategic action and response. As a result, relations among the three sectors are constantly developing.

In terms of nonprofit-market relations, nonprofits serve specialized economic functions by compensating for imperfections in the market economy associated with inadequate demands or hidden producer exploitation. By doing so, nonprofits change market structures and reduce their own competitive advantages. Nonprofit and market organizations also manipulate one another for strategic advantages in resource relations, as a result of which nonprofits come to

serve as an arena in which economic elites consolidate their power.

In terms of nonprofit-government relations, nonprofits have vested interests in the scope and structure of public sector activities. As nonprofits act to protect those interests, they engage in interest group politics. Where they come to share in the delivery of public goods, their political interests become especially well focused and their relations with the public sector institutionalized and difficult to restructure.

The character of these strategic structures and dynamic processes is most clearly evident from a comparison of industries that differ in the relative dominance of market and public sectors. Where the market sector is relatively weak, nonprofits have few incentives or occasions to pursue market activities themselves. In such fields, nonprofits are likely to be of less strategic relevance to market sector actors and present few opportunities for the exercise of elite power. Such nonprofits will therefore face difficulties in establishing resource relations with private firms.

Where the public sector is relatively undeveloped, nonprofits have legitimate occasions for pursuing political actions that focus on the scope and general structure of public sector mandates. They also, however, have few opportunities to become an integral part of the delivery of public goods and to benefit from the legitimacy, financial resources, and entry to negotiations about crucial administrative details that flow from such participation.

In this chapter, I first characterize the political economy of the United States with specific reference to social services and community development and argue that this economy differentially shapes the role of nonprofits vis-à-vis public and market sector organizations in their respective fields. I use findings from case studies of six social service and seven community development organizations[1] in the Chicago area to illustrate variations in the structure and dynamics of sectoral relations that result from these differences. Finally, I extend this approach and point to systematic variations in manifestations of the United States political economy across other industries and argue that there are corresponding differences in how nonprofits relate to market and state organizations in these fields.

The Role of Social Service and Community Development Nonprofits in the U.S. Political Economy

The political economy of the United States is shaped by the joint operation of two driving forces. The first of these is the ideological dominance of a classical economic model which defines free markets and competing market organizations as the fundamental institutions of society, leaving government and nonprofits to play secondary and supportive roles. The second and closely related force is deeply ingrained suspicion of virtually all public programs and authorities, which are viewed as inefficient, subject to favoritism, and antagonistic to the much-preferred system of private initiative, unless carefully controlled and monitored.

The result is a persistent preoccupation with and celebration of market forces, a relative absence of strong restraints on private initiatives, and a system of public policy mandates that have developed late and remain narrow, contentious, and incomplete, especially in the area

of social policy.[2] The combination of these outcomes may have produced the world's most powerful economy as measured by gross national product or similar monetary standards, but it has been at the expense of addressing fundamental social issues.

Nonprofits play a critical role in the U.S. political economy. As voluntary associations, they suit the American preference for private auspices. As institutions established for charitable or common purposes, they alleviate the need for such action under public auspices. Yet nonprofit organizations do not have the economic and political clout of private and public sector organizations.

Relationships with the Private Sector

The prominence of private market activities in the United States (and their protection in law and public policy) means that private sector organizations dominate the economy and condition the economic and social needs that nonprofits seek to address. As I show below, however, nonprofits also have specialized economic functions in the market economy and may serve as an arena in which economic elites exercise power. Both of these features differ among social service and community development organizations.

Nonprofit Functions in the Market Economy

Economic theories of nonprofit organizations (Hansmann 1980, 1987; Rose-Ackerman 1986; Weisbrod 1975, 1977, 1988) usually imply that nonprofits fulfill narrow but important functions in compensating for imperfections in standard market relationships, in which informed customers shop for the best bargain and producers seek the largest profit. Nonprofits solve two kinds of problems in these relations: market failure and contract failure. Market failure occurs when demands for a product or service are so low or thin that private firms cannot generate sufficiently high profits to stay in business by meeting the demand. Because nonprofits have access to private donations and are exempt from certain taxes and fees, they can subsidize service activities or products and still meet operating costs in spite of low demand.

Contract failure occurs when the customer does not have sufficient information to evaluate the quality or competitive value of goods and services available in the marketplace. This may occur if the quality of the service is difficult to determine (for example, counseling) or the customer possesses only limited ability to exercise judgment (for example, because of age or impairment or ignorance). In these cases, market transactions occur under conditions of asymmetric information that impede the free operation of market forces. That is, if customers do not know what they are buying, providers can exploit their ignorance to maximize profit without affecting demand. Nonprofits avoid these inefficient tendencies because they are legally restricted from distributing any economic gains to private individuals. Because nonprofits have no incentives to exploit customer ignorance, they are more likely to deliver high-quality services and warrant the consumer trust made necessary by asymmetric information under conditions of contract failure.

Case studies show nonprofit social service agencies serving the specialized functions of overcoming both market and contract failure. One nonprofit social service agency, Minority Search, which defined itself as a nonprofit business, exemplifies the ability of nonprofits to overcome market failure. It charged major corporations a flat annual fee for providing long-term training to minority college students who worked in internship positions with the corporations during the summer.

Another social service agency, Christian Therapists, provided therapy to born-again Christians. This service is a classic example of a thin market operating under conditions of asymmetric information. The market is thin because born-again Christians are reluctant to seek help from secular organizations for fear that their Christian faith will be ignored or subverted in the process. The information is asymmetric because the quality of therapy is notoriously difficult for clients to evaluate.

As at many other social service organizations and among professional therapists generally, the agency required clients to pay a fee for services received. It argued that the willingness to pay a fee is evidence of commitment to therapy. Only clients who are committed to therapy are likely to obtain full benefit from the treatment received. Payment of a fee, even just a token amount, is taken to demonstrate a minimum level of commitment to treatment.

Clients who are willing to pay fees, of course, also serve another important function for the agency: They confirm that they find the agency's services of value. The result is a self-reinforcing process by which counselors or other staff members of an agency, by serving fee-paying clients, find personal and professional rewards and the agency obtains revenues (Hasenfeld 1978).

Commercial actions of community development organizations fit mainly the market failure model of thin or inadequate demand. Inner-city neighborhoods experienced major, prolonged decline as middle-class families, businesses, and manufacturing firms moved to the suburbs after World War II. The more recent economic decline of the Northeast and the Midwest has accelerated that process for these regions. The absence of commercial investments has forced increasing numbers of community organizations in cities like Chicago to devote sustained attention to housing and economic development in their communities to counteract these trends.

Several of the community organizations I studied have participated in construction projects (for example, of housing developments and strip malls) in partnership with local businesses, real estate developers, and manufacturing firms, at times also involving governmental units as active or passive partners. In some cases, they have created formally incorporated joint ventures with proprietary firms, receiving a share of the profit.

Federal regulatory developments such as community reinvestment requirements for financial institutions and efforts to eliminate redlining have opened up new market niches and sources of earnings for nonprofit community development organizations. Thus, several of the case study organizations discussed here have worked closely with financial institutions to help local commercial establishments negotiate the borrowing process in return for loan-packaging fees.

Special events constitute another market niche created by nonprofit organizations of all types, catering to increasingly sophisticated demands for recreation and entertainment while at the same time affording new sources of revenues to many nonprofits. Three of the community development organizations, Hispanic Neighbors, New Town Sponsors, and Community Preservation Council, obtained the bulk of their revenues from major neighborhood festivals, attracting tens of thousands of visitors and clearing hundreds of thousands of dollars. This market niche has expanded greatly in recent years to the point where some commercial enterprises now specialize in organizing and catering events like the leasing of luxury boats for casino excursions.

These commercial explorations by nonprofits are part of a dynamic, iterative process so that over time, the availability of commercial services and products from nonprofits helps change consumer tastes and stimulate demand.[3] At some point, the demand increases sufficiently to entice entrepreneurs or profit-making organizations into the newly created market niche.

Community organizations face increasing competition from for-profit providers in their efforts to generate fee income. On the one hand, those that seek to support and provide services to private sector firms benefit from the expectations of local businesses to pay for services received. They encounter few, if any, protests by community residents, board members, or clients if they charge for their services. By the same token, however, once the loan-packaging market is established, local lending institutions or enterprising consultants easily enter the market.

By creating new markets in this way, nonprofits attract private firms into the fray. By establishing standards for organizational behavior that reassure uneasy customers about the quality of services they receive, as in the case of Christian Therapy, nonprofits allow private sector firms to overcome customer fears of ex-

ploitation. These dynamics are likely to intensify as the private economy continues to restructure and shift away from manufacturing toward a service economy.

At the same time, both social service and community organizations are increasingly turning to fees and other commercial receipts to supplement their revenues. The combination of these developments—the intrusions by for-profit organizations into nonprofit market niches and the cultivation by nonprofits of for-profit revenue streams—suggests that the boundary between the two sectors may become increasingly blurred and contentious. So far, representatives from the for-profit sector have been most vocal in defending their territory. They claim that nonprofit organizations compete unfairly with small businesses (Bennett and DiLorenzo 1989) because their access to donations and avoidance of tax payments allow them to operate at lower costs.

Nonprofits as Arenas for Economic Elites

In addition to performing these specific economic functions, nonprofit social service and community development organizations serve other strategic purposes for market organizations as they seek to use such firms for their benefit. Given the dominance of private firms in American society and the financial resources they control, it is not surprising that nonprofits have sought to establish explicit linkages with the for-profit sector. Nonprofits pursue such relations when they solicit corporate donations or sponsorship of special events, and they formalize the linkages when they appoint corporate leaders to serve on their boards of directors.

The nonprofit organization's size and prestige and the opportunities it provides for networking or exercise of leadership will influence the degree of interest corporate leaders have in joining the board. Such large, well-established nonprofit organizations as United Ways, foundations, universities, hospitals, and major cultural institutions have been quite successful in attracting corporate support and corporate leaders (or their spouses) to board memberships

(Ostrander 1984; Odendahl 1990; Schiller 1989; Useem 1984; Brilliant 1990).

Most social service organizations, by contrast, find it difficult to be equally successful. They are too small and numerous to stand out in the pack of major nonprofits seeking corporate contacts at the highest level of the firm. More important, in contrast to the services offered by institutions of higher education and major cultural organizations, theirs are rarely of key interest to major corporations. Although disadvantaged by their smallness, community organizations present specific strategic advantages to firms and institutions located in a given community. Although few of the community organizations attracted any top corporate executives to their board, most were successful in involving the local managers of major firms with operations in their community or executives of such important local institutions as banks, real estate firms, hospitals, universities, and churches.

There are good reasons for their success. Three of the case study organizations, New Town Sponsors, Economic Development Commission, and United Residents, had access to local banks, large businesses, major employers, and institutions of higher education in their communities; they had cultivated relationships with the cast of community institutions.[4] The three had also developed special mechanisms to institutionalize the financial support involved, for example, by varying the membership dues of commercial property owners according to the assessed evaluation of the real estate involved.

Major community institutions are important actors in community development organizations. The former have vested, legitimate interests in the community, and community organizations cannot oppose or ignore them without incurring potential costs. The relationship is reciprocal in that each sees the other as providing an opportunity to influence development without having to take full responsibility for direct and aggressive community action.

Because of the variety of strong local institutions in the communities, these three community development organizations defined their role as one of providing opportunities to air and resolve diverse community interests. They

sought to supply a forum in which local community actors could interact and kept their direct political involvement focused on issues of direct local impact around which negotiated positions could be developed. Had they attempted to play a more forceful role, they would have risked offending portions of their constituency and losing donations or dues.

Community Renewal illustrates the process by which community organizations serve the interest of local institutions. This group obtained the bulk of its funding from a single institution with major investments in the community and approached a condition of co-optation. The institution had devoted significant resources to expanding and protecting its interests in the community. Rather than undertaking these activities internally, however, it delegated much of its visible activities to Community Renewal. The decoupled structural arrangement ensured that the efforts received full-time management attention, while protecting the institution from controversy and risk of failure; the institution remained separate from such controversial, forceful efforts as lawsuits against local property owners that might have entailed substantial financial or symbolic costs.

Only a narrow range of community institutions are likely to want to influence or control a community development organization to the point of co-optation. Factories, hospitals, universities, major commercial establishments, leading banks, and large corporate headquarters all exercise direct control over sizable portions of local real estate holdings if they are located in a small community. They cannot avoid having a major impact on local communities in managing these holdings. They also have vested interests in many of the arenas in which community development organizations are active: decisions on land use patterns, enforcement of building codes, and crime control. These types of community institutions therefore have major incentives to define their interests in the community broadly and to pursue them actively by collaborating with or co-opting community development organizations.

As these examples show, corporate participation in nonprofit boards serves the direct economic interests of both parties. Well-con-nected boards of directors afford nonprofits per-sonalized access to such important resources as corporate and foundation grants, in-kind sup-port for special events and marketing efforts, and financial and legal advice. For corporate leaders, financial support of nonprofit organizations and membership on nonprofit boards of directors are indirect opportunities to promote corporate interests and extend their sphere of influence.[5]

These opportunities develop as corporate leaders interact with one another in the neutral settings offered by nonprofits and through spe-cific actions by individual firms. The latter in-clude efforts to create goodwill and market recognition (that is, cause-related marketing), shape policy agendas and definitions of prob-lems, and, more generally, ensure that corporate positions and interests are known and incorpo-rated into nonprofit activities as well as in the corporate world (Useem 1984; Schiller 1987).

Such attempts at mutual exploitation may take on a life of their own and become difficult for either party to control. For nonprofits, the risk is one of dependence on fickle corporate goodwill, if not actual co-optation. For corpo-rate actors, participation in nonprofit social ser-vice and community development activities may risk involvement in controversies that antago-nize potential customers or complicate already thorny business relations.[6]

Relations with the Public Sector

Nonprofit social service and community devel-opment organizations also maintain distinctive relationships with the public sector. The pecu-liar nature of the American welfare state is espe-cially important to social service agencies and relevant to community development organiza-tions as well.

National social welfare policies developed late in the United States and continue to be beset—for ideological and other reasons that run counter to the celebration of private initiative and free markets noted earlier—by a general re-luctance to expand public mandates. These fea-tures help explain the emergence of a welfare

system in which non-public service providers play an important role in executing public man-dates (Grønbjerg, Street, and Suttles 1978; Sosin 1990; Wilensky and Lebeaux 1965). Indeed, nonprofits are the main providers of nonpublic services in the social service field but have more complex relations with the public sector in the community development field.

Nonprofits and Indirect Demand Structures

The public sector uses a combination of fiscal and monetary policies to guide the nation's eco-nomic and social development and to meet the needs for specific public services.

The nature of monetary policies (for exam-ple, Federal Reserve Bank discount rates) and the structure and size of tax systems indirectly modify demands for services by both social ser-vice and community development nonprofits. In the case of social services, monetary policies influence the general state of the economy and therefore overall employment and wage levels.

The structure of tax systems affects the vol-ume of discretionary income and financial secu-rity available to different income groups. Mid-dle- and upper-income groups receive extensive asset-building support in the form of tax de-ductibility of mortgage interest payments, real estate taxes, and employment-related retirement savings (Sherraden 1991). These income groups therefore have a greater capacity than low-in-come earners to make donations to nonprofits and to pay near-market fees for nonprofit ser-vices, thereby encouraging nonprofits to pro-vide services of particular interest to these groups.

Monetary and tax policies also affect the de-mand for community development efforts. The United States still does not effectively distin-guish between productive investments and leveraged buyouts and has only recently begun to use monetary and tax policies to encourage reinvestment in existing structures as opposed to new infrastructures. Widespread celebration of growth and newness tends to favor the latter, leaving older communities with deteriorating infrastructures and cumulative disinvestment, thus increasing the need for community devel-

opment organizations to take action to counteract or overcome these trends.

Nonprofits and Direct Public Spending

The amounts and purposes of public spending
directly shape the community needs and service
demands that nonprofits encounter, whether or
not they have any public funding themselves.
The United States has a fairly limited definition
of public goods. It lags behind most other industrial nations in the proportion of gross national product allocated to public welfare
spending, especially outside the area of health
care, and still lacks universal health insurance or
family allowance programs (Palmer, Smeeding,
and Torrey 1988).

Means-tested income-assistance programs
(for example, Aid to Families with Dependent
Children) and other services for the poor have
increased only modestly, barely doubling in
constant per capita dollars, and jointly account
for only about one-tenth of total public welfare
spending. Low levels of spending for traditional
welfare purposes mean that nonprofits are faced
with meeting a wide range of basic needs which
are not directly addressed by public spending.

All other welfare services targeted at low-income groups accounted for only about 3 percent
of total public welfare expenditures in 1984, although that percentage represented more than a
tripling of real spending per capita in 1950.
Nonprofit social service and community development organizations obtain most of their public funding from this latter, smallest, and slow-
growing component of public welfare spending.

The structure of public policy and priorities
means that the United States has major service
needs and service gaps. Nonprofit social service
and community development organizations
benefit from these patterns in monetary, tax,
and fiscal policies because they leave them with
an important role to play in addressing major
societal problems.

Direct Nonprofit-Public Linkages

Although the volume of public spending is
clearly important, assessing the form that
spending takes is even more critical for under-

standing how nonprofit and public sectors interact. Some public spending takes the form of
direct payments to individuals (for example,
public aid and social security payments) or
vouchers that individuals exchange for specified
services (for example, food stamps, student
loans, Medicare, Medicaid, Section 8 Housing
vouchers). These payment systems are of interest to nonprofits because they give individuals
discretion over where to obtain services. Consequently, nonprofits must compete with free
public services (in the case of direct public provision) and with each other and for-profit organizations for fee-paying or credit-bearing
clients. Nonprofits therefore have a vested interest in limiting the scope and quality of these
payment systems because lack of competition
makes their own program activities more attractive and needed.

A third payment structure, public subsidies to
private providers, usually in the form of grants
or contracts, is of greater direct interest to nonprofits because they tend to be the preferred recipients of such support.

The contract system lends hidden support to
persistent suspicions about the deservingness of
low-income clients in the United States—beliefs
that they are at fault for their predicament and
should not be entitled to free services at taxpayer expense. By channeling public spending
targeted at such clients through nonprofit subcontractors, the system avoids leaving service
decisions in the hands of clients assumed to be
ill-informed or unworthy or both. Instead,
nonprofits come to act as gatekeepers, able to
provide the most appropriate service and to
weed out those with questionable claims to
legitimacy.

The contract system not only provides nonprofits with revenues and gives them a culturally
approved role to play, but also simplifies some
management tasks. It reduces the need of nonprofits to compete for and satisfy, in the case of
social agencies, a large number of individual
clients with fickle interests or, in the case of
community organizations, apathetic or warring
community residents and institutions. Instead,
nonprofits with public contracts must satisfy
only a limited number of funders, over whom
they can exercise some degree of control, and

they obtain substantial levels of funding, secure for the duration of the contract and often beyond.

Cooperation in Social Services. The dependence is mutual: public agencies depend on nonprofits to deliver their social services, and public funding is a major source of revenue for social service nonprofits.

The spending structure is strengthened by the dynamics under which public-nonprofit resource relationships play themselves out in the social policy arena. Once the public-nonprofit grants or contract funding system is established, public agencies purchase more than service capacities and access to infrastructures, and nonprofits obtain more than revenues. The relationship comes to involve also the exchange of legitimacy, knowledge, and influence (Saidel 1991). The result is a self-reinforcing process in which nonprofit social service agencies develop complex interorganizational relations with public sector agencies.

The linkage is evident from tendencies toward isomorphism between the two sectors and the types of operational practices that public funding encourages in or imposes on the nonprofit partners. The receipt of public funding by nonprofit social service agencies means that they must track the fallout from budget negotiations and shifting priorities up and down the paths of intergovernmental transfers. They must adhere to rules and regulations that limit internal management discretion, meet work-intensive reporting requirements, and survive cost control and cost sharing. They must also overcome their built-in proclivities toward fragmentation and the ad hoc planning associated with managing multiple contracts with idiosyncratic requirements and timetables. Finally, they must weigh opportunity costs associated with pursuing alternative sources of funding.

In return for accepting these contingencies, nonprofit social service agencies obtain sizable, dependable funding. The four Chicago-area social service agencies with public funding that I studied—Youth Outreach, Hispanic Youth Services, Immigrant Welfare League, and Alcohol Treatment—rarely lost an existing public grant

or contract.[7] Indeed, the evidence shows that it is difficult for public agencies to terminate funding relations. For example, in late 1987, the Illinois Department of Children and Family Services (DCFS) decided to allow new agencies to bid for certain counseling contracts in competition with existing subcontractors. When DCFS awarded contracts to several new agencies (including Youth Outreach) with higher proposal review scores than existing providers, the latter took their case to the governor and forced DCFS to cancel the contracts the day before services were supposed to start.

On the other hand, nonprofit social service agencies do obtain access to new opportunities for public contracts as the information network alerts them to leftover funding or newly created funding streams and as public agency administrators come to accept them as reliable subcontractors. In fact, one public agency not only alerted Immigrant Welfare League of a new source of funding in another public agency, but advised it on how to write the application.

There is other evidence that important state agencies have come to depend on access to a reliable, cooperative infrastructure of nonprofit organizations in order to carry out their mandates, especially in child welfare, community mental health, and substance abuse treatment and prevention. For example, membership in key nonprofit coalitions is the best single predictor of the amount of funding that nonprofits received from the Illinois DCFS in 1989 (Grønbjerg, Chen, and Stagner 1992).

Indeed, nonprofit statewide coalitions and major child welfare agencies remain among the organizations most called upon to help formulate or comment upon social policies. They view themselves as the indispensable partners of public agencies, providing high-quality, professional social services, and believe they are entitled to adequate public (that is, state) reimbursements for those services. The state has accepted these claims, at least in the child welfare field, and established a formal structure for negotiating rate setting with nonprofit child welfare agencies.

The nonprofit-public relationship in social services thus approximates a pattern of cooperation because the public sector depends on nonprofit service providers to execute public mandates. This dependence derives from and bolsters shared goals. The absence of strong for-profit competitors in the field supports the assumption of good faith in contractual relations. Yet the process is a self-reinforcing one. Funding relations become increasingly institutionalized as either party becomes reluctant or unable to undertake major modifications. At the same time, the relationships become increasingly complex and costly to the participants because both parties seek to exploit available opportunities to exercise control over the relationship. Neither party appears to be fully successful in doing so.

Symbiosis in Community Development.   The relationship of nonprofit community development organizations with the public sector differs notably from that of the social services. From a fiscal point of view, nonprofits are much less important to public sector activities in community development than they are in delivering publicly financed social and mental health services.

In spite of low reliance by the public sector on nonprofits in community development, these nonprofits still depend on public funding for a significant portion of their revenues. The dependence is therefore not symmetric: Nonprofits in the field depend much more on government for their resources than government depends on them for program activities.[8]

This helps explain why in the community development field, the pattern of relationship to the public sector approximates symbiosis. Rather than functioning as a critical part of the publicly funded service infrastructure, nonprofits in the community development field play an intervening or mediating role in the overwhelmingly political interactions between public and market organizations. These two each attempt to enlist community organizations on their side, just as community organizations may negotiate alliances with either.

In contrast to social service agencies, community development organizations rarely have the capacity or resources to carry out relevant activities themselves, for example, build or repair housing and create new jobs. Only recently have new sources of public support become available to them for such purposes, and not in large amounts. Instead, the role of community development organizations has centered on identifying needs or gaps in public services and on closely related efforts to promote or resist public or private sector developments. Some engage in limited partnerships with the public or private sectors, especially in the planning phases of housing and community development projects (for example, commercial strip development and incubator ventures) but also as managers or coordinators of ongoing efforts.

Such brick and mortar projects highlight land use and geographic considerations and therefore local politics. That makes involvement in party politics a highly salient and legitimate activity for community development organizations. Their claim to represent the interest of a geographic community further propels them into political involvement. They often find themselves mediating or directly involved in politics as partisans in inter- or intra-community conflicts. Many such conflicts mobilize local politicians who may use their control over public spending for community development to reward supporters and punish opponents.

In fact, among the case study organizations, each community development organization with public funding had been caught in the political process. African-American Neighbors, for example, dropped from $612,000 in city grants and contracts to $19,000 two years later because the organization took a lead role in the boycott of a favored event sponsored by then-mayor Jane Byrne. When the mayor retaliated and pulled the organization's public contracts, African-American Neighbors protested in vain, and other community development organizations were reluctant to enter the fracas.

This is a drastic example, but community development organizations do encounter greater uncertainty in securing access to stable public funding than social service agencies and must expect to encounter terminated public contracts.[9]

Even so, public funding for community development organizations is more certain than most other sources of funding available to nonprofits.[10] And, although some public grants and contracts are fairly small, few revenue sources offer a similar scale of funding to these types of organizations.

As in the case of social service agencies, there are major costs to community development organizations associated with the receipt of public funding. The costs are quite similar because the grants and contract system operates under comparable principles. However, community development organizations have less certain access to continued funding, greater need for paying careful attention to party politics, and less severe problems of coordination because of their smaller scale of operation.

In short, there are important divergences in how nonprofit social service and community development organizations relate to market and public sector actors. Social service agencies have less direct utility to private firms than community development organizations and have fewer opportunities to develop institutionalized linkages or ongoing support from such firms. There are, however, many more and somewhat larger social service agencies than community development organizations, and they are more likely to rely on public funding and to have institutionalized relationships with public agencies as well as other nonprofit organizations.

More important, social service agencies are of greater significance to public agencies and have greater control and leverage over public funding. This is shown by their better access to stable, continued funding than community development organizations and by their acceptance as legitimate, expert participants in the technical debate on how to administer public human service programs. Community development organizations, by contrast, are more likely to be viewed as organized, local constituency groups, among the many with which local politicians have to contend, albeit ones with potentially powerful allies in the local business community.

Industry Variations in the U.S. Political Economy

The differences in how nonprofit social service agencies and community development organi-

zations relate to state and market organizations have broad applicability and are useful for understanding interactions among the three sectors in other industries as well. Indeed, nonprofits are active in a variety of fields, as the National Taxonomy of Exempt Entities illustrates: health care, civil rights, public affairs, religion, education, environmental protection, employment and training, social services, youth development, housing, arts and culture, community organizing, philanthropy, research, and so forth (Hodgkinson et al. 1992). These industries are also influenced by the two major driving forces in American society: the dominance of market models and the scope and structure of public sector activities, although the political economy manifests itself differently across industries.[11]

Nonprofit Relations to the Market Sector

The relationships between nonprofits and private sector organizations differ from industry to industry. In some industries, nonprofits compete directly with market organizations, while corporate support for nonprofits in some fields offers strategic advantages to private firms. There are costs to the firms associated with such support: valuable executive time, direct outlays in the form of corporate grants or sponsorships, and inability to escape the fallout when nonprofit partners undertake controversial activities.

In some fields, nonprofits do not compete directly with private firms and afford access mainly to expertise and technology (for example, higher education and medical research) or enhance the quality of life for corporate staff and leadership (for example, through arts and cultural institutions and some health organizations). Not surprisingly, these fields tend to receive the bulk of corporate donations and to have strong corporate linkages on their boards.[12]

In fields such as social services, for-profit organizations are relatively few and unimportant, with the exception of day care and homemaker services, and public and nonprofits dominate the service fields. Market organizations may supply funding for nonprofits in the form of smaller donations and other subsidies because they view themselves as benefiting at least marginally from the array of services that they provide. Their funding for any specific non-profit organization is therefore likely to be episodic, uncertain, and difficult for the non-profit organization to influence or control.

In service fields like health and job training, nonprofits compete directly with market organizations or are vertically integrated with them. Thus for-profit health clinics refer patients to nonprofit hospitals, or nonprofit job training agencies seek private sector placements for their trainees. In health care, individual providers like doctors and pharmacists, group practices, and major corporations such as insurance companies and pharmaceutical industries traditionally have dominated the field, while for-profit hospitals and long-term care facilities have gained prominence in recent years.

The active participation of the for-profit sector imposes marketlike transactions on non-profits as well, blurs the line between the two sectors, and imposes greater complexity on their interactions. Even public subsidies take market-like forms. For example, the Medicare and Medicaid systems both incorporate critical elements of consumer choice, while the Job Training Part-nership Act uses a performance-based payment system.

In still other fields, including housing and community development, environmental control, and civil rights, the for-profit sector also has a vested interest in nonprofit activities. The basis for nonprofit-market interactions, however, is not direct competition between the two sectors or corporate desire for nonprofit services, but the likelihood that nonprofit actions will impose external control over the market sector's own productive capacity, discretion, and access to critical opportunities. That is the case when nonprofit community organizations oppose (or support) private sector development projects, when environmental groups seek restrictions on industrial pollution, and when civil rights organizations press for affirmative action in private sector employment.

Under these circumstances, relationships between nonprofit and for-profit organizations become highly complex, with either party view-ing the other as a potential opponent, constituent, or customer (that is, a purchaser of technical expertise in the field). To the extent that for-profit organizations become constituents or customers of nonprofits, they are likely to be stable and fairly controllable sources of market transactions or subsidies for nonprofits. Even so, the relationships are rarely static but subject to continuing negotiations and strategic action by either party. Relationships are likely to become particularly contentious in fields in which nonprofits are changing the market structure by creating new markets or standardizing products, as appears to be the case in health and social services.

Nonprofit Relations to Public Sector

Although deep suspicion surrounds virtually all government action in the United States, the size and structure of public sector activities differ significantly across policy arenas. There are also local variations within specific service fields, reflecting timings, patterns of settlement, and other special circumstances. Nevertheless, for historical and ideological reasons, the public sector has been involved earlier, more extensively, and more directly in the provision of some services than others.

In social services, the infrastructure has been largely controlled by the nonprofit sector, and in health, by a combination of nonprofit and for-profit entities (hospitals, pharmaceutical firms, medical practitioners). In job training, the infrastructure has been located mainly in for-profit organizations that train their own workers, although the capacity for job training of most direct relevance to low-income or other specialized groups is located in public schools and nonprofit social service agencies.

In still other fields, such as environmental control, arts and culture, civil rights, housing, and community development, public sector responsibilities are even more recent and limited in scope. As a result, they have not been fully institutionalized and are still subject to considerable debate, focusing mainly on the proper role of government vis-à-vis that of the private sector, with only minimal attention to the non-profit sector. Finally, public sector activities are more or less completely absent from such fields as philanthropy and religion.

Partly for these reasons, the mechanisms by which public-nonprofit funding relationships operate also differ greatly among service fields, and these variations in the scope and structure of public sector activities exert marked control over the organizational environment in which different types of nonprofit organizations operate. In education and health, the payment structure gives extensive control to market forces and to the mutual selection process at work between service recipients and providers. The amount of public funds received by nonprofits in these fields depends on the degree to which they attract and accept clients who carry cash or credit from public sources, that is, tuition grants, student loans, and eligibility for Medicare or Medicaid reimbursements.[13]

Public-nonprofit payment structures in most other fields (social service, employment and training, housing and community development, arts and culture) are organized more along the lines of formal grants and contracts that link provider agencies directly to their respective public funders. In this case, clients have little to say about the size of the public-nonprofit exchange, and market forces are correspondingly attenuated.

Public sector dependence on nonprofit infrastructures varies along parallel lines, and the type and degree of dependence determine not only whether and how much public sector funding is available to nonprofits but also the leverage that nonprofits are likely to have over public sector agencies. Thus, the dependence may be low and nonprofit leverage minimal because the public sector maintains its own infrastructure (education). In this case, nonprofits are likely to focus mainly on keeping public sector outlays sufficiently low and narrow in focus to protect their own competitiveness. At the other extreme, public sector dependence may be direct and fairly high (social service). Nonprofit leverage is then extensive because the public sector needs access to nonprofit infrastructures to meet its own mandates.

Alternatively, public sector dependence on nonprofits may be direct and mixed with dependence on for-profit infrastructures (that is, health, job training). Nonprofit leverage is important here but lower than if dependence was extensive and limited to nonprofits because the public sector does not rely exclusively on nonprofit infrastructures. Finally, the public sector's dependence may be low, indirect, and limited to setting and shaping agendas (civil rights, community development, environmental issues). As a result, nonprofit leverage is also indirect and highly politicized because the public sector seeks to induce actions in the private sector and does not require direct access to nonprofit service infrastructures of any kind, although nonprofit advocacy and other political efforts are highly relevant.

Conclusion

I have argued that nonprofits have distinctive relations with market and public sector organizations and documented differences in these relationships for social service and community development organizations. These patterns have broad applicability and are useful for understanding interactions among the nonprofit, market, and public sectors in other industries as well. There are major differences in how nonprofits relate to market organizations. In some industries, nonprofits compete with private firms (health), are vertically integrated with them (job training), or otherwise provide important services to them (education, arts/culture), have potential consequences for their internal decision making (civil rights, environmental issues), or are mainly neutral arenas for elite interaction (social services).

There are also major industry variations in how nonprofits relate to the public sector. They either compete with public sector organizations (for example, education), operate in partnerships with them through subsidy relations (for example, social service, health), define them as forces to be mobilized (for example, civil rights, environmental issues, community development), or view them as alien to the primary purpose of the organization (for example, philanthropy, religion).[14]

Equally important, these economic and political interactions are dynamic and ongoing. They reflect the configuration of strategic opportunities that the sectors present to one another. Individual organizations active in a given field make use of these opportunities to actively promote their own interests and secure stable resources, expanding markets, and increased power. There are several implications that should be highlighted. First, nonprofits are not passive targets for market or public sector interests but take active roles in shaping their environment and resource opportunities. Second, over time, the division of labor among the three sectors will shift as some strategies are more effective than others. Third, in the process of pursuing organizational self-interests, a good deal of public goods are delivered, although not necessarily in the most efficient manner or in ways that assure effective attention to major social issues.

Notes

1. All were medium-sized organizations with revenues between $250,000 and $1.5 million in 1987 and located in the Chicago area. They were selected to allow for systematic comparisons by field and by major type (commercial, public, donations) and stability of funding (stable, turbulent).

2. The United States remains one of the few developed nations to not have universal health insurance or family allowance program.

3. Such commercial activities may also subvert the charitable mission of nonprofits and endanger other resources. Both Minority Search and Christian Therapists pursued fee strategies to the point of disengaging themselves from low-income individuals with complex problems (Cloward and Epstein 1965; Grønbjerg 1990).

4. Some communities are so impoverished that organizations obtain little business support locally. This was the case for Hispanic Neighbors and African-American Neighbors.

5. In Granovetter's terms (1973), nonprofit boards provide the opportunities for corporate leaders to develop and maintain weak ties with one another.

6. This is most evident in the insistence by corporate board members that United Way organizations, which they dominate, stay out of controversies (e.g.,

abortion services, affirmative action on behalf of gays and lesbians) as much as possible.

7. For Hispanic Youth Services and Immigrant Welfare League, terminated or one-time contracts amounted to only 5 to 6 percent of total public funding received over a five-year period. Neither Alcohol Treatment nor Youth Outreach had any such awards.

8. That pattern is possible because community development organizations are relatively few in number and small in size.

9. Although none of the four social service agencies with public grants or contracts had more than 6 percent of such funding in the form of terminated or one-time awards over a five-year period, the corresponding proportions ranged between 24 and 45 percent for three community development organizations.

10. The thirteen case study organizations provided year-by-year data on twenty-nine aggregated streams of private donations (e.g., all individual gifts). More than half (sixteen) of these streams have annual fluctuations of more than 50 percent, including one-third (nine) with annual fluctuations of 100 percent or more. Only those donation streams that involve highly institutionalized relationships with particular donors (e.g., the United Way, affiliated churches, co-opting institutions) tend to provide stable funding.

11. There are other important differences among nonprofit industry fields that I do not discuss here. For example, they differ in terms of the nature of activities involved, the size and composition of organizations active in the fields, and the extent to which the industry itself is highly institutionalized. These differences both reflect and influence how attractive the field is or might be to public, nonprofit, or market organizations respectively.

12. Since the early 1980s, education has accounted for roughly 40 percent of corporate donations, with health about one-quarter to one-third. Arts and culture have received a stable 10 percent of corporate funding.

13. This pattern is fully understandable for the health field, given the prominence of market institutions noted earlier. The pattern is more interesting for higher education, given the dominance of nonprofit institutions. Why has the public funding that benefits nonprofit colleges and universities not been channeled into grants and contracts as it was for social service agencies? I speculate that several factors are important. First, nonprofit colleges and universities have traditionally relied extensively on well-established market resources (e.g., tuition fees), while social service agencies traditionally relied on donations.

Hence, the public funding structures were adapted to existing resource patterns. In addition, colleges and universities have always competed with one another for students and are large and well established. Most likely, they could successfully resist special subsidies to their competitors.

14. These generalizations are, of course, simplistic. For example, nonprofits are involved in advocacy efforts across all industries. However, I believe these descriptions capture the dominant character of how the respective industries interact with the public sector.

References

Bennett, James T., and Thomas J. DiLorenzo. 1989. *Unfair Competition: The Profits of Nonprofits.* Lanham: Hamilton Press.

Brilliant, Eleanor L. 1990. *The United Way: Dilemmas of Organized Charity.* New York: Columbia University Press.

Chen, Ted H., Kirsten A. Grønbjerg, and Matthew W. Stagner. 1992. *An Analysis of Financial Payments to Service Providers of the Illinois Department of Children and Family Services.* Report prepared for the Children's Policy Project. Chicago: Chapin Hall Center for Children.

Cloward, Richard A., and Irwin Epstein. 1965. "Private Social Welfare's Disengagement from the Poor: The Case of Family Adjustment Agencies." In *Proceedings of the Annual Social Work Day Institute.* Buffalo: State University of New York at Buffalo, School of Social Welfare.

Granovetter, Mark. 1973. "The Strength of Weak Ties." *American Journal of Sociology* 78:1360–80.

Grønbjerg, Kirsten A. 1990. "Poverty and Nonprofit Organizational Behavior, Contingencies, and Linkages." *Social Service Review* 64:208–43.

_____. 1993. *Understanding Nonprofit Funding: Managing Revenues in Social Service and Community Development Organizations.* San Francisco: Jossey-Bass.

Grønbjerg, Kirsten A., Ted Chen, and Matthew Stagner. 1992. "Market Forces and Leverage: Contracting Relations in a Child Welfare System." Paper presented at the American Political Science Association meetings, Chicago, September 4, 1992.

Grønbjerg, Kirsten A., James Musselwhite, Jr., and Lester M. Salamon. 1984. *Government Spending and the Nonprofit Sector in Cook County/Chicago.* Washington, D.C.: Urban Institute Press.

Grønbjerg, Kirsten A., Ami Nagle, Lauree Garvin, and Lori Wingate. 1992. *Nonprofit Human Service Facilities in Illinois: Structure, Adequacy, and Management.* Report prepared for the Illinois Facilities Fund.

Grønbjerg, Kirsten A., David P. Street, and Gerald Suttles. 1978. *Poverty and Social Change.* Chicago: University of Chicago Press.

Hansmann, Henry. 1980. "The Role of Nonprofit Enterprise." *Yale Law Journal* 89:835–901.

_____. 1987. "Economic Theories of Nonprofit Organization." In *The Nonprofit Sector: A Research Handbook,* ed. W. W. Powell, 27–42. New Haven: Yale University Press.

Hasenfeld, Yeheskel. 1978. "Client-Organization Relations: A System Perspective." In *The Management of Human Services,* ed. Rosemary C. Sarri and Yeheskel Hasenfeld, 184–206. New York: Columbia University Press.

Hodgkinson, Virginia A., Murray S. Weitzman, Christopher M. Toppe, and Stephen M. Noga. 1992. *Nonprofit Almanac, 1992–1993: Dimensions of the Independent Sector.* San Francisco: Jossey-Bass.

Odendahl, Teresa. 1990. *Charity Begins at Home: Generosity and Self-Interest among the Philanthropic Elite.* New York: Basic Books.

Ostrander, Susan A. 1984. *Women of the Upper Class.* Philadelphia: Temple University Press.

Palmer, John L., Timothy Smeeding, and Barbara Boyle Torrey, eds. 1988. *The Vulnerable.* Washington, D.C.: Urban Institute Press.

Rose-Ackerman, Susan. 1986. *The Economics of Nonprofit Institutions: Studies in Structure and Polity.* New York: Oxford University Press.

Saidel, Judith. 1991. "Resource Interdependence: The Relationship between State Agencies and Nonprofit Organizations." *Public Administration Review* 51:543–53.

Schiller, Herbert I. 1989. *Culture, Inc. The Corporate Takeover of Public Expression.* New York: Oxford University Press.

Sherraden, Michael. 1991. *Assets and the Poor: A New American Welfare Policy.* Armonk, N.Y.: M. E. Sharpe.

Sosin, Michael R. 1990. "Decentralizing the Social Service System: A Reassessment. *Social Service Review* 64:617–36.

Useem, Michael. 1984. *The Inner Circle: Large Corporations and the Rise of Business Political Activity in the U.S. and U.K.* New York: Oxford University Press.

Weisbrod, Burton. 1985. "Toward a Theory of the Voluntary Non-Profit Sector in a Three-Sector Economy." In *Altruism, Morality, and Economic Theory,* ed. E. S. Phelps, 171–95. New York: Russell Sage.

_____. 1977. *The Voluntary Nonprofit Sector.* Lexington, Mass.: Lexington Books.

_____. 1988. *The Nonprofit Economy.* Cambridge: Harvard University Press.

Wilensky, Harold L., and Charles N. Lebeaux. 1965. *Industrial Society and Social Welfare: The Impact of Industrialization on the Supply and Organization of Social Welfare Services in the U.S.* New York: Free Press.

PART 7

SOCIAL AND COMMUNITY THEORIES OF THE NONPROFIT SECTOR

Nonprofit organizations do not simply exist in communities; they are essential elements of communities and community life. Voluntary nonprofits[1] (or, as they sometimes are called, "donative nonprofits")[2] in particular draw volunteer time and effort, leadership, donations of money and supplies, government contracts, credibility, and membership in community networks from their communities. They give back to their communities directly through the services and programs they provide, but also indirectly by creating opportunities for citizens to associate, to express their creativity, and to develop their civic leadership abilities.

Sociological theories tend to be "rich theories" that incorporate numerous phenomena. They tend to examine questions that are quite different from those of economists and (to a lesser degree) political scientists (Part 6). For example, sociologists have contributed theories and research findings that help to explain the "place" of nonprofits in communities, the complexity of relationships among nonprofit organizations, and interaction patterns among their numerous constituencies and other community institutions. Sociological theories have identified and explained the roles of community networks of individuals, groups, and organizations; niches; and the importance of community elites and influentials for nonprofits. Because communities, civics, politics, government, the economy, and nonprofit organizations are inexorably intertwined, economists, political scientists, and public administration scholars also have contributed to our knowledge and understanding of community.

Voluntary Association in Communities

In the colonial era, people could not rely on government for assistance. They had to do things for themselves. When the task at hand was more than one family could do, they had to turn to each

233

other for assistance. They had no alternative. Families had to work together to survive and to carve out lives in the hostile environment. When Alexis de Tocqueville, the "founder of a sociology of politics,"[3] visited the United States in the 1830s, "it was the Americans' propensity for civic association that impressed him the most as the key to their unprecedented ability to make democracy work."[4] Tocqueville's fascination with the American tendency to associate voluntarily is evident:

> Americans of all ages, all stations in life, and all types of disposition are forever forming associations. There are not only commercial and industrial in which all take part, but others of a thousand different types—religious, moral, serious, futile, very general and very limited, immensely large and very minute. Americans combine to give fêtes, found seminaries, build churches, distribute books, and send missionaries to the antipodes. Hospitals, prisons, and schools take shape in that way. Finally, if they want to proclaim a truth or propagate some feeling by the encouragement of a great example, they form an association. In every case, at the head of any new undertaking, where in France you would find the government or in England some Territorial magnate, in the United States you are sure to find an association.[5]

The lessons of the colonial days were learned well. The tradition of mutual support has lasted through the centuries, and Americans have always turned to voluntary associations as the primary institutions through which "community" finds expression and is enacted. It can be argued that voluntary nonprofit organizations are so pervasive in our society and are accepted so unquestioningly as community institutions in the United States because participation has always been an integral part of our history.

Strengthening Civil Life: Social Capital Formation

Tocqueville continued:

> I shall have occasion hereafter to show the effects of association in civil life; I confine myself for the present to the political world. . . .
>   The second degree in the exercise of the right of association is the power of meeting. When an association is allowed to establish centers of action at certain important points in the country, its activity is increased and its influence extended. Men have the opportunity of seeing one another; means of execution are combined; *and opinions are maintained with a warmth and energy that written language can never attain* [emphasis added].[6]

Tocqueville observed what is known today as *social capital*, "the change in relations among persons that facilitate actions" that is formed through ongoing association.[7] Social capital is highly intangible: It exists in the relationships among people. It is the warmth and trust Tocqueville described, the bonds of trust and goodwill that are created among community members while they work together to accomplish purposes they care about as individuals, and the by-product of their side activities—their conversations and sharing of joys and concerns. Social capital decreases transaction costs and thereby facilitates getting tasks done easily, comfortably, and with mutual trust.[8] When there is social capital, there is no need to rely on formal contracts, written agreements, rigid rules, inflexible policies, or bureaucratic controls. "A group within which there is extensive trustworthiness and extensive trust is able to accomplish much more than a comparable group without that trustworthiness and trust."[9]

As volunteers associate at regular meetings of a board of trustees, to build props for a community theater, to coordinate a neighborhood watch program, or to help the local PTA offer children a safe Halloween experience, they are creating social capital—without ever consciously thinking about this "secondary benefit" that flows unintended from their association. All they care about at the moment is the program they are working on, the set they are building, or the problem they are solving. The benefits of social capital come later to the participating individuals, to the "networks" to which they belong, and to the community—as a side effect of the associations.

> In a housing project built during World War II in an eastern city of the United States, there were many physical problems caused by poor construction: faulty plumbing, crumbling sidewalks, and other defects. . . . Residents organized to confront the builders and to address these problems in other ways. Later, when the problems were solved, the organization remained as available social capital that improved the quality of life for residents. Residents had resources available that they had seen as unavailable where they had lived before. (For example, despite the fact that the number of teenagers in the community was smaller, residents were *more* likely to express satisfaction with the availability of teenage babysitters.) [Emphasis in the original.][10]

Interestingly, *obligations* contribute to and play a part in social capital formation. When I ask you for a favor, an obligation is created. Your granted favor, however, does not benefit only me, and the existence of my obligation to you is not necessarily a negative state. You (the grantor of the favor) also benefit by "adding to a drawing fund of social capital available in a time of [future] need. If the [asker] can satisfy his need through self-sufficiency, or through aid from some official source without incurring an obligation, he will do so—and thus fail to add to the social capital outstanding in the community."[11]

Information and trustworthiness are other forms of social capital. Most persons acquire information primarily for their own use. Once we have information, however, we become information sources for others, which creates obligations and thus social capital. When a nonprofit, for example, becomes known as a source of accurate and reliable information, it benefits other individuals and organizations who ask for and use the information. The obligation that is created strengthens the broader community by creating social capital.

Although social capital can be created in any type of organization, nonprofits—particularly voluntary nonprofits—are ideal settings. We spend some of our leisure time with nonprofits because we care enough about "something" to give of our time.[12] No one tells us we must volunteer (usually), and most of us do not choose to associate with a nonprofit or its cause in order to increase our income.[13] When we care about something, we join together (associate), put energy and emotion into a task, and make things happen. While we are getting things done, we also create social capital and strengthen our community. Future problems will be easier to solve and future tasks will be easier to accomplish, because social capital has been created and we are now members of networks.

Networks

Networking, one of my mother's old phrases, musty slang of yesteryear. Even in her sixties she still did something she called that, though as far as I could see all it meant was having lunch with some other woman.[14]

Networks are "connections" that are created through stable, recurrent, formal, or informal interactions among individuals. "Network structures serve both as important opportunities and barriers to actors' performances and their realization of ends. The fundamental assumption of network analysis is that the social structures generated by networks of social ties have important consequences both for the individual actors and for the system within which they are embedded."[15]

Nonprofits play important roles in initiating and maintaining networks of community organizations. Nonprofits often serve as intermediary community structures. They help create and maintain networks of organizations in and between the three sectors. Nonprofits often initiative endeavors that bring together individuals from private businesses, government agencies, and other nonprofits (sometimes including foundations) to solve community problems and capitalize on opportunities—individuals and organizations who would not ordinarily know each other or work together. Powell, for example, notes the existence of network nonprofit organizations—organizations that consist of nothing other than horizontal links and relationships based on trust, reciprocity, and reputation. There is no hierarchy.[16]

Niches and Community Integration

In the language of sociology, a *niche* is a "property space for people and/or organizations, defined partially by the characteristics and preferences of members but also by other stakeholders."[17] Nonprofit organizations and individuals seek niches in communities for reasons of comfort and survival. *Niche-width* defines an organization's identity—its distinctiveness—and thus the community niche that it may call "its own."[18] The ability of nonprofit organizations to attract and retain diverse groups of volunteers, is the most important application of niche theory for the nonprofit sector. David Horton Smith thus posits that *social integration* is one of the most important community social benefits the voluntary sector provides:

[It links] together individuals, groups, institutions and even nations that otherwise would be in greater conflict, or at least competition, with each other. At the community level, a variety of voluntary associations will each tend to have as members a set of two or more individuals representing differing and often opposing political, religious, cultural, or social perspectives and backgrounds. The coparticipation of this set of individuals in the same voluntary association can have significant moderating effects on the relationships among these individuals.[19]

Some recent research findings based on niche theory, unfortunately, do not support Smith's optimistic vision. (See, for example, the reading reprinted in this part by Popielarz and McPherson.)

Readings Reprinted in This Part

Although Peter Berger and John Neuhaus's book *To Empower People: The Role of Mediating Structures in Public Policy* is more than twenty years old now, its central argument about the need for "mediating structures" in communities remains highly applicable today.[20] When *To Empower People* was first published, it was expected to provide the Reagan administration with the philosophical justification for massive diffusion of public service programs to the nonprofit sector—a key component in Reagan's agenda to shrink government. But the expectation did not materialize. The Reagan administration never used the Berger and Neuhaus argument effectively.[21] The essence of their argument is: In a complex society such as ours, individuals need buffers—mediating structures—to help them cope with large public and private bureaucracies when they are trying to get problems solved. Community needs can be met best when citizens utilize neighborhood, family, church, and voluntary associations as these mediating structures.

> Without institutionally reliable processes of mediation, the political order becomes detached from the values and realities of individual life. . . . When that happens, the political order must be secured by coercion rather than by consent. And when that happens, democracy disappears. . . . Such mediation cannot be sporadic and occasional; it must be institutionalized in *structures*. . . . The structures we have chosen . . . exist where people are, and that is where sound public policy should always begin [emphasis in original].

Steven Smith and Michael Lipsky's chapter, "Nonprofit Organizations and Community, examines nonprofit-community relationships mostly as foundation building for their analyses of the impacts that contracting with government has on nonprofits—the focus of their book, *Nonprofits for Hire*.[22] The authors use Robert Bellah's definition of "a community [as] a group of people who are socially interdependent, who participate together in discussion and decision-making, and who share certain *practices* that both define the community and are nurtured by it" (emphasis in original).[23] They then expand on the Berger and Neuhaus sociopolitical argument summarized above: Nonprofits are "manifestations of community," a concept that is essential for "understanding why changes in the relationship between nonprofit organizations and governments are consequential for public values." Smith and Lipsky posit that three qualities are essential for understanding the significance of community for nonprofit organizations: a "community is self-identifying"; "communities are fueled by voluntary action"; and "communities are important because it is in their midst that our most deeply held values are expressed. . . . Moreover, communities give expression to those values through the development of informal and formal organizations . . . , schools, charity organizations, orphanages, youth groups, and the like." In order for community to be enacted, "it must show itself in the activities people undertake to express those shared values. These activities include problem solving service agencies that communities incorporate as nonprofit organizations: *They are communities made manifest*" (emphasis added).

Smith and Lipsky's categories of nonprofit organizations include the following: (1) traditional, old-line, social service agencies; (2) nonprofits that "derive most if not all of their revenues from government"; and (3) "grassroots agencies" that are founded out of strong personal feelings and commitment, "in response to unmet neighborhood or other community needs."

This part's final chapter, "On the Edge or In Between: Niche Position, Niche Overlap, and the Duration of Voluntary Association Memberships," by Pamela Popielarz and Miller McPherson, presents an interesting, counterintuitive, argument: Voluntary associations serve as barriers to community social integration. "Voluntary associations are overwhelmingly homogenous, promoting relations between similar people but inhibiting contact between dissimilar ones. . . . Since the relations that people form can be only as heterogeneous as the structures within which they meet other people, voluntary group homogeneity acts as a barrier to societal integration." Popielarz and McPherson arrive at their conclusion through research findings indicating that "voluntary organizations lose fastest those members who are either atypical of the group (the niche edge hypothesis) or subject to competition from other groups (the niche overlap hypothesis)—and thus they conclude that voluntary associations are not sources of community social integration.

Notes

1. See Steven R. Smith and Michael Lipsky, "Nonprofit Organizations and Community," reprinted in this part; and J. Steven Ott, "Perspectives on Organizational Governance: Some Effects on Government-Nonprofit Relations," reprinted in Part 8.

2. Henry Hansmann, "The Two Nonprofit Sectors: Fee for Service Versus Donative Organizations," in V. A. Hodgkinson and R. W. Lyman, eds., *The Future of the Nonprofit Sector,* pp. 91–102 (San Francisco: Jossey-Bass, 1989).

3. Whitney Pope, *Alexis de Tocqueville: His Social and Political Theory* (Beverly Hills, Calif.: Sage, 1986), p. 12. Whitney cites A. Salomon, "Tocqueville, 1959," *Social Research* 27, 1960, 449–470.

4. Robert D. Putnam, "Bowling Alone: America's Declining Social Capital," *Journal of Democracy* 6 (1), January 1995, 65; and Robert D. Putnam, *Bowling Alone: The Collapse and Revival of American Community.* New York: Simon and Schuster, 2000.

5. Alexis de Tocqueville, "On the Use Which the Americans Make of Associations in Civil Life," in A. de Tocqueville, *Democracy in America,* vol. 2 (New York: Doubleday, Anchor, 1969), p. 513.

6. Alexis de Tocqueville, "Political Associations in the United States," in A. de Tocqueville, *Democracy in America,* vol. 1 (New York: Vintage, 1945), p. 199.

7. James S. Coleman, "Social Capital in the Creation of Human Capital," *American Journal of Sociology* 94, Supplement, 1988, S100.

8. See Part 6, "Economic and Political Theories."

9. Coleman, "Social Capital," S101.

10. Ibid., S108.

11. Ibid., S117.

12. I use "leisure" broadly here, to include "serious leisure." See, for example, Robert A. Stebbins, "Volunteering: A Serious Leisure Perspective," *Nonprofit and Voluntary Sector Quarterly* 25 (2), June 1996, 211–224.

13. This is not to deny that sometimes people are motivated to volunteer primarily for resumé building and business networking purposes. See Jone L. Pearce, *Volunteers: The Organizational Behavior of Unpaid Workers* (London: Routledge, 1993).

14. From Margaret Atwood, *The Handmaid's Tale.* Cited in David Knoke and Miguel Guilarte, "Networks in Organizational Structures and Strategies," *Current Perspectives in Social Theory: Recent Developments in the Theory of Social Structure,* Supplement 1 (Greenwood, Conn.: JAI Press, 1994), p. 77.

15. Ibid., pp. 77, 78.

16. Walter W. Powell, "Hybrid Organizational Arrangements: New Form or Transitional Development?" *California Management Review* 30, 1987, 67–87.

17. Pamela A. Popielarz and J. Miller McPherson, "On the Edge or In Between: Niche Position, Niche Overlap, and the Duration of Voluntary Association Memberships," *American Journal of Sociology* 101 (3), November 1995, 698–720 (reprinted in this part).
18. Michael T. Hannan and John Freeman, "The Population Ecology of Organizations," *American Journal of Sociology* 88, 1977, 1116–1145.
19. David Horton Smith, "The Impact of the Volunteer Sector on Society." Reprinted in Part 2.
20. Peter L. Berger and John Neuhaus, *To Empower People: The Role of Mediating Structures in Public Policy* (Washington, D.C.: American Enterprise Institute for Public Policy Research, 1977). The text that is reprinted in this part has been edited substantially in order to highlight the roles of voluntary associations (including churches).
21. Lester M. Salamon, "Nonprofit Organizations: The Lost Opportunity," in J. L. Palmer and I. V. Sawhill, eds., *The Reagan Record*, pp. 261–284 (Cambridge, Mass.: Ballinger, 1984).
22. Steven Rathgeb Smith and Michael Lipsky, "Nonprofit Organizations and Community," in S. R. Smith and M. Lipsky, *Nonprofits for Hire: The Welfare State in the Age of Contracting*, pp. 20–40 (Cambridge: Harvard University Press, 1993).
23. Robert N. Bellah et al., *Habits of the Heart: Individualism and Commitment in American Life* (New York: Harper and Row, 1985), p. 333.

References

Berger, Peter L., and John Neuhaus. *To Empower People: The Role of Mediating Structures in Public Policy.* Washington, D.C.: American Enterprise Institute for Public Policy Research, 1977.
Coleman, James S. "Social Capital in the Creation of Human Capital." *American Journal of Sociology* 94, Supplement, 1988, S95–S120.
Heimovics, Richard D. "Neighborhood-Based Organizations (NBOs)." In Jay M. Shafritz, ed., *International Journal of Public Policy and Administration*, pp. 1486–1488. Boulder: Westview Press, 1998.
Knoke, David, and Miguel Guilarte. "Networks in Organizational Structures and Strategies." In J. David Knottnerus and Christopher Prendergast, eds., *Current Perspectives in Social Theory: Recent Developments in the Theory of Social Structure*, Supplement 1, pp. 77–115. Greenwood, Conn.: JAI Press, 1994.
Lohmann, Roger A. *The Commons.* San Francisco: Jossey-Bass, 1992.
McPherson, J. Miller. "Evolution in Communities of Voluntary Associations." In J. V. Singh, ed., *Organizational Evolution: New Directions*, pp. 224–245. Newbury Park, Calif.: Sage, 1990.
Milofsky, Carl. "Neighborhood-Based Organization: A Market Analogy." In Walter W. Powell, ed., *The Nonprofit Sector: A Research Handbook*, pp. 277–295. New Haven: Yale University Press, 1987.
Oliver-Lumerman, Amalya. "At-Risk Populations." In Jay M. Shafritz, ed., *International Journal of Public Policy and Administration*, pp. 149–153. Boulder: Westview Press, 1998.
Popielarz, Pamela A., and J. Miller McPherson. "On the Edge or In Between: Niche Position, Niche Overlap, and the Duration of Voluntary Association Memberships." *American Journal of Sociology* 101 (3), November 1995, 698–720.
Putnam, Robert D. *Bowling Alone: The Collapse and Revival of American Community.* New York: Simon and Schuster, 2000.
_____. "Bowling Alone: America's Declining Social Capital." *Journal of Democracy* 6 (1), January 1995, 65–78.
_____. "The Prosperous Community: Social Capital and Public Life." *American Prospect* 13, 1993, 35–42.
Smith, Steven Rathgeb, and Michael Lipsky. *Nonprofits for Hire: The Welfare State in the Age of Contracting.* Cambridge: Harvard University Press, 1993.
Stebbins, Robert A. "Volunteering: A Serious Leisure Perspective." *Nonprofit and Voluntary Sector Quarterly* 25 (2), June 1996, 211–224.
Tocqueville, Alexis de. "On the Use Which the Americans Make of Associations in Civil Life." In A. de Tocqueville, *Democracy in America*, vol. 2, pp. 513–517. New York: Doubleday, Anchor, 1969.

CHAPTER 20

To Empower People: The Role of Mediating Structures in Public Policy

PETER L. BERGER AND RICHARD JOHN NEUHAUS

I. Mediating Structures and the Dilemmas of the Welfare State

Two seemingly contradictory tendencies are evident in current thinking about public policy in America. First, there is a continuing desire for the services provided by the modern welfare state. Partisan rhetoric aside, few people seriously envisage dismantling the welfare state. The serious debate is over how and to what extent it should be expanded. The second tendency is one of strong animus against government, bureaucracy, and bigness as such. This animus is directed not only toward Washington but toward government at all levels. Although this essay is addressed to the American situation, it should be noted that a similar ambiguity about the modern welfare state exists in other democratic societies, notably in Western Europe.

Perhaps this is just another case of people wanting to eat their cake and have it too. It would hardly be the first time in history that the people wanted benefits without paying the requisite costs. Nor are politicians above exploiting ambiguities by promising increased services while reducing expenditures. The extravagant rhetoric of the modern state and the surrealistic vastness of its taxation system encourage magical expectations that make contradictory measures seem possible. As long as some of the people can be fooled some of the time, some politicians will continue to ride into office on such magic.

But this is not the whole story. The contradiction between wanting more government services and less government may be only apparent. More precisely, we suggest that the modern welfare state is here to stay, indeed that it ought to expand the benefits it provides—but that *alternative mechanisms are possible to provide welfare-state services.*

The current anti-government, anti-bigness mood is not irrational. Complaints about impersonality, unresponsiveness, and excessive interference, as well as the perception of rising costs and deteriorating service—these are based upon empirical and widespread experience. What first appears as contradiction, then, is the sum of equally justified aspirations. The public policy goal is to address human needs without exacerbating the reasons for animus against the welfare state.

Of course there are no panaceas. The alternatives proposed here, we believe, can solve *some* problems.

The basic concept is that of what we are calling mediating structures. The concept in various forms has been around for a long time.

What is new is the systematic effort to translate it into specific public policies. For purposes of this study, mediating structures are defined as *those institutions standing between the individual in his private life and the large institutions of public life.*

Modernization brings about an historically unprecedented dichotomy between public and private life. The most important large institution in the ordering of modern society is the modern state itself. In addition, there are the large economic conglomerates of capitalist enterprise, big labor, and the growing bureaucracies that administer wide sectors of the society, such as in education and the organized professions. All these institutions we call the *megastructures.*

Then there is that modern phenomenon called private life. It is a curious kind of preserve left over by the large institutions and in which individuals carry on a bewildering variety of activities with only fragile institutional support.

For the individual in modern society, life is an ongoing migration between these two spheres, public and private. The megastructures are typically alienating, that is, they are not helpful in providing meaning and identity for individual existence. Meaning, fulfillment, and personal identity are to be realized in the private sphere. While the two spheres interact in many ways, in private life the individual is left very much to his own devices, and thus is uncertain and anxious. Where modern society is "hard," as in the megastructures, it is personally unsatisfactory; where it is "soft," as in private life, it cannot be relied upon. Compare, for example, the social realities of employment with those of marriage.

The dichotomy poses a double crisis. It is a crisis for the individual who must carry on a balancing act between the demands of the two spheres. It is a political crisis because the megastructures (notably the state) come to be devoid of personal meaning and are therefore viewed as unreal or even malignant. Not everyone experiences this crisis in the same way. Many who handle it more successfully than most have access to institutions that *mediate* between the two spheres. Such institutions have a private face, giving private life a measure of stability, and

they have a public face, transferring meaning and value to the megastructures. Thus, mediating structures alleviate each facet of the double crisis of modern society. Their strategic position derives from their reducing both the anomic precariousness of individual existence in isolation from society and the threat of alienation to the public order.

Our focus is on four such mediating structures—neighborhood, family, church, and voluntary association. This is by no means an exhaustive list, but these institutions were selected for two reasons: first, they figure prominently in the lives of most Americans and, second, they are most relevant to the problems of the welfare state with which we are concerned. The proposal is that, if these institutions could be more imaginatively recognized in public policy, individuals would be more "at home" in society, and the political order would be more "meaningful."

Without institutionally reliable processes of mediation, the political order becomes detached from the values and realities of individual life. Deprived of its moral foundation, the political order is "delegitimated." When that happens, the political order must be secured by coercion rather than by consent. And when that happens, democracy disappears.

Democracy is "handicapped" by being vulnerable to the erosion of meaning in its institutions. Cynicism threatens it; wholesale cynicism can destroy it. That is why mediation is so crucial to democracy. Such mediation cannot be sporadic and occasional; it must be institutionalized in *structures.* The structures we have chosen to study have demonstrated a great capacity for adapting and innovating under changing conditions. Most important, they exist where people are, and that is where sound public policy should always begin.

This understanding of mediating structures is sympathetic to Edmund Burke's well-known claim: "To be attached to the subdivision, to love the little platoon we belong to in society, is the first principle (the germ as it were) of public affections." And it is sympathetic to Alexis de Tocqueville's conclusion drawn from his observation of Americans: "In democratic countries the science of association is the mother of science;

the progress of all the rest depends upon the progress it has made." Marx too was concerned about the destruction of community, and the glimpse he gives us of post-revolutionary society is strongly reminiscent of Burke's "little platoons." The emphasis is even sharper in the anarcho-syndicalist tradition of social thought.

In his classic study of suicide, Emile Durkheim describes the "tempest" of modernization sweeping away the "little aggregations" in which people formerly found community, leaving only the state on the one hand and a mass of individuals, "like so many liquid molecules," on the other. Although using different terminologies, others in the sociological tradition—Ferdinand Toennies, Max Weber, Georg Simmel, Charles Cooley, Thorstein Veblen—have analyzed aspects of the same dilemma. Today Robert Nisbet has most persuasively argued that the loss of community threatens the future of American democracy.

Also, on the practical political level, it might seem that mediating structures have universal endorsement. There is, for example, little political mileage in being anti-family or anti-church. But the reality is not so simple. Liberalism— which constitutes the broad center of American politics, whether or not it calls itself by that name—has tended to be blind to the political (as distinct from private) functions of mediating structures. The main feature of liberalism, as we intend the term, is a commitment to government action toward greater social justice within the existing system.

American liberalism has been vigorous in the defense of the private rights of individuals, and has tended to dismiss the argument that private behavior can have public consequences. Private rights are frequently defended *against* mediating structures—children's rights against the family, the rights of sexual deviants against neighborhood or small-town sentiment, and so forth. Similarly, American liberals are virtually faultless in their commitment to the religious liberty of individuals. But the liberty to be defended is always that of privatized religion. Supported by a very narrow understanding of the separation of church and state, liberals are typically hostile to the claim that institutional religion might

have public rights and public functions. As a consequence of this "geometrical" outlook, liberalism has a hard time coming to terms with the alienating effects of the abstract structures it has multiplied since the New Deal. This may be the Achilles heel of the liberal state today.

The left, understood as some version of the socialist vision, has been less blind to the problem of mediation. Indeed the term alienation derives from Marxism. The weakness of the left, however, is its exclusive or nearly exclusive focus on the capitalist economy as the source of this evil, when in fact the alienations of the socialist states, insofar as there are socialist states, are much more severe than those of the capitalist states.

On the right of the political broad center, we also find little that is helpful. To be sure, classical European conservatism had high regard for mediating structures, but, from the eighteenth century on, this tradition has been marred by a romantic urge to revoke modernity—a prospect that is, we think, neither likely nor desirable. On the other hand, what is now called conservatism in America is in fact old-style liberalism. It is the laissez-faire ideology of the period before the New Deal, which is roughly the time when liberalism shifted its faith from the market to government. *Both* the old faith in the market *and* the new faith in government share the abstract thought patterns of the Enlightenment. In addition, today's conservatism typically exhibits the weakness of the left in reverse: it is highly sensitive to the alienations of big government, but blind to the analogous effects of big business. Such one-sidedness, whether left or right, is not helpful.

As is now being widely recognized, we need new approaches free of the ideological baggage of the past. The mediating structures paradigm cuts across current ideological and political divides.

The argument of this essay—and the focus of the research project it is designed to introduce— can be subsumed under three propositions. The first proposition is analytical: *Mediating structures are essential for a vital democratic society.* The other two are broad programmatic recommendations: *Public policy should protect and foster mediating structures,* and *Wherever possible, public policy should utilize mediating structures for the realization of social purposes.*

The analytical proposition assumes that mediating structures are the value-generating and value-maintaining agencies in society. Without them, values become another function of the megastructures, notably of the state, and this is a hallmark of totalitarianism. In the totalitarian case, the individual becomes the object rather than the subject of the value-propagating processes of society.

The two programmatic propositions are, respectively, minimalist and maximalist. Minimally, public policy should cease and desist from damaging mediating structures.

The maximalist proposition ("utilize mediating structures") is much riskier. There is the real danger that such structures might be "co-opted" by the government in a too eager embrace that would destroy the very distinctiveness of their function. The prospect of government control of the family, for example, is clearly the exact opposite of our intention. The goal in utilizing mediating structures is to expand government services without producing government oppressiveness.

Our point is not to attack the megastructures but to find better ways in which they can relate to the "little platoons" in our common life.

The theme is *empowerment.* One of the most debilitating results of modernization is a feeling of powerlessness in the face of institutions controlled by those whom we do not know and whose values we often do not share. Lest there be any doubt, our belief is that human beings, whoever they are, understand their own needs better than anyone else—in, say, 99 percent of all cases. The mediating structures under discussion here are the principal expressions of the real values and the real needs of people in our society. They are, for the most part, the people-sized institutions. Public policy should recognize, respect, and, where possible, empower these institutions.

II. Neighborhood

At first blush, it seems the defense of neighborhood is a motherhood issue. The neighborhood is the place of relatively intact and secure existence, protecting us against the disjointed and threatening big world "out there." Around the idea of neighborhood gravitate warm feelings of nostalgia and the hope for community.

While no doubt influenced by such sentiments, the new interest in neighborhoods today goes far beyond sentimentality. The neighborhood should be seen as a key mediating structure in the reordering of our national life. As is evident in fears and confusions surrounding such phrases as ethnic purity or neighborhood integrity, the focus on neighborhood touches some of the most urgent and sensitive issues of social policy.

To put it simply, real community development must begin where people are.

For public policy purposes, there is no useful definition of what makes a good neighborhood, though we can agree on what constitutes a bad neighborhood. With respect to so-called bad neighborhoods, we have essentially three public policy choices: we can ignore them, we can attempt to dismantle them and spread their problems around more equitably, or we can try to transform the bad into the better on the way to becoming good. The first option, although common, should be intolerable. The second is massively threatening to the nonpoor, and therefore not feasible short of revolution. The third holds most promise for a public policy that can gain the support of the American people.

One pays the price for the neighborhood of one's choice. Making that choice possible is the function of the *idea* of neighborhood as it is embodied in many actual neighborhoods. It is not possible to create the benefits of each kind of neighborhood in every neighborhood. One cannot devise a compromise between the cohesion of a New England small town and the anonymity of the East Village without destroying both options.

The mediating structures paradigm requires that we take seriously the structures, values, and habits by which people order their lives in neighborhoods, wherever those neighborhoods may be, and no matter whether they are cohesive or individualistic, elective or hereditary.

The empowerment of people in neighborhoods is hardly the answer to all our social problems. Neighborhoods empowered to impose their values upon individual behavior and expression can be both coercive and cruel. Government that transcends neighborhoods must intervene to protect elementary human rights. Here again, however, the distinction between public and private spheres is critically important. In recent years an unbalanced emphasis upon individual rights has seriously eroded the community's power to sustain its democratically determined values in the public sphere. It is ironic, for example, to find people who support landmark commissions that exercise aesthetic censorship—for example, by forbidding owners of landmark properties to change so much as a step or a bay window without legal permission—and who, at the same time, oppose public control of pornography, prostitution, gambling, and other "victimless crimes" that violate neighborhood values more basic than mere aesthetics.

Many different streams flow into the current enthusiasms for neighborhood government. Sometimes the neighborhood government movement is dubbed "the new Jeffersonianism." After two centuries of massive immigration and urbanization, we cannot share Jefferson's bucolic vision of rural and small-town America, just as we do not indulge the re-medievalizing fantasies associated in some quarters with the acclaim for smallness. Our argument is not against modernity but in favor of exploring the ways in which modernity can be made more humane.

If neighborhoods are to be key to public policy, governmental action is necessary to fund neighborhood improvement. Without a direct assault upon the free enterprise system, the possibilities of evasion and subterfuge in order to invest money where it is safest or most profitable are almost infinite. To strengthen the mediating role of neighborhoods we need to look to new versions of the Federal Housing Administration assistance programs that played such a large part in the burgeoning suburbs after World War II. Such programs can, we believe, be developed to sustain and rehabilitate old communities, as they have been used to build new ones. The idea of urban homesteading, for example, although afflicted with corruption and

confusion in recent years, is a move in the right direction. At a very elementary level, property tax regulations should be changed to encourage rather than discourage home improvement.

Neighborhoods will also be strengthened as people in the neighborhood assume more and more responsibility for law enforcement, especially in the effort to stem the tide of criminal terrorism.

We should examine the informal "law enforcement agents" that exist in every community—the woman who runs the local candy store, the people who walk their dogs, or the old people who sit on park benches or observe the streets from their windows.

All of which is to say that the goal of making and keeping life human, of sustaining a people-sized society, depends upon our learning again that parochialism is not a nasty word. Like the word parish, it comes from the Greek, *para* plus *oikos,* the place next door. Because we all want some choice and all have a great stake in the place where we live, it is in the common interest to empower our own places and the places next door.

III. Family

For most Americans, neighborhood and community are closely linked to the family as an institution.

Of course, modernization has already had a major impact on the family. It has largely stripped the family of earlier functions in the areas of education and economics, for example. But in other ways, modernization has made the family more important than ever before. It is the major institution within the private sphere, and thus for many people the most valuable thing in their lives. Here they make their moral commitments, invest their emotions, plan for the future, and perhaps even hope for immortality.

We can take positive measures to protect and foster the family institution, so that it is not defenseless before the forces of modernity.

This means public recognition of the family *as an institution*. It is not enough to be concerned for individuals more or less incidentally related to the family as institution. Public recognition of the family as an institution is imperative because every society has an inescapable interest in how children are raised, how values are transmitted to the next generation.

The sovereignty of the family over children has limits—as does any sovereignty in the modern world—and these limits are already defined in laws regarding abuse, criminal neglect, and so on. The onus of proof, however, must be placed on policies or laws that foster state interference rather than on those that protect family autonomy. In saying this we affirm what has been the major legal tradition in this country.

Conversely, we oppose policies that expose the child directly to state intervention, without the mediation of the family. We are skeptical about much current discussion of children's rights—especially when such rights are asserted *against* the family. Children do have rights, among which is the right to a functionally strong family.

The implications of our policy concept may be clarified by looking briefly at three currently discussed issues—education vouchers, day care, and the care of the handicapped. The idea of education vouchers has been around for a while and has had its ups and downs, but it remains one of the most intriguing possibilities for radical reform in the area of education. In this proposal, public funding of education shifts from disbursement to schools to disbursement to individuals. Parents (or, at a certain age, their children) choose the schools where they will cash in their vouchers, the schools then being reimbursed by the state. Essentially the proposal applies the paradigm of the GI Bill to younger students at earlier periods of education. This proposal would break the coercive monopoly of the present education system and empower individuals in relating to the megastructures of bureaucracy and professionalism, with special benefits going to lower-income people. In addition, it would enhance the diversity of American life by fostering particularist communities of value—whether of life style, ideology, religion, or ethnicity.

Turning to our second example, we note that day care has become a public issue, as more

and more mothers of small children have entered the labor force and as many people, spurred by the feminist movement, have begun to claim that working mothers have a right to public services designed to meet their special needs.

Three positions on national day-care policy can be discerned at present. One is that the government should, quite simply, stay out of this area. Another position endorses a federally funded, comprehensive child-care system attached to the public schools. A third position is much like the second, except that the national program would be less closely linked to the public school system.

It should come as no surprise that we favor the third position. We do so because there is a real need and because the need should be met in a way that is as inexpensive and as unintrusive as possible. The mediating structures concept is ideally suited to the latter purpose and may also advance the former. Vouchers would facilitate day-care centers that are small, not professionalized, under the control of parents, and therefore highly diversified.

The third issue mentioned is care of the handicapped. An important case in this area is the so-called special child—special children being those who, for a broad range of nonphysical reasons, are handicapped in their educational development.

Innovative thinking today moves toward using the family as a therapeutic context *as much as possible*. This means viewing the professional as *ancillary* to, rather than as a substitute for, the resources of the family. It may mean paying families to care for a handicapped child, enabling a parent to work less or not at all, or to employ others.

The principal public policy interest in the family concerns children, not adults. This interest is common to all societies, but in democratic society there is an additional and urgent interest in fostering socialization patterns and values that allow individual autonomy. That interest implies enhanced protection of the family in relation to the state, and it implies trusting people to be responsible for their own children in a world of their own making.

IV. Church

Religious institutions form by far the largest network of voluntary associations in American society. Yet, for reasons both ideological and historical, their role is frequently belittled or totally overlooked in discussions of social policy. Whatever may be one's attitude to organized religion, this blind spot must be reckoned a serious weakness in much thinking about public policy. The churches and synagogues of America can no more be omitted from responsible social analysis than can big labor, business corporations, or the communications media. Not only are religious institutions significant "players" in the public realm, but they are singularly important to the way people order their lives and values at the most local and concrete levels of their existence. Thus they are crucial to understanding family, neighborhood, and other mediating structures of empowerment.

From the beginning, we have emphasized the importance of mediating structures in generating and maintaining values. Within the family, and between the family and the larger society, the church is a primary agent for bearing and transmitting the operative values of our society. This is true not only in the sense that most Americans identify their most important values as being religious in character, but also in the sense that the values that inform our public discourse are inseparably related to specific religious traditions. In the absence of the church and other mediating structures that articulate these values, the result is not that the society is left without operative values; the result is that the state has an unchallenged monopoly on the generation and maintenance of values. Needless to say, we would find this a very unhappy condition indeed.

Our proposal is that the institutions of religion should be unfettered to make their maximum contribution to the public interest. In some areas of social service and education, this means these institutions should be free to continue doing what they have historically done.

Again, and in accord with our maximalist proposition, we expect increased public funding for the meeting of human needs in a wide range of policy areas; our particular contention is that mediating institutions, including religious institutions, be utilized as much as possible as the implementing agencies of policy goals. Contrary to some public policy and legal thinking today, such increased funding need not require an increase in governmental control and a consequent war on pluralism.

V. Voluntary Association

There is a history of debate over what is meant by a voluntary association. For our present purposes, a voluntary association is a body of people who have voluntarily organized themselves in pursuit of particular goals. (Following common usage, we exclude business corporations and other primarily economic associations.) Important to the present discussion is the subject of volunteer service. Many voluntary associations have both paid and volunteer staffing. For our purposes, the crucial point is the free association of people for some collective purpose, the fact that they may pay some individuals for doing work to this end not being decisive.

At least since de Tocqueville the importance of voluntary associations in American democracy has been widely recognized. Voluntarism has flourished in America more than in any other Western society and it is reasonable to believe this may have something to do with American political institutions. Associations create statutes, elect officers, debate, vote courses of action, and otherwise serve as schools for democracy. However trivial, wrongheaded, or bizarre we may think the purpose of some associations to be, they nonetheless perform this vital function.

Apart from this political role, voluntary associations are enormously important for what they have actually done. Before the advent of the modern welfare state, almost everything in the realm of social services was under the aegis of voluntary associations, usually religious in character. We are interested in one type within the vast array of voluntary associations—namely, associations that render social services relevant to recognized public responsibilities.

Assaults on voluntary associations come from several directions, from both the right and left of the political spectrum. Some condemn them as inefficient, corrupt, divisive, and even subversive. Many subscribe to the axiom that public services should not be under private control. From the far left comes the challenge that such associations supply mere palliatives, perpetuate the notion of charity, and otherwise manipulate people into acceptance of the status quo.

The problem confronting us arises when the vested interests in question use coercive state power to repress individual freedom, initiative, and social diversity. We are not impressed by the argument that this is necessary because voluntary associations often overlap with the functions of government agencies. Overlap may in fact provide creative competition, incentives for performance, and increased choice. But our more basic contention is against the notion that anything public must *ipso facto* be governmental. That notion is profoundly contrary to the American political tradition and is, in its consequences, antidemocratic.

Our present problem is also closely linked with the trend toward professionalization. Whether in government or nongovernment agencies, professionals attack allegedly substandard services, and substandard generally means nonprofessional. Through organizations and lobbies, professionals increasingly persuade the state to legislate standards and certifications that hit voluntary associations hard, especially those given to employing volunteers. The end result is that the trend toward government monopoly operates in tandem with the trend toward professional monopoly over social services. The connection between such monopoly control and the actual quality of services delivered is doubtful indeed.

Professional standards are of course important in some areas. But they must be viewed with robust skepticism when expertise claims jurisdiction, as it were, over the way people run their own lives. Again, ordinary people are the best experts on themselves.

So long as voluntary work is genuinely voluntary—is undertaken by free choice—it should be cherished and not maligned. It is of enormous value in terms of both the useful activity offered to volunteers and the actual services rendered. In addition, because of their relative freedom from bureaucratic controls, voluntary associations are important laboratories of innovation in social services; and, of course, they sustain the expression of the rich pluralism of American life.

The policy implications of our approach touch also on the role of nonprofit foundations in our society. Technically, there are different kinds of foundations—strictly private, publicly supported, operating, and so on—but the current assault applies to all of them. The argument is summed up in the words of the late Wright Patman whose crusade against foundations led to Title I of the Tax Reform Act of 1969:

> Today I shall introduce a bill to end a gross inequity which this country and its citizens can no longer afford: the tax-exempt status of the so-called privately controlled charitable foundations, and their propensity for domination of business and accumulation of wealth. . . . Put most bluntly, philanthropy—one of mankind's more noble instincts—has been perverted into a vehicle for institutionalized deliberate evasion of fiscal and moral responsibility to the nation. (*Congressional Record,* August 6, 1969)

Of course, foundations have engaged in abuses that need to be curbed, but the resentment and hostility manifested by the curbers also needs to be curbed if we are not to harm the society very severely. The curbers of foundations make up an odd coalition. Right-wing forces are hostile to foundations because of their social experimentation (such as the Ford Foundation's programs among inner-city blacks), while others are hostile because of the role of big business ("the establishment") in funding foundations.

While large foundations would seem to be remote from the mediating structures under discussion, in fact they are often important to such structures at the most local level, especially in the areas of education and health. Were all these institutions taken over by the government, there might be a more uniform imposition of standards and greater financial accountability than now exists (although the monumental corruption in various government social services does not make one sanguine about the latter), but the price would be high. Massive bureaucratization, the proliferation of legal procedures that generate both public resentment and business for lawyers, the atrophying of the humane impulse, the increase of alienation—these would be some of the costs. Minimally, it should be public policy to encourage the voluntarism that, in our society, has at least slowed down these costs of modernity.

As always, the maximalist side of our approach—that is, using voluntary associations as agents of public policies—is more problematic than the minimalist. One thinks, for example, of the use of foster homes and half-way houses in the treatment and prevention of drug addiction, juvenile delinquency, and mental illness. There is reason to believe such approaches are both less costly and more effective than using bureaucratized megastructures (and their local outlets). Or one thinks of the successful resettlement of more than 100,000 Vietnam refugees in 1975, accomplished not by setting up a government agency but by working through voluntary agencies (mainly religious). This instance of using voluntary associations for public policy purposes deserves careful study. Yet another instance is the growth of the women's health movement, which in some areas is effectively challenging the monopolistic practices of the medical establishment. The ideas of people such as Ivan Illich and Victor Fuchs should be examined for their potential to empower people to reassume responsibility for their own health care. Existing experiments in decentralizing medical delivery systems should also be encouraged, with a view toward moving from decentralization to genuine empowerment.

VI. Empowerment Through Pluralism

The theme of pluralism has recurred many times in this essay. This final section aims simply to tie up a few loose ends, to anticipate some objections to a public policy designed to sustain

pluralism through mediating structures, and to underscore some facts of *American* society that suggest both the potentials and limitations of the approach advanced here.

It should be obvious that by pluralism we mean much more than regional accents, St. Patrick's Day, and Black Pride Days, as important as all these are. Beyond providing the variety of color, costume, and custom, pluralism makes possible a tension within worlds and between worlds of meaning. Worlds of meaning put reality together in a distinctive way. Whether the participants in these worlds see themselves as mainline or subcultural, as establishment or revolutionary, they are each but part of the cultural whole. Yet the paradox is that wholeness is experienced through affirmation of the part in which one participates. This relates to the aforementioned insight of Burke regarding "the little platoon." In more contemporary psychological jargon it relates to the "identity crisis" which results from "identity diffusion" in mass society. Within one's group—whether it be racial, national, political, religious, or all of these—one discovers an answer to the elementary question, "Who am I?" and is supported in living out that answer. Psychologically and sociologically, we would propose the axiom that any identity is better than none. Politically, we would argue that it is not the business of public policy to make value judgments regarding the merits or demerits of various identity solutions, so long as all groups abide by the minimal rules that make a pluralistic society possible. It is the business of public policy not to undercut, and indeed to enhance, the identity choices available to the American people (our minimalist and maximalist propositions throughout).

This approach assumes that the process symbolized by "E Pluribus Unum" is not a zero-sum game. That is, the *unum* is not to be achieved at the expense of the *plures*. To put it positively, the national purpose indicated by the *unum* is precisely to sustain the *plures*. Of course there are tensions, and accommodations are necessary if the structures necessary to national existence are to be maintained. But in the art of pluralistic politics, such tensions are not to be eliminated but are to be welcomed as the catalysts of more imaginative accommodations. Public policy in the areas discussed in this essay has in recent decades, we believe, been too negative in its approach to the tensions of diversity and therefore too ready to impose uniform solutions on what are perceived as national social problems. In this approach, pluralism is viewed as an enemy of social policy planning rather than as a source of more diversified solutions to problems that are, after all, diversely caused and diversely defined.

Throughout this paper, we have emphasized that our proposal contains no animus toward those charged with designing and implementing social policy nor any indictment of their good intentions. The reasons for present pluralism-eroding policies are to be discovered in part in the very processes implicit in the metaphors of modernization, rationalization, and bureaucratization. The management mindset of the megastructure—whether of HEW, Sears Roebuck, or the AFL-CIO—is biased toward the unitary solution. The neat and comprehensive answer is impatient of "irrational" particularities and can only be forced to yield to greater nuance when it encounters resistance, whether from the economic market of consumer wants or from the political market of organized special interest groups. The challenge of public policy is to anticipate such resistance and, beyond that, to cast aside its adversary posture toward particularism and embrace as its goal the advancement of the multitude of particular interests that in fact constitute the common weal. Thus, far from denigrating social planning, our proposal challenges the policy maker with a much more complicated and exciting task than today's approach.

Throughout this essay we have frequently referred to democratic values and warned against their authoritarian and totalitarian alternatives. We are keenly aware of the limitations in any notion of "the people" actually exercising the *kratein,* the effective authority, in public policy. And we are keenly aware of how far the American polity is from demonstrating what is possible in the democratic idea. The result of political manipulation, media distortion, and the sheer weight of indifference is that the great majority of Americans have little or no political will, in the sense that term is used in democratic theory, on

the great questions of domestic and international policy. Within the formal framework of democratic polity, these questions will perforce be answered by a more politicized elite. But it is precisely with respect to mediating structures that most people do have, in the most exact sense, a political will. On matters of family, church, neighborhood, hobbies, working place, and recreation, most people have a very clear idea of what is in their interest. If we are truly committed to the democratic process, it is *their* political will that public policy should be designed to empower. It may be lamentable that most Americans have no political will with respect to U.S. relations with Brazil, but that is hardly reason to undercut their very clear political will about how their children should be educated.

The subculture that envisages its values as universal and its style as cosmopolitan is no less a subculture for all that. The tribal patterns evident at an Upper West Side cocktail party are no less tribal than those evident at a Polish dance in Greenpoint, Brooklyn. That the former is produced by the interaction of people trying to transcend many particularisms simply results in a new, and not necessarily more interesting, particularism. People at the cocktail party may think of themselves as liberated, and indeed they may have elected to leave behind certain particularisms into which they were born. They have, in effect, elected a new particularism. *Liberation is not escape from particularity but discovery of the particularity that fits.* The goal of public policy in a pluralistic society is to sustain as many particularities as possible, in the hope that most people will accept, discover, or devise one that fits.

While our proposal is, we hope, relevant to modern industrialized society in general, whether socialist or capitalist, its possibilities are peculiarly attuned to the United States. (We might say, to North America, including Canada, but some aspects of particularism in Canada—for example, binationalism between French- and English-speaking Canadians—are beyond the scope of this essay.) There are at least five characteristics of American society that make it the most likely laboratory for public policy designed to enhance mediating structures and the pluralism that mediating structures make possible. First is the immigrant nature of American society. The implications of that fact for pluralism need no elaboration. Second, ours is a relatively affluent society. We have the resources to experiment toward a more humane order—for example, to place a floor of economic decency under every American. Third, this is a relatively stable society. Confronted by the prospects of neither revolution nor certain and rapid decline, we do not face the crises that call for total or definitive answers to social problems. Fourth, American society is effectively pervaded by the democratic idea and by the sense of tolerance and fair play that make the democratic process possible. This makes our society ideologically hospitable to pluralism. And fifth, however

weakened they may be, we still have relatively strong institutions—political, economic, religious, and cultural—that supply countervailing forces in the shaping of social policy. Aspirations toward monopoly can, at least in theory, be challenged. And our history demonstrates that the theory has, more often than not, been acted out in practice.

Of *this* we are convinced: America has a singular opportunity to contest the predictions of the inevitability of mass society with its anomic individuals, alienated and impotent, excluded from the ordering of a polity that is no longer theirs. And we are convinced that mediating structures might be the agencies for a new empowerment of people in America's renewed experiment in democratic pluralism.

CHAPTER 21

Nonprofit Organizations and Community

STEVEN RATHGEB SMITH AND MICHAEL LIPSKY

Every advanced industrial society has its particular signature, determined by how that nation balances government, community, and market responsibilities. In some countries radio and television outlets are owned by the government, in others the communications industry is privately owned. Some governments run the airlines and railroads, some do not.[1] Where private ownership prevails, countries also differ in the degree of influence the public sector has over private affairs through regulations, subsidies, and infrastructural development.

Citizens of the industrialized countries receive income and social services not only from government but from the business and community sectors as well. In different measures, for example, elderly people may receive income support from private pensions, governmental supplements, or family and nonprofit institutions.[2] In the area of social services, alcoholics may receive counseling through their employers or public agencies, or from chapters of Alcoholics Anonymous, a self-financing voluntary association, or their church.

In every country the particular mix of government, market, and community responsibility can and does change over time. Over the last several decades, social policy in the United States has evolved in ways that favor increased public responsibility in some areas (for example, educating handicapped children, preventing physical abuse and neglect among household members, and providing additional land for recreation). At the same time, the country has been reducing the degree of public responsibility for providing or regulating services in other areas, for example, in family planning counseling.

Each sector emphasizes different values and operates according to different norms.

It is consequential whether governmental norms, market practices, or community associations govern social welfare provision in the broadest sense. It is also consequential if the balance in sectoral provision changes. If society sought to depend more on markets and less on government for health insurance, it would likely be seeking greater variety of options and possibilities of cost reductions through competition. But it would probably be trading off reduced standardization of coverage and greater reliance on employment status as a factor in the distribution of health coverage.

Our concerns are consistent with the view that any changes in the relations of the state and the economy (say, deregulation in transportation), the economy and community (business takeovers of proprietary hospitals), or the state and community (the focus of this effort), deserve attention because they are likely to be accompanied by changes in degrees of equity, responsiveness, flexibility, and liberty that one or another of these sectors promotes as dominant concerns.

Nonprofits as Manifestations of Community

The term "community" often used very loosely, is for our purposes defined well by Robert Bellah and his colleagues. In *Habits of the Heart* they write that "a community is a group of people who are socially interdependent, who participate together in discussion and decision-making, and who share certain *practices* that both define the community and are nurtured by it."[3] Nonprofit service organizations, in this definition, are tangible, significant manifestations of community. This central proposition is essential to understanding why changes in the relationship between nonprofit organizations and governments are consequential for public values.

Three qualities of community are especially important in understanding the significance of community to nonprofit organizations and public policy. First, a community is self-identifying. People belong in communities if they think of themselves as members. Unlike individuals defined by congressional districts, tribes, professional societies, commodity futures markets, and other forms of social organization, community members are those who elect to consider themselves part of a larger collectivity.

Sometimes community overlaps with other forms of organization, such as a neighborhood or ethnic fraternity. When this happens the impression is conveyed that the two are the same, but they are not.

The second quality of communities is that they are fueled by voluntary action. People contribute time and money, extend their influence, and otherwise make community organizations work because they want to make a difference.[4] Such voluntary organizations may be particularly strong precisely because they are au-

tonomous and not subject to market vagaries or changing governmental priorities. They also enjoy a special sort of legitimacy because their existence derives from free association rather than law or anticipation of profit, and because they are thought to arise from the sort of passionate convictions that tend to be respected in politics disproportionately to the number of people who hold the beliefs.

Third, communities are important because it is in their midst that our most deeply held values are expressed—literally so, since it is where we engage with other people in common enterprises of the highest salience. Religious communities, for example, facilitate worship by providing a safe and supportive haven. Moreover, communities give expression to those values through the development of informal and formal organizations. For example, religious communities make possible the realization of strongly felt "core" values by establishing schools, charity organizations, orphanages, youth groups, and the like.

Communities are not only self-conscious collectivities of shared sentiment. They also take on activities that are consistent with those sentiments. They establish churches, radio stations, study groups, newspapers, community centers, block clubs, and other activities that allow them to inject their values into the society for the benefit of themselves, or others. Communities thus provide the context within which groups can organize to solve common problems. Communities of workers give rise to unions. Women's groups sponsor shelters and advocate for public policy dealing with spouse abuse. Neighbors brought together by environmental threats turn to organizations such as the Sierra Club.

If "community" is to signify more than general feelings about common concerns, it must show itself in the activities people undertake to express those shared values. These activities include problem-solving service agencies that communities incorporate as nonprofit organizations: they are communities made manifest.

Not every community organization incorporates itself as a nonprofit. The nonprofit designation is a legal category that requires an organization to file forms with the Internal Revenue

Service and adhere to regulations on the distribution of earnings and political activity.

Legal status is also a way of joining two important aspects of community: the moral community, in which individuals share certain values and social concerns, and the legal community, which defines the rules of governance and participation for the organization.[5] This distinction is integral to our discussion because we view nonprofit service organizations not only as service-providing institutions but also as political organizations that play key roles in citizen representation and governance.

All these voluntary organizations embody some of the most prominent ways by which the rest of the world comes to know communities, and many have assumed nonprofit status. And it is through such organizational expressions that political elites are able to contact and interact with communities when they attempt to aid or contain them.[6] In short, these organizations provide a key link between the citizenry and their government, and changes in their character may produce major shifts in the citizen-government relationship.[7]

Pathways to Participation

The most straightforward way to demonstrate that nonprofit service organizations are manifestations of community is to recount the role of individuals in the organizations. These roles are discussed elsewhere in this book and so will be treated only briefly here.

First, their boards of directors are drawn from community notables who support the organizations' objectives and are expected to provide leadership. Boards are constructed when organizations are established; later the composition of boards is altered incrementally depending upon the organization's goals and the perceived strengths of the rest of the board. Members are typically chosen for their potential contribution to advancing the organization's mission, including their expected financial contribution, their reputation, or their expertise. A hospital, museum, or orchestra may recruit to its board prominent individuals who will themselves contribute financially to the institution and induce generosity among their friends. A new job training center or youth development agency may recruit socially minded people in business whose ties to banks will help in establishing credit and getting the advice of lawyers and experts in the agency's policy field. An agency with government contracts may recruit individuals with influential political connections to help them retain their contracts and attract new ones.

Second, nonprofit organizations make extensive use of volunteers. Hospitals depend upon volunteers to staff gift shops and cafeterias and to greet and direct patients and visitors. Shelters depend upon volunteers to serve meals and make guests feel welcome. Rape crisis centers depend upon volunteers to provide counseling and other support services. From door-to-door solicitations to taking calls during annual telephone drives, volunteers are central to mass solicitation efforts. Moreover, low pay lends a degree of voluntarism to paid work in nonprofit organizations.

Third, many nonprofits raise significant parts of their annual budgets from individuals who believe they are supporting community institutions. People walk to raise money for hunger or AIDS relief programs. They contribute to Christmas funds for the homeless or the destitute. They give toys, food, or clothing to a local children's agency. In short, the cash and in-kind donations support the view that these nonprofit organizations are manifestations of community.

Community and the Theory of Nonprofit Organizations

Political theorists recognize that social life tends to be held together by "mediating" institutions, including family structures and community organizations, that provide services outside the mandates and force of law implicit in government programs.[8] For such theorists, community organization is prior to government provision of service, coexists with public service provision, and plays a social role that cannot fully be taken over by government. In the absence of government-sponsored daycare programs, for example, families, friends, and neighbors invent childcare arrangements. Without nursing homes, the sick and frail are cared for at home. Without welfare programs, destitute people find succor through church programs for the poor.

This theory of "mediating institutions" highlights the capacity of communities to solve their own problems and warns against the danger that government efforts to provide parallel services may undermine spontaneous community initiatives,[9] while public efforts to subsidize them may result in loss of vitality and character.[10] Moreover, these organizations are considered to be an important buffer for the individual against excessive government penetration of society. In this view—which harks back to Tocqueville—mediating institutions are essential to a democratic way of life.[11]

This instructive perspective is properly cautionary about the dangers of government intrusion into community affairs, but it can be misguided in failing to understand the need for large-scale responses to widespread social need. It is one thing to recognize, consistent with the theory of mediating institutions, that the rise of food banks and soup kitchens were spontaneous community responses to the needs of hungry people. It is another to suggest that food banks using private food donations might be able to feed the hungry and eliminate the need for food stamps.

Two views of nonprofits that arise out of the economist's perspective also support our understanding of them as manifestations of community. One question economic theorists seek to answer is why certain goods that benefit large numbers of people are produced by society when their production cannot be explained by market-oriented behavior. To many economists, governments produce collective goods such as roads and lighthouses because these necessary goods cannot be produced by markets. No individual can afford to produce them, nor do people have incentives voluntarily to pay their share, since they can be "free riders" and enjoy these collective goods (if they exist) without contributing to their production or maintenance. Government is able to overcome this "market failure" because it acts through legitimate political processes to force the participa-

tion of everyone in contributing to the production of collective goods.

In a democracy government is limited to producing only those collective goods which are either accessible to all, or, if targeted to benefit certain groups, enjoy the support of the majority.[12] Other goods and services, such as orchestras and ethnic-specific burial societies, are not candidates for public policy because, while perhaps desired by many, they are not preferred by a critical mass. In such cases the "market failure" to produce collective goods is solved by private collective action.

It would follow that the number of nonprofits would be directly related to ethnic and cultural heterogeneity. As economist Estelle James argues, the more diverse a society, the more difficult it is to reach consensus on the provision of collective goods.[13] (However, this view overlooks the possibility of pork-barrel policymaking: support for benefits to one narrow group is implicitly exchanged in legislatures for support for other projects benefiting other narrow groups.)

This perspective on nonprofits is descriptively insightful. It supports our contention that communities desiring collective action establish organizations to meet their needs. It also structures analysis in such a way as to offer an explanation for the intrusion of government into some previously untouched areas. As the popular conception of the role and scope of government has changed, activities once regarded as inappropriate for public collective action are now undertaken by the state. Relatively recent federal support for the arts and for social policy concerns such as special education and child abuse illustrate how conceptions of the proper scope of public action change over time.

Expectations of Others

The history of the nonprofit sector and the experiences of individuals and organizations that interact with it establish certain expectations. People of vital importance to an organization's environment may come to expect that organizations of certain sorts will be nonprofit organizations; new organizations then conform to those expectations reflexively. For example, counseling services for children and families for many years were almost exclusively the domain of nonprofit and public service organizations; no models of for-profit service organizations existed in this area. Another example is battered women shelters. Nothing prevents a shelter from being operated under for-profit auspices; however, the expectations of the community and government are that these shelters should be nonprofit.

Three Types of Nonprofit Service Agencies

The world of nonprofit organizations is vast. It ranges from enormous hospitals and philanthropic foundations to the smallest legally incorporated storefront service centers. It encompasses multinational relief organizations such as the Red Cross and CARE, and food banks on a single site. It includes multifunction organizations such as universities, with their colleges, research centers, libraries, theaters, athletic teams and real estate operations, to single-purpose organizations such as Voices of the Homeless, an arts organization. It embraces complexities and variations so numerous that they would appear to defeat all efforts to generalize.

We propose to distinguish among three types of nonprofit service agencies, each with very different connections to community. One type is the traditional social service agency, the old-line service association such as the Massachusetts Society for the Prevention of Cruelty to Children (MSPCC), established in 1878 and based in Boston. Founded by affluent civic leaders, this and similar agencies typically were established many decades before the New Deal. They usually have endowments (sometimes very substantial ones), and therefore tend to be less dependent on government funds than other agencies. Often they offer many different services and programs and thus are also less dependent than other agencies on demand for any single service. Typically, these agencies have relatively large boards of directors (30 to 40 members) drawn from the political and economic elite of a com-

munity. Sectarian agencies such as Catholic Charities also fall under this category.

A second type of nonprofit social service organization is the agency founded within the last twenty years, directly in response to the availability of government funds for job training, mental health, and other contemporary services. An example is the Key Program, a large youth services agency established in Boston in 1970 to provide community and residential services for delinquent youth. These agencies usually derive most if not all of their revenues from government. Their boards are often small (fewer than 10 members) by comparison to the traditional agencies. Typically, these agencies do not exist as nonprofit organizations for very long prior to receiving a government contract. And in some instances the founders will reach an understanding about a contract prior to the creation of the agency. In the case of the Key Program, founded by Scott and Bill Wolfe, the Massachusetts Commissioner of Youth Services "hammered out a loose contract with the Wolfe brothers while they were still in the process of creating a nonprofit entity."[14]

A third type of organization is the agency founded in response to unmet neighborhood or other community needs. These may be organizations devoted to solving problems experienced as local concerns, such as homelessness, hunger, or runaway youth. Or they may be established to solve problems for communities of people who are less identifiable by geography than by some other characteristic: battered women, developmentally disabled individuals, or AIDS patients. Organizations formed to aid these groups tend to be started and staffed by volunteers or underpaid workers out of strong personal commitments to alleviate suffering or to help other people realize their potential when it is otherwise thwarted by social conditions. Particularly at their start, they are typically shoestring operations built on shaky financial grounds.

Seen from the perspective of their relationship to government these three types of organizations form something of a continuum: at one extreme are the new community-based organizations that tend to act most like volunteer associations—they are nonbureaucratic and held together by the freely given commitments of their members.[15] At the other end are the organizations founded in response to the availability of government funds. These tend to be rule-bound, concerned with consistency, and highly responsive to the priorities of the government agencies whose grant programs were the occasion for their establishment and development in the first place. These distinctions are important because they suggest that different types of nonprofits are affected by government funding priorities in different ways. The most pronounced shifts and the greatest conflicts with government occur among those agencies that initially resemble government least.

This does not imply that the motivations of the founders of the second and third type of organization, or their *initial* ties to the community, need be dissimilar. Both government-funded and volunteer organizations of the 1960s and 1970s often represented the efforts of social reformers to change society's response to particular problems or policy issues. Whether or not a group of individuals comes together as an all-volunteer organization or a primarily government-funded organization may depend on existing structural factors. In situations where government funding was initially quite scarce, as in the case of shelters for battered women, individual activists organized along all-volunteer lines. Where government funding was ample, as in the case of youth training initiatives in recent years, activists did not form all-volunteers organizations prior to receiving government funding: the funds came simultaneously with the founding of the organization.

Once an organization is founded, though, the relationship to the community depends upon the relationship to government. In organizations established through government auspices, the impact of contracting is likely to be relatively modest because the organizations started out having conformed to contracting requirements. In contrast, the newly founded volunteer organizations are not only, by necessity, oriented toward the community, but they also will have had an extended period as autonomous bodies before accepting government funds.

For all agency types, however, some degree of change is virtually inevitable as government contracting increases and evolves. As we shall see, government contracts eventually bring administrative and accountability demands which may be at odds with the agencies' original visions.

Notes

1. E. S. Savas, *Privatizing the Public Sector* (Chatham, N.J.: Chatham House, 1981), p. 168; Anthony King, "Ideas, Institutions and the Policies of Governments: A Comparative Analysis: Parts I, II, and III," *British Journal of Political Science*, 3 (1973): 291–313, 409–423.

2. Martin Rein and Lee Rainwater, eds., *Public/Private Interplay in Social Protection: A Comparative Study* (Armonk, N.Y.: M.E. Sharpe, 1986).

3. Bellah et al., *Habits of the Heart*, p. 333.

4. The willingness to donate time and money is an important characteristic of community organizations distinguishing them from organizations based on self-interest. For more on the latter organizations see Mancur Olson, *The Logic of Collective Action* (Cambridge, Mass.: Harvard University Press, 1965).

5. This distinction is discussed by Walzer, *Spheres of Justice,* especially chapters 1–3. Walzer's arguments are reviewed by William A. Galston, *Liberal Purposes: Goods, Virtues and Diversity in the Liberal State* (Cambridge: Cambridge University Press, 1991), p. 44.

6. Some of the greatest controversies relating to communities occur when nonprofit organizations are found to be unrepresentative of the communities to which they lay claim. In this vein, G. William Domhoff argues that many community organizations are really elite entities that facilitate and promote upper class social dominance. See G. William Domhoff, *Who Really Rules? New Haven and Community Power Reexamined* (New Brunswick, N.J.: Transaction Books, 1978).

7. See Jurgen Habermas, *The Legitimation Crisis* (Boston: Beacon Press, 1975); Claus Offe, *The Contradictions of the Welfare State* (Cambridge, Mass.: The MIT Press, 1984), pp. 179–206.

8. Berger and Neuhaus, *To Empower People;* Robert A. Nisbet, *Community and Power* (New York: Oxford University Press, 1962).

9. See Jack E. Meyer, ed., *Meeting Human Needs: Toward a New Social Philosophy* (Washington, D.C.: American Enterprise Institute, 1982).

10. Glazer, "The Self-Service Society."

11. Alexis de Tocqueville, "Of the Use Which Americans Make of Public Associations in Civil Life," in *Democracy in America*, ed. Richard D. Heffner (New York: New American Library, 1956), pp. 198–202. See also David L. Sills, "Voluntary Associations: Sociological Aspects," in *International Encyclopedia of the Social Sciences*, ed. David L. Sills (New York: Macmillan, 1968), XVI, p. 376.

12. See Burton Weisbrod, *The Nonprofit Economy*, chap. 2; Anthony Downs, "Why the Government Budget Is Too Small in a Democracy," *World Politics*, 12, 4 (July 1960): 540–563.

13. James, "The Nonprofit Sector in Comparative Perspective," in *The Nonprofit Sector*, pp. 397–415.

14. Jerome G. Miller, *Last One Over the Wall: The Massachusetts Experiment in Closing Reform Schools* (Columbus, Ohio: Ohio State University Press, 1991), p. 187.

15. For a very useful typology which elaborates upon our category of community-based organizations, see Gabriel Chanan, *Taken for Granted: Community Activity and the Crisis of the Voluntary Sector* (London: The Community Development Foundation, 1991), pp. 8–9.

On the Edge or In Between: Niche Position, Niche Overlap, and the Duration of Voluntary Association Memberships

PAMELA A. POPIELARZ AND J. MILLER MCPHERSON

Introduction

Blau tells us that societal integration depends on intergroup relations (Blau 1977, 1987, 1994; Blau and Schwartz 1984). Organizations, particularly voluntary associations, should be perfect arenas for such integration (Babchuk and Edwards 1965; Tocqueville [1835] 1961), but they are not.[1] Instead, voluntary associations are overwhelmingly homogeneous, promoting relations between similar people but inhibiting contact between dissimilar ones (McPherson and Smith-Lovin 1986, 1987; Popielarz 1990, 1992). Since the relations that people form can be only as heterogeneous as the structures within which they meet other people, voluntary group homogeneity acts as a barrier to societal integration.

Voluntary association homogeneity magnifies social differences, rather than mitigating them. When people are segregated into homogeneous groups, access to the important resources that these groups afford inevitably becomes concentrated in small social circles rather than dispersed in the general population. These re-

sources include new social network ties (and the information and support that they provide), as well as other forms of social capital and political influence.

In this article we address the structural mechanisms (Mayhew 1980) by which voluntary organizations maintain homogeneity. We argue that group homogeneity results from the fact that members who are typical of the association stay in the group longer, while atypical members leave the group at a higher rate. In addition, individuals who are in demand by multiple groups leave their voluntary organizations more quickly. We analyze an event-history data set of 1,050 individuals containing information on the timing of entry to and exit from voluntary associations to show how groups maintain their homogeneity through these simple mechanisms.

Individuals and Organizations in Social Space

The theoretical tool we use to organize our explanation of how groups remain homogeneous is a multidimensional property space, which we call "social space."[2] The dimensions of social space are those salient sociodemographic characteristics of individuals that influence social interaction (e.g., age, education, sex, and race). Individuals occupy points in this space, defined by their values on each of the dimensions. In social space, groups and associations occupy multidimensional shapes, represented most simply by rectangular boxes (in two dimensions) or hyperboxes (in more than two dimensions). These boxes constitute the niches of the groups, as has been discussed in detail elsewhere (McPherson 1983). Variation in members' characteristics determines the distance each group occupies along each dimension. Figure 22.1 illustrates two hypothetical groups in social space. The members of group 1 are indicated by stars, the members of group 2 are pluses, and nonmembers are points. As the figure shows, not all individuals in a group's niche will belong to a group. A group whose members are spread widely in social space, such as group 2, is heterogeneous in member characteristics and is called a generalist (McPherson 1983). Group 1, more restricted in its membership in social space, is a specialist. If all groups were

maximally generalist, they would share the same niche, centered in social space and extending equally far in all directions. The main purpose of this article is to show why this does not happen.

Networks in Social Space

Just as individuals in society affect one another, the points in social space are interconnected. The fabric of connections between individuals is the global social network in the community. These connections consist of social network ties of all types: strong, weak, kin, nonkin, symmetric, asymmetric, and so forth (see Burt [1990] and Bernard et al. [1990] for a review of network ties).

Social network ties are not distributed randomly in social space. As Blau (1977, 1987, 1994; Blau and Schwartz 1984) points out, people associate with others who are similar in sociodemographic characteristics. This tendency for network relations to form between those who have similar social characteristics is known as the "homophily principle." Since individuals close to one another on a dimension of social space are similar, homophily implies that ties are local in social space. As a result of homophily, the probability of a tie between two individuals decreases with social dissimilarity—their distance from one another in social space. In social space, ties tend to connect close neighbors, spanning relatively short distances. In fact, as Marsden (1987, 1988) shows convincingly, homophily accounts for most of the structure in large social networks.

Distance in social space is multidimensional. A homophilous tie may connect points that are close to one another in social space by spanning a relatively large distance on one dimension but only a small distance on other dimensions. This explains apparent exceptions to the homophily principle for some combinations of relations and dimensions. For instance, marriage ties cross sex categories, and parents are older than their children, but the members of these dyads are homophilous on other dimensions: spouses are often of the same educational and socioeconomic

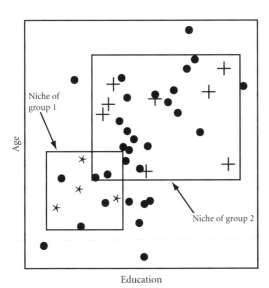

FIGURE 22.1   Niches in Social Space

background; parents and children are usually the same race, religion, and so forth. Homophily affects voluntary association homogeneity by localizing organizational recruitment through network ties.

Recruitment to Voluntary Associations

Voluntary associations recruit through the network ties of their members (Booth and Babchuk 1969), as do firms (Granovetter 1974), social movements (Fernandez and McAdam 1988; Snow, Zurcher, and Ekland-Olson 1980), and religious cults (Stark and Bainbridge 1980). As a result, new members replicate the sociodemographic characteristics of old ones. Those friends and acquaintances who join the group through their connections to present members will be very similar to their contacts within the organization, because of the homophily principle.

Recruitment through homophilous ties guarantees that the new recruits to a group are never a random sample of people. Instead, each organization recruits from a characteristic region of social space, the organization's niche. At any time, individuals in the niche are at the highest risk of becoming members because they are most likely to be connected by a homophilous network tie to a present member. New members of the group come predominantly from within the niche, rooting the organization in that neighborhood of social space.

Yet, if only recruitment governed group membership, eventually all groups would spread throughout social space, since the homophilous ties of a group's members yield some slightly different new members from just beyond the niche boundaries. As a result of this tendency to expand across social space, all organizations would be extreme generalists in the absence of some additional mechanism. This article proposes a simple explanation for the fact that voluntary associations stay localized in social space. We argue that groups lose members at the edge of the niche faster than in the center. This differential loss of members at the edge of the niche

keeps groups from spreading unchecked in social space. The next sections outline two basic reasons for this fact: social network ties and interorganizational competition.

Network Ties and Membership Duration

Social network ties help determine membership duration in voluntary groups (McPherson, Popielarz, and DrobniO (1992). First, ties between comembers in an organization lengthen the memberships of both members. If a member is connected to another member of the organization, the membership lasts an average of 66% longer than without the intraorganizational tie. Second, ties between members and nonmembers shorten the durations of the memberships. If a member shares a tie with someone who is not a member of the group, the membership lasts an average of 14% less time than without the extraorganizational tie. Both effects are cumulative: the more such ties, the greater the effects on membership duration.

The balance between these effects—internal network ties keeping members in the group and external ties pulling members out of the group—produces different results for individuals in the center of the niche than for those at the edge of the niche. Since the homophily principle implies that most of an individual's social network ties will be nearby in social space, people in the center of the niche will be connected mostly to others in the niche of the group, whereas people at the edge of the niche are more likely to have connections outside the niche.

Niche position is the opportunity structure for the homophilous social ties that shape membership; it acts as a proxy for all kinds of social network ties—strong, weak, kin, acquaintance, and so forth. Thus, members at the edge of the organization's niche will have higher turnover than members at the center of the organization's niche, as a result of their higher proportion of extraorganizational ties and their lower proportion of intraorganizational ties.[3] The forces acting on members at the edge of the niche are centrifugal, while those acting on members at the center of the niche are centripetal. To summarize the niche edge hypothesis: Members near the edge of the association's niche leave the group at a higher rate than members at the center of the niche.

This hypothesis is related to Kanter's (1977) token hypothesis. Kanter argues that people of a social type that is heavily underrepresented in an organization will suffer various detrimental effects, ranging from being stereotyped to experiencing high levels of stress. In addition, she says, these individuals are "more likely to be excluded from informal peer networks" (Kanter 1977, p. 249). This lack of ties within the group is exactly what we assert shortens peripheral members' length of stay in organizations.

Thus, the organization's activities are reinforced by the coherence of the social world at the center of the niche and are dissipated by the focus of the social world on things outside the organization at the edge of the niche. For individuals at the center of the niche, the group is an integral part of the social structure of relations. But for those at the edge of the niche, the group divides the social world rather than reinforces it. In this sense, the edge of the niche is a boundary milieu in which individuals constantly experience pressures pulling in different directions. However, network ties are not the only important mechanism governing membership duration.

Intergroup Competition and Membership Duration

Voluntary associations compete for the limited time and attention of members (McPherson 1983; McPherson and Rotolo 1996).[4] Empirical evidence suggests that voluntary association recruitment works through homophilous network ties (McPherson et al. 1992), such that new organizational recruits tend to come from within the niche of the group in social space. Competition between voluntary associations occurs when niches overlap—when groups recruit the same kind of members.[5] The more groups recruiting in an individual's neighborhood in social space, the more organizational competition operating on the individual. An individual in an

area of social space where the niches of two or more organizations overlap risks being recruited by each of these organizations. The conflicting forces created by intergroup competition lead to shorter membership durations for the individuals who experience them, because of the zero-sum character of members' time and other resources. In other words, individuals whose position in social space puts them in demand for multiple groups quickly run out of the time, money, and attention important for voluntary association participation. As a result, they have higher membership turnover than people who are less in demand.

Figure 22.2 illustrates the competitive forces in a simple two organization system. Individuals in the area where both organizations recruit, where the niches overlap, are subject to the highest intergroup competitive pressure.[6] Multiple opportunities for organizational membership make their affiliation with any one group tenuous. The availability of an alternative shortens the stay of a member in either group, since individuals have finite amounts of time, money and other resources. Individuals in areas covered by only one organizational niche experience less demand for their resources. The lack of

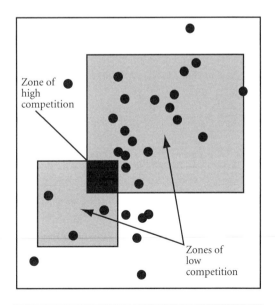

FIGURE 22.2   Competition in Social Space

conflicting demands for their time makes memberships among such people relatively durable, ceteris paribus. To summarize the niche overlap hypothesis: Members in areas of social space where many organizational niches overlap leave the group at a higher rate than members in areas where few niches overlap.

Combining the Two Mechanisms

It is important to recognize that these hypotheses are independent of one another; that is, we expect to find the niche edge effect when we take into account the niche overlap, and vice versa. In particular, rates of leaving should be highest among members who are both near the edge of an association and in an area of multiple organizational overlap.

Although both of the formal hypotheses deal directly with the rates at which individuals leave groups, our ultimate purpose in developing and testing these hypotheses is to be able to draw conclusions about organizational-level processes, in particular those leading to voluntary association homogeneity. The organizational effect of the niche edge hypothesis is to remove from the group members who are unlike typical group members. Clearly this process works in favor of group homogeneity. The niche overlap hypothesis similarly implies the systematic sorting out of members from areas of the organization's niche that overlap with many other organizational niches. But where do these multiple overlaps occur? In most cases, since groups grow at the edges, they will encounter each other at their intersection in multidimensional social space. Thus, while in general the edges of the organization's niche are scenes of high membership turnover, this effect reaches its peak on those niche boundaries that intersect with the boundaries of other groups. The combination of these effects is crucial for group homogeneity: the niche edge effect generally curtails expansion of the organization's niche, but the niche overlap effect guarantees that this pattern is especially acute along shared niche boundaries. The result is that the community of volun-

tary associations resembles a scatter of various specialist and generalist associations spread across social space, and not a stack of perfectly overlapping maximal generalists.

Data and Methods

The data for this study come from the second wave of the Ten Towns Project, collected during the summer and fall of 1989 (McPherson 1988).[7] This survey made use of the hypernetwork sampling method (McPherson 1982) in order to generate a random sample of voluntary associations from a random sample of individuals. The project has three stages, each focusing on a different level of analysis. This article makes use of the first stage of the survey, in which 1,050 individuals (aged 18–89 years) were interviewed in ten towns in Nebraska.

The unit of analysis here is the membership—not the individual or the organization.

Each respondent generates as many records, or spells, as memberships reported. The focus on the individual membership, as opposed to the individual, highlights the fact that we are most interested in the intersections of individual actors with organizations. Through the medium of the membership, the individual and the organization are duals of one another (Breiger 1974). The characteristics of the membership include the union of the characteristics of both the individual and the association. The resulting membership-level data set includes records of 2,983 memberships generated by the 1,050 respondents.

Event-History Analysis and Censoring

Our basic analytical tool is event-history analysis of the rate at which members leave their voluntary association memberships.[8] Duration of membership is measured in months; the average membership duration is 140 months, or 11 years and 8 months. Of the 2,983 membership spells in the data set, 2,087 of them (70%), represent memberships that were current at the time of the survey.

Measuring Niche Position and Niche Overlap

The niche of the organization is defined by the distribution of all of the group members along the niche dimension (McPherson 1983). A member's position in the niche is relative to that distribution. Each member's niche position is therefore constructed in comparison to the other members of the group. In this study we focus on education and sex as the relevant dimensions of the resource space of members, since these dimensions are salient, relatively stable, and easily measured and interpreted.

Previous work on sex segregation in various institutional settings (McPherson and Smith-Lovin 1986; Bielby and Baron 1986; Jacobs 1989 Mayhew et al. 1995) convinces us that sex is a highly salient dimension of social space.

We construct our measure of niche position in the education dimension by calculating the standard score of each member's distance from the mean education of the group type. The or-

ganizations sampled in our study are classified into 17 types.[9]

The education niches presented in Table 22.1 summarize the years of education for members in each type of association in 1989. Niche breadth extends one standard deviation in either direction from the center, or mean, for that type. Members are placed in the niches of their organizations on the basis of their 1989 educational level.[10]

Discussion

We ultimately seek an explanation for homogeneity in organizations themselves. The true import of our results lies in their implication that voluntary organizations lose fastest those members who are either atypical of the group (the niche edge effect) or subject to competition from other groups (the niche overlap effect). In fact, given the independence of these two effects, an organization most risks losing members who

TABLE 22.1   Education Niches of Sixteen Types of Voluntary Associations

Type	Current Memberships	Total Memberships	Niche Center (Years of Education)	Niche Width[a]	Niche Breadth (Years of Education)
All	2,083	2,983	13.89	2.95	10.94–16.84
Church	414	588	13.03	2.58	10.45–15.61
Professional	284	373	16.05	2.80	13.25–18.85
Veterans/patriotic	197	215	12.95	2.96	9.99–15.91
Recreational	230	432	13.95	2.77	11.18–16.72
Social	102	137	14.18	2.77	11.41–16.95
Youth	111	225	14.33	2.59	11.74–16.92
Elderly	144	154	12.56	2.42	10.14–14.98
Charity	77	106	14.13	3.38	10.75–17.51
Public interest	65	99	14.77	3.18	11.59–17.95
Ethnic	6	10	13.50	3.45	10.05–16.95
Hobby	64	95	13.89	3.26	10.63–17.15
Political	8	16	14.50	2.67	11.83–17.17
Fraternal/service	207	264	14.01	3.07	10.94–17.08
Union	28	41	12.64	1.64	11.00–14.28
Farm	51	76	13.12	2.20	10.92–15.32
Civic	47	89	13.36	2.13	11.23–15.49
Other	48	63			

[a] 1 SD.

are both atypical of that group and typical of many other groups. Put this way, the membership-level effects explain why voluntary associations are homogeneous.

It is crucial for the general theory of organizational evolution (McPherson 1990; McPherson and Ranger-Moore 1991; McPherson and Rotolo 1996) that retention of memberships is not random, but dictated by position in the niche. The results here suggest that when an organization acquires a member who is unlike other members, that member does not last for long. These atypical members are mutants in the membership pool of the organization. Both the lack of ties between peripheral members and central members and exposure to competing organizations select against these atypical memberships. Selection against extreme members keeps the niche boundaries of the organization in focus. In other words, the process of selection, acting through the niche edge effect and the niche overlap effect, acts as a homogenizing mechanism for voluntary associations.

The strong support for the niche position hypothesis adds in an interesting way to the ongoing debate about the relative explanatory power of the attributes of individuals versus the relations between them (Wellman 1979, 1988). The results here show that the relative positions of individuals in social space can act as a proxy for the network connections between them. Through the organizing structure of social space, the attributes of individuals summarize their homophilous relations with others who are near and distant in social space. In the present theory, attributes are not essential characteristics of individuals, but measures of the structural position of individuals relative to one another (see McPherson et al. 1992, fig. 1).

Conclusion

In this article, we explain and test two simple mechanisms by which voluntary associations maintain homogeneity. In Blau's (1977, 1994) terms, the niche edge and niche overlap effects help prevent population heterogeneity (in sex) and inequality (in education) from penetrating

to the level of voluntary associations. Since many social network ties form within voluntary groups (Marsden 1990; Feld 1981), this process constricts opportunities for cross-category contact.

From Tocqueville ([1835] 1961) to the present (Curtis, Grabb, and Baer 1992), the voluntary association literature has long concerned itself with individual integration into society through voluntary affiliation. This literature ignores that fact that homogeneous voluntary organizations segregate the population along important sociodemographic lines (Popielarz 1992; cf. Granovetter 1973). Since segregation is a well-known foundation on which to base inequality, our theory addresses very basic sociological questions about stratification.

The most interesting feature of our results is the conclusion that maintenance of homogeneity in voluntary associations may rest purely on niche structure, intergroup competition, and the homophily principle. We do not appeal to rational choice mechanisms or discrimination by the organization, nor do we interpret these effects as the result of institutional forces. Rather, the emergent structure of network connections and the community of voluntary associations in social space can account for the homogeneity of these social groups. This line of evidence provides support for the argument that blind evolution, rather than human agency, may structure the fundamental character of social groups.

Notes

1. For the purpose of this work, voluntary associations are those formal and informal social groups that are not directly part of family, government, religion, or economic firms.

2. Elsewhere we use the term "Blau space" to acknowledge the contribution of Blau's *Inequality and Heterogeneity* (1977) to our work (McPherson and Ranger-Moore 1991).

3. Notice that rate of turnover and duration of membership are related to one another negatively; i.e., a high rate of turnover implies short membership durations.

4. Competition need not be consciously undertaken or obvious to those involved.

5. Each group competes with other groups in that area of social space, and with more generalized competitors, such as families, occupations, and other activities, for the resources of the individual.

6. Of course, the figure assumes that the omitted generalized competitors, such as families, are averaged out across social space; this assumption is discussed more fully in McPherson and Ranger-Moore (1991) and McPherson et al. (1992). DrobniO (1992) studies the competitive relationship between organizational careers in these groups and careers in firms.

7. See McPherson and Smith-Lovin (1986, 1987) for a discussion of the 1983 study design and results.

8. Respondents were asked, "What month/year did you leave the organization? By leaving the organization we mean the time when you stopped attending meetings or stopped paying dues."

9. The types are church, professional, veteran's/patriotic, recreational, social, youth, elderly, charity, public interest, ethnic, hobby, political, fraternal/service, union, farm, civic, and other.

10. Educational level typically changes only during a limited portion of the life cycle. The mean education in our sample is 14 years. Most people reach this level by the time they are 20 years old. If a respondent was 20 years old in 1974, then she would have been 35 at the time of the study. Since less than a quarter of our sample is age 35 or under, a large majority of our respondents most likely remained at the same educational level throughout the study period. Discarding students and respondents under the age of 35 from the sample did not qualitatively alter the conclusions we present.

References

Babchuk, Nicholas, and John N. Edwards. 1965. "Voluntary Associations and the Integration Hypothesis." *Sociological Inquiry* 35:149–62.

Bernard, H. Russell, Eugene C. Johnson, Peter D. Killworth, Christopher McCarty, Gene A. Shelley, and Scott Robinson. 1990. "Comparing Four Different Methods for Measuring Personal Social Networks." *Social Networks* 12:179–215.

Bielby, William T., and James N. Baron. 1986. "Men and Women at Work: Sex Segregation and Statistical Discrimination." *American Journal of Sociology* 91:759–99.

Blau, Peter M. 1970. "A Formal Theory of Differentiation in Organizations." *American Sociological Review* 35:201–18.

_____. 1977. *Inequality and Heterogeneity: A Primitive Theory of Social Structure.* New York: Free Press.

_____. 1987. "Microprocess and Macrostructure." Pp. 83–100 in *Social Exchange Theory,* edited by K. Cook. Newbury Park, Calif.: Sage.

_____. 1994. *Structural Contexts of Opportunities.* Chicago: University of Chicago Press.

Blau, Peter M., and Joseph Schwartz. 1984. *Crosscutting Social Circles.* New York: Free Press.

Booth, Alan, and Nicholas Babchuk. 1969. "Personal Influence Networks and Voluntary Association Affiliation." *Sociological Inquiry* 39:179–88.

Breiger, Ronald L. 1974. "The Duality of Persons and Groups." *Social Forces* 53:181–90.

Burt, Ronald S. 1990. "Kinds of Relations in American Discussion Networks." Pp. 411–51 in *Structures of Power and Constraint: Papers in Honor of Peter Blau,* edited by C. Calhoun, M. W. Meyer, and W. R. Scott. New York: Cambridge University Press.

Curtis, James E., Edward G. Grabb, and Douglas E. Baer. 1992. "Voluntary Association Membership in Fifteen Countries: A Comparative Analysis." *American Sociological Review* 57:139–52.

Drobnič, Sonja. 1992. "Voluntary Associations and Firms: A Study in Organizational Careers." Ph.D. dissertation. Cornell University, Sociology Department.

Fernandez, Roberto M., and Doug McAdam. 1988. "Social Networks and Social Movements: Multiorganizational Fields and Recruitment to Mississippi Freedom Summer." *Sociological Forum* 3:357–832.

Granovetter, Mark. 1973. "The Strength of Weak Ties." *American Journal of Sociology* 78:1360–80.

_____. 1974. *Getting a Job: A Study of Contacts and Careers.* Cambridge, Mass.: Harvard University Press.

Jacobs, Jerry A. 1989. *Revolving Doors: Sex Segregation and Women's Careers.* Stanford, Calif.: Stanford University Press.

Kanter, Rosabeth Moss. 1977. *Men and Women of the Corporation.* New York: Basic.

Marsden, Peter V. 1987. "Core Discussion Networks of Americans." *American Sociological Review* 52: 122–31.

_____. 1988. "Homogeneity in Confiding Relations." *Social Networks* 10:57–76.

Mayhew, Bruce H. 1980. "Structuralism Versus Individualism: Part I, Shadowboxing in the Dark." *Social Forces* 59:335–75.

Mayhew, Bruce H., J. Miller McPherson, Thomas Rotolo, and Lynn Smith-Lovin. 1995. "Sex and

Race Heterogeneity in Face to Face Groups." *Social Forces,* in press.

McPherson, Miller. 1982. "Hypernetwork Sampling: Duality and Differentiation among Voluntary Organizations." *Social Networks* 3:225–49.

_____. 1983. "An Ecology of Affiliation." *American Sociological Review* 48:519–32.

_____. 1988. "Niches and Networks: An Ecological Evolutionary Model of Voluntary Organization." Proposal submitted to the National Science Foundation. University of Arizona, Department of Sociology.

_____. 1990. "Evolution in Communities of Voluntary Associations." Pp. 224–45 in *Organizational Evolution: New Directions,* edited by J. V. Singh. Newbury Park, Calif.: Sage.

McPherson, J. Miller, Pamela A. Popielarz, and Sonja Drobnič. 1992. "Social Networks and Organizational Dynamics." *American Sociological Review* 57:153–70.

McPherson, J. Miller, and James R. Ranger-Moore. 1991. "Evolution on a Dancing Landscape." *Social Forces* 70:19–42.

McPherson, J. Miller, and Thomas Rotolo. 1996. "Testing a Dynamic Model of Social Composition: Diversity and Change in Voluntary Groups." *American Sociological Review,* in press.

McPherson, J. Miller, and Lynn Smith-Lovin. 1986. "Sex Segregation in Voluntary Associations." *American Sociological Review* 51:61–79.

_____. 1987. "Homophily in Voluntary Organizations: Status Distance and the Composition of Face to Face Groups." *American Sociological Review* 52:370–79.

Popielarz, Pamela A. 1990. "On the Edge: Niche Position and Membership Duration in Voluntary Associations." M.A. thesis. Cornell University, Department of Sociology.

_____. 1992. "Connection and Competition: A Structural Theory of Sex Segregation in Voluntary Associations." Ph.D. dissertation. Cornell University.

Snow, David A., Louis A. Zurcher, Jr., and Sheldon Ekland-Olson. 1980. "Social Networks and Social Movements: A Microstructural Approach to Differential Recruitment." *American Sociological Review* 45:787–801.

Stark, Rodney, and William Sims Bainbridge. 1980. "Secularization, Revival, and Cult Formation." *Annual Review of the Social Sciences of Religion* 4:85–119.

Tocqueville, Alexis de. (1835) 1961. *Democracy in America.* New York: Knopf.

Wellman, Barry. 1979. "The Community Question: The Intimate Networks of East Yorkers." *American Journal of Sociology* 84:1201–31.

_____. 1988. "Structural Analysis: From Method and Metaphor to Theory and Substance." Pp. 19–61 in *Social Structures: A Network Approach,* edited by B. Wellman and S. D. Berkowitz. New York: Cambridge University Press.

PART 8

ORGANIZATION THEORIES OF THE NONPROFIT SECTOR

Why do nonprofit organizations make the strategic decisions they do? What causes nonprofits to act in certain ways? Why are organizations in the nonprofit sector designed and structured as they are? How *should* nonprofits be organized and thus managed? To what extent should nonprofit organization structures, processes, and controls "look like" government and business organizations? Organization theories attempt to answer questions such as these.

An Organization

An *organization* is simply a social unit with some particular purposes. "The most common formal definition of an organization is a collection of people engaged in specialized and interdependent activity to accomplish a goal or mission."[1] The essential components of organizations have remained surprisingly constant over the centuries and across all three sectors. All organizations have explicit or implicit purposes, attract participants, acquire and allocate resources to accomplish their purposes, establish a structure to coordinate tasks, and permit some members to lead or manage others.[2]

A few neighbors who decide to establish a neighborhood watch program or to fight for speed bumps on a busy street probably will form a simple organization without giving much thought to the fact that they are doing so. Fielding a Little League baseball team or establishing a homeowners' association requires a slightly more complex organization. The organizers probably will want to create an organization structure, with officers, a board, lines of authority and responsibility, a means for orderly replacement of officers, fiscal and program responsibilities, and a procedure for resolving disagreements. As the purposes and tasks that people want to accomplish with their organizations become more complex, more costly, require more people with special skills, and last for longer periods of time, the organizations they create also become more complex.

Organization Theory

A theory is "any intellectual construct that enables someone to make sense of a situation or problem."[3] Simply stated, a *theory* is a proposition or set of propositions that seeks to explain or predict something.[4] For *organization theory,* that "something" is an aspect of how organizations or groupings of organizations make decisions or act in different sets of circumstances. Organization theorists thus are interested in "macro" concerns, such as "organizational structure, organizational design, or organizational culture. That is, organization theory tries to understand the organization as a unit of analysis, as opposed to the 'micro' approach that concentrates on individual behavior in organizations."[5] In practice, nonprofit organization theories usually are concerned with the effects of interrelationships among factors and forces in a nonprofit organization's environment.

The Evolution of Organization Theory

Until recent decades, organization theory was almost entirely concerned with large, bureaucratic, centrally controlled business and government organizations—not fluid nonprofits or networks of community associations. Early twentieth-century legends such as Frederick Winslow Taylor (scientific management)[6], Max Weber (bureaucracy)[7], and Henri Fayol,[8] and Luther Gulick (general principles of organization)[9] authored the foundation concepts.

Organization theories do not develop or exist in vacuums, however. (Neither do organization structures, processes, or norms.) Organizations and organization theories reflect their environments in their eras. They adapt to changes in cultures over time. "Thus . . . the advent of the factory system, World War II, the 'flower child'/antiestablishment/self-development era of the 1960s, the computer/information society of the 1970s, and the pervasive uncertainties of the 1980s and 1990s all substantially influenced the evolution of organization theory."[10]

For all practical purposes, *classical organization theory* was the only theory of organization until World War II, and it remains the most common form of organization of governments and businesses around the world. Weber's bureaucracy, Taylor's scientific management, and Fayol's and Gulick's general principles of administration are the foundation concepts of classical organization theory and thus also for essentially all long-standing theories of government and business organization. The basic tenets of classical organization theory—tenets that continue to have high credence in many organizations today—include the following:

- Organizations exist to accomplish production-related and economic goals.
- There is one best way to organize for production, and that way can be found through systematic, scientific inquiry.
- Production is maximized through specialization and division of labor.
- People and organizations act in accordance with rational economic principles.[11]

These tenets may have been appropriate for the realities of business and government organizations in the 1700s, 1800s, and the first half of the 1900s. As the world around them changed, however, and as the importance of the nonprofit sector emerged, organizations and organization theory also adapted—but never completely let go of the tenets and features of classical organization theory, particularly of bureaucracy.[12]

Organization Theory for Nonprofits

A lot can be learned about nonprofit organizations by studying theories that were developed for and about government and business organizations. All nonprofits share some characteristics with organizations in the other sectors—simply because they are organizations. And often it is difficult to discern differences between larger, older, well-established bureaucratic nonprofits and organizations in the other two sectors. Commercial nonprofits, for example, often are all but indistinguishable from for-profit businesses; and nonprofits that derive most of their income from contracts with government agencies often look, act, and "feel" very much like government agencies.[13] Therefore, the decisions and actions of nonprofit organizations often can be explained well by using general theories of organization.

As we have seen in earlier chapters, however, nonprofit sector organizations have distinctive features, components, and values that require theories of their own. A veritable wave of useful nonprofit organization theories has been published in recent years, particularly in the literature of sociology, economics, psychology, cultural anthropology, and organization studies (mostly in public and business administration). It is important to understand, however, that there is not, cannot be, and should not be a single theory of nonprofit organizations. There are—and need to be—many theories to explain and predict how nonprofit organizations will act under a variety of circumstances and with different organizational purposes, structures, and cultures.[14]

Readings Reprinted in This Part

The theories presented in the readings that follow are from the fields of sociology, organizational behavior, and organization theory. They present an array of perspectives, but they all have the same purpose: to increase understanding about the distinctive factors that influence nonprofit organizational decisions and actions.

"The Sociology of Nonprofit Organizations and Sectors," by Paul DiMaggio and Helmut Anheier, is a meta-study of mostly sociological research and theories about nonprofit organizations.[15] Two questions that are central concerns of organization theory are addressed at the organization, industry, and nation-state levels:

- Why (and where) are there nonprofit organizations?
- What difference does nonprofitness make? To what extent, and why, do nonprofits' performance, structures, services and client mix, strategies, and human-resource policies differ from those of other forms of organization?

Combining these two questions with the three levels of analysis produces six questions, which DiMaggio and Anheier then answer systematically through an exhaustive search of the literature:

Origins 1:   Why are some organizations nonprofit, others for-profit, and still others public?

Origins 2:   What explains differences among industries in the division of labor among nonprofit, government, and for-profit forms?

Origins 3:   How can one explain cross-national variation in the definition, prevalence, and role of the nonprofit form?

Behavior 1:   Within industries, what if any behavioral differences exist between nonprofit organizations and for-profit organizations or government agencies?

Behavior 2:   What, if any, differences in the structure and performance of industries are associated with the division of labor among public, for-profit, and nonprofit enterprises?

Behavior 3:   What, if any, are the implications for national societies of the prevalence and distribution of nonprofit organizations?

In "Perspectives on Organizational Governance," Steven Ott uses an *organizational model* to help explain practical differences between nonprofit organizations that receive significant voluntary support (i.e., open system organizations) and government agencies (i.e., more closed system organizations), and why the use of "inappropriate mental models" cause relations between government agencies and some contracted nonprofits to become uncomfortable.[16] Thus, system theory *and* the nature of the relationships between government and nonprofit organizations (and their members) can be useful for explaining differences among organizations' actions.

A *model* is a form of organization theory that is presented in a way that attempts to represent real life. Models are created from theories and basic assumptions important for understanding, explaining, and perhaps predicting organizational behavior. A *practical theory* is a theory or model "that either illuminates possibilities for action that would not otherwise be apparent *or* stimulates greater understanding of what the person has been doing."[17] Ott argues that the mental image ("model") of voluntary nonprofit organizations as atoms "is more useful [than the bureaucratic pyramidal model] for understanding relationships among its components and constituencies, and therefore its decisions and actions." Applicability of this particular model is limited, however, to voluntary nonprofit organizations, "a nonprofit organization that receives significant support from voluntary contributions of time, effort, and/or money, and its organizational culture contains beliefs, values, and basic assumptions associated with voluntary participation." This "atom model" postulates that

- Constituencies of voluntary nonprofit organizations are not ordered in neat, hierarchical positions or slots.
- A voluntary nonprofit organization will survive as long as its activities continue to satisfy the interests of its constituencies.
- Just as an atom does not depend on the presence of any particular individual electron for its existence, the ongoing survival of a voluntary nonprofit organization does not depend upon the continuing participation of any one or two specific constituencies.

- A voluntary nonprofit organization's identity is altered when the paths of some constituencies' orbits alternately move closer and farther away from the core, other constituencies leave the atom's field, or new constituencies choose to associate.

There are major differences between nonprofit organizations and government organizations.

> The rational instrumental hierarchical model of bureaucratic organization—the government organizational model—is not applicable to voluntary nonprofit organizations. Failure to understand these differences can cause misunderstanding, confusion, frustration, and even anger, in an organization and between people who must work together in organizations in different sectors.

"Nonprofit Organizations in an Age of Uncertainty," by sociologists Joseph Galaskiewicz and Wolfgang Bielefeld is about the comparative usefulness of different and often competing organization theories for explaining changes in nonprofit organizations from 1980 through 1994.[18] "We wanted to see what organizational theory could do today to explain change in a panel of nonprofits." The authors formulated hypotheses from several competing organizational theories, collected data about changes in these nonprofit organizations over the twelve-year period, tested the hypotheses, and summarized the results. The authors then "tried to evaluate [each] theory and how well it did in explaining organizational change." The reading is divided into three sections, one for each of the three sets of organization theories they examine: selection models, adaptation models, and structural embeddedness models. The sections

1. define the core characteristics of the theory and describe the types of variables and questions the particular theory attempts to address;
2. present hypotheses, findings, and discussions about the following:
   - the growth and decline of these nonprofit organizations;
   - tactics they employed, including, for example, their competitive, revenue-generating, "niche" tactics;
   - quality of life in the organizations, including the tendency to centralize decisionmaking authority, disagreements while making decisions, conflict with employees, the degree of employee alienation, and the quality of the creative or innovative work environment.

"Nonprofit Organizations in an Age of Uncertainty" reports on a rich study of organization theories that incorporates myriad complex environmental factors influencing nonprofit organizations. The authors introduce variables to test theories primarily from sociology, economics, and political science. For example, they conclude that although

> the sociological literature has often taken a dim view of elite participation in nonprofits, . . . over the fifteen years of our study, elite contacts resulted in more donations and volunteers, an increase in the use of political and managerial tactics (which, in turn, resulted in an increase in donated and commercial income), less alienation among participants, and a work environment more sympathetic to creativity and innovation.

These are important findings for nonprofit practitioners as well as scholars.

Notes

1. Phillip J. Cooper, Linda P. Brady, Olivia Hidalgo-Hardeman, Albert C. Hyde, Katherine C. Naff, J. Steven Ott, and Harvey White, *Public Administration for the Twenty-First Century* (Fort Worth, Tex.: Harcourt Brace, 1998), p. 203.

2. A parallel discussion of organization theory in the public sector is included in J. Steven Ott and E. W. Russell, eds., *Introduction to Public Administration: A Book of Readings* (New York: Addison Wesley Longman, 2001).

3. Michael M. Harmon and Richard T. Mayer, *Organization Theory for Public Administration* (Boston: Little, Brown, 1986), p. 61.

4. For a more complete discussion of theories in general, see Part 5.

5. Robert B. Denhardt, "Organization Theory," in Jay M. Shafritz, ed., *International Encyclopedia of Public Policy and Administration* (Boulder: Westview Press, 1998), p. 1554.

6. Frederick W. Taylor, *The Principles of Scientific Management* (New York: Norton, 1911).

7. Max Weber, "Bureaucracy," in *Essays in Sociology,* edited and translated by H. H. Gerth and C. Wright Mills (1922; reprint, Oxford: Oxford University Press, 1946).

8. Henri Fayol, *General and Industrial Management* (1916; reprint, London: Pitman, 1949).

9. Luther Gulick, "Notes on the Theory of Organization," in Luther Gulick and Lyndall Urwick, eds., *Papers on the Science of Administration* (New York: Institute of Public Administration, 1937), pp. 3–13.

10. Jay M. Shafritz and J. Steven Ott, "Introduction," in Shafritz and Ott, eds., *Classics of Organization Theory,* 5th ed. (Fort Worth, Tex.: Harcourt Brace, 2001), p. 2.

11. Lee G. Bolman and Terrence E. Deal, *Reframing Organizations: Artistry, Choice, and Leadership,* 2nd ed. (San Francisco: Jossey-Bass, 1997).

12. Excellent examples are in B. Guy Peters, *The Future of Governing: Four Emerging Models* (Lawrence: University Press of Kansas, 1996).

13. Steven Rathgeb Smith and Michael Lipsky, *Nonprofits for Hire* (Cambridge: Harvard University Press, 1993).

14. Shafritz and Ott, "Introduction."

15. A meta-study is a study of research studies that have been done previously on a subject.

16. J. Steven Ott, "Perspectives on Organizational Governance: Some Effects on Government-Nonprofit Relations," *Southeastern Political Review* 21 (1), Winter 1993, pp. 3–21.

17. Michael M. Harmon and Richard T. Mayer, *Organization Theory for Public Administration* (Boston: Little, Brown, 1986), p. 61.

18. Joseph Galaskiewicz and Wolfgang Bielefeld, *Nonprofit Organizations in an Age of Uncertainty* (New York: Aldine-DeGruyter, 1998).

References

Alexander, Victoria D. "Environmental Constraints and Organizational Strategies: Complexity, Conflict, and Coping in the Nonprofit Sector." In Walter W. Powell and Elisabeth S. Clemens, eds., *Private Action and the Public Good,* pp. 272–290. New Haven: Yale University Press, 1998.

Anthony, Robert N., and David W. Young. *Management Control in Nonprofit Organizations,* 6th ed. Homewood, Ill.: Irwin/McGraw-Hill, 1999.

DiMaggio, Paul J., and Helmut K. Anheier. "The Sociology of Nonprofit Organizations and Sectors." In W. Richard Scott and Judith Blake, eds., *Annual Review of Sociology* 16, pp. 137–159. Palo Alto: Annual Reviews, 1990.

Donaldson, Lex. *For Positivist Organization Theory.* London: Sage, 1996.

Galaskiewicz, Joseph, and Wolfgang Bielefeld. *Nonprofit Organizations in an Age of Uncertainty.* New York: Aldine-DeGruyter, 1998.

Gortner, Harold F., Julianne Mahler, and Jeanne Bell Nicholson. *Organization Theory: A Public Perspective.* Fort Worth, Tex.: Harcourt Brace, 1997.

Handy, Charles. *Understanding Organizations.* New York: Oxford University Press, 1993.

Harmon, Michael M., and Richard T. Mayer. *Organization Theory for Public Administration.* Boston: Little, Brown, 1986.

Keidel, Robert W. *Seeing Organizational Patterns: A New Theory and Language of Organizational Design.* San Francisco: Berrett-Koehler, 1995.

March, James G., and Herbert A. Simon. *Organizations,* 2nd ed. Cambridge, Mass.: Blackwell, 1993.

Ott, J. Steven. "Perspectives on Organizational Governance: Some Effects on Government-Nonprofit Relations." *Southeastern Political Review* 21 (1), Winter 1993, 3–21.

Scott, W. Richard. *Organizations: Rational, Natural, and Open Systems,* 4th ed. Upper Saddle River, N.J.: Prentice Hall, 1998.

_____. *Institutions and Organizations.* Thousand Oaks, Calif.: Sage, 1995.

Shafritz, Jay M., and J. Steven Ott, eds. *Classics of Organization Theory,* 5th ed. Fort Worth, Tex.: Harcourt Brace, 2001.

Simon, Herbert A. *Administrative Behavior,* 4th ed. New York: Free Press, 1997.

Soichet, Richard. "An Organization Design Model for Nonprofits." *Nonprofit Management and Leadership* 9 (1), Fall 1998, 71–88.

Weick, Karl E. *Sensemaking in Organizations.* Thousand Oaks, Calif.: Sage, 1995.

> ▶ CHAPTER 23

The Sociology of Nonprofit Organizations and Sectors

Paul J. DiMaggio and Helmut K. Anheier

Introduction

The past two decades have witnessed a groundswell of interest in nonprofit organizations (NPOs) and nonprofit sectors (NPSs). For social scientists, the origin and behavior of sectors that stand outside market and state are tantalizing puzzles. The curiosity of US scholars has been piqued by rapid post-war nonprofit sector growth: Increased regulation has accompanied growth, stimulating sector-level political mobilization by NPOs formerly organized only at the level of their own industries. Such efforts have supported research and conferences, improved the quality of aggregate data, and encouraged scholars to think in sectoral terms. This review develops a sociological perspective on the nonprofit form, emphasizing comparison among NPOs in different industries and societies. Thus we draw very selectively on voluminous specialized literatures (e.g. on health, the arts, voluntary associations, social services, community organizations, churches, social movement organizations), and we emphasize research focussing on "non-profitness" per se, including work in other disciplines.

For the United States, unless otherwise specified, "nonprofit organizations" are those falling under section 501(c)3 of the Internal Revenue Code (a category including most nonprofit hospitals, cultural organizations, traditional charities, foundations, schools, daycare centers and foundations, among others), or the smaller, related 501(c)4 category (civic leagues and social welfare organizations, which are denied tax-deductible contributions but which may engage in some political or commercial activities from which (c)3s are barred): these do *not* include such mutual-benefit associations as labor unions, workers or consumers cooperatives, veterans organizations, or political parties, which the law treats separately. 501(c)3s and 4s are subject to the nondistribution constraint (which proscribes distributing net income as dividends or above-market remuneration); they must serve one of several broadly defined collective purposes; and they receive certain tax advantages (Simon 1987). In discussing nonprofit sectors *outside* the United States, we vary terminology according to national legal and political traditions.

The Issues

Two problems are fundamental. First, *origin:* why do nonprofit organizations exist? This question concerns the intersectoral division of

274

labor: the distribution of functions among for-profits (FPs), NPOs, and public agencies. Given the apparent disadvantages of NPOs with respect to incentives (compared to for-profits) and revenue generation (compared to government), why are there so many of them? Second, there is the issue of organizational *behavior*. To what extent, and why, do NPOs' performance, structures, service and client mix, strategies, and human-resource policies differ from those of other forms? We may pose each problem at three levels of analysis: (*a*) organization, (*b*) industry and (*c*) nation-state (with the understanding that structural features at any level will influence processes at lower levels). Cross-classifying problems and levels yields six questions, which structure this review:

Origins 1: Why are some organizations nonprofit, and others for profit, and still others public?

Origins 2: What explains differences among industries in the division of labor among NP, government, and FP forms?

Origins 3: How can one explain cross-national variation in the definition, prevalence, and role of the nonprofit form?

Behavior 1: Within industries, what if any behavioral differences exist between NPOs and FPs or government agencies?

Behavior 2: What, if any, differences in the structure and performance of industries are associated with the division of labor among public, FP and NP enterprises?

Behavior 3: What, if any, are the implications for national societies of the prevalence and distribution of NPOs?

Why Are There Nonprofit Organizations?

Organization Level

One can predict the legal form of most organizations if one knows the industry and nation-state in which they operate. Residual variation (and NPOs) are encapsulated in a relatively small, albeit important, set of industries where

two or more forms are well represented: in the United States, hospitals, daycare, museums, universities, home health care, social services, broadcasting, and a few others.

Many such industries comprise well-defined niches (commercial television and public broadcasting). Given an account of activities and official goals, one can identify legal form with almost complete accuracy. In some (hospitals, daycare), NP and FP forms compete within the same niche, a situation likely to be unstable. In a few cases (local arts agencies, which include NP, public, and hybrid specimens), form is weakly related to niche but competition is minimal. Few studies explore why entrepreneurs select particular legal forms when they have a choice, or why some organizations change form. Factors suggested in the literature include founder dispositions [e.g. religious values, profit-mindedness, risk averseness, or altruism (James & Rose-Ackerman 1986)], access to capital markets (Hollingsworth & Hollingsworth 1987), and eligibility rules for government aid (DiMaggio 1987).

Industry Level: The Division of Labor Among Forms

Economic theory. Economists have done much on this topic (Hansmann 1987, Rose-Ackerman 1986). Their arguments go far to explain which industries are likely to have NPSs. But their capacity to explain variation in NP activity within industries over time and space is limited. First they neglect supply-side factors, especially social cohesion among potential beneficiaries or entrepreneurs (Ben-Ner & Van Hoomissen 1989), that influence the capacity of NPOs to respond to demand. Second they view states as competing providers rather than (as is often the case) financiers or consumers of NP services. Third, they neglect such institutional factors as state policy, organizing norms, ideology and religion.

Historical perspective. In historical perspective, US NPOs appear less a single form than a kind of cuckoo's nest occupied by different kinds of entrepreneurs for different purposes.

Three entities—status groups, professions, and the state—have been particularly active.

Status groups. US NPOs were differentiated from for-profit firms over the course of the nineteenth century (Hall 1982). In the late 1800s, impetus for the formation of NPOs came from emerging upper classes eager to control unruly urban environments and to define social boundaries. The charitable and cultural enterprises of the Gilded Age performed such new public functions as social welfare and aesthetic improvement in ways the market could not support and the polity might not tolerate (McCarthy 1982, Story 1980).

Urban elites remain prominent in NPO governance, largely as members of boards of trustees and volunteer committees. Evidence suggests that such activities promote and maintain upper-class solidarity and permit elites to monitor and control NP policies (Salzman & Domhoff 1983, Ostrander 1987, Daniels 1988). The character of elite influence may be changing, however. Local upper-class patrons and trustees are losing influence in many fields due to declining dependence on donations, increased support from government, and managerial professionalization. Greater demand for trustees as the number of NPOs has risen renders some boards more heterogeneous than in the past. Most important, the central role in elite participation has moved from local upper classes to corporate managers, who are recruited on the basis not of kin but of company affiliation (Useem 1984). Although demographically similar to traditional trustees, many are "corporate rationalizers" (Alford 1975), impatient with communal governance styles and supportive of managerial reform (DiMaggio 1991). And direct company giving has become more generous and systematic (Useem 1987, Galaskiewicz 1985). Attracting prestigious trustees and corporate support sustains NPOs' legitimacy and revenues (Zald 1967, Provan 1980).

Other status groups (workers, ethnic and religious communities) form NPOs. [The number of churches strongly predicts intercounty variation in the NP share of employment in four New York State multiform industries (Ben-Ner & Van

Hoomissen 1989)]. Although lacking definitive data, we suspect that such NPOs are often less stable, less likely to incorporate, and less likely to claim community-wide missions than those created by the wealthy. Many status-based NPOs (including those attached to upper classes) resemble bureaucracies less than formal structures draped around the ongoing life of densely connected networks, geared to producing "goods" (solidarity, self-esteem, distinction, work experience, opportunities for association) external to formal missions (Rothschild-Whitt 1979, Milofsky 1987). [For economic models of NPOs emphasizing status groups, see Ben-Ner 1986, Hansmann 1986; see also reviews of specialized literatures on social movement organizations (Jenkins 1987) and voluntarism (Van Til 1988).]

Professionals. During the Progressive Era the organizing impulse shifted from local upper classes to nationally mobilizing professionals. Majone (1984) notes a similarity between the justifying ideologies of professions and of NPOs: service ethos, autonomy from market values, and exercise of expertise on behalf of the common good. Although some professionals (lawyers, accountants) found the FP form suited to their needs, most turned to NPOs. In hospitals, universities, and social-service agencies, by the 1920s professionals employed by NPOs dominated national discourse and organization, while sharing local authority with upper-class trustees (Perrow 1963, Starr 1982).

Professionals retain much influence in many NPOs. Hospitals vie for doctors, who bring prestige and patients; some economists view NP hospitals as, in effect, physicians' cooperatives (Pauly & Redisch 1973). But scholars agree that medical authority has declined due to supply factors, regulatory and competitive pressures, and changes in administrative rules and structures (Gray 1990, Starr 1982). Declines are also noted in the organizational power of social workers (Kramer 1987), professors (Freidson 1986), and curators (Peterson 1986).

Nonetheless, in most fields nonprofit organizations remain more conducive than for-profits to professional autonomy by virtue of their charters, which mirror professional ideologies;

governance systems, which often include professional participation; and revenue structures, which empower professionals with access to private donors—doctors, curators—or funding agencies—academics. Moreover, the declining influence of particular professions often reflects increased competition for organizational authority—Scott (1983) reports that hospitals employ workers in up to 200 professions—and the gravitation of power in many NPOs from service to technobureaucratic professions (Larson 1977). The persistent elective affinity between NPOs and professionals is reflected in the greater propensity of NPO-employed than of other professionals to espouse "new class" social and political views (Brint 1987, Macy 1988).

The state. By 1960 the engine of voluntarism had shifted again, this time, ironically, to the state, with the growth of "third-party government," that is, state delegation of functions by grant or contract to NPOs (Salamon 1981). Far from competing over a fixed set of functions, the US domestic state and NPS grew in tandem, the former expanding domains of public responsibility and financing programs the latter implemented. By 1975, government had replaced private donors as the largest source of NPO revenues.

Although early work noted increased interdependence between public and NP sectors (Smith 1975, Kramer 1981), Reagan administration domestic budget cuts provided stimulus to and a laboratory setting for research. Studies have documented the financial dependence of NPOs on the state (Salamon & Abrahamson 1982), investigated effects of federal cutbacks (Altheide 1988, Wolch 1990, reviewed in Salamon 1987) and proposed theoretical accounts (Kramer 1987, Gronbjerg 1987).

Institutions. An historical perspective brings into focus explanatory factors that play little role in economic models (which in turn possess an elegance that more historically attentive explanations lack). Specifically, the prevalence of NPOs within industries is related to three aspects of institutional structure.

Key decisions. Pivotal decisions by organizational entrepreneurs are institutionalized in models that raise the cost of new forms while making it inexpensive to adhere to tradition (Stinchcombe 1965, DiMaggio & Powell 1983). Mechanisms reproducing existing forms include interorganizational networks seeking state restraint of entry by new kinds of providers; scale economies in organizing due to availability of models and experienced participants (Marrett 1980, Wievel & Hunter 1985); and consumer expectations resistant to change. Thus, initial choices of form, which may be subject to large stochastic elements, exert long-term effects.

Public policy. Comparing US states, Hansmann (1985) reports significant relationships between tax policy and the NP proportion of schools and nursing homes. Econometric studies summarized by Jencks (1987) reveal the influence of tax rates on private donations. Within industries, narrow decisions are consequential: the Supreme Court's *Thor* ruling on inventory depreciation made NP publishers more attractive to authors who want to keep their books in print, benefitting university presses that had experienced severe competitive pressures (Powell 1985).

Climates of opinion. Perceptions of the trustworthiness of forms (rather than measurable differences) shape decisions of consumers and policy makers (Hansmann 1987). Certain goods are seen as inappropriate for market exchange or requiring special protection from corruption by the profit motive (Titmuss 1971, Hansmann 1989), and definitions of "public goods" and "community needs" vary over time (Gronbjerg 1986).

Ecology. The arguments reviewed have been implicitly ecological: they portray for-profit, nonprofit, and public forms as competing or cooperating within industries, the success of each determined by material and ideological environments. It follows that an ecological approach (McPherson 1983, Hannan & Freeman 1989) is well suited to test theories about the intersectoral division of labor. One must transform such arguments from hypotheses about proportions of activity (in which form they have thus far been tested) into propositions about change over time in birth and death rates of NP, FP, and public firms and transition rates from one form to another. Although such rates *may* move in tandem (e.g. the same factors may simultaneously generate high death and low birth rates for NPOs and low death and high birth rates for FPs) it is likely that different factors influence different rates and that no one theory of industry composition will suffice.

Explaining Cross-National Variation

Organizational and sectoral equivalence.   Few countries use the term "nonprofit sector." Nonetheless, comparative researchers assume implicitly, that the French *économie sociale* (Forsé 1984), the United Kingdom's *voluntary sector* (Knapp et al 1990, Ware 1989), the German *gemeinnützige Organisationen* (Anheier 1988), and the US *nonprofit sector* share many central features. Comparativists face difficulty in establishing cross-national equivalence, however.

Differences in legal tradition further confound comparison.

Heterogeneity.   Following Weisbrod, James (1987b) argues that society's religious, ethnic, and ideological heterogeneity generates differentiated demand for collective goods and stocks of religious entrepreneurs. James finds substantial, if qualified, support for this position in research on cross-national variation in the size and scope of NP primary and secondary education.

Value rationality.   NPOs are often based on strong ideological, especially religious, orientations: value-rational rather than means-rational, in Weber's terms. Cross-national variation in such values and in religious traditions influences the size and form of NPSs: in the only cross-national quantitative analysis, James & Levin (1986) found religious factors significant predictors of the proportionate role of private schools.

Historical contingencies.   Because NPOs adapt less quickly to environmental change than do FPs (which are subject to market discipline) or government agencies (which are politically accountable), NPSs incorporate and preserve responses to historical political and social conflicts.

Intersectoral relations.   Variations in relations between nonprofit organizations and state and corporate sectors also influence cross-national variation in NPO prevalence and role. For example, US corporations make substantial donations to certain NP subsectors, a practice far less common in most of Europe. The structure of state/NP relations is also crucial: e.g. whether NPOs are subject to fragmented centralization coordinated through grants (Scott & Meyer 1990) or are integrated into corporatist systems of interest mediation and conflict accommodation (Lijphart 1984).

Polity structure.   National societies develop distinctive political traditions and institutional models that are imprinted in national dispositions toward organizing (Jepperson & Meyer 1990). Definitions of public and private, and the division of labor between public and private sectors, are neither stable nor formalized, but rather tend to shift over time (Kramer 1981). Bauer (1987) contends that NPSs' political orientations reflect the regulatory regimes under which they operate.

Cross-national research underscores the limits of economic explanation and the centrality of institutional factors. Microeconomic approaches cannot explain cross-national variation in the size and composition of NPSs because they take account of neither religious nor political factors (James 1987b).

Behavioral Effects of Nonprofitness

Organization Level

Research has centered on hospitals (Gray 1986, 1990) and schools (Levy 1986b, James & Levin

1986, James 1987a), with comparisons by organizational form in structure, services provided, clients served, and various measures of performance.

Efficiency. Contrary to orthodox economic theory, research on hospitals reports that NPOs are less expensive (in per-diem patient cost) and thus ostensibly more efficient than FPs; by contrast, nursing-home studies find that FPs are cheaper (Gray 1990, Marmor et al 1987). There are many reasons to question if such studies really tap efficiency (Steinberg 1987, Gray 1990). Weisbrod (1988) dismisses comparative efficiency research as systematically biased by failure to take into account subtle differences in output mix and clientele.

Service and client mix. Research on hospitals demonstrates that NPOs have lower prices and offer slightly more unprofitable services and care to nonpaying patients than do FPs (though not as much as publics), but care quality (as measured) is not systematically influenced by form (Gray 1986, 1990; Marmor et al 1987). Several studies report NP nursing homes superior to FP in care-quality measures (Gray 1986). Weisbrod suggests that FPs attend to easily observable aspects of quality (which may influence revenues), but economize (and are thus inferior to NPs) on less visible quality aspects: he and Schlesinger (1986) interpret findings that FP nursing homes have fewer code violations but more customer complaints than do secular NPOs as supporting this view. (Church-owned NPOs have fewer than either.) Private schools have lower student-teacher ratios than public, a sign of either higher quality or lower productivity (Levy 1987). Coleman et al (1982) found that comparable students learn somewhat more in NP than in public schools, although effects differ by student type and between Catholic and other NPOs. Institutional context is critical: NP hospitals accepting federal Hill-Burton construction funds were obliged to provide services to the indigent; by contrast, reliance of NP hospitals on bond issues for capital places a premium on minimizing financial risk (Gray 1990).

Human resources. Each of two contrary hypotheses receives some support. (Possible heterogeneity of samples and unmeasured sources of variation dictate caution in interpretation.) *Rent theories* reason that NPOs use tax savings to pay higher wages than FP competitors. Most hospital studies find wages higher in NPOs than in FPs (Steinberg 1987): *Recruitment theories* hold that NPO employees are willing to work for less because their values differ systematically from those of employees of FP firms: Religious nursing homes pay lower wages than FPs (or secular NPOs) (Borjas et al 1983); teachers forego much income to teach in NP rather than public schools (Chambers 1984). Using sophisticated estimation methods, Preston (1985, 1988) reports that NP employees value job quality more and wages less than FP staff.

Four studies of colleges and universities have explored the relationship between form and inequality. Tolbert found the ratio of female to male faculty members higher in NP than in public institutions (even controlling for female student-body share), but discovered no systematic relationship between form and gender inequality in salary (1982, 1986). Two studies (Pfeffer & Davis-Blake 1987, Pfeffer & Langton 1988) report significantly higher levels of overall salary inequality in NP than in public institutions.

Structure. Structural differences among forms reflect differences in institutional systems or environments that vary among industries (Scott & Meyer 1988). Public schools, for example, are much more likely than NPOs to be part of complex hierarchal systems; FP hospitals are more likely than NPOs to belong to large chains. Such variation has consequences at the organizational level: Public schools are structurally more complex, less coherent, and more intensely administered than NPOs (Scott & Meyer 1988). Research on structural differences in similar environments tends to report weaker effects. NP hospitals have larger and more diverse boards than do FPs (Fennell & Alexander 1987); anecdotal accounts suggest that NP board meetings are more contentious than those of FPs, and NP trustees more likely than FP directors to try to influence staff and administrators directly (Middleton 1987).

Strategy.   NPOs are believed to respond less readily than FPs to market changes, owing to different goals and less access to capital (Hansmann 1987, Steinberg 1987). NPs are larger than FPs in most industries, perhaps evidence of relative generalism (Ben-Ner & Van Hoomissen 1989). Results of several studies suggest that NPOs are less central than FPs and publics in interorganizational exchange networks (Galaskiewicz 1979, Knoke & Rogers 1979, Knoke & Wood 1981); whether this reflects the NPOs' desire for autonomy or their unattractiveness as partners (Kramer 1987) is uncertain. NPOs pursue cartelization strategies that (because they aim at donors rather than consumers) are defined as cooperation rather than restraint of trade: united fund-raising bodies are prominent vehicles (Seeley et al 1957, Polivy 1982). Again, ecological factors appear more important than generic differences.

Comment.   The research literature is vast and inconclusive. We suggest that the quest for generalizable differences among NPOs, proprietaries, and public agencies is problematic for several reasons.

Heterogeneity.   Variation *within* populations defined by legal form may swamp variation between them. Heterogeneity is also produced by variation among NPOs in resource-dependence patterns, e.g. extent of reliance on private donations (and whether these are from a few big donors or many small ones), sale of services (and whether sales are to consumers or third parties), and government assistance [and the mechanisms—grant, contract, vouchers— through which such support is tendered (Kramer 1981, Salamon 1987)]. Studies that distinguish between religious and secular NPOs often find systematic differences between them.

Unclear boundaries.   Lines between public. NP, and FP enterprise are often unclear: indeed

"publicness" is better viewed as a continuous variable than as a category (Starr & Immergut 1987, Levy 1987). Is a NP hospital run by a FP management company as "nonprofit" as one that is not? Are NPOs funded through closely monitored contracts as "private" as those receiving categorical entitlements with only superficial financial monitoring? When regulation is both detailed and uniform across provider types, behavioral correlates of form are likely to be weak.

Compositional effects.   Most important, differences in the behavior of NP and other firms in the same industry often flow from industry composition. Cross-national research makes this especially apparent: Geiger (1986) and Levy (1986a) report dramatic variation in the niches occupied by NP and FP higher education in different societies. In industries with significant direct provision by government, NPOs tend to specialize by service and clientele, and measurable differences between NP and FP providers are modest. When the state delegates service provision to NPOs, they are more heavily regulated, provide a wider range of services to a broader clientele, and differ more sharply from FPs.

A corollary is that it is hazardous to extract policy implications even from well-designed comparative performance studies. Reviewing research on comparative performance of NP and FP hospitals and nursing homes, Gray (1990) warns that we cannot assume that processes generating differences and similarities will persist far into the future.

Goals and constituencies.   If generic NP/FP differences exist, they may derive from the greater number and abstractness of the former's goals and their more complex and varied constituencies. Multiple, ambiguous goals and environmental heterogeneity yield complex administrative structures (Scott & Meyer 1990), difficulty in evaluation (Kanter & Summers 1987), internal conflict and demanding publics (Zolberg 1986), concern with legitimacy (Grønbjerg 1986), weak external boundaries (Middleton 1987), and frequent goal displacement (Sills

1957, Powell & Friedkin 1987). Whether such differences, which vary by field with regulatory policy, influence the kinds of measures upon which research has focussed is unclear. Given available evidence, one can conclude only that legal form *does* make a difference, but the difference it makes depends on the institutional and ecological structures of the industry in question.

Industry Level

In most industries, routines, programs, goals, public accounts, and structures are subject to both competitive and institutional isomorphic pressures (Hannan & Freeman 1989, DiMaggio & Powell 1983). Such pressures presumably dampen such behavioral consequences of legal form as might otherwise exist. Competition among FP and NP health-care providers, for example, is said to make the latter more socially responsible and the former more efficient than they would otherwise be (Gray 1991). Hollingsworth & Hollingsworth (1987) report declining differences on a range of structural and performance variables of NP, FP, and public hospitals between 1935 and 1979. Competition among NP and public universities yield advantages to those in each form that adopt fundraising structures pioneered by the other (Tolbert 1985).

Thus form-related differences might emerge more strongly in comparisons among industries with differing compositions in one society, or between the same industries in different places. Nonetheless, the possibility that the division of labor among forms within an industry influences all firms in similar ways merits pursuit, perhaps through qualitative and quantitative historical studies of industries during periods of change.

Societal Level

NPSs are often described as sources of diversity and innovation. They contribute to pluralism by creating centers of influence outside the state and provide vehicles through which disenfranchised groups may organize. They enlarge the menu of models among which policy makers may choose when experimenting locally with solutions to social ills (Douglas 1983, 1987; Simon 1978).

Other authors portray NPSs as reflecting elite interests (Arnove 1980, Cookson & Persell 1985, Stanfield 1984). Collins (1987) suggests that because of tax advantages accruing to donations, charity represents a form of regressive redistribution in which the rich exchange donations for entry into prestigious charitable activities; this entry in turn enhances and legitimates their social status (Ostrander 1984).

Each of these images can be amply illustrated: social movement organizations, progressive foundations, some religious schools and human-rights organizations boost diversity; boarding schools, business-supported policy research centers, and some arts organizations may reproduce patterns of inequality. (Many NPOs sustain diversity *and* privilege.) What is less clear is whether such varied activities have any *net* effect on societies, what the effect is, and how it varies cross-nationally.

Streeck & Schmitter (1985) argue that interest-mediating organizations (a category that overlaps NPOs) produce, as well as reflect, differentiated tastes and values. But the relationship between interest mediation and diversity depends on state and polity structures. Whereas in pluralist systems NPOs may enhance diversity, in corporatist systems they may develop "welfare cartels" or "supply oligopolies" of social services (Heinze & Olk 1981). Thus, under corporatism, structures meant to accommodate social conflicts and to integrate society also exercise domination and control. By contrast, in the consociational democracies of the Netherlands and Belgium, NPOs provide institutional infrastructure to segmented and potentially antagonistic publics.

In corporatist *and* consociational democracies, NPO self-governance enables the state to delegate sensitive issues to specialized agencies outside the political center. Seibel (1989) describes the NPS's "mellow weakness" as a politically attractive but ineffectual safety-valve, to which the state offloads insoluble problems (e.g. the alleviation of poverty) that would otherwise threaten its legitimacy. Estes & Alford (1990) contend that service to the state has made US NPOs more bureaucratic and, at times, more market-oriented than they would otherwise be, thus undermining their legitimacy. At the other extreme, delegating public tasks to NPOs or QUANGOs (quasi-autonomous nongovernmental organizations) may result in the emergence of policymaking circuits that compete with government (Billiet 1984).

NPOs are active in politically sensitive policy areas in liberal polities, too (Jenkins & Eckert 1986, Laumann & Knoke 1988). Meyer (1987) views NPOs as rationalizers in societies (like the United States) with weak or weakened state centers: The often-latent political functions of voluntary associations become manifest in institutionalized negotiations of organizational status groups, in which NPOs, public agencies, QUANGOs, and firms are major actors. Several political theorists warn that dense networks of private associations may contribute to the paralysis of social and political action (Lowi 1969, Olson 1982).

A variant of this theme can be found in the work of European scholars who discuss NPOs under such rubrics as "the crisis of the welfare state" (Offe 1985). In order to maintain stability and legitimacy, so the argument goes, the Keynesian welfare state delegates more and more functions to private and semipublic organizations. The state, its sovereignty over specialized constituencies reduced, then faces "steering problems" and is unable to govern. Thus, whereas Tocqueville viewed voluntary associations as indicators of the robustness of liberal democracy, such theorists see in their proliferation a sign of legitimation crisis.

Research on the role of NPOs in nonwestern societies offers support for the "diversity" argument. Fruhling (1989, 1987) describes the role of NP human-rights organizations as vehicles for opposition to Latin American authoritarian regimes and their capacity to maintain networks that are mobilized during transitions to democracy. A large literature focusses on the role of Third-World "nongovernmental" organizations in social and economic development (Anheier 1987, Smith 1990).

Comment.   NPSs are seen as protectors of both pluralism and privilege, sites of democracy and control, sources of innovation and paralysis, instruments of and competitors to states. Such arguments must be formulated more rigorously for systematic cross-national research to assess their merits. We hazard only two generalizations. First, the extent to which such roles are played depends on the manner in which NPSs are constituted in particular societies and on their relationships to other sectors. Second, NPSs are unlikely to exert strong causal effects on features of states and polities. Elites may use NPOs to further their interests but usually have more effective vehicles, e.g. laws permitting the private mobilization of dynastic capital for public purposes seem more likely to stem from than to cause upper-class power.

Conclusions

Developing a sociological theory of NPOs is difficult not just because these sectors are internally diverse, but because the nonprofit label is culturally loaded, often evoking ideological reactions. Some critics view NPOs as instruments of capital; others scorn them for evading the laws of the marketplace. For the most part, however, sociology remains a liberal discipline, and the NPS is often seen as the locus of values—voluntarism, pluralism, altruism, participation—that liberals hold dear. If academics are the prototype of the "new class," NPOs (including the universities in which they work) are prototypical new class institutions. No wonder many scholars have been too quick to apply complimentary but misleading adjectives ("voluntary," "independent," "private") to this complex and heterogeneous region of the organizational universe (Alexander 1987).

We hope the reader will take three lessons from this review, each of which militates away from broad generalization:

1. The origins and behavior of NPOs reflect not just incentive structures and utility functions, which economists emphasize,

but also institutional structures and state policies.

2. Research on NPOs can profit from an ecological approach, both conceptually (viewing differences among forms as reflecting the division of labor among them) and methodologically.

3. Modern NPSs are constituted as adjuncts to, or in opposition to, states; "nonprofit-ness" has little consistent transnational or transhistorical meaning.

Many resources are available: Balkanized literatures on specific industries and organizational data sets with neglected measures of legal form are two of the most important. Although we are skeptical about the plausibility of any *general* "theory of nonprofit organizations," we are optimistic about sociology's potential for developing a more sophisticated and more empirically informed understanding of the origins and behavior of NPOs.

Literature Cited

Aldrich, H., Staber, U., Zimmer, C., Beggs, J. 1989. *Minimalism and mortality: Patterns of disbandings among American trade associations in the 20th century.* Ms. Univ. N. Carolina

Alexander, J. A., Amburgey, T. L. 1987. The dynamics of change in the American hospital industry: Transformation or selection? *Med. Care Rev.* 44:279–321

Alexander, J. C. 1987. The social requisites for altruism and voluntarism: Some notes on what makes a sector independent. *Sociol. Theory* 5:165–71

Alford, R. R. 1975. *Health Care Politics: Ideological and Interest-Group Barriers to Reform.* Chicago: Univ. Chicago Press

Altheide, D. L. 1988. Mediating cutbacks in human services: A case study in the negotiated order. *Sociol. Q.* 29:339–55

Anheier, H. K. 1987. Indigenous voluntary associations, nonprofits and development in Africa. See Powell 1987, pp. 416–33

Anheier, H. K. 1988. *The third sector in West Germany.* Pres. Symp. on Religion and the Independent Sector. Princeton Univ., Princeton. NJ

Anheier, H. K. 1990. Themes in international research on the nonprofit sector. *The Nonprofit and Voluntary Sector Q.* 19: Forthcoming.

Anheier, H. K., Seibel, W., eds. 1990. *The Third Sector: Comparative Studies of Nonprofit Organizations.* New York: DeGruyter

Archambault, E. 1990. Decentralization and the nonprofit sector in France. In *The Third Sector: Comparative Studies of Nonprofit Organizations.* ed. H. K. Anheier, W. Seibel. New York: DeGruyter

Arnove, R. S. ed. 1980. *Philanthropy and Cultural Imperialism: Foundations at Home and Abroad.* Bloomington: Indiana Univ. Press

Bauer, R. 1987. Intermediäre Hilfesysteme personenbezogener Dienstleistungen in zehn Ländern. In *Verbandliche Wohlfahrtspflege im internationalen Vergleich.* ed. R. Bauer, A. Thränhardt, pp. 9–30. Opladen: Westdeutscher Verlag

Ben-Ner, A. 1986. Non-Profit Organizations: Why do they exist in market economies? In *The Economics of Nonprofit Institutions: Studies in Structure and Policy,* ed. S. Rose-Ackerman, pp. 94–113. New York: Oxford Univ. Press

Ben-Ner, A., Van Hoomissen, T. 1989. The relative size of the nonprofit sector in the mixed economy: Theory and estimation, Ms. Univ. Minn., Minneapolis

Billiet, J. 1984. On Belgian pillerization: Changing patterns. *Acta Politica* 19:117–28

Blau, J. 1989. The disjunctive history of U.S. museums, 1869–1959. Ms. Univ., N. Carolina, Chapel Hill

Blau, P. M. 1977. *Inequality and Heterogeneity: A Primitive Theory of Social Structure.* New York: Free

Borjas, G. J., Frech, H., Ginsburg, P. B. 1983. Property rights and wages: The case of nursing homes. *J. Human Res.* 17:231–46

Bozeman, B. 1987. *All Organizations Are Public: Bridging Public and Private Organization Theory.* San Francisco: Jossey-Bass

Brint, S. 1987. The occupational class identifications of professionals: Evidence from cluster analysis. *Res. Soc. Strat. Mobility* 6:35–57

Chambers, J. G. 1984. Patterns of compensation of public and private school teachers. Stanford Univ., Proj. Rep. No. 84–A18, Inst. Res. Educ. Finance Govern.

Coleman, J., Kilgore, S., Hoffer, T. 1982. *High School Achievement: Public, Catholic and Private Schools Compared.* New York: Basic

Collins, R. 1987. The independent sector: Altruism and culture as social products. Pres. Conf. on the Sociol. of Independent Sector, Princeton Univ. NJ

Cookson, P., Persell, C. H. 1985. *Preparing for Power: America's Elite Boarding Schools.* New York: Basic

Daniels, A. K. 1988. *Invisible Careers: Women Civic Leaders from the Volunteer World.* Chicago: Univ. Chicago Press

DiMaggio, P. J. 1987. Nonprofit organizations in the production and distribution of culture. See Powell 1987, pp. 195–220

DiMaggio, P. J. 1991. Social structure, institutions and cultural goods: The case of the U.S. In *Social Theory and Emerging Issues in a Changing Society,* ed. J. Coleman, P. Bourdieu, Forthcoming

DiMaggio, P. J., Powell, W. W. 1983. The iron cage revisited: Institutional isomorphism and collective rationality in organizational fields. *Am. Sociol. Rev.* 82:147–60

DiMaggio, P. J., Romo, F. P. 1984. The determinants of humanities educational programming in U.S. art and history museums. Rep. Natl. Endowment for the Humanities, Off. Planning Policy Assess.

Douglas, J. 1983. *Why Charity? The Case for the Third Sector.* Beverly Hills: Sage

Douglas, J. 1987. Political theories of nonprofit organization. See Powell 1987, pp. 43–54

Esping-Anderson, G. 1988. *Politics Against Markets: The Social Democratic Road to Power.* Princeton, NJ: Princeton Univ. Press

Estes, C. L., Alford R. R. 1990. Systemic crisis and the nonprofit sector: Toward a political economy of the nonprofit service health and social services sector. *Theory & Society.* Forthcoming

Fennell, M. L., Alexander, J. A. 1987. Organizational boundary spanning in institutionalized environments. *Acad. Manage. J.* 30:456–76

Forsé, M. 1984. Le création d'associations: Un indicateur de changement social. *Observations et Diagnostics Economiques* 6:125–45

Freidson, E. 1986. *Professional Powers: A Study of the Institutionalization of Formal Knowledge.* Chicago: Univ. Chicago Press

Fruhling, H. 1987. Non-governmental human rights organizations and redemocratization in Brazil. Yale Prog. Non-Profit Organ. Work. Pap. No. 124

Fruhling, H. 1989. Nonprofit organizations as opposition to authoritarian rule: The case of human rights organizations in Chile. In *The Nonprofit Sector in International Perspective: Studies in Comparative Culture and Policy,* ed. E. James, pp. 358–76. New York: Oxford Univ. Press

Galaskiewicz, J. 1979. *Exchange Networks and Community Politics.* Beverly Hills: Sage

Galaskiewicz, J. 1985. *Social Organization of an Urban Grants Economy: A Study of Business Philanthropy and Nonprofit Organizations.* Orlando: Academic Press

Geiger, R. 1986. *Private Sectors in Higher Education: Structure, Function and Change in Eight Countries.* Ann Arbor: Univ. Michigan Press

Gray, B. H., ed. 1986. *For-Profit Enterprise in Health Care.* Washington: National Acad. Press

Gray, B. H. 1990. *Profit, Corporate Change and Accountability in American Health.* Rep. Submitted 20th Century Fund

Grønbjerg, K. A. 1986. Communities and nonprofit organizations: Interlocking ecological systems. Pap. pres. ann. meet. Am. Sociol. Assoc.

Grønbjerg, K. A. 1987. Patterns of institutional relations in the welfare state: Public mandates and the nonprofit sector. *J. Voluntary Action Res.* 16:64–80

Grosfeld, I., Smolar, A. 1988. The independent sector in Poland: Between omnipresent state and weak market. Presented at Symp. on Religious and the Independent Sector. Princeton Univ., NJ

Hall, P. D. 1982. *The Organization of American Culture, 1700–1900: Institutions, Elites, and the Origins of American Nationality.* New York: New York Univ. Press

Hannan, M., J. Freeman. 1989. *Organizational Ecology.* Cambridge: Harvard Univ. Press

Hansmann, H. 1980. The role of nonprofit enterprise. *Yale Law J.* 89:835–901

Hansmann, H. 1981. Nonprofit enterprise in the performing arts. *Bell J. Econ.* 12:341–61

Hansmann, H. 1985. The effect of tax exemption and other factors on competition between nonprofit and for-profit enterprise. Yale Prog. on Non-Profit Organ. Work. Pap. No. 65

Hansmann, H. 1986. Status organizations. *J. Law. Econ., Organ.* 2:119–30

Hansmann, H. 1987. Economic theories of nonprofit organization. See Powell 1987, pp. 27–42

Hansmann, H. 1989. The economics and ethics of markets for human organs. *J. Health Policy, Politics Law.* Forthcoming

Heinze, R., Olk, T. 1981. Die Wohlfahrtsverbände im System sozialer Dienstleistungspoduktion: Zur Entstehung und Struktur der bundesrepublikanischen Verbändewohlfahrt. *Kölner Zeitschr. für Soziol Sozialpsychol.* 33:94–114

Hodgkinson, V., Weitzman, M. 1986. *Dimensions of the Independent Sector.* Washington: Ind. Sector

Hollingsworth, R., Hollingsworth, M. E. 1987. *Controversy about American Hospitals: Funding, Own-*

ership and Performance. Washington: Am. Enterprise Inst.

Hood, C., Schuppert G., eds. 1988. *Delivering Public Services in Western Europe: Sharing Western European Experience of Para-Government Organization.* London: Sage

Hunter, A. 1981. The neighborhood movement as communal class politics. Ms. Northwestern Univ.

James, E. 1987a. The public/private division of responsibility for education: An international comparison. *Econ. Educ. Rev.* 6:1–14

James, E. 1987b. The nonprofit sector in comparative perspective. See Powell 1987, pp. 397–415

James, E., ed. 1989. *Nonprofit Organizations in International Perspective: Studies in Comparative Culture and Policy.* New York: Oxford Univ. Press

James, E., Rose-Ackerman, S. 1986. *The Nonprofit Enterprise in Market Economies.* London: Harwood Acad. Publishers.

James, T., Levin, H. M. 1986. *Comparing Public and Private Schools.* London: Falmer

Jencks, C. 1987. Who gives to what? See Powell 1987, pp. 321–39

Jenkins, J. C., Eckert, C. M. 1986. Channeling black insurgency: Elite patronage and professional social movement organizations in the development of the black civil-rights movement. *Am. Sociol. Rev.* 51:812–29

Jenkins, J. C. 1987. Nonprofit organizations and policy advocacy. See Powell 1987, pp. 289–318. New Haven: Yale Univ. Press

Jepperson, R., Meyer, J. W. 1990. The public order and the construction of formal organizations. In *The New Institutionalism in Organization Theory,* ed. W. W. Powell & P. J. DiMaggio, Chicago: Univ. Chicago Press. Forthcoming

Kanter, R. M., Summers, D. V. 1987. Doing well while doing good: Dilemmas of performance measurement in nonprofit organizations and the need for a multiple constituency approach. See Powell 1987, pp. 154–66

Katzenstein, P. 1984. *Corporatism and Change: Austria, Switzerland and the Politics of Industry.* Ithaca: Cornell Univ. Press

Knapp, M., Robertson, E., Thomason, C. 1990. Public money, voluntary action: Whose welfare? In *The Third Sector: Comparative Studies of Nonprofit Organizations,* ed. H. K. Anheier, W. Seibel. New York: DeGruyter

Knoke, D., Rogers, D. L. 1979. A block model analysis of interorganizational relations. *Sociol. Soc. Res.* 64:28–50

Knoke, D., Wood, J. B. 1981. *Organized for Action: Commitment in Voluntary Associations.* New Brunswick: Rutgers Univ. Press

Kramer, R. M. 1981. *Voluntary Agencies in the Welfare State.* Berkeley: Univ. Calif. Press

Kramer, R. M. 1987. Voluntary agencies and personal social services. See Powell 1987, pp. 240–57

Larson, M. S. 1977. *The Rise of Professionalism: A Sociological Analysis.* Berkeley: Univ. California Press

Laumann, E. O., Knoke, D. 1988. *The Organizational State.* Madison: Univ. Wisconsin Press

Levy, D. C. 1986a. *Higher Education and the State in Latin America: Private Challenges to Public Dominance.* Chicago: Univ. Chicago Press

Levy, D. C., ed. 1986b. *Private Education: Studies in Choice and Public Policy.* New York: Oxford Univ. Press

Levy, D. C. 1987. A comparison of private and public educational organizations. See Powell 1987, pp. 258–76

Lijphart, A. 1984. *Democracies: Patterns of Majoritarian and Consensus Government in 21 Countries.* New Haven: Yale Univ. Press

Lowi, T. J. 1969. *The End of Liberalism: Ideology, Politics and the Crisis of Public Authority.* New York: Norton

Macy, M. 1988. New-class dissent among social-cultural specialists: The effects of occupational self-direction and location in the public sector. *Sociol. Forum* 3:325–56

Majone, G. 1984. Professionalism and nonprofit organizations. *J. Health Policy, Politics and Law* 8:639–59

Marmor, T. R., Schlesinger, M., Smithey, R. 1987. Nonprofit organizations and health care. See Powell 1987. pp. 221–39

Marrett, C.B. 1980. Influences on the rise of new organizations: The formation of women's medical societies. *Admin. Sci. Q.* 25:185–99

Marschall, M. 1990. The nonprofit sector in a centrally planned economy. In *The Third Sector: Comparative Studies of Nonprofit Organizations,* ed. H. K. Anheier, W. Seibel. New York: DeGruyter

McCarthy, K. 1982. *Noblesse Oblige: Charity and Cultural Philanthropy in Chicago, 1849–1929.* Chicago: Univ. Chicago Press

McPherson, J. M. 1983. An ecology of affiliation. *Am. Sociol. R.* 48:519–32

Meyer, J. W. 1987. The independent sector: Tocquevillian centralization. Pres. Symp. on Sociol. Ind. Sector. Princeton Univ., NJ

Meyer, J. W., Scott, W. R. 1983. *Organizational Environments: Ritual and Rationality.* Beverly Hills: Sage

Middleton, M. 1987. Nonprofit boards of directors: Beyond the governance function. In *The Nonprofit Sector: A Research Handbook,* ed. W. W. Powell, pp. 141–53. New Haven: Yale Univ. Press

Milofsky, C. 1987. Neighborhood based organizations: A market analogy. See Powell 1987, pp. 277–95

Minkoff, D. 1988. From service provision to institutional advocacy: The shifting legitimacy of organizational forms, 1955–78. Pres. at 1989 Annu. Meet. Am. Sociol. Assoc.

Murnane, R. J. 1986. Comparisons of private and public schools: The critical role of regulations. In *Private Education: Studies in Choice and Public Policy,* ed. D. Levy. pp. 138–52. New York: Oxford Univ. Press

Offe, C. 1985. *Disorganized Capitalism.* Cambridge: MIT Press

Olson, M. 1982. *The Rise and Decline of Nations: Economic Growth, Stagflation, and Social Rigidities.* New Haven: Yale Univ. Press

Ostrander, S. A. 1984. *Women of the Upper Class.* Philadelphia: Temple Univ. Press

Ostrander, S. A. 1987. Elite domination in private social agencies: How it happens and how it is challenged. In *Power Elites and Organizations,* ed. G. W. Domhoff, T. R. Dye, pp. 85–102. Newbury Park: Sage

Pauly, M. P., Redisch, M. R. 1973. The not-for-profit hospital as a physician's cooperative. *Am. Econ. Rev.* 63:87–99

Perrow, C. 1963. Goals and power structures: A historical case study. In *The Hospital in Modern Society,* ed. E. Friedson, pp. 112–46. New York: Macmillan.

Peterson, R. A. 1986. From impressario to arts administrator: Formal accountability in nonprofit cultural organizations. In *Nonprofit Enterprise in the Arts: Studies in Mission and Constraint,* ed. P. J. DiMaggio, pp. 161–83. New York: Oxford Univ. Press

Pfeffer, J., Davis-Blake, A. 1987. *Determinants of salary inequality in organizations.* Ms. Stanford Univ., Calif.

Pfeffer, J., Langton, N. 1988. Wage inequality and the organization of work: The case of academic departments. *Admin. Sci. Q.* 33:588–606

Polivy, D. K. 1982. A study of the admissions policies and practices of eight local United Way organizations. Yale Program on Non-Profit Organ. Work. Pap. No. 62 New Haven

Powell, W. W. 1985. *Getting into Print: The Decision-Making Process in Scholarly Publishing.* Chicago: Univ. of Chicago Press

Powell, W. W. ed. 1987. *The Nonprofit Sector: A Research Handbook.* New Haven: Yale Univ. Press

Powell, W. W., Friedkin, R. J. 1987. Organizational change in nonprofit organizations. See Powell 1987, pp. 180–94

Preston, A. 1985. Women in the white collar nonprofit sector: The best option or the only option? Yale Prog. Non-Profit Organ. Work. Pap. No. 101

Preston, A. 1988. The effects of property rights on labor costs of nonprofit firms: An application to the day care industry. *J. Industrial Econ.* 36:337–50

Provan, K. C. 1980. Board power and organizational effectiveness among human service agencies. *Acad. Manage. J.* 23:221–36

Rosas, A. 1984. Notes on the legal status of national Red Cross Societies. In *Studies and Essays on International Humanitarian Law and Red Cross Principles,* ed. C. Swinarski, pp. 954–73. Geneva: Nijhoff

Rose-Ackerman, S., ed. 1986. *The Economics of Nonprofit Institutions: Studies in Structure and Policy.* New York: Oxford Univ. Press

Rothschild-Whitt, J. 1999. The collectivist organization. *Am. Sociol. R.* 44:509–28

Salamon, L. M. 1981. Rethinking public management: Third-party government and the changing forms of public action. *Public Policy* 29:255–75

Salamon, L. M. 1987. Partners in public service: The scope and theory of government-nonprofit relations. See Powell 1987, pp. 99–117

Salamon, L. M., Abrahamson. A. J. 1982. *The Federal Budget and the Nonprofit Sector.* Washington: Urban Inst. Press

Salzman, H., Domhoff, G. W. 1983. Nonprofit organizations and the corporate community. *Soc. Sci. Hist.* 7:205–16

Scott, W. R. 1983. Health care organizations in the 1980s: The convergence of public and professional control systems. In *Organizational Environments: Ritual and Rationality,* ed. J. W. Meyer, W. R. Scott, pp. 99–127. Beverly Hills: Sage

Scott, W. R., Meyer, J. W. 1988. Environmental linkages and organizational complexity: Public and private schools. In *Comparing Public and Private Schools: Vol. 1, Institutions and Organizations,* ed. T. James, H. M, Levin., pp. 128–160. New York: Falmer

Scott, W. R., Meyer, J. W. 1990. The organization of societal sectors: Propositions and early evidence. In *The New Institutionalism in Organization Theory,* ed. W. W. Powell and P. J. DiMaggio. Chicago: Univ. Chicago Press. Forthcoming

Seeley, J. R., Junker, B. R., James, R. W. 1957. *Community Chest.* Toronto: Univ. Toronto Press

Seibel, W. 1989. The function of mellow weakness: Nonprofit organizations as problem nonsolvers in Germany. In *The Nonprofit Sector in International Perspective: Studies in Comparative Culture and Policy.* ed. E. James., p. 177–92. New York: Oxford Univ. Press.

Sills, D. L. 1957. *The Volunteers: Means and Ends in a National Organization.* Glencoe: Free

Simon, J. G. 1978. Charity and dynasty under the federal tax system. *Probate Lawyer* 5:1–92

Simon, J. G. 1987. The tax treatment of nonprofit organizations: A review of federal and state policies. See Powell 1987, pp. 67–98

Singh, J., Tucker, D., Meinhard, A. 1990. Institutional change and ecological dynamics. In *The New Institutionalism in Organizational Theory,* ed. W. W. Powell, P. J. DiMaggio. Chicago: Univ. of Chicago Press. Forthcoming.

Smith, B. 1990. *More than Altruism: The Politics of Private Foreign Aid.* Princeton, NJ: Princeton Univ. Press

Smith, B. L. R. ed. 1975. *The New Political Economy: The Public Use of the Private Sector.* New York: Wiley

Stanfield, J. S. 1984. *Philanthropy and Jim Crow in American Social Science.* Westport: Greenwood

Starr. P. 1982. *The Social Transformation of American Medicine.* New York: Basic

Starr, P., Immergut, E. 1987. Health care and the boundaries of politics. In *The Changing Boundaries of the Political,* ed. C. Maier. New York: Cambridge Univ. Press

Steinberg, R. 1987. Nonprofit organizations and the market. See Powell 1987, pp. 118–38

Stinchcombe, A. J. 1965. Organizations and social structure. In *Handbook of Organizations,* ed. J. G. March, pp. 142–93. Chicago: Rand McNally

Story, R. 1980. *The Forging of an Aristocracy: Harvard and Boston's Upper Class, 1800–1870.* Middletown, Conn.: Wesleyan Univ. Press

Streek, W., Schmitter, P. C. 1985. *Private Interest Government: Beyond Market and State.* Beverly Hills: Sage

Titmuss, R. 1971. *The Gift Relationship: From Human Blood to Social Policy.* New York: Vintage

Tolbert, P. S. 1982. *Sources of organizational demography: Faculty sex ratios in colleges and universities.* Ms. Cornell Univ., Ithaca

Tolbert, P. S. 1985. Resource dependence and institutional environments: Sources of administrative structure in institutions of higher education. *Admin. Sci. Q.* 30:1–13

Tolbert, P. S. 1986. Organizations and inequality: Sources of earnings differences among male and female faculty. *Sociol. Educ.* 59:227–36

Useem, M. 1984. *The Inner Circle: Business and Politics in the U.S. and U.K.* New York: Oxford Univ. Press

Useem, M. 1987. Corporate philanthropy. See Powell 1987, pp. 340–59

Van Til, J. 1988. *Mapping the Third Sector: Voluntarism in a Changing Social Economy.* New York: Foundation Ctr.

Venanzoni, G. 1981. *Private Non-Profit Institutions Serving Households.* Final Rep. to Statist. Off. Eur. Commun., Luxembourg

Ware, A. 1989. *Between Profit and State: Intermediate Organizations in Britain and the United States.* Cambridge: Polity

Weisbrod, B. A. 1975. Toward a theory of the voluntary non-profit sector in a three sector economy. In *Altruism, Morality and Economic Theory,* ed. E. Phelps, pp. 171–96. New York: Russell Sage

Weisbrod, B. A. 1977. *The Voluntary Nonprofit Sector: An Economic Analysis.* Lexington: Heath

Weisbrod, B. A. 1988. *The Nonprofit Economy.* Cambridge: Harvard Univ. Press

Weisbrod, B. A., Schlesinger, M. 1986. Public, private, nonprofit ownership and the response to asymmetric information: The case of nursing homes. In *The Economics of Nonprofit Institutions: Studies in Structure and Policy,* ed. S. Rose-Ackerman, pp. 133–51.

Wievel, W., Hunter, A. 1985. The interorganizational network as a resource: A comparative case study on organizational genesis. *Admin. Sci. Q.* 30:482–96

Wolch, J. R. 1990. *The Shadow State: Government and the Voluntary Sector in Transition.* New York: Foundation Ctr.

Zald, M. N. 1967. Urban differentiation, characteristics of boards of directors and organizational effectiveness. *Am. J. Sociol.* 73:261–71

Zolberg, V. L. 1986. Tensions of mission in American art museums. In *Nonprofit Enterprise in the Arts: Studies in Mission and Constraint,* ed. P. J. DiMaggio, pp. 184–198. New York: Oxford Univ. Press

Zucker, L. G., Taka, P. L. 1987. Modeling institutional and task environment change: Period and cohort effects on innovation in hospital organizations, 1959–1979. Pap. pres. NSF/ASA conference on institutional theory. Center for Advanced Study in the Behav. Sci. Stanford, Calif.

CHAPTER 24

Perspectives on Organizational Governance: Some Effects on Government-Nonprofit Relations

J. STEVEN OTT

Without question, the distinction between government and nonprofit organizations has faded and become more blurred in recent years (Cnaan 1990; Ferris and Graddy 1989; Van Til 1988), at least partially because of recent trends toward increased interdependence (Ostrander, Langton, and Van Til 1987) and coproduction (Brudney 1990a). Yet, many distinctions have not been erased, particularly around nonprofit organizations that involve volunteers extensively in their activities and whose organizational cultures contain beliefs, values, and basic assumptions associated with voluntary participation. People who have spent time in and around voluntary nonprofit organizations know that these organizations seldom operate, feel, or act like government agencies. Key actors do not relate to each other or to the organization in the same ways as they do in the more instrumentally rational (Simon 1976), bureaucratic-type organizations that are characteristic of public sector organizations. Things usually do not get done in the same ways, people and groups do not fill similar roles, possess similar power, or share the same service- or bureaucracy-related values (Brudney 1990b).

Our own personal experiences affirm what many theoreticians and researchers have been telling us: Despite the blurring between sectors, voluntary nonprofit organizations are not the same things as government organizations (De-Hoog 1986; Kettl 1988; Kettner and Martin 1989; Morgan and England 1988; NAPA 1989). Yet, consciously or unconsciously our mental images and our expectations often are of pyramidal, bureaucratic, goal-oriented, instrumental organizations. This expectation is particularly ironic considering the overwhelming evidence that even the most bureaucratic of our organizations—government agencies—seldom act in ways the rational, instrumental organizational theories would have us believe. However, our mental images and expectations of organizations are deeply ingrained because they are products of our culture and traditions. We cling tenaciously to the "deeply embedded cultural assumption . . . that all organizations are fundamentally **hierarchial** in nature" (Schein 1989, 63). The hierarchical goal-oriented model matches well with our Western cultural norms and expectations. We are a logical, scientific, purposeful, rationally oriented society. Thus, for symbolic reasons (as well as rational reasons), people in and around government agencies and nonprofit organizations alike appear to need to conceive—to believe in—our public and nonprofit organizations and officials as agents in diligent, efficient, and effective pursuit of rational goals. The goal-oriented, instrumental model is comfortable and comforting both for people who support them and people who benefit from them.

This paper presents a theory or perspective to help in understanding voluntary nonprofit organizations—a type of nonprofit organization with which many units of government contract to provide services. It proposes that rational instrumental hierarchical theories of organization are not applicable. Instead, the mental image of a voluntary nonprofit organization as an atom is more useful for understanding relationships among its components and constituencies, and therefore its decisions and actions. The practical implications are substantial for governance roles, allocations of power, resources, rights, and functions among activities and groups. Thus, the theory presented in this paper is an attempt to help make sense of the sometimes confusing and apparently irrational behavior that government administrators, new members of boards of directors, and others may experience working with voluntary nonprofit organizations.

Definitions (and Concepts)

A *voluntary nonprofit organization* is defined here as a nonprofit organization that receives significant support from voluntary contributions of time, effort, and/or money, and its organizational culture contains beliefs, values, and basic assumptions associated with voluntary participation.[1] This definition includes many large, well established donatively supported organizations as well as countless small safe-houses, counseling centers, cause advocacy groups, support networks, crisis intervention hot-lines, and employment training centers that use volunteers as trainers or counselors and which attract charitable contributions.

In contrast, *commercial nonprofit organizations* derive their "income from the sale of services and

frequently compete with for-profit firms" (Hansmann 1989, 91). Some nonprofit organizations are purely voluntary, and many are purely commercial. Most, however, have some elements of both types, and it is useful to think of nonprofit organizations as being at points along a continuum from voluntary to commercial, rather than as absolute types. The lack of purity does not invalidate the reason for drawing the distinction. The history, traditions, and culture of organizations influence the way constituencies see and relate to them (Ott 1989a; Schein 1992). We should expect a nonprofit organization that operated for decades as a voluntary nonprofit, but that recently has become involved in commercial activities, to act more like a voluntary nonprofit organization than a nonprofit organization would that is engaged in the same commercial activities but lacks a history, tradition, and culture steeped in the values of voluntarism.

This paper's exclusive focus on voluntary nonprofit organizations does not exclude the many nonprofit organizations with long histories, deep traditions, and cultures steeped in voluntaristic values, that are responding to current fiscal pressures by aggressively pursuing opportunities to provide human services through contracts with government agencies (Hansmann 1989; Hodgkinson and Weitzman 1988).

Governance is:

> The state of being under the control of higher legal or political authority. Thus citizens are under the governance of their national government, agencies are under the governance of their jurisdictions, and police officers are under the governance of their department.
>
> The collective actions of a board of directors, board of trustees, or a board of governors in providing policy guidance to the organization that the board was established to manage (Shafritz 1988, 249).
>
> The function of oversight and administration that takes place when a group of people come together to legally incorporate under the laws of a state for a nonprofit organizational purpose (Gies, Ott, and Shafritz 1990, 178).

Constituencies is used here in its broad sense to mean people, groupings of people, and groups who have a stake in an organization—who affect and/or are affected by it. Constituencies include external groups (for example, contracting agencies and suppliers) as well as internal participants, clients, and members of clients' families. Thus the term is similar in use to Mitroff's (1983) *stakeholders.*

A Theory of Voluntary Nonprofit Organizations: Atoms As an Analogy (or Model)

Voluntary nonprofit organizations are easier to understand if one thinks of them as being constructed and acting more like atoms than pyramids. Constituencies circle the central core of an organization in patterned "orbiting paths" analogous to electrons orbiting the nucleus of an atom. The organization consists of the core (activities), circling constituencies, and the spaces (as well as the distances) in and among the component elements. The orbiting path of some constituencies remains closer to the core than others, reflecting higher levels of involvement, commitment, self-perceived centrality, and psychological ownership. The orbital paths of most constituencies are elliptical rather than circular, because people alternately move closer and farther away from a voluntary nonprofit organization's activities (core).[2]

The atom analogy is used in this paper to help communicate a theory or model of voluntary nonprofit organizations, but it is only an analogy (see Figure 24.1). Analogies are partial similarities between like features of two things on which a comparison may be based. As is true of all analogies, the atom analogy is an imperfect representation. The movements of atoms, nuclei, and electrons are regular because they are governed by physical laws. The actions of human constituencies around voluntary organizations are not. Thus, despite the communicative usefulness of the analogy, it has limitations.

In this analogous model, the structure, offices, goals, or fiscal resources *are not* its core. Instead, the nucleus is its activities: the myriad

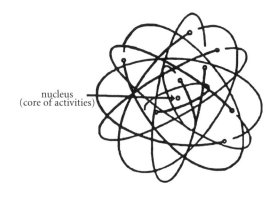

FIGURE 24.1   The Atom Analogy Model

events, programs, meetings, and functions in which constituencies engage to satisfy their interests. This imagery of an atom has many advantages over the pyramidal bureaucratic form of organization for visualizing and understanding behavior and relationships in and of voluntary nonprofit organizations.

1. Constituencies of voluntary nonprofit organizations are not ordered in neat, hierarchical positions or slots. They and their behavior are messy and usually patterned mostly by chance. They circle, move in and out; they are "all over and all around." Voluntary nonprofit organization rarely can be understood by looking "up" the organization chart.

2. An atom continues to exist as long as electrons are held in orbit by their attraction to the nucleus' positive charge. Likewise, a voluntary nonprofit organization will survive as long as its activities continue to satisfy the interests of its constituencies, As a corollary, when an organization's activities no longer satisfy constituencies' interests, its activities must change or it will cease to exist. This is how voluntary nonprofit organizations "die."

3. Just as an atom does not depend on the presence of any particular individual electron for its existence, the ongoing survival of a voluntary nonprofit organization does not depend upon the continuing

participation of any one or two specific constituencies. Obviously, it must have **some** constituencies, and the withdrawal of a group or groups will affect its character, nature, size, shape, and style. However, the organization will continue to exist (in some altered form) as long as constituencies perceive that they are benefiting from its activities and thus continue to orbit in its field.

The board of directors in most voluntary nonprofit organizations is not the small tip of an organization pyramid with authority over staff members and volunteers that is based on dependence (Herman and Heimovics 1991; Pearce 1982). In reality, the board of directors exercises authority over the staff and volunteers only occasionally and under unusual circumstances (Harris 1989). The directors are only one of many (albeit usually important) constituencies orbiting the organization's activities. Under ordinary circumstances, staff usually prepares budgets, drafts board policy, and engineers board decisions. However, members of the board and employees usually act or role play as though an authority relationship exists, because it is simply assumed this is the way things should be. I propose that we have great difficulty conceiving of a nonprofit organization that does not have a board of directors with the "divine right" (Schein 1989) to make fundamental decisions that affect other constituencies' abilities to satisfy their interests—whether or not the directors have credibility, sensitivity, or knowledge of the issues they decide. We simply assume that boards are responsible for core identity-creating and maintaining functions including strategic planning, and establishing and articulating organizational goals and policy. And, assumptions create realities.

4. A voluntary nonprofit organization's identity is altered when the paths of some constituencies' orbits alternately move closer and farther away from the core, other constituencies leave the atom's field

(temporarily or permanently dissociate), and new constituencies choose to associate. Obviously, when staff turns over, board members resign and are replaced, volunteers withdraw, new volunteers with different interests associate, or clients decide not to participate in programs, a voluntary nonprofit organization undergoes changes. New coalitions of constituencies may cause changes in activities, programs, goals, the culture or character of the organization, or the process by which resources are allocated (Ott 1989b). Not even an organization's mission statement or its original cause is necessarily safe from alteration. Despite the amount or importance of the changes, however, a voluntary nonprofit organization will continue to exist, even if it is in an altered form, for as long as some of its constituencies continue to benefit from its activities. Activities are the nucleus of a voluntary nonprofit organization.

There are convincing theoretical reasons why the atom-analogy theory is highly applicable to voluntary nonprofit organizations, the most important of which is the voluntary nature of relationships between constituencies and an organization. Constituencies can—and frequently do—initiate and withdraw, reduce and increase their participation. Voluntary participation is a prerequisite to feelings of involvement with and psychological ownership of an organization. Without feelings of involvement and psychological ownership, conflict often surfaces among constituencies. It becomes difficult for them to reach agreement on shared activities. Lack of agreement on shared activities jeopardizes the ability of constituencies to satisfy their personal interests, and causes them to limit or withdraw their participation. When constituencies withdraw, established patterns of interdependence are disrupted, power arrangements are realigned and, most importantly, a voluntary nonprofit organization's reason for existence is jeopardized. Voluntariness is essential to the survival of organizations, and the preservation of voluntary relations may be a more basic issue for voluntary nonprofit organizations than is goal attainment (Keeley 1988).

Basic Purposes of Voluntary Nonprofit Organizations— Per the Atom-Analogy Model

People (and groupings of people) with similar interests (**constituencies**) associate with a voluntary nonprofit organization for two primary reasons: (1) They support and want to advance its broadly defined common cause or mission (instrumental purpose), and (2) to satisfy their own personal interests through its activities. Although voluntary nonprofit organizations are established and sustained by people who share a broad common purpose or cause, **activities** are their reason for being (Keeley 1988). A statement of general purpose is always included in founding documents, such as the articles of incorporation, bylaws, and application for tax-exempt status, and in the mission statement. The purpose as stated in these documents, however, is rarely more than minimally limiting. Unlike public agencies, nonprofit organizations are not legislatively mandated to provide specific types of services to identified populations. Mission statements do not even bind an organization or its future participants to a current identity or general direction. Rather, they reflect the current vision of mission as articulated by current constituencies. Within a voluntary nonprofit organization's original purpose and its mission statement, there is extensive latitude to engage in a smorgasbord of activities and to pursue a broad spectrum of ends.

The notion of **satisfaction of interests** or **personal interests** is central to the model of voluntary nonprofit organization proposed here. It is not used with negative connotations, such as **selfishness.** Instead, **satisfaction of personal interests** connotes the broad range of needs and wants that cause people and constituencies to join and remain associated with a voluntary nonprofit organization. It is a neutral concept, somewhat akin to the economist's **utilitarian behavior.** Almost without exception, con-

stituencies of voluntary nonprofit organizations seek to satisfy multiple interests, and the interests virtually always overlap somewhat with those of other constituencies. However, most constituencies also have interests that are unique to them—that they alone seek to satisfy through association with the organization (Connolly, Conlon, and Deutsch 1980). Most constituencies' interests fall into three broad categories:

- *A desire to advance the cause or purpose that is the organization's object of concern* or purpose, most typically involving the prevention or elimination of the causes or ameliorating the impacts of a particular disease, condition, or behavior, such as hunger, child abuse, ongoing support to families of people with mental illness, the level of pollution in the air or water, or a family temporarily in distress.
- *A desire to improve the quality of life and social democracy in a community* through participative action. For example, "bring the citizens together to solve the problem in city hall, and in the process strengthen the community bonds;" or, "get people from the different neighborhoods to work together on allocating grant funds and, while they are doing it, learn about each other and how they think and see things."
- *A desire to advance one's own circumstances.* For example, spend time with people who value the same things or share similar concerns or circumstances, develop one's own leadership skills, earn a living as a professional in an organization that is more flexible and caring than a government agency, build a grass-roots base for a political campaign, or learn how a service delivery system works in order to be a better advocate for a disabled family member.

Most voluntary nonprofit organizations are only secondarily instruments for accomplishing instrumentally rational goals and objectives.

This is not their primary purpose, as the rational, goal-oriented theories of organization would have us believe. It is more accurate to speak of constituencies' goals **for** an organization rather than of **organizational goals.** Organizations do not have goals; organizations are not living organisms (Keeley 1980, 1988). They are artificial entities (March and Simon 1958; Simon 1981)—creations of our collective minds and of laws. An organization's goals are nothing more than the goals **for** it as espoused by a currently dominant coalition of constituencies. In contrast, the diverse interests (goals) of people who choose to associate with a voluntary nonprofit organization are real in their behavioral consequences (Berger and Luckmann 1966; Thomas 1923). They explain why constituencies join and remain associated with a particular voluntary organization. The interests of constituencies—their goals **for** an organization—are satisfied primarily through its activities. Even though constituencies' goals for an organization usually differ widely, their interests are met through shared common organizational activities, within the broad parameters of its broad purpose and mission.

This perspective, that organizations are essentially unwritten agreements for the satisfaction of constituencies' interests through activities, is not new. Thirty years ago, Cyert and March (1963) described organizations as coalitions of self-interested participants and the behavior of firms as the result of agreements to cooperate among participant groups. In a similar vein, the "negotiated order theorists" (Day and Day 1977; Strauss, Schatzman, Bucher, et al. 1963) view organizations as legal fictions within which "contractual relations" provide a framework for the complex negotiation processes through which conflicting objectives of constituencies are brought into equilibrium (Jensen and Meckling 1976). Even everyday working relations are seen as the products of tentative agreements about lines of behavior that are reached through bargaining (Strauss 1978). Recently, several authors have described the multiple and conflicting constituencies that comprise nonprofit organizations, each with its own goals and its criteria of effectiveness (Connolly, Conlon and Deutsch 1980; Hatten 1982; Kanter and Summers 1987; Wortman 1983).

Unfortunately, theorists who describe organizations as coalitions of self-interested participants, including Cyert and March and the negotiated order theorists, overlook an important issue: voluntary association. They require (Strauss 1978) or simply assume (Hessen 1979a, 1979b; Pilon 1979) the existence of voluntary relations between constituencies and organizations. Even though some constituencies of public agencies enjoy somewhat voluntary relationships (ability to associate and withdraw), it is naive to assume that voluntary constituency-to-organization relations are commonplace around governmental organizations. Voluntary relations can only be assumed to exist widely among constituency groups of voluntary nonprofit organizations. Most constituencies of voluntary nonprofit organizations can, and often do, withdraw their support and participation when their psychological contracts with the organization are violated in fact or in perception. Even paid employees, who typically are among the least voluntary constituencies of organizations, tend to view their participation in nonprofit voluntary organizations as at least quasi-voluntary. Employee commitment to voluntary nonprofit organizations and their general causes usually is high. People work here first for **psychic income** (O'Neill 1989, 272). They care professionally about the organization's clientele and its cause. In Etzioni's typology, staff involvement is **moral** rather than **alienative** or **calculative** (1975, 12). This unique characteristic—voluntary association with freedom to withdraw from participation—is what renders the instrumentally rational bureaucratic theories inapplicable and requires an alternate, more applicable, and practical theory of voluntary nonprofit organization.

Conclusion

The analogy of an atom provides a practical framework for thinking about the structure, relationships, rights and privileges, and thus behavior of voluntary nonprofit organizations. The rational instrumental hierarchical model of bureaucratic organization that reflects our culture's dominant expectation about how those organizations **should** look and act is not applicable to voluntary nonprofit organizations. It simply does not fit the realities. Under this model, boards of directors do not necessarily speak for or act with authority on behalf of a voluntary nonprofit organization. All constituencies—including boards of directors— must earn the right to participate (and the level of participation) in deciding an organization's activities and directions, under rules (norms and criteria) that reflect the organization's most important values, beliefs, and assumptions (organizational cultures) as well as its survival needs.

Notes

1. This definition is narrower than "voluntary agency," as the term is used in Great Britain to mean "nongovernment, non-profit-seeking organizations that have their own governing bodies composed of people who serve in a voluntary capacity. Voluntary agencies may or may not use volunteers to carry out the work of the organization" (Harris 1989, 331).

2. The model and its assumptions are detailed in Ott 1991. However, three assumptions are absolutely basic to the model and need to be introduced here. First, the most fundamental assumption involves the extent to which important constituencies associate voluntarily with and are free to disassociate from an organization. The second basic assumption concerns the level of involvement with "psychological ownership" of, or "stake" in an organization's activities that important constituencies perceive they have. The third involves the extent to which an organization's goals and activities are imposed on it by external constituencies (e.g., a legislature) versus developed by various coalitions of internal, semi-internal, and external constituencies. The three assumptions should be considered simultaneously. Thus, if the important constituencies (for example, an organization's employees and clients) are not free to withdraw from their relationship with the organization, these constituencies do not perceive that they have high

"stakes" in and "psychological ownership" of its activities, and the organization's goals and activities are imposed on it, the instrumental goal-oriented hierarchical model will "fit" better than the theory of voluntary organization that is presented in this paper, i.e., the behavior of an organization can be predicted or explained more accurately using the instrumental goal-oriented model. On the other hand, if key constituencies are associated voluntarily and feel high involvement and psychological ownership of an organization's activities, the model of voluntar organization probably will "fit" better.

References

Berger, Peter L., and Thomas Luckmann. 1966. *The Social Construction of Reality.* Garden City, NY: Doubleday.

Brudney, Jeffrey L. 1990a. *Fostering Volunteer Programs in the Public Sector: Planning, Initiating, and Managing Voluntary Activities.* San Francisco: Jossey-Bass.

Brudney, Jeffrey L. 1990b. "Expanding the Government-by-Proxy Construct: Volunteers in the Delivery of Public Services." *Nonprofit and Voluntary Sector Quarterly* 19:315–28.

Cnaan, Ram A. 1990. "Volunteers in Public and Nonpublic Settings." *Nonprofit and Voluntary Sector Quarterly* 19:311–14.

Connolly, Terry, Edward J. Conlon, and Stuart Jay Deutsch. 1980. "Organizational Effectiveness: A Multiple Constituency Approach." *Academy of Management Review* 5:211–17.

Cyert, Richard M., and James G. March. 1963. *A Behavioral Theory of the Firm.* Englewood Cliffs, NJ: Prentice-Hall.

Day, Robert, and JoAnne V. Day. 1977. "A Review of the Current State of Negotiated Order Theory: An Appreciation and a Critique." *Sociological Quarterly* 18:126–42.

DeHoog, Ruth H. 1986. "Evaluating Human Service Contracting: Managers, Professionals, and Politicos." *State and Local Government Review* 37–44.

Denhardt, Robert B. 1993. *Theories of Public Organization,* 2d ed. Belmont, CA: Wadsworth.

Etzioni, Amitai. 1975. *A Comparative Analysis of Complex Organizations* (rev. ed.). New York: The Free Press.

Ferris, James M., and Elizabeth Graddy. 1989. "Fading Distinctions Among the Nonprofit, Government, and For-profit Sectors," in V. A.

Hodgkinson and R. W. Lyman, eds., *The Future of the Nonprofit Sector.* San Francisco: Jossey-Bass.

Gies, David L., J. Steven Ott, and Jay M. Shafritz, eds. 1990. *The Nonprofit Organization: Essential Readings.* Pacific Grove, CA: Brooks/Cole.

Hansmann, Henry. 1989. "The Two Nonprofit Sectors: Fee for Service Versus Donative Organizations," in V. A. Hodgkinson and R. W. Lyman, eds., *The Future of the Nonprofit Sector: Challenges, Changes, and Policy Considerations.* San Francisco: Jossey-Bass.

Harmon, Michael M., and Richard T. Mayer. 1986. *Organization Theory for Public Administration.* Boston: Little, Brown and Company.

Harris, Margaret. 1989. "The Governing Body Role: Problems and Perceptions in Implementation." *Journal of Nonprofit and Voluntary Sector Quarterly* 18:317–33.

Hatten, M. L. 1982. "Strategic Management in Not-for-Profit Organizations." *Strategic Management Journal* 3:89–104.

Herman, Robert D., and Richard D. Heimovics. 1991. *Executive Leadership in Nonprofit Organizations.* San Francisco: Jossey-Bass.

Hessen, Robert. 1979a. *In Defense of the Corporation.* Stanford, CA: Hoover Institution.

Hessen, Robert. 1979b. "A New Concept of Corporations: A Contractual and Private Property Model." *Hastings Law Journal* 13:1327–350.

Hodgkinson, Virginia A., and Murray S. Weitzman. 1988. *Dimensions of the Independent Sector: A Statistical Profile—Interim Update.* Washington, DC: Independent Sector.

Jensen, Michael C., and William H. Meckling. 1976. "Theory of the Firm: Managerial Behavior, Agency Costs and Ownership Structure." *Journal of Financial Economics* 3:305–60.

Kanter, Rosabeth M., and David V. Summers. 1987. "Doing Well While Doing Good," in W. W. Powell, ed., *The Nonprofit Sector: A Research Handbook.* New Haven, CT: Yale University Press.

Keeley, Michael. 1980. "Organizational Analogy: A Comparison of Organismic and Social Contract Models." *Administrative Science Quarterly* 25: 337–62.

Keeley, Michael. 1988. *A Social-Contract Theory of Organizations.* Notre Dame, IN: University of Notre Dame Press.

Kettl, Donald F. 1988. *Government by Proxy: [Mis?]managing Federal Programs.* Washington, DC: CQ Press.

Kettner, P. M., and L. L. Martin. 1989. "Contracting for Services: Is Politics a Factor?" *New England Journal of Human Services* 9:15–20.

March, James G., and Herbert A. Simon. 1958. *Organizations.* New York: Wiley.

Mitroff, Ian I. 1983. *Stakeholders of the Organizational Mind.* San Francisco: Jossey-Bass.

Morgan, D. R., and R. E. England. 1988. "The Two Faces of Privatization." *Public Administration Review* 48:979–87.

National Academy of Public Administration. 1989. "The Management Challenges of Privatization," in NAPA *Privatization: The Challenge to Public Management.* Washington, DC: National Academy of Public Administration.

O'Neill, Michael. 1989. "Responsible Management in the Nonprofit Sector," in V. A. Hodgkinson and R. W. Lyman, eds., *The Future of the Nonprofit Sector.* San Francisco: Jossey-Bass.

Ostrander, Susan A., Stuart Langton, and Jon Van Til. 1987. *Shifting the Debate: Public/Private Relations in the Modern Welfare State.* New Brunswick, NJ: Transaction Press.

Ott, J. Steven. 1989a. *The Organizational Culture Perspective.* Pacific Grove, CA: Brooks/Cole.

Ott, J. Steven. 1989b. "Power and Influence," in J. S. Ott, ed., *Classic Readings in Organizational Behavior.* Pacific Grove, CA: Brooks/Cole.

Ott, J. Steven. 1991. "A Model of Voluntary Organization." University of Maine. Unpublished manuscript.

Pearce, Jone L. 1982. "Leading and Following Volunteers: Implications for a Changing Society." *Journal of Applied Behavioral Science* 18:385–94.

Pilon, Roger. 1979. "Corporations and Rights: On Treating Corporate People Justly." *Georgia Law Review* 13:1245–1370.

Salancik, Gerald R., and Jeffrey Pfeffer. 1977. "Who Gets Power—and How They Hold On To It: A Strategic-Contingency Model of Power." *Organizational Dynamics* 5:2–21.

Schein, Edgar H. 1989. "Reassessing the 'Divine Rights' of Managers." *Sloan Management Review* 30:63–68.

Schein, Edgar H. 1992. *Organizational Culture and Leadership,* 2d ed. San Francisco: Jossey-Bass.

Shafritz, Jay M. 1988. *The Dorsey Dictionary of American Government and Politics.* Pacific Grove, CA: Brooks/Cole.

Simon, Herbert A. 1976. *Administrative Behavior: A Study of Decision-Making Processes in Administrative Organization,* 3d ed. New York: Free Press.

Simon, Herbert A. 1981. *The Sciences of the Artificial,* 2d ed. Cambridge, MA: MIT Press.

Strauss, Anselm. 1978. *Negotiations.* San Francisco: Jossey-Bass.

Strauss, Anselm, Leonard Schatzman, Rue Bucher, Damita Ehrlich, and Melvin Sabshin. 1963. "The Hospital and Its Negotiated Order," in E. Freidson, ed., *The Hospital in Modern Society.* New York: Free Press.

Thomas, W. I. 1923. *The Unadjusted Girl.* New York: Harper Torchbooks, 1967.

Van Til, Jon. 1988. *Mapping the Third Sector: Voluntarism in a Changing Social Economy.* New York: Foundation Center.

Wortman, Max. 1983. "Strategic Planning in Voluntary Enterprises," in M. Moyer, ed., *Managing Voluntary Organizations.* Proceedings of a conference held at York University, Toronto, Ontario, October 19–21.

► CHAPTER 25

Nonprofit Organizations in an Age of Uncertainty

JOSEPH GALASKIEWICZ AND
WOLFGANG BIELEFELD

The purpose of this monograph was to see how well different theories developed in the fields of organizational sociology and management science could explain changes in a panel of nonprofit organizations. We wanted to see what organizational theory could do today to explain change in a panel of nonprofits. Indeed, our findings were not always as strong as some of our colleagues in the field would have liked. Yet we found enough results to convince us of the utility of organizational theory in helping scholars understand changes in the not-for-profit organization, and we hope that applied researchers will pay more attention to this literature and body of work in the future.

Explaining Organizational Change: A Contest of Ideas

The bottom line is that no one theory of organizational change dominated our results. There was something to say for each of them, and, in all likelihood, they all will survive to see another day.

We discuss each theory in turn and the relevant results. We recount what we thought we should find if the theory was correct (i.e., we give hypotheses). Then we look at our results to see if the hypotheses were supported.

A. Selection Models

Selection refers to a change in the composition of a set of organizations as one form is replaced by another simply because the former is unable to reproduce itself while the latter can (Hannan and Carroll 1995a). Organizations and their managers, however, do not have much say in the matter. Depending upon conditions in the larger environment, some organizations will grow and prosper, while others will decline and wither away. Most selection models are formulated at the population level of analysis, predicting changes within populations, e.g., birth and death rates, using variables that are also measured at the population level, e.g., density. Sometimes these theories focus on industries (e.g., Carroll and Hannan 1995); other times they study organizational fields (e.g., Powell and DiMaggio 1991). This is true for both organizational ecology and institutional theory in organizational sociology. Our goal was to test selection theory using individual organizations as the units of analysis and environmental conditions as contextual effects.

To aid us in bridging the gap between the environmental and the organizational levels, we focused on organizational niches. We defined a niche as that arena of action in which organizations competed for scare resources, e.g., money, information, support, authority, and focused on the competition among incumbents. However, one could also study actors in the broader organizational field or ecological community that provided the resources (e.g., customers and/or grantmakers), regulated the competition (e.g., government agencies and the courts), and observed the action (e.g., community and environmental groups). These players are as crucial in understanding what goes on within niches as those who compete against one another. However, we focused only on competitors.

Niches were conceptualized as structurally equivalent action sets that emerged out of the day-to-day competition for scarce resources. The niche could be defined in terms of products, types of revenue sources, organizational capabilities (e.g., organizational size), types of labor inputs, client/consumer/member characteristics (i.e., market segment), technology, or locale. We delimited our niche boundaries focusing on products (or activities), revenue sources, size of organization, and labor inputs.

We measured several features of organizational niches. We proceeded to operationalize the niche space of nonprofits in the Twin Cities using data from four random samples of public charities in 1980, 1984, 1988, and 1992. We focused on where organizations received their revenues (donations, commercial income, government grants and contracts, and miscellaneous income), their type of labor inputs (employees, volunteers), their products (welfare/health, cultural/recreational, educational, other), and their capabilities (size measured as expenditures) and created structurally equivalent sets from these data.

Now is the time to see how well selection theory did in explaining organizational change in our panel of nonprofits. Our strategy is to state the hypotheses derived from the theory and

then review the findings. The more hypotheses supported, the more confidence we can have in the theory. The fewer hypotheses supported, the less confidence.

Growth and decline. We offered four hypotheses that used ecological and institutional variables to explain the growth and decline of nonprofits in our panel. To summarize briefly,

> *Organizations in more dense niches are likely to increase commercial income, donated income, employees, and volunteers, up to a point, after which they are likely to lose commercial income, donated income, employees, and volunteers over time.*
> *Organizations in more concentrated niches are likely to increase commercial income, donated income, employees, and volunteers over time.*
> *Organizations in niches with greater sociopolitical legitimacy are likely to increase commercial income, donated income, employees, and volunteers over time.*
> *Organizations that are specialists are likely to increase commercial income, donated income, employees, and volunteers over time, while organizations that are generalists should lose resources over time.*

Density had negative effects on growth in earned income and employees between 1980 and 1984 ($p < .05$).[1] Density had a nonmonotonic effect on changes in earned income and employees between 1988 and 1994 in the shape of an inverted U ($p < .10$; $p < .10$), but this was the only evidence of density dependence in the eight models.

Organizations in niches that were marked by high levels of resource concentration increased their commercial income and employees between 1980 and 1984 ($p < .10$) and between 1984 and 1988 ($p < .05$), but concentration had little effect on changes between 1988 and 1992 or between 1988 and 1994. Organizations in niches occupied by highly legitimate actors were likely to increase their commercial income and employees between 1988 and 1992 ($p < .01$) and 1988 and 1994 ($p < .05$).[2] Furthermore, specialists increased their commercial income and employees between 1980 and 1984 (*p* < .10), 1984 and 1988 (*p* < .01), and 1988 and 1994 (*p* < .001). However, these three variables had no statistically significant effect on changes in donated income and volunteers in any of the periods.

Tactics. We argued that niche conditions would be important in the selection of tactics. Two competing models were offered. The first said that competition would drive organizations out of their niche. This we borrowed from contingency theory. Operationally this meant that under competitive conditions organizations would embrace new tactics, change their products or activities, and retrench operations.

In more competitive niches, organizations that are more dependent on commercial income and employees are likely to increase their use of political tactics over time.

Organizations that reside in more competitive niches are more likely to change their products and services over time.

Organizations that reside in more competitive niches are likely to increase their use of retrenchment tactics over time.

The second model derived from organizational ecology (inertia theory) said that competition would prompt organizations to step up their efforts, i.e., increase their use of resource tactics, but organizations would stay in their niche, not venture into other niches.

In more competitive niches, organizations that are more dependent on commercial income and employees are likely to increase their use of managerial tactics over time.

In more competitive niches, organizations that are more dependent on donated income and volunteers are likely to increase their use of political tactics over time.

In more competitive niches, organizations that are more dependent on donated income and volunteers are likely to increase their use of managerial tactics over time.

We found little evidence that niche conditions prompted organizations to change niche position. In neither our OLS nor our Poisson regressions did we find niche conditions having an effect on the relationship between commercial income and employees and increases in the use of political tactics in our test of niche flight. In the Poisson regressions, however, we found that if their niche was sparsely populated or resources were less concentrated, organizations that were dependent upon commercial income and employees increased their managerial tactics (in three out of four tests), and organizations that were dependent upon donated income and volunteers increased their political and managerial tactics (in four out of eight tests).

We also found that between 1984 and 1988 and between 1988 and 1992 organizations were very reluctant to change their products or services—even when facing a hostile or competitive environment. However, niche conditions had some effect on the use of retrenchment tactics.

We had sketched out two scenarios. Facing competitive environments, organizations could respond either by escalating commitments to the tactics employed in the past or by changing their niche position. Our results showed that in less legitimate or less concentrated niches, organizations increased their efforts to extract resources from familiar sources and did not change their mix of products and services. However, some did downsize their operations. Thus when faced with hostile niche conditions, organizations continued to do what they had done in the past but on a somewhat smaller scale.

Quality of life. In our exploratory analysis there was only one hypothesis that linked niche conditions to the quality of life within organizations. However, it was an important hypothesis. We argued that the effect of growth and decline on conditions within an organization would be contingent on niche conditions. In particular, decline in a competitive environment should result in more "negatives" than decline in a noncompetitive context.

Organizations that experience a decline in resources in highly competitive resource niches are more likely to centralize decision-making authority, have disagreements while making decisions, conflict with employees, alienation, and a less creative or innovative work environment than organizations that experience a decline in resources in less competitive niches.

Testing this hypothesis required that we estimate five models and test for five interaction effects, since there were five dependent variables. For the most part, growth and decline were neither important, nor contingent upon conditions in local niches, in explaining changes in the quality of organizational life. We did find, however, that organizations in more crowded niches decentralized their decision-making between 1988 and 1994 ($p < .01$) and had more conflicts with employees in 1994 than in 1988 ($p < .05$), but reasons for this remain unclear.

Discussion.   Clearly ecological theory worked better explaining changes in arenas where organizations competed for customers and employees than in arenas where they competed for donors and volunteers. In all periods niche conditions explained growth and decline in commercial income and employees but not donated income and volunteers. Perhaps we should not be surprised, since competition is an important value in market arenas. Yet extensive research on nonprofits found density dependence effects (e.g., Baum and his associates, and Singh and his associates), so we had thought that donative transactions (i.e., donations and volunteering) would also be affected by niche conditions. Perhaps the organizations studied by the ecologists were heavily dependent upon fees and program service revenues. We do not know. But if we can trust our results, they suggest that organizations in niches with strong process controls were immune to selection. This, of course, implies that selection theories have limited utility for studying nonprofit organizations, as many rely heavily on donations and volunteers.

Although restricted to explaining growth and decline in commercial income and employees, we were surprised that specialists so decidedly outcompeted generalists. This was perhaps one of the most consistent ecological effects we

found. It is noteworthy, because it goes against common sense. Oftentimes organizations are told to diversify, spread their risks, and ensure that they do not become too dependent on any one source of funds. Yet we found that organizations that drew their resources from a narrower range of sources and had fewer products grew at a faster rate than those that had funding from multiple sources and provided many different products. Here ecological theory clearly won out over common sense.

Selection theory clearly scored points in the flight vs. fight debate, but it did not record a knockout. As inertia theory would predict, niche conditions did not prompt organizations to change their funding source or go into new product lines; as adaptation theory would predict, niche conditions resulted in some retrenchment. For the most part (although not in all periods), hostile environmental conditions prompted organizations to fight back and do more of what they were doing but on a smaller scale. Thus niche conditions had a modifying effect on the relationship between funding source and tactics. Apparently the ecologists—and two streetwise business consultants—were right. Smart organizations "stick to the knitting" and don't stray too far from home.

B. Adaptation Models

The adaptation approach argued that organizations could and would take measures to achieve their goals or ensure their survival. The adaption model is more proactive and finds expression in what has come to be called the "strategy" literature in management science. Whereas selection models are often criticized for being overly deterministic, ignoring the agency of organizational actors, adaptation theories are often criticized for being "under-socialized," that is, too willing to make managers and administrators omnipotent. Reality probably resides somewhere between these two extremes, and organizations are both affected by the environment and formulate strategies and implement tactics that help to ensure their well-being.

For adaptation theory, the unit of analysis is the organization and thus this theory is more appropriate to our study than selection theory, yet there are still problems. Many of the standard problems that plague organizational analysis plague adaptation theory as well. Organizational goals are often in conflict, interest groups and coalitions sometimes displace organizational goals with their own agendas, and at times the survival (or systems) needs of the organization seem to mitigate any effort to pursue organizational goals in a rational manner (Scott 1998). Still when asked why organizations change—for better or worse, most would reply that it is because management has done something different (Barnett and Carroll 1995:220). It seems obvious and responds to our need to make someone accountable.

In order to pit variables derived from the selection and adaptation literatures against one another in an empirical contest, we returned to the niche. Our general theoretical argument was that resources were allocated through different kinds of mechanisms across niches. The upshot of all this was that the dynamics—or you could say processes—within each segment of a niche space were going to be different depending upon the type of controls. For example, organizations that were seeking to attract donors or contributors to their organization went about it differently than organizations that were trying to attract customers. The incentives offered each were different; the meaning of the relationship was different; the obligations of the organization to funding sources were different.

The basic assumption behind our discussion was that organizations and their leaders were striving to optimize resources or inputs. This is implicit in selection theory and explicit in adaptation theory. Some sought more resources to better attain organizational goals (e.g., world peace, social equality, shareholder return on equity), others sought more resources to ensure organizational survival (even if at the expense of goals), some sought more resources to serve managerial utilities, and some sought more resources just to accumulate more resources. Whatever the motivation, the assumption was that organizations would do what they had to do in order to accumulate more inputs.

Clearly this relates directly back to the above discussion. If an organization was in a niche segment where it sought donations from wealthy philanthropists, it would do what it had to, e.g., demonstrate its public regardingness or trustworthiness, to get those donations. If an organization was in a niche segment where it taught English as a second language to immigrants who paid their own tuition, it would do what it had to do to get their business, e.g., advertise its services or improve teaching techniques. In other words, depending upon where they were situated in the resource space, organizations had to do certain things to procure the resources they needed.

To link this argument to the strategy literature, we then argued that organizations, their boards, and their managers have different orientations. Some were oriented toward growth, others toward consolidation. We next moved to the level of tactics, which we defined as operational initiatives or techniques aimed at achieving certain strategic ends. Here we called efforts to consolidate operations, retrenchment tactics. We then distinguished between tactics geared at achieving growth in niches with strong output controls and tactics oriented toward realizing growth in niches with strong process controls. We called the former managerial tactics, the latter political or legitimation tactics.

Managerial tactics were institutionally approved techniques to realize growth in niches where resources were procured through competitive bidding, the pursuit of self-interest, and exchange processes. We further distinguished between internal tactics aimed at reducing overhead and production costs, improving product quality, and making systems more reliable without reducing organizational capabilities, and external tactics aimed at reducing transaction costs, marketing products better, and competing more effectively against other providers. These tactics were standard for business organizations, but we argued that they were appropriate for any type of organization—for-profit or nonprofit—that sold its products to customers, secured its labor inputs from the marketplace, and produced easy-to-evaluate goods and services.

Political tactics were institutionally approved techniques to realize growth in niches where resources were procured by supplicants demonstrating commitment to collective or public interest goals, institutional gatekeepers evaluating their sincerity and trustworthiness, and resources being allocated through donative processes. We again distinguished between internal and external tactics. The former aimed at strengthening the organization's moral capital, ensuring loyalty to mission, and safeguarding its integrity. External tactics included convincing key stakeholders of the organizations' credibility, changing stakeholders' perceptions and priorities, and getting others to testify on behalf of the organization. These tactics were standard for charitable or communal organizations, but we argued that they were useful for any organization that relied on donations and volunteer help, sold hard-to-evaluate trust goods and services, or provided collective or public goods.

As noted above, an organization would do whatever it thought necessary—within institutional bounds—to procure the resources it needed. If it found itself dependent upon sales to consumers, employees, and selling easy-to-evaluate goods and services, it would utilize more managerial tactics and, in turn, it would increase its commercial income and employees. On the other hand, if it found itself dependent upon donors (or grantmakers) and volunteers, and either sold hard-to-evaluate trust goods or produced collective or public goods, it would utilize more political tactics and, in turn, increase its donated income and volunteers. This was why organizations—whether for-profit or nonprofit—would come to look more like prototypical business organizations over time, if they were heavily dependent upon market transactions; and why organizations—whether for-profit or nonprofit—would come to look more like prototypical charitable organizations over time, if they were heavily dependent upon donative transfers for their resources. In other words, we hypothesize competitive isomorphism (DiMaggio and Powell 1983).

Now again it is time to see how well the theory did. As we did for selection theory, we will present the various hypotheses derived from extant theory and review our results. More empirical support for the hypotheses strengthens our faith in adaptation theory; less weakens it.

Growth and decline. The first set of hypotheses closely mirrored the arguments made above, focusing on the employment of certain tactics and the subsequent increases or decreases in different types of resources. The first two are a restatement of basic adaptation theory. The third came from DiMaggio and Powell's (1983) discussion of how institutional gatekeepers often regard managerial tactics as indicators of organizations' accountability, reliability, and trustworthiness. It demonstrates a commitment to rationality. We introduced the fourth as a further test of adaptation theory, where organizations intentionally attempted to reduce their scale of operations.

> *Organizations that employ more managerial tactics are likely to increase commercial income and employees over time.*
> *Organizations that employ more political tactics are likely to increase donated income and volunteers over time.*
> *Organizations that employ more managerial tactics are likely to increase donated income and volunteers over time.*
> *Organizations that employ more retrenchment tactics are likely to lose commercial income, donated income, employees, and volunteers over time.*

The results were straightforward. The use of more managerial tactics increased commercial income and employees between 1980 and 1984 ($p < .05$), 1984 and 1988 ($p < .001$), and 1988 and 1994 ($p < .01$). Managerial tactics also led to an increase in donated income and volunteers between 1980 and 1984 ($p < .10$), 1984 and 1988 ($p < .05$), and 1988 and 1992 ($p < .05$). Thus our position and that of DiMaggio and Powell (1983) were both strongly supported by the data. We also saw that political tactics increased donations and volunteers between 1980 and 1984 ($p < .05$) and between 1988 and 1994 ($p < .01$) and in a later analysis political tactics led to an increase in commercial income and employees between 1980 and 1984 ($p < .05$). Thus the recent attention given to political or legitimation tactics (e.g., Suchman 1995; Oliver 1991) is well deserved.

Retrenchment sometimes resulted in a decline in resources (commercial revenues and employees between 1980 and 1984 ($p < .05$) and donated income and volunteers between 1984 and 1988 ($p < .05$)), but most of the time it did not. This was a remarkable finding: One of two things was happening. First, organizations were reducing their costs without hurting their income streams. That is, they fired staff, reduced pay, eliminated programs, or did all those other ugly things without jeopardizing either their commercial income or their donated income. They created for themselves a windfall situation that may have returned some of these organizations to solvency and feathered the nest of others. Alternatively, retrenchment was simply a process that organizations routinely engaged in as part of their day-to-day housekeeping. They eliminated programs but started others; they cut some people's pay and benefits but later gave raises to others; they reduced service delivery staff and hired more administrators; or they fired administrators and hired more service delivery staff. Needless to say, this nonfinding was intriguing and worthy of further investigation.

Tactics. We also offered several hypotheses that speculated on when organizations would utilize different tactics. There were certainly irrational explanations for why organizations selected the tactics they did, and these will be discussed in our discussion of embeddedness effects. Here we present and evaluate hypotheses aimed at explaining the use of tactics from the adaptation perspective.

> *Organizations that are more dependent on commercial income and employees are likely to increase their use of managerial tactics over time.*
>
> *Organizations that are more dependent on donated income and volunteers are likely to increase their use of political and managerial tactics over time.*

All three hypotheses were supported. We found that between 1984 and 1988 and between 1988 and 1992, organizations that were more dependent upon fees and employees increased their use of managerial tactics ($p < .01$; $p < .01$) and that organizations more dependent upon private donations and volunteers increased their use of political tactics ($p < .01$; $p < .001$). We also saw that organizations more dependent upon private donations and volunteers increased their use of managerial tactics between 1988 and 1992 ($p < .05$) (but not between 1984 and 1988). Thus organizations took on the appropriate trappings of the arenas upon which they were heavily dependent for resources. Those dependent upon fees and employees came to look more "businesslike" over time, while those dependent upon donations and volunteers came to look more "charitable" and "businesslike."

The anomaly was that between 1988 and 1992 we also found that organizations that were more dependent upon commercial income and employees in 1988 increased their use of political tactics as well ($p < .01$). Perhaps we overestimated the importance of niche identities and the different effects they have on the procurement of different kinds of resources and that now large organizations—regardless of their funding type—are becoming more managerial *and* more political. Needless to say, more research is needed to address this issue.

Quality of life. In our exploratory analysis we offered four hypotheses linking the use of different tactics with the various quality of life indicators that we identified. The first two dealt with retrenchment tactics. This time we wanted to see if they affected organizational behaviors. The second two addressed a very interesting proposition that came out of both the ecological and management literatures. Did organizations that employed tactics that were incongruent with their current niche position suffer any negative behavioral consequences?

> *Organizations that retrench operations are more likely to have disagreements while making decisions, conflict with employees, alienation, and a less creative or innovative work environment than organizations that do not retrench operations.*

Organizations that retrench operations are more likely to centralize decision-making patterns.

Organizations that use managerial tactics are more likely to have disagreements while making decisions, conflict with employees, alienation, and a less creative or innovative work environment, if they were more heavily reliant on donated income and volunteers in the past.

Organizations that use political tactics are more likely to have disagreements while making decisions, conflict with employees, alienation, and a less creative or innovative work environment, if they were more heavily reliant on commercial income and employees in the past.

The analysis showed that retrenchment had a much greater impact on decision-making patterns and quality of life than growth and decline. Retrenchment led to more conflicts with employees ($p < .01$), less value being placed on creativity and innovativeness ($p < .10$), and more centralized decision-making patterns ($p < .05$) between 1988 and 1994. These findings, of course, were especially impressive because they were independent of growth and decline in resources. One of the reasons we tested these hypotheses was that we wanted to see if growth and decline or the use of retrenchment tactics were more important in deciding organizational behavioral outcomes. The data suggest the latter, not the former. Decline per se had no negative effects on the organizations we studied, although it did interact with niche density and alienation, as noted earlier. In fact, it led to *fewer* conflicts with employees ($p < .05$). Retrenchment was another matter. These findings were also important in light of our earlier findings that retrenchment had no consistent negative effect on growth in resources and was a seemingly favorite tactic of nonprofits reliant on commercial income and employees. Managers who employed more retrenchment tactics did not jeopardize the flow of resources into the organization, but they surely opened themselves up to problems nonetheless.

Support for the other two hypotheses was much weaker. We found that organizations that utilized more political tactics had more disagreements if they were more heavily dependent upon fees and employees ($p < .001$), and organizations that utilized more managerial tactics had more disagreements if they were more heavily dependent upon donations and volunteers ($p < .01$). We only found these effects for disagreements, but then it may only be in decision-making that the problems caused by switching identities come out. Indeed, it was in policymaking situations that Hall (1990) saw the conflict between an executive director who wanted to protect what he felt to be the mission and integrity of the organization and a board chair and his executive committee that was pushing the organization to be more businesslike.[3]

Discussion. What can we say about adaptation theory and its contribution to our understanding of organizational change among nonprofits? Of all three theoretical perspectives, it garnered the most support. Perhaps the popular perception is accurate that administrative initiatives are important in explaining organizational behavior and change.

Retrenchment tactics were intriguing. While having only limited impact on the growth/decline in resources, they produced negative behavioral outcomes. These latter findings were crucial, because they substantiated our theoretical argument that administrative tactics or choices, i.e., the use of retrenchment tactics, had more to do with the quality of life within organizations than the growth or decline in resources. It also placed the blame for the negative externalities on managers' tactics instead of on the lack of resources.

With a few notable exceptions, organizations adopted tactics that were appropriate for the resource niche in which they were dependent for resources, and, if they utilized more of these tactics, they were rewarded with more resources from that arena. First, receiving donated income and having more volunteers led an organization to become more charitablelike in the sense of employing more political tactics, and employing more political tactics garnered an organization more donations and volunteers. We also found some evidence (between 1980 and 1984) that they increased commercial income and employees as well. However, they produced some nasty externalities in the process. Second, receiving commercial income and having more employees led an organization to become more businesslike, and employing more managerial tactics garnered one more earned income/employees and donated income/volunteers. It produced both positive and negative externalities.

Earlier we talked about the possibility of their being a dedifferentiation of the market and grants economies. That is, to get either commercial income or donations may require hefty doses of managerialism *and* politics. Yes, normative charities were coming to look more like business organizations; but nonprofits heavily dependent upon commercial income were coming to look more like charities (i.e., by increasing their political tactics). The bottom line is that by the end of our study, large, successful organizations now did both, regardless of their funding source.

While this may have been driven simply by the resource needs of organizations, the spread of political tactics could be replacing the spread of managerial tactics as an institutional process (DiMaggio and Powell 1983). This could be attributed to a creeping politicalization of all organizational life. Fombrun (1996) argued that all organizations have to worry about their legitimacy and reputation. It is in their enlightened self-interest. He argues that an organization's reputational capital is a valuable asset that has an impact on the bottom line either in the short term or long term. This is also the implicit lesson to managers in the work of the neoinstitutionalists (e.g., W. R. Scott 1995) and made explicit in the work of their students (Suchman 1995). Indeed, someday we may find managerial tactics decoupled from earned income and employees but still coupled to donated income and volunteers, while political tactics are tightly coupled to earned income and employees but decoupled from donated income and volunteers. In all likelihood, however, we expect the differentiation between managerial and political tactics to become less, a higher correlation between earned income/employees and donated in-

come/volunteers, and simply a "tactics" effect on growth and decline of all kinds.

C. Structural Embeddedness Models

The structural embeddedness perspective was the least developed of the three general models we reviewed, and it produced fewer clear-cut hypotheses. In fact, most of the hypotheses mused on how social structural variables could modify the effect of either environmental conditions or tactics on organizational changes.

The attractiveness of the embeddedness approach lies in the identification of "clutter" within an otherwise sterile and sanitized organizational world. The social structural factors identified in this monograph included formal properties of the organization—its size, age, and pattern of decision-making—as well as informal structures—social networks. We equated social structure with clutter, because sometimes it gets in the way and sometimes it is quite useful. For example, large organizations are often difficult to manage or communicate with, but they can be quite useful when fighting off a hostile takeover attempt and one is trying to garner political support at the state legislature (e.g., Davis and Thompson 1994). Age can also be an asset or liability depending upon the circumstances, as can decision-making structures. We focused on two types of social networks. The first was the network of linkages among nonprofit organizations in the community. The second was the use and support of the organization by local or community elites. Maintaining the organization's position in both networks is costly in terms of time and sometimes money, but the possible benefits of drawing on network contacts in crisis situations far outweighs the costs. Yet the organization may never have a crisis, so it is not clear that attending all those breakfast meetings or hosting those receptions for local celebrities will ever pay off. One is never too sure how much to invest in their social networks.

Informal social structures or networks are especially attractive to both scholars and practitioners today (see, for example, Mackay 1997), since they seem to hold some "secrets to success" that we have not yet discovered.

Our view of social networks was more modest, for we viewed them as auxiliary features—maybe even "clutter"—within and between organizations. The hypotheses tested in this monograph reflected this more temperate perspective on social structure.[4]

Growth and decline. All the hypotheses looked for modifying effects. That is, social structure was seen as either facilitating strategy implementation or blocking it. The first two focused on the impact of size and age. Larger organizations were assumed to be more bureaucratized with a more elaborate set of rules and regulations, control systems, and more established routines. Older organizations were assumed to have more wisdom or, at least, more accumulated knowledge. Both fit the image of structure as clutter. Bureaucracy could get in the way of change, but having some extra knowledge and experience around could help an organization get through some tough times and over some new terrain.

> *The effects of managerial tactics on increases in commercial income and employees and political tactics on increases in donated income and volunteers will be stronger, the smaller the organization.*
> *The effects of managerial tactics on increases in commercial income and employees and political tactics on increases in donated income and volunteers will be stronger, the older the organization.*

We also developed a hypothesis that focused on decision-making structures. We derived a measure of how centralized or decentralized decision-making authority was within the organization. Our inspection of these scores showed us that within organizations where few positions had authority to make formal decisions, the board of directors dominated. This was the centralized organization. Where decision-making was decentralized, many different functionaries (e.g., administrators, professional staff, volunteers, even clients) had to be consulted before decisions could become policies. Again, we viewed social structure as clutter. Once the

board decided on a tactic to implement, it could proceed without delay if other folks in the organization did not have to be listened to or coopted or brought on board.

> *The effects of managerial tactics on increases in commercial income and employees and political tactics on increases in donated income and volunteers will be stronger, the more centralized decision-making authority.*

The third set of embedded effects involved interorganizational network ties as well as ties to local elites. However, they only addressed the coupling of political tactics to increases in donated income and volunteers. The argument was that organizations that had ties to many other organizations and/or more members of the local community elite were able to realize greater returns on their efforts to convince others of their public regardingness and trustworthiness. They had more folks to tap for favors, more folks to make introductions, and more folks to be references, i.e., actors who would vouch for them and back up their claims.

> *The effects of political tactics on increases in donated income and volunteers will be stronger, the greater the number of network ties to other organizations.*
> *The effects of political tactics on increases in donated income and volunteers will be stronger, the greater the number of network ties to the local community elite and the more the elite values the organizations.*

The results were simple to summarize. Among middle-aged and older organizations, the use of managerial tactics increased commercial income and employees between 1980 and 1984, but not among younger organizations ($p < .10$). Among medium-size and smaller organizations, the use of political tactics increased donated income and volunteers between 1988 and 1992 ($p < .05$), and between 1988 and 1994 ($p < .01$). But that was all. For the most part, large organizations were as successful as small organizations, young organizations were as successful as old organizations, decentralized organizations were as successful as centralized organizations, and socially isolated organizations were as success as heavily networked organizations in implementing tactics. There was not enough support to argue that strategy implementation was contingent or modified by social structural variables.

However, the network variables did have some independent effects on growth in donated income and volunteers. Organizations more embedded in interorganizational networks in 1984 increased their donated income between 1980 and 1984 ($p = .133$) and between 1984 and 1988 ($p < .10$). Organizations more embedded in elite networks in 1980 increased their donated income between 1980 and 1984 ($p < .10$) and between 1984 and 1988 ($p < .05$). Also, if organizations utilized fewer political tactics, elite network ties had a significant effect on growth in donated income and volunteers between 1988 and 1994 ($p < .05$). Thus there was some evidence that social networks did have a direct effect on the growth and decline of donated income and volunteers.

Tactics. Basically the thesis was that the choice of tactics was a function of the tactics of one's social network contacts and role models. That is, organizations would adopt the tactics of those whom they knew and trusted. They would also mimic the tactics of those they thought were successful especially under conditions of environmental uncertainty.

> *Organizations are likely to increase their use of political and/or managerial tactics, if they had direct resource exchanges with other organizations that used political and/or managerial tactics extensively in the past.*
>
> *Organizations are likely to increase their use of political and/or managerial tactics, if managers knew personally other managers who used political and/or managerial tactics extensively in the past.*
>
> *Under conditions of uncertainty, organizations are likely to increase their use of political and/or managerial tactics, if managers perceived other organizations as successful who used political and/or managerial tactics extensively in the past.*

Organizations increased their managerial tactics between 1984 and 1988, if organizations with which they exchanged resources or information utilized more managerial tactics in 1984 ($p < .05$). Organizations also increased their political tactics between 1984 and 1988 if organizations with which they exchanged resource or information utilized more political tactics in 1984 ($p < .10$). Organizations increased their managerial tactics between 1988 and 1992 if organizations where they knew someone personally utilized more managerial tactics in 1988 ($p < .05$). And organizations increased their political tactics between 1988 and 1992 if organizations where they knew someone personally utilized more political tactics in 1988 ($p < .05$). Except in one single case[5] organizations did not mimic the tactics of those whom they believed were more successful.

We also offered a hypothesis that stated that contact with more members of the local community elite would result in the organization utilizing more managerial tactics. The gist of our argument was that elites, as champions of the "business model," coerced organizations into adopting this management style with the implicit threat that they would abandon the organization if it refused (e.g., Hall 1990).

> *Organizations are likely to increase their use of managerial tactics, if more members of the community elite personally used or supported their organizations with donations, volunteer help, board memberships, and consulting services.*

We found that organizations increased their use of both managerial ($p < .10$) and political tactics ($p < .05$) between 1988 and 1992, if more members of the community elite used their services or supported their efforts with time and money.

Quality of life. In our exploratory study we speculated that organizations that were embedded in social network ties would have less "rancorous" disruptions and become better work environments over time. The argument was that organizations deeply embedded in a network of interorganizational or elite ties would be more moderate or temperate and might even be more benevolent toward participants, because "others" were watching. This was a crude test of Coleman's (1988) thesis that networks are vehicles that exercise social control over participants.

> *Organizations that are embedded in elite community networks are less likely to have disagreements while making decisions, conflict with employees, and alienation, and more likely to have a creative or innovative work environment.*
>
> *Organizations that are embedded in community interorganizational resource exchange networks are less likely to have disagreements while making decisions, conflict with employees, and alienation, and more likely to have a creative or innovative work environment.*

Centrality in community interorganizational resource exchange networks had no effect whatsoever on any of the quality of life indicators. We found, however, that having more members of the elite supporting and/or using the organization for services resulted in organizations becoming more creative and receptive to innovations ($p < .05$) and less alienated ($p < .05$). Elite presence had no affect on the number of disagreements or conflicts with employees.

Discussion. What can we now say about embeddedness theory? Were we unfair in equating social structure with clutter? Probably. The clutter hypotheses received little support. With a few exceptions, social structures did not modify the effect of tactics on growth and decline. Thus organizational size, age, decision-making structures, and network ties did not increase or decrease the chances of successfully implementing tactics.

Did social structure then have an independent effect on organizational change? For the most part, yes.

These findings suggest that there was a complicated interaction between elite contacts, political and managerial tactics, donations and volunteers, and time. Our suspicion is that the elite's role in nonprofit organizations changed over time. In the earlier period the elite was a market signal that nonprofits used to show funders that they were reliable, accountable, and worthy of support. Ties to the elite were rewarded with more donations and volunteers. In turn, it was the elite's job to monitor the organization. The negative effects that we found in the Poisson regressions suggest that earlier in the study period, nonprofits may have felt they could shed both political and managerial tactics, if they had strong ties to the local elite. In the 1990s things changed. Instead of being a market signal and watchdog for the rest of the donor community, elites became more like extension agents, spreading the gospel of strategic management. Their presence was important to procure donations and recruit volunteers, if the organization did not employ political tactics, but was no longer important if they did. Rather the elite was there to teach nonprofit boards and managers how to behave proactively—both in a managerial and political way.

The sociological literature has often taken a dim view of elite participation in nonprofits (for an exception, see Ostrander 1995). Maybe this position should be reevaluated. Over the fifteen years of our study, elite contacts resulted in more donations and volunteers, an increase in the use of political and managerial tactics (which, in turn, resulted in an increase in donated and commercial income), less alienation among participants, and a work environment more sympathetic to creativity and innovation. Of course, this does not speak to what happened to organizations' mission, outputs, or client base with greater elite involvement. This is still an empirical question. Yet, in all fairness to our data, contact with the elite had numerous beneficial effects on organizations.

We also found that interorganizational networks influenced the choice of organizational tactics, independent of organizations' patterns of resource dependencies. Organizations adopted tactics that were used by organizations in their resource exchange networks and managers in their acquaintanceship networks. This was not good news for rational choice theorists and those who believe that tactics should be tightly coupled to the resource needs of organizations. The social influence findings were impressive precisely because they were independent of the organization's dependency upon different resource streams, mimetic variables, and funding uncertainty. This suggested that these effects were important and played an ongoing role in influencing the tactics used by organizations. Whether this is a "problem" or not is something others can decide.

This brings us to our final point. Earlier we argued that we might better interpret social network effects using selection theory rather than adaptation theory. Network ties tend to be unobtrusive and "taken for granted." A manager and/or her organization interact with other managers and other organizations on a day-to-day basis. Not much thought goes into these exchanges, yet our data suggested that these network ties had subtle influences over growth and decline, the selection of tactics, and even the quality of organizational life. In addition to seeing elites as a kind of resource tactic used by organizations, we interpreted the effect of elite ties on donated income and volunteers as a kind of inertial effect where organizations that received donations and volunteer support in the past would receive donations and volunteer support in the future. Similarly we would say that organizations that do things certain ways, say, employ managerial or political tactics, cluster together and reinforce one another's choices and habits. The network did not so much bring about change as it may have "bonded" actors that tended to do things similarly. In this respect network effects are longstanding and difficult to dislodge and may have long-term (and unanticipated) positive and negative effects on organizations.

Notes

1. Density also had a negative effect on changes in donated income and volunteers between 1988 and 1992 in our initial analysis. However, this effect weakened when we controlled for the network variables.

2. Note that we included niche legitimacy in only three analyses: 1980–1984, 1988–1992, and 1988–1994, because we did not have data on niche legitimacy for 1984.

3. Even if political tactics resulted in growth in commercial income and employees and managerial tactics resulted in growth in donated income and volunteers, this does not mean that everyone in the organization would be happy about it. It's a cultural and not a resource argument that we proffer here.

4. Perhaps one reason that both academics and practitioners get so excited about networks and social capital imagery is that some of that clutter (or social inventory) that the organization has had to carry can finally be valuated and thus rationalized as part of the asset base of the organization.

5. In one Poisson regression, measuring change in tactics between 1988 and 1992, we did find that organizations increased their use of managerial tactics if those which they perceived to be successful utilized more managerial tactics in 1988 ($p < .10$).

References

Barnett, William P. and Glenn R. Carroll. 1995. "Modeling Internal Organizational Change." *Annual Review of Sociology* 21:217–36.

Barney, Jay B. and William G. Ouchi (Eds.). 1986. *Organizational Economics.* San Francisco: Jossey-Bass.

Baum, Joel A. C. and Jane E. Dutton. 1996. "The Embeddedness of Strategy." Pp. 1–15 in *Advances in Strategic Management,* Volume 13, edited by Paul Shrivastava, Anne S. Huff, and Jane E. Dutton. Greenwich, CT: JAI.

Baum, Joel A. C. and Heather A. Haveman. 1997. "Love Thy Neighbor? Differentiation and Agglomeration in the Manhattan Hotel Industry, 1898–1990." *Administrative Science Quarterly* 42:304–38.

Baum, Joel A. and Stephen J. Mezias. 1993. "Competition, Institutional Linkages, and Organizational Growth." *Social Science Research* 22:131–64.

Baum, Joel A. C. and Christine Oliver. 1991. "Institutional Linkages and Organizational Mortality." *Administrative Science Quarterly* 36:187–218.

Baum, Joel A. C. and Christine Oliver. 1992. "Institutional Embeddedness and the Dynamics of Organizational Populations." *American Sociological Review* 57:540–59.

Baum, Joel A. C. and Christine Oliver. 1996. "Toward an Institutional Ecology of Organizational

Foundings." *Academy of Management Journal* 39:1378–1427.

Baum, Joel A. C. and Walter W. Powell. 1995. "Cultivating an Institutional Ecology of Organizations." *American Sociological Review* 60:529–38.

Baum, Joel A. C. and Jitendra V. Singh. 1994a. "Organizational Niche Overlap and the Dynamics of Organizational Mortality." *American Journal of Sociology* 100:346–80.

Baum, Joel A. C. and Jitendra V. Singh. 1994b. "Organizational Niche Overlap and the Dynamics of Organizational Founding." *Organization Science* 5:483–502.

Baum, Joel A. C. and Jitendra V. Singh. 1996. "Dynamics of Organizational Response to Competition." *Social Forces* 74:1261–97.

Carroll, Glenn R. and Michael T. Hannan (Eds.). 1995. *Organizations in Industry: Strategy, Structure and Selection.* New York: Oxford University Press.

Coleman, James S. 1988. "Social Capital in the Creation of Human Capital." *American Journal of Sociology* 94(Supplement):S95-S120.

Davis, Gerald F. and Tracy A. Thompson. 1994. "A Social Movement Perspective on Corporate Control." *Administrative Science Quarterly* 39:141–73.

DiMaggio, Paul and Walter W. Powell. 1983. "The Iron Cage Revisited: Institutional Isomorphism and Collective Rationality in Organizational Fields." *American Sociological Review* 48:147–60.

Fombrun, Charles J. 1996. *Reputation: Realizing Value from the Corporate Image.* Boston: Harvard University Business School Press.

Hall, Peter D. 1990. "Conflicting Managerial Cultures in Nonprofit Organizations." *Nonprofit Management and Leadership* 1:153–65.

Hannan, Michael T. and Glenn R. Carroll. 1995a. "An Introduction to Organizational Ecology." Pp. 17–31 in *Organizations in Industry: Strategy, Structure and Selection,* edited by Glenn R. Carroll and Michael T. Hannan. New York: Oxford University Press.

Hannan, Michael T. and Glenn R. Carroll. 1995b. "Theory Building and Cheap Talk about Legiti-

mation: Reply to Baum and Powell." *American Sociological Review* 60:539–44.

Mackay, Harvey. 1997. *Dig Your Well Before You're Thirsty: The Only Networking Book You'll Ever Need.* New York: Currency/Doubleday.

Oliver, Christine. 1991. "Strategic Responses to Institutional Processes." *Academy of Management Review* 16:145–79.

Ostrander, Susan A. 1995. *Money for Change: Social Movement Philanthropy at Haymarket People's Fund.* Philadelphia, PA: Temple University Press.

Powell, Walter W. and Paul J. DiMaggio (Eds.). 1991. *The New Institutionalism in Organizational Analysis.* Chicago: University of Chicago Press.

Scott, W. Richard. 1995. *Institutions and Organizations: Theory and Research.* Thousand Oaks, CA: Sage.

Scott, W. Richard. 1998. *Organizations: Rational, Natural, and Open Systems,* 4th edition. Upper Saddle River, NJ: Prentice-Hall.

Singh, Jitendra V. 1986. "Performance, Slack, and Risk Taking in Organizational Decision-Making." *Academy of Management Journal* 29(September):562–85.

Singh, Jitendra V., Robert J. House, and David J. Tucker. 1986. "Organizational Change and Organizational Mortality." *Administrative Science Quarterly* 31:587–611.

Singh, Jitendra V. and Charles J. Lumsden. 1990. "Theory and Research in Organizational Ecology." *Annual Review of Sociology* 16:161–95.

Singh, Jitendra V., David J. Tucker, and Robert J. House. 1986. "Organizational Legitimacy and the Liability of Newness." *Administrative Science Quarterly* 31:171–93.

Singh, Jitendra V., David J. Tucker, and Agnes G. Meinhard. 1991. "Institutional Change and Ecological Dynamics." Pp. 390–422 in *The New Institutionalism in Organizational Analysis,* edited by Walter W. Powell and Paul J. DiMaggio. Chicago: University of Chicago Press.

Suchman, Mark C. 1995. "Managing Legitimacy: Strategic and Institutional Approaches." *Academy of Management Review* 20:571–610.

PART 9

GIVING THEORIES OF THE NONPROFIT SECTOR

Why do people give—of their money, time, and effort? Why do some people give more than others do? To what extent is giving driven or influenced by sympathy, empathy, a sense of justice, to alleviate guilt, or by rational calculation of personal utility? Is altruism—or egoism—a characteristic of human nature that emanates from genetic structure? Is giving an inherited personality trait—a "drive"? Or is altruism learned from others around us, developmentally over years? Why do people give more to some organizations and purposes than they do to others? How and why do people's giving patterns differ at various life stages? How is philanthropy similar and different in other countries?

These types of questions are the essence and focus of theories of giving. A variety of diverse theories of giving are needed in order to understand the distinctiveness and the complexities of the nonprofit sector. And at a practical level, they also should be of vital importance to the trustees and executives of the thousands of nonprofit organizations that rely on philanthropy for substantial portions of their revenue.

Giving theories inform us about an important aspect of human behavior—donating voluntarily to support the establishment, operations, and survival of organizations and programs in the nonprofit sector. Giving theories also help us to know what causes who to give how much to which particular types of charitable purposes and organizations—knowledge that is vital for the survival and growth of nonprofit organizations.

The myriad existing theories of giving present contrasting views about what is important to understand about giving, what causes people to give to what, and the degree to which giving is shaped by internalized motivations or social pressures. They even differ in their assumptions about the nature of human beings. Do people rationally calculate utilities before deciding to give, or do emotions impulsively "trigger" acts of giving? These diversities in assumptions reflect the differences between the three academic disciplines that have produced most of the theories: psychology, sociology, and economics. *Psychological theories* of giving focus mostly on individual motivations for giving; *sociological theories* on cultural influences, including socialization processes, group norms, and the role of institutionalized religion; *economic theories* on rational public choices—decision processes that lead people to donate instead of allocating their resources to other ends.

Please remember that giving is not the topic of this chapter alone. Giving is one of the most distinctive features of the nonprofit sector, and theories of giving are integral elements of the sector's history—especially in the United States. Readers who are particularly interested in giving theory should consider reviewing the closely related readings in other parts of the book, including the following: "Voluntarism," by Jeffrey Brudney; "The Gospel of Wealth," by Andrew Carnegie; and "A Brief History of Tax Policy Changes Affecting Charitable Organizations," by Gary Scrivner.

This part's readings introduce some of the most interesting and often-competing theories of giving. First, however, I define several concepts that are central to theories of giving, review a few practical implications of giving theories, and briefly introduce some thoughts about giving that were espoused by Benjamin Franklin and Maimonides—philosophies that continue to have applicability and influence in the twenty-first century.

Definitions

Giving theory is an umbrella term that incorporates and builds on four interrelated concepts and four bodies of literature: *philanthropy, altruism, charity,* and *voluntarism.*[1] The definitions of these concepts are the cause of disagreement among practitioners and theorists alike. But the disagreement about these cornerstone concepts highlights the main differences among many of the various alternative theories.

Jeffrey Brudney defines *philanthropy* (in a reading reprinted in Part 2) as the following:

> Voluntary giving, voluntary serving, and voluntary association to achieve some vision of the public good; includes charity, patronage, and civil society. . . . The usual inclusive contemporary definition of philanthropy is "values, organizations, and practices that entail voluntary action to achieve some vision or the public good" or the "private" production of "public goods."

Rubin's definition is largely consistent with Brudney's but introduces additional notions:

> Systems of beliefs and related actions that result in benevolence toward others, that serve a public good, and that do not entail expectations of disproportionate reciprocity. . . . (1) Action or behavior based on a belief system stressing benevolence toward others; (2) the practice of making contribution(s) of monetary value to a humane cause or a common good.[2]

Foundations are the primary institutions for philanthropy, "nonprofit, nongovernmental organizations that promote charitable giving and other public purposes usually by giving grants of money to nonprofit organizations, qualified individuals, and other entities. . . . Foundations are formed by individuals, families, and business corporations, which usually donate money, property, or other financial assets."[3] Since the turn of the twentieth century, foundations have joined churches in serving as intermediaries between donors and recipients of philanthropy, a role that in Maimonides' era was reserved for churches alone. This should not be surprising, however, be-cause foundations developed out of long traditions of secular and religious giving. Research has shown that donors create foundations for reasons that are quite similar to the ones espoused in recent years by sociological, psychological, and economic theories of giving—several of which are reprinted in this part.

> Donors' reasons for creating foundations were found to vary significantly. Some had a deeply felt reli-gious background or a tradition of a family social responsibility and concern for the poor, and others had political or ideological beliefs they wished to advance. Some donors desired to create a memorial to themselves or their families. Other donors felt a commitment to a community or pressure from their peers to be philanthropic. Relatively few formed foundations because of tax incentives, although the existence of tax incentives often influenced the size of the contribution to the foundation.[4]

Ott and Shafritz[5] explain that the concept of *charity* overlaps with philanthropy but also differs in emphasis:

> Overlap: "Philanthropy: Donations and gifts of money, property, and time or effort to needy and/or socially desirable purposes. Philanthropy is a broader term than charity."
> Differences: "Whereas charity traditionally has been used to mean the alleviation of individual cases of physical illness, poverty, etc., philanthropy has referred to efforts to eliminate the causes of those problems that charity seeks to alleviate."

Cnaan, Handy, and Wadsworth offer an assortment of definitions of *volunteer* that range from the "broadest" to the "purest" on four key dimensions: the voluntary nature of the act; the nature of the reward; the context or auspices under which the volunteer activity is performed; and who benefits (this fourth dimension follows directly from the Code of Maimonides).[6] In analyzing about three hundred articles on voluntarism, Cnaan, Handy, and Wadsworth found that each di-mension had "steps" that differentiated between volunteers and nonvolunteers.

> For example, in the dimension of free choice, we identified three key categories: (1) free will (the abil-ity to voluntarily choose), (2) relatively uncoerced, and (3) obligation to volunteer. Whereas all defini-tions would accept category 1 (free will) as relevant in defining a volunteer, pure definitions would not accept category 2 (relatively coerced), and only the broadest definition would define court-ordered volunteers or students in a required service program as volunteers.[7]

These dimensions and "steps" that separate volunteers from nonvolunteers highlight the impor-tance of definitions for giving theories. Alan Wolfe's explanation of behavioral, motivational, and environmental theories of *altruism* (reprinted in this part) demonstrates how theoretical per-spectives drive definitions. "Behavioral approaches [to altruism] examine what an organism does, irrespective of the state of mind." In contrast, the motivational theorists argue: "The missing ingredient in behavioral accounts . . . is *intent:* to be altruistic, an act must be directed specifically toward an altruistic end" (emphasis in original).[8]

I find Jeffrey Brudney's definition of *voluntarism* (reprinted in Part 2) to be particularly useful: "Actions undertaken freely by individuals, groups, or organizations that are not compelled by biological need or social convention, mandated or coerced by government, or directed principally at financial or economic gain, regarded as beneficial by participants or the larger society."[9]

"Philosophies of Giving" from Benjamin Franklin and Maimonides

Many implicit theories of giving are reflected in the insightful and sage advice of Benjamin Franklin and Maimonides.

Benjamin Franklin

"[The Speaker of the House of Representatives] is hereby required to sign an Order on the Provincial Treasurer for the Payment of Two Thousand Pounds in two yearly Payments, to the treasurer of the said Hospital, to be applied to the Founding, Building and Finishing of the same." This Condition carried the Bill through. . . . And then in soliciting Subscriptions among the People we urg'd the conditional Promise of the Law as an additional Motive to give, since every Man's Donation would be doubled. Thus the Clause work'd both ways. The Subscriptions accordingly soon exceeded the requisite sum, and we claim'd and receiv'd the Public Gift which enabled us to carry the Design into Execution. A convenient and handsome Building was soon erected, the Institution has by constant Experience been found useful, and flourishes to this Day. And I do not remember any of my political Manoeuvres, the Success of which gave me at the time more Pleasure. . . .

It was about this time that another Projector, the Revd. Gilbert Tennent, came to me, with a Request that I would assist him in procuring a Subscription for erecting a new Meeting-house. . . . Unwilling to make myself disagreeable to my fellow Citizens, by too frequently soliciting their Contributions, I absolutely refus'd. He then desir'd I would furnish him with a List of the Names of Persons I knew by Experience to be generous and public-spirited. I thought it would be unbecoming in me, after their kind Compliance with my Solicitations, to mark them out to be worried by other Beggars, and therefore refus'd also to give such a List. He then desir'd I would at least give him my Advice. That I will readily do, said I; and, in the first Place, I advise you to apply to all those whom you know will give something; next to those whom you are uncertain whether they will give any thing or not; and show them the List of those who have given; and lastly, do not neglect those who you are sure will give nothing; for in some of them you may be mistaken. He laugh'd, thank'd me, and said he would take my Advice. He did so, for he ask'd *every body;* and he obtain'd a much larger Sum than he expected, with which he erected the capacious and very elegant Meeting-house that stands in Arch Street. (NOTE: The Second Presbyterian Church, organized in 1743, opened its new building at Arch (Mulberry) and Third Streets in 1752) [emphasis in original].[10]

Maimonides

Maimonides, a Jewish scholastic philosopher and rabbi who was born in Spain, is believed to have lived from 1135 to 1204. Maimonides' "code" was one of the earliest recorded attempts to identify degrees of goodness in giving or, if you will, to articulate a theory of giving. The values that differentiate Maimonides' levels of giving are reflected in many of the theories reprinted in this book. For example, Maimonides' highest level of "almsgiving" is a gift or loan made to another to "strengthen his hand"—a gift that allows the recipient to become employed or open a business, become self-sufficient, and not need to beg again. Centuries later, Andrew Carnegie echoed this theme in his stern admonitions: "In bestowing charity, the main consideration should be to help those who will help themselves; to provide part of the means by which those who desire to improve may do so; to give to those who desire the aids by which they may rise. . . . Neither the individual nor the race is improved by alms-giving" (Carnegie's "The Gospel of Wealth" is reprinted in Part 2). And like the philosophy of Andrew Carnegie's contemporary, John D. Rockefeller,[11] Maimonides saw the primary purpose for giving as ensuring one's place in the afterlife: "Whosoever serves food and drink to poor men and orphans at his table, will, when he calls to God, receive an answer and find delight in it."

> 7. There are eight degrees of almsgiving, each one superior to the other. The highest degree, than which there is none higher, is one who upholds the hand of an Israelite reduced to poverty by handing him a gift or a loan, or entering into a partnership with him, or finding work for him, in order to strengthen his hand, so that he would have no need to beg from other people. Concerning such a one Scripture says, *Thou shalt uphold him; as a stranger and a settler shall he live with thee* (Lev. 25:35), meaning uphold him, so that he would not lapse into want.
>
> 8. Below this is he who gives alms to the poor in such a way that he does not know to whom he has given, nor does the poor man know from whom he has received. This constitutes the fulfilling of a religious duty for its own sake, and for such there was a Chamber of Secrets in the Temple, whereunto the righteous would contribute secretly, and wherefrom the poor of good families would draw the sustenance in equal secrecy. Close to such a person is he who contributes directly to the alms fund. . . .
>
> 9. Below this is he who knows to whom he is giving, while the poor man does not know from whom he is receiving. He is thus like the great among the Sages who were wont to set out secretly and throw the money down at the doors of the poor. . . .
>
> 10. Below this is the case where the poor man knows from whom he is receiving, but himself remains unknown to the giver. He is thus like the great among the Sages who used to place the money in the fold of a linen sheet which they would throw over their shoulder, whereupon the poor would come behind them and take the money without being exposed to humiliation.
>
> 11. Below this is he who hands the alms to the poor man before being asked for them.
>
> 12. Below this is he who hands the alms to the poor man after the latter has asked for them.
>
> 13. Below this is he who gives the poor man less than what is proper, but with a friendly countenance.
>
> 14. Below this is he who gives alms with a frowning countenance. . . .
>
> 16. He who provides maintenance for his grown sons and daughters—whom he is not obligated to maintain . . . , and likewise he who provides maintenance for his father and mother, is accounted as performing an act of charity. Indeed it is an outstanding act of charity, since one's relative has precedence over other people.[12]

The values that separate Maimonides' seven lower degrees of almsgiving are anonymity of the donor, anonymity of the recipient, giving before being asked, and giving cheerfully. The first two presage current theories, research studies, and debates about, for example, the relative worth of giving "out of true altruism" versus giving to receive public recognition and acclaim, or giving because of sympathy or empathy for the plight of recipients versus giving to advance a principle or a cause.

Readings Included in This Part

Alan Wolfe introduces the essence and intensity of the competing approaches to giving theories in the opening sentences of his overview article, "What Is Altruism?"

> A debate over the relative importance of altruism and egoism is the latest chapter in the long-running story of how social scientists think about human behavior. That story . . . has pitted an economic conception of human beings against a sociological one. The economic conception views the individual as a utilitarian calculator of self-interest, the sociological as an other-regarding member of some larger group or society.[13]

"What Is Altruism?" distinguishes between three concepts of altruism—behavioral, motivational, and environmental; identifies their assumptions and disciplinary bases; and assesses the advantages and risks of the three approaches. The *behavioral approach to altruism* examines "what an organism does, irrespective of the state of mind." It views altruism as a predetermined reality, not as behavior that can be developed and learned. Further, the behavioral approach ignores the possibility of an altruistic personality. "Altruism is not a state waiting to be activated but rather something that requires aspects of mind . . . before it can be said to exist." Altruism is not predetermined—as the behaviorists assume. "We do not, when we act altruistically, respond to hardwired programs for sacrificial behavior that have been written into our genes through millennia of evolutionary response."

In contrast, the *motivational approach to altruism* argues that "the missing ingredient in behavioral accounts . . . is *intent;* to be altruistic, an act must be directed specifically toward an altruistic end." A distinction is needed between "purity of motives" and "purity of behavior." Motivational theories thus are usually advocated by psychologists, are individualistic, and often overlook the importance of social influences on individual motivations. "The incompleteness of many of the psychological accounts of altruism indicates that the larger social environment may well be an important factor in encouraging or discouraging altruism." The *environmental approach to altruism* thus stresses the roles that culture and institutions play in influencing altruism. Wolfe argues for a pluralistic approach that incorporates behavioral, motivational, and environmental approaches. "Altruism requires that an individual make choices in the context of particular situations," and thus no single approach can be universally adequate. "Such choices must be a reflection of the way individuals think and develop as they confront contexts within which they must make decisions."

Joan Mount's article, "Why Donors Give," reports on psychological and social-psychological motives that influenced individual alumni/ae givers (and nongivers) to a publicly financed Canadian university.[14] Mount's questionnaire study "examines motives that lie behind personal philanthropy in the educational sphere, explores how donors are different from nondonors, and why donors give the amounts they do." The importance of the study, however, extends beyond higher education, because it "continues the quest for a general theory of individual philanthropy." The motives included in her study were a belief in the cause, joy of giving, liking to be asked, altruism, sympathy, pride or self-respect, obligation, reciprocity, nostalgia, commemoration, appreciation (gratitude from the recipient), recognition (public acknowledgment), and tax credit. "Why

Donors Give" identifies donor motivations, differences between givers and nongivers, and differences that affected the size of gifts. From these findings, Mount proposes a model that uses five variables to predict "largesse": involvement, predominance, self-interest, means, and past behavior.

The introductory essay in Part 2 advises that Andrew Carnegie's article, "The Gospel of Wealth," is included there but that Milton Goldin's analysis of the philosophies of Carnegie and John D. Rockefeller, "The Founding Fathers of Modern Philanthropy," is reproduced here because it does more than describe two groundbreaking philosophies of philanthropy.[15] It also provides important insights into the differences between two enduring philosophies of philanthropy.[16] Carnegie and Rockefeller, both turn-of-the-century giants of industry and philanthropy, accumulated enormous wealth and gave great amounts to improve social ills in post–Civil War America. Their giving was stimulated, however, by different sets of beliefs, expectations, and motivations. Despite their differences, they gave at least in part out of "a broader concern for the permanent economic and social viability of capitalist society."

"The Call of Service: Satisfactions," by Robert Coles, offers an emotional look at the satisfactions people have derived from volunteering.[17] "The Call of Service" is a series of vignettes about individuals who have given themselves to others, their self-reported reasons for volunteering, and the satisfactions they have reaped. Whereas the articles reprinted here on giving theories by Wolfe, Brown, Mount, and Clary et al. are rationally analytical, "The Call of Service" relates theory through poignant personal accounts that are interrupted occasionally with analysis. "Theories of volunteer giving" are told in story form by a young, northern, black civil rights activist and SNCC member who registered voters in Louisiana—and often spent time in southern jails; a college student who became a Big Brother to a youngster whose family had recently immigrated from the Dominican Republic; a housewife who "missed the hospital" when she was away for a few days; a working-class "man's man" who after adapting to the reality that his long-awaited first son had Downs syndrome, volunteered regularly with older youth at a state school for children with developmental disabilities; a middle-aged black mother who taught children as she drove her school bus; and a Harvard undergraduate who tutored children in the Roxbury section of Boston. "The Call of Service" is more than a series of vignettes. Coles uses his interviewees' words to convey the pain that accompanies wrestling with thorny issues: To what extent are these persons drawn to volunteering by egoism or by altruism, or by the desire to learn about a side of life they don't know? One of Coles's volunteers answered the question, "Hey, what's in it for you?" for himself only after he "worked all of the ironies and complexities, really, of a privileged life into a few sentences: the satisfactions of doing community service work and the additional satisfaction that went with knowing that his work would no doubt advance the further work he hoped to do as a lawyer or businessman."

Notes

1. Most students of the nonprofit sector define philanthropy as an overarching term that includes both charity and voluntarism. They are listed separately here as a reminder that all three concepts are included in our usage of the term *giving theory*. These terms are used almost interchangeably in this part, however.

2. Hank Rubin, "Philanthropy: Historical and Philosophical Foundations," in Jay M. Shafritz, ed., *International Encyclopedia of Public Policy and Administration* (Boulder: Westview Press, 1998), p. 928.

3. Elizabeth T. Boris, "Foundations," in Jay M. Shafritz, ed., *International Encyclopedia of Public Policy and Administration* (Boulder: Westview Press, 1998), p. 928.

4. Boris, "Foundations," pp. 931, 932, reporting on John Edie's study in "Congress and Foundations: Historical Summary," in Teresa Odendahl, ed., *America's Wealthy and the Future of Foundations* (New York: Foundation Center, 1987).

5. J. Steven Ott and Jay M. Shafritz, *The Facts on File Dictionary of Nonprofit Organization Management* (New York: Facts on File, 1986), p. 284.

6. Ram A. Cnaan, Femida Handy, and Margaret Wadsworth, "Defining Who Is a Volunteer: Conceptual and Empirical Considerations," *Nonprofit and Voluntary Sector Quarterly* 25 (3), September 1996, 364–383.

7. Ibid., p. 370.

8. Alan Wolfe, "What Is Altruism?" in Walter W. Powell and Elisabeth S. Clemens, eds., *Private Action and the Public Good* (New Haven: Yale University Press, 1998), pp. 39 and 37 respectively.

9. Jeffrey L. Brudney, "Voluntarism," in Jay M. Shafritz, ed., *International Encyclopedia of Public Policy and Administration* (Boulder: Westview Press, 1998), p. 2343.

10. Benjamin Franklin, *The Autobiography of Benjamin Franklin,* ed. Ralph L. Ketcham, Helen C. Boatfield, and Helene H. Fineman (New Haven: Yale University Press, 1964), pp. 201, 202.

11. See Milton Goldin's comparative analysis of the philosophies of Carnegie and Rockefeller in "The Founding Fathers of Philanthropy," reprinted in this part.

12. Maimonides, *The Code of Maimonides,* Book Seven, *The Book of Agriculture,* trans. from the Hebrew by Isaac Klein (New Haven: Yale University Press, 1979), pp. 91, 92.

13. Wolfe, Alan, "What Is Altruism," in Walter W. Powell and Elisabeth S. Clemens, eds., *Private Action and the Public Good* (New Haven: Yale University Press, 1998), p. 36.

14. Joan Mount, "Why Donors Give," *Journal of Nonprofit Management and Leadership* 7 (1), Fall 1996, 3–14.

15. Milton Goldin, "The Founding Fathers of Modern Philanthropy," *Fund Raising Management* 99, June 1988, 48–50.

16. Readers are urged to review the readings by Stephen Block, Peter Dobkin Hall, and Gary Scrivner, reprinted in Part 3.

17. Robert Coles, "Satisfactions," in Robert Coles, *The Call of Service: A Witness to Idealism* (Boston: Houghton Mifflin, 1993), pp. 68–94.

References

Block, Stephen R. "Nonprofit Organization." In Jay M. Shafritz, ed., *International Encyclopedia of Public Policy and Administration,* pp. 1509–1514. Boulder: Westview Press, 1998.

Boris, Elizabeth T. "Foundations." In Jay M. Shafritz, ed., *International Encyclopedia of Public Policy and Administration,* pp. 928–935. Boulder: Westview Press, 1998.

Brown, Eleanor. "Altruism Toward Groups: The Charitable Provision of Private Goods." *Nonprofit and Voluntary Sector Quarterly* 26 (2), June 1997, 175–184.

Brudney, Jeffrey L. "Voluntarism." In Jay M. Shafritz, ed., *International Encyclopedia of Public Policy and Administration,* pp. 2343–2349. Boulder: Westview Press, 1998.

Clary, E. Gil, Mark Snyder, and Robert Ridge. "Volunteers' Motivations: A Functional Strategy for the Recruitment, Placement, and Retention of Volunteers." *Journal of Nonprofit Management and Leadership* 2 (4), Summer 1992, 333–350.

Cnaan, Ram A., Femida Handy, and Margaret Wadsworth. "Defining Who Is a Volunteer: Conceptual and Empirical Considerations." *Nonprofit and Voluntary Sector Quarterly* 25 (3), September 1996, 364–383.

Coles, Robert. *The Call of Service: A Witness to Idealism.* Boston: Houghton Mifflin, 1993.

Franklin, Benjamin. *The Autobiography of Benjamin Franklin,* ed. Leonard W. Labaree, Ralph L. Ketcham, Helen C. Boatfield, and Helene H. Fineman. New Haven: Yale University Press, 1964.

Freund, Gerald. *Narcissism and Philanthropy: Ideas and Talent Denied.* New York: Viking, 1996.

Goldin, Milton. "The Founding Fathers of Modern Philanthropy." *Fund Raising Management* 99, June 1988, 48–50.

Ilchman, Warren F. "Philanthropy." In Jay M. Shafritz, ed., *International Encyclopedia of Public Policy and Administration,* pp. 1654–1661. Boulder: Westview Press, 1998.

Maimonides. *The Code of Maimonides,* Book Seven, *The Book of Agriculture,* trans. and ed. Isaac Klein. New Haven: Yale University Press, 1979.

Mount, Joan. "Why Donors Give." *Journal of Nonprofit Management and Leadership* 7 (1), Fall 1996, 3–14.

Odendahl, Teresa. *Charity Begins at Home.* New York: Basic Books, 1990.

Payton, Robert L. *Philanthropy: Voluntary Action for the Public Good.* New York: American Council on Education/Macmillan, 1988.

Prince, Russ Alan, and Karen Maru File. "Profiling the Seven Faces of Philanthropy." In Prince and File, *The Seven Faces of Philanthropy.* San Francisco: Jossey-Bass, 1994.

Rubin, Hank. "Philanthropy: Historical and Philosophical Foundations." In Jay M. Shafritz, ed., *International Encyclopedia of Public Policy and Administration,* pp. 1661–1667. Boulder: Westview Press, 1998.

Scott, Jacquelyn Thayer. "Voluntary Sector." In Jay M. Shafritz, ed., *International Encyclopedia of Public Policy and Administration,* pp. 2358–2362. Boulder: Westview Press, 1998.

Stebbins, Robert A. "Volunteering: A Serious Leisure Perspective." *Nonprofit and Voluntary Sector Quarterly* 25 (2), June 1996, 211–224.

Wolf, Alan. "What Is Altruism?" In Walter W. Powell and Elisabeth S. Clemens, eds., *Private Action and the Public Good,* pp. 36–46. New Haven: Yale University Press, 1998.

CHAPTER 26

What Is Altruism?

Alan Wolfe

A debate over the relative importance of altruism and egoism is the latest chapter in the long-running story of how social scientists think about human behavior. That story, since at least the nineteenth century, has pitted an economic conception of human beings against a sociological one. The economic conception views the individual as a utilitarian calculator of self-interest, the sociological as an other-regarding member of some larger group or society. This battle has never stopped (Schwartz 1986), and it is not likely to do so in the future. The economistic version has, in recent years, won numerous adherents, often in fields far removed from economics, including sociology (Coleman 1990). But the more popular rational choice theory becomes, the more contested it is; many see rational choice theory as increasingly limited, which raises the possibility of the emergence of a new paradigm that once again pays attention to altruism (Piliavin and Charg 1990; Batson 1990, 1991; Simmons 1991).

It is no longer possible to argue, as it was just a decade or two ago, that assumptions of self-regarding behavior are more realistic or predictive than assumptions of other-regarding behavior. To be open to the world around them, social scientists need to go beyond monocausal explana-

tions of human behavior that achieve a certain formal elegance, but do so at the price of prematurely closing off the complexities of human behavior.

If the need for a theoretical appreciation of altruistic behavior is increasingly accepted by social scientists, problems of conceptualization remain formidable. Altruism is a far more tricky concept philosophically than self-interest, for it involves not only defining the motives of an individual actor, but also dealing with the consequences of those actions for a multitude of other actors.

These difficulties suggest the need for some stock-taking with respect to the way social scientists have tried to theorize about and understand altruistic behavior. Such a task could be carried out in two ways. One would be to examine the theoretical and conceptual difficulties facing any attempt to operationalize what altruistic behavior might be. The other is to put such conceptual issues on hold, at least for a while, in an attempt to examine presumptively altruistic behavior in real world or approximate real world conditions. My aim in this chapter is to start with real world or approximate real world efforts to understand altruism, and from them to generalize back to theoretical and conceptual problems rather than the other way around.

Daniel Bar-Tal (1985/86) has distinguished between behavioral and motivational conceptions of altruism. To these I would add a third: environmental. Each approach to altruism carries both advantages and risks.

Behavioral Altruism

Behavioral approaches examine what an organism does, irrespective of the state of mind of the organism that does it. (Indeed, some organisms can act altruistically without having any state of mind at all, if by *state of mind* we mean the complex cognition associated with humans and perhaps some other primates). "Altruism," J. Phillipe Rushton writes, "is defined as social behavior carried out to achieve positive outcomes for another rather than for the self" (1980, 8). Behavioral definitions of altruism thus have a seemingly great contribution to make; they seem to prove that, despite Hobbesian pessimism, there are solutions to prisoners' dilemma situations that are based on something more solid than temporary agreements or contingent contracts.

It is a short step from a behavioral definition of altruism to the conclusion that human beings are by nature cooperative, social, or even, in some accounts, moral (Wilson 1993). Considering the fact that nineteenth-century intellectual traditions left us with a legacy of claims that self-interest is biologically based, it is refreshing to believe that the opposite may be the case. Refreshing though such a case may be, it is not, however, persuasive. Do human beings act altruistically without having altruistic motives? This is an impossible question to answer definitively, given the notorious problems of establishing what motives are, but there are sufficient hints in what we know about altruistic behavior to suggest that the behavioral model has serious empirical flaws.

First, the behavioral approach imagines altruism as a state that is activated by a genetic switch. There are two reasons to question such an approach. One is that altruism possesses clear *developmental* features. One can quibble with Jean Piaget's or Lawrence Kohlberg's account of the stages of moral development, but there is little doubt that as human beings mature, they become more capable of taking the position of an abstract other (Zahn-Waxler 1991). Similarly, we know that altruistic behavior varies from one society to another. The question is not so much whether, in any given organism (or society), altruism exists or not, but rather, how much of a disposition to altruism (or, for that matter, egoism) exists?

In addition, it is by no means clear that a precise conceptualization of altruism, one which imagines such behavior as being turned on automatically, corresponds with the way in which individuals pursue activities that have public-regarding intentions or consequences. Such a point of view imagines altruistic behavior as an emerging reality, whereas behavioral approaches to altruism imagine it as a determined reality.

A second problem with behavioral approaches to altruism is that they ignore the existence of an altruistic personality. Altruism is not a state waiting to be activated but rather something that requires aspects of mind—cognition, self-perception, identity formation, empathy—before it can be said to exist. What differentiated rescuers of Jews from nonrescuers in the study by Samuel and Pearl Oliner was their state of mind: altruistic people tend to believe in the existence of a just world, are more inward looking, and tend to be the children of parents who emphasized similar values. These findings have been replicated in laboratory and everyday life situations by social psychologists (Carlo et al. 1991; Bierhoff, Klein, and Kramp 1991). Mental activity is a dynamic component of altruistic behavior: altruism happens because people use their minds to interpret the world around them and, basing themselves on that information, decide to act in one way rather than another.

Third, although altruism is learned, it does not take heroic amounts of education or training to instill it. To be sure, there will always be saints whose altruism stands as an unattainable ideal for ordinary people, but most real world altruism is learned through others in the course of everyday life. Altruism, for one thing, usually involves a substantial amount of conformist behavior. For example, people are more likely to give money to the Salvation Army if they see others do it (Hurley and Allen 1974; Krebs 1970). A variety of laboratory studies indicate that when some people act altruistically, others do as well (Reykowski 1980). Even heroic acts of altruism can have a conformist dimension. Rescuers of Jews in Nazi Europe, for example, were more likely to appear in parts of Europe where the moral climate credited their activities. And although rescue was by its very nature secret—and therefore not likely to be conformist—there is evidence that rescuers' neighbors knew of many rescue activities and silently acknowledged them, an indirect form of social approval (Oliner and Oliner 1988, 125).

Altruism, like selfishness, is facilitated by rewards; the reward of selfishness may be increased material benefit, while that of altruism is attachment to group norms. Group solidarity can be as important as individual conscience in contributing to prosocial behavior (Dawes, van de Kragt, and Orbell 1988). Moreover, just as altruism has a conformist dimension, interestingly, so does nonaltruism: the famous bystander effect—that is, people will be more likely not to act altruistically when they know that others are present—demonstrates the importance of conformity in nonaltruistic responses (Latané and Darley 1970). Learning from others—watching what they do and then deciding to do something similar—is a constitutive feature of altruistic behavior.

Taken together, all these factors are indirect evidence that, at least in human beings, altruism is not a product of preconscious or unconscious drives. We do not, when we act altruistically, respond to hard-wired programs for sacrificial behavior that have been written into our genes through millennia of evolutionary response. What is most important about altruism is precisely what behaviorism leaves out, namely, the activating factors that transform an instinct into something worth knowing about. When altruism exists, something happens. Behavioral definitions willfully choose to ignore what that something might be.

Whatever the empirical problems facing a naturalistic explanation of altruism, there are normative problems as well. Because hard-wired explanations of human behavior are usually associated with such notions as those of a "selfish gene" (Dawkins 1976), we usually think of biological theories as insufficiently altruistic because they allow little room for imagining people as making complex moral choices. Ironically, such theories are also problematic because they are, in a sense, too altruistic. Altruism in and of itself is not a good. The fact that animals sacrifice themselves for the sake of their offspring does not mean that a human being who did so would be acting in an altruistically appropriate way. Society would face as much trouble reproducing itself if everyone were other-regarding all the time as it would if everyone were self-regarding all the time.

This is not the place for asserting my own normative commitments and judging any particular approach to altruism a failure because it fails to appreciate them. But I do think it appropriate to argue that a minimum normative standard can be developed from empirical grounds. If altruism means an effort to do good for others, then the minimal normative principle that a definition of altruism should meet is respect for pluralism, given that conceptions of the good will be contested (Mansbridge, 1998). A pluralistic perspective on human behavior would be suspicious of any kind of moral perfection or imperfection. People are by nature neither saints nor sinners. Behavioral approaches to altruism are insufficiently appreciative of those problems. A society that was perfectly altruistic but that, as a result, lacked a human capacity to err would not necessarily be a good society. We might well prefer a society in which there was some cruelty to others—crime, for example—to one in which such cruelty was completely abolished if the former contained the freedom that makes such things as crime possible.

Assumptions of psychological pluralism, then, raise questions about behavioral approaches to altruism on both empirical and normative grounds. At a time when psychologists themselves have moved well beyond behaviorism, it makes little sense for other social scientists to adopt their discarded models in seeking to understand a phenomenon as complex as human altruism.

Motivational Altruism

Some experimental social psychologists trying to understand prosocial behavior have turned to an examination of the motives people have for taking others into account. The missing ingredient in behavioral accounts, they argue, is *intent;* to be altruistic, an act must be directed specifically toward an altruistic end. The most parsimonious definition of motivational altruism comes from Daniel Batson and Laura Shaw: "Altruism is a motivational state with the ultimate goal of increasing another's welfare" (Batson and Shaw 1991, 108).

Batson makes a distinction between purity of motives and purity of behavior. Batson and his colleagues have tried to show that altruistic goals will be more likely to be chosen when an individual identifies empathically with other people (Batson, Batson, Slingsby, Harrell, et al. 1991; Batson, Oleson, Weeks, Healy, et al. 1989; Batson, Batson, Griffitt, Barrientos, et al. 1989; Batson, Dyck, Brandt, Batson, et al. 1988; Dovidio, Allen, and Schroeder 1990). Such empathy is not the by-product of benefits to the self, such as the relief brought about by minimizing another's distress. There is such a thing as pure motivational altruism, Batson claims. We really are capable of caring for others (Batson 1990).

Batson's work has not been universally accepted by social psychologists. Some are critical of his work because the concept of a motive does not seem to account either for behavior that is without motives or behavior that is guided by motives that cannot be fully articulated.

Nancy Eisenberg (Eisenberg, Miller, Schaller, Fabes, et al. 1989; Eisenberg 1991, 29) makes an important distinction in this context between empathy, which in her view involves feeling what the other feels, and sympathy, which involves wanting the other person to feel better. To the degree that altruism involves empathy, it involves sentiments which are not quite the same as conscious motivations; generally speaking, we feel what another person feels not after considering the matter and being motivated to do so, but out of a spontaneous emotional reaction. From this point of view, Batson's motivational account of altruism is too demanding; to meet its standard, human beings must not only react empathically to another, but do so by meeting a standard of rationality that is rarely found in real world situations.

Yet from another point of view, Batson's definition does not set a high enough standard of rational conduct. One of the most fully elaborated theoretical accounts of how morality develops is that of Kolhberg, who argues that the most moral acts are those which rise beyond convention and situation to principled reasoning in line with the essentially impersonal Kantian criterion of judgment (Kohlberg 1981). Whatever one thinks of such an account, altruism, in the higher stages of moral development, would not be produced by motives that grow out of empathic identification with the other. It would instead be a reflective response to norms of justice that have been internalized by a particular individual (Eisenberg 1991, 128–29). As every Kantian knows, there are occasions in which the upholding of a norm of justice requires cruelty in specific circumstances; that is, to achieve a higher form of altruism, one must *resist* the desire to act out of empathy in a particular situation. Batson's definition, which tends to exclude emotional identification with a specific other, also tends to exclude rationalized identification with a general principle.

One way of combining these critiques of purely motivational theories of altruism is to point out that motives, like altruism in general, are rarely in one state or another. When we act altruistically, we can be responding at a number of levels and attempting to meet a variety of mixed goals (Mansbridge 1998). Our inclination to act altruistically could originate in an emotion, as when, confronted with another's pain, we want to do something for that person. At the same time, such a response to another's pain can reflect a principled, cognitive commitment, namely, that it is right that we respond to the pain of another. Not surprisingly, emotions usually accompany altruistic acts: we think of the sacrifices people make for their children, which generally grow out of love, as the most altruistic of acts. Surprising as it may seem, however, altruistic acts are also often motivated by a commitment to principle.

Emotional appeals without any appeal to principle, for one thing, can backfire, exhibiting what has been called psychological reactance (Brehm 1966). When door-to-door solicitors for a charity showed potential contributors pictures of handicapped children, they did find such an effect (Isen and Noonberg 1979). In most cases, showing pictures did not bring about additional contributions; the best that could be said in support of emotional appeals to altruism was that they did not hurt contributions (Thorton, Kirchner, and Jacobs 1991). In addition, much real world altruistic behavior is motivated by commitments to abstract norms of justice. Psychologists have demonstrated that altruistic behavior *is* associated with an orientation toward norms; those who help others usually possess a strong sense that they *ought* to act in ways to help others (Schwartz 1977; Schwartz and Howard 1982). These internalized norms have important real world consequences. We know, for example, that those who have a strong sense of moral obligation are more likely to be blood donors (Zuckerman and Reiss 1978) and that repeat blood donors are more likely to act on the basis of principle than first-time blood donors (Charg, Piliavin, and Callero 1988). Similarly, individuals are more likely to ignore opportunities to act as free riders when they have a strong sense of moral obligation. For example, individuals are more likely to participate in a recycling program when they believe it is the right thing to do (Hopper and Nielsen 1991).

Because the motives that lie behind altruistic acts are complex, combining, as they do, both emotion and principle, motivational theories of altruism can be faulted, not because they all pay attention to motives, but because they reduce all motives to one thing. Batson is surely correct to stress the importance of motivation; behavior that has altruistic consequences without any altruistic motive is less altruistic than behavior which is intended to help others but which actually harms them. We would be more likely to view the action of someone who tries to save a drowning man but fails as altruistic than the actions of someone whose passing boat acts as a life raft to bring a drowning person to shore. Moreover, there are clear normative advantages

to a motivational account; one generally wants to believe that individuals are responsible for their acts and that when they act well it is because they were motivated to achieve the goal of acting well. But Batson runs into problems when he identifies motives with the pursuit of one goal only, for such an account does not give full appreciation to real world, as opposed to laboratory, conditions.

Motivational theories ought to be viewed as establishing necessary but not sufficient conditions for an understanding of altruism. Perhaps because they are usually advocated by psychologists, motivational theories tend to be individualistic, stressing how motives are internally arrived at as people examine the world around them. In this way, motivational theories accept a distinction between a private realm in which motives matter and a public realm in which people act on the basis of their motives. But this distinction, as Calhoun argues, is problematic (Calhoun, 1998). His point applies as much to theories of motivation as it does to other efforts to draw a sharp line between private and public activity. Motives come from somewhere. To the degree that the place from which they come lies outside individuals and their particular cognitive or emotional makeup, to that extent is a motivational account of altruism unsatisfactory.

Some evidence exists that the normative principles associated with altruistic acts *do* come from outside individuals themselves. In her study of blood donations in specific communities, Jane Piliavin found that personal norms did not account fully for variations in altruistic behavior. Any particular individuals' motives for giving blood were reenforced in those communities which were perceived as valuing such acts. In other words, personal norms were connected to social norms and could not be fully understood without an appreciation of the connection (Piliavin and Libby 1985/86). One need not take a Durkheimian position that society stands outside the individual and acts as a conscience for individuals; it is sufficient to recognize that individual motives toward altruism are influenced by the degree to which the society in which the individual lives values altruism. Obviously, as the examples of the rescue of European

Jews illustrate, societies that denigrate altruism can still manifest it. Still, real world conditions underscore the point that motivations come from somewhere. We are more likely to see altruism occurring in societies that give social approval to altruism, just as we are more likely to see extreme egoism in cultures that, because they lack the rudiments of self-sufficiency, cannot make care of others a primary goal (Turnbull 1972).

Environmental Altruism

The incompleteness of many of the psychological accounts of altruism indicates that the larger social environment may well be an important factor in encouraging or discouraging altruism. (In using the term *environment* in this context, I am not referring to the natural or ecological environment).

One way to illustrate the role that environmental factors play in encouraging or discouraging altruistic behavior is to consider the question of religion because religious beliefs and institutions, since Durkheim, have been understood to be part of the larger social structure—what I am calling the environment—that influences individual conduct. We would generally expect that the more religious people are, the more altruistic their behavior.

Somewhat to their surprise, the Oliners discovered that rescuers could not be distinguished from nonrescuers on the basis of religious belief (1988, 156). Similarly, the sociologist Robert Wuthnow wrote, "Participation in religious organizations, it appears, has a genuine, but limited, effect on charitable behavior" (1991, 126). If this were the end of the story, Chaves's argument that religion is a public good which contributes directly and indirectly to philanthropic activity would be hard to explain (Chaves, 1998). But in fact, religion is an important factor in encouraging altruism, even if the relation is indirect.

This indirect relation can be best understood if we think of religious beliefs and institutions as frameworks that enable people to understand the meaning and consequences of altruism. In order to grasp what altruistic behaviors are, Wuthnow argues, we need to look beyond those behaviors themselves to "the languages we use to make sense of such behaviors, the cultural understandings that transform them from physical motions into human action" (1991, 45). Chaves argues against the notion that religious organizations engage in charitable behavior in order to hold on to or gain members. But he does not go completely in the opposite direction of arguing that religious organizations are directly altruistic. Rather, he suggests, religious organizations generally have "unclear goals, unclear technologies, and fluid participants." The role of religion in encouraging altruism is indirect because organizations, like individuals, have multiple objectives and pursue the good in a variety of ways.

One must be careful about relying too much on environmental explanations of altruistic variation. We have already seen that religious belief does not correlate strongly with altruism; neither, in the Oliners' study, did political affiliation or social class (1988, 156–59). Other environmental factors, however, do seem to correlate with altruistic behavior. For all their methodological difficulties, many studies demonstrate that women tend to be more altruistic than men (Russell and Mentzel 1990; Mills, Pedersen, and Grusec 1989). There are stages in the life cycle which suggest that people's level of altruism is correlated with age (Midlarsky and Hannah 1989). Cross-cultural variations in the degree of altruism have frequently been observed (Johnson et al. 1989). Altruism is more frequent in rural areas than in urban ones (Kamal, Mehta, and Jain 1987). Gender may account for the fact that lesbians tend to be much more altruistic than male homosexuals (Weller and Benozio 1987)—and, for that matter, nurses usually more than doctors (Chambliss 1996)—but questions of lifestyle and cultural choice are also involved. Because some things seem to explain altruism better than others, we ought to remind ourselves that environmental explanations of altruism do not offer a foolproof guide to empirical observations; they play a major role, but they always have to be interpreted with some caution.

Environmental approaches to altruism stress the role to be played, not only by culture, but also by social institutions. Bureaucratic organization can make it possible for altruism to exist in the absence of altruists. Sweden is often viewed as a very altruistic society composed of people who do not want to take any *personal* responsibility for the fate of their neighbors. When altruism is embodied in institutions, as Merton and Gieryn have pointed out, "the institutional arrangements of the professions tend to make it a matter of self-interest for individual practitioners to act altruistically" (1982, 119). From an institutional perspective, motives are the raw materials that are transformed by the institutions into something else, including behavior quite at variance with the original motive. As Selznick has argued, organizations can produce immoral outcomes from the intentions of moral people, but they can also do the opposite, create moral responsibility out of indifferent or even ill-intentioned persons (1992, 265–80). Just as markets can channel a disposition to act for the sake of others into a tendency to act out of self-interest, social institutions can transform selfish intentions into a collectively altruistic result.

There seems little question. then, that a good deal of real world altruistic behavior is related to the strength of social factors like culture and institutions. No empirical account of altruism can be complete without moving from the psychological level to the social. It would, I believe, be a mistake to move from extreme psychological accounts of altruism that emphasize what individuals do and ignore social and environmental factors to extreme environmental explanations in which individuals' motives are downplayed. Although environmental explanations are polar opposites of genetic ones, both have a tendency to downplay individual acts in favor of determinations at another level: either below the individual in the genes or above the individual in a Durkheimian reification of society. Moreover, it is a hotly contested question—one that cannot be resolved here—whether it would be preferable to live in a nonaltruistic society filled with altruists or in an altruistic society filled with indifference. On both empirical and normative

grounds, there is much to say for environmental accounts of altruism, but such accounts should be used judiciously.

Conclusion

People will always act in a variety of ways: any theory which reduces their behavior to one way of acting is therefore problematic on scientific grounds. But even more, people should act in multiple ways. The best way to avoid the twin extremes of pure value relativism and preaching is to recognize the complexity of human objectives.

Respect for pluralism can be illustrated in two ways from the literature on altruism. In the first place, any theory of human behavior should not posit that egoism always rules over altruism or vice versa. What emerges from the literature in many forms is a sense that altruism and egoism do not constitute mutually exclusive categories. In experimental social psychology, it is recognized that human beings do respond out of empathy for the plight of others, as Batson has shown (for an overview of his work, see Batson and Shaw 1991), but at the same time that empathy often satisfies the relatively selfish function of stress reduction, as Batson's main critic, Cialdini (1991), has argued. (For a compromise position, see Stiff et al. 1988). Likewise, the sociological study of real world altruism, such as blood or kidney donation, indicates that, in the words of Roberta Simmons, "it is very difficult to untangle altruistic and egoistic motives" (1991, 5).

Much the same mixture of motives seems to underlie altruistic professions and institutions. Altruistic professions are caught between many imperatives, not all of them altruistic. On the one hand, those usually helped by such professions increasingly reject altruism as a model that gives meaning to the help provided them; among the deaf, for example, there has been a clear rejection of the notion of giving, replaced by an assertion of rights (Lane 1992). On the other hand, those who entered altruistic professions in order to give end up organizing themselves into unions, engaging in efforts to prevent their exploitation in the name of altruism, and feeling burned out by the demands placed upon them (Chambliss 1996).

Even the most extraordinary altruistic behavior—such as the acts of those who rescued the European Jews—supports the idea that altruism and its opposite exist in a kind of uneasy simultaneity. In their study of rescuers, the Oliners point out that

> they were and are "ordinary" people. They were farmers and teachers, entrepreneurs and factory workers, rich and poor, parents and single people, Protestants and Catholics. Most had done nothing extraordinary before the war nor have they done much that is extraordinary since. Most were marked neither by exceptional leadership qualities nor by unconventional behavior. They were not heroes cast in larger-than-life molds. What most distinguished them were their connections with others in relationships of commitment and care. (259)

So "normal" were the people who rescued Jews, often at great risk to themselves, that, when interviewed many years later, a number of them appeared to be completely conventional, some even vaguely anti-Semitic.

If the models we develop to represent reality are to be as complex as the reality we want to represent, such models should be pluralistic in nature. A pluralistic model would make the following assumptions about human behavior: both egoism and altruism exist; most real world examples of human behavior contain elements of both simultaneously; efforts to attribute to one or the other the determining role in explaining human behavior are inevitably contrived; and as a result, social scientists should use a wide variety of techniques, methods, and approaches to gain insights to how human beings actually act.

Just as we ought to assume a pluralistic position when it comes to identifying egoism and altruism, so we ought to be pluralistic with respect to the approaches to altruism discussed in this chapter. It may be that a combination of these approaches best fulfills a commitment to pluralism. Although there are valuable aspects

associated with behavioral approaches, they tend to be difficult to incorporate into a pluralistic theory because they tend to reduce all behavior to one thing. We ought, therefore, to think of altruism as containing primarily motivational and environmental components compared to behavioral ones. Most altruistic acts occur in an environment friendly to altruism but require the normative motivation that only individuals can provide.

I think of altruism—or, for that matter, of selfishness—as a template, a preframed response that guides but does not determine individual behavior. When we are called upon to make a decision, these bundles of responses called altruism are out there, available to us, helping us frame the complex reality we confront. In most situations, we are fully aware of which reactions are selfish and which are altruistic, and this makes it possible for us to reflect on how we make our decisions as we are in the process of making them.

But it is not culture that determines whether any particular choice we make will be selfish or altruistic. Only our individual attributes—the way we think, the lessons we have internalized, the reactions to past experience—shape how we will respond to the preexisting templates available to us. Only on the rarest possible occasions will we choose either template in its entirety. Most of the time, what we do involves an uneasy combination of motives and intentions, some of them selfish, others altruistic. Indeed, it is precisely because there is nearly always a gap between how we act and the ways that our culture tells us we should act that we have such a thing as a conscience.

Altruism, then, represents that bundle of cultural practices which insist that the decisions we take be made in the light of their consequences for others. In this sense, altruism is primarily an environmental phenomenon; it exists in the stories, traditions, beliefs, and institutional memories of a society, handed down from generation to generation. The giving of accounts will be influenced by the norms of the society, norms which themselves are derived from the cultural practices that establish standards of altruism. But every individual will have a different relation to those social norms. There will never be clear markers of who is likely to be more altruistic and who is likely to be less. It is theoretically possible for a particular individual to lack any degree of altruism at all. But for society as a whole, there will always be both altruistic codes and altruistic behavior or else there will be no society.

This is a relatively weak definition of altruism, one that seems to downplay the heroically altruistic—the rescuers of the European Jews, for example. But I think it worth emphasizing that with both self-interest and altruism, we generally find as much as our definitions allow. If social scientists define self-interest broadly and altruism narrowly, they will certainly find more self-interest than altruism.

There are, I believe, two major threats to a pluralistic understanding of altruism contained in recent social science and social theory. On the one hand, strongly individualistic theories are based on the notion that people already know their preferences, making it unnecessary for them to have strong social institutions and structures that help shape preferences. Individuals under such a construct are singular; we generally know what they want because their preferences are either constant or transitive. On the other hand, certain communitarian tendencies, presumably the opposite of individualistic ones, can, as Calhoun argues (1998) emphasize national values in ways that reduce all people to singularity as well; we know what they want because we know the country to which they belong.

Both points of view overtheorize. Both approach individuals as people whose behavior and choices are already shaped. But altruistic acts, as one of the most important things that people do, may not be shaped at all. Altruism requires that an individual make choices in the context of particular situations. Such choices must be a reflection of the way individuals think and develop as they confront contexts within which they must make decisions. Weak definitions of altruism are important because they tend to produce stronger conceptions of individual choice. If we know what altruism is, we need to know little about individuals who act al-

truistically. If we leave the definition of altruism relatively open, both our understanding of people and our appreciation for their multiple objectives are likely to be enhanced.

References

Bar-Tal, Daniel. 1985/86. "Altruistic Motivation to Help: Definition, Utility, and Operationalization." *Humboldt Journal of Social Relations* 13:3–14.

Batson, C. Daniel. 1990. "How Social an Animal? The Human Capacity for Caring." *American Psychologist* 45:336–46.

_____. 1991. *The Altruism Question: Towards a Social-Psychological Answer.* Hillsdale, N.J.: Erlbaum Associates.

Batson, C. Daniel, Judy G. Batson, Jacqueline K. Slingsby, Kevin Harrell, et al. 1991. "Empathic Joy and the Empathy-Altruism Hypothesis." *Journal of Personality and Social Psychology* 61:413–26.

Batson, C. Daniel, Kathryn C. Oleson. Joy L. Weeks, Sean P. Healy, et al. 1989. "Religious Prosocial Motivation: Is It Altruistic or Egoistic?" *Journal of Personality and Social Psychology* 57:873–84.

Batson, C. Daniel, Judy G. Batson, Cari A. Griffitt, Sergio Barrientos, et al. 1989. "Negative-state Relief and the Empathy-Altruism Hypothesis." *Journal of Personality and Social Psychology* 56:922–33.

Batson, C. Daniel, Janine L. Dyck, Randall J. Brandt, Judy G. Batson, et al. 1988. "Five Studies Testing Two New Egoistic Alternatives to the Empathy-Altruism Hypothesis." *Journal of Personality and Social Psychology* 55:52–77.

Batson, C. Daniel, and Laura L. Shaw. 1991. "Evidence for Altruism: Toward a Pluralism of Prosocial Motives." *Psychological Inquiry* 2:107–22.

Bierhoff, Hans W., Renate Klein, and Peter Kramp. 1991. "Evidence for the Altruistic Personality from Data on Accident Research." *Journal of Personality* 59:263–80.

Brehm, J. W. 1966. *A Theory of Psychological Reactance.* New York: Academic Press.

Calhoun, Craig. 1998. "The Public Good as a Social and Cultural Project." In Walter W. Powell and Elisabeth S. Clemens, *Private Action and the Public Good*, ed., 20–35. New Haven, Conn.: Yale University Press.

Carlo, Gustavo, Nancy Eisenberg, Debra Troyer, and Galen Switzer. 1991. "The Altruistic Personality:

In What Contexts Is It Apparent?" *Journal of Personality and Social Psychology* 61:450–58.

Chambliss, Dan. 1996. *Beyond Caring: Hospitals, Nurses, and the Social Organization of Ethics.* Chicago: University of Chicago Press.

Charg, H. V., J. A. Piliavin, and P. L. Callero. 1988. "Role Identity and Reasoned Action in the Prediction of Repeated Behavior." *Social Psychology Quarterly* 51:303–17.

Chaves, Mark. 1998. "The Religious Ethic and the Spirit of Nonprofit Entrepreneurship." In Walter W. Powell and Elisabeth S. Clemens, ed., *Private Action and the Public Good,* 47–65. New Haven, Conn.: Yale University Press.

Cialdini, Robert B. 1991. "Altruism or Egoism? That Is (Still) the Question." *Psychological Inquiry* 2:124–26.

Coleman, James S. 1990. *Foundations of Social Theory.* Cambridge: Harvard University Press.

Dawes, Robyn M., Alphons J. C. van de Kragt, and John M. Orbell. 1988. "Not Me or Thee but We: The Importance of Group Identity in Eliciting Cooperation in Dilemma Situations: Experimental Manipulations." *Acta Psychologica* 68:83–97.

Dawkins, Richard. 1976. *The Selfish Gene.* New York: Oxford University Press.

Dovidio, John F., Judith L. Allen, and David A. Schroeder. 1990. "Specificity of Empathy-Induced Helping: Evidence for Altruistic Motivation." *Journal of Personality and Social Psychology* 59:249–60.

Eisenberg, Nancy. 1991. "Values, Sympathy, and Individual Differences: Toward a Pluralism of Factors Influencing Altruism and Empathy." *Psychological Inquiry* 2:128–31.

Eisenberg, Nancy, Paul A. Miller, Mark Schaller, Richard Fabes, et al. 1989. "The Role of Sympathy and Altruistic Personality Traits in Helping: A Reexamination." *Journal of Personality* 57:41–67.

Hopper, Joseph R., and Joyce M. Nielsen. 1991. "Recycling as Altruistic Behavior: Normative and Behavioral Strategies to Expand Participation in a Community Recycling Program." *Environment and Behavior* 23:195–220.

Hurley, Dennis, and Bern Allen. 1974. "The Effect of the Number of People Present in Nonemergency Situations." *Journal of Social Psychology* 92:27–29.

Isen, A. M., and A. Noonberg. 1979. "The Effect of Photographs of the Handicapped on Donations to Charity: When a Thousand Words May Be Too Much." *Journal of Applied Social Psychology* 9:426–31.

Johnson, Ronald C., George P. Danko, Thomas J. Darvill, Stephen Bochner, et al. 1989. "Cross-Cultural Assessment of Altruism and Its Correlates." *Personality and Individual Differences* 10:855–68.

Kamal, Preet, Manju Mehta, and Uday Jain. 1987. "Altruism in Urban and Rural Environment." *Indian Psychological Review* 32:35–42.

Kohlberg, Lawrence. 1981. *The Philosophy of Moral Development.* New York: Harper and Row.

Krebs, Dennis L. 1970. "Altruism — An Examination of the Concept and a Review of the Literature." *Psychological Bulletin* 73:258–302.

Lane, Harlan. 1992. *The Mask of Benevolence: Disabling the Deaf Community.* New York: Knopf.

Latané, Bibb, and John Darley. 1970. *The Unresponsive Bystander: Why Doesn't He Help?* Englewood Cliffs: Prentice-Hall.

Mansbridge, Jane. 1998. "On the Contested Nature of the Public Good." In Walter W. Powell and Elisabeth S. Clemens, *Private Action and the Public Good,* ed., 3–19. New Haven, Conn.: Yale University Press.

Merton Robert K., and Thomas F. Gieryn. 1982. "Institutional Altruism: The Case of the Professions." In Robert K. Merton, *Social Research and the Practicing Professions,* ed. with an introduction by Aaron Rosenblatt and Thomas F. Gieryn, 109–34. Cambridge, Mass.: Apt Books.

Midlarsky, Elizabeth and Mary E. Hannah. 1989. "The Generous Elderly: Naturalistic Studies of Donations across the Life Span." *Psychology and Aging* 4:346–51.

Mills, Rosemary S., Jan Pedersen, and Joan E. Grusec. 1989. "Sex Differences in Reasoning and Emotion about Altruism." *Sex Roles* 20:603–21.

Oliner, Samuel P., and Pearl M. Oliner. 1988. *The Altruistic Personality: Rescuers of Jews in Nazi Europe.* New York: Free Press.

Piliavin, Jane Allyn, and Hong-Wen Charg. 1990. "Altruism: A Review of Recent Theory and Research." *Annual Review of Sociology* 16:27–65.

Piliavin, Jane Allyn, and Donald Libby. 1985/86. "Personal Norms, Perceived Social Norms, and Blood Donation." *Humboldt Journal of Social Relations* 13:159–94.

Putnam, Robert. 1993. *Making Democracy Work: Civic Traditions in Modern Italy.* Princeton: Princeton University Press.

Reykowski, Janusz. 1980. "Origin of Prosocial Motivation: Heterogeneity of Personality Development." *Studia Psychologia* 22:91–106.

Rushton, J. Phillipe. 1980. *Altruism, Socialization, and Society.* Englewood Cliffs, Prentice-Hall.

Russell, Gordon W., and Robert K. Mentzel. 1990. "Sympathy and Altruism in Response to Disasters." *Journal of Social Psychology* 1990:309–16.

Schwartz, Barry. 1986. *The Battle for Human Nature.* New York: Norton.

Schwartz, S. H. 1977. "Normative Influences on Altruism." In *Advances in Experimental Social Psychology,* ed. L. Berkowitz, 221–79. New York: Academic Press.

Schwartz, S. H., and J. A. Howard. 1982. "Helping and Cooperation: A Self-Based Motivational Model." In *Cooperation and Helping Behavior: Theories and Research,* ed. J. Derlega and J. Grzelak, 327–53. New York: Academic Press.

Selznick, Philip. 1992. *The Moral Commonwealth: Social Theory and the Promise of Community.* Berkeley: University of California Press.

Simmons, Roberta G. 1991. "Altruism and Sociology." *The Sociological Quarterly* 32:1–22.

Stiff, J. B., J. P. Dillard, L. Somera, H. Kim, and C. Sleight. 1988. "Empathy, Communication, and Prosocial Behavior." *Communication Monographs* 55:198–213.

Thorton, Bill, Gayle Kirchner, and Jacqueline Jacobs. 1991. "Influence of a Photograph on a Charitable Appeal: A Picture May Be Worth a Thousand Words When It Has to Speak for Itself." *Journal of Applied Social Psychology* 21:433–45.

Turnbull, Colin M. 1972. *The Mountain People.* New York: Simon and Schuster.

Weller, Leonard, and Motti Benozio. 1987. "Homosexuals' and Lesbians' Philosophies of Human Nature." *Social Behavior and Personality* 15:221–24.

Wilson, James Q. 1993. *The Moral Sense.* New York: Free Press.

Wuthnow, Robert. 1991. *Acts of Compassion: Caring for Others and Helping Ourselves.* Princeton: Princeton University Press.

Zahn-Waxler, Carolyn. 1991. "The Case for Empathy: A Developmental Perspective." *Psychological Inquiry* 2:155–58.

Zuckerman, M., and H. Y. Reiss. 1978. "Comparison of Three Models for Predicting Altruistic Behavior." *Journal of Personality and Social Psychology* 36:468–510.

CHAPTER 27

Why Donors Give

Joan Mount

Appeals for worthy causes come throughout the year by telephone and in person, and hardly a week goes by without a mail solicitation. Individuals and households are canvassed by both privately and publicly funded organizations. Individuals in North America contribute far more than do corporations; recent figures suggest over seventeen times more in the United States (Kaplan, 1992, p. 15), and in excess of six times more in Canada (Sharpe, 1994, p. 26). If we look at the available U.S. figures over the past decade, we see a close correspondence between the percentage change in individual giving and the percentage change in philanthropy overall. This is not surprising when we consider that private donations make up the largest element—over eighty cents out of every dollar. In 1993, for example, individual philanthropy expressed in inflation-adjusted dollars accounted for $102.6 billion (81.2 percent) of the reported overall $126.2 billion (Kaplan, 1994, p. 27).

Yet, reported individual givings are but a small percentage of total personal spending. This fact is affirmed by Sharpe (1994), who found that individual charitable giving is only 2 percent of personal expenditure in Canada's national economy. Moreover, the Canadian Centre for Philanthropy (1990) found that no more than 12 percent of respondents budgeted to support secular causes. At a time of government cutbacks the implications for fundraisers are clear. Increasing emphasis on individual contributions makes it timely to explore the motives of this donor pool.

Background

In an omnibus survey of more than one thousand health, education, religious, recreational, and cultural organizations, Panas (1984) discovered that the two most important considerations overall related to belief in the cause (that is, belief in the mission of the institution or, more narrowly, great interest in a specific program within the project), followed by memorial opportunity. Other motives were tax credit, recognition of the gift, and competition, in descending order of importance. The findings specific to the educational sphere showed competition slightly ahead of tax credit and recognition of the gift but were otherwise identical.

Some investigators, such as Rosenblatt, Cusson, and McGowan (1986), have researched donorship to medical causes and have tied their findings to the health belief model (M. Becker, 1974). Moreover, these particular researchers have believed that their model of donating behavior can be applied to personal giving *in general*. This attempt to extend a model of personal philanthropy constructed around the health belief model to donating behavior in general raises interesting questions. The health belief model per se tries to predict individual willingness to take steps to maintain or enhance health and presents self-preservation as the prime motive. Derived from this model, the Rosenblatt, Cusson, and McGowan model of personal philanthropy proposes four explanatory variables: *involvement*, emanating from a sense of being at risk; *severity*, or perceived seriousness of the cause; *alleviation*, based on the belief that one's contribution can make some difference; and *predominance*, associated with the visibility of the cause. These four variables mediate the *importance of giving*, which in turn predicts *donating behavior*.

A close examination of Rosenblatt, Cusson, and McGowan's (1986) model, however, prompts counterargument. In particular, the motive of reduced risk to self and self-preservation embodied in the model's involvement construct is not present in all cases of giving. An example is a donation to a local theater group or to an international relief organization. Similarly, the predominance of a cause may arise not solely from the external visibility of the cause. There is also the visibility of the donation itself, associated with the social reward that goes with being seen to be a supporter. Further, it may be that the cause itself is not particularly visible but is nonetheless prominently lodged in some internal hierarchy of causes embraced by the donor. A parent whose child dies of crib death may routinely support Sudden Infant Death Syndrome research, with no external prompt needed.

In their model, Rosenblatt, Cusson, and McGowan present severity or seriousness of the cause as yet another predictor variable, and certainly Leslie and others (1983) and Leslie and Ramey (1988) found that "demonstration of critical financial need will be productive" in prompting alumni giving. There are other views, however. Panas (1984) argued that it is far better to stress positive goals that fire the potential donor's imagination.

In conclusion, the interpretation of donating behavior within the context of the health belief model is thought-provoking, but also subject to challenge. The present study continues the quest for a general theory of individual philanthropy by examining personal donating behavior in a domain unrelated to the medical sphere, or even to care giving broadly.

This article examines motives that lie behind personal philanthropy in the educational sphere, explores how donors are different from nondonors, and why donors give the amounts they do. Extrapolating from these findings, I propose a general model of individual donating behavior and suggest some of the implications of this model for fundraisers.

Data and Methodology

A fundraising campaign was conducted in 1987 among the alumni of a relatively new, publicly financed Canadian university. This campaign was part of a larger initiative involving corporate donors. Personal donations were received from 545 alumni, representing 27 percent of those canvassed by both telephone and mail. Within the year, these 545 donors were contacted by the university to fill out a questionnaire designed to produce a profile of the people who gave, their motivations for giving, and their responsiveness to certain features of the solicitation. A sample of identical size was then selected at random from people who were approached but who did not give. The questionnaire was sent without change to this second group as well.

The survey instrument reflects a dyad: soliciting organization and prospective individual donor.

To better understand the person side of the interaction and, in particular, what might prompt donating behavior, thirteen motive variables were extracted from the fundraising literature. This array of motive variables included belief in the cause, joy of giving (referring to psychological reward), liking to be asked (the "ask factor," implying a resultant feeling of being important or special), altruism (alluding to a general desire to help others), sympathy (implying a response to some perceived deprivation), pride or self-respect (stemming from ability to give), obligation (rooted in social responsibility), reciprocity (paying back for benefits received), nostalgia (springing from thoughts of one's past), and commemoration (responding to a memorial opportunity). Three other motives relating to externally administered rewards were also identified: appreciation (in the form of expressions of gratitude from the recipient), recognition (referring to public acknowledgment), and tax credit.

Two long-time fundraisers in the community were consulted about the face validity of the motives selected. They agreed on all of the above and also suggested two more: Some people respond to pressure ("the hard sell"), and some are impelled by an urge to compete, as Panas (1984) affirmed, by matching the gifts of an earlier time or those of other donors in the present. This latter element may lead to friendly rivalry encouraged by fundraisers, as between teams in a workplace; it may also take the form of individual donors covertly competing to match or outstrip others.

The research questionnaire contained a number of statements reflecting these fifteen motives. The survey recipients were invited to agree or disagree with each on a 7-point Likert scale. A score of 1 corresponded to complete disagreement, and 7 denoted complete agreement. For each potential motive there were three statements scattered throughout a total of forty-five items. For example, pride or self-respect was addressed in the following three assertions: "I like to be reminded that I am an achiever who is being asked to help others achieve also." "It gives me a feeling of pride in myself to be able to give to my alma mater." "I feel good about myself knowing that I am now in a position to give financially to my university."

With respect to the educational institution's part in the individual-organization dyad, a central issue concerned the kind of solicitation that would be most compelling to the greatest number of potential donors. When framing the appeal, the fundraisers considered two very diverse approaches, one featuring individuals as beneficiaries receiving needed support, and the other centered on impersonal goals of "doing the job on behalf of the collective," for example, funding of facilities (library, laboratory, and so on). The research questionnaire was designed to discover which emphasis would generate the most effective campaign. In the solicitation, the donor was cast in the role of investing in the cause "in order to effect change," and hence as exhibiting leadership behavior. Accordingly, a standard leadership behavior test was embedded in the research instrument in order to answer the following question: "If put in charge of some activity, would your focus be more on task-related matters or, alternatively, on people-related ones?

The third and final section of this survey contained questions related to a variety of sociodemographic variables: age, sex, principal language, current household income, years after graduation, and attendance at another university. It concluded by inquiring about support for another university, and support for other causes.

Both donors and nondonors were surveyed by mail within twelve months of the 1987 fundraising campaign. The response was 242 usable questionnaires from donors and 77 from nondonors. Their sociodemographic characteristics were similar.

Donor Motives

Because at least some of the fifteen donorship motives covered by the questionnaire could be interrelated, a factor analysis was conducted on the data in order to identify the underlying constructs. The factors thus revealed were labeled joy of giving, public recognition, commemoration, tax incentive, nostalgia, and help for the needy. The statements associated with each of these factors had loadings above .50. The internal consistency was computed in order to measure the association of the variables that constructed these factors and was found to be high in every case, ranging from a Cronbach alpha of .93 for joy of giving to .70 for commemoration.

The first factor, joy of giving, was found to explain 26.3 percent of the variance. Joy of giving describes how donors feel after giving to a cause that they believe in.

The second, third, and fourth factors—public recognition, commemoration (through memorial donations), and tax incentive—represent other types of rewards to the donor. These factors together accounted for another 18 percent of the variance. Insofar as the donor can accomplish one or more goals extraneous to the cause itself, such as decreasing personal taxes, donorship assumes a utility value as a means to an end. However, these factors are arguably less central to the act of giving than is the inner satisfaction from supporting a cause one believes in.

The fifth and sixth factors, nostalgia and help for the needy, explained only 8 percent of the variance. It may be that nostalgia was a weak factor because of the nature of the particular institution. The median length of time since graduation from this relatively young institution, founded in 1960, was only ten years. Results of other research suggest that fond remembrance of one's student days correlates directly with years since graduation: the longer, the fonder. The motive value of nostalgia begs further study. Perhaps the factor identified as help for the needy was relatively weak also because of the donorship sphere examined. Evoking sympathy goes well with a care-giving cause such as the Save the Children Fund, but the same fit is not as apparent for the educational sphere.

How Donors Are Different from Nondonors

The differentiating factors were joy of giving, tax incentive, and commemoration. Joy of giving, which incorporates the notion of deriving pleasure from the ability to give to causes that one believes in, characterized donors markedly more than it did nondonors. The importance of this inner satisfaction has been identified and affirmed by other researchers. The facilitative role of the tax incentive concurs with the findings of Feldstein's (1975a, 1975b) in-depth study. The present study suggests also that emphasis on a permanent remembrance has a negative impact on both donors and nondonors,

but more so on nondonors; this finding may be an artifact, however, of the relatively youthful alumni pool that was canvassed (again, the median length of time since graduation was only ten years).

Donors were found to be more inclined to support other causes, in particular, other universities, and more task-oriented than nondonors. The discriminant function consisting of these three variables correctly classified 70 percent of the cases in a holdout sample.

Why Donors Give the Amounts They Do

. . . Donors who gave more than $50 were likely to be older (mean age of forty-three compared with thirty-seven), to have a higher family income (between $60,000 and $70,000 rather than between $40,000 and $50,000), to have been out longer (twelve years versus nine, on average), to be male, and to be more task-oriented. As indicated earlier, this preeminence of task orientation was deemed to affirm the efficacy of substantial and enduring goals tied into the principal functions of the university.

Formulating the Model

The study described here allows one to conceptualize individual donating behavior in terms of largesse, which, according to *Webster's New Twentieth Century Dictionary,* is a "gift or donation generously given." This concept is operationalized by the size of the gift. To predict this largesse, I propose five variables (see Figure 27.1). These predictors derive from the present findings and are supported by earlier research on personal donating behavior, which I discuss below.

Involvement

. . . The Rosenblatt, Cusson, and McGowan (1986) model . . . posits that involvement, severity, alleviation, and predominance mediate personal philanthropy. The current study suggests that psychological rewards from giving can in-

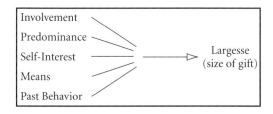

FIGURE 27.1   Empirically Based Model of Personal Donorship

spire donations with no trace of self-preservation, which is the driving force in Rosenblatt, Cusson, and McGowan's notion of involvement. The satisfaction derived from being able to support causes in which one believes (recall that most donors to universities support other causes as well) may explain why people give to quite disparate social (political, cultural, and so on) causes where risk to self and self-preservation plays no part. We can speculate that donating to causes that one considers worthy offers a way to feel useful and is even a form of self-actualization (Maslow, 1954). Inasmuch as a self-preservation element, central to Rosenblatt, Cusson, and McGowan's notion of involvement, need not be present, this research suggests that the concept of involvement is best recast in relation to anticipated psychological reward, that is, joy of giving. Involvement springs from expected satisfaction.

It may also be that the belief that one's gift can make a difference is a precondition of the warm glow known as the joy of giving (for example, Panas, 1984). Without a belief that one's gift will help to effect change, can the prospective donor genuinely anticipate an outcome from the act of giving, either a resulting satisfaction and joy or, as in the earlier conceptualization, a lessening of risk to self? I propose that the conviction that one's donation can make a difference (Rosenblatt, Cusson, and McGowan's notion of alleviation) is necessary to fuel the element of expectation inherent to the involvement construct and hence is a precondition of the latter.

A task orientation was found to distinguish givers from nongivers, and larger givers from lesser. This suggests the wisdom of fundraising goals that relate to the provision of sound educational services and benefits to the collective rather than to the individual (such as a new library). Campaigns directed toward broad educational ends appear to carry weight and, accordingly, to trigger an anticipated joy of giving and hence involvement within the prospective donor. A people orientation, by contrast, might suggest an alumni solicitation couched in terms of the needy beneficiary, stressing the financial plight of students or researchers. Such solicitations, however, would arguably be less effective in the arena of personal misfortunes than in the arena of medical causes and other life threats that compete for the potential donor's discretionary dollars; hence the response might fall short. This finding is in keeping with Rosenblatt, Cusson, and McGowan's emphasis on the severity of seriousness of the cause.

Predominance

Panas (1984) asserted that potential donors warm to large targets that require substantial sums, and he advocated a bold appeal. Clearly, a large goal is more likely to have the objective visibility needed to secure predominance among other causes. I propose, however, that the predominance of a cause, as defined by Rosenblatt, Cusson, and McGowan (1986), be reinterpreted as a subjective measure of the degree to which a cause stands out in an individual's personal hierarchy of philanthropic options, whether because of its perceived gravity or other reasons, perhaps including enhanced social standing from being a supporter.

Self-Interest

This study supports the role of elements directly linked to the donor's self-interest, such as the tax incentive. Here an extraneous goal is served by the act of giving.

Means

The present study revealed that donors whose gifts surpassed $50 were likely to be older and to have higher household incomes than those who gave less. It seems, therefore, that means is an important determinant of the size of the donation, referred to here as largesse, and a factor that no canvasser is likely to overlook.

Past Behavior

This study reveals that people who give to a particular cause are likely to be donors to other causes. One can infer that past donating behavior is a signal of what a fundraiser can expect. This association is strongly supported by the findings of Lindahl and Winship (1992), whose research indicates that past giving to a cause is the best single predictor of future giving to the *same* cause. This observation is consistent with the findings of researchers working within the framework of Fishbein and Ajzen's (1975) widely recognized theory of reasoned action (Ajzen and Fishbein, 1980), who have found that past behavior exerts a direct effect on subsequent behavioral intention and hence on behavior. It should hardly seem surprising that satisfaction and joy derived from past donations generate an expectation of satisfaction on each new occasion, and that this positive expectation reinforces one's inclination to say yes again.

Implications of the Model for Fundraisers and Researchers

This study, with its findings concerning involvement and predominance, suggests the importance of big campaign projects that are visible and lead to permanent outcomes that cannot be dismissed as trivial. Clearly, the campaign should stress the relative importance and urgency of the project. If the potential donor is led to see his or her gift as an "investment" and valued contribution toward some worthy campaign project, then hopefully he or she will anticipate satisfaction and joy of giving from making the donation. Expectation of this satisfaction prompts involvement.

Second, the importance of cultivating predominance cannot be overstated given the barrage of charitable requests that bombard the potential donor. This overwhelming number represents a "clutter" that can easily diminish the impact of any particular cause. When presented to a potential donor, the project must sufficiently grab that person's imagination so as to take on the necessary predominance among competing causes.

Third, this research supports the role of elements that serve the donor's self-interest. On the strength of this study, we can conclude that the tax incentive is not generally as robust a motive as the anticipated joy of giving. Yet, Seymour (1966) made the point that the timing of discussion of this dimension is critical. He recommended that discussion of the tax incentive in any personal solicitation take place after extracting a commitment to give, but before the donor has decided how much to give. This advice implies that a tax credit does not produce the generic decision to give but can influence the size of the donation.

Fourth, the ability to give, or means, is crucial. Moreover, other research suggests that donors who give large amounts tend to be more likely to budget their charitable givings than those who give less (Canadian Centre for Philanthropy, 1990, pp. 122–123). Organizations that depend on private philanthropy would do well to stress the notion of "thoughtful and proportionate" donations through whatever avenues at their disposal. It clearly behooves the fundraiser to try to persuade the prospective donor to budget deliberately for personal philanthropy.

Finally, past experience in which a donor derived pleasure from giving will reinforce his or her expectation of similar gratification on each new occasion; anticipated satisfaction may be the key to explaining the pattern that fundraisers have long observed, namely, a link between past and present giving. Lindahl and Winship (1992) confirmed what fundraisers know: The best prospects are those individuals who have already given. Further, as Seymour (1966) pointed out, the more a person gives, the more likely he or she is to give more. It is therefore arguably the case that past donors will be most receptive to the notion of proportional giving.

Amidst these implications of my empirically based model of personal giving there is one caveat: People seldom give serious sums without being asked to do so. Understanding and accommodating the donor's motives are not enough: *There must be an ask.*

A useful follow-up to this research on individual donorship would be to extend it by testing the ability of the model to predict individual allocations of scarce resources in many spheres, across a variety of causes, ranging from preservation of life to buying new uniforms for the university football team. Further, while the present model has been formulated with monetary gifts in mind, it could apply to volunteer time donations as well and, again, could be tested across domains beyond care giving and education. Finally, largesse has been operationalized as the size of gift; additional research must expand on this operationalization to examine the frequency and regularity of giving.

References

Ajzen, I., and Fishbein, M. *Understanding Attitudes and Predicting Social Behavior.* Englewood Cliffs, N.J.: Prentice Hall, 1980.

Becker, M. H. "The Health Belief Model and Sick Role Behavior." *Health Education Monographs,* 1974, *2,* 409–419.

Canadian Centre for Philanthropy. *Law, Tax and Charities: The Legislative and Regulatory Environment for Charitable Non-Profit Organizations.* Toronto, Ontario: Canadian Centre for Philanthropy, 1990.

Feldstein, M. "The Income Tax and Charitable Contributions. Part 1: Aggregate and Distributional Effects." *National Tax Journal,* 1975a, *28,* 81–99.

Feldstein, M. "The Income Tax and Charitable Contributions. Part 2: The Impact on Religious, Edu-cational and Other Organizations." *National Tax Journal,* 1975b, *28,* 209–226.

Fishbein, M., and Ajzen, I. *Belief, Attitude, and Behavior: An Introduction to Theory and Research.* Reading, Mass.: Addison-Wesley, 1975.

Kaplan, A. E. (ed.). *Giving USA: The Annual Report on Philanthropy for the Year 1991.* New York: American Association of Fund-Raising Counsel Trust for Philanthropy, 1992.

Kaplan, A. E. (ed.). *Giving USA: The Annual Report on Philanthropy for the Year 1993.* New York: American Association of Fund-Raising Counsel Trust for Philanthropy, 1994.

Leslie, L. L., and Ramey, G. "Donor Behavior and Voluntary Support for Higher Education Institutions." *Journal of Higher Education,* 1988, *59,* 115–132.

Leslie, L. L., and others. "Factors Accounting for Variations Over Time in Voluntary Support for Colleges and Universities." *Journal of Education Finance,* 1983, *9,* 213–225.

Lindahl, W. E., and Winship, C. "Predictive Models for Annual Fundraising and Major Gift Fundraising." *Nonprofit Management and Leadership,* 1992, *3* (1), 43–64.

Maslow, A. *Motivation and Personality.* New York: HarperCollins, 1954.

National Easter Seal Society. *Donor Profile 1983 Easter Seal Telethon.* Chicago: National Easter Seal Society, 1983.

Panas, J. *Megagifts: Who Gives Them, Who Gets Them?* Chicago: Pluribus Press, 1984.

Rosenblatt, J. A., Cusson, A. J., and McGowan, L. "A Model to Explain Charitable Donations: Health Consumer Behavior." In R. J. Lutz (ed.), *Advances in Consumer Research.* Vol. 12. Ann Arbor, Mich.: Association for Consumer Research, 1986.

Seymour, H. J. *Designs for Fund-Raising: Principles, Patterns, Techniques.* New York: McGraw-Hill, 1966.

Sharpe, D. *A Portrait of Canada's Charities: The Size, Scope and Financing of Registered Charities.* Toronto, Ontario: Canadian Centre for Philanthropy, 1994.

CHAPTER 28

The Founding Fathers of Modern Philanthropy

MILTON GOLDIN

By 1889, neither church-related charities dating from the Colonial period, nor corrupt public welfare agencies established during the 1870s and 1880s, could deal with the human costs of the post-Civil War industrial revolution. Unemployment, illness and the need to care for the elderly at home, devastated families accustomed to the settled ways of America's prewar agrarian society. Waves of immigrants further confused and then angered them, by appearing to compound problems.

In an article entitled "Wealth" in the June 1889 issue of *The North American Review,* Andrew Carnegie argued with impressive skill the thesis that "the problem of our age is the proper administration of wealth . . ." Critics agreed with him that rich and poor must enter into a "harmonious relationship." Differences between the writer and his critics stemmed mainly from his fulsome admiration of the rich and his insistence that charitable giving could solve acute social problems.

Carnegie wrote that it was the "duty" of a rich man to use "all [of his] surplus revenues . . . in the manner which, in his judgment, is best calculated to produce the most beneficial results for the community." Unpersuaded by the rhetoric, the Reverand William Jewett Tucker, professor of religion at Andover and later president of Dartmouth, responded that he could "conceive of no greater mistake, more disastrous in the end to religion if not to society, than that of trying to make charity do the work of justice . . . "

What further complicated the discussion of philanthropy (then as now) was the problem of separating the generosity of robber barons from a larger issue: How did men, whose stupendous fortunes no one before had dreamed possible, relate to American society? Neither the ruthlessness and duplicity of which the muckraker Ida Tarbell accused John D. Rockefeller in her monumental *The History of the Standard Oil Company* (1904), nor the genius and benefactions for which later generations of writers would acclaim him, deal with this issue satisfactorily. While the former fall into the category of accusation, the latter fall into the category of apology.

The only useful determinants in explaining the philanthropies of Carnegie and Rockefeller are strains in American society between the end of the Civil War and the beginning of World War I, proposed solutions, and how successfully the two men who organized the "business of benevolence" responded to both the strains and the proposals.

Elect of God

Political, business, educational, and religious leaders urged the population to become rich as quickly as possible. A wealthy man was the elect of God. Anyone poor in the midst of so much economic opportunity must deserve his or her condition, including newcomers to America on the Lower East Side of Manhattan, where more people lived per acre than in the worst slums of Calcutta.

Not unnaturally, solid citizens, born in the country during less hectic times, felt that the America they knew was slipping away. Among them, members of the gentry saw their status and influence decline in direct proportion to the rise of robber barons. Also held responsible for lawlessness and societal breakdowns were the immigrants, who spoke Slavic and Mediterranean languages (or Yiddish), and who brought with them such beliefs as socialism, Catholicism, and Orthodox Judaism.

As social conditions worsened in the cities, the gentry saw itself as a caste rather than a class, a small band of the faithful everywhere surrounded by ragged newcomers and aggressive entrepreneurs. Socialist insurrection was considered a distinct possibility. During the Panic of 1873, unemployment reached new heights, state after state called out militias to end strikes, and federal troops were mobilized.

Thanks to widespread political corruption in every city and particularly in Washington, the gentry eschewed political action and focused on education as the solution to society's problems. Ivy League colleges became bases of operation. Social Darwinism—the belief that because animals engage in a struggle for existence, societies are destined to rise or fall in the same fashion—and the desirability of converting all Americans to Protestant outlooks, were two establishment *desiderata*. Social Darwinism's most articulate American spokesman, William Graham Sumner, professor of political and social science at Yale, lumped together as equally benighted trade unions, socialism, philanthropy, and monopolists such as Carnegie and Rockefeller. Each union, he declared, implied deliberate interference with personal liberty and the "natural or- der," although robber barons proved the validity of the phrase, "survival of the fittest."

The impact of Social Darwinism on American society can hardly be overemphasized. Intellectuals, as well as rabble-rousers, proclaimed the moral superiority of native-born Americans, rationalized Sumner's contradictions, and counseled that the poor should be left to their just desserts. Still, abandoning the poor ignored Judeo-Christian concepts of charity, and the gentry, charitable bodies, and public authorities alike reacted to the crisis with soup kitchens, baskets of food, used clothing, and lodging houses. Admittedly, these were palliatives. But how to respond on a meaningful scale, prove the superiority of the rich, and yet avoid corruption?

Moneymakers

For both Carnegie and Rockefeller, the Panic of 1873 provided new opportunities to further increase their already substantial fortunes. Carnegie's extensive interests in bridge building, telegraphy, and sleeping cars, made possible his entry into the steel industry, which, in turn, would make him the richest man in the world for a brief period before Rockefeller took the title in the early 1900s.

Rockefeller was the other side of the coin, neither a salesman nor an intellectual, certainly no sycophant, and above all, a master of strategic planning. Secretive and withdrawn, he was determined early in his career to control every process remotely connected with refining oil. In 1870, Rockefeller incorporated Standard Oil of Ohio, and began driving competitors from the field. In 1882, he and his associates founded the Standard Oil of Ohio Trust, which promptly sold $70 million worth of securities on the strength of his highly-respected, money-making abilities. Trusts were illegal under laws then in force and were further outlawed by the Sherman Antitrust Act in 1890. By that time, however, attempting to restrain monopolies was like attempting to control the weather. "Individualism has gone, never to return," concluded Rockefeller.

In 1901, aged 65 and with another 18 years of life ahead of him, Carnegie retired from business to devote himself to benevolence, and to prove another of his dicta, "The man who dies rich dies disgraced." The year before, he had set a price of $158 million for the Carnegie Steel Company. When Rockefeller displayed some interest in buying him out, Carnegie inflated the price to $250 million, whereupon the oil magnate dropped out of the bidding. The next year, Carnegie sold the company to J.P. Morgan for $447 million, taking stock, bonds, and a mortgage on United States Steel, the successor corporation.

By this time, Carnegie sensed to a greater extent than when he wrote "Wealth," that if the American establishment failed to address social problems, the alternative of a socialist takeover might not be academic. He had begun his giving in the late 1860s with grants for swimming pools in the Scottish town of Dunferline, where he was born, but soon ignored recreational, spiritual (except for church organs), and medical causes in favor of colleges and libraries—a move that generated warm approval among establishments on both sides of the Atlantic.

Among those waiting impatiently to help him dispose of surplus revenues when he returned from his castle in Scotland in 1901, were the presidents of Cornell, Harvard, Princeton, and Johns Hopkins. Carnegie called for a national university in Washington, an idea that thrilled only the president of Johns Hopkins, who thereupon discovered that his institution would not qualify (the trust that had established Johns Hopkins would not permit the campus to be moved) and also became miffed.

Carnegie never built the national university, but his scant interest in Ivy League colleges was only one surprise for the gentry. A second surprise was that Carnegie favored small colleges and black colleges in his giving, which seems curious, given his constant need for publicity, his strong espousal of Social Darwinism, and his obvious adoration of wealth.

His logic in making these gifts provides a fascinating insight into contradictory motivations. He liked both the curricula and the composition of small college student bodies—white youths

(and black youths) making sacrifices to get an education—people who would one day serve as executives of corporations of the type that he had worked to create. Carnegie had begun his career as an immigrant youth with no education; but the America of the future would be dependent on highly-educated and motivated men and women able to manage an industrial society. Therefore it was critical to encourage the best and the brightest of every group. In this respect, his thinking was 100 years ahead of his time, and he grasped a truth still dimly perceived in the 1980s—that the dedication of professors and the talents of students, as much as the sheer numbers of people enrolled in institutions of higher learning, distinguish educational systems.

Not quite true to his dictum about dying rich, Carnegie left $23 million to his family and gave the rest of his fortune to a variety of foundations and educational institutions that he established between 1901 and 1911. Just as his great fortune had come from a supertrust, United States Steel, his largest single gift, $125 million, went to the first superfoundation in America, the Carnegie Corporation of New York, formed "to promote the advancement and diffusion of knowledge among the people of the United States . . . "

Even the gentry could hardly quarrel with this last achievement, but he and aristocrats made one discovery they found hard to accept: It was not necessarily the rich man who could decide what was best for society. Carnegie had begun his major philanthropic activities making all decisions himself in his New York mansion at 2 East 91st Street. He ended by employing dozens of experts at his foundations to advise him on what was best for mankind.

Bearing Fruit

A month before "Wealth" appeared, Rockefeller made an initial contribution of $600,000 (eventually he would give a total of $35 million) to the Baptist seminary that became the University of Chicago. "I would that more men of wealth were doing as you are doing with your money," he wrote Carnegie admiringly in January 1896, "but, be assured your example will bear fruits . . ." Carnegie's example bore fruits, but Rockefeller did not follow his mentor's philanthropic model.

Unlike Carnegie, who was an agnostic, Rockefeller, a giver from his youth, based his philanthropy on strict religious precepts. America's first billionaire tithed, swept floors, and cleaned windows at the Erie Street Baptist Church in Cleveland, the city in which he grew up. Indeed, his entire life centered on three locations—his office, his home, and the Baptist Church, for which he was an asker as well as a giver. ("I cannot understand why some men say, 'I am not a beggar,'" he wrote, recalling a fund-raising campaign to save the church building in 1859. "Any man should be proud to beg in such a good cause.")

It is startling not only how little his ideas changed during his lifetime but how liberal many of them were. The same man who brought modern medicine to millions smoked mullein leaves in a clay pipe when he was ill. He transferred the evangelistic fervor of frontier religion to philanthropy. As a youth, he contributed to the Underground Railroad in the sincere belief that black men were as deserving of freedom as white men. He was a constant and generous giver to black colleges. When he died in Florida in 1937, Rockefeller was the only white member of a black congregation in that state.

The year of his first major gift, 1889, was also the beginning of a period of great personal travail. Because it violated antitrust laws, the federal government would eventually order the dissolution of the Standard Oil Trust, and Judge Kenesaw Mountain Landis would levy a $29 million fine on the corporation. One consequence was that the industrialist developed a rare disease, alopecia, which causes the loss of hair.

Embarrassed by his disfigurement, Rockefeller retired to a 4,180-acre Pocantico Hills estate in Westchester County, where he was visited by Frederick T. Gates, a former Baptist minister who was now head of the American Baptist Education Society. Gates not only solicited the ini-

tial gift for the University of Chicago, but warned the dispirited capitalist that at the rate his wealth was increasing, his family would figuratively "drown" in money.

Gates had a point. The Rockefeller fortune, $40 million in 1892, quadrupled by 1898 and quintupled by 1900, despite antitrust actions and thanks to strategic planning. Agreeing on the danger Gates described and hounded by solicitors, Rockefeller made Gates his almoner. Both men firmly believed that God had directed the industrialist's career, but Gates credited himself with introducing Rockefeller to "the principles of scientific giving," in which the country's most hated robber baron gave up "retail giving almost wholy . . . [to enter] safely and pleasurably into the field of wholesale philanthropy."

What was "wholesale philanthropy?" A smokescreen to mask intentions, according to muckrakers. Not giving in a vacuum, according to Rockefeller and Gates, but devoting major gifts to causes that could produce solutions to major problems.

Consider the Rockefeller Sanitary Commission's first public health endeavor, dealing with hookworm in the South. In the early 1900s, possibly half the population of North Carolina and some 6 million people in eight other Southern states suffered from hook-worm, a parasite identified 10 centuries before Hippocrates. Victims became lethargic, and onlookers elsewhere in the country described southerners as shiftless and lazy. The cause (bad hygiene) and an available cure (thymol capsules and salt) had long been known, but in Washington, the Treasury Department declined to pay for experiments in public hygiene.

On Gates' advice, Rockefeller financed Charles Wardwell Stiles, an early public health scientist, who worked with evangelical determination and finally ended the scourge with a cure costing less than 50 cents per dose. For $800,000, dramatic results occurred almost overnight. The success led Gates to encourage Rockefeller to make grants in the area of medical education. Medical schools of the time were not inclined to closely examine instructors' qualifications or students' preparation. Many were money-making sidelines run by local physicians. Gates wanted "scientific medicine," through which highly-trained professionals would deal with health problems.

Using the Johns Hopkins medical school as a prototype, Rockefeller provided philanthropic financing on a scale unheard of in the early 1900s. Gates insisted on conditions: Each recipient institution was to have a full-time faculty whose members could do research. There was even talk that a dissertation should be made part of the medical doctor requirement. The net result was the creation of systems of health care and medical education that survive to this day.

Combining Effort

Today we know that private sector giving, even by billionaires, has limits to its effectiveness. No circumstance exists for which it is preferable that donations replace taxes as a main source of financing for essential public services. Even Ronald Reagan has learned this. Nor has it been found wise to leave choices for the public welfare to any one group, whether it be the rich, the poor, experts at foundations, or public officials. Evidently, the best results can be obtained only through combination of public and private efforts.

If Carnegie's and Rockefeller's giving was motivated at least in part by "a broader concern for the permanent economic and social viability of capitalist society," as one writer recently argued, the achievements must be seen against the backdrop of the 1890s to truly measure their importance. Perhaps the time has come to let go of the myth of the 1960s that great philanthropic institutions must be conceived and guided by saints determined to save sinners. Only then can the roles of Carnegie and Rockefeller be fully appreciated and their legacies understood.

CHAPTER 29

The Call of Service: Satisfactions

R O B E R T   C O L E S

The first civil rights activist and SNCC member I met did not belong to the "office group," as some called it, who worked out of Atlanta, but was a young black student, Dion Diamond, who had taken leave from the University of Wisconsin to work in Louisiana, where he had relatives. Dion had been jailed on grounds of "disturbing the peace"—for attempting to have lunch at a restaurant that wanted no part of black customers. I was to testify on his behalf. Curiously, the local prosecutor had decided to call him "unstable" and possessed of an "anti-social personality," hence his lawyer's decision to ask me to interview him and later tell the court what I thought of his "personality."[1]

As I sat in the prison's visiting room and heard the tall, thoughtful, sensitive, hard-working man tell of the extreme danger he'd been facing, voluntarily, in hopes of seeing an end to segregation in Louisiana, I wondered, first to myself and then out loud, what gave him the strength to keep going. He was in constant danger, and in 1962 there wasn't the national backing and attention that coalesced behind the Mississippi Summer Project of 1964. Often he was working alone, and there was a distinct possibility that one day he'd be found alone and dead.

The psychiatrist in me was posing questions to him, for I knew that in court similar questions would be posed. I said, "Dion, your ideals and values apart, I'm wondering why you keep at this, given the danger and the obstacles." In fact, I had a lengthier wind-up to the question, because I didn't want him to think I was insinuating that there was anything psychologically wrong with his choice of activity—the line of reasoning that the county prosecutor was pursuing.

In any event, I was stopped in my well-meaning tracks by the young man's three-word reply: "The satisfaction, man." I'm afraid my imagination then was rather limited. I could think of few possible satisfactions for him. Dion had been telling me about how tough his work was, how lonely at times, how frightening at other times, and, worst of all, how discouraging—the suspicion he encountered from black people, who knew well the dangers of trying to integrate a lunch counter or a motel and who were not reluctant to be psychologically skeptical of him: Why *are* you here among us, urging us to do what might eventually mean that we get shot at or arrested?

When I asked him about those "satisfactions," he said, "I'm meeting some really fine people. I'm listening to them tell me a lot about their lives. I'm hearing them stop and think about what they're willing to do to change this world here in Louisiana. Isn't that enough—isn't that a

343

good reason to feel satisfied? If you can spend some of your life doing work like this, then you're lucky! There may be a sheriff out there waiting for me with a gun, but if he gets me, I'll die thinking: Dion, you actually *did* something—you were part of something much bigger than yourself, and you saw people beginning to change, right before your eyes, and that was a real achievement, and that's what I mean by 'satisfaction.'"

Something Done, Someone Reached

To this day I go back to that young man's appraisal of himself and others—of a volunteer effort and its satisfactions. Dion kept telling me what he was trying to *do;* he kept describing for me the various individuals he was getting to know—the lives he was affecting, even as his own life had already been deeply affected. I wanted to know about his earlier life. I asked about any "troubles" he may have had, any brushes with the law (or with my kind of doctor); about the ways he was handling the terrible stresses of being, in essence, a front-line warrior, taking on tough, sometimes murderous, local and state power.

Eventually I testified in court, as did others, and he was let free—with a warning from the bench that he would do well to return to Wisconsin and college life. Shortly afterward, I took Dion up on his suggestion to accompany him. Our visits to the rural homes of the "folks" he had mentioned were not easy ones to make. I left my car in Baton Rouge and went with him in his car—followed, almost always, by a police car. I knew the police were looking for any excuse to arrest him again. He made light of it, called them "my friends." He drove so circumspectly that I became aware of every road sign and of the speed he was maintaining, however low. He kept looking in his rear-view mirror, smiling. When he signaled a coming turn with his left arm and hand, I had the feeling he was trying hard to be the obliging child to fiercely punitive parents, ever ready to take out the strap—or their pistols.

He was also turning the whole exercise into a parody, but not a joke; he was the "suspect," and they were his pursuers, constantly on his trail.

These families, a number of them tenant farmers, were nearly penniless, living hand to mouth. Because of our escort, the police, we brought along plenty of fear and anxiety—as if those folks didn't already have enough to worry about with the daily insults and threats that constituted their experience of "law and order" in that segregationist world.

Yet in no time, as we sat and nursed our Cokes and Pepsis and 7-Ups and orange sodas ("Now, Mister Doctor, what can we do you with . . . "), I began to see legs stretching, arms folding or falling back in relaxation, facial muscles constructing smiles; I began to hear jokes and stories and laughter—some of it the sharp, dry, bitter laughter of people who didn't know whether to be amused by their difficult lives or cry out their hearts on that account. I also began to hear music: people singing, strumming guitars, hitting old upright pianos. I began to hear, finally, plenty of exhortation: the Old and New Testaments summoned lest, as one field hand put it, "we forget all those who knew pain before we were ever even near being born." The biblical themes of exile and return, of suffering and redemption, of mystery and revelation, and the biblical view of the powerful as suspect, the lowly as destined to sit close to God, in His kingdom—these were subjects close to the heart of men, women, and children caught in the most unpromising of earthly lives.

As we went from home to home—it was summer, the weather was hot and humid, and there were no air conditioners to help out—I began to understand how much this young activist from up North meant to the people receiving us and, conversely, how much they meant to him. I also learned to appreciate what he meant when he spoke from deep within himself.

"I tell you, this is a real *privilege;* I am doing something useful with people who are the salt of the earth! Every day I thank my lucky stars—I thank God—for the good fortune to be here, going from home to home, sitting and listening to these folks tell their stories, being fed by them, being taught by them. You asked me yesterday why I do this, and I could recite the civil rights line, and I believe it—that our people aren't free, and that we have to fight for our freedom, especially here in the segregated South. To be absolutely honest, I came here to spend a month working on a voter registration project, but I've stayed here because I love what happens when I go visit these folks. Every day I learn something from them—about gospel music, about how to put in a good vegetable garden, about the history of the Mississippi Delta and upstate Louisiana, about all the tricks of the local whites, and remember, the Negroes here know *everything:* they have eyes and ears in every white home, and the reports come filtering back every night.

"It's what I get accomplished, the people I reach and who get to me: that's why I'm here. We have a growing movement here of men and women who really want to work together to break the back of the whole segregationist power structure. They meet in the basement of a church, and they sing and pray—and they also talk hard, tough politics. 'It's your baby,' one of the men said to me, about the 'club,' they call it, 'the freedom club.' Talk about why I do this work! I'll have to leave—but I'll never really leave for good. The way I see it, this is the most important educational experience I'll ever have. People say, 'Hey, man, you're into fighting with cops.' I answer, If you don't take on the cops, then you're into something else: surrendering to cops! So we're for sticking to our original purpose here—getting more and more people to become voters—and I'm staying because I get the satisfaction of seeing the baby grow and being with all the folks, a huge family.

"You know what? You look at those cops now—they've begun to respect us! They don't give us that big belly laugh anymore, they don't spit at us or sneer at us. They look real serious when they follow us around. And the other day, I couldn't believe it, one of them, he nodded at me and two of my buddies when we came out of the store. It was as if—well, hey, we sure do know each other! I thought I saw just the beginning of a smile on his face—just the start of one. You want to know why I do this work? To see that look on that cop's face!"

Over the years I have heard his sentiments echoed many times—the enthusiasm and pleasure, the exhilaration that accompany action taken, and the consequences of such action: deeds done, people very much touched, and in return, quite eager to return the favor, through dozens of reciprocal gestures, remarks, initiatives.

Moral Purpose

In a modest, unselfconscious way, Dion was regarding himself and that policeman as historical figures: a pair of protagonists worthy of a moment of notice—each of them a witness to social change as well as a participant in it. No question that for many volunteers the considerable satisfaction that goes with making a connection with a fellow human being is enhanced by the overall context of the service being rendered. They have sought, found, and fulfilled a moral purpose. For this young political activist, the moral purpose was obvious: he was engaged in a struggle against the tyranny of segregation. But all service is directly or indirectly ethical activity, a reply to a moral call within, one that answers a moral need in the world.[2]

The manner in which a moral purpose is worked into a particular volunteer's life will vary enormously. Some volunteers are at pains to insist (to themselves, let alone others) that what they are doing *is* a moral effort and that what they get from their actions is a kind of moral satisfaction or peace—a moral hunger assuaged. Others wave aside the moral underpinnings of their actions, emphasizing instead the friendships they have made, the boredom overcome. Even when pressed about the good they are doing, they demur, as did Gary, a college student who became a Big Brother to a youngster whose family had recently arrived from the Dominican Republic.

"I enjoy leaving this place [a college community] and I love going to the neighborhood where he lives—the sights and sounds and smells. I suppose some people would want me to wear my heart on my sleeve and to say I feel sorry for all the people there and I'm trying to help them—but I don't like that word 'help,' I really don't. When people tell me they admire what I'm doing, I go ballistic; I say they should compliment my friend Juan and his family for being nice enough to put up with me! They let me come visit them. They feed me. They help me with my Spanish. I've always wanted to work in Latin America—a business, a bank, maybe. This way I sharpen my street Spanish. I get to shoot baskets; I learn all about a neighborhood—who makes money doing this or doing that. I know where to place bets. I know where to buy the best food, and where the best places to eat are. When I go to visit Juan, I learn by walking, listening to him and his friends, seeing all there is to see through his eyes and through my own."

"We take walks—that's the best. He acts like he owns the whole world. He points out everything to me—it's better than a lecture here. But all of a sudden, he'll see someone, or he'll notice something in a store window, and he becomes a different person. He looks so grim! He doesn't talk, he just stares ahead. Then I try to draw him out. I talk. *I* start pointing things out. I ask him questions—anything to get him, get *us* out of this mood. It works, but it takes a lot out of me. It's then that I begin to realize how hard this kid's life is. I know that the man he calls Dad is his stepfather, and he beats him up really badly; that his mother is a heavy drinker, and she tunes out, to the point that they all don't know what to do with her. It sounds like she goes into a trance and then, all of a sudden, she clears, and she's back to normal. His sister is sleeping around at fifteen, having dropped out of school; and a younger brother has epilepsy, the serious kind. Not a pretty picture!

"I'll be honest—I'm surprised at myself some days, because I'll hear me giving Juan a really strong lecture. I'll tell him that he's fighting for his life and that if he doesn't watch out, he'll end up drowning. You may think I'm stepping outside my bounds; I'm only nineteen years old, and I'm a history major, and I've never even taken a psychology course, so what do I know! But when you see someone floundering, and you're afraid he's going to go under, then you sure try your damnedest to throw out every lifesaver you can think of!

"I have been trying to be a friend to Juan, and I've tried to give him some direction. I don't mean that I preach sermons, rant and rave. I wouldn't last a minute with him or his neighborhood friends, if I *told* him what to do, told them. But I play basketball with him and his friends, and there are times when we just stand around after some serious playing, shooting the breeze, and it's then that I show my hand. I start in casually, talking about how you've got to realize that you either take responsibility for your life and try to find some direction you're headed for or, if you don't, you'll be at the mercy of other people, and believe me, if *they're* going to be deciding what you're going to do—then *forget it!*

"The gist of my message is that you either get pushed and pulled by all these other folks, or you take charge yourself. That's what I keep hitting Juan with, and he does listen. The more I talk, the more I realize *I'm* listening, too! A lot of what I'll tell him and his buddies—it's what my dad told me, and my mom, and her dad. Basically I'm trying to connect those kids with the middle-class world I come from. I don't say it the way I heard it at home, but the heart and soul of my own values, that's what I'm advocating. I have no illusion that I'm this kid's savior. I'm not sure Sigmund Freud could save him either. There's only one person who can save him—that's what I keep hammering away at. When I come at him like that, Juan listens. He even nods his head. I feel a little optimistic. But hell, I know the odds, and the more I come to see him, the better I know the odds.

"When I'm through, and we've had our pizza or something, and I'm ready to say good-bye, I look him right in the eye, and I say, 'Keep trucking, man'; and he says, 'Yeah.' Once in a while he'll say, 'I will.' That makes my day—my week! I feel I've actually done something with my life—for someone else, not just me, me, me: the big me that we all celebrate in this place!³

"The more I say what I think, what I believe—well, the more I really *do* believe it! That's the big irony, and I'm afraid to mention it even: that all of this volunteering, this 'do-good work,' one of my cynical friends calls it, will end up being a big boost for my morale and my life. That same guy says, 'You're doing that for your brag-sheet.' I get really furious at him, but I don't give him the pleasure of seeing how I feel. It's true—sure, it'll be nice to list this on my CV; but damn it, I could just go through the motions here. I could show up every week—every *other* week, every third week—and buy my way out by going to a pool hall with Juan and playing pool, or playing cards, or just having a Coke, and pretty soon I could say, 'I have to go, Juan, so have a nice week.' I'd have my community service record for the CV. Maybe that's part of what motivates us [to do such work], but it doesn't take long (I'll speak for myself, and I'm not bragging, I'm *worrying*, actually), it doesn't take too long for something else to get going: what I've been talking about. You become a link for these kids, but you become self-conscious about it, and that means you're putting yourself on the ropes, asking yourself the big questions, so you'll be able to do the same with your Little Brother."

Gary kept addressing the irony that he himself was the moral beneficiary of an involvement with a Little Brother. He was looking intensely inward, groping hard to clarify his own beliefs and values so that he could try to stand by them in his conversations with Juan, and so that he could speak not just out of self-knowledge and a common sense that is, actually, fate's, luck's gift to him, but out of a sincere conviction, a moral earnestness, the expression of which he had come to realize might well be his main chance, his only hope, of reaching, of persuading Juan: "Somehow I think I'm trying to get to him, so he'll pick my values, when he's facing a choice, rather than those he gets from the street and, I hate to say it, at home. That's a tall order. I don't mean to put it like that—we're back to this ego thing: a big temptation. But there's a conflict, a struggle in everyone: what do you decide about all sorts of things? I just hope Juan picks up some of the determination I picked up from my parents, picks it up through our time together. I try to tell him what I believe, and I've even told him that when I talk with him, it helps me because I realize that what I believe is important!"

As I've listened to this student of mine I've learned how much stronger he has become as a Big Brother, a tutor, an older friend to Juan. (He would eventually earn a doctorate in education and help teach in an undergraduate course I offer.) It is as if the weekly meetings, often two or so hours long, enable in each of the two another kind of coming together than that of a shared activity, even a shared conversation. The volunteer, on his own, is given pause: what does he uphold to himself, and why? If he is to be a convincing friend and teacher and guide it is such a question he will have to answer—hence the moral introspection he pursues. Juan's need for a kind of moral purpose that will carry him through any number of critical moments becomes for his older friend, who lives across the proverbial railroad tracks, a reason to locate more explicitly and consolidate his own moral purpose as a prelude to sharing it, however gingerly and indirectly.

Naturally, guile always matters in moral exchanges: how do you get something across without souring the entire enterprise by stirring up annoyance, irritation, resentment?[4] That question, too, haunted this young volunteer—how should he "deliver" moral energy to another person? The longer he struggled to convey his moral strength to Juan, and the more clearly he became aware of that moral strength, the more solid his sense of his own purpose in life became. This gift surprised him, even embarrassed him, but he had to learn to accept it if he was to keep at it with Juan. He did indeed persist with the boy, much to the benefit of both of them.

Personal Affirmation

Not all people who work with or on behalf of others become moralists (in the nonpejorative sense). For many volunteers there is obviously a moral purpose at work. Yet those people do not find themselves morally challenged as they do their volunteer work, do not think of it as bringing a moral bonus. Many even make a contrast between the obvious moral nature of their work and their own sense that they are getting "quite a bargain," as one middle-aged suburban hospital volunteer put it.

"I go to the hospital because I enjoy doing the work there. I love the nurses and the doctors, and I love the patients. I feel lucky to be able to spend part of my week that way. I hesitate to say I'm there because I feel I *should* be there. I don't deny that if I were a different person, with other values than the kind I have—we should be useful to others!—I probably would be elsewhere: maybe playing golf all spring, summer, autumn, like some of my friends do. But I have to be honest: I don't really judge someone playing golf or tennis, which I love to play, as doing something any less worthy of my time and energy than working as a hospital volunteer. I don't mean to sound selfish, but if you asked me what it means to me to do my work—why I do it—I'd have to say that I do it because I enjoy the world there, and, frankly, it's a tremendous educational experience. Not a day goes by that I don't learn something from the doctors, listening to them, and from the patients I meet.

"I used to think I was weak; I had a slight anemia, and my thyroid was on the low side. But since I've learned the ropes there at the hospital, I find myself really pitching in—until the next thing I know, people are telling me it's time to go home! I'm glad to leave, but I'm glad to come back in a day or two. I have to say it: I *miss* the hospital. There's a sense of excitement—lives are at stake! For me, it's a place where I feel myself needed and where I can live up to the expectations of others. Now this job is a big part of my life. I put a lot of myself into it; but I get back so much more. The people I meet who are struggling with pain and uncertainty—they help me realize that you can take things for granted until you get sick, and then you stop and think about what life really means."

What she was saying was not all that surprising. At times she came across as the slightly restless suburban housewife whose service smacked of condescension toward those who have fallen into sickness—their suffering an excuse for her to count her blessings! But when I watched her in the hospital or heard her recounting a most active, exhausting, giving day, it was certainly possible to overlook what she said and remember what she did week after week, often with great tact and sensitivity.

She was perhaps speaking most accurately when she emphasized the discoveries her work offered—all the people she met, all the stories she heard. "I remember what I hear in the evening; I talk to my husband about what I hear, and he says it's changed me a lot, what I do there on those wards."

Modesty—like arrogance—is no one's exclusive property by virtue of class or race. A woman from a quite genteel world, on her knees cleaning up after a patient who had fallen and then vomited, took the experience to heart and became quieter, less self-regarding, more reflective, more modest. Thirty miles away a tough working-class man, who never pretended to be soft-spoken or self-effacing, found a way to cope with disappointment when his son was born with Down syndrome. To make ends meet, he worked long hours as an automobile mechanic, then pumped gas at night. When his son was first born, a boy at last after five girls, he was not sad, anxious, or self-pitying, only angry.

His wife understood her husband well. "He's always been a man's man—he has his buddies, and they drink a lot of beer on Fridays. Otherwise, he's sober and very hard-working—two jobs, and never more than six hours' sleep. He's been a good husband and a good father: he loves those girls! But I'd be lying if I told you he didn't want a son. Oh, he was crazy for a boy, and when we decided to give it one last chance and he kept telling me he knew we'd have a sixth girl, he knew it, I knew something myself—how much he wanted a boy.

"Then I delivered, and we all were in ecstasy because it was a boy. Then came the news there was something wrong, that the boy, Ben, wasn't so good, that he wasn't passing the tests these doctors have when they examine babies. The rest—it's a nightmare. I don't know how to tell it—all we went through, but especially him."

The father's dreams of raising a son had to be surrendered.

"He used to be full of energy, and now he's lost a lot of it. He used to jump out of bed, and he'd be ready for the day, even if it was five in the morning and dark, in coldest winter. These days he's sleeping hard, and the alarm goes off, and he wants to go back to sleep. He must feel terrible—real guilty, because he's a decent guy ordinarily.

"That's the trouble, this is not an ordinary time! He's heartbroken. We both are, only I seem to be taking it much better. I say a dozen times to myself: God's will. If the good Lord wanted to send a retarded child here, and a boy, then that's His decision. For me the church is a big help. You know something? When he was at his lowest, he even stopped going [to church]. I said, 'It's bad enough, our troubles, and now you're going to send yourself to hell?' He looked at me, and you know what he said? He said, 'I'm already in hell.' *I* was ready to throw a glass at the wall when I heard that! I thought to myself, I'm fed up with all this feeling sorry for yourself that's coming out of his mouth! I just grabbed my raincoat and I left the house, and I slammed that door so hard I was afraid the roof would cave in. Then I realized I'd forgotten my pocketbook, so I ran back in and I grabbed it and ran out, and I slammed the door again, even harder, if that was possible! The only thing was, I saw out of the corner of my eye that he was crying, that he was wiping his eyes with a handkerchief.

"I was in the car, and I was ready to go, and then I said to myself, Hey, stop a minute. What's more important—to go to church and sit there and fume and ask Jesus to feel sorry for you and to condemn your husband or to skip church and go back inside and sit with him and hope he'll really break down and cry and cry, so all that disappointment in him will come out, and then he can talk with me, and we can try to figure out a way that we can pick up from here."

She chose to go home and take the chance that her husband would resolve his growing desperation—his disappointments, as she kept calling them, which were struggling to "express themselves," as she put it. She went into the kitchen and busied herself making fresh coffee, started cooking corn bread for lunch, one of his favorites, and said nothing. Finally he began to sob openly, and they began to talk.

"He didn't need to say much. All he needed to do was show me what he was feeling—I guess you could say show *himself*, because he'd been biting his lip and pushing himself like mad, as though there was nothing eating away at him, when everything he did showed that in a while there'd be nothing left of him at the rate he was going!

"All of a sudden, I broke my silence, and I said, 'Honey, you're as busy as anyone in the world can be, I know, but you've got to find some time for yourself, not for me and the kids, as much as we want you and need you. You've got to find some way of doing something that will give you some peace.' He looked up at me, and I could see he knew what I was saying, but he was helpless; he didn't know what to do. I racked my brains, and then I thought, Why not a doctor? I just blurted it out, the name of the pediatrician. I didn't say anything else, I just said his name. I didn't have to go further, or maybe I was afraid to, or I didn't know what words to use."

A week later he and the pediatrician had a long talk. The doctor took the lead, told his patient's father that he needed to become part of Ben's life and that one way to do so was to work with older retarded children. That way, when the boy was no longer a baby, the father would have some experience with children who needed special education. A month later, with the doctor's help, this father began volunteering on weekends at a state school for retarded and disabled children.

"I was 'slow' myself: I was 'disabled,'" he would recall a year later. He was also anxious, frightened, ready to give up and flee or to break down and cry. But he also wanted "some way out of the trap" he'd built for himself. He intuitively knew that his tears were a kind of grief, evidence of a mind in mourning. "I've been crying for all the hopes and dreams I once had—they're not going to happen. It's only gradually occurring to me that the only way out of this corner I'm in—like I keep saying, it's a trap, and I've made it myself—the only way out is for me to find some other place to go, some new hopes for myself."

By then he had already begun to build up some "hopes"—not for himself or, least of all, his son, but for the three or four youngsters he was learning to engage with, challenge to activities, help restrain and excite to action.

He didn't lose his wistfulness about what might have been. Rather, he let those thoughts ignite in him the fierce willfulness he had always possessed as a worker. Once the sight of boys playing in a Little League game had been unbearable. The time would come when he would organize his own son's Little League team. When a neighbor once called the team "special," he flinched. "I didn't like the way he used that word. I felt myself getting weak. I was a little teary for a second, and my knees felt as though if someone just touched me, I'd fall over. But in another second I was up for anything. I said, 'You bet we're special.' I meant it. Me and the kids, we were doing great, and we'd show him, we'd be thrilled to show him! It was then I knew I'd crossed some big street, and I was walking on the other side and my head was up, not down, and it was working with those kids that did it. They're the ones who got me across to the other side—do you see?"

I nodded, grateful to a man who had shown what it can mean to fall down, then pick himself up, not through hours of psychological talk or the support of a "group," and not even through the healing that time itself offers. In the end, his willfulness responded to his wife's loyalty and affection and to a doctor's sensible suggestion. But in the end, also, his pain responded to the visible, concrete opportunities a few children offered him. The gifts he brought on their birthdays and at Christmas signaled not only what these children had come to mean to him, but what they had enabled him to find and affirm in himself. They walked him "across," to a place where he was able to manage on his own. He became once again the assertive, capable, resourceful person he'd been before his setback, a setback that was followed by a breakthrough. As I heard him talk about the "choice" he had made, as I heard him remember "wishing" with each visit to that state school for the strength to make the best of his time with those children, I remembered the Latin I had learned many years earlier: the very root of the word "volunteer," *voluntas*—a choice—comes from *velle*, to wish.

Stoic Endurance

Some people exert themselves in a manner less directly personal than the man described above. In many years of work among poor families in Boston and Cambridge, I have met individuals who have wondered why they engage in volunteer work, and to what effect. They say simply that they do what they do—but for no particular reason that they care to spell out and with no particular personal consequences. They claim no affirmation for themselves, though an outsider, watching them in action and overhearing what they say, might disagree. They don't even assert the restricted satisfaction of friendships. Sometimes they acknowledge a motivation that does scant credit to their depth of commitment. An aside such as "I just get a kick out of it" hardly conveys the satisfaction achieved from a voluntary obligation taken on with great seriousness.

In Roxbury I met a middle-aged black mother who did her fair share of listening to children. She worked as a bus driver, taking children to and from school every weekday.[5] After her husband died of a stroke at the age of forty-four, she was tempted to immerse herself in the troubled lives of her two daughters and their four children. She had encouraged both daughters to finish high school and take courses at a nearby community college to become nurses or computer programmers or teachers, whatever might catch their interest. The daughters adamantly refused: they wanted no more school, even though they were not always happy as mothers. One went dancing a lot (her boyfriend, the father of her one son, had left her and gone to the West Coast). The other, who had three children, moved in and out of serious depressive states, even as she tried occasionally to work in a fast-food chain. Her husband had been hurt in an automobile accident but received no compensation because he had been drinking and was responsible for the crash.

In these unpromising family circumstances this bus-driving mother and grandmother went out of her way to keep an eye on many of the children whom she transported to school. She volunteered at an elementary school as a teacher's assistant, and even on the bus she did far more than drive. I first heard about her from a mother whose son and daughter I was getting to know. She told me that her children's bus driver "taught" her charges all the way to school and all the way back.

Once I took the liberty of inquiring about her reasons for doing this teaching. She warmed to the question but wasn't sure she knew how to answer. "I wish I could tell you more," she said almost plaintively. Then she said, "I want to see these kids make it in life. I want to see them survive." As she spoke, I thought that she was also expressing her own persistence, her capacity for stoic survival. She was a wise woman, earthy and intelligent and determined with regard to those children she tried to assist.

"I had an aunt who would come and help us out, she was a maiden lady, my momma called her. This aunt, Josephine, would sing gospel music, and she'd start her declaring. She'd tell us that we had to do something God would notice, or else we'd just get lost in the big shuffle! I can still hear her saying that now. I can still see myself staring at her and getting more and more worried by the second! What would happen to me if God just overlooked me while He was paying attention to some others, who'd been smart enough to make sure they captured His attention? Why, I'd end up in one of those big fires 'down there' that don't get put out by any men with hoses shooting out water!

"So I'd try to figure out how to get His attention, and I had some ideas. One, I'd go to church *alone* sometimes, and that way He'd see me being loyal, and He'd remember me from all the others. Two, if I did something, got a job, I'd try to do it a little better and different from other folks; that way the Lord up there would spot me, or maybe He'd hear from others what I was doing. Three, I'd try to go the extra mile so I could show Him that I'm not just running with the crowd. That's the worst, my aunt used to tell us, when you just sit there and let yourself be traveling like the other folks around you.

"When I'm driving the bus, I call some kids to be up there near me, sitting, and I've done my homework—I've checked into *their* homework!—and I'm ready for them. I'll quiz them. I'll try to give them hints about how to do better in school. I'll teach them about obeying and keeping quiet and speaking out at the right time. If they're doing good, I reach into my bag, and I give them a chocolate bar—and it's extra good, not just the five-and-dime-store

kind! 'Made in England' is what it says on the wrapper—and I get them to read it.

"The teachers have called me an 'honorary' one, and that's fine. I go to school and sit there in a class, and try to get those kids to pay attention and study as hard as they can. When a kid does well, I feel great! It's my reward—and I hope the good Lord is taking it all down. A lot of times, though, I don't get my hopes too high—about the kids or about myself, either. A lot of times I'm saying to myself that I've seen so much trouble hereabouts, and it's not getting the slightest better, and sometimes it's worse. So if a kid learns to spell a little bit better, and he does his figuring, his arithmetic a little better, and he writes his sentences right, it still won't prove much down the road, because there's a trap he'll fall into—drugs, or a bullet that hits him even if it's meant for someone else, or sickness."

Such a mix of continuing energy, spent generously on children, and a stoic endurance that forswears self-importance or even a conviction of one's significance in the lives of others is not altogether rare in certain older volunteers, even if they don't attribute their condition to the Lord's presence (a threatened presence?) in their lives. This woman took great pleasure in asking children to do a lot and yet not expecting a world-shattering miracle as a consequence of what happened between her and them. She hoped (and prayed daily) for a "touch of wisdom"—a quiet acceptance of what would be. She did hope to contribute to what would be, yet she had a sense of history that was almost Tolstoyan in nature: she was mindful of all the forces that conspire to make us turn out as we do.

I think of that bus driver when I watch several older people visit sick children in a pediatric ward or when I watch schoolchildren visiting the elderly in a nursing home not far from an urban middle school.[6] Some of the older people are not unlike that bus-driving woman: energetic and forceful, yet glad to feel detached. They try to help others even though they themselves are ailing a bit.

"I couldn't do this work if I was too involved with those children," one woman remarked to me. "I've learned that if you exhaust yourself, if you overcommit yourself, you lose rather than win. The children pull back—and why shouldn't they! You have to learn just the right attitude with them, and when you've got it, then you really can enjoy this work. It doesn't become a chore or a burden, and yet you do get close to the kids. It's a matter of tone, you could say: you know enough to persist, but not feel the world hangs on your every word!"

A Boost to Success

For a person to remain committed to service despite the outcome, he or she must have felt a prior sense of accomplishment. Some people who work at community service or enlist in privately sponsored or government service programs are also anxious to help launch a career. They hope to become doctors or lawyers or to enter the world of business or to teach. They look ahead to applications, interviews, committee evaluations and decisions. The ladder upward beckons toward college or graduate school, toward a hospital appointment, law clerkship, business or teaching position. It is not easy to understand the complex mixture of ideas, concerns, and motives that informs the decisions of such volunteers. Any discussion of the satisfactions of service ought to mention the dilemmas many students feel as they balance their idealistic motivations with the practicalities required as they contemplate their future occupation or profession.

Not all young volunteers are as forthcoming—as relentlessly able and willing to enter into self-scrutiny and share the results—as one young man who as a Harvard undergraduate worked for two years tutoring children in the Roxbury section of Boston. He worked hard to earn the children's trust, but he still felt he was "on trial."

"A month ago, one child suddenly shot this question at me: 'Hey, what's in it for you?' At first I wasn't sure what he meant—what 'it' was supposed to be. He saw me trying to figure out what I was being asked, how to ask for some kind of clarification. So he expanded his ques-

tion. 'You come out here a lot, and you're nice to us, and a few of us were wondering, Why does he come here, and what will he get out of it?' I didn't answer right away. I could have spouted a big line: how much it means to me to be able to help others, and the tremendous satisfaction I get when I see someone improving in school, and my parents' Christian beliefs that you give to others, try to do the best you can to share what you have with people who are in need. Then I could have added that I have *fun*, that I like coming here and meeting people, and we have a good time, and I feel better, frankly, when I return because I have a sense of accomplishment, and I've enjoyed being with friends, and I remember the stories I've heard, and the jokes.

"Instead I sat there, and I guess I was silent *too* long, because a couple of kids laughed nervously, and one kid said I didn't have to answer the question. 'Besides,' she added, 'we like you, and we don't care what your reasons are for coming here.' I sure was relieved to hear that!

"Finally I said the truth; I said that it was a real hard one to put to me, what they'd asked. I said, 'Look, I like coming here—you've become friends of mine, I hope, and I hope you feel the same way, that I'm a friend of yours. I love getting a pizza and bowling, and I love trying to help out with your work so you can do better, just the way certain teachers helped me out in high school, and before that too.' I said, 'If you can see someone doing better and better in school, and you've been able to be part of that— of the person improving in English or math— then you feel good, or at least I do.' Then I tried to be honest, to level with them. I said, 'Hey, I can't deny that it helps me to come out here. I like doing it and feel proud to be able to be with you and make friends and do the teaching. But yes, I wouldn't want to deny it, I'll put this down on my record, what I've done here, and that will help me—people like to see that, admissions people. I won't deny it!'

"That's about it, word for word, what I said. I was grabbing hard for words, and I was afraid that I was falling down and making a mess of everything! But they were very nice to me. They told me to forget it, and they told me I was cool, and they told me it was time to go get one of those pizzas, since I just mentioned them. Later, when we were eating our pizzas, and everyone was talking about other things, my mind was still on that question I'd been asked, and what the right answer to it is, and how you phrase your answer."

He was certainly not alone in the moral quandary he expressed. He spent a long time trying to settle in his mind exactly what he *was* doing in Roxbury as a tutor and what his reasons and expectations were. Some others who did similar community service, he felt, were "crudely opportunistic." When I asked him to explain, he was terser than usual. "They want to list their community service work on their CV." Then he added, after a very short pause, "So do I. It's self-serving for me to distinguish myself from them—me the good guy, they the clever frauds. It's so damn complicated. I don't know how to begin to look at all this—what our motives are."

He had turned that youth's question into an excuse for a far-reaching kind of self-arraignment, I began to realize. It is important to note under the rubric of satisfactions the unquestionable pleasure many young men and women have taken, not only in the value to others of their community service work but in the value it can have for themselves as well.

That value is not only a moral one (so much learned from others in tutoring them) but also a personal one, as this young man said quite pointedly: "This work I do will help me, I sometimes think, more than it will help the kids. I guess I ought to say that the work will give a boost to my success, and that I know it, and that when you ask me about the satisfactions I get from this kind of work—well, if I left that out, I'd be leaving something out that's part of the picture!"

His expression was singularly candid and quite telling. He worked all of the ironies and complexities, really, of a privileged life into a few sentences: the satisfactions of doing community service work and the additional satisfaction that went with knowing that his work would no doubt advance the further work he hoped to do as a lawyer or businessman (he hadn't yet settled that question). In our many further talks de-

voted to this matter, we brought in other students to ponder the awkward yet important implications of a quite human ethical issue first given shape (speaking of irony) by the question of a boy in a ghetto school who was having an exceedingly hard time of it educationally.

Those who took part in this discussion were outspokenly idealistic and at the same time self-critically assertive of their own rights and needs—a rather tense and complicated attitude. Again and again I heard comments that were apologetically self-serving—sinners proclaiming with melancholy insistence their necessary wrong-doing!

"I live in a world where you have to play all the angles," a young woman announced, and then she denounced such an imperative with considerable vehemence. "I'd like to work at public-interest law, but first I have to get into law school, and so if I work at helping public interest lawyers now, I'll have a better chance of becoming one later." Minutes afterward, those words prompted her conscience to rebel: such talk was "sleazy," she wanted it known, and she didn't so much ask for forgiveness as hope that "one day there will be an end to it [the kind of remarks she'd just made], at least for me. Maybe they [on the admissions committee] see through all this. Maybe they remember their own chicanery." Her good work as a teacher of needy children had now become a manifest confidence trick, at least with respect to what she had intended when she began the service work. Still, the work had its own worth, most of these ambitious, able young men and women remembered, and their tutees would agree.

Notes

1. This episode is described at length in "Serpents and Doves: Nonviolent Youth in the South."

2. I report on this "moral call," as students give voice to it, in *The Call of Stories*. Of course, the person being called does not always take the step from having a sense of what ought be done to making a commitment of time and effort.

3. He had been reading and taking to heart Christopher Lasch's *The Culture of Narcissism* (New York: Norton, 1978).

4. I remember well Reinhold Niebuhr's frequent and unapologetic use of the word "guile" in a course I audited at Union Theological Seminary in 1952, and in sermons at Harvard when he was a visiting teacher there in the 1960s. I recall my work as a student of his in "Reinhold Niebuhr's Nature and Destiny of Man," *Daedalus,* Winter 1974.

5. I allude to the matters discussed in this section in a children's book of fiction based on the Boston school desegregation struggle: *Dead End School* (Boston: Atlantic-Little, Brown, 1968).

6. My work, done in conjunction with college volunteers, will eventually be described in a study on resiliency in the elderly.

PART 10

THE BLENDING AND BLURRING OF THE SECTORS

The relationships among the public, business, and nonprofit sectors are undergoing major change in the United States as well as in a number of other countries. Government reliance on nonprofits for the provision of public goods and services continues to grow, particularly for persons with mental illness, disabilities, youths and gangs, families, victims of abuse; to support and coordinate the arts; and to provide financial and political support, for example, for national parks, seashores, and rivers. States such as Massachusetts and New Jersey, in particular, provide essentially no direct human services. Virtually all such services have been contracted, mostly into the nonprofit sector.[1] At the same time, the percentage of the sector's income from selling services and products has increased (see Part 1), and many nonprofits have become aggressively commercial. They compete for business directly with for-profit firms (see Part 6). This chapter addresses what we *believe* we know about the blurring and blending of sector and organizational boundaries, as well as many of the issues where considerable disagreement remains.

The nonprofit sector has always been positioned rather delicately between the business sector's profit motive and the government sector's drive to meet social needs. Its existence, roles, and functions thus are impacted by changes in the other two sectors, and changes in the other two sectors became quite dramatic as we entered the new millennium. Although the trend toward "blurring and blending" is quite universally acknowledged, the magnitude and shape of the implications for the business, nonprofit, and public sectors are not at all clear. Indeed, the implications are not clear for democratic government and civil society. The privatization of human services raises a far more complex set of issues than simply getting people off welfare. Our notions of democracy, citizenship, and accountability also are at stake.

Growing numbers of nonprofits have become reliant on government funding in many functional areas at a period in time when government funding appears to be on a long-term decline (see Part 11). Republicans and Democrats alike in Washington, D.C., and statehouses are clamoring for governments to be *downsized* (government budgets, in particular); for the *devolution* of government services and fiscal responsibility to state, county, and municipal governments; and for the *diffusion* of services and responsibility out of government and into the private sector.[2] This downsizing, devolution, and diffusion "movement" arrived at a time when individual and corporate donations to nonprofit organizations have been stagnant and, by some measures, declining.

Nonprofits are told that they must therefore be more businesslike if they hope to survive. They must be more entrepreneurial in pursuing alternative sources of revenue, and they need to manage their resources and programs more efficiently. To make this happen, there need to be more business representatives on their boards and more professionalism in their management staff. During the 1980s and 1990s, nonprofits were surprisingly successful at meeting these challenges.[3] Their successes, however, have created new problems and challenges.

Blurring Between the Public and Nonprofit Sectors

As the nonprofit sector has emerged over the past several decades as the preferred deliverer of public services, government has become the primary source of revenue for many nonprofits.[4] The percent of total income that nonprofits receive from government varies by organizational purpose and program function, from a high of 42 percent in social and legal services and 36 percent in health services, to a low of 17 percent in education and 11 percent in the arts.[5] Smith and Lipsky have been among the most outspoken about the marked effect that dependence on government funding is having on the governance, leadership, management, and character of the nonprofit sector.[6] As this dependence has grown, it is possible that the lines that separate the sectors may have become more blurred than is good for government, the nonprofit sector, or society. There is substantial disagreement, however, about this conclusion.

During the "Great Society" era of the 1970s, the U.S. government imposed numerous administrative requirements on states as conditions for receiving categorical grants, including personnel systems and practices, budgeting procedures, and financial reporting standards.[7] Although these requirements probably improved the administration of grants, in truth they were only part of a larger public policy agenda in Washington. The federal government wanted to strengthen the administrative practices of state governments. The "feds" were determined to make the administration of state governments similar in process and substance to U.S. government practices.

Units of government at all levels used the same approach and tactics with nonprofit organizations in the 1980s and 1990s. Eligibility for contracts and contract awards were conditioned upon nonprofits adopting government-like systems, policies, procedures, and practices. The substance of the requirements varied, but most were intended to protect the rights of employees, clients, unserved individuals, records, and fiscal resources.

Smith and Lipsky argue that the requirements and resource dependence diminished the independence of nonprofits. Ferris counters that reliance on government funding does not necessarily decrease the ability of contracted nonprofits to remain true to their missions or to their community roots.[8] Other observers disagree with Ferris.[9] Smith and Lipsky counterargue that government's influence on the administration of a contracted nonprofit far exceeds the percent of income received from government. Kramer cautions that the effects of resource dependence may be powerful and pervasive: "The source of resources determines the type of and standards for success and failure, the character of decision making, accountability, and the external relations of an organization."[10] There is no consensus. The standards and requirements that government agencies have imposed on contracted nonprofits can be stifling, but the resources provided by government contracts also can provide freedoms.[11]

Some effects of resource dependence appear to be predictable: The longer a nonprofit relies extensively on government contracts, the more it will tend to look, think, feel, and act like a small (or not so small) government agency.[12] And thus, as Judith Saidel notes, "one of the necessary shifts in intersectoral theory . . . is the abandonment of the notion of the third sector as independent."[13]

Other factors and trends have also contributed to the blurring of the lines between the government and nonprofit sectors. As services have shifted from government to nongovernmental providers, "where the action is" for employees also has moved to the nonprofits.[14] Employees reportedly are moving back and forth between the sectors frequently. The government funders of today may be the nonprofit service deliverers of tomorrow, and vice versa. If so, the historic differences in perspectives between employees in the two sectors eventually will vanish.[15]

Also, contracting relationships—the interorganizational means through which contracts are administered and monitored—have been evolving away from traditional arms-length, legalistic contract relationships and toward public-private partnerships.[16] In many human services systems, the contract relationship is developing into a collaborative, problem-solving type of partnership. Inevitably, close working partnerships lead to shared perceptions, values, expectations, and standards.[17] There is growing *interdependence* among organizations in the two sectors. The dependence is *not* one-way, which is potentially both "good news" and "bad news" for nonprofits, government, clients, and for democratic civil society.[18]

The literature in the fields of political science and public administration has noted the massive changes that contracting is causing in the government sector worldwide. The effects of the changes will be felt most immediately by civil service employees and lower- to middle-level public administrators, but they will extend much farther.

> Reinventing government's ["reinventing government" includes but is not limited to contracting with nonprofits] progress may bring with it a weakening of neutral competence, merit, professionalism, and related values. . . .
>
> If we assume the worst, then reinventing government as political ideology suggests the disempowerment of public employees and the career civil service. Privatization, debureaucratization, and decentralization reduce the size and scope of government; managerialism makes public servants more like corporate workers . . . and reinstates the politics/administration dichotomy. When central government is downsized and load shedding shifts government activities to the private or nonprofit sectors, public employees and organizations that represent them lose numbers, standing, influence and power. . . . Reinventing government tends to strengthen the hand of private sector forces, and to cause reallocations of power from legislative to executive branches.[19]

The blurring between the two sectors has not been caused solely by changes in the nonprofit sector. Milward and his associates,[20] Smith and Lipsky, and others have warned about the "hollow state" and the "gutting" of government's historic roles and functions that has occurred as nongovernmental organizations have "taken over" service delivery. "The issue of privatizing welfare raises the question and challenges the notion of what constitutes the public arena and what responsibilities lie there."[21] Alexander, Stivers, and Nank ask whether the blurring may indeed threaten the future of civil society.[22]

At the same time that many nonprofits have increased their reliance on government contracts, however, the total amount of U.S. government money flowing into the human services, the arts, and environmental protection has declined steadily, sometimes dramatically.[23] States, counties, and cities have not been anxious to replace these declining federal funds when tax and deficit reductions continue to command high public support. And individual and corporate donations, historically the largest source of nonprofit sector revenues, have remained level and actually declined as a percentage of income. (See Parts 1 and 11.)

Blurring Between the Business and Nonprofit Sectors

Because of these downward trends in all of the sector's longtime revenue sources, the pressure has been increasing on nonprofits to be more businesslike, entrepreneurial, and innovative. They have been challenged to find and develop new sources of income, increase their efficiency, bring more business executives onto their boards, create venture partnerships with business—to *be more like businesses* in all respects. Nonprofits have done surprisingly well at meeting this challenge since early in the 1980s.

Nonprofit organizations in many subsectors have ventured out aggressively into a wide assortment of commercial markets. Numbers and percentages vary with different definitions and sources of information, but in 1992, charitable nonprofits overall raised an estimated 54 percent of their income from dues, fees, and other charges for services and products—from businesslike activities.[24] Nonprofits in the health care subsector have been competing directly and aggressively with for-profit businesses since the 1970s.[25] Nonprofit hospitals and clinics own for-profit subsidiaries that provide corporate wellness programs, own condominium physicians' offices, and manage private health clubs. Mental health agencies and other nonprofits that serve mostly low-income populations regularly buy, manage, and sell companies that operate apartment houses, pet stores, laundries, and many other historically low-wage service businesses. Many of these commercial ventures by nonprofits have proven to be enormously successful by almost any measures.

Commercial-type ventures usually provide multiple benefits for the clients who receive services and for the nonprofit organizations as well. They often create employment opportunities and make more hard-to-find services available for clients. They also generate revenues that can be "plowed" back into more or better services and thereby benefit clients and advance the nonprofit's mission. Careful legal lines must be drawn and business strategies followed, however, in order to limit Unrelated Business Income Taxes (UBIT) and to preserve an organization's tax-exempt status with the IRS and state taxing authorities (see Part 4). However, it is easy to understand why nonprofit organizations' commercial ventures have incited vociferous cries of "unfair competition," particularly from small businesses.[26]

Other developments have also contributed to the blurring of the line between the business and nonprofit sectors. First, for-profit businesses are "invading turf" that has historically "belonged" to the nonprofit sector. For-profit chains have replaced nonprofits as the primary providers of hospital care in the United States. Private emergency medical services (EMS) companies have all but driven nonprofits out of urban and suburban markets and have made major inroads in many rural areas. For-profits also have made aggressive entries in the fields of mental health, substance abuse, and youth and adult corrections. Nonprofits and for-profits thus are competing with each other in fields that used to be each other's "turf."

Second, the professionalism of the managers of nonprofit organizations has increased dramatically since 1985. The numbers of professional master's degree programs and students have expanded nearly exponentially during the past twenty years.[27] Nonprofit executives are often recruited now from businesses, and in some subsectors they are being paid *Fortune 500* wages.[28]

Third, a larger percentage of nonprofit organization trustees—the individuals who have policymaking responsibility—reportedly are employed in businesses while fewer are from government agencies and other nonprofit organizations. Finally, mutually beneficial venture partnerships between businesses and nonprofits became commonplace in the 1990s. Planned giving programs, cause-related marketing ventures,[29] and businesses using nonprofit higher education research facilities and faculty rather than investing in their own are only a few examples of this type of intertwining relationship.

Conclusion

In sum, nonprofit organizations are becoming more like businesses:

- Nonprofit organizations are becoming more businesslike in their revenue-generating activities as they compete directly with profit-making businesses.
- Nonprofit organizations have been learning more about the "ways" of business from trustees and executives who have been recruited from businesses.
- Nonprofit organizations are gaining in their management sophistication as managers and executives earn MBAs (master of business administration), MPAs (master of public administration), MNMs (master of nonprofit management), MFAAs (master of fine arts administration), administrative tracks in MSWs (master of social work), and professional certificates.
- Nonprofit organizations are partnering with businesses at a rapidly increasing rate.

In "The Current Crisis" (reprinted in Part 11), Lester Salamon warns that nonprofit organizations are in danger of losing public support and favored treatment from government because they have been too successful in becoming like businesses. Likewise, Burton Weisbrod asks: "As the nonprofit sector grows in size and commercial activities, is it becoming indistinguishable from the private sector? . . . This question is significant because at root is whether the organizations in the rapidly growing nonprofit sector deserve the subsidies and tax exemptions they receive from individuals and from the federal, state, and local governments."[30]

The issues in this essay are a synthesis of many questions and issues that have been raised in earlier chapters, including the justifications for tax exemption and tax deductible contributions (Part

4); the many theories of the sector's existence, roles, and functions, primarily from economics, political science, psychology, sociology, and organization theory/public administration (Parts 5 through 9); and both the history (Part 3) and the "distinctiveness" of the sector (Part 2). These issues also lead directly to a discussion of the challenges facing the sector, which is the topic of Part 11.

Readings Reprinted in This Part

According to Dennis R. Young, "Third Party Government" is "a term coined by Lester Salamon in 1981 to describe the pattern of relationships between government and the private sector in the delivery of public services in the United States."[31] *Third party government* refers to the various forms of collaborative government-nonprofit relationships in which "government typically provides the finances and influences service policies, while nonprofits deliver the services." Young argues that Salamon's "voluntary failure" theory is a more useful theory for explaining government-nonprofit contracting relationships than "contract failure" and "government failure" theories.

In "Voluntary Agencies and the Contract Culture: 'Dream or Nightmare?'" Ralph M. Kramer provides a comprehensive overview of the major concepts and public policy concerns associated with *purchase of service contracting* (POSC).[32] He addresses four major issues: the rationale and incentives for POSC; processes, transaction costs, and strategies; consequences for the service delivery system and for the governmental and voluntary nonprofit organizations involved; and implications for policy, management, and future research. In discussing the policy context, Kramer observes that POSC can "be viewed as part of the 'crisis of the welfare state,' . . . accompanied by the policies of privatization, decentralization, deregulation, and deinstitutionalization. One outcome has been a pervasive blurring of the boundaries between the public and private sectors." Government contracts most of its social services for several identifiable reasons: legislative mandates, political and social ideology, as the result of rational decisionmaking, and as a pragmatic expedient. The consequences of POSC for service delivery systems, for government, and for contracted nonprofit organizations are not well known. "Clearly, a New Age has emerged of blurred organizational boundaries in which public and nongovernmental organizations need and depend on each other more than ever. It is necessary, however, to get beyond the usual rhetoric of collaboration and to recognize not only the mutual dependency but also the significance of the unequal distribution of power in these public-private 'partnerships.'"

Judith R. Saidel has been in the forefront of researchers who have been examining the complex web of relationships between government agencies and contracted nonprofit service providers. "Resource Interdependence: The Relationship Between State Agencies and Nonprofit Organizations" reports information collected from nonprofit and state agency managers who work together in the subfields of the arts, health, developmental disabilities, and human services.[33] Saidel characterizes the relationship as one of "substantial and symmetrical resource interdependence"—of "dependence of public agencies and nonprofit agencies on each other for resources." The resources that "flow from state agencies to nonprofit organizations are revenues; information, including expertise and technical assistance; political support and legitimacy . . . ; and access to the nonlegislative policy process." In turn, nonprofit organizations "supply their service-delivery capacity, information, political support, and legitimacy to state agencies." The three dimensions of dependence—and thus the sources of power each sector holds over the other—are the importance of the resource; the availability of alternative sources of the resource; and "the ability to compel provision of the resource."

Saidel raises important concerns: "The activities of nonprofit organizations do not appear to be at the margins . . . but rather at the center of public services. . . . Symmetrical resource dependence [which Saidel found to characterize the relationship] may not allow sufficient nonprofit or public organizational autonomy. Some autonomy is necessarily lost by both parties in an interdependent relationship." She also notes that public agencies tend to become more dependent on nonprofits "when nonprofit providers who deliver high priority services are scarce and/or politically powerful," and thus the agencies tend to have less autonomy.

James M. Ferris has been less concerned about the potential effects of contracting on nonprofits than most other writers. In "The Double-Edged Sword of Social Service Contracting: Public Accountability Versus Nonprofit Autonomy," Ferris uses transaction cost theory and resource dependence to argue that the resources nonprofit organizations provide to government ("their trustworthiness and experience") should cause governments to continue their preference for contracting with them.[34] "Although the fear that such organizations [nonprofits] might jeopardize their autonomy by becoming too reliant on government contracts cannot be entirely discounted, the attractiveness of nonprofits as a contracting option should allay some of these concerns." Ferris also believes that government will "be inclined to contract with nonprofit organizations [in preference to for-profit businesses] in order to limit the transaction costs associated with contract monitoring and enforcement." Despite Ferris's inclination to dismiss concerns about contracting and nonprofit autonomy, he concludes that "nonprofit organizations should be mindful that too heavy a dependence on public funding threatens their identity."

Burton Weisbrod's article "The Future of the Nonprofit Sector: Its Entwining with Private Enterprise and Government" addresses three questions: Why is the nonprofit sector expanding in the United States and in other nations? How has the growth of nonprofits affected other segments of the economy? What evidence is there that nonprofits make a difference—that they perform functions that private firms or government cannot perform?[35] Weisbrod analyzes the effects of competitive and cooperative nonprofit activities on the private sector, government, consumers, and other nonprofit organizations, respectively. He also uses a series of "tests" to assess whether nonprofit organizations behave differently than for-profit businesses and government agencies. His tests include efficiency, output quality, trustworthiness, pricing policies, waiting lists, opportunities to volunteer, and managerial compensation. Weisbrod is one of many students of the sector who are concerned that "increased user fees and commercial activities all bring troubling side effects. . . . The growth of nonprofit sectors throughout the world is thrusting nonprofits into the central debate over the organization of society. . . . Success has its price!"

Notes

1. Steven R. Smith and Michael Lipsky, *Nonprofits for Hire* (Cambridge: Harvard University Press, 1993).

2. J. Steven Ott and Lisa A. Dicke, "HRM in an Era of Downsizing, Devolution, Diffusion, and Empowerment . . . and Accountability??" in A. Farazmand, ed., *Strategic Public Personnel Administration/HRM: Building Human Capital for the 21st Century* (Praeger/Greenwood Press, forthcoming).

3. Lester M. Salamon, "The Current Crisis: Holding the Center," reprinted in Part 11.

4. Steven R. Smith, "Transforming Public Services: Contracting for Social and Health Services in the U.S.," *Public Administration 74*, Spring 1996, 113–127.

5. Julian Wolpert, "How Federal Cutbacks Affect the Charitable Sector," in Lynn A Staeheli, Janet E. Kodras, and Colin Flint, eds., *State Devolution in America: Implications for a Diverse Society* (Thousand Oaks, Calif.: Sage, 1997), p. 100.

6. Steven R. Smith and Michael Lipsky, *Nonprofits for Hire* (Cambridge: Harvard University Press, 1993).

7. See, for example, chapters 4 and 5 in Phillip J. Cooper et al., *Public Administration for the Twenty-First Century* (Fort Worth, Tex.: Harcourt Brace, 1998); chapter 4 in Jay M. Shafritz and E. William Russell, *Introducing Public Administration* (New York: Longman, 1997).

8. See James Ferris, "The Double-Edged Sword of Social Service Contracting," reprinted in this part.

9. See Melissa Middleton Stone, "Competing Contexts: The Evolution of a Nonprofit Organization's Governance System in Multiple Environments," *Administration and Society* 28 (1), May 1996, 61–89.

10. Ralph M. Kramer, "Voluntary Agencies and the Contract Culture," *Social Service Review* 68 (1), March 1994, 33–60. (Reprinted in this part.)

11. Lisa A. Dicke and J. Steven Ott, "Public Agency Accountability in Human Services Contracting," *Public Productivity and Management Review* 22 (4), June 1999, 502–516.

12. Smith and Lipsky, *Nonprofits for Hire.*

13. Judith R. Saidel, "Dimensions of Interdependence: The State and Voluntary-Sector Relationship," *Nonprofit and Voluntary Sector Quarterly* 18 (4), Winter 1989, p. 336.

14. Ott and Dicke, "HRM in an Era of Downsizing."

15. Smith and Lipsky, *Nonprofits for Hire.*

16. Ruth H. DeHoog, "Competition, Negotiation, or Cooperation: Three Models for Service Contracting," *Administration and Society* 22 (3), November 1990, 317–340; and Lester M. Salmon, "Partners in Public Service: The Scope and Theory of Government-Nonprofit Relations," in Walter W. Powell, ed., *The Nonprofit Sector: A Research Handbook* (New Haven: Yale University Press, 1987), pp. 99–117.

17. These relationships are the focus of a research project being conducted by Lisa A. Dicke, Department of Political Science, Texas Tech University.

18. Judith R. Saidel, "Devolution and the Politics of Interdependence: Management and Policy Trade-Offs in Government-Nonprofit Contracting," paper presented at the American Society for Public Administration, Seattle, Wash., May 9–12, 1998.

19. Richard C. Kearney and Steven W. Hays, "Reinventing Government, the New Public Management and Civil Service Systems in International Perspective," *Review of Public Personnel Administration* 18 (4), Fall 1998, pp. 39, 46.

20. H. Brinton Milward, Barbara A. Else, and Jakob T. Raskob, "Managing the Hollow State," paper presented at the 1991 American Political Science Association, Washington, D.C., August 29—September 1, 1991; and H. Brinton Milward, "Non-profit Contracting and the Hollow State," *Public Administration Review* 54 (1), January/February 1994, 73–76.

21. Meghan Cope, "Responsibility, Regulation, and Retrenchment: The End of Welfare?" in Lynn A Staeheli, Janet E. Kodras, and Colin Flint, eds., *State Devolution in America: Implications for a Diverse Society* (Thousand Oaks, Calif.: Sage, 1997), p. 200.

22. Jennifer Alexander, Camilla Stivers, and Renee Nank, "Implications of Welfare Reform: Do Nonprofit Survival Strategies Threaten Civil Society?" *Nonprofit and Voluntary Sector Quarterly* 28 (4), December 1999, 452–475.

23. Lester M. Salamon, "The Current Crises" (reprinted in Part 10); also see Virginia A. Hodgkinson and Richard Lyman, "The State of the Independent Sector" (reprinted in Part 1).

24. Virginia A. Hodgkinson, Murray Weitzman, et al., *Dimensions of the Independent Sector, 1992–1993* (San Francisco: Jossey-Bass, 1992).

25. Since about 1995, however, the nonprofit hospitals have been "losing" in the competition.

26. U.S. Small Business Administration, *Unfair Competition by Nonprofit Organizations with Small Business: An Issue for the 1980s,* 3rd ed. (Washington, D.C.: U.S. Government Printing Office, June 1984). And nonprofit credit unions have been a huge "thorn in the side" of commercial banks for decades.

27. Naomi Wish and Roseanne M. Mirabella, "Educational Impact on Graduate Nonprofit Degree Programs: Perspectives of Multiple Stake Holders," *Nonprofit Management and Leadership* 9 (3), Spring 1999, 329–340.

28. For example, *U.S. News and World Report*'s October 2, 1995, cover story exclaimed: "Tax Exempt! Many Nonprofits Look and Act Like Normal Companies—Running Businesses, Making Money. So Why Aren't They Paying Uncle Sam?"

29. See, for example, Alan R. Andreasen, "Profits for Nonprofits: Find a Corporate Partner," *Harvard Business Review,* November/December 1996, 47–59; and William P. Ryan, "The New Landscape for Nonprofits," *Harvard Business Review,* January/February 1999, 127–136.

30. Burton A. Weisbrod, "The Nonprofit Mission and Its Financing: Growing Links Between Nonprofits and the Rest of the Economy," in Burton A. Weisbrod, ed., *To Profit or Not to Profit: The Commercial Transformation of the Nonprofit Sector* (Cambridge: Cambridge University Press, 1998), p. 4.

31. Dennis R. Young, "Third Party Government," in Jay M. Shafritz, ed., *International Encyclopedia of Public Policy and Administration,* pp. 2252–2254 (Boulder: Westview Press, 1998).

32. Ralph M. Kramer, "Voluntary Agencies and the Contract Culture," *Social Service Review* 68 (1), March 1994, 33–60.

33. Judith Saidel, "Resource Interdependence: The Relationship Between State Agencies and Nonprofit Organizations," *Public Administration Review,* November/December 1991, 543–553.

34. James M. Ferris, "The Double-Edged Sword of Social Service Contracting: Public Accountability Versus Nonprofit Autonomy," *Nonprofit Management and Leadership* 3 (4), Summer 1993, 363–376.

35. Burton A. Weisbrod, "The Future of the Nonprofit Sector: Its Entwining with Private Enterprise and Government," *Journal of Policy Analysis and Management* 16 (4), 1997, 541–555.

References

Alexander, Jennifer, Camilla Stivers, and Renee Nank. "Implications of Welfare Reform: Do Nonprofit Survival Strategies Threaten Civil Society?" *Nonprofit and Voluntary Sector* 28 (4), December 1999, 452–475.

Bennett, James T., and Thomas J. DiLorenzo. *Unfair Competition: The Profits of Nonprofits.* Lanham, Md.: Hamilton Press, 1989.

Bernstein, Susan R. *Managing Contracted Services in the Nonprofit Agency: Administrative, Ethical, and Political Issues.* Philadelphia: Temple University Press, 1991.

Cope, Meghan. "Responsibility, Regulation, and Retrenchment: The End of Welfare?" In Lynn A. Staeheli, Janet E. Kodras, and Colin Flint, eds., *State Devolution in America: Implications for a Diverse Society,* pp. 181–205. Thousand Oaks, Calif.: Sage, 1997.

Dicke, Lisa A., and J. Steven Ott. "Public Agency Accountability in Human Services Contracting." *Public Productivity and Management Review* 22 (4), June 1999, 502–516.

Donahue, John D. *The Privatization Decision: Public Ends, Private Means.* New York: Basic Books, 1989.

Ferris, James M. "The Double-Edged Sword of Social Service Contracting: Public Accountability Versus Nonprofit Autonomy." *Nonprofit Management and Leadership* 3 (4), Summer 1993, 363–376.

Ferris, James M., and Elizabeth Graddy. "Fading Distinctions Among the Nonprofit, Government, and For-profit Sectors." In Virginia A. Hodgkinson and Richard W. Lyman, eds., *The Future of the Nonprofit Sector,* pp. 123–139. San Francisco: Jossey-Bass, 1989.

Government Accounting Office (GAO). *Privatization: Lessons Learned by State and Local Governments.* Washington, D.C.: United States General Accounting Office, 1997 (GAO/GGD–97–48).

Handler, Joel F. *Down from Bureaucracy: The Ambiguity of Privatization and Empowerment.* Princeton: Princeton University Press, 1996.

Jabbra, Joseph G., and O. P. Dwivedi, eds.. *Public Service Accountability.* West Hartford, Conn.: Kumarian Press, 1988.

Kearney, Richard C., and Steven W. Hays. "Reinventing Government, the New Public Management and Civil Service Systems in International Perspective." *Review of Public Personnel Administration* 18 (4), Fall 1998, 38–54.

Kearns, Kevin P. *Managing for Accountability: Preserving the Public Trust in Public and Nonprofit Organizations.* San Francisco: Jossey-Bass, 1996.

Koch, Deborah, and Sarah Boehm. *The Nonprofit Policy Agenda: Recommendations for State and Local Action.* Washington, D.C.: Union Institute, Center for Public Policy, February 12, 1992.

Kramer, Ralph M. "Voluntary Agencies and the Contract Culture: 'Dream or Nightmare?'" *Social Service Review* 68 (1), March 1994, 33–60.

Osborne, David, and Ted Gaebler. *Reinventing Government.* Reading, Mass.: Addison-Wesley, 1992.

Ott, J. Steven, and Lisa A. Dicke. "Important but Largely Unanswered Questions About Accountability in Contracted Public Human Services." *International Journal of Organization Theory and Behavior* 3 (3 and 4), Summer 2000, 283–317.

Prager, Jonas, and Swati Desai. "Privatizing Local Government Operations: Lessons from Federal Contracting Out Methodology." *Public Productivity and Management Review* 20 (2), December 1996, 185–203.

Rekart, Josephine. *Public Funds, Private Provision: The Role of the Voluntary Sector.* Vancouver: University of British Columbia Press, 1993.

Saidel, Judith R. "Devolution and the Politics of Interdependence: Management and Policy Trade-Offs in Government-Nonprofit Contracting." Paper presented at the 1998 National Conference of the American Society for Public Administration, Seattle, Wash., May 9–12, 1998.

_____. "Resource Interdependence: The Relationship Between State Agencies and Nonprofit Organizations." *Public Administration Review,* November/December 1991, 543–553.

Scotchmer, Kristin L. *Nonprofit/Government Contracting and Sectoral Relationships: An Annotated Bibliography.* Washington, D.C.: Union Institute, Center for Public Policy, 1995.

Smith, Steven R., and Lipsky, Michael. *Nonprofits for Hire: The Welfare State in the Age of Contracting.* Cambridge: Harvard University Press, 1993.

Stone, Melissa Middleton. "Competing Contexts: The Evolution of a Nonprofit Organization's Governance System in Multiple Environments." *Administration and Society* 28 (1), May 1996, 61–89.

Van Riper, Paul P. "Why Public Administration: When *Not* to Privatize. *Administrative Theory and Praxis* 21 (3), September 1999, 362–370.

View, Jenice. *A Means to an End: The Role of Nonprofit/Government Contracting in Sustaining the Social Contract.* Washington, D.C.: Union Institute, Center for Public Policy, 1995.

Weisbrod, Burton A. "The Future of the Nonprofit Sector: Its Entwining with Private Enterprise and Government." *Journal of Policy Analysis and Management* 16 (4), 1997, 541–555.

Weisbrod, Burton A., ed. *To Profit or Not to Profit: The Commercial Transformation of the Nonprofit Sector.* Cambridge: Cambridge University Press, 1998.

Wolpert, Julian. "How Federal Cutbacks Affect the Charitable Sector." In Lynn A. Staeheli, Janet E. Kodras, and Colin Flint, eds., *State Devolution in America: Implications for a Diverse Society,* pp. 97–117. Thousand Oaks, Calif.: Sage, 1997.

Young, Dennis. "Third Party Government." In Jay M. Shafritz, ed., *International Encyclopedia of Public Policy and Administration,* pp. 2252–2254. Boulder: Westview Press, 1998.

► CHAPTER 30

Third Party Government

DENNIS R. YOUNG

Third Pary Government. A term coined by Lester Salamon in 1981 to describe the fundamental pattern of relationships between government and the private sector in the delivery of public services in the United States: "The central characteristic of this pattern is the use of nongovernmental, or at least non-federal governmental, entities to carry out governmental purposes, and the exercise by these entities of a substantial degree of discretion over the spending of public funds and the exercise of public authority" (Salamon 1987, p. 110). The concept of third party government serves as a counter-weight to theories of the private, nonprofit sector that view the nonprofit as a residual sector that fills in where government or commercial businesses fail. In the third party government model, private, nonprofit organizations serve as partners with government in the provision of public services rather than as substitutes or gap fillers. In this view, government typically provides the finances and influences service policies, while nonprofits deliver the services. The precise mechanisms used to finance these arrangements vary considerably. They include governmental grants, contracts and loan guarantees, and demand-side subsidies such as consumer vouchers, reimbursements, or tax deductions (Salamon 1987).

Considerable empirical evidence exists for the third party government view of the role of nonprofit organizations. Salamon (1987) documents that the governmental nonprofit sector partnership arrangements enjoy a long history in the United States. However, the 1960s was the watershed era in which the United States emphatically embraced the third party government model by significantly expanding expenditures on social programs without commensurate enlargement of government employment. Rather than delivered through government bureaucracy, new services were implemented largely through arrangements with private, nonprofit suppliers. Not incidentally, the expansion of government social programs in the late 1960s and 1970s corresponded to the period of fastest growth for the U.S. nonprofit sector (Hodgkinson et al. 1992).

The theory of third party government, that is, nonprofits as a partner to rather than substitute for government, is based on an assessment of the comparative advantages of government and nonprofit organizations in carrying out the tasks associated with delivering public services. Overall, government is seen as relatively more efficient in raising and distributing funds, formulating policies for the benefit of the entire society, and in redistributing resources to correct for inequities and externalities. Alternatively, non-profits are seen to be more efficient at customizing services to local preferences and delivering them at lower cost or higher quality. Salamon (1987) also points out that third party government arrangements are effective in reconciling the American public's preference for pluralism and its ideological antagonism toward large government with its demands for public services.

Salamon (1987) developed an alternative theory of third party government to explain the role of the American nonprofit sector by directly challenging the premises of the "contract failure" and "government failure" theories of the nonprofit sector. In particular, Salamon postulates that the voluntary, nonprofit sector should be the primary point of reference and that government intervenes in the delivery of public services only to compensate for the weaknesses of the voluntary sector. In this connection, he (1987) describes four ways in which voluntary organizations can fall short:

1. *Philanthropic insufficiency* reflects the free rider problem associated with voluntary support of public goods and argues for governmental financing through taxation to provide adequate funding.
2. *Philanthropic particularism* recognizes that voluntary action depends on the efforts of cohesive groups and may miss important segments of society that are not addressed by such groups. This deficiency argues for government to ensure more complete coverage. Government may also have a role in increasing efficiency by exploiting economies of scale not achievable by smaller organizations individually and by providing coordination to avoid unnecessary duplication of services supplied by individual voluntary agencies.
3. *Philanthropic paternalism* recognizes that the allocation of voluntary resources is influenced primarily by those wealthy enough to donate them. This deficiency argues for government intervention and support to allow a wider spectrum of views to influence the allocation of nonprofit sector resources.

4. *Philanthropic amateurism* recognizes that a substantial portion of the work of nonprofit organizations is carried out by volunteers or well-meaning amateurs who may not have the time or training to provide services in the most effective way. This weakness argues for government regulation and support to allow nonprofits to become more professional in their approaches to providing the services and in the quality of their workforces.

Overall, Salamon's "voluntary failure" theory articulates how government and voluntary agencies can serve as complementary partners to one another in the delivery of public services. Although voluntary organizations can be responsive to the grassroots needs of local groups and causes that enjoy sufficient private support, they cannot be counted on to generate adequate levels of resources or coordinate those resources to achieve efficient and equitable levels of service provision. Conversely, governments cannot be relied upon to be responsive to variations in local needs and preferences, but they are able to generate and redistribute necessary resources through taxation and expenditure policies and to take a wide view of societal needs. Thus, government, according to the theory, can serve the complementary roles of financing, coordinating, and regulating the services that nonprofits can best deliver.

This ideal of the nonprofit-government partnership has been questioned on a number of grounds:

- that contracting with private agencies results in a loss of accountability for expenditure of public resources (Smith and Lipsky 1993; Bernstein 1991);
- that the government-nonprofit partnership transforms nonprofit organizations into "vendors," undermining their autonomy and independence and distorting their missions to conform with government requirements (Salamon 1987; Kramer 1980);
- that the partnership model leads to the bureaucratization and professionalization

of nonprofit organizations, making them more costly and less responsive to community needs (Salamon 1987);

- that the partnership model results in the devolvement of political power and authority from government to private parties, raising fundamental questions of democratic governance (Smith and Lipsky 1993);
- that the partnership model creates series problems of managing nonprofit organizations, including constraints on cash flow and budgeting caused by governmental regulations and practices (Bernstein 1991; Grossman 1992).

The severity of these problems and their long-run implications for the viability of nonprofit organizations and their partnership arrangements with government remain important issues of debate and continuing research.

One of the main contributions of third party government theory is to provide a sobering perspective on the implications of cutbacks in governmental expenditures for public services. An inference commonly made from the alternative theory of "government failure" is that the nonprofit sector serves essentially as a substitute for government in the provision of public goods. In this view, cutbacks in government can be expected to result in compensatory growth of the nonprofit sector. However, the third party government model suggests the opposite effect—that government cutbacks may result in reductions in support of nonprofit organizations and the services they provide.

This debate is not merely of theoretical interest. The view that government and the nonprofit sector are essentially competitors in conflict with one another, rather than collaborating partners, drove the policies of the Reagan administration in its quest to pare down the federal budget (Salamon and Abramson 1982). Empirical analysis shows these policies to have been based on questionable premises. According to Salamon and Abramson's (1994) analysis of federal spending reductions in the 1980s, "The changes in federal spending . . . not only increased the demand for services from private,

nonprofit organizations. . . . They simultaneously made it more difficult for nonprofits to meet this increased demand because they reduced the revenues that nonprofit organizations receive from federal programs" (p. 7). In that same report, Salamon and Abramson analyzed whether private contributions have replaced lost government funds. For selected areas of social services over the 1980–1995 period, they found only partial compensation: "Private giving has fortunately risen sufficiently to offset the direct revenue losses to nonprofit organizations during this period, but it has not grown enough to offset the cumulative overall reduction in real federal spending in these fields or to cope with the residue of unmet needs that have amassed during the decade" (p. 15).

The issue of government's relationship to nonprofits goes far beyond the borders of the United States. Analyzing studies of the nonprofit sector in nine different European countries, Benjamin Gidron, Ralph Kramer, and Lester Salamon (1992) identified a variety of ways in which government and the nonprofit sector combine to finance and deliver public services. Although the collaborative third party government model is most prominent in the United States, the questions it raises about the appropriate juxtaposition of the two sectors apply elsewhere. In particular, as governments everywhere, in their quests to become more efficient and democratic, reexamine the ways in which they provide public welfare and other services, the experience with third party government in the United States grows in interest.

In the United Kingdom, the Thatcher government, intent on reducing the role of government, adopted an ideology similar to that of the Reagan administration in the United States. However, the starting point for placing greater reliance on the nonprofit sector was considerably different (Taylor 1992). In the United Kingdom, both the finance and the delivery of social welfare services were dominated by government and the voluntary sector played an essentially residual role, assisted modestly by government grants-in-aid. The thrust of the Conservative government policy has been to contract out the delivery of services to private organizations, thus making the role of the nonprofit sector more prominent and the arrangements for service delivery more similar to those in the United States. The changes in Britain have stirred controversies familiar to those heard in the United States. First, there is concern over the degree to which government will maintain its financial support as it privatizes service delivery. Second, there is concern that the new contractual regime will undermine the integrity of voluntary organizations, reducing their diversity, innovativeness, and independence and making them more like businesses or extensions of governmental bureaucracy.

The contemporary experiences of the United States and the United Kingdom demonstrate that the third party government paradigm remains an important construct for analyzing the implications for nonprofits, as governments respond to pervasive pressures to streamline their services and respond more effectively to diverse political constituencies. The model also serves as an important beacon to governments as they seek to become more efficient without damaging the capacities of nonprofit organizations to deliver services to vulnerable populations.

References

Bernstein, Susan R., 1991. *Managing Contracted Services in the Nonprofit Agency.* Philadelphia, PA: Temple University Press.

Gidron, Benjamin, Ralph M. Kramer, and Lester M. Salamon, eds., 1992. *Government and the Third Sector.* San Francisco, CA: Jossey-Bass.

Grossman, David A., 1992. "Paying Nonprofits: Streamlining the New York State System." *Nonprofit Management and Leadership,* vol. 3, no. 1, (Fall): 81–91.

Hodgkinson, Virginia A., Murray S. Weitzman, Christopher M. Toppe, and Stephen M. Noga, eds., 1992. *Nonprofit Almanac 1992–1993.* San Francisco, CA: Jossey-Bass.

Kramer, Ralph, 1980. *Voluntary Agencies in the Welfare State.* Berkeley: University of California Press.

Salamon, Lester M., 1981. "Rethinking Public Management: Third-Party Government and the Changing Forms of Public Action." *Public Policy,* vol. 29:255–275.

_____, 1987. "Partners in Public Service." Chapter 6 in Walter W. Powell, *The Nonprofit Sector: A Research Handbook.* New Haven, CT: Yale University Press, 99–117.

_____, 1992. *America's Nonprofit Sector.* New York: Foundation Center.

Salamon, Lester M. and Alan J. Abramson, 1982. *The Federal Budget and the Nonprofit Sector.* Washington, D.C.: Urban Institute Press.

_____, 1994. "The Federal Budget and the Nonprofit Sector: FY 1995." A Report to Independent Sector. Baltimore: Institute for Policy Studies, Johns Hopkins University.

Salamon, Lester M., and Helmut K. Anheier, 1994. *The Emerging Sector: An Overview.* Baltimore: Institute for Policy Studies, Johns Hopkins University.

Smith, Steven R., and Michael Lipsky, 1993. *Nonprofits for Hire.* Cambridge, MA: Harvard University Press.

Taylor, Marilyn, 1992. "The Changing Role of the Nonprofit Sector in Britain." Chapter 7 in Benjamin Gidron, Ralph M. Kramer, and Lester M. Salamon, eds., *Government and the Third Sector.* San Francisco, CA: Jossey-Bass, 147–175.

CHAPTER 31

Voluntary Agencies and the Contract Culture: "Dream or Nightmare"?

RALPH M. KRAMER

In the past 5 years, there has been a remarkable resurgence of interest in purchase of service contracting (POSC), now the primary method of financing and delivering the personal social services in the United States. It is also likely to become much more significant in Europe and particularly in Britain, where there is great concern whether it will turn out to be a "dream or a nightmare."[1] What follows is a preliminary overview of the subject, a necessary first step toward a more systematic and comprehensive assessment. While the focus is primarily on contracting, most of the analysis is relevant to other fiscal transfers between government and nonprofit organizations in the form of grants and payments, except that POSC, because of its legal status, involves a greater degree of specificity and accountability.

After a brief description of the policy context and three dominant paradigms used in the recent research on POSC, we review its contribution to our understanding of (1) the rationale or the incentives to enter into POSC by both government and the nonprofit organizations; (2) the dynamics of the process, including the problems at various stages and the strategies used to cope with them; (3) the effects of POSC

on the organizations involved and on the service delivery system; and (4) some implications for social policy, management, and future research.

The Policy Context of the Contract State

Purchase of service contracting is part of a larger context in which the welfare state during the past 25 years has become much more of an "enabler," whereby the funding and production of social services have been administratively separated.[2] Public responsibility has been retained for policy and planning, financing, regulating, monitoring, and audit, whereas nongovernmental providers, both nonprofit and commercial organizations, are increasingly used to deliver a growing number of social services.

This has meant that, as part of the public service delivery system of the personal social services, nonprofit organizations function more often as a substitute for government rather than in their traditional roles as an alternative, a supplement, or a complement. Michael Sosin and others have pointed out how POSC enabled the extension of the welfare state, particularly since the 1970s, when it has been under attack in the face of a declining economy.[3] A growing interdependence has developed over a period of 25 years between government and nonprofit organizations, with little planning or evaluation of the implications of their becoming "agents of the expansion of the welfare state" and with their future so closely bound to its fate.[4]

The growth of POSC with its greater reliance on nonprofit organizations can also be viewed as part of the "crisis of the welfare state," during which the virtues of voluntarism were rediscovered in the 1980s, accompanied by the policies of privatization, decentralization, deregulation, and deinstitutionalization.[5] One outcome has been a pervasive blurring of the boundaries between the public and private sectors, whose interpenetration and mutual dependence is reflected in numerous metaphors such as third-party government, indirect public administration, the contract state, nonprofit federalism, the new or mixed political economy of welfare, and so forth. Although new roles and relationships (administrative, fiscal, regulatory, and political) between government and nonprofit organizations have developed, we still lack concepts, models, research paradigms, and data useful for policy and management.

The Future of Nonprofit Organizations

Despite its pervasiveness, POSC is still viewed as a controversial issue in social policy, particularly in the voluntary sector. There are many persons in both the United States and the United Kingdom who have become greatly concerned about the impact of contracting on the character, goals, and role of nonprofit organizations in the personal social services. They fear that the public policy of contracting for the social services will undermine the essential and distinctive contribution of voluntarism to a pluralist democracy. Contracting is viewed as transforming nonprofit organizations into quasi-nongovernmental organizations or into wholly owned subsidiaries of a governmental agency

with a quasi-public staff. Funds from government, whether as a partner, patron, or purchaser, are often viewed as inherently controlling, co-opting, and contaminating the mission of nonprofit organizations. Some observers see a process of "devoluntarization" and goal distortion as one of the organizational costs of POSC.[6] Is this true? For what types of organizations? Under what conditions? Others, however, tend to minimize these dangers but are concerned about the difficulties of securing public accountability from large numbers of nonprofit organizations, particularly in states like Massachusetts and New Jersey, where virtually all human services are contracted out.[7] Also worrisome is the dubious ability of nongovernmental and specialized providers to assure the equity, universalism, and entitlements associated with public services. Finally, it is questioned whether POSC is really cost-effective, whether it provides more flexibility and greater choice in the service delivery system, or whether it perpetuates the present array of services, limiting the meeting of new social needs.

Overview of Research on POSC

What do we really know about POSC? A commentary once made on the state of organization theory is apt: not much is known, but it has been said over and over again in many different ways.[8]

Perhaps because much of the debate about POSC has been ideological, usually stressing the virtues of privatization that favor market transactions over governmental bureaucracies, relatively few empirical data have been gathered until the past decade.

Research Paradigms

Three basic models or metaphors are embedded in the recent research on POSC: (1) a partnership, stressing cooperation between government and nonprofit organizations, but including negotiation; (2) a market in which competition is assumed but in which it occurs infrequently; and (3) an interactional process conceptualized as a game or as a regime.[9] In the few studies that have been guided by a theoretical framework, the dominant research paradigms are resource dependency and political economy models, with a nod toward the "new institutionalism."[10] The following overview of recent POSC research begins with its rationale and then analyzes the process, consequences, and implications.

Rationale for POSC

Why does government contract out most of the personal social services? The explanations fall into these categories: legislative mandate, ideology, rational decision making, and pragmatic expedient.

Legislative Mandate

In many programs in fields such as aging, mental health, alcohol and drug abuse, food distribution, or Head Start, the governmental agency has no option because it is prohibited by law from offering the service itself: it must contract with a nonprofit organization, although, in many instances, commercial organizations may be used. Even under these conditions, the contract can be designed and implemented in a competitive, negotiated, or cooperative framework, dependent on the availability and resources of nonprofit organizations.[11] Similar provisions are now also found in England, requiring the Local Authority Social Service Departments to contract out a fixed amount of community care or face fiscal sanctions.[12]

Ideology

The ideological argument is based on a series of organizational characteristics attributed to government and to nonprofit organizations, which are generally in the form of invidious stereotypes of private virtues and public vices, many of which have their origin in the nineteenth-century subsidy system. Typically, there is a deep distrust of government, accompanied by exaggerated, idealized notions about the advantages of nongovernmental organizations. Viewed as a moderate form of privatization, POSC is seen as a way of dealing with the inherent costliness and inefficiencies of government. More positively, POSC is sometimes viewed as an opportunity to optimize choice, promote citizen participation, and provide specialized, innovative services in a more flexible way, closer to the user.

Ideologically, there is an unusual consensus on both the Right and Left for the use of voluntary organizations to implement public policy, though their motivations and organizational referents are quite different. On the Right, voluntary organizations are seen as a bulwark against further governmental intervention, or at least as an alternative to, if not as a substitute for, such intervention. On the Left, voluntary organizations are often viewed nostalgically, as a means of recovering a lost sense of community through greater citizen participation. Additional support for POSC has come from relatively new, community-based organizations, particularly those representing groups not previously part of the urban polity such as gays, feminists, and ethnic and racial minorities. Part of this ideological consensus may be due to a failure to distinguish between various forms of voluntarism: between volunteers as unpaid staff and as peer self-help and between community-based grassroots associations and service bureaucracies staffed by professionals.

Rational Decision Making

The choice of POSC as the outcome of a rational decision-making process in government is one of the most frequently found models, both descriptively and normatively. It assumes that officials can or will systematically assess the relative costs and benefits of internal versus external production of the social services and then will choose the appropriate sector on the basis of an objective evaluation of relative advantages and disadvantages.

Ferris and Graddy, using a 1982 survey of contracting in 1,780 cities and counties, found support for their hypothesis that nonprofit providers were selected more often if they had a good reputation for service delivery; factors also considered important were cost-efficiency, access, and quality. They inferred from a statistical analysis of the data that government takes into account both production and transaction costs in considering POSC and that nonprofit organizations or other governmental agencies are preferred for hard-to-monitor services, particularly in the social services.[13]

Perhaps the most systematic and complex of the rational decision-making models has been developed by Peter Kettner and Lawrence Martin, who proposed a set of criteria for government to consider before it embarks on POSC. These criteria include cost-effectiveness, productivity, and fiscal control; provider vulnerabilities; monitoring abilities; barriers to planning, design, and funding; impact on clients; public policy and legal considerations; and politics and agency loyalties.[14]

Pragmatic Expedient

Apart from mandated services, contracting as a pragmatic expedient seems to be the most frequent explanation for POSC for both government and the voluntary agency. The imperatives of legislation and administrative realities predominate rather than a commitment to a set of principles or the outcome of a methodical, rational process of evaluative decision making, as suggested above. This can be summed up in the generalization that POSC will occur when one agency has something that the other needs or wants and can provide it at a price that is acceptable. Primary determinants in this quasi market seem to be supply, including competition; demand; the nature of the service technology; and the politics and history of the community.[15] Concerning the latter, there is a tendency to underestimate the role of politics in POSC, particularly as it operates in urban communities with social service agencies under the auspices of emerging ethnic constituencies of Hispanic, Asian, and African-American groups.

Kirsten Grønbjerg, in her intensive case studies of a small number of Chicago nonprofit organizations, came to the conclusion that the actual operation of POSC does not con-

form to the beliefs of either its supporters or critics.[16]

Consequences of POSC for the Service Delivery System, Government, and Nonprofit Organizations

Valid and reliable information about the consequences of POSC for the agencies involved, the service delivery system and the users, is scarce, controversial, and generally of a poorer quality.

Many of the generalizations about the impact of POSC or governmental funds on nonprofit organizations or the service delivery system are inferred from findings that are often equivocal, anecdotal, or impressionistic.

Many of the findings could, however, constitute a series of hypotheses for further testing and thus guide the design of future research. They could also sensitize policymakers and managers to what might occur in POSC; that is, the findings can suggest some of the possible outcomes that could be taken into account in considering contracting as a policy option.

Impact on the Service Delivery System

In general, relatively little is known directly about the effects of POSC on access or what difference it makes to clients if the service is provided by a governmental, for-profit, or nonprofit agency.[17] It is widely believed, however, that nonprofit organizations are particularly well suited to serve clientele with highly specialized needs or who are ineligible for or unlikely to use governmental services. Although it seems likely that POSC has made it possible for many public social services to be extended without high fixed costs, the evidence about relative cost-effectiveness is not very substantial.

Martin Knapp concluded that "it is impossible to generalize about the presence or direction of cost-effectiveness differences between the sectors," that conclusions reached for one industry or country are not transportable to others, and that often there are more cost differences among voluntary agencies than between them and the statutory bodies.[18]

Because neither government nor nonprofit organizations ordinarily know or calculate their indirect costs, the "real" production and transaction costs are rarely used in the determination of rates of payment and in comparing direct provision by government with the purported economies of POSC. Indeed, it could be said that the supply of voluntary agency services and the demand of government intersect at a price that is below the real cost for both parties. The conventional wisdom is that most of the cost savings in POSC, at least in the short run, come from the use of lower-paid and part-time staff, as well as from unpaid volunteers, who are not entitled to the same package of benefits received by civil service workers. In the long run, however, there is a tendency for such costs to increase, particularly as nonprofit organizations become subject to the same rules and standards of governmental agencies.[19]

A recent review of POSC research in the United States by a British observer concluded that there was no evidence that POSC was any better than other modes of service delivery.[20]

David Austin is among the few scholars who have included "accountability structures" and the proportion of income from governmental sources as part of his analysis of the political economy of human service programs.[21] Yet other researchers ascribe certain dysfunctional aspects of the service delivery system specifically to POSC with nonprofit organizations. For example, Sosin, drawing on his study of homelessness in Chicago, claims that POSC has resulted in less flexibility and responsiveness to new needs because of the vested interest that both the providers and government develop in the status quo, a point also made by Ruth DeHoog and Kirsten Grønbjerg.[22]

It is widely believed that contracting has made it possible for many public social services to be extended without high fixed costs and that it has provided more flexibility in the administration of these programs. Yet the inevitable decentralization of services and the use of multiple providers have been described as "fragmentation" by detractors and as "pluralism" or "diver-

sity" by supporters of POSC. Similarly, as we shall see, what is "accountability" to some is "control" to others. This accounts for an often bewildering array of contracts and grants in a nonprofit organization, each based on a separate piece of legislation, and with different governmental agencies on three levels funding various components of a single-agency program. In this way, POSC is one of the major factors militating against coherence, continuity, coordination, and planning, which are the basic elements of a more rational service delivery system.[23]

Consequences of POSC for Government

As with the service delivery system, there are a number of widely held beliefs but relatively few empirical or research data except for a few surveys of POSC on the state level. There is general recognition of the paradox that POSC does not lessen the role of government in the delivery of public social services; rather, it heightens and transforms governmental functions into a new, complex, technical, and political arena where government is involved in mutually dependent relationships with nonprofit organizations with which it has contracted to purchase personal social services. In the process, however, government also may benefit from its reduced visibility and responsibility for direct provision of services.

Because there is less competition in the personal social services than in some other fields of service, governmental agencies are even more reluctant to seek new providers.[24] Consequently, the dominant pattern is to renew contracts, heightening the dependency on a small group of nonprofit organizations, and furthering bureaucratic symbiosis. Attempts to change the provisions of the contract or to award it to another agency usually meet with considerable resistance and political pressures, which are resented by the staff of the governmental agency. Thus, POSC can presumably result in a loss of autonomy, not only for the nonprofit organization as is frequently claimed, but also for government, whose freedom of choice becomes more limited.

The most problematic area for government relates to its requirements for accountability.

Increased oversight is the cost of decentralizing or delegating public functions, and monitoring is expensive and elusive, subjecting the governmental agency to charges of unnecessary red tape and unwanted intrusions. Assuring accountability and contract compliance are not tasks in which government has traditionally excelled. Every survey of POSC on the state level identified the loss of control and difficulties of securing accountability as the major weakness of POSC for government.

Furthermore, it is usually overlooked that few governmental agencies and their staff members have high regard for the role of accountability (or monitoring), and it is rarely one for which staff members are trained. In the personal social services, POSC alters the role of professional staff in government to case management, rather than direct work with clients. On the organizational level, government struggles with the lack of centralized administrative oversight and planning, the absence of consistent standards, and its control of some inputs for nonprofit organizations' accountability.

Effects on the Nonprofit Organization

There are two schools of thought regarding the impact of POSC on the autonomy and the identity of nonprofit organizations. There are those who claim that the controlling influence of governmental funding has resulted in widespread distortion of the mission and role of nonprofit organizations, that such organizations have lost much of their autonomy and distinctiveness in becoming public agents who deliver social services according to government specifications on client eligibility, staffing, and service patterns. In addition, POSC is also held responsible for nonprofit organizations' dependency, co-optation, and dilution of advocacy because of governmental control over their programs. These trends are believed to be reinforced and result in "devoluntarization" by the increased formalization, bureaucratization, and professionalization required of a public agent.[25]

Others maintain, however, that the alleged loss of autonomy of nonprofit organizations is exaggerated, that, in the POSC process, which is more one of mutual dependence, public accountability is more likely to suffer. Changes in the organizational structure and performance of nonprofit organizations that have been criticized are believed to be part of broader trends in the society and not just a response to POSC.[26] Which view is correct? For which type of nonprofit organizations?

The positive side of POSC is the recognition that it has enabled many nonprofit organizations to maintain, expand, and diversify their regular services in ways that would not have been possible without governmental funding. As Grønbjerg somewhat reluctantly concluded, "The overall advantages outweigh the disadvantages or are at least more obvious and certain than for alternative funding sources."[27] A distinction between nonprofit organizations on the basis of size and age, in addition to field of service and type of technology, is important here because POSC probably has a differential impact on them. For example, for more traditional, larger, and older agencies, it may have displaced philanthropic funds that were not able to keep up with the demand beginning in the 1960s. For smaller, newer, and community-based organizations, creatures of the 1960s that perhaps were born too late to have a supporting constituency and who were dependent on government from the beginning, grants and contracts are often the primary, if not the only, source of funds.

The major trends in the internal organizational structure of nonprofit organizations that have been observed during the last 10–15 years are increased size and scale of operations and greater formalization and bureaucratization, although it is not clear to what extent these changes can be attributed to public funding such as POSC. Generally, the bigger organizations get even larger, and the smaller ones get bigger, if they survive. There are, however, contrasting tendencies of centralization and decentralization based on size.

It is ironic that smaller community-based organizations survive in the contract culture by modifying the very qualities that might have made them attractive as contractors in the first place: being smaller, more informal, and more accessible to a population that would be difficult for government to serve.

Other internal changes that have been observed are also responses to the demands of the grants economy that nurtures grantsmanship and its preemption of administrative tasks. It is claimed that management has become more entrepreneurial and that boards of directors look more to the corporate world for models of administrative behavior.

Related to these structural changes are other trends in the fiscal resource system of nonprofit organizations such as the increased reliance on fees and income from various commercial ventures, in many cases undertaken to replace the loss of governmental funds or to provide for growth when other sources are unavailable. A survey by Carolyn Adams and Felice Perlmutter of more than 100 nonprofit organizations in Philadelphia found that many agencies embarked on "venturism" as a means of obtaining funds with fewer restrictions than POSC. This extensive cultivation of revenue from the sale of services and products by nonprofit organizations has added to the controversies with the Internal Revenue Service over "unrelated business income," and it has led to additional challenges to the tax exemption for non-profit organizations.[28]

Externally, there has been a growth in structures such as provider coalitions that exert pressure on local and state government for increased rates of reimbursement and regulatory change. Some believe that this indicates a shift from advocacy on behalf of clients to organizational self-interest, although the nature of the evidence makes it very difficult to separate the two interests. There is no doubt that POSC thrusts nonprofit organizations into the public arena and requires the ability to maneuver politically. Although some public officials resent this intrusion into their domain because they then have to deal with another lobby, others have learned how to utilize the political influence of provider organizations to support their own agendas.[29] This is part of the give-and-take of the uneasy "partnership" between government and its contractors, which is sometimes "cozy," other times more adversarial.

Four concepts are involved in this debate, all of which can be described as "unanalyzed abstractions": goal deflection/distortion, autonomy, accountability, and "devoluntarization."

Goal distortion or deflection. Bernstein noted that, for the executives in her study, the mission of their agencies was the most crucial factor in their decision making.[30] Similarly, in another case study of the influence of public funding policies on nonprofit organizations during the 1980s, Sarah Liebshutz concluded that there was no goal deflection during this period; agencies found a variety of ways to cope with the changes in the character of their funding sources without having to abandon their goals.[31]

Although changes in service delivery may occur under POSC, this is not necessarily a matter of goal deflection. What is diminished somewhat is the discretion of nonprofit organizations to make certain decisions about the type of clientele, staff, and mode of service without having to take into account the funding source.

In POSC, as in other resource exchanges, there is a trade-off: some decision making must be shared with government if a nonprofit organization wants to be funded. If it is unwilling to comply with the standards and procedures of the contract or to try to negotiate more acceptable terms, then it is not required to enter into such an arrangement.[32]

Autonomy. All organizations are dependent on their environment and are embedded in larger systems of relations.[33] Nonprofit organizations, however, may be more vulnerable to external constraints because they have no mandated existence or legal claim to public funds. At the same time, the autonomy of governmental agencies is also limited, often by the actions of nonprofit organizations on whom they have become dependent.[34]

Evidence collected during the past decade in the United States, England, Australia, Israel, the Netherlands, and Germany suggests that the control of government funding on the behavior of nonprofit organizations is much less than is commonly believed.[35] A manager of a nonprofit organization receiving 80 percent of its funds from governmental agencies was interviewed by Bernstein and expressed it as follows: "We have more autonomy because we contract with several different government agencies, and we do make decisions that the city can't make. We decide to stop providing a service because we decided that it was not the best use of our effort at that time. We decide not to serve certain clients because they're not appropriate for our program. We decide to have different standards than the city."

Accountability.   Accountability is frequently understood to conflict with the autonomy of the nonprofit organization, particularly because it implies some form of external control. Accountability means, at a minimum, having to answer to those who control a necessary resource. Accordingly, nonprofit organizations have multiple accountability: to their boards, bylaws, clients, staff, contributors, and other funding sources, such as foundations and United Ways, which also constrain their discretionary behavior. This is further complicated by the diffuse goals and technologies of nonprofit organizations, making it difficult to produce evidence of effectiveness.

Therefore, the conventional dualism between autonomy and accountability for a nonprofit organization may be more artificial than real. Perhaps the issue should be rephrased, not in terms of preserving the autonomy of nonprofit organizations, but rather in terms of how to make them more accountable without restricting the very qualities of flexibility and responsiveness that make them useful providers of public services. How can the organizational interests of government and its nonprofit providers be balanced? How can their organizational strengths be integrated to overcome their distinctive vulnerabilities?[36]

"Devoluntarization."   Purchase of service contracting is believed to have also contributed to a process of "devoluntarization," that is, to the increased formalization, bureaucratization, and professionalization of nonprofit organizations and to downplaying the role of volunteers in service giving and in governance. Purchase of service contracting thus promotes the loss of the distinctive identity of nonprofit organizations, blurring the differences between the sectors so that it can be claimed that "all organizations are public."[37]

Finally, there is an underlying assumption that there once was a golden age of voluntarism, before governmental funds were so readily available, when small, informal community-based organizations were able to rely on contributions and volunteers to provide essential personal social services. Apart from being more myth than history, this belief ignores the developmental stages through which most nonprofit organizations move.

Even without the strong incentive of public funding, it is characteristic of nonprofit organizations to begin their life cycle as voluntary associations and then become more complex and formalized if and when they seek to provide some social service in the community and to influence public policy.

Summary and Conclusions

The preceding overview of recent research on POSC suggests the following: there are strong incentives stemming both from legislative mandates and practical administrative and fiscal considerations for government to contract with nonprofit organizations. For voluntary agencies, government has become a primary source of funds, exceeding contributions and more traditional revenues. Although ideology does not seem to play a significant part—both the supporters and opponents of government favor contracting—decisions concerning the choice of POSC and the renewal of contracts are often part of a highly politicized process in the community.

Although the POSC regime can occasionally function as a partnership, more often it operates as a quasi market that has a game-like character that is shaped by the power relationships between government and its service providers.

What, then, are some of the implications for policy, management, and future research?

As a policy, POSC has become institutionalized in the personal social services; clearly, it is here to stay, and the question is less *whether* government should contract but *how* POSC can operate to optimize service delivery values such as access, accountability, choice, equity, and effectiveness. Framing the question in this manner presupposes continuation of the mixed economy of welfare, which, by separating financing from production and distribution, utilizes the distinctive organizational capabilities of government and nonprofit organizations as part of the evolving "contract state." At the same time, this policy environment poses a serious challenge to many nonprofit organizations: how can they avoid becoming just another public agent and a substitute for government? How can they preserve their traditional roles as alternatives, supplementing and complementing the public services?

Clearly, a New Age has emerged of blurred organizational boundaries in which public and nongovernmental organizations need and depend on each other more than ever. It is necessary, however, to get beyond the usual rhetoric of collaboration and to recognize not only the mutual dependency but also the significance of the unequal distribution of power in these public-private "partnerships." Coming to terms with the politics of contracting is particularly important in any attempt to institutionalize these interorganizational relationships with appropriate structures, incentives, norms, and rules for planning and coordination.

In the future, the demand for greater efficiency and accountability in the expenditure of public funds could produce a nightmare of overregulation or it could lead to new structures and realize the dream of more productive patterns of interorganizational relations between government and nonprofit organizations.

But perhaps the contract culture in the United States will be neither a dream nor a nightmare, but a little of each at the same time. Research should, in any case, reflect the daytime reality of experience as we know it.

Notes

1. Both terms in the title of this article originate from the United Kingdom. After the publication of the Griffiths Report in 1989 on community care, there was widespread concern, and some apprehension, about the impact of the "contract culture," which would emerge as local authorities would be required to make increasing use of voluntary agencies to deliver the personal social services instead of providing the service themselves as part of what became the Community Care Act of 1992. From 1988 on, the Community Care Project of the National Council for Voluntary Organisations produced a stream of publications, including one on which the title of this article is based, as part of a planned approach to contracting, in contrast to the drift of the voluntary sector in the United States into a grants economy in the 1960s. As part of a process of learning from the U.S. experience, see Richard Gutch, *Contracting Lessons from the United States* (London: National Council for Voluntary Organisations, 1992); and Robin Currie, "Contracting: Facing Up to Difficulties—Report on US Study Tour, April/May 1993" (Liverpool: Personal Service Society, 1993).

2. Neil Gilbert and Barbara Gilbert, *The Enabling State: Modern Welfare Capitalism in America* (New York: Oxford University Press, 1989).

3. Michael R. Sosin, "Decentralizing the Social Service System: A Reassessment," *Social Service Review* 64, no. 4 (December 1990): 617–36. See also Susan Ostrander, "Private Social Service: Obstacle to the Welfare State," *Nonprofit and Voluntary Sector Quarterly* 18, no. 1 (1989): 25–35.

4. Smith and Lipsky, pp. 98–100. A somewhat different perspective is Judith Saidel, "Dimensions of Interdependence: The State and Voluntary Sector Relationships," *Nonprofit and Voluntary Sector Quarterly* 8, no. 4 (1989): 335–48.

5. Ralph M. Kramer, Hakon Lorentzen, Willem B. Melief, and Sergio Pasquinelli, *Privatization in Four European Countries: Comparative Studies in Government-Third Sector Relationships* (Armonk, N.Y.: M.E. Sharpe, 1993), pp. 1–5; see also Michael K. Brown, "Remaking the Welfare State: A Comparative Perspective," in *Remaking the Welfare State: Retrenchment and Social Policy in America and Europe,* ed. Michael K. Brown (Philadelphia: Temple University Press, 1988), pp. 3–28.

6. Smith and Lipsky, pp. 111–15.

7. Demone and Gibelman, eds. pp. 210–14, 310–24; Aileen Hart, "Contracting for Child Welfare

Services in Massachusetts: Emerging Issues for Policy and Practice," *Social Work* 33, no. 6 (1988): 511–15.

8. The observation is attributed to James G. March.

9. An American counterpart of the "contract culture" in Britain is the concept of a contract "regime" as used by Smith and Lipsky to refer to "a set of principles, norms, rules, and decision-making procedures around which actor expectations converge in a given issue-area" (p. 43). It consists of a "regularized pattern of behavior, relying on long term relationships rather than episodic ones." Although the term originated in political science, it has much in common with the game metaphor used by Bernstein in her ethnographic study of POSC in New York City.

10. Walter W. Powell, Jr., and Paul DiMaggio, eds., *The New Institutionalism in Organizational Analysis* (Chicago: University of Chicago Press, 1991).

11. Ruth H. DeHoog, "Competition, Negotiation, or Cooperation: Three Models for Service Contracting," *Administration and Society* 22, no. 3 (1990): 317–40. See also her earlier book, *Contracting Out for Human Services: Economic, Political and Organizational Perspectives* (Albany, N.Y.: SUNY Press, 1984).

12. Gutch (n. 1 above); Jane Lewis, "Developing the Mixed Economy of Care: Emerging Issues for Voluntary Organizations," *Journal of Social Policy* 22, no. 2 (1993): 173–92.

13. James Ferris and Elizabeth Graddy, "Production Costs, Transaction Costs, and Local Government Contractor Choice," *Economic Inquiry* 29 (July 1991): 541–54.

14. Kettner and Martin. The classification of the factors to take into account in the decision to contract was based on responses to a survey of state agency executives in five states that were among the first to use POSC for human services during the 1970s.

15. Ralph M. Kramer and Bart Grossman, "Contracting for Social Services: Process Management and Resource Dependencies," *Social Service Review* 61, no. 1 (March 1987): 32–55.

16. Kirsten A. Grønbjerg, "Managing Grants and Contracts: The Case of Four Nonprofit Organizations," *Nonprofit and Voluntary Sector Quarterly* 20, no. 1 (1991): 5–24.

17. Donna Hardina, "The Effect of Funding Sources on Client Access to Services," *Administration in Social Work* 14, no. 3 (1990): 33–46.

18. Martin Knapp, "Intersectoral Differences in Cost-Effectiveness: Residential Child Care in England and Wales," in *The Nonprofit Sector in International Perspective,* ed. Estelle James (New York: Oxford University Press, 1988), pp. 193–216.

19. Ibid., p. 7.

20. Gutch (n. 1 above).

21. David Austin, *The Political Economy of Human Service Programs* (Greenwich, Conn.: JAI Press, 1988).

22. Sosin (n. 4 above); DeHoog, *Contracting Out for Human Services* (n. 11 above); and Grønbjerg, *Understanding Nonprofit Funding.*

23. Curiously, there is much more concern evident in England than in the United States about the necessity of integrating nonprofit provider organizations into a planning process with governmental agencies. Some of the attempts to establish suitable structures under governmental auspices are noted in Demone and Gibelman, eds. pp. 408–9. A critical view of such efforts at coordination is Janet Weiss, "Substance Versus Symbol in Administrative Reform: The Case of Human Services Coordination," in *Community Organizations: Studies in Resource Mobilization and Exchange,* ed. Carl Milofsky (New York: Oxford University Press, 1988), pp. 103–22.

24. See n. 22 above.

25. Representative of these views are Harold L. Nixon II, "Organizational Subversion in Voluntary Rehabilitation Associations," *American Behavioral Scientist* 28, no. 1 (1985): 347–66; Smith and Lipsky; Michael B. Fabricant and Steven Burghardt, *The Welfare State Crisis and the Transformation of Social Service Work* (Armonk, N.Y.: M. E. Sharpe, 1992); and Wolch.

26. See Ralph M. Kramer, *Voluntary Agencies in the Welfare State* (Berkeley and Los Angeles: University of California Press, 1981), and "Voluntary Agencies and the Personal Social Services, in *The Nonprofit Sector: A Research Handbook,* ed. W. W. Powell (New Haven, Conn.: Yale University Press, 1987), pp. 240–57; Lester M. Salamon, "Partners in Public Service: The Scope and Theory of Government-Nonprofit Relations," in Powell, ed., pp. 99–117; Michael Krashinsky, "Management Implications of Government Funding of Nonprofit Organizations: Views from the United States and Canada," *Nonprofit Management and Leadership* 1, no. 1. (1990): 39–53.

27. Grønbjerg, *Understanding Nonprofit Funding* p. 260.

28. Carolyn Adams and Felice Perlmutter, "Commercial Venturing and the Transformation of American Voluntary Social Welfare Agencies," *Nonprofit and Voluntary Sector Quarterly* 20, no. 1 (1991): 25–38. A comprehensive perspective on these trends is Lester M. Salamon, "The Marketization of Welfare: Changing Nonprofit and For-Profit Roles in the American Welfare State," *Social Service Review* 67, no. 1 (March 1993): 16–39.

29. James Drew, "The Dynamics of Human Services Sub-contracting: Service Delivery in Chicago,

Detroit and Philadelphia," *Policy Science Journal* 13 (1984): 67–89.

30. Bernstein.

31. Sarah Liebshutz, "Coping by Nonprofit Organizations during the Reagan Years," *Nonprofit Management and Leadership* 2, no. 4 (1992): 363–80.

32. Grønbjerg, *Understanding Nonprofit Funding* p. 49.

33. John W. Meyer and W. Richard Scott, *Organizational Environments: Ritual and Rationality* (Beverly Hills, Calif.: Sage, 1983).

34. Salamon, "Partners in Public Service" (n. 26 above), p. 116.

35. Kramer et al. (n. 5 above); Heinz-Dieter Horch, "Does Government Financing Have a Detrimental Effect on the Autonomy of Voluntary Associations?" (paper presented at the Third International Conference of Research on Voluntary and Nonprofit Orga-

nizations, University of Indiana, Center on Philanthropy, Indianapolis, March 18, 1992).

36. This is essentially the meaning of Salamon's concept of "third-party government," which can be described as a form of compensatory complementarity, in which the strengths of one type of organization compensate for the failings of the other type. For example, the particularism of voluntary organizations is balanced by the universalism of public agencies, the paternalism of the former by the democratic policy-making of the latter, and the uncertain fund-raising ability of nonprofit organizations is complemented by the more reliable funding of government. Others, such as Smith and Lipsky, view these differences as more problematic.

37. Barry Bozeman, *All Organizations Are Public: Bridging Public and Private Organization Theories* (San Francisco: Jossey-Bass, 1987).

Resource Interdependence: The Relationship Between State Agencies and Nonprofit Organizations

JUDITH R. SAIDEL

The relationship between government agencies and nonprofit organizations is the focus of increasing attention within the public administration community. Practitioners recognize that the organization of public services relies to a substantial degree upon what we have come to call third-party government (Salamon, 1981). Nongovernmental actors not only deliver government-funded services but also actively participate throughout the policy process. Often the third-party is a nonprofit organization.[1]

Within this context of extensive sharing of responsibility between governmental and nongovernmental actors for operating public programs, the government/nonprofit relationship is widely acknowledged as a critical element.

Research findings reported here describe that relationship in terms of the dependence of public agencies and nonprofit organizations on each other for resources and their resulting interdependence. The results document a relationship of substantial and symmetrical resource interdependence. The implications of this finding are explored later in this article.[2]

Methodology

The statewide sample on which these findings are based included 80 nonprofit organizations in four service areas and four state agencies with whom these nonprofit organizations contract. In most instances, the state agency was the principal source of state revenues for the nonprofit agency. It should be noted, however, that just under 75 percent of the 80 nonprofit agencies had contracts with more than one state agency. Almost 25 percent contracted with four or more agencies. The service areas were: arts, culture, humanities; general health; mental retardation and developmental disabilities; and human services.

The Survey

Response categories were strongly disagree, generally disagree, disagree a little, agree a little, generally agree, strongly agree.

The conceptual anchors of each scale were (1) independence and (6) dependence. Three scales—importance, alternative availability, pressure—measured the dependence of state agencies on nonprofit organizations for resources. Three parallel scales measured the same dimensions for resource dependence in the other direction. Items were predominantly attitudinal; some were behavioral.

Scale scores were the average of the item scores. Table 32.1 reports reliability and discriminant validity results for the six scales. Alpha reliability coefficients are listed in bold-face type. Discriminant validity may be measured by the inter-scale correlation coefficients shown on the diagonal in that table.

The average of the three individual scale scores measuring state agency dependence on nonprofit agencies became Dsn in the model. The average of the three individual scale scores measuring nonprofit agency dependence on state agencies became Dns. These reciprocal resource flows, understood together, became the basis for a model of resource dependence between sectors, between sectors further subdivided into service areas, and between service areas without regard to sectors.

Sample and Framework

The study focused on New York State executive branch agencies and public benefit nonprofit organizations (classified as 501c3 in the Internal Revenue Code) that contract with state government for the delivery of public services.

Building Resource Dependence Equations

The two elements necessary to build resource dependence equations are (1) the resources that flow between the sectors; and (2) the criteria by which resource dependence is measured. In the context of this research on reciprocal resource dependence between organizations, "resource" is defined as anything of value, tangible or intangible, that can be exchanged between organizations.[3]

Resources

What resources, common across service areas, are exchanged between state government bureaucracies and public-benefit Nonprofit organizations? Figure 32.1 presents the resources in this framework that were either suggested spontaneously or confirmed in the model refinement interviews. Resources that flow from state agencies to nonprofit organizations are: revenues; information, including expertise and technical assistance; political support and legitimacy, in the sense of external validation (Galaskiewicz, 1985); and access to the nonlegislative policy process (Rourke, 1984).[4]

Nonprofit organizations supply their service-delivery capacity, information, political support, and legitimacy to state agencies. Nonprofit organization service-delivery capacity was documented as a substantial resource to government in the Urban Institute Nonprofit Sector Project

TABLE 32.1 Resource Dependence Scales: Reliabilities and Intercorrelations (133 < N < 143)

	1	*2*	*3*	*4*	*5*	*6*
1 S-Importance	**.67**					
2 S-Alternative availability	.25	**.73**				
3 S-Pressure	−.10	.09	**.63**			
4 N-Importance	.56	.01	−.14	**.70**		
5 N-Alternative availability	.16	.34	−.01	.35	**.70**	
6 N-Pressure	−.34	.17	.22	−.22	−.22	**.75**

S = State.
N = Nonprofit.

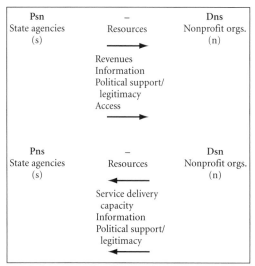

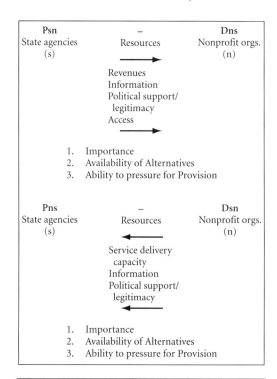

Psn is the resource-based power of state agencies over
nonprofit organizations.
Dns is the dependence of nonprofits on state agencies
for resources.
Pns is the resource-based power of nonprofits over state
agencies.
Dsn is the dependence of state agencies on nonprofits
for resources.

FIGURE 32.1   State Agency/Nonprofit Agency
Resource Dependence Equations

FIGURE 32.2   Dimensions of Resource Dependence

finding that "nonprofit organizations actually
deliver a larger share of the services government
finances than do government agencies themselves" (Salamon, 1987, p. 30). Two state agency
interviewees captured the revenue/service-
delivery capacity part of this exchange rather
succinctly:

> New York State agencies make dollars available
> to nonprofits. . . . They provide a service to the
> clients in whom we have an interest.
>
>   It's pretty straightforward. What we're doing
> is buying service which would otherwise not be
> available or which we would have to provide
> directly.

Political support and legitimacy are included
as resources because of the public arena in
which resource relationships between state
agencies and nonprofit organizations are forged.
In their dealings with the legislature, governor's
office, and division of the budget, nonprofit or-

ganizations can be influential actors on behalf of
the interests of state agencies.

Dimensions of Dependence

Three resource dependence criteria or dimensions of dependence (Bacharach and Lawler,
1981) can be specified: (1) the importance of
the resource; (2) the availability of alternatives;
and (3) the ability to compel provision of the resource (Figure 32.2).

   The importance, or essentiality of a resource
to an organization, consists of the organization's
need for the resource in order to function, to
operate, or to deliver programs or services
(Levine and White, 1961; Emerson, 1962; Blau,
1964; Jacobs, 1974; Thompson, 1967; Cook,
1977; Pfeffer and Salancik, 1978; Brudney, 1978;
Aldrich, 1979; Provan, Beyer, and Kruytbosch,
1980; Provan and Skinner, 1989). The importance dimension incorporates the elements of
substitutability and criticality or the organiza-

tion's ability to forego the resource and still continue operating (Jacobs, 1974; Pfeffer and Salancik, 1978; Aldrich, 1979).

The availability of the same resource from another supplier is widely acknowledged as a dimension of dependence (Levine and White, 1961; Emerson, 1962; Blau, 1964; Thompson, 1967; Jacobs, 1974; Cook, 1977; Pfeffer and Salancik, 1978; Brudney, 1978; Provan and Skinner, 1989). Cook's explanation is representative: "To the extent that alternative sources are available to an organization in an exchange network, dependence is less . . . " (1977, p. 66).

Insofar as organization A can compel, pressure, or force organization B to provide needed resources, A is less dependent on B. In contrast to the availability of alternatives, this dimension appears much less frequently in the literature (Blau, 1964; Aldrich, 1979; Provan, Beyer, and Kruytbosch, 1980). In the context of third-party government research, the ability to compel provision of a resource includes statutory and regulatory sanctions as well as the use of less formal kinds of pressure to force resource provision. This expanded scope is appropriate to the complex political environment within which inter organizational resource exchanges occur across sectors.[5]

Dimensions of Dependence Scales

To measure reciprocal resource dependence of state agencies and nonprofit organizations, six Likert-type scales were constructed with a number of items to which the respondent indicated intensity of agreement or disagreement on a six-point scale.

Analysis by Sector

The picture of resource dependence that emerged from a comparison by sector was somewhat surprising. Public-sector agencies and nonprofit sector organizations reported virtually identical resource dependence on each other. Out of a maximum 100 percent dependence, public-sector agencies reported that they are 61 percent dependent on nonprofit organi-

zations for resources. Nonprofit organizations reported that they are 62 percent dependent on state agencies for resources. Of the total theoretical dependence possible, each sector saw itself as dependent for resources on the other at about the same level.[6]

Sectoral differences in reported or perceived dependence became apparent at the dimension of dependence level. On four out of six dimensions, statistically significant differences were found in sectoral views. Public-sector agencies reported that they had more alternative sources for resources than nonprofit organizations thought they had (S-Alt, p < .001); nonprofit organizations reported that state agency resources were less important to them than state agencies thought they were (N-Imp, p < .01).

Divergent sectoral views were found on both pressure dimensions. Each sector reported that it was *less* able to exert pressure for resources than the other sector reported (S-Press, p < .01; N-Press, p < .001). In other words, both state and nonprofit organizations underestimated their ability to pressure for resources in the eyes of the other sector.

At the same time, both sectors agreed that, relative to independence measured any other way, state agencies were less dependent on nonprofit organizations because of their ability to pressure nonprofit organizations for resources. These responses appeared to reflect the regulatory, licensing, and certification authority of government and the powerful effect of state contracts on nonprofit contractors.

In summary, public-sector agencies and third-sector organizations described, in the aggregate, a similar relationship of reciprocal dependence. Of the total theoretical dependence possible, each sector saw itself as about 60 percent dependent for resources on the other (Figure 32.3). Although this suggests considerable inter-sectoral dependence, it also indicates that each sector perceived that it retained substantial resource autonomy relative to the other sector.

State agencies and nonprofit organizations differed with respect to certain elements of resource dependence. These included the uniqueness to state agencies of nonprofit agency-provided resources, the importance to nonprofit organiza-

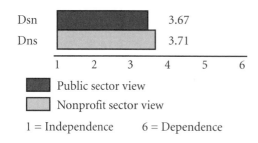

FIGURE 32.3   Resource Dependence: A Sectoral View

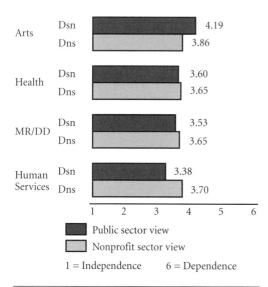

FIGURE 32.4   Resource Dependence by Sector and Service Areas

tions of state agency-provided resources, and the pressure each sector was able to exert on the other (Figure 32.4). Some of these findings reoccurred in the analysis from a different perspective reported in the following section.

Analysis by Sector and Service Area

When the data were analyzed from the perspective of public-sector agencies and nonprofit-sector organizations further subdivided into the

four service areas, some striking similarities and some important contrasts appeared in perceived resource dependence.

The measure of the dependence of state agencies on nonprofit organizations (Dsn) varied from 3.38 for the human service state agency to 4.19 for the arts state agency (p<.001). These were the lowest and highest reported means of dependence by state agencies on nonprofit organizations in the data set, regardless of how the data were partitioned. . . .

The other noteworthy similarity in reported resource dependence was the dependence of nonprofit organizations on public agencies for resources (Dns). Here the data indicated a shared view of the extent of that dependence among all respondents, regardless of sector or service area. Mean Dns scores in the four service areas ranged from 3.53 to 3.86. In other words, regardless of the kind of public services nonprofit organizations were producing, both sectors assessed the extent of nonprofit agency dependence on state agencies for resources at about the same level, from 58.8 percent to 64.3 percent dependent.

This was particularly interesting in the light of large differences in the actual percent of revenues derived from New York State sources by nonprofit organizations. Table 32.2 presents the medians and ranges of the percent of revenues from state government in 1988 reported by nonprofit organizations in the four service areas.

How can this contrast between reported resource dependence and the actual flow of revenues be explained? One possible explanation is that the model of resource dependence explored in this study incorporates information, support/legitimacy, and access as public resources in addition to revenues. It may be that, based on an assessment of their dependence on all these resources taken together, nonprofit organizations evaluate their dependence similarly. For instance, one nonprofit agency executive director observed, "We're extremely dependent upon the state agency for resources, mostly financial, secondly technical assistance and political pressure."

A second possible explanation, rooted in methodological considerations, is the issue of

TABLE 32.2 Nonprofit Organization Revenues from State Government Sources in 1988

	Arts N = 20	Health N = 20	MR/DD N = 20	Human Service N = 20
Median percent	9	33	75	26
Percent ranges	0–46[a]	8–97	30–100	0–90[a]

[a] 4 of the sample 80 nonprofit agencies had no state revenues in 1988. The original random sample was drawn from nonprofit agencies with state contracts in 1985.

objective versus subjective data. . . . Researchers who have used the Emerson formulation maintain that decisions are made and actions undertaken on the basis of perceived power dependence, which may or may not correlate highly with other objective measures (Brudney, 1978; Bacharach and Lawler, 1981).

The interviews shed additional light on the contrast between reported resource dependence and the actual flow of revenues, especially with respect to how managers think about the dependence of their organizations on the state for resources. For instance, almost one-quarter of nonprofit agency managers described their organizations' resource dependence in terms of specific programs. "Our dependence is minimal in terms of the overall budget," said one manager, "but we're very dependent if we're talking about a specific program." Another responded, "To a great extent we depend on them. It's more than the percentage of the budget; without state support we'd be very diminished in our services."

Third, heavy dependence on nonmonetary resources may compensate for less dependence on public funds in certain subsectors. For instance, in the arts service area that had the smallest median percent of revenues from New York State, several nonprofit agency managers mentioned the particular importance of the legitimacy that goes along with state funding.

> In a rural upstate area, arts council funding has provided a level of credibility for programs and projects. We have used it here to stimulate community support of the museum.

> The arts council is in the forefront of any one of our funders. Also their seal of approval helps leverage other private and public funds.

One human service nonprofit agency received no state dollars but relied on the social service agency for information.

> Right now in terms of financial resources, there is zero dependence. Certainly for our research, we make substantial data and program requests for information. Therefore, there is considerable dependence in terms of research.

Another element of resource dependence is the stability of the resource. Bozeman (1987) argues that government-provided resources are, over time, more stable than many have believed. Grønbjerg's (1990) research and the comments of several nonprofit agency executive directors in this study substantiate that contention.

> It's not so much the quantity but what they give it for and the reliability of the funding. It's not just the dollar amount.
>
> I think this organization relies heavily because it is ongoing funds, as opposed to grants from other places which you never know whether they're going to continue.

The next section reports results from an analysis of the data divided into the four service areas of arts, general health, mental retardation/developmental disabilities, and human services. When the sector category is removed as a basis of comparison, some parallel findings remain.

Analysis by Service Area

When all participant responses were partitioned only by the four service areas or subsectors included in this study, an interesting picture of resource dependence emerged.

Although there were statistically significant differences in Dsn and Dns among the four service areas, Tukey Post-Hoc test results indicated that the arts, culture, and humanities service area was unique on these measures. The general health, mental retardation/developmental disabilities (MR/DD), and human service subsectors described the reciprocal resource dependence of state agencies and nonprofit agency in virtually the same way. Again, both public and nonprofit managers in three different fields of public service activity reported substantial mutual resource dependence between state agencies and nonprofits.

Figure 32.5 shows that the arts service area reported higher levels of resource dependence in both directions. It was also the only service area in which state agency dependence on nonprofit organizations for resources exceeded nonprofit agency dependence on the agency.

In contrast, variation among all the service areas was much more evident at the dimension of dependence or individual scale level where statistically significant differences were found along each dimension (Table 32.3). All four service areas figured in these differences. It was particularly interesting to note that, of the 26 pairs of means that differed, only one involved a public-sector agency and nonprofit agency from the same service area. In other words, along the six dimensions of dependence, almost no differ-

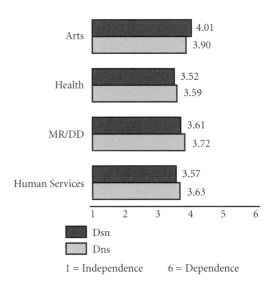

FIGURE 32.5   Resource Dependence by Service Areas

ence existed in the assessment of state agencies and nonprofit organizations in the same service area. This finding reinforced the notion of shared views in policy or issue networks (Heclo, 1978) that evolve in particular policy areas.

TABLE 32.3   Analyses of Variance by Service Area for Resource Dependence Scales

		State and Nonprofit Agencies				
		Arts N = 38	Health N = 38	MR/DD N = 39	Human Service N = 38	F Ratio
S-Importance	Mean	5.11	4.76	4.90	4.50	6.52[a]
	(SD)	(.55)	(.58)	(.48)	(.71)	
S-Alternative availability	Mean	4.03	3.31	3.58	3.41	5.38[b]
	(SD)	(.79)	(.69)	(.76)	(.92)	
S-Pressure	Mean	2.89	2.49	2.35	2.80	4.34[b]
	(SD)	(.91)	(.74)	(.59)	(.57)	
N-Importance	Mean	5.01	4.62	4.85	4.46	4.98[b]
	(SD)	(.55)	(.59)	(.51)	(.82)	
N-Alternative	Mean	3.00	2.96	3.59	2.96	5.65[a]
	(SD)	(.79)	(.72)	(.66)	(.83)	
N-Pressure	Mean	3.66	3.18	2.72	3.45	7.90[a]
	(SD)	(.83)	(.75)	(.74)	(.96)	

[a] $p < .001$.
[b] $p < .01$.

Resource Interdependence Findings

Operationalization of the dependence of state agencies on nonprofit organizations and vice versa yielded two measures of resource *dependence.* In order to describe the simultaneous two-way flow of resources or resource *interdependence,* dependence variables were combined into magnitude and distribution measures.

Magnitude

Magnitude refers to the extent of interdependence, that is, how much interdependence exists in a particular relationship. It can be measured by adding the dependences of the two actors. There could be resource relationships of low, moderate, or high interdependence.[7] Magnitude is equivalent to the total power concept, "the sum total of dependence in the relationship," explored by Bacharach and Lawler (1981, p. 221) in their analysis of the cognitive processes involved in collective bargaining. Regardless of how the data were categorized, every magnitude score was in the moderate range. . . . Although this suggests considerable interdependence, it also indicates that each sector retains, relative to the other sector, substantial resource autonomy.

Distribution

This measure captures the relative dependence in a relationship. How dependent are state agencies on nonprofit organizations compared to the dependence of nonprofit organizations on state agencies? Distribution is measured by a ratio of one actor's dependence to the magnitude of dependence in the relationship. This is similar to Bacharach and Lawler's relative power concept, "the ratio of one party's dependence to the other's dependence" (1981, p. 221).

Analysis by sector revealed that each sector assessed relative resource dependence at precisely the same levels. Both judged nonprofit organizations to be slightly more dependent on state agencies than vice versa. . . .

Symmetry and Asymmetry

. . . Symmetry is defined as situations in which two or more organizations are *equally* dependent upon one another for the resources each has access to or controls. A relationship of asymmetrical interdependence is one in which two or more organizations are *not equally dependent* upon one another for the resources each has access to or controls.

Perhaps the single most striking finding of this study was the symmetry in the distribution of resource dependence between state agencies and nonprofit organizations at all levels of analysis—sector, sector/service area, service area. Relationships of resource interdependence in all four subsectors were characterized by resource flows upon which public agencies and nonprofit organizations are equally dependent. Whether nonprofit organizations were producing cultural events, delivering health care, or providing social services, public and nonprofit administrators assessed the distribution of dependence at about the same level.[8]

Implications

Based on the magnitude and distribution of resource inter-dependence reported in this study, it is clear that the government/nonprofit relationship in four service areas within New York State is a critical axis in the modern welfare state (Table 32.4). The activities of nonprofit organizations do not appear to be at the margins (Sharkansky, 1975) but rather at the center of public services. Emergent institutional relationships, noted by Weidenbaum (1969) several decades ago, are so firmly in place that an important part of policy discussion and research should focus at least as much on *public services,* developed and delivered through interactions across sectors, as on the unitary *public sector.*

Still, the government/nonprofit axis is precarious for several fundamental reasons. First, symmetrical resource dependence may not allow sufficient nonprofit or public organizational autonomy. Some autonomy is necessarily

TABLE 32.4   Differences in Distribution of
Dependence

	Public Sector More Dependent	Nonprofit Sector More Dependent
Arts agency	Yes	No
Arts nonprofits	No	Yes
Health agency	Yes	No
Health nonprofits	No	Yes
MR/DD agency	No	Yes
MR/DD nonprofits	Yes	No
Human service agency	No	Yes
Human service nonprofits	Yes	No

lost by both parties in an interdependent relationship. The question is whether the magnitude of exchange, although symmetrically distributed, is at too high a level. For instance, Wolch argues that the increasing reliance of nonprofit organizations on public revenues has extended the reach of the state into the management and goal-setting processes of nonprofit organizations (1990, p. 15). Weidenbaum warned about this development, describing it as "the public assumption of private decisionmaking" (1969, p. 48).

Public bureaucracies also experience reduced autonomy when nonprofit providers who deliver high priority services are scarce and/or politically powerful. In a Michigan study, DeHoog described a scenario in which contractors, completely dependent on state funds to deliver services to needy clients, effectively mobilized political influence and thereby limited state agency discretion. "Consequently, the Department of Social Services would be contracting for services that were determined, not by service priorities and performance, but by the very fact of contractor dependence" (1984, p. 41).

Linked to this point is the key issue of accountability. Mosher (1980) and others (Seidman and Gilmour, 1986; Kettl, 1987; Moe, 1987) maintain that public accountability, a goal at the heart of representative government, is increasingly more difficult to achieve because of the in-

volvement of nongovernmental parties as implementors of public services. This reflects both the increased complexity and blurred lines of authority inherent in indirect service provision (Sharkansky, 1975; Goodsell, 1985). A number of important questions remain to be explored. A primary issue is the larger relationship of interdependence between state and nonprofit organizations. It has been suggested elsewhere (Saidel, 1989) that, in addition to resource exchanges, other political and administrative interactions constitute two major dimensions of intersectoral relations. . . .

Another important issue concerns the sharing of governmental authority with third-parties involved in public services. What kinds of authority are and are not shared? Where are the boundaries between sectors? Do boundaries disappear because they become less distinct? These issues gain considerable saliency because of the web of interdependence depicted in this research.

Notes

I acknowledge with deep appreciation the contributions of Phillip J. Cooper, Ronald B. Hoskins, and David C. McCaffrey to this research. I would also like to thank David H. Rosenbloom and the anonymous reviewers for very useful suggestions. Another explanation that may account in part for symmetrical resource dependence distribution comes from institutional theory. One version of this theory defines institutionalization as "the process by which actions become repeated over time and are assigned similar meanings" (Scott, 1987, p. 495). In general, the four subsectors examined here are characterized by government/nonprofit interactions over several decades. It is possible that institutionalization processes have resulted in a shared view of these interactions.

1. The terms "nonprofit," "voluntary," and "third-sector" are used as synonyms for "nonprofit." Although nonprofit is not legally precise in the sense that nonprofit organizations can earn a surplus of revenues over expenditures, the term is widely used among both academics and practitioners for ease of communication.

2. Several words of caution are in order. Whereas state agencies are often at the front line of interactions with the voluntary sector, this is not the only

point of intersection or resource interdependence between sectors. In addition, the exchange of resources between government and voluntary organizations, while fundamental to their interactions, is only one aspect of a larger relationship of interdependence described elsewhere (Saidel, 1989).

3. This meaning is narrower than Hall's generic definition of resources as "the contents of the many transactions among organizations" (1982, p. 256) and broader than Cook's definition of resource as "any valued activity, service or commodity" (1977, p. 64).

4. Client referrals—a resource mentioned in earlier studies (Hasenfeld, 1983; Kramer and Grossman, 1987)—was not suggested in any of the model refinement interviews.

5. This modification of the pressure dimension may make it more usable in an interorganizational setting than the original notion described by Blau (1964). Brudney (1978) notes the difficulty for intraorganizational research inherent in the Blau formulation.

6. The variance in perception within each sector, as expressed in standard deviations, was not very great and was well within the expected range for a normal distribution.

7. As noted earlier, the operationalization of resource dependence was the mean of scale scores based on a 1 to 6-point scale. Therefore, low magnitude scores were 2.0–5.3, moderate scores were 5.4–8.7, and high scores were 8.8–12.

8. Pfeffer and Salancik made the important point that asymmetry may occur in one direction in relation to a particular resource while, at the same time, there may be other asymmetries in the other direction for different resources (1978, p. 53). The distribution measure in this study describes interdependent relationships, when resources are considered together. It does not differentiate between levels of dependence relative to individual resources.

References

Aldrich, Howard E., 1979. *Organizations and Environments.* Englewood Cliffs, NJ: Prentice-Hall.

Bacharach, Samuel B. and Edward J. Lawler, 1981. "Power and Tactics in Bargaining." *Industrial and Labor Relations Review,* vol. 34 (January), pp. 219–233.

Blau, Peter M., 1964. *Exchange and Power in Social Life.* New York: John Wiley and Sons.

Bozeman, Barry, 1987. *All Organizations Are Public: Bridging Public and Private Organizational Theories.* San Francisco: Jossey-Bass.

Brudney, Jeffrey L., 1978. "An Exchange Approach to Intraorganizational Power." Unpublished dissertation, University of Michigan.

Cook, Karen S., 1977. "Exchange and Power in Networks of Interorganizational Relations." *The Sociological Quarterly,* vol. 18 (Winter), pp. 62–82.

DeHoog, Ruth H., 1984. *Contracting Out for Human Services: Economic, Political, and Organization Perspectives.* Albany, NY: State University of New York Press.

DeHoog, Ruth H., 1990. "Competition, Negotiation, or Cooperation: Three Models for Service Contracting." *Administration and Society,* vol. 22 (November), pp. 317–340.

Emerson, Richard H., 1962. "Power-Dependence Relations." *American Sociological Review,* vol. 27, (February), pp. 31–41.

Galaskiewicz, Joseph, 1985. *Social Organization in an Urban Grants Economy.* Orlando, FL: Academic Press.

Goodsell, Charles T., 1985. *The Case for Bureaucracy: A Public Administration Polemic,* 2d ed. Chatham, NJ: Chatham House Publishers.

Grønbjerg, Kirsten A., 1987. "Patterns of Institutional Relations in the Welfare State: Public Mandates and the Nonprofit Sector." *Journal of Voluntary Action Research,* vol. 16, pp. 64–80.

Grønbjerg, Kirsten A., 1990. "Managing Nonprofit Funding Relations: Case Studies of Six Human Service Organizations." PONPO Working Paper No. 156. New Haven: Yale University.

Heclo, Hugh, 1978. "Issue Networks and the Executive Establishment." In Anthony King, ed., *The New American Political System.* Washington, DC: American Enterprise Institute.

Jacobs, David, 1974. "Dependency and Vulnerability: An Exchange Approach to the Control of Organizations." *Administrative Science Quarterly,* vol. 19, pp. 45–59.

Kettl, Donald F., ed., 1987. *Third Party Government and the Public Manager: The Changing Forms of Government Action.* Washington, DC: National Academy of Public Administration.

Levine, Sol and Paul E. White, 1961. "Exchange as a Conceptual Framework for the Study of Interorganizational Relationships." *Administrative Science Quarterly,* vol. 5 (March), pp. 583–601.

Moe, Ronald C., 1987. "Exploring the Limits of Privatization." *Public Administration Review,* vol. 47 (November/December), pp. 454–460.

Mosher, Frederick C., 1980. "The Changing Responsibilities and Tactics of the Federal Government." *Public Administration Review,* vol. 40, pp. 541–548.

Pfeffer, Jeffrey, and Gerald R. Salancik, 1978. *The External Control of Organizations: A Resource Dependence Perspective.* New York: Harper and Row.

Provan, Keith G., Janice M. Beyer, and Carlos Kruytbosch, 1980. "Environmental Linkages and Power in Resource-Dependence Relations Between Organizations." *Administrative Science Quarterly,* vol. 25 (June), pp. 200–225.

Provan, Keith G., and Steven J. Skinner, 1989. Interorganizational Dependence and Control as Predictors of Opportunism in Dealer-Supplier Relations." *Academy of Management Journal,* vol. 32 (March), pp. 202–212.

Rourke, Francis E., 1984. *Bureaucracy, Politics, and Public Policy,* 3d ed. Boston: Little, Brown and Co.

Saidel, Judith R., 1989. "Dimensions of Interdependence: The State-Voluntary Sector Relationship." *Nonprofit and Voluntary Sector Quarterly,* vol. 18 (Winter), pp. 335–347.

Saidel, Judith R., 1991. "Managing Interdependence between Sectors: Public Agency and Nonprofit Organizational Strategies." Paper presented at the 1991 American Society for Public Administration Annual Conference, Washington, DC, March 23–27.

Salamon, Lester M., 1981. "Rethinking Public Management: Third-Party Government and the Changing Forms of Government Action." *Public Policy,* vol. 29, pp. 255–275.

Salamon, Lester M., 1987. "Of Market Failure, Voluntary Failure, and Third-Party Government: Toward a Theory of Government-Nonprofit Relations in the Modern Welfare State." *Journal of Voluntary Action Research,* vol. 16, pp. 29–49.

Seidman, Harold and Robert Gilmour, 1986. *Politics, Position, and Power, From the Positive to the Regulatory State,* 4th ed. New York: Oxford University Press.

Sharkansky, Ira, 1975. *Whither the State? Politics and Public Enterprise in Three Countries.* Chatham, NJ: Chatham House Publishers.

Thompson, James D., 1967. *Organizations in Action.* New York: McGraw-Hill.

Weidenbaum, Murray L., 1969. *The Modern Public Sector.* New York: Basic Books.

Wolch, Jennifer R., 1990. *The Shadow State: Government and Voluntary Sector in Transition.* New York: The Foundation Center.

The Double-Edged Sword of Social Service Contracting: Public Accountability Versus Nonprofit Autonomy

JAMES M. FERRIS

Much attention has been focused in recent years on the relationship between nonprofit organizations and the public sector. Government often uses nonprofit organizations as an instrument for carrying out public policies, in particular with the expansion of welfare state expenditures at the national level (Salamon, 1987). The increasing recognition of this trend has heightened concern about the threat to nonprofit autonomy in the United States as the contract state has evolved (Gibelman and Demone, 1989).

Maintaining the independence of nonprofit organizations in the face of government contracting is an issue that has developed as nonprofits have diversified their revenue sources and government has expanded its involvement in social services. This situation in the United States is in contrast, as Krashinsky (1990) has noted, to the situation in other countries such as Canada, where government funding of nonprofit organizations has been an accepted tradition. It should be apparent, however, that there is no absolute autonomy in the nonprofit sector, just as there is none in the public or business sectors. All organizations are required to be accountable to their constituencies, in particular those who provide the necessary funds that support their existence.

To fully understand how government contracts affect nonprofit organizations, particularly in terms of their autonomy, it is essential to understand the motives, incentives, and constraints under which both sides of the social service market operate. This article seeks to illuminate the double-edged sword of government contracts, suggest that it is not as sharp as is often perceived, and recommend ways in which nonprofit managers might act strategically to blunt its negative effects.

I will first examine the government's contracting decision to highlight the fact that in many instances nonprofit organizations will be a preferred organizational choice. I then turn my attention to the behavior of nonprofit organizations in responding to government contract demands. By focusing on the motivations of both sides of the social service contract "market," I can examine the comparative advantage of nonprofit organizations in social service delivery and the implications of government contracts for the behavior, performance, and autonomy of nonprofit organizations.

The Government Contracting Decision

Once a government chooses to finance a social service, it must decide how to produce it. It has an array of institutional arrangements from which it may choose—internal production as well as contracts with other governments, for-profit firms, or nonprofit organizations. Indeed, the possibilities of contracting were underscored by the Title XX amendments in the mid 1970s that encouraged contracts with nonprofit organizations (Kramer, 1985).

Ferris and Graddy (1986, 1991) have developed a model of the local government's production decisions that frames the organizational choices for social service delivery. They assume that local governments try to minimize the costs of service delivery, subject to political and legal constraints. Service delivery costs include production costs (that is, the cost of the inputs such as labor and capital) and transaction costs (that is, the cost of the contracting process in terms of contractor selection and contract enforcement). The various organizational forms have different implications for these two types of costs. Recognition of these differences together with an understanding of contract market competitiveness underscore the importance of the nonprofit organization as a contract option for social services.

Service Delivery Costs and Organizational Choice

In this section we consider how production costs and transaction costs vary with the choice of public, nonprofit, and for-profit contractors.

Production costs.   Several factors suggest that contracting might lead to production cost savings; these factors include scale economies, managerial incentives, and managerial discretion. The ability to realize these savings through

contracting is likely to vary by the type of contractor chosen.

The efficiency incentives of managers are likely to vary with the form of their organization. In public agencies, there are few incentives for managers to minimize costs.

Private-sector organizations have stronger managerial incentives. In for-profit organizations the manager can be given a share of the profits. The calculation of profits (revenues minus costs) and their distribution to managers enables owners to reward management for performing in accordance with the owner's desire to maximize profits. This system provides strong incentives for production efficiency.

The nonprofit organization can make profits, but it cannot distribute them (Hansmann, 1987). Revenues in excess of costs can be used to expand services, enhance quality, or subsidize unprofitable activities. Moreover, the lack of a singular objective for nonprofit organizations analogous to profit maximization in the for-profit sector makes it difficult to generalize about the incentives inherent in nonprofit organizations (James and Rose-Ackerman, 1986). Nevertheless, there is more opportunity to devise incentives in nonprofit organizations than in public agencies. Thus, in terms of strength of managerial incentives for cost savings, nonprofit organizations seem to fall between for-profit and external public organizations.

The ability of organizations to achieve cost efficiency also depends on managerial discretion in selecting inputs and production technologies. Public organizations are subject to civil service rulès and public budgeting systems that inhibit the selection of the optimal mix of inputs. Public personnel policies limit the discretion of managers in selecting the optimal combination of labor inputs for a given output. Constraints on hiring, firing, promotions, and compensation levels make it difficult for managers to rearrange their staffs and their skills composition to deliver services at minimum costs. In addition, public managers, faced with separate budgetary processes for capital and operating expenditures, do not always have the flexibility necessary to acquire the level of capital they desire.

Private organizations, both for-profit and nonprofit, lack these constraints on input selection. The for-profit sector, however, with its easier access to financing, does have an input control advantage over the nonprofit sector. The magnitude of this advantage is limited to the extent that nonprofits benefit from their tax-exempt status and are able to secure funding from charitable contributions, foundation grants, or government tax-exempt bonds.

In summary, the production cost savings gained from choosing external production are expected to vary by the organizational form of the contractor. Based on differences in managerial incentives and input rigidities, the for-profit firm should offer the greatest production cost savings, the nonprofit organization somewhat less, and the public bureau the least.

Transaction costs. Just as production costs are likely to vary by organizational type, so too are transaction costs. While there are transaction costs associated with internal production, the transaction costs associated with external production are probably greater. Failure to effectively implement contracting can jeopardize public accountability (the responsibility for ensuring that public funds are spent effectively for public purposes). This is likely to make public officials concerned about potentially high transaction costs.

The contracting government incurs transaction costs to ensure that the contractor will behave so as to meet the government's objectives. The contracting government is not likely to have complete information on the capacity of the different bidders to perform to contract specifications. To increase the likelihood of selecting the best contractor, the contracting government incurs costs to gather information. In addition, the government will incur costs in monitoring the performance of the contractor. Without monitoring, the contractor may be inclined to perform at a level below contract specifications.

The magnitude of these costs relates to the type of service and the contractor's organizational form. Contract specification requires that one can define and measure the quantity and quality of the service, and can describe the conditions under which the service will be delivered. Such tasks are facilitated when the service is characterized by relatively constant citizen preferences and relatively stable cost conditions. Once a contract is written, it must be monitored and enforced. The feasibility of measuring performance is critical. It must be technically possible to measure outputs, both quantitatively and qualitatively, and to do so at a reasonable cost. For social services, such measurement is typically difficult. Although it is possible to develop quantity measures, for example, the number of individuals served, the issue of determining quality is more vexing.

Transaction costs also vary by organizational type. Nonprofit organizations can reduce transaction costs at both the contract writing and monitoring stages. A hallmark of the nonprofit sector is its ability to respond to diverse demands for collective goods (Weisbrod, 1988). If nonprofits have responded effectively to community demands, then the contract-writing costs for government are likely to be decreased, either because the nonprofit organization's record of service provision is satisfactory or because the nonprofit organization helps write the contract through cooperative negotiations (DeHoog, 1990).

The nonprofit form may even be more attractive in terms of monitoring cost savings. First, due to their inability to distribute profits, they are assumed to be more trustworthy than for-profit organizations. Second, many nonprofit organizations were created as a result of a keen interest in the quantity or quality of the service. Third, the fact that nonprofit organizations often receive considerable donations creates the possibility that individuals making such donations may be in a position to monitor these organizations, especially when donations take the form of volunteering (Schiff, 1990). Consequently, nonprofits may be preferred to for-profit firms when monitoring is difficult (Krashinsky, 1986). Similar reasoning suggests that external public organizations will be preferred to for-profit organizations.

Market Conditions

The incentives and constraints embedded in the different organizational forms are not all that matter. A key consideration is the competitiveness of the contract market. Although public, nonprofit, and for-profit organizations differ with respect to constraints and incentives, they all tend to be more efficient when subject to competitive forces, whether within a sector or across sectors. For example, public agencies exposed to competitive forces, as when they serve as a supplier to other governmental units, exhibit more efficient behavior (Mehay and Gonzalez, 1985).

Most contracting discussions assume a competitive model. In effect, this model assumes such a large number of buyers and sellers that no one actor can influence the price charged for services. However, a blind application of a competitive model for social services is suspect. The degree to which there are large numbers of actors on either side of the market will vary by service type. For some social services, there is a long history with a multitude of providers. In these cases, the market does approximate a competitive model. In other instances, however, the demand for a particular social service might have been so recently voiced that the market is not fully developed—for instance, in the case of social services for individuals with AIDS.

Another important consideration, in addition to the number of suppliers, is the options available across sectors. The set of supply options is limited to one or two sectors. For example, while there are a large number of hospital service suppliers in all three sectors, shelters for battered women are almost exclusively the realm of nonprofit organizations. It is also possible that the service might be so specialized, as with trauma centers, that there are few, if any, external options. The competitiveness of the market has significant impact on the cost savings that contracting can achieve as well as implications for the effects on nonprofit organizations.

Competitive conditions.   In instances where there are multiple providers and these providers are distributed across sectors, the government has a full array of contract options from which to choose. If the service is characterized by high transaction costs, the government may find that the most efficient contract option, considering both production and transaction costs, is a nonprofit producer. On the other hand, if transaction costs for the service are minimal, it may select a for-profit producer with greater cost-minimization incentives (Ferris and Graddy, 1991).

Even if the contracting process is initially competitive, with a large number of bidders, there is no guarantee that subsequent bidding processes will be competitive. Once a producer receives a contract, it will invest in a variety of resources. To the extent that these organizational resources are specific to the production of the contracted service, the existing contractor will have an advantage over potential contractors in the future. Likewise, to the extent that the contracting government is pleased with the performance of the contractor, that government is likely to be unwilling to switch contractors. Consequently, one might expect that the production cost savings generated by competitive markets might dissipate over time (Williamson, 1985). On the other hand, it is possible that there are transaction cost savings that will accrue as the contracting government and the contractor become more familiar with each other.

Limited supply options.   If the government is entering a service arena for the first time and the private, nonprofit, or for-profit sectors have not previously supplied it, the government has a limited set of choices. The providing government may develop the production capability internally, or it may wish to stimulate a supply capacity through negotiations with existing nonprofit organizations in related fields or the incubation of autonomous, nonprofit organizations. This latter option is what Kettner and Martin (1989) refer to as the partnership model. DeHoog (1984) gives numerous cases in which local governments, in introducing new social services to their responsibilities, cultivated nonprofit organizations to begin supplying such services.

With a limited number of suppliers, it is unlikely that all of the benefits that are often ascribed to contracting will be realized. Thus the contracting government is likely to turn to the nonprofit sector.

Summary

This framework presumes that contracting decisions are driven by efficiency considerations. But there are other factors, such as legal constraints and political forces, that motivate the service delivery choices of local governments. Legal prohibitions on particular types of contractors constrain organizational choices. These vary by service and by jurisdiction.

Citizen preferences are also an important influence on service delivery choices. If organized, a service's constituency can play a pivotal role. For example, the constituency may prefer internal production if they perceive that government has a higher commitment to the provision of services produced in-house. Contracted services are, in fact, easier to terminate. This fact is not lost on nonprofit contractors who worry about government funding uncertainty. Nonprofit organizations may lobby not only for increased public spending but for increased support for the activities of nonprofit organizations. But the interests of those served by the organization are not the only ones that matter. There are broader constituencies within the community that have particular preferences about the local political economy (that is, attitudes toward the public sector's fiscal roles) that also shape local government service delivery decisions. For example, a community might prefer private-sector alternatives for ideological reasons, or a community might have a predisposition against services that are redistributive in nature.

Nonprofit Organizations as a Preferred Contracting Option

This discussion of local government production decisions underscores the attractiveness of non-profit organizations as a contracting option for social services. This preference derives from the ability of nonprofit organizations to limit transaction costs through their presumed trustworthiness, experience in service delivery, and responsiveness to diverse client groups Although their capacity to minimize production costs

might not be as sharp as that of for-profit organizations, they offer a balance of the production efficiencies of private organizations and the public accountability of public agencies. Moreover, the fact that the nonprofit sector is often the first to respond to preferences for collective goods implies in many instances that they are not only the preferred option, but the only option.

The nonprofit sector is the prominent contracting option for social services. A survey of local service delivery arrangements, conducted by the International City Management Association in 1982, indicates that at least half of the contracting governments surveyed relied on nonprofit organizations for the production of day care, child welfare, elderly services, public health, substance abuse, and mental health programs (Ferris and Graddy, 1986). These data suggest that governments find nonprofit organizations an attractive contracting option. To the extent that competition for these services exists, it comes primarily from the for-profit sector. Yet, with the notable exceptions of day care and hospitals, for-profits are typically the choice of only about 20 percent of the contracting governments. This suggests that nonprofit organizations have considerable power to influence the conditions of government contracts. This is particularly true in instances where they do not face competition from the for-profit and public sectors.

Implications for the Nonprofit Sector

The dependence of nonprofit organizations on government funding has produced much anxiety in the nonprofit community. Kramer and Grossman (1987) identify several sources of anxiety for nonprofits that rely heavily on government contracts: funding uncertainty, goal deflection due to resources expended in contract acquisition and compliance, and reduced fiscal flexibility. Although the fear that such organizations might jeopardize their autonomy by becoming too reliant on government contracts cannot be entirely discounted, the attractiveness of nonprofits as a contracting option should allay some of these concerns. The principal advantages of nonprofit organizations as external production options are their trustworthiness and experience. Governments are likely to prefer contracting with nonprofits for services where these attributes are salient, thus minimizing threats to public accountability.

The government will be inclined to select nonprofits, particularly those with a proven record, in order to reduce the risk of choosing contractors without the ability and intent to meet contract specifications. However, the selection of a contractor goes beyond organizational form to the merits of the particular organization. An important attribute for awarding contracts is the organization's history of service delivery. Contracting governments are likely to prefer an organization with an established reputation over one without a track record, both in terms of service delivery and charitable support, to enhance the likelihood that the contractor will produce the desired service outcome.

The government will also be inclined to contract with nonprofit organizations in order to limit the transaction costs associated with contract monitoring and enforcement. The government's fiduciary responsibility requires careful monitoring of expenditures of public funds. However, because of the problems of outcome measurement, the monitoring that takes place focuses more on fiscal accountability than on performance accountability (Kramer and Terrell, 1984). The difficulties of performance monitoring induce contracting governments to choose nonprofit contractors over for-profit contractors. Thus, the possibility that contract monitoring substantially reduces autonomy seems overstated. This contention is consistent with Kramer's (1981) observation that complaints about government monitoring stem more from the inconvenience of frequent reporting and the excessiveness of regulations than the distortion of organizational goals.

In addition to the attractiveness of nonprofit contractors to the government, market conditions also have implications for the impact of government contracts on nonprofit organizations. There is an assumption in discussions of

government contracting that supply is competitive, giving the government the ability to dictate terms to its contractors. However, in instances where the number of available suppliers is limited, the power of the contracting government is also limited. In fact, the contracting government must sometimes seek out potential contractors. As long as the nonprofits have an independent financial base, the concern about undue government influence should not be major. The influence of the government is a more prominent issue in instances where the organization has been nurtured on government funding.

Summary

The threat that government funding poses for nonprofit autonomy depends on nonprofit behavior as much as that of contracting governments. There is reason to believe that the experience, trust-worthiness, and flexibility of nonprofit organizations make them an attractive contract option. The extent to which government funding detracts from the autonomy of nonprofit organizations and encroaches on their uniqueness will depend on the behavior of contracting governments as well as that of nonprofit organizations. The diversity of nonprofit organizations suggests that the threat to nonprofit autonomy is likely to be greatest for those nonprofits that were created and nurtured on public funding.

Conclusion

The heightened concern over the threat of increased public funding to nonprofit autonomy is understandable given the increased trend in the public funding of nonprofit organizations. However, this concern seems to be exaggerated in many instances. Governments find nonprofit organizations to be an attractive partner in social service delivery because they combine the efficiencies of the private sector with regard to production costs and the efficiencies of not-for-profit (nonprofit and public) organizations with regard to transaction costs. The desire to achieve efficiency and public accountability is not inherently contradictory to the goals and objectives of social service organizations. Indeed, in many instances government contracts present an opportunity for nonprofit organizations to increase the breadth of their service delivery role and expand their influence over the quantity and quality of the services being provided.

There are no guarantees that government funding will not infringe on nonprofit autonomy. Governments should be mindful that funding and the conditions that are attached to funding have the potential to diminish the qualities of the nonprofit sector they find desirable (Grønbjerg, 1990). Yet the ultimate responsibility for protecting nonprofit autonomy rests with the nonprofit organizations themselves. The analysis of the different types of nonprofit organizations suggests that nonprofit organizations should be mindful that too heavy a dependence on public funding threatens their identity. It is their responsibility to make strategic choices in seeking or not seeking funding sources. They must be cognizant of the truth that to simply substitute public funding for charitable markets is to risk a real threat to their autonomy and their distinctiveness.

References

DeHoog, R. H. *Contracting Out for Human Services: Economic, Political and Organization Perspectives.* Albany: State University of New York Press, 1984.

DeHoog, R. H. "Competition, Negotiating, or Cooperation: Three Models for Service Contracting." *Administration and Society,* 1990, *22* (3), 317–340.

Douglas, J. "Political Theories of Nonprofit Organizations." In W. W. Powell (ed.), *The Nonprofit Sector: A Research Handbook.* New Haven, Conn.: Yale University Press, 1987.

Ferris, J., and Graddy, E. "Contracting Out: For What? With Whom?" *Public Administration Review,* 1986, *46* (4), 332–344.

Ferris, J., and Graddy, E. "Production Costs, Transaction Costs and Local Government Contractor Choice." *Economic Inquiry,* 1991, *29* (3), 541–554.

Gibelman, M., and Demone, H., Jr. "The Evolving Contract State." In H. W. Demone, Jr., and M. Gibelman (eds.), *Services for Sale.* New Brunswick, N.J.: Rutgers University Press, 1989.

Grønbjerg, K. *Managing Nonprofit Funding Relations.* Working paper no. 156, Program on Non-Profit Organizations, Yale University, 1990.

Hansmann, H. B. "Economic Theories of Nonprofit Organization." In W. W. Powell (ed.), *The Nonprofit Sector: A Research Handbook.* New Haven, Conn.: Yale University Press, 1987.

James, E., and Rose-Ackerman, S. *The Nonprofit Enterprise in Market Economies.* New York: Harwood, 1986.

Kettner, P., and Martin, L. "Making Decisions about Purchase of Service Contracting." In H. W. Demone, Jr., and M. Gibelman (eds.), *Services for Sale.* New Brunswick, N.J.: Rutgers University Press, 1989.

Kramer, R. *Voluntary Agencies in the Welfare State.* Berkeley: University of California Press, 1981.

Kramer, R. "The Future of the Voluntary Agency in a Mixed Economy." *Journal of Applied Behavioral Science,* 1985, *21* (4), 377–391.

Kramer, R., and Grossman, B. "Contracting for Social Services: Process Management and Resource Dependencies." *Social Service Review,* Mar. 1987, pp. 32–55.

Kramer, R., and Terrell, P. *Social Service Contracting in the Bay Area.* Berkeley, Calif.: Institute of Governmental Studies, 1984.

Krashinsky, M. "Transaction Costs and a Theory of the Nonprofit Organization." In S. Rose-Ackerman (ed.), *The Economics of Nonprofit Institutions.* New York: Oxford University Press, 1986.

Krashinsky, M. "Management Implications of Government Funding of Nonprofit Organizations: Views from the United States and Canada." *Nonprofit Management and Leadership,* 1990, *1* (1), 39–53.

Lipsky, M., and Smith, S. "When Social Problems Are Treated as Emergencies." *Social Service Review,* Mar. 1989, pp. 5–25.

Lipsky, M., and Smith, S. "Nonprofit Organizations, Government, and the Welfare State." *Political Science Quarterly,* 1989–1990, *104* (4), 625–648.

Mehay, S. L., and Gonzalez, R. A. "Economic Incentives under Contract Supply of Local Government Services." *Public Choice,* 1985, *46* (1), 79–86.

Rudney, G. "The Scope and the Dimensions of Nonprofit Activity." In W. W. Powell (ed.), *The Nonprofit Sector: A Research Handbook.* New Haven, Conn.: Yale University Press, 1987.

Salamon, L. "Partners in Public Service: The Scope and Theory of Government Nonprofit Relations." In W. W. Powell (ed.), *The Nonprofit Sector: A Research Handbook.* New Haven, Conn.: Yale University Press, 1987.

Schiff, J. *Charitable Giving and Government Policy: An Economic Analysis.* New York: Greenwood Press, 1990.

Smith, S. "Federal Funding, Nonprofit Agencies, and Victim Services." In H. W. Demone, Jr., and M. Gibelman (eds.), *Services for Sale.* New Brunswick, N.J.: Rutgers University Press, 1989.

Weisbrod, B. *The Nonprofit Economy.* Cambridge, Mass.: Harvard University Press, 1988.

Williamson, O. E. *The Economic Institutions of Capitalism.* New York: Basic Books, 1985.

The Future of the Nonprofit Sector: Its Entwining with Private Enterprise and Government

BURTON A. WEISBROD

Introduction

Nonprofits are increasingly around us—providing day care for our children, medical care for our sick, and nursing home care for our elderly; operating museums; assisting the poor; supporting basic medical research; and far more. Yet they are largely overlooked, except when they are pleading for funds or someone is complaining about their competition with private firms or governments are trying to tax them.

Only rarely does anyone ask the fundamental questions: Does society need nonprofits? If so, in what parts of the economic system are they most useful? In what ways are they better than private firms and government?

I pose three questions about the nonprofit sector: (a) Why are they expanding worldwide? (b) How is the growth affecting other parts of the economy? and (c) What evidence is there that nonprofits make a difference, that they perform functions which private firms or government cannot perform?

Why Is the Nonprofit Sector Growing?

Why is the nonprofit sector growing? The answer, I believe, is this: Nonprofits perform the kinds of functions typically identified with government—helping the disadvantaged, providing social services, supporting collective services such as museums and schools, preserving the environment, funding medical research, and the like. When government provides these services in forms and amounts that voters want, there will be little role for nonprofits. However, when populations are very diverse, services that satisfy the majority may leave many people severely undersatisfied; nonprofits are thus understandable as an alternative mechanism for providing collective services. The more homogeneous a society is—the more similar are its citizens' preferences—the smaller the need for nonprofit organizations. In countries with relatively homogeneous populations, such as in Scandinavia, government can meet the wants of its citizens for the various collective services, and so we find that *governments* are in fact considerably larger in those countries, whereas the *nonprofit sectors* are relatively unimportant. This helps to explain two phenomena that have been widely observed: first, the far greater importance of the nonprofit sector in the United States than in other countries; and second, the growing importance of nonprofits everywhere, as population migration and the flow of information through television and computers have the effect of magnifying diversity in country after country (Weisbrod, 1975).

This growing diversity of societies is bringing, everywhere, retrenchment of government and increased reliance on the nonprofit sector. Nonprofits, however, face an enormous obstacle: They lack government's power to tax, and so when they are confronted by increased demands, they do not have the commensurate resources to meet those demands. The result is that nonprofits search for new sources of revenue, and this brings them into increasingly complex relationships with the rest of the economy. They have been successful, overall, in finding ways to increase revenues, but that success has brought side effects, for nonprofits have become more and more "commercial."

What Are the Effects of Nonprofit Sector Growth— On Private Firms, Government, Consumers, and on Nonprofits Themselves?

As nonprofit organizations struggle to offset declining governmental support, they reach out for new markets, trying to find things they can sell profitably. The result is that nonprofits have thrust themselves into new arenas, generating increased competition and growing political attention. Tension has escalated between nonprofits and both private firms and governments, as *competition* between nonprofits and these other sectors has increased.

At the same time, there has also been growing *cooperation* between nonprofits and these other organizations. There has been scarcely any public recognition of the alliances between nonprofits and private enterprises, and between nonprofits and government, but these are generating behavior that is no less troubling than nonprofits' aggressive *competitive* behavior. Whatever the specific form of entanglement between nonprofits and the rest of the economy, problems and stresses emerge. Whenever nonprofits enter new markets, there are consequences.

What are those consequences—for private enterprise, for government, and for the nonprofit sector itself? Both the nonprofit activities that *compete* with the private and public sectors, and those that involve *cooperation* with them, pose problems.

Effects on the Private Sector

Competition and tension with private enterprise. The more the nonprofit organizations expand, the more they encounter resistance— for example, charges that they are guilty of "unfair competition" with private enterprise because they receive subsidies (Emshwiller, 1995; U.S. Small Business Administration, 1983). What is clear is that nonprofits are competing increasingly with for-profit firms, and in an amazing variety of forms. Here are some examples:

- The nonprofit Metropolitan Museum of Art operates 16 museum shops in the United States and 21 abroad, in addition to its catalog of items for sale (Cronin, 1995).
- The nonprofit Duke University Medical Center is establishing a business unit to "compete with private-sector companies that run trials for drug and medical-device companies" (Winslow, 1995, p. B6).
- Nonprofit food banks established to feed the poor are building food-dehydrating plants that compete with private firms (Lewin, 1994).
- Nonprofit churches are running tours in competition with for-profit travel agencies (Brannigan, 1995).

- Nonprofit zoos are developing creative ways to attract support from paying tourists; for example, one zoo constructed a high wire for orangutans to show off their ability to climb and swing (Molotsky, 1995).

The competition between nonprofits and private firms is made even more complex by the fact that, at the same time nonprofits are moving into activities that have previously been the domain of for-profit firms, private firms are expanding into traditionally nonprofit areas. Thus, private health clubs have entered an industry long the preserve of the nonprofit YMCAs and YWCAs in the United States, and for-profit amusement parks "are encroaching on [nonprofit] museum turf by adding educational aspects to their entertainment products" (Becker, 1995, p. 7). There is very little understanding of the dynamic forces causing the expansion of each sector into areas long dominated by the other, and equally little understanding of the effects.

Cooperation with private enterprise. The "growing commercialism" of nonprofits is also occurring through *cooperative* mechanisms in which nonprofits and private firms join forces. Between 1980 and 1981 and 1987 and 1988, for example, private industry support for university research more than doubled in real terms in France, Japan, the United Kingdom, and the United States, and it more than tripled in Germany (Webster, 1994). Virtually every major U.S. university has joined forces in some manner with large multinational firms, especially pharmaceutical and chemical firms (Blumenthal et al., 1996). For instance, Harvard University has contracted with the German chemical company, Hoechst A.G.; Washington University with Monsanto Chemical Company; and Northwestern University with Dow Chemical.

Scientific research is not the only area in which nonprofit universities are becoming allied with private firms. Athletics is another. The University of Michigan recently reached a multimillion dollar agreement to advertise athletic shoes for Nike; in a masterful obfuscation, Nike agreed

to "help" the university design its uniforms! Even charities are engaging in such alliances: The March of Dimes (MOD) recently teamed up with Kellogg's, the manufacturer of breakfast cereals; the MOD received $100,000 in return for what amounts to an endorsement of Kellogg's Product 19—a cereal that contains folic acid, which helps prevent birth defects of the spine and brain. This is no isolated example; the nonprofit MOD even has a senior staff member with the title, Director of Strategic Alliances, National Promotions, to develop such money-generating arrangements (McIver, 1995).

Why are nonprofits engaging in such symbiotic relationships with private firms? Because there are potentially massive financial benefits from collaboration—benefits that are not occasional and random, but are systematic consequences of powerful economic forces. Universities and other nonprofits such as hospitals, museums, and charities receive many subsidies, and if the nonprofits are clever, they can convert those benefits into something that is salable to private firms. *It is increasingly difficult to evaluate the social contribution of nonprofits in the modern world where barriers between nonprofit and for-profit firms are crumbling.* The increased fuzziness of the boundary between nonprofit and for-profit organizations is not accidental; there are forces breaking down these borders. Wise public policy must recognize them.

Nonprofits' drive for revenue and private firms' drive for profit present great opportunities for both to gain from collaboration. But whether nonprofits are collaborating with private firms or competing with them, there is a critical question: *Are nonprofits acting more and more like private firms, and by doing so, forfeiting their claim of special status and privilege?* I will return to this theme.

Now I turn from the ways that growth of the nonprofit sector is affecting private firms to its effects on government.

Effects on Government

Competition and tension with government. When nonprofits expand, government loses revenue. In the United States, the loss is particularly important for local governments. Property taxation is their major source of revenue, and every parcel of land that moves out of the taxed, private enterprise sector and into the untaxed, nonprofit sector means more loss of tax revenue. At a time when governments are searching desperately for new sources of revenue to deal with the growing problems of crime and poverty and the loss of revenues from the federal government, the expansion of nonprofits is a serious fiscal threat. The most recent report by the U.S. Treasury Department noted that 10 percent of all property in the country was held by tax-exempt nonprofits in 1977 (Arenson, 1995c); the figure is surely higher today. Indeed, as of 1993, the city of Buffalo, New York, found that 34 percent of its real estate was tax exempt, and for Syracuse, New York, it was 59 percent (Glaberson, 1996).

Local governments are responding to this erosion of their tax base. They are developing innovative ways to circumvent state laws that grant exemptions from local government taxation, in order to collect revenue from nonprofit organizations. For example, cities are withholding zoning approval and building permits for new buildings unless the nonprofit university, hospital, or symphony orchestra agrees to pay a "voluntary" tax. Tension between nonprofits and governments is becoming so intense that lawmakers are searching for reasons to withdraw tax-exempt status altogether. The tension has escalated as evidence has surfaced that nonprofit executives were receiving levels of pay that were unseemly for charitable organizations. When most Americans learned of compensation of over $500,000 per year for nonprofit organization executives such as the president of United Way of America, William Aramony, the chief executive of the PTL Ministry, the Reverend Jim Bakker, and the president of Adelphi University, Peter Diamondopoulos (Hancock, 1996), they were shocked. Both Aramony and Bakker went to prison, but in the process the public faith in nonprofits has been shaken (Arenson, 1995b; Gaul and Borowski, 1993). *Nonprofits are increasingly being seen not as public-spirited philanthropies but as self-serving entities that pursue the interests of their top officials and board members.*

Another form of tension between nonprofits and government involves the application of antitrust laws to nonprofits whose activities have traditionally been regarded as benevolent. In 1991 the U.S. Department of Justice brought an antitrust action against a group of nonprofit universities for price-fixing in their granting of financial aid to prospective students. One of the schools refused to abandon the practice, contending that the price-fixing—which it admitted—actually promoted social welfare because it increased overall opportunities for low-income students ["M.I.T. Wins a New Trial in Price-Fixing Case," 1993]. In effect, the university was saying that its collusion with other schools was socially valuable, whereas collusion in the private enterprise sector was not. The Justice Department disagreed. Neither side, however, could call upon a solid research base to buttress its case. Nonprofit hospitals, too, have fallen victim to antitrust laws, as proposed mergers have been held to be anticompetitive. Again, public policy hangs on matters about which little is known—whether nonprofit and for-profit organizations use monopoly power in materially different ways. Although little is known, one recent study indicates that nonprofit hospitals that gain greater market power are likely to reduce prices, while for-profits are more likely to raise them (Lynk, 1995).

Cooperation with government. Nonprofits' search for revenue does not always hurt government. Sometimes governments benefit. For example, nonprofits in the United States have discovered money-making opportunities in working with state governments to market automobile license plates. Thirty-six states now permit some nonprofits to benefit from specialty license plates that advertise arts organizations, universities, environmental groups, and garden clubs. The University of California, Los Angeles (UCLA), is collaborating with the state of California to sell a license plate that finances student scholarships (Herman, 1995). Such cases of what amount to joint ventures between nonprofits and governments appear to be rare, but fiscal pressures on both types of organizations are bound to generate more such novel alliances in the future.

Effects on Consumers

Change within the nonprofit sector is taking many forms. Among hospitals in the United States, where nonprofits dominate the industry, pressures to reduce costs are leading to mergers and closings that are increasing hospitals' market power—as noted earlier. But there has been little research on the effectiveness of competition in industries with a large nonprofit sector. How are consumers affected when nonprofits dominate an industry? Just a few years ago, hospital executives in five states of the United States were doing what was previously "unthinkable, and possibly illegal"—talking to one another about cooperation and joint ventures that would earlier have violated antitrust laws (Felsenthal, 1993). Two years later the U.S. Justice Department shifted its position and instituted antitrust suits against four hospitals and physician groups for cooperating too much, contending that they formed monopolistic alliances to maintain high prices, to the detriment of consumers (Simpson, 1995). Is public policy right now in discouraging nonprofits' expansion? Or was it right earlier in encouraging it? We simply do not know.

Effects on Nonprofits

Tension is growing inside the nonprofit sector, too. As nonprofits become increasingly commercial in their activities, they are doing things not customarily identified with the genteel approaches of benevolent organizations. Charities are bringing lawsuits for breach of contract against people who pledge donations but do not fulfill them (Schmitt, 1995), and universities are sending recruiters (some might term them "salespeople") around the world in search of tuition-paying students (Hancock and Roberts, 1994).

Nonprofit organizations are also developing for-profit subsidiaries. At Northwestern University, for example, its Institute for Learning Sciences has started a for-profit firm to market a customized computer program that allows the user to hold conversations with experts in a field, and the director of the Institute is also

the acting president of the new corporation (*PARKprogress*, 1995). There is absolutely nothing illegal about such arrangements, but they do blur the distinctions between nonprofits and private firms, and they need to be assessed (Kramer, 1995; Young, 1994).

In the case of university-industry cooperation in research, the key question is whether these financial arrangements change the direction of university research and researchers' interpretation of findings. A new study of nearly 200 companies engaged in collaborative research with universities disclosed numerous agreements to keep research results secret, even beyond the time required to file for a patent (Blumenthal et al., 1996). Was the Internal Revenue Service in the United States justified in claiming that in some partnership arrangements the nonprofit partner was sacrificing the interests of charity and hence violating the tax code requirement that it be "operated exclusively for . . . charitable purposes" (Simon, 1987, p. 93)? The issues are subtle and complex.

Why Do Interactions Occur Across Sectors, and Are They Increasing?

I predict that the increased fiscal pressure on nonprofits will lead them to generate new, more creative forms of commercial activities, and that these new forms will further blur the distinctions between nonprofit organizations and private firms. In the process I expect reconsideration of many existing public policies regarding nonprofits: their subsidization and restrictions on their freedom to lobby government; to engage in joint ventures with private firms; and to compete with private firms. I also expect increased pressure from government to require nonprofits to disclose more publicly their compensation of executives, and I anticipate the applicability of antitrust laws to nonprofits to emerge as a political issue.

There is a potent force behind these forecasts. This force was not unleashed earlier because of the availability of government support. With that support withering, however, nonprofits face the choice of either reducing their activities, at the very time that social need is growing because of government retrenchment, or finding ways to increase revenues from nongovernmental sources. If they choose the latter, which most are doing, they can pursue two avenues—try to increase private donations or find ways to generate more income through the sale of goods or services—that is, commercial activity.

Increasing donations is generally not promising. Although some new and imaginative forms of appeals for donations are being developed—a recent advertisement by a charitable nonprofit said, "Donate your car, truck, motorcycle, boat (any condition)," emphasizing that it was tax deductible (*JUF News,* 1995)—there is little reason to expect that donations can be significantly increased unless tax laws are changed substantially. Such changes, however, are being discussed—particularly the granting of tax *credits* to encourage charitable donations.

New commercial activities are the major path open to nonprofits to generate additional revenue. And once nonprofits enter the realm of finding salable outputs, they are in the domain of private enterprise, for selling goods and services is *the* preeminent source of private sector revenue. Nonprofits that pursue revenue in the same ways that private firms do are likely to emulate those firms, and by becoming more like them, they undermine the fundamental justification for the special social and economic role they have played. Why, it is increasingly being asked, should society give subsidies and tax exemptions to nonprofit organizations that are less and less distinguishable from private firms?

The key to understanding the interrelatedness of nonprofits with other parts of the economic system is to recognize that nonprofits operate according to rules and constraints that differ from those on government and private enterprise. This underscores a fundamental economic proposition: *Whenever "rules"—for example, regulations, taxes, or prices—differ among sectors of an economic system, organizations can gain from exchanges between sectors.* Non-profit and for-profit organizations face differential restrictions on whether their income is taxed, differential availability of resources such as volunteer labor, differential restrictions on their freedom to lobby legislators (Arenson, 1995a), and differential access to private and public subsidies.

The "gains from exchange" between taxed (for-profit) and "untaxed" (non-profit) organizations apparently benefit the organizations involved, but they do not necessarily benefit society. The managerial "creativity" can be brilliant but socially inefficient. Consider the following illustration.

In 1983, the president of Bennington College, a small college in Vermont, made a discovery: Because Bennington was a nonprofit organization that paid no corporate profits taxes, it did not benefit from being allowed to charge depreciation as a cost of production; private firms, by contrast, did benefit, because depreciation reduced their tax liabilities. Eureka! The college had found an opportunity to gain from exchange between sectors that differed in their tax rules. Soon Bennington agreed to sell all its buildings to an alumni group, for $3 million to $8 million annually, and lease them back for 99 years. "In effect, the college would get an interest-free loan and the alumni would reap tax benefits" (Biddle and Slade, 1983, p. 9). Both the college and the real estate purchaser benefited—as inevitably occurs when organizations face differential prices for the same commodity (Galper and Toder, 1983).

Did *everyone* gain? Not really. Taxpayers lost, as tax revenues declined. In effect, tax benefits were being sold. Congress subsequently prohibited such "sale-leaseback" arrangements, which have no economic justification but to reduce taxes. Nevertheless, the potential for mutual gain for the taxed and untaxed sectors remains. One skirmish with tax authorities had ended, but the "war" was far from over. Other novel exchanges between the nonprofit and private enterprise sectors are predictable. After all, because organizations in both sectors can benefit from the differential rules under which they operate, the incentive to find ways to overcome the barriers to trade across sectors remains.

The fact that nonprofits are entwined with private enterprise and government is important for a number of reasons, but they all lead to a central question: Are the contributions of the nonprofit sector sufficient to justify their preferential treatment? Thus, I move to the third of my three questions: Do nonprofit organizations behave differently, and "better," than private firms and government agencies?

Do Nonprofit Organizations Behave Differently Than Private Firms and Government Agencies? What Is the Evidence?

Nonprofits have been viewed in sharply contrasting ways. Some prominent economic analysts see nonprofits as little more than inefficient private firms that, without the lure of profit and private gain, waste resources and perform no socially desirable role (Alchian and Demsetz, 1972). Others, however, see a significant role for nonprofits in light of "failures" of both private enterprise and government (Hansmann, 1980; Weisbrod, 1975; Wolf, 1988). Both views may well be right. Some nonprofits may be inefficient, doing little to justify their existence but surviving because of subsidies. Others may be highly efficient providers of services that meet important social needs.

The list of criteria for gauging nonprofit organization performance is lengthy. It includes: (a) efficiency and output quality, particularly in dimensions that are difficult for consumers to observe (Ben-Ner, 1986; Hansmann, 1980; Weisbrod, 1988); (b) access by consumers regardless of ability to pay (Schlesinger, in press); (c) provision of collective goods that complement those of government (Weisbrod, 1975); (d) encouragement of altruistic values such as the opportunity to volunteer (Wuthnow, 1995); (e) alternatives to "monolithic" government in the social welfare arena; and (f) preserving national identity (Schuster, 1994). I will focus primarily on the first two—efficiency and quality of output, particularly in dimensions that consumers find difficult to monitor, and methods used to control access to services—but I will also touch on volunteering. Do nonprofits and for-profits differ?

Efficiency, Output Quality, and Trustworthiness

There is some available evidence about quality in nonprofit and for-profit sectors in industries in which they coexist.[1] One indicator of quality that is difficult for consumers to monitor is the use of sedatives in nursing homes. It is virtually impossible for family members to determine whether a patient is being sedated because of medical need or simply to reduce the labor costs associated with patients that are more active. In nursing homes in the United States; the use of sedatives was found to be more than four times as great at for-profit facilities as at church-related nonprofit facilities—12.5 compared with 3.0 units per month (Svarstad and Bond, 1984), and medical "need" appeared to be similar. We do not know, however, whether the for-profit firms were providing too much sedation, or the nonprofits too little.

Although there is some evidence available on institutional quality, it is in forms that consumers often have difficulty in assessing. Focusing on the nursing home and mentally handicapped facilities industries in the United States, I utilized the Survey of Institutionalized Persons (SIP). I used two proxies for output quality: (a) the amounts of labor inputs per 100 patients; and (b) consumer satisfaction with services.[2]

The findings strongly indicate that, in both industries, *satisfaction is consistently highest at church-related nonprofit facilities and lowest at for-profit facilities.* Satisfaction is typically 8 to 17 percent higher at church-related nonprofits than at proprietary facilities. Moreover, *the nonchurch nonprofits are indistinguishable from for-profit facilities.* Again we find that nonprofit organizations are not homogeneous.

Access to Services: Pricing Policies and Waiting Lists

Nonprofit organizations may be socially valuable not only because of the kinds of outputs they produce but also because of the ways they distribute their services. Society often has distributional goals that are inconsistent with unbridled private market behavior. Sale of human organ transplants, for example, has been prohibited in a number of countries.

I have examined patient access in two ways—the organization's pricing practices, specifically, its price-cost margin (the difference between its charges and its average cost), and its use of a waiting list. The findings are that nonprofit and for-profit organizations use quite different ways of distributing their services in both the nursing home and mentally handicapped industries.

Price-cost margins differ materially. Other things being equal, both church and nonchurch nonprofits have profit margins that are significantly smaller than at proprietary facilities. Price-cost margins average $80 per month less at mentally handicapped facilities and $120 per month less at nursing homes. These differences are 12 to 20 percent of the average costs in the two industries—around $600 per month.

Waiting lists are also used differentially to control access. Even for-profit firms find it useful to employ waiting lists on occasion, but their principal distributional mechanism is price. In both industries, church-related facilities are far more likely to have a waiting list—92 percent compared to 65 percent among nursing homes, and 92 percent compared to 60 percent among facilities for the mentally handicapped.

Nonprofits that are not church-related are more like proprietary facilities in their use of waiting lists. Among nursing homes these "other" nonprofits have an estimated 73 percent frequency of maintaining a waiting list, which is not significantly more than the 65 percent at for-profit facilities.

Another Measure of Performance—Opportunities to Volunteer

One of the performance measures I noted earlier was the opportunity that organizations provide for people who wished to volunteer. In the child day-care industry, where nonprofits involve parents as volunteers far more than do for-profit facilities. In a recent survey, only 14 percent of parents with children in for-profit centers reported that they volunteer, compared with 51 percent of parents at church-related nonprofits. Moreover, at nonprofits, nearly 50

percent of parents who volunteered worked directly in the classroom, compared with 25 percent of the volunteers at proprietary facilities (Mauser, 1993, chapter 6, p. 10).

Managerial Compensation

Still another way to shed light on the behavior of nonprofit organizations relative to other forms of institutions is to examine the ways they compensate their top executives, whose decisions affect organization behavior. A number of studies of labor compensation have found lower wages in nonprofit organizations. Some workers appear willing to work for less pay at an organization that is engaged in public-serving activities. In the U.S. legal services industry, for example, lawyers in nonprofit "public interest" law firms were found to receive pay that is some 15 percent lower than what they could have received in private enterprise, given their experience, gender, law school class rank, and law school quality (Weisbrod, 1983). In the hospital industry, top management was again found to receive 15 to 20 percent lower pay in nonprofit hospitals than in their for-profit counterparts, even though the jobs were found to be more complex at the lower paying nonprofit hospitals (Roomkin and Weisbrod, 1997). Not every study has found this pattern (Preston, 1988), however, and so the issue of whether pay differentials reflect greater willingness to work for a nonprofit because of its activities, or differential worker productivity, is not resolved.

Policy Implications and Directions for Future Research

Assertions about the contributions as well as the shortcomings of private firms and nonprofit organizations abound, and they give rise to conflicting public policy prescriptions. Doubts concerning the social desirability of private enterprise have been expressed about many industries—hospitals, day-care centers, and certain legal services (Mansnerus, 1993)—where output quality is difficult to monitor and write into a contract. Now the debate has expanded to the desirability of for-profit prisons; they already exist in Australia, Britain, New Zealand, and the United States, and are being considered in Canada, France, The Netherlands, and the Czech Republic (Butterfield, 1995; Kettl and Winnick, 1995; Weisbrod, 1988). Perhaps they should be nonprofits.

What is the future of the nonprofit sector? That depends on nonprofits' success in finding new sources of revenue. Donations are a very limited source. Volunteer time is important but not easily substituted for money. Increased user fees and commercial activities all bring troubling side effects. The non-profit sector is entwined with the rest of the economy and is likely to become even more entwined in the future.

One matter is both clear and critical: Competition for resources is driving all organizations—nonprofit, for-profit, and government—to search for new markets, and a market that is new to one type of organization is quite likely to be occupied already by another. The growth of nonprofit sectors throughout the world is thrusting nonprofits into the central debate over the organization of society. Until now, the nonprofit sector has benefited from being small and largely out of sight. Success has changed this, with growing demands for accountability. Success has its price!

Notes

1. When commodities are complex, so that it is costly for consumers to gauge performance and, hence, for sellers to warrant the quality of output, organizational form may provide a signal of quality. Zeckhauser and Viscusi (1990) have pointed out that, in a world of positive costs of obtaining information, it may be efficient to utilize a proxy for information. Specifically, they note that "mandatory requirements may be preferable to . . . information efforts." Institutional form could perform an analogous informational role.

2. If systematic behavioral differences were not observed, that would not imply that institutional form is irrelevant to public policy. It could be the case that competition forces all surviving forms of institutions to behave in similar ways (Hirth, 1993; Wolff and Schlesinger, 1994).

References

Alchian, Armen and Harold Demsetz (1972), "Production, Information Costs, and Economic Organization," *American Economic Review* 62, pp. 777–795.

Arenson, Karen W. (1995a), "Law Would Tighten Limits on Political Advocacy by Charities," *New York Times*, August 7, p. A9.

Arenson, Karen W. (1995b), "Large Charities Pay Well, Survey Finds," *New York Times*, September 5, p. A7.

Arenson, Karen W. (1995c), "A Small College's Tax-Exempt Status Challenged," *New York Times*, September 26, p. A14.

Becker, T. J. (1995), "Opening Door to Synergy," *Chicago Tribune*, May 16, section 5, pp. 1, 7.

Ben-Ner, Avner (1986), "Nonprofit Organizations: Why Do They Exist in Market Economies?" in Susan Rose-Ackerman (ed.), *The Economics of Nonprofit Institutions* (New York: Oxford University Press).

Biddle, Wayne and Margot Slade (1983), "Ideas and Trends: Bennington's Mutual Aid Idea," *New York Times*, April 10, section 4, p. 9.

Blumenthal, David, Nancyanne Causino, Eric Campbell, and Karen Seashore Louis (1996), "Relationships between Academic Institutions and Industry in the Life Sciences—An Industry Survey," *New England Journal of Medicine* 334 (February), pp. 368–373.

Brannigan, Martha (1995), "Church-Run Tours Collide with Travel Agents," *Wall Street Journal*, September 18, pp. B1–B2.

Butterfield, Fox (1995), "Private Tennessee Prison is Praised in State Studies," *New York Times*, August 19, p. Y6.

Cronin, Anne (1995), "Museums: The Sluggers of the Culture Lineup," *New York Times*, August 9, pp. A1, B2.

Emshwiller, John R. (1995), "More Small Firms Complain about Tax-Exempt Rivals," *Wall Street Journal*, August 8, p. B1.

Felsenthal, Edward (1993), "New Rules Let Hospitals Start Joint Ventures," *Wall Street Journal*, May 14, pp. B1, B5.

Galper, Harvey and Eric Toder (1983), "Owning or Leasing: Bennington College, and the U.S. Tax System," *National Tax Journal* 36, pp. 257–261.

Gaul, Gilbert M. and Neill A. Borowski (1993), "In High-Level Jobs at Nonprofits, Charity Really Pays," *The Philadelphia Inquirer*, April 22, pp. A18–A20.

Glaberson, William (1996), "In Era of Fiscal Damage Control, Cities Fight Idea of 'Tax Exempt,'" *New York Times,* February 21, pp. A1, C17.

Hancock, LynNell and Melissa Roberts (1994), "Fishing for Freshmen," *Newsweek,* November 21, pp. 104–105.

Hancock, LynNell (1996), "All the President's Perks," *Newsweek,* January 22, p. 56.

Hansmann, Henry (1980), "The Role of Nonprofit Enterprise," *Yale Law Review* 89(April), pp. 835–899.

Hansmann, Henry (1995), "The Changing Roles of Public, Private, and Nonprofit Enterprise in Education, Health Care, and Other Human Services," Working Paper, School of Law, Yale University.

Herman, Tom (1995), "Got a Message, Do You? You Can Send It by Plate," *Wall Street Journal,* February 8, p. A1.

Hirth, Richard A. (1993), "Information and Ownership in the Nursing Home Industry," Ph.D. dissertation, University of Pennsylvania.

Hodgkinson, Virginia A. and Murray S. Weitzman (1994), *Giving and Volunteering in the United States* (Washington, DC: Independent Sector).

Israel Finance Ministry (1996), *Non-Profit Institutions in Israel, 1991,* Publication 1016 (Jerusalem, Israel: Central Bureau of Statistics).

JUF News 4 (1995), advertisement (New York: Jewish United Fund).

Kettl, Donald F. and Louis Winnick (1995), "Privatize City Jails? Here's the Hitch," *New York Times,* August 22, p. A11.

Kramer, Ralph (1995), "Is the Sector Concept Obsolete?" *Inside ISTR* (Bulletin of the International Society for Third-Sector Research, Johns Hopkins University) 3(1), p. 6.

Lewin, Tamar (1994), "Dehydrated-Food Plant in Texas Is Dedicated to Effort to Feed the Hungry," *New York Times,* October 25, p. A14.

Lynk, William J. (1995), "Nonprofit Hospital Mergers and the Exercise of Market Power," *Journal of Law and Economics* 38(October), pp. 437–461.

Mansnerus, Laura (1993), "Bar Groups Are Happy to Find You a Lawyer," *New York Times,* February 27, p. A30.

Mauser, Elizabeth (1993), "Is Organizational Form Important to Consumers and Managers? An Application to the Day-Care Industry," Ph.D. dissertation, University of Wisconsin-Madison.

McIver, LaVonne (1995), "March of Dimes to Receive $100,000 for Health Message," *Nonprofit Times* (September), p. 5.

"M.I.T. Wins a New Trial in Price-Fixing Case" (1993), *New York Times,* September 18, p. A6.

Molotsky, Irvin (1995), "National Zoo Puts Six Orangutans to Work in a High-Wire Act," *New York Times,* August 21, p. A7.

PARKprogress 5 (1995), newsletter, Northwestern University—Evanston Research Park.

Preston, Anne E. (1988), "The Effects of Property Rights on Labor Costs of Nonprofit Firms: An Application to the Day Care Industry," *Journal of Industrial Economics* 36, pp. 337–350.

Roomkin, Myron and Burton A. Weisbrod (1997), "Managerial Compensation in For-Profit, Nonprofit, and Government Hospitals," Working Paper, Department of Economics, Northwestern University.

Salamon, Lester M. and Helmut Anheier (1994), *The Emerging Sector* (Baltimore: Johns Hopkins University Institute for Policy Studies).

Salamon, Lester M. and Helmut Anheier (1995), "The Emerging Sector: A Statistical Supplement," Working Paper, The Johns Hopkins Comparative Nonprofit Sector Project.

Schlesinger, Mark (in press), "Mismeasuring the Consequences of Ownership: External Influences and the Comparative Performance of Public, For-Profit, and Private Nonprofit Organizations," in Walter W. Powell and Elizabeth Clemens (eds.), *Private Action and the Public Good* (New Haven, CT: Yale University Press).

Schmitt, Richard B. (1995), "Uncharitable Acts: If Donors Fail to Give, More Nonprofit Groups Take Them to Court," *Wall Street Journal,* July 27, pp. 1, 5.

Schuster, J. Mark Davidson (1994), "Arguing for Government Support of the Arts: An American View," in Olin Robison, Robert Freeman, and Charles A. Riley (eds.), *The Arts in the World Economy,* Salzburg Seminar (Hanover, NH: University Press of New England).

Simon, John (1987), "Tax Treatment of Nonprofit Organizations," in Walter W. Powell (ed.), *The Nonprofit Sector: A Research Handbook* (New Haven, CT: Yale University Press).

Simpson, Glenn (1995), "U.S. Says Hospitals, Doctors in 2 Areas Tried to Block Managed-Care Providers," *Wall Street Journal,* September 14, p. A5.

Svarstad, Bonnie L. and Chester A. Bond (1984), "The Use of Hypnotics in Proprietary and Church-Related Nursing Homes," School of Pharmacy, University of Wisconsin-Madison.

U.S. Council of Economic Advisers (1995), *Economic Indicators* (Washington, DC: U.S. Council of Economic Advisers).

U.S. Small Business Administration (1983), *Unfair Competition by Nonprofit Organizations with Small Business: An Issue for the 1980's* (Washington, DC: U.S. Small Business Administration).

Webster, Andrew (1994), "University-Corporate Ties and the Construction of Research Agendas," *Sociology* 28, pp. 123–142.

Weisbrod, Burton A. (1975), "Toward a Theory of the Voluntary Nonprofit Sector in a Three Sector Economy," in Edmund S. Phelps (ed.), *Altruism, Morality, and Economic Theory* (New York: Russell Sage Foundation).

Weisbrod, Burton A. (1983), "Nonprofit and Proprietary Sector Behavior: Wage Differentials among Lawyers," *Journal of Labor Economics* 1, pp. 246–263.

Weisbrod, Burton A. (1988), *The Nonprofit Economy* (Cambridge, MA: Harvard University Press).

Weisbrod, Burton A. (1996), "Do Private Firms, Church-Related Nonprofits, and Other Nonprofits Behave Differently?" Working Paper, Department of Economics, Northwestern University.

Winslow, Ron (1995), "Getting Down to Business at Duke's Medical School," *Wall Street Journal,* August 29, pp. B1, B6.

Wolf, Charles Jr. (1988), *Markets or Governments: Choosing Between Imperfect Alternatives* (Cambridge, MA: MIT Press).

Wolff, Nancy and Mark Schlesinger (1994), "Changes in Ownership-Related Differences in Hospital Performance in Response to Intersectoral Competition," Working Paper, Institute for Health Care Policy, and Aging Research, Rutgers University.

Wuthnow, Robert (1995), *What It Means to Volunteer: Lessons from America's Youth* (Washington, DC: Independent Sector).

Young, Dennis R. (1994), "Through the Looking Glass: When Businesses and Not-for-Profits Act Alike," *Advancing Philanthropy* (Summer), pp. 13ff.

Zeckhauser, Richard J. and W. Kip Viscusi (1990), "Risk Within Reason," *Science* 248 (May), pp. 559–564.

PART 11

CHALLENGES FACING THE NONPROFIT SECTOR

The headline for a 1995 *Time* magazine article[1] asked rhetorically, "Can Charity Fill the Gap? Groups That Help the Poor Are Bracing for a Double Hardship; Surging Need and Federal Budget Cuts."* The message of this story was not much different than it would be if it were to be published today: Federal budget cuts in social programs are looming. Nonprofits will be expected to provide the "social safety net," but there will be less government money available to fund their programs. *Time* quotes Glenn Bailey, Executive Director of Crossroads Urban Center in Salt Lake City, the largest emergency food pantry in Utah and a charity that accepts almost no government funding:

> "It's simple mathematics," he says. The number of clients will go up because "people won't be eligible for welfare at a time when they need [it]." If the other local food pantries, which rely heavily on federal funds, were "crippled and had to close, folks would not quit being hungry," he observes. And he's not sure his donors will jump at the chance to make up the difference. "Churches and private charities are already stretched to the maximum," Bailey says wearily. "They are not going to be able to make up billions of dollars. There is no way private [giving] can handle that. It's a bad argument."[2]

Most nonprofits survived the threatened budget cuts that year. In 1996, however, Congress placed a five-year lifetime limit on individuals' eligibility for welfare benefits. Thousands of persons will be removed involuntarily from the welfare roles on December 31, 2001.[3]

Will charities across the United States be able to meet the demands? Will giving by private individuals, corporations, foundations, and churches rise enough to offset the billions of dollars in reduced government social program funding? Few observers of the sector believe that charities will be able to make up for the lost government funds. "Congress is engaged in sociological speculation, fueled by ideological wishfulness, that if they cut back on government, more private

---

*Jared C. Bennett, University of Utah, contributed significantly to this essay.

giving will take place. But there has been no test, no experiment, no trial basis in one state. It's just a blanket guess."[4] Or perhaps Marvin Olasky is correct in his observation: There is so much waste and inefficiency in the welfare programs of government and big charities that the thousands of smaller nonprofits will indeed be able to "do the job" with less.[5]

Or will nonprofits need to become even more aggressively entrepreneurial in pursuing funds through commercial business ventures? If so, how long will it take the small business trade associations and the U.S. Small Business Administration to successfully lobby Congress and state legislatures to enact more stringent limits and restrictions on nonprofits' business activities and income?

The threat of massive funding cuts is not limited to the human services, and the "villains" are not all housed in a single political party or espouse the same political ideology. Government funding of programs in the arts and humanities, environmental protection, health care, and education are all at risk. Perhaps the challenges have advanced from problems into true crises. "'It's like asking folks to prepare for a hurricane,' says Gordon Raley, executive director of the National Assembly of National Voluntary Health and Social Welfare Organizations, of the anticipated cuts. 'The nature of what is about to happen is nearly impossible to prepare for. It is incomprehensible to suggest that we could pick up the burden that government is getting ready to drop.'"[6] Some would argue that the challenges are insurmountable now, and the nonprofit sector will be forced to undergo fundamental restructuring. Many 501(c)(3) nonprofits will not survive, particularly public charities. Others believe that the warning cries are nothing more than self-serving hysteria. The government funding cuts are needed to start an overdue "shaking out" of inefficient nonprofits that have been at "the government trough" too long. No one, however, questions the magnitude of the challenge that confronts the sector.

As huge as the challenge may be to fill the voids left by declining government services and funding, it is only one of many serious challenges that confront the nonprofit sector at the start of this century. The cover story in the October 2, 1995, issue of *U.S. News and World Report* "exposes" what may be yet a more serious challenge for the sector—its credibility. The headline shouts provocatively: "TAX EXEMPT! Many nonprofits look and act like normal companies—running businesses, making money. So why aren't they paying Uncle Sam?"[7]

> Today, 1.1 million organizations claim tax-exempt status—and many bear little resemblance to traditional charities. They include powerful Washington lobbies, liberal and conservative advocacy groups, professional sports leagues, even companies that sell burial plots. Some are very rich. The J. Paul Getty Trust has $5.7 billion in assets. It owns two hilltops in Los Angeles and is building a sprawling art museum complex on one of them. Some nonprofits are unusual—a trade organization composed of hot-rod racers, for example, and the Breeders' Cup, which promotes thoroughbred racing.
>
> Questionable money-making ventures have given some nonprofits a black eye. The IRS is examining tax deductions of the National Rifle Association. Congress is scrutinizing the business practices of the American Association of Retired Persons. A *U.S. News* review of tax filings, property records, and personnel-compensation arrangements found that nonprofits of all kinds sheltered billions of dollars in profits while paying executives six- and seven-figure salaries. Many nonprofits also use their wealth to lobby Congress for still more favorable treatment. . . . *U.S. News*'s four-month investigation shows that [America] has become the land of the free ride.

This *U.S. News and World Report* story is not an anomaly. It reflects the depth and intensity of the doubts, concerns, and frustrations that the sector now faces in some quarters. It serves as an indicator of a rising tide of lost confidence and growing distrust of the nonprofit sector. Could there be any greater challenge for the sector than regaining lost public confidence? Nonprofit organizations are dependent on public trust. How can nonprofit organizations possibly work successfully to meet other challenges if their credibility is being questioned by those who provide their revenue and who define the boundaries of their revenue-generating activities?

> In Washington, some lawmakers hear stories [of abuses] and lose patience. Flouting government regulations, fat salaries for executives, cozy deal making with for-profit companies through private contracting arrangements—none of that, says a plainly disgusted Rep. Fourtney Pete Stark, a California Democrat, is what the Congress envisioned when it created these exemptions to the Internal Revenue Code so many years ago. The other day, Stark put in legislation to tighten the government's grip on hospitals and others that might be abusing their tax-exempt status. "It's time," Stark says, "to close down the personal piggy banks."[8]

Readings Included in This Part

In "Nonprofits at the Brink," Patrick J. McCormack serves a warning for nonprofits in the social services arena. McCormack's pessimistic predictions are based on two political trends: drastic cuts in the federal government's budget for social services, and the devolution of decisionmaking powers to state and local governments. (See Part 10.)

Cuts in social programs mean that people's needs will be expanding while money will become scarcer. And in this climate of "doing more with less," decisions about social programs are moving from Washington, D.C., out to the states. Cities, states, and counties are being handed control over programs that used to be run by the federal government. State legislators and county commissioners face difficult decisions about how to allocate block grants and whether to cut budgets or raise taxes to make up for the shrinking federal funds. Cutting budgets is far more politically advantageous than raising taxes these days. Elected officials may well opt to cut social service budgets in order to avoid being punished at the polls for raising taxes.

McCormack offers two "survival prescriptions." First, the nonprofit sector must coalesce if it is to succeed in persuading state and local government decisionmakers to allocate "a slice" of the dwindling budgetary "pie" to the types of causes that nonprofit organizations serve. Second, he cautions that even if a relatively large piece of the budgetary pie were to be allocated, money will still be scarce. Nonprofits thus must practice "cutback management" principles now—even though more needs to be done. Without sector unity to influence public policy decisions *and* without implementation of cutback management by individual nonprofits, many organizations in the sector face possible demise.

Lester M. Salamon is perhaps more worried about the sector's future than McCormack is. In "The Current Crisis," Salamon asserts that the nonprofit sector is facing numerous challenges of great severity and magnitude and that any one challenge by itself would represent a stern test for the sector's ability to survive. Salamon groups these challenges into four categories of crises: *fiscal, economic, effectiveness,* and *legitimacy.*

Salamon's *fiscal crisis* mirrors McCormack's analysis. This crisis has been caused by three factors: cuts in government funding; the inability of nonprofits to raise enough money from charitable donors to make up for lost government revenue; and increasing needs of constituents. Thus, nonprofits are expected to serve more people, in more ways, with less money.

The *economic crisis* has developed as nonprofits have turned to businesslike practices in order to supplement dwindling funding from government and stagnant giving by donors. Many nonprofit organizations have entered markets that had been dominated by for-profit firms, and vice versa. Firms in the two sectors often compete directly, and thus the line that once separated the two sectors is becoming hard to discern. (See Part 10.) Citizens and public policymakers are listening to small businesses' cries of "unfair competition" and are questioning whether tax exemption for nonprofits is warranted. Does the nonprofit sector possibly face severe restrictions—or perhaps elimination—of tax exemptions and tax deductibility? If so, how many nonprofits will be forced to close their doors permanently?

The *crisis of effectiveness* has several components. First, many social problems have not been solved that nonprofits have set out to "fix." Some problems may have become worse—or more visible—including poverty, illiteracy, homelessness, youth gangs and their senseless crimes, teenage pregnancies, rape, spouse and child abuse. A public perception of nonprofit ineffectiveness has been growing. At the most cynical level, nonprofits are perceived to have not dealt successfully with problems purposefully—to ensure that they always will have work.

Second, nonprofits are viewed as ineffective because they are "overprofessionalized." Overprofessionalization, particularly in the human services, alienates nonprofits from the populations they serve. Overprofessionalization has created large, cold, impersonal, self-perpetuating bureaucracies. Nonprofits have evolved into the same type of government-like bureaucracies that they were expected to replace.

Third, nonprofits are perceived as ineffective because they have difficulty demonstrating the value of the services they perform, regardless of whether they perform their services well. For example, how do you quantify the value of serving meals to the elderly, and how do you know whether you are providing the service well? These types of questions are difficult for many nonprofits to answer with any degree of certainty, and it costs money to get answers—money that could be used to provide more or better services.

Collectively, the nonprofit sector's financial, economic, and ineffectiveness crises have caused the fourth crisis, a *crisis of legitimacy.* Citizens and elected officials are questioning whether the nonprofit sector should be entitled to favorable tax treatment and preferred contracting status. Salamon argues that the sector's inability to define its role in our current mixed economy is the single greatest force behind this crisis. We still envision a nonprofit as a community-based organization that organizes volunteers to administer to the needy—not as a multistate conglomerate with a director who earns a six-digit salary. Unless the nonprofit sector is able to (re)define its role in the minds and perceptions of citizens and elected officials, the crisis of legitimacy eventually will disable it.

Notes

1. David Van Biema, "Can Charity Fill the Gap? Groups That Help the Poor Are Bracing for a Double Hardship; Surging Need and Federal Budget Cuts," *Time,* December 4, 1995, 44–53.

2. Ibid., p. 53.

3. In Glenn Bailey's home state of Utah, the legislature decided that five years was too generous and opted instead for three years. The first "round" of welfare roll purges in that state began on December 31, 1999.

4. Fred Kammer, president of Catholic Charities USA, quoted in Heather R. McLeod, "The Devolution Revolution—Are Nonprofits Ready?" *WhoCares,* Fall 1995, p. 40.

5. Marvin Olasky, *The Tragedy of American Compassion* (Washington, D.C.: Regnery, 1992).

6. McLeod, "The Devolution Revolution."

7. Edward T. Pound, Gary Cohen, and Penny Loeb, "Tax Exempt! Many Nonprofits Look and Act Like Normal Companies—Running Businesses, Making Money. So Why Aren't They Paying Uncle Sam?" *U.S. News & World Report* October 2, 1995, 36–39, 42–46, 51.

8. Ibid., p. 51.

References

Brown, Montague. "Commentary: The Commercialization of America's Voluntary Health Care System." *Health Care Management Review* 21 (3), 1996, 13–18.

Hasan, Malik. "Let's End the Nonprofit Charade." *New England Journal of Medicine* 334 (16), April 18, 1996, 1055–1058.

McCormack, Patrick J. "Nonprofits at the Brink: Lean Budgets, Growing Needs, and the Fate of Nonprofits. *Northwest Report* 20, April 1996.

McLeod, Heather R. "The Devolution Revolution—Are Nonprofits Ready?" *WhoCares,* Fall 1995, 36–42.

Olasky, Marvin. *The Tragedy of American Compassion.* Washington, D.C.: Regnery, 1992.

Pound, Edward T., Gary Cohen, and Penny Loeb. "Tax Exempt! Many Nonprofits Look and Act Like Normal Companies—Running Businesses, Making Money. So Why Aren't They Paying Uncle Sam?" *U.S. News & World Report,* October 2, 1995, 36–39, 42–46, 51.

Salamon, Lester M., *Holding the Center: America's Nonprofit Sector at a Crossroads.* New York: Nathan Cummings Foundation, 1997.

Van Biema, David. "Can Charity Fill the Gap? Groups That Help the Poor Are Bracing for a Double Hardship; Surging Need and Federal Budget Cuts." *Time,* December 4, 1995, 44–53.

CHAPTER 35

Nonprofits at the Brink: Lean Budgets, Growing Needs, and the Fate of Nonprofits

PATRICK J. MCCORMACK

The world of community and nonprofit organizations is about to undergo a sea change. Budget cuts are inevitable and old familiar ways of doing business are ending. The seven lean years will now commence, and there will be no seven fat years to follow. The result will be a division within the nonprofit community, into lions and lambs, the savvy and the slow to change, the survivors and the well-meaning folks down the road whose doors are closing.

Republican Congressional budget proposals envision cuts totaling more than $500 billion over the next seven years. These are cuts in the rate of anticipated growth, but that anticipation of larger federal budget increases was not hollow or silly. Cutting the growth rate in federal programs leaves barely enough funds for existing needs. Demographic changes are imminent that will swamp social service programs. Yet states wish to adopt *more* cuts in their budgets, on top of federal cuts. We are about to lower the seawall when flood warnings have been posted.

Nonprofits receive between 15 and 20 percent of their funding directly from federal grants, and another 20 to 40 percent through indirect fees generated by federal programs. Federal cuts will be compounded by state budget cuts in many states, as governors try to prevent tax increases. There is no way that charity, foundation support, or the private sector can replace the lost state and federal funds.

The challenge for the next 10 years will not simply be surviving the loss of money. The structural changes in federal commitment and the demographic changes in American society are about to create a pincer movement that will grip most tightly upon the nonprofit community. Can a way be found to continue helping people? This is the challenge that awaits, when the fear subsides and the smoke clears and the social service community finds itself cash poor amid clamoring needs.

Real Cuts Are Needed

The key is that federal cuts are inevitable, this year or next, and have been called for by responsible Democrats of all sorts.

Yes, Democrats. For example, the Clinton budget proposals envision cuts in Medicare of just under $100 billion by the year 2002. Moderate Congressional Democrats envision cuts for all programs totaling well over $300 billion over the next seven years. Senator Bob Kerry, a Democrat from Nebraska, was a crucial member of a national commission on entitlements that called for drastic changes in social spending. Minnesota Congressman Martin Sabo has found himself this year working behind the scenes in the Capitol to find smaller, more palatable *cuts*.

Now, throw in the Republicans, who have framed the debate and brought all sides to the cutting room. The result is a consensus on cutting, and even a consensus on the general amount of the cuts to be made.

This is because the need for change is real, and undeniable. Entitlements as a percentage of the federal budget have grown from 23 percent in 1963 to 47 percent in 1993, and will swallow the entire federal budget whole, 100 percent, by the year 2030. This is a product of the baby boom generation, who will require senior services at an alarming rate. Bluntly put, entitlements must be cut, and cut even deeper than current Republican proposals, if the federal government is to survive. The most drastic Medicare cuts yet envisioned only keep the system solvent until around the year 2010.

How Deep Are the Cuts?

It is clear that either the Clinton or the Congressional budget will require major reductions in growth. The cash is impressive, but the real story lies in who is cut, and how the changes in money affect the changes in program incentives. The budget cuts will be accompanied by programmatic changes, including new requirements for efficiency, outcome measurement, and responsiveness to state, or even county, demands.

The budget cuts will fall on users of federal services, and it is fair to say that the affected people are of lower income and higher vulnerability than the general population. However, some of the sufferers are hospitals, schools, daycare centers, federal offices, military bases, rural areas, and inner cities . . . there is enough pain to go around.

A number of struggling rural hospitals will fail, close, or consolidate. The urban hospitals will not escape this trend, and consolidations, specialization, and integration with larger health companies will continue.

Health care will move to managed care at unprecedented rates, meaning that capitation will reign. Capitation is the payment of a fixed rate for a set of services, regardless of loss or claims experience. This will be the model for all social services in the coming years. Nonprofits will be contractors and will receive a check, and be held accountable for all needed services for the year. If the check runs out, tough luck. Capitation also means outcome measurement, as governments demand that measures of success be compiled and that funding be tied to accurate research.

As money dwindles needs will blossom. An example: The number of people who will qualify for social services is projected to increase at a rate of between 8 and 11 percent per year in the next five years, according to Congressional and census estimates. The Congressional budget envisions growth of between 2 and 4 percent per year, possibly not even enough to offset inflation, much less address growing demographic needs. This wedge between needs and federal commitments will grow each year into the next decade.

At this moment some states and nonprofits are fooled, because even the most stringent Congressional budgets really don't hurt programs in 1996. Small cuts are compounded in later years by the cap placed under Congressional budgets. In other words, programs will no longer expand when needs increase, but will grow only at a capped percentage, making the budget shortfalls worse each and every year.

States Become Real Players

When federal funds come into state legislatures, the dollars typically have long strings attached. How can Oregon or Idaho spend the money they received this year? Only in accordance with federal rules that spell out who gets the money, how it can be spent in various areas of the state, and even what color pencils are used to fill out forms (a *slight* exaggeration). This is changing under the block grants proposed for Medicaid, welfare reform, jobs and training, education, and other parts of the social services budget. Block grants are lumps of cash that are given for a general purpose, such as welfare, and that allow states great leeway regarding how the cash can be spent. Block grants typically grow at some capped percentage, which saves money for the federal government but ignores inflation or increases in needs.

States will assume new powers and responsibilities. In addition to block grants, simple relaxation of federal rules will permit new latitude for the states. Latitude means decisions made by states, some of which will infuriate nonprofits.

Many federal programs require that equal services be given to all program participants. These and other federal requirements will go by the board, resulting in a new environment. When states decide the how, who, and what of budgets, they might also decide to fund nonprofit A and not nonprofit B. Or they might turn the entire industry over to a for-profit bidder.

The states will have to make up their minds about how these programs should operate. This in itself is a change. States have often relied upon the federal rules and requirements to forestall any bickering about who gets what, or who operates what. Those decisions are coming to the states—and to the counties.

The Impact on Community and Nonprofit Organizations

If funds are increasingly fungible between programs and purposes, nonprofits will have to compete for their funding with other community organizations, and with for-profit firms that want to slice up the existing social services market. If states or counties are going to be deciding how services are delivered, they might also be picking winners or losers among the service delivery industry.

The budget cuts are real, and imminent. Fiscal analysts in several states were interviewed for this article. Most were sanguine about the short term, and some even expected short-term increases in transportation and other funds. This faux optimism means that the near future is a time akin to the Phony War between Germany and France in 1940, before the shooting started.

The initial need is for cutback management. Political analyst Robert Behn wrote a seminal article on the politics of cutbacks in the public sector ("Cutback Management," *Journal of Policy Analysis and Management,* Winter 1985), but any private sector firm that has survived the past decade can provide a blueprint on cutting back. Nonprofits will see cuts in budgets, staff reductions, shifts to part-time or temporary staff, consolidations, and elimination of middle managers.

There are some discomforting parallels between the community and nonprofit sectors and other industries that have suffered budget shortfalls. Every industry that has lost income or market share begins by cutting middle levels, from AT&T laying off 50 percent of middle management in 1995 to the nonprofit sector's coming shake-out in the late nineties. The first option is always belt tightening, a move that lacks imagination but is absolutely necessary and establishes a manager's credibility for later, more imaginative steps.

Behn calls for a reexamination of the central mission of the organization, as a first step towards directing the cutbacks.

The blunt reality: After seeking these paltry management savings there are only three remaining ways to cut. Payments to providers can be lowered, but only to an extent. Benefits can be reduced to some lower level, if the community agrees. Eligibility can be tightened, and as a result people can be turned away.

How will the social service industry respond? More or less intelligently. More or less efficiently. People run these organizations, and people do not like to admit that times are changing. There was a time when being a middle manager at AT&T ensured a 35-year career. Now the telecommunications business is cutthroat, with competitive profit margins. The nonprofit sector will change itself, or be changed.

The Dark Side

If you have read this far, you might think I have already covered the dark side. Hardly. The history of the social service industry over the past 30 years has been one of generally rising federal funding, even during the Reagan years. The most stringent cuts ever achieved by President Reagan were a bare fraction of the cuts called for in the *Clinton* budget proposal. There are a number of storm clouds on the horizon.

The first dark cloud: *Less money means less money.* If I would underline this point and put it in extra large type, the point would still not be made as forcefully as necessary. Less money means that the incentives within the current system will change. Does it make sense now to close that rural hospital? Shall we cut medical school sizes? Will capitation mean risk-sharing by nonprofits, meaning bankruptcies?

The second storm cloud: *States and counties have flexibility.* Legislators or county board members can take funds from welfare and spend it on nursing homes, or roads, or cops. This means the state legislature or county board will become the nexus for political wars. It will be my need against your need, county against state, a nonprofit that measures against a nonprofit that is not sophisticated and cannot provide outcome measures.

The third cloud: *Nonprofits will need to be their own best advocates.* They will need to actively promote themselves and the issues and constituents they represent. They will need to bid for contracts. They will need to become sophisticated. Lobbying and advocacy in the broadest sense are sophisticated arts, and nonprofits are neophytes.

The fourth, and this is a real thunderhead: *Needs will explode.* Demographics suggest that the elderly population in all states will soon double and triple—especially in rural areas. For example, the most conservative of three census projections estimates that there will be 9.8 million persons over age 85 living in the United States in the year 2050, triple the figure of 3.5 million in 1995. The most pessimistic estimate is that almost 17 million people over age 85 will be alive and needing services. These people use social services at an alarming rate. There is no credible example of state or federal recognition of this demographic reality.

The final thunder-banger for the late 1990s: *The middle class will be restless.* Politicians will be faced with competing interests between the middle class and those in need. Traditional political favorites, such as tax cuts, property tax buy-backs, higher-education grants, and other middle-class entitlements, will be expanded only at a direct cost to programs aimed at the needs of the poor, the elderly, and children. There is a sad truth: County boards and legislatures tend to represent the interests of the middle-class voter over those of the poor nonvoter.

Changes or Opportunities?

One of the most banal claims, oft repeated by every would-be futurist with a laptop, is that changes are coming. Well, changes are coming. The key for the long-term survival of the nonprofit community will be in understanding the subtexts and underlying realities behind the big headlines. This is a task for statewide and multistate organizations of nonprofits and community groups. Perhaps a broad coalition of interested nonprofits can avoid being bamboozled by clever budget analysts and legislative staffers.

Will nonprofits be companionable, and seek joint answers to the problems they face? Creating a well-staffed statewide or multistate response seems like one hopeful answer to the new competitive pressures that are coming. But it is entirely likely that even with such cooperation, a war of the nonprofits will break out. When the folks down the road bid on *your* contract, a bit of friendliness will be lost.

I'm always struck by the before and after snapshots of people on diets. Something has happened to change those folks, something determinative. This is the short-term future for the social service industry. A diet is coming, and the sad fact is, most "before" pictures of the nonprofit community look pretty skinny already.

► CHAPTER 36

The Current Crisis

LESTER M. SALAMON

For a variety of reasons, this set of institutions that is so crucial to the preservation of the American experience now faces an extraordinary series of challenges. Each of these challenges by itself would tax the staying power of this sector. What makes the current situation particularly troubling is that several different challenges are hitting the sector at once. The degrees of freedom available to nonprofit managers are therefore declining dramatically, leading many to give up on the nonprofit form altogether.

It seems clear to this author that an unusual series of challenges *does* confront the American nonprofit sector at the present time, that these challenges affect a significant portion of the sector, and that considerable harm could be done to a set of institutions in which Americans have a crucial stake if these challenges are not effectively addressed. More particularly, four such challenges seem especially prevalent. Together they constitute an emerging crisis of the American nonprofit sector.

The Fiscal Crisis

The most visible of these crises is fiscal in character: *Key portions of the nonprofit sector face a*

continuing decline in one of their most important sources of support—i.e., government revenue—and seem unlikely to be able to make it up from the source that is widely assumed to be the most likely alternative—i.e., private charitable giving. This is taking place, moreover, at a time of increased need for the services that nonprofits provide.

Background: Nonprofit Federalism

To understand the nature of this challenge, it is necessary to review briefly the recent history of nonprofit finances. Perhaps the most salient feature of this history has been the vast expansion of governmental support to nonprofit organizations, particularly during the 20 years that began with the Great Society era of the mid–1960s. Faced with expanding pressures to alleviate the serious poverty and distress that became increasingly visible in the late 1950s and early 1960s, the federal government responded with a host of new programs that relied extensively on private, nonprofit organizations for their implementation. The result was the emergence of an elaborate and widespread partnership between government and the nonprofit sector in a wide variety of fields.[1]

The Reagan Cutbacks

Against this background, the election of Ronald Reagan in 1980 produced a significant reversal. Justifying its moves as an effort to get government out of the nonprofit sector's way, the Reagan administration significantly reduced government spending in many of the fields where nonprofits are active. In the process, however, it also reduced a significant source of nonprofit revenue and hence the ability of nonprofit organizations to meet the expanded need. Although federal spending continued to grow in the health field, elsewhere it declined by approximately 25 percent in the early 1980s and had not returned to its 1980 level in inflation-adjusted terms by fiscal year 1994.

Although spending in many of these fields began to increase again in the late 1980s and early 1990s, nonprofit organizations outside of the health field nevertheless lost a cumulative total of $38 billion in federal revenue between 1982 and 1994 compared to what they would have had available if 1980 spending levels had been maintained.

The "Contract with America" Cuts

With the election of a Republican majority in Congress in 1994, the pressures on nonprofit revenues from government returned with a vengeance. Committed through their *Contract with America* not only to eliminate the Reagan-

era federal deficit but also to accommodate a further massive tax cut, Republican budget planners targeted not only the "discretionary" programs that had been the object of Reagan-era cuts, but key facets of the Federal government's "entitlement" protections as well, including Medicaid, Medicare, and Aid to Families with Dependent Children.[2]

These cutbacks reduced federal support for nonprofit organizations under these programs by an estimated $1.7 billion, or about 10 percent, in FY 1996 alone. In addition to this, the welfare reform bill adopted in the summer of 1996 eliminated one of the major entitlement programs providing assistance to the poor, thus potentially putting further demand on the services available through nonprofit organizations.[3]

Complicating matters further, while state governments proved able to offset at least some of the cutbacks in federal discretionary spending during the 1980s, this time the advocates of retrenchment are firmly ensconced at the state level as well, even in states such as New York and New Jersey that have traditionally supported generally progressive social policies. All of these factors increase the likelihood that cuts at the federal level will be sustained in the states.

These projected reductions in federal spending mean further increases in the demands on nonprofit agencies. At the same time, however, they also mean further reductions in the *revenues* nonprofit agencies have available to meet those demands. Thus, as shown in Table 36.1,

TABLE 36.1   Projected Changes in Nonprofit Revenues from Federal Sources, FY 1997–2002: FY 1997 Congressional Budget Resolution vs. Actual FY 1995 Spending (in billions of 1995 dollars)

	Proposed vs. FY 1995 Actual		Cumulative Change Proposed FY 1997–2002 vs. FY 1995
	Amount	%	
Education, Training, Social Services	−3.6	−24%	−13.1
Community and Regional Development	−0.4	−51%	−1.4
Health	−19.7	−17%	−67.6
International Affairs	−0.5	−45%	−2.0
Total	−$24.1	−18%	−$89.1

SOURCE: Alan J. Abramson and Lester M. Salamon, "FY 1997 Federal Budget: Implications for the Nonprofit Sector," (June 1996).

the FY 1997 budget resolution projects an 18 percent reduction below FY 1995 levels in the inflation-adjusted value of federal support to nonprofit organizations as of FY 2002. Indeed, if Congress follows the guidelines it has established for itself in this budget resolution, nonprofit organizations stand to lose a cumulative total of close to $90 billion in Federal support over the FY 1997–2002 period. This would significantly reduce federal support to nonprofit organizations in such fields as education and training, employment, social services, community development, health, international assistance, and arts and culture.

Constraints on Private Charitable Growth

To what extent can we reasonably expect increases in private giving to offset these reductions in federal expenditures on programs of interest to nonprofit organizations, and ultimately in federal support to nonprofit organizations, as advocates of the cuts have hoped? The answer, it seems, is not very much. For one thing, the scale of increases required is overwhelming. In order to offset just the direct revenue losses that nonprofits will endure if even the FY 1997 Congressional Budget Resolution, let alone the original *Contract with America* Budget Resolution, is implemented, private giving would have to grow by 12 percent above the rate of inflation in fiscal year 1997, by 16 percent in fiscal year 1998, and by 32 percent as of fiscal year 2002. Yet the recent growth has rarely exceeded the inflation rate by even 3 percent.

The history of private giving growth in the 1980s, the last time giving was called on to offset significant budget cuts, is hardly encouraging, however. In fact:

- Individual giving as a share of personal income actually declined during the 1980s, from an average of 1.81 percent per year over the period 1973–82 to 1.76 percent over the period 1983–1992.[4]
- One reason for this may have been the increase in the standard deduction on the federal income tax forms and the resulting

decline in the share of taxpayers who itemize their deductions, including their charitable deductions. By 1992, the proportion of itemizers was down to 29 percent and the proportion claiming charitable deductions down to 26 percent.[5] Since research has shown that itemizers tend to give more to charity than do non-itemizers, this reduction in the share of taxpayers itemizing their deductions has a negative impact on charitable giving.

- At the same time, the liberalization of tax rates during the 1980s, particularly at the upper income levels, seems to have reduced the incentives to give among upper income taxpayers, who received the greatest benefits from the tax changes. This result runs counter to the hopes of those who claimed that the 1986 tax act, by reducing marginal tax rates for upper income taxpayers and thus leaving more money in their hands, would encourage these taxpayers to contribute more to charity. The actual outcome seems more consistent with econometric models suggesting that when the out-of-pocket "cost" of giving increases, as it does when tax rates fall, the incentive to give declines and giving falls off.

- Changes in tax law also seem to have affected *bequest* giving. Well over 80 percent of all estates make no provision for charitable bequests; this share seems to be falling; and so is the share of all estate wealth that finds its way into charitable bequests.[6] This is sobering news indeed for those who have looked to the inter-generational transfer of wealth that now seems to be under way as a source of immense new income for charitable institutions.

- In the case of corporations, increased giving in the early 1980s was not sustained in the latter 1980s, and actually reversed course and declined in real terms in the early 1990s.

Reflecting these various developments, private giving, far from filling in for government cutbacks, actually lost ground as a source of nonprofit revenue during the decade that began with the Reagan budget cuts. In particular, as reflected in Table 36.2, giving fell from 15 percent of total nonprofit revenue in 1982 to 11 percent in 1992. In only two fields (civic and culture), in fact, did giving gain ground during this period, but these are relatively small components of the sector.

Complicating things further is the fact that the *composition,* as opposed to the scale, of giving does not seem to match the profile of government spending sufficiently to suggest that one could be a substitute for the other *even if the amounts were equivalent.* Generally speaking, giving is greatest where wealth is greatest, rather than where the need is greatest. What is more, much of private giving flows not to those in greatest need but to functions with a significant "amenity" value to the givers (e.g., education, culture).

Recent Tax Overhaul Proposals

Despite the recent rhetoric in Congress about the need to devolve power to the local level, moreover, recent proposals for major tax reform would likely impose additional burdens on nonprofit organizations and further reduce the financial incentives for giving. Essentially, these proposals would shift the basis of federal taxation from income to consumption. Not only would this expose nonprofit organizations to taxation on at least some of their activities (since nonprofits "consume" even though they

do not "earn" income), but also it could seriously disrupt, and most likely considerably weaken, the current incentives for charitable contributions. For example:

- A proposal by Congressman Armey to replace the federal income tax with a "flat tax" would eliminate the charitable deduction for both individuals and businesses.
- The proposal originally advanced by Senators Nunn and Domenici to replace the federal income tax with a so-called "Value Added Tax" would eliminate the deductibility of charitable contributions for businesses.
- A proposed National Retail Sales Tax would also eliminate the charitable deduction for income, estate, and gift taxes. In addition, it would treat any property or personal services received as a result of contributions or dues to not-for-profit organizations as purchases that would be taxed at their fair market value.[7]

In addition to their likely negative impact on charitable contributions, and hence on the *revenues* of nonprofit organizations, these proposals would also expose nonprofit organizations to direct taxes on some of their activities, thus increasing their *costs.*

As this writing, it seems unlikely that any of these overhaul proposals will be enacted in the foreseeable future. At the same time, as least some of the concepts embodied in these proposals may see the light of day. For example, small business leaders seem likely to push for establishment of a "commerciality test" in deciding which nonprofit activities are subject to taxation. Under such a provision, any nonprofit activity for which there is a commercially available alternative would be subject to tax, regardless of whether it is a "related" or "unrelated" activity.

Other Tax Measures

Beyond these proposals for federal tax restructuring, moreover, nonprofit organizations are also confronting mounting opposition to the

TABLE 36.2 Private Giving as a Share of Nonprofit Revenue, 1982–1992 (as % of Total Nonprofit Revenues)

Subsector	1982	1992
Health	11	5
Education	15	15
Social services	26	21
Civic	31	32
Arts, culture	40	47
Total	15%	11%

NOTE: Private giving includes giving from individuals, foundations, corporations, and bequests.

SOURCE: Computed from data in *Nonprofit Almanac*, 1996.

definition of what constitutes a "charity" for tax purposes, restricting it, for example, to organizations that primarily or exclusively serve the poor. These are the proposals either to replace the current charitable deduction system, or to augment it, with a system of *tax credits*. Unlike tax deductions, which deliver their benefits by reducing the taxable income on which taxpayers compute their tax obligations, tax credits deliver their benefits by directly reducing the taxes a taxpayer owes by the full amount, or a given fraction of the amount, of the charitable gift. Under a tax credit, therefore, the tax benefit resulting from a given gift does not vary with the tax bracket of the taxpayer, as it does under the current tax deduction system.

Whether these various issues can be worked out in the near term and a tax credit program put in place is far from certain at this writing. More likely is a continued fiscal squeeze, particularly on agencies serving those in greatest need.

The Economic Crisis

In addition to the fiscal crisis facing nonprofit organizations as a consequence of reduced government support and tepid growth in private giving is a broader economic crisis in which these organizations also find themselves. In fact, these two crises are interrelated. Fiscal pressures resulting from decreased or uncertain government support have induced nonprofit organizations to seek alternative sources of financial support. Finding inadequate support from private charity, they have turned increasingly to fees and service charges, often with quite good effect. This source alone accounted for 52 percent of the growth of the nonprofit sector during the 1982–92 period.

While this "marketization" has enabled nonprofit organizations to survive the Reagan-era budget cuts and prosper, it nevertheless has also exposed them to significant new challenges. In a sense, the nonprofit sector may be the victim of its own success. Having created, or newly entered, markets that could yield substantial commercial returns, it is now encountering massive competition from for-profit providers attracted

to these same markets. In addition, service purchasers in many of these markets are squeezing profit margins severely, undermining the ability of the nonprofit providers to subsidize the "mission-related" activities such as charity care or research that pushed them into these markets in the first place. This, in turn, has narrowed the differences between the nonprofit and for-profit providers, obscuring the distinctive image of the nonprofit providers and raising fundamental questions about the justification for the tax advantages that nonprofit organizations enjoy. What is more, it has begun to induce nonprofits to convert to for-profit status in order to attract the capital required to survive. In this way, through a series of incremental steps, the basic viability of the nonprofit form appears to be under challenge in a number of fields. While it may be premature to conclude, paraphrasing T. S. Eliot, that this is the way the nonprofit sector will end, "not with a bang but a whimper," the fact remains that numerous nonprofit organizations are facing serious challenges of precisely this sort.

Health Care Shifts

These developments are perhaps most clearly evident in the health field. Already by 1977, well over half (54 percent) of all nonprofit health-organization income came from commercial fees and charges, much of it from third-party insurance payments. Along with the growth of the federal Medicare and Medicaid programs, which pumped immense resources into the health care sector, this commercial activity attracted for-profit providers into the field.

While this trend toward for-profit expansion in the hospital field slowed in the latter 1980s and early 1990s, it has recently resumed with a vengeance. This time, however, the vehicle is not the establishment of new for-profit institutions but the take-over of nonprofit institutions or their conversion into for-profit status. Thus, thirty-one nonprofit hospitals shifted from nonprofit to for-profit status in 1994, usually through acquisitions by for-profit chains; and this number increased to 59 in 1995, with another 200 reported in active discussion.[8] What is more, nonprofit Blue Cross and Blue Shield in-surance organizations are under-going similar transformations in major markets from Califor-nia to New York.[9]

What lies behind these changes is a series of profound shifts in the basic structure of the health care market, which have greatly intensi-fied competitive pressures and put nonprofit providers at a distinct disadvantage. Because of their inability to offer investors a return on their equity, nonprofit hospitals find it increasingly difficult to compete. This has led some ob-servers to conclude, as one recent article in the *New England Journal of Medicine* put it, that "nonprofit health plans are a byproduct of the past."[10] While such a conclusion would seem premature, the pressures on nonprofit health providers are severe.

Human Services

While the economic pressures on nonprofit health providers are especially salient, similar pressures are also confronting other types of nonprofit organizations, including those pro-viding social services. As noted above, nonprofit social service agencies experienced especially ro-bust growth during the 1980s. One reason for this was the ability of these agencies to tap into the government's health care reimbursement and other entitlement programs to offer home health, day care, and related services. At least as important, however, was the growth of fee income.

As with the health care field, however, non-profit providers have not been free to pursue these sources of support on their own. To the contrary, intense competition has emerged from for-profit providers. What is more, the for-profit providers seem to be gaining the edge in a num-ber of crucial areas. For-profit firms accounted for 80 percent of the growth in *day care* estab-lishments and 70 percent of the growth in day care employees between 1977 and 1992, even though they started the period with only 57 per-cent of the centers and 46 percent of the em-ployees. In the *home health* field, one of the most explosive in recent years, for-profits essentially displaced nonprofit providers during this pe-riod, accounting for all of the growth in estab-lishments and 74 percent of the growth in em-ployment, although they started the period with well under 50 percent of both. It is therefore no real surprise that the ink was hardly dry on the recent welfare reform bill before stories began to circulate of huge state contracts with for-profit companies, including giants like Lockheed Mar-tin and Andersen Consulting, to manage the complex process involved in moving millions of welfare recipients into jobs.[11] In this field, as in many others, the assumption of nonprofit dom-inance is therefore clearly a thing of the past.

Arts and Education

Nonprofit arts and education institutions have also found themselves drawn into difficult com-petitive dilemmas. For arts institutions, the sig-nificant slowing of federal support along with increased difficulties in attracting corporate and foundation support have necessitated a wide variety of innovative "marketing" efforts, in-cluding substantial increases in ticket prices, de-velopment of varied outreach programs at shopping malls or outdoor venues, and the mar-keting of various related products, such as books, reproductions of paintings, and compact discs. In addition, the competition from the commercial entertainment industry has led many nonprofit groups to emphasize popular, and therefore more remunerative, activities over those with potentially greater artistic value. Taken together, these activities are increasingly exposing arts organizations as well to growing challenges about the legitimacy of their tax exemptions.

The case of higher education is more com-plex, but also revealing. The growth of nonprofit education has lagged behind that of other seg-ments of the nonprofit sector.

To offset these fiscal pressures, nonprofit in-stitutions of higher education, like their coun-terparts elsewhere in the nonprofit sector, are increasingly moving into essentially commercial markets. Medical schools have already paved the way for this in the form of clinical practice, which provides a significant share of medical school income nationwide.[12] As part of this general thrust, universities are actively exploring partnerships with private business under which the businesses will invest in university-based research and then share the proceeds of any discoveries that result.

Whether this new commercial involvement by higher education institutions will prove to be blessing or a curse is still far from clear. For one thing, corporate support is likely to be no more reliable than governmental support, and probably less so. Second, heavy reliance on this source of support could seriously distort research priorities and undercut the more basic research that has proved to be the foundation for the success of American higher education. Finally, higher education institutions may find themselves challenged by competing research organizations that can demonstrate more cost-effective ways to carry out the research that corporations need. Indeed, many university professors, newly acquainted with business entrepreneurs, may find it more advantageous to handle their research grants through separate for-profit labs than through the university system, thus denying universities the benefits they seek through these arrangements. If this were to occur on a significant scale, it could fundamentally challenge the whole concept of the modern research university and return the university to its pre-nineteenth-century form as essentially a teaching institution.

Summary

In short, the fiscal pressures nonprofits face have induced them to enter fields of activity in which they encounter increasing competition from for-profit providers. In the process, many of the most crucial features of this sector have been put at risk, including the sector's gap-filling role, its willingness to address unmet needs, its innovativeness, its altruism, and its trustworthiness. Indeed, many of these activities have placed nonprofit organizations on a slippery slope that has led them to begin abandoning the nonprofit form altogether. While this may not have negative consequences in the short run, the long-term consequences could be severe, eliminating a crucial element of diversity and weakening a

vital mechanism for promoting the values of community.

The Crisis of Effectiveness

In addition to the fiscal and economic crises facing the nonprofit sector at the present time, a significant *crisis of effectiveness* has surfaced in recent years. Because they do not meet a "market test," nonprofits are always vulnerable to charges that they are inefficient in their use of resources and ineffective in their approaches to problems. The scope and severity of these charges have grown massively in recent years, however. In fact, the competence of the nonprofit sector has been challenged on at least three different grounds.

Programmatic Opposition

In the first place, nonprofit organizations, particularly in the human service field, have been implicated in the general assault on public social programs that has animated national political debate for more than a decade now. Despite considerable contrary evidence,[13] the persistence of poverty, the alarming growth of urban crime, the epidemic of teen-age pregnancy, and the continuation of welfare dependency have been taken as evidence that these programs not only do not work, but actually make the problems worse. The resulting open season on government social programs has caught major components of the nonprofit sector in the crossfire, particularly since the sector has been involved in administering many of the programs that are being attacked. Worse than that, the very motives of the nonprofit agencies have been called into question. Involvement in government programs "changes charities' incentives," charges one recent critique, "giving them reasons to keep caseloads up instead of getting them down by successfully turning around peoples' lives."[14] That the assault on these programs has failed to differentiate clearly between the successful and the unsuccessful, that the levels of resources committed to the programs have actually been far less than assumed, and that many of the difficulties these programs have encountered have resulted less from the incapacities of the agencies charged with administering them than with the complex administrative arrangements through which they were forced to operate—all of these factors have not diminished in the least the intensity of the criticisms. In the process, much of the nonprofit human service delivery system has been discredited as a viable instrument for coping with poverty and distress.[15]

The Professionalization Critique

Beyond the political assault on Great Society social programs lies a more profound line of criticism that takes nonprofit organizations to task for becoming a principal locus for the "overprofessionalization" of societal problem-solving. The emergence of a therapeutically oriented casework pattern in social work led social workers away from social diagnosis, community organizing, and social reform—tasks that social workers were uniquely in a position to perform—leaving "a vacuum which remains unfilled."[16] The upshot, widely recognized in the 1960s and 1970s, was a growing alienation of the social work profession and the human service organizations employing them from the impoverished people they were supposed to serve.[17]

A similar process of alienation has been identified in the case of nonprofit hospitals as they were transformed from small community institutions into large, professionalized bureaucracies early in this century.

This critique of professionalism has gained increased force in recent years, however, as a product of political developments on both the political Left and the political Right. On the Left, the critique of professionalism has figured prominently in the new search for "community." According to this line of thinking, the professionalization of social concerns, by redefining basic human needs as "problems" that only professionals can resolve, has alienated people from the helping relationships they could establish with their neighbors and kin. Not only does this undermine community, but it also typically fails

to meet the need. Far from fostering social capital and building a sense of community, in other words, nonprofit organizations, by embracing professionalism, have become an enemy of community instead.

Critics on the Right have been equally contemptuous of the professionalized human service apparatus, charging it with inflating the cost of dealing with social problems by "crowding out" lower-cost alternative approaches involving informal networks of families and friends.[18] Similar arguments have been lodged, moreover, against nonprofit educational institutions and cultural institutions. In both cases, the institutions are faulted for being run by and for the professionals who inhabit them rather than for the society that supports them or those, such as students, who need their help.[19]

The Accountability Movement

Complicating matters further is the fact that nonprofit organizations generally lack meaningful bases for demonstrating the value of what they do. Indeed, nonprofit organizations have often resisted demands for greater accountability on grounds that responding to such demands might interfere with the independence that gives the sector its special character. Instead, nonprofits have tended to point to their not-for-profit status as *ipso facto* evidence of their trustworthiness and effectiveness. Indeed, the trustworthiness supposedly bequeathed by this "nondistribution constraint" has long been one of the principal rationales claimed for the nonprofit form. According to this line of argument, nonprofit organizations are needed precisely to overcome the inherent limitations of the market in situations where information is lacking to allow consumers to make informed choices in the marketplace, and where a higher element of trust is therefore required.[20]

Increasingly, however, these implicit claims by nonprofit providers have been subjected to serious challenge as a result not only of several recent scandals, but also of growing questions about the basic efficiency and effectiveness of nonprofit agencies. "Unlike publicly traded companies," management expert Regina

Herzlinger has thus noted, "the performance of nonprofits and governments is shrouded behind a veil of secrecy that is lifted only when blatant disasters occur."[21] This is problematic, she argues, because nonprofit organizations generally lack the three basic accountability mechanisms of business: the self-interest of owners, competition, and the ultimate bottom-line measure of profitability. Nor do the existing reporting requirements on nonprofit organizations offer much help. The Form 990 that nonprofits must file annually with the Internal Revenue Service contains precious little performance information, and even the basic financial data that organizations file have been found to contain massive error rates. Since the Internal Revenue Service generates no revenue from careful scrutiny of these filings, it naturally devotes little energy to auditing them. Nor do federated fundraising organizations such as United Way systematically review and publicize the performance of their member organizations. Even if they did, the overall impact would be slight since the number of member organizations in any community is quite small.

These concerns have prompted a serious re-evaluation of accountability mechanisms within the nonprofit sector.[22] One line of response has been to strengthen the formal mechanisms for penalizing nonprofit agencies that violate prohibitions against "private inurement," i.e., the use of the nonprofit form for private gain. Thus, in an effort to facilitate greater enforcement of these prohibitions, the Taxpayers' Bill of Rights enacted in the summer of 1996 gives the IRS "intermediate sanctions" in the form of penalty taxes to impose on organizations that violate the "private inurement" rules. However, private inurement is only the most egregious of the accountability problems the nonprofit sector faces, and attention to the other aspects of organizational performance remains a pressing concern.

Crisis of Legitimacy

Behind the fiscal, economic, and competence issues facing the nonprofit sector at the present time, finally, is a much more fundamental moral or political challenge, a veritable crisis of legitimacy that has raised basic questions about the whole concept of the nonprofit sector and about the sector's entitlement to the special tax and other advantages it enjoys.

In a sense, the nonprofit sector's success at adjusting to the realities of postwar American society may ironically be costing it the support of significant elements of the American public, who remain wedded to a nineteenth-century image of charity and altruism, of small voluntary groups ministering to the needy and downtrodden. The nonprofit sector is thus being hoisted on its own mythology. Having failed to make clear to the American public what its role should be in a mature mixed economy, the sector has been thrown on the defensive by revelations that it is not operating the way its own mythology would suggest. A massive gap has thus opened between the modern reality of a sector intimately involved with government and moving into commercial activities in the wake of governmental cutbacks, and the popular image of a set of community-based institutions mobilizing purely voluntary energies to assist those in need. Against this backdrop, disclosures of the sort involved in the United Way and New Era Philanthropy scandals, and revelations about the salaries of some nonprofit executives, have fallen on unusually fertile ground. The upshot has been a series of fundamental challenges to the sector's credibility and privileged position. These challenges are evident in at least four different forums.

Public Attitudes

In the first place, there is evidence of a deterioration in public confidence in charitable institutions. Recent Gallup surveys of giving and volunteering reveal that as of 1994 only about one-third of the American population expressed "a great deal" or "quite a lot" of confidence in nonprofit organizations outside of religion and education.

This apparent weakening of the attachment Americans feel towards private charitable institutions has not been entirely spontaneous. It has been encouraged by a strident conservative assault against key components of the nonprofit sector. Conservative critics have come to recognize the significant role that nonprofit organizations have played in surfacing public problems and mobilizing public support for their resolution. Rather than applauding this crucial advocacy function of nonprofit organizations as a sign of the vibrancy of American democracy, however, they deplore it as a potent mechanism for fueling the continued growth of the modern welfare state. Entire organizations have thus been formed to challenge the presumed emergence of a "new kind of nonprofit organization, dedicated not to voluntary action, but to an expanded government role in our lives."[23] Attacks on nonprofit organizations have thus become a staple of conservative talk radio and fodder for conservative columnists. Of special focus, moreover, has been the growth of government-nonprofit cooperation, which, in the eyes of conservative critics, has transformed nonprofit organizations into just another group of supplicants "feasting at the public trough" and therefore unable to represent the public interest with objectivity.[24] Given this kind of assault, it is perhaps no wonder that significant portions of the public might begin to question what the nonprofit sector truly represents.

Tax Exemption Challenge

Squeezed by the same budget cuts and growing service needs that are affecting nonprofit organizations, state and local governments have increasingly begun looking at tax-exempt charitable institutions as a potential source not just of programmatic, but also of fiscal, relief. The upshot has been a marked escalation of state and local government challenges to the property and income tax exemptions that nonprofit organizations have long enjoyed at the local level.[25]

- Health organizations, perhaps the most exposed part of the nonprofit sector because of their scale and commercial prowess, were among the first to feel the effects of this sentiment.[26] Nonprofit Health Maintenance Organizations faced threats to their tax-exempt status early on,

and this proved to be one of the factors leading most of them to convert to the for-profit form over the past 20 years. Blue Cross health insurance organizations lost most of their federal tax benefits in the 1986 Tax Reform Act, and many of them are now following the HMOs into the for-profit world. Now assaults are being mounted against the tax exemptions of hospitals. Such challenges were "unheard of in decades past,"[27] yet they have recently surfaced in more than 20 states.

- In the course of challenging the tax exemptions of hospitals, states are establishing legal precedents that could have far wider implications. Recent state supreme court decisions in Utah and Pennsylvania, for example, have explicitly rejected the prevailing Federal common law concept of "charity" so far as hospitals are concerned. Under this common law precept, the promotion of health is considered to be an inherently charitable activity. Nonprofit hospitals thus qualify for charitable status even if their patients pay for their care so long as the institutions use all profits for "the maintenance or improvement of the institution or some other charitable purpose."[28] Instead of this standard, the Utah Supreme Court established a *quid pro quo* test under which a hospital can lose its exemption from state and local property taxes unless it meets three conditions: (a) it is supported mainly by donations and gifts, (b) most of its patients receive their care for free or reduced cost, and (c) income is sufficient only to cover operating and long-term maintenance costs.[29] Using this standard, most nonprofit hospitals involved in the Medicare program would likely be vulnerable to a loss of-tax exempt status.
- This same logic has now been applied in Pennsylvania not only to hospitals, but also to institutions of higher education, despite the fact that education is explicitly identified in the most authoritative summary of the English common law concept

of charity as an inherently "charitable" purpose.[30]

• What is more, the scope of such challenges appears to be widening. Using a combination of three principal arguments—(a) that local tax exemptions should be available only to organizations that primarily serve the poor; (b) that all "commercial income," including that from fees and charges, as well as the property used to produce it, should be taxed; and (c) that local tax exemptions should be limited to organizations that primarily serve people who live in the same town or state,[31] assessors in a wide assortment of states have launched challenges against local nonprofit institutions. A recent ballot initiative in Colorado would have denied tax exemption to all but a handful of charitable institutions, including all churches. Although this provision was roundly defeated, opponents fear that a revised version, preserving the exemption for churches, could ultimately win broader support.

• Many of these same issues are now surfacing at the federal level as well. Thus, as noted earlier, the so-called "commerciality" test has been built into the proposed national sales tax, so that nonprofits providing services that are "commercially available" would be subject to tax on these sales. Despite the ambiguity of the concept of "commercially available," efforts are under way to introduce this concept into the existing income tax system as a substitute for the existing "relatedness" test.

Zoning Restrictions

Nonprofit organizations are also being targeted increasingly in NMBY (Not in My Backyard) regulations at the local level. The Hartford City Council, for example, approved an ordinance in November 1995 establishing a moratorium on all new homeless shelters, rehabilitation homes, and other treatment or social service centers in the city. A recent study revealed that at least 30 cities have similar statutes or regulations that employ zoning or building codes to exclude service agencies.[32]

Anti-Advocacy Legislation

Finally, the so-called Istook Amendment at the Federal level (and counterpart legislation at the state level) has brought the same kind of challenge to one of the other fundamental functions of the voluntary sector—namely, its advocacy and representational function. Under this amendment, which came close to passage in the 104th Congress, nonprofit organizations receiving federal grants would be severely limited in using even their private revenues to engage in a broad range of advocacy and representational activities. This would undercut one of the major rationales for the existence of a nonprofit sector—that is, to give voice to the underrepresented and to bring new issues to public attention. That this provision made the headway it did is testimony to the vulnerability of the nonprofit sector at the present time. Having joined with government to respond to public needs, nonprofit organizations are now in the uncomfortable position of appearing to be advocating not on behalf of the clients and communities they serve, but in their own self interest, for the budgets and programs that support their own operations. This has opened them to the kind of attack recently leveled by Heritage Foundation President Edwin Feulner, who has sought to discredit nonprofit support for expanded public benefits to the poor on grounds that the agencies advancing these claims are themselves "on the public take" and therefore advocating not for their clientele but for their own organizational budgets. It is this vulnerability that proposals of the sort embodied in the Istook Amendment seek to exploit.

Summary

In short, a significant challenge confronts the American nonprofit sector at the present time. This challenge is part fiscal, part economic, part political, and part philosophical and moral.

Nonprofit organizations are being forced or enticed into modes of behavior that diverge increasingly sharply from public expectations and norms, and too little is being done to bring either the reality back into alignment with expectations, or expectations into better alignment with reality. The upshot is a dangerous crisis of confidence and legitimacy for one of the oldest, most venerated, and most critical components of our national heritage.

Notes

1. This development and its resulting scope and structure are explored more fully in: Lester M. Salamon, *Partners in Public Service: Government-Nonprofit Relations in the Modern Welfare State,* (Baltimore: Johns Hopkins University Press, 1995).

2. Most federal programs are "discretionary programs" that receive their funding through annual appropriations bills passed by the Congress and approved by the President. Included here are programs such as Head Start, Community Development Block Grants (CDBG), Social Service Block Grants, job training. However, most federal domestic spending flows through so-called "entitlement programs," which do not require annual appropriations. Rather, spending levels in these programs are determined by the authorizing legislation for the programs, which sets eligibility standards for receipt of benefits. Anybody meeting these standards is automatically "entitled" to the benefits so that the spending levels are determined by the number of people eligible and the share of these who show up and demand the benefits.

Prior to 1984, Congress had no mechanism for considering spending levels for both the discretionary and the entitlement programs together. Beginning that year, however, Congress established a budget process that requires the passage of an initial Budget Resolution in the spring and a final Budget Resolution in the Fall addressing both sets of programs. Under Congressional procedures, appropriations committees and legislative authorizing committees are then obliged to meet the targets set in the Budget Resolution for their respective sets of programs. If they do not, Congress can pass a "Reconciliation Bill" that incorporates the necessary changes in both appropriations and entitlement program benefit and eligibility levels.

The budget resolutions apply to Congressional action only and do not require presidential approval.

Reconciliation bills, however, must be approved by the President to become law, unless they are passed over his veto.

3. Under the welfare reform bill, the federal government's automatic guarantee to match state payments to eligible fatherless families with dependent children was ended and replaced with a fixed grant to states. In addition, this grant was conditioned on state termination of assistance to families which had received these benefits for more than five years and assistance to immigrants was restricted.

4. Computed from data in Virginia Ann Hodgkinson and Murray S. Weitzman with John Abrahams, Eric Crutchfield, and David R. Stevenson, *Nonprofit Almanac, 1996–1997: Dimensions of the Independent Sector* (San Francisco: Jossey-Bass Publishers, 1996), p. 81. (Cited hereafter as Hodgkinson and Weitzman, *Nonprofit Almanac.*)

5. Internal Revenue Service, *Statistics of Income Bulletin,* various editions, as reported in Hodgkinson and Weitzman, *Nonprofit Almanac,* 1996, p. 89.

6. Based on data in Barry W. Johnson, "Estate Tax Returns," *Statistics of Income,* various years, as reported in Independent Sector, *Nonprofit Almanac,* 1996, Table 2.7, p. 91.

7. The discussion here draws on: Council on Foundations/Independent Sector, Working Group on Tax Restructuring. "Impact of Tax Restructuring Proposals on Charitable Entities," mimeo, September 1996.

8. See, for example: Harris Meyer, Terese Hudson, James E. Cain, Stewart L. Carr, and David Zacharias, "Selling . . . or Selling Out," *Hospitals and Health Networks* (June 5, 1996), p. 22; Montague Brown, "Commentary: The Commercialization of America's Voluntary Health Care System," *Health Care Management Review* (1996), 21 (3), pp. 13–18; Malik Hasan, "Let's End the Nonprofit Charade," *New England Journal of Medicine* (April 18, 1996), Vol 334, No. 16, pp. 1055–8; Anne Lowrey Bailey, "Health Care's Merger Mania," *Chronicle of Philanthropy* (November 16, 1995), p. 1.

9. See, for example: Milt Freudenheim, "Health Plans in New Jersey Face Rivalries," *New York Times* (May 30, 1996); Milt Freudenheim, "For Blue Cross, at Crossroads, A Fight to Save Role for System," *New York Times* (June 15, 1996); Milt Freudenheim, "Empire Blue Cross Seeks Permission to Earn Profits," *New York Times* (September 26, 1996).

10. Dr. Malik Hasan, "Let's End the Nonprofit Charade," *New England Journal of Medicine* (April 18, 1996), Vol 334, No. 16, pp. 1055–8.

11. Nina Bernstein, "Giant Companies Entering Race to Run State Welfare Programs," *The New York Times* (September 15, 1996), p. A1.

12. One source puts the value of clinical practice fees at 40 percent of the income at medical schools nationwide. William Richardson, "The Appropriate Scale of the Health Sciences Enterprise," *Daedalus* (Fall 1993), p. 186.

13. Lisbeth Schorr, *Within Our Reach: Breaking the Cycle of Disadvantage* (New York: Anchor books, 1988).

14. Kimberly Dennis, "Charities on the Dole," *Policy Review: The Journal of American Citizenship,* No. 76 (March–April 1996).

15. See, for example: Marvin Olasky, *The Tragedy of American Compassion* (Washington, D.C.: Regnery Publishing, Inc., 1992).

16. Roy Lubove, *The Professional Altruist* (Cambridge: Harvard University Pres, 1965), p. 220.

17. H. Hasenfeld and English, *Human Service Organizations* (Englewood Cliffs: Prentice Hall, 1974), p. 19.

18. Stuart Butler, *Privatizing Federal Spending* (New York: Universe Books, 1985).

19. See, for example: Martin Anderson, *Imposters in the Temple: American Intellectuals Are Destroying Our Universities and Cheating Our Students* (Englewood Cliffs, N.J.: Simon and Schuster, 1992).

20. This line of argument is developed most forcefully in Henry Hansman, "The Role of Nonprofit Enterprise," *Yale Law Journal* 89 (1980), pp. 835–901.

21. Regina Herzlinger, "Can Public Trust in Nonprofits and Governments Be Restored?" *Harvard Business Review* (March-April 1996), p. 98.

22. See, for example, the special issue on "accountability of nonprofit organizations" in *Nonprofit Management and Leadership,* Volume 6, No. 2 (Winter 1995), pp. 121–196.

23. Capital Research Center, "Our Mission," Capital Research Center World Wide Web Site (November 1996).

24. See, for example: Edwin Feulner, "Truth in Testimony," *Heritage Foundation Testimony* (August 22, 1996).

25. Historically, state and local governments have extended property and income tax exemptions to organizations that qualify for tax exemption under federal income tax rules. However, the state treatment of the tax status of nonprofit organizations is completely independent of the treatment these organizations receive under federal law. States are therefore free to tax or not tax organizations that are exempt from federal income taxation, so long as they otherwise do not infringe on federal constitutional prohibitions against interfering with interstate commerce and denial of "equal protection of the laws."

26. The material here draws heavily on: Bradford H. Gray, "Challenges Facing Nonprofit Health Care Organizations," unpublished memorandum (September 1996), p. 6.

27. Margaret A. Potter and Beaufort B. Longest, Jr., "The Divergence of Federal and State Policies on the Charitable Tax Exemption of Nonprofit Hospitals," *Journal of Health Politics, Policy, and Law,* Vol. 19, No. 2 (Summer 1994), p. 394.

28. American Law Institute, *Restatement of the Law of Trusts 2d* (1959), quoted in Potter and Longest, "Divergence," p. 397.

29. *Utah County v. Intermountain Health Care* 709 P. 2d 265 (Utah 1985), cited in Potter and Longest, (1994), p. 411.

30. In *Pemsel's Case* (1891), British Lord Mac-Naghten provided what has come to be the definitive summary of the meaning of the term "charitable" in the British common law tradition by identifying "four principal divisions"—i.e., relief of poverty, advancement of education, advancement of religion, and "other purposes beneficial to the community . . . "

31. *State Tax Trends for Nonprofits,* Vol 4, No. 2 (Spring 1996), p. 9.

32. Jonathan Rabinovitz, "Fighting Poverty Programs," *New York Times* (March 24, 1996).

Credits

Chapter 1: Hodgkinson and Weitzman, "Overview and Executive Summary: The State of the Independent Sector." In Hodgkinson, Weitzman, et al. (eds.), *Nonprofit Almanac 1996—1997.* Copyright © 1996 Jossey-Bass Inc., Publishers.

Chapter 2: Lester M. Salamon, "Scope and Structure: The Anatomy of America's Nonprofit Sector." In Salamon, *America's Nonprofit Sector: A Primer,* 2nd ed. (pp. 21–47). Washington, D.C.: The Foundation Center, 1999.

Chapters 3, 4, 11, 12, 15, 16, 30: From *The International Encyclopedia Of Public Policy and Administration,* by Jay Shafritz. Copyright © 1989 by Jay Shafritz. Reprinted by permission of Westview Press, a member of Perseus Books, L.L.C.

Chapter 5: Andrew Carnegie, "The Gospel of Wealth" (Published originally as "Wealth"). *North American Review,* 147, June 1889, pp. 653–664 and 149, December 1889, pp. 682–698. Reprinted from the *North American Review* with the permission of the University of Northern Iowa.

Chapter 6: John H. Filer, *Report of the Commission on Private Philanthropy and Public Needs* ("The Filer Commission Report"). Washington, D.C.: National Commission, 1975.

Chapter 7: David H. Smith, "The Impact of the Volunteer Sector on Society." In D. H. Smith, *Voluntary Action Research.* Lexington, Mass: Lexington Books, 1973. Reprinted with the permission of the author.

Chapter 8: David L. Gies, J. Steven Ott, and Jay M. Shafritz, eds., *The Nonprofit Organization: Essential Readings.* Pacific Grove, CA: Brooks/Cole, 1990. Reprinted with permission of the author.

Chapter 9: Hall, *Inventing the Nonprofit Sector and Other Essays on Philanthropy, Voluntarism, and Nonprofit Organizations.* Pp. 13–16, 66–83. Copyright © The Johns Hopkins University Press.

Chapter 10: Gary N. Scrivner, "A Brief History of Tax Policy Changes Affecting Charitable Organizations." Reprinted with the permission of the author.

Chapter 13: Lester M. Salamon, "What Is the Nonprofit Sector and Why Do We Have It?" In Salamon, *America's Nonprofit Sector: A Primer,* 2nd ed. (pp. 7–19). Washington, D.C.: The Foundation Center, 1999.

Chapter 14: R. A. Lohmann, *The Commons,* pp. 46–82. Copyright © 1992 Jossey-Bass Inc., Publishers.

Chapter 17: "And Lettuce Is Nonanimal," in *Nonprofit & Voluntary Sector Quarterly* 18 (4) pp. 367–383. Copyright © 1989 by Sage Publications Inc.

Chapter 18: James Douglas. "Political Theories of Nonprofit Organizations," in Walter W. Powell (Ed.), *The Nonprofit Sector: A Research Handbook,* © 1987. reprinted with the permission of Yale University Press.

Chapter 19: Kirsten A. Grønbjerg, *Private Action and the Public Good* (1998), "Markets, Politics, and Charity: Nonprofits in the Political Economy," pp. 137–150. Reprinted with the permission of Yale University Press.

Chapter 20: Peter L. Berger and Richard John Neuhaus, *To Empower People: The Role of Mediating Structures in Public Policy.* Washington, D.C.: American Enterprise Institute for Public Policy Research, 1977.

Chapter 21: Reprinted by permission of the publisher from *Nonprofits for Hire* by